I0823748

MIDDLE BABYLONIAN TEXTS IN THE CORNELL COLLECTIONS

The publication of
CORNELL UNIVERSITY STUDIES IN ASSYRIOLOGY AND SUMEROLOGY
Volume 37

was made possible thanks to a generous subvention from an anonymous donor

Cornell University Studies in
Assyriology and Sumerology
(CUSAS)

Volume 37

# Middle Babylonian Texts in the Cornell Collections

## Part Two
## The Earlier Kings

by

Elena Devecchi

Eisenbrauns
University Park, Pennsylvania

Library of Congress Cataloging-in-Publication Data
Names: Devecchi, Elena, author.
Title: Middle Babylonian texts in the Cornell collections : part 2 : the earlier kings / Elena Devecchi.
Description: University Park, Pennsylvania : Eisenbrauns, [2020] | Series: Cornell University studies in Assyriology and Sumerology (CUSAS) ; volume 37. | Includes bibliographical references and index.
Summary: "Translation, transliteration, and commentary of cuneiform documents from Babylonia dating to the Kassite period, the middle of the second millennium BCE, in ancient Iraq"—Provided by publisher.
Identifiers: LCCN 2020936680 | ISBN 9781575067490 (cloth)
Subjects: LCSH: Cornell University. Department of Near Eastern Studies—Catalogs. | Sumerian language—Texts—Catalogs. | Akkadian language—Texts—Catalogs. | Cuneiform inscriptions, Sumerian—Catalogs. | Cuneiform inscriptions, Akkadian—Catalogs. | Cuneiform tablets—Iraq—Catalogs. | Babylonia—Antiquities—Catalogs.
Classification: PJ4053.C67 S65 2020 | DDC 231.7/65—dc23
LC record available at https://lccn.loc.gov/2020936680


Printed in the United States of America
Published by The Pennsylvania State University Press,
University Park, PA 16802-1003

Eisenbrauns is an imprint of The Pennsylvania State University Press.

The Pennsylvania State University Press is a member
of the Association of University Presses.

It is the policy of The Pennsylvania State University Press to use acid-free paper. Publications on uncoated stock satisfy the minimum requirements of American National Standard for Information Sciences—Permanence of Paper for Printed Library Material, ANSI Z39.48-1992.

# Contents

Series Editor's Preface ix
Acknowledgments xi
Abbreviations and Conventions xiii
Catalog 1
Concordances 7

Introduction 17
1. Origin of the Tablets 17
1.1 The Nippur Area 17
1.2 Dūr-Enlilē? 19
1.3 House of Enlil-Kidinnī or Bīt-Enlil-Kidinnī? 20
2. Remarks on Selected Text Groups 21
2.1 Accounts of Agricultural Revenues 21
2.2 Expenditures 28
2.3 Flock Records 32
3. Economic Activities 33
3.1 Primary Production 33
3.1.1 Agriculture 33
3.1.2 Animal Husbandry 34
3.2 Secondary Production 35
3.2.1 Milling 35
3.2.2 Brewing 35
3.2.3 Textile Industry 37
4. Administrative Structure 38
4.1 The Main Actors 38
4.2 Further Officials 42
4.3 Administrative Units 45
4.4 Storage Facilities 46
4.5 Temples 46
4.6 Interactions with the Royal and Provincial Government 47

## Texts

1. Administration of Agricultural Products .......... 51
1.1 Accounts of Agricultural Revenues .......... 51
1.1.1 Annual *tēlītu*-Accounts for One Town .......... 51
i. Barley Together with Other Cereals, Pulses, and Cress (1–16) .......... 51
ii. Sesame (17–21) .......... 73
1.1.2 Annual *tēlītu*-Accounts for Several Towns .......... 78
i. Barley Together with Other Cereals, Pulses, and Cress (22–23) .......... 78
ii. Sesame (24) .......... 80
iii. Wheat (25) .......... 81
1.1.3 Annual edin-Accounts for One Town (26–36) .......... 81
1.1.4 Accounts of "Shares" (37–39) .......... 92
1.1.5 Other Accounts of Revenues (40–46) .......... 95
1.2 Stored Goods .......... 102
1.2.1 "Stored Barley/Grain" (47–57) .......... 102
1.2.2 "Rest of the Stores" (58–60) .......... 113
1.2.3 Stored Flour (61) .......... 115
1.3 Expenditures .......... 116
1.3.1 Single Expenditures (62–91) .......... 116
1.3.2 Multiple Expenditures for One Purpose .......... 136
i. Rations (92–104) .......... 136
ii. Fodder (105–7) .......... 150
iii. Seed (108–9) .......... 153
iv. Production Supplies (110–17) .......... 154
v. Supplies for Temples (118–19) .......... 161
vi. Loan with Interest (120–22) .......... 163
vii. "Delivery" (123) .......... 166
viii. Gifts (124–25) .......... 167
ix. "Exchange" (126) .......... 169
1.3.3 Multiple Expenditures for Various Purposes (127–90) .......... 170
1.3.4 *aklu*-Expenditures of Foodstuffs .......... 239
i. Single *aklu*-Expenditures (191–235) .......... 239
ii. Summaries of *aklu*-Expenditures (236–45) .......... 256
2. Administration of Animal Husbandry .......... 264
2.1 Sheep (246–53) .......... 264
2.2 Goats (254) .......... 269
2.3 Sheep and Goats (255–62) .......... 269
2.4 Cattle (263–66) .......... 275

3. Textile Production ........ 280
3.1 Allocation of Wool as Work Material (267–72) ........ 280
3.2 Garments and Textiles (273–90) ........ 284
4. Miscellaneous Administrative Texts ........ 300
4.1 Personnel Lists (291–92) ........ 300
4.2 Beer (293) ........ 301
4.3 Beer and Bread (294) ........ 302
4.4 Beer and Draff (295) ........ 303
4.5 Pig's Fat (296) ........ 304
4.6 Receipt of Aromatics and Disbursement of Cereals (297) ........ 304
4.7 Hides (298–99) ........ 306
4.8 Bricks (300) ........ 307
4.9 Paint (301) ........ 308
4.10 Wood (302) ........ 309
4.11 Sickles (303) ........ 310
4.12 Sacks (304) ........ 311
4.13 Metal (305) ........ 312
4.14 Inventory of Precious Goods (306) ........ 313
4.15 Uncertain (307–23) ........ 314
5. Legal Documents ........ 324
5.1 *tuppi aḫūzati* (324) ........ 324
5.2 Contract of Exchange (325) ........ 326
5.3 Purchase of an Ox (326) ........ 328
5.4 Settlements of Disputes (327–28) ........ 330
5.5 Loans (329–31) ........ 334
5.6 Uncertain (332–34) ........ 337
6. Letters (335–38) ........ 339

7. References ........ 345

8. Indexes ........ 349
Personal Names ........ 349
Professions ........ 381
Geographic Names and Ethnonyms ........ 384
Temples ........ 386
Cuneiform Sources ........ 387

9. Plates ........ 391

# Series Editor's Preface

Elena Devecchi's CUSAS 37 completes the publication of the second half of Cornell Rosen Collection's Middle Babylonian tablets just five years after the publication of CUSAS 30 (2015) by Wilfred van Soldt. Together they add nearly 800 additional economic texts to the available corpus from the Middle Babylonian period, thereby providing substantial new data to scholars and students to facilitate the study of the Kassite period in Mesopotamia. These two volumes include full transliterations, translations, and extended commentaries on these new texts. They expand significantly our previous knowledge of the Nippur region under Kassite rule hitherto based on published sources that came primarily from Nippur itself. Devecchi's comprehensive treatment expands upon van Soldt's initial publication of a later series of texts from the same source, updating and expanding upon his substantive analysis of those texts. Although the text corpus lacks provenance and archaeological context, the size and coherence of the archival groups nevertheless preserve substantial data that indicate their likely common source from a site in the Nippur region, likely to have been Dūr-Enlilē, as proposed initially by van Soldt and tentatively confirmed by Devecchi's current study. In addition, their respective and thorough studies reflect the importance that the recording, prompt publication, and dissemination of these data will have to promote progress in the study of the Kassite period and to diminish somewhat the tragic effect that the looting and destruction of sites in Iraq have had. This editor remains committed to a continuing effort to rescue and, particularly, to publish these and other sources in the CUSAS series to further these goals.

Unfortunately, while the CUSAS series continues to provide unique material for Assyriological research from the Rosen Collection, the current and former deans of the College of Arts and Sciences at Cornell University have closed down the Jonathan and Jeannette Rosen Ancient Near Eastern Studies Seminar and Tablet Conservation Laboratory and terminated all work on the conservation and photography of the remaining unpublished tablets that are being sent to the Iraq Museum, where continued access and publication will no longer be possible.

We are grateful to Elena Devecchi for undertaking the publication of this important corpus of Middle Babylonian tablets and to Laura Johnson-Kelly, Alexandra Kleinerman, and the assistants at the Rosen Seminar who together facilitated the publication of these texts. They undertook the conservation, cataloguing, and photography while providing helpful support to all visiting scholars at this unique facility. None of this would be possible without Jonathan and Jeannette Rosen and the Rosen Foundation, whose continued interest and generous support for the ongoing study and publication of the Rosen Collection at Cornell University. For nearly nineteen years, the Rosen Seminar has been a magnet for scholars and provided unprecedented access to unpublished texts and support for their respective publications. From 2007 to 2019, the CUSAS series has produced ca. 40 volumes under the auspices of the CDL Press, and I am pleased to note that the series will continue now with Eisenbrauns—an imprint of the Pennsylvania State University Press. While it is regrettable that university politics, political correctness, and a hostile faculty caused the termination of our facility, the ongoing contributions of the CUSAS series remain as a monument to its success. We owe the Rosen family and all those who have participated in the Rosen Seminar and its publications a great debt for their collective input and support.

David I. Owen, Director
The Jonathan and Jeannette Rosen Ancient Near Eastern Studies Seminar and Tablet Conservation Laboratory
Cornell University, Ithaca, NY
July 2019

# *Acknowledgments*

It is a great pleasure to express my gratitude to the several persons and institutions who made this publication possible.

First and foremost, I would like to thank David I. Owen, former curator of tablet collections in the Jonathan and Jeannette Rosen Ancient Near Eastern Studies Seminar and Tablet Conservation Laboratory at Cornell University in Ithaca, New York, for having offered me the opportunity to work on the texts published in this volume and for the trust and patience he showed while waiting for the book to be completed. I also thank Laura W. Johnson-Kelly, collection manager and head photographer/conservator of the collections, as well as Jeffrey R. Zorn, Anna Keeton, and Alexander Kracht for providing me with excellent photographs of the tablets and kindly assisting me both during and after my research visits to the collection. Several other people helped to ensure that my time in Ithaca was enjoyable. I am especially grateful to Laura W. Johnson-Kelly and Alexandra Kleinerman for their friendliness and to Karel Van Lerberghe and Gabriella Voet for generously allowing me to stay at their lovely house in Trumansburg, New York, in fall 2015.

I am indebted to a number of institutions that provided financial support for this project. The Fonds Wetenschappelijk Onderzoek–Vlaanderen (FWO) funded my initial visit to Cornell in September 2009. I was able to dedicate myself to the full-time study of the tablets in 2013 thanks to a postdoctoral grant from the Bayerische Gleichstellungsförderung in support of the project "Neue Keilschrifturkunden der Kassitenzeit (1359–1264 v. Chr.) in der Cornell University, NY," which I conducted at the Institute for Assyriology and Hittitology of the Ludwig Maximilian University of Munich. A travel grant from the Thyssen Foundation made possible a second visit to Cornell in fall 2013. Thanks to the funding of the project "Managing the Harvest: The Administration of Agricultural Production in Kassite Babylonia," financed by the Deutsche Forschungsgemeinschaft, I could visit the Penn Museum and the Yale Babylonian Collection to work on the Middle Babylonian tablets kept there, which provided important reference material to the texts from the Rosen Collection.

As a newcomer to the field of Kassite studies and to Mesopotamian administration in general, I benefited enormously from the generosity of more experienced colleagues.

First of all, I am deeply indebted to Wilfred van Soldt, who kindly helped and guided me in my first steps in the world of Middle Babylonian texts and since then has always been ready to share his knowledge with me.

This book would not have been possible without the support of Walther Sallaberger, whom I should thank for all the time he spent discussing with me major and minor issues arising from the work on the texts, ranging from philological problems to the more general understanding of the administrative system.

I consulted on several occasions John A. Brinkman, whom I sincerely thank for his valuable suggestions on several text passages and for bringing to my attention some unpublished Nippur tablets.

It was a pleasure to discuss several topics covered by the texts published here with Susanne Paulus, whom I particularly thank for her expertise on the legal documents.

Aron Dornauer, Palmiro Notizia, and Zsombor Földi deserve my sincere gratitude for having made useful comments on groups of texts or parts of this work.

Klaus Wagensonner was so kind as to provide me with "last-minute" collations of some tablets in August 2018.

I am very grateful to Giuseppe F. Del Monte for having generously shared with me the material he collected during his researches on the Kassite period, which made the consultation of the Nippur texts much easier.

Special thanks go to Anne Löhnert and Paola Paoletti for their inspiring and motivating talks. They proved to be the best peers one could ever wish for during my postdoctoral years in Munich.

Over the years I could always count on the encouragement and advice of Lucio Milano and Stefano de Martino, to whom I would like to express once again my deepest gratitude.

I would also like to thank Eugene McGarry for being very professional and collaborative in correcting the English and editing the manuscript.

The plates were prepared by Laura W. Johnson-Kelly and Maria Letizia Ferri, whom I would like to thank for their careful work.

Last but not least, I must thank my family and friends for always being there when I need them and apologize to them for the endless occasions when I had to excuse myself with the words "Sorry, I have to finish a book." It took longer than we probably all expected, and it is also thanks to them that this work finally reached an end.

Turin, October 2018

# *Abbreviations and Conventions*

## Abbreviations

acc. — accession year
*AfO* — *Archiv für Orientforschung*
AHw — W. von Soden, *Akkadisches Handwörterbuch*, Wiesbaden 1965–1981
Akk. — Akkadian
AnOr — Analecta Orientalia (Roma)
AOAT — Alter Orient und Altes Testament (Münster)
*AoF* — *Altorientalische Forschungen*
AOS — American Oriental Series (New Haven)
ARM — Archives royales de Mari
AS — Assyriological Studies (Chicago)
BaF — Baghdader Forschungen (Mainz am Rhein)
*BaM* — *Baghdader Mitteilungen*
BATSH — Berichte der Ausgrabung Tall Seh Hamad / Dur-Katlimmu (Berlin)
BB — Burna-Buriaš
BBVO — Berliner Beiträge zum Vorderer Orient Texte (Berlin)
BE — The Babylonian Expedition of the University of Pennsylvania (Philadelphia)
BE 14 — texts from Nippur published by Clay 1906a
BE 15 — texts from Nippur published by Clay 1906b
BE 17 — texts from Nippur published by Radau 1908
*BiOr* — *Bibliotheca Orientalis*
*BSA* — *Bulletin of Sumerian Agriculture*
CAD — *The Assyrian Dictionary of the University of Chicago* (Chicago)
CBS — Museum siglum of the University Museum in Philadelphia (Catalog of the Babylonian Section)
CDLI — Cuneiform Digital Library Initiative
CUNES — Museum siglum of the Jonathan and Jeannette Rosen Ancient Near Eastern Seminar in the Department of Near Eastern Studies at Cornell University
CUSAS — Cornell University Studies in Assyriology and Sumerology (Bethesda, MD)
CUSAS 30 — Texts from the Rosen Collection published by van Soldt 2015
D-K — Texts from Dūr-Kurigalzu published by Gurney 1949
DN — Divine name
GN — Geographic name
HANE/S — History of the Ancient Near East / Studies (Padova)
Iml. — Texts from Tell Imlihiye published by Kessler 1982
*JAOS* — *Journal of the American Oriental Society*
*JCS* — *Journal of Cuneiform Studies*
*JNES* — *Journal of Near Eastern Studies*
KaE — Kadašman-Enlil
KT — Kadašman-Turgu
KuE — Kudur-Enlil
LB — Late Babylonian
L.e. — Lower edge
Le.e. — Left edge
MA — Middle Assyrian
MB — Middle Babylonian
MBTU — Texts from Ur published by Gurney 1983
MC — Mesopotamian Civilizations (Winona Lake, IN)
MesZL — See Borger 2010

| | |
|---|---|
| MRWH | texts from Nippur published by Petschow 1974 |
| MUN | texts from Nippur published by Sassmannshausen 2001 |
| NA | Neo-Assyrian |
| NB | Neo-Babylonian |
| n.d. | not dated |
| NM | Nazi-Maruttaš |
| OAkk. | Old Akkadian |
| OB | Old Babylonian |
| OBO | Orbis Biblicus et Orientalis (Freiburg) |
| Obv. | Obverse |
| OIC | Oriental Institute Communications (Chicago) |
| OIP | Oriental Institute Publications (Chicago) |
| OIS | Oriental Institute Seminars (Chicago) |
| PBS | University of Pennsylvania, Publications of the Babylonian Section (Philadelphia) |
| PBS 1/2 | texts from Nippur published by Lutz 1919 |
| PBS 2/2 | texts from Nippur published by Clay 1912 |
| PBS 13 | texts from Nippur published by Legrain 1922 |
| PIHANS | Publications de l'Institut historique-archéologique néerlandais de Stamboul (Istanbul and Leiden) |
| PN | Personal name |
| *RA* | *Revue d'Assyriologie et d'Archéologie Orientale* |
| Rev. | Reverse |
| RGTC | Répertoire géographique des textes cunéiformes (Wiesbaden) |
| RGTC 3 | See Groneberg 1980 |
| RGTC 5 | See Nashef 1982 |
| *RlA* | *Reallexikon der Assyriologie und vorderasiatischen Archäologie* (Berlin and Leipzig) |
| SANER | Studies in Ancient Near Eastern Records (Boston and Berlin) |
| SCCNH | Studies on the Civilization and Culture of Nuzi and the Hurrians (Winona Lake, IN, and Bethesda, MD) |
| ŠŠ | Šagarakti-Šuriaš |
| StOr | Studia Orientalia (Helsinki) |
| UAVA | Untersuchungen zur Assyriologie und Vorderasiatischen Archäologie. Ergänzungsbände zu ZA (Berlin) |
| UDBD | Texts published by Peiser 1905 |
| U.e. | Upper edge |
| VAT | Vorderasiatische Abteilung, Tontafeln (museum siglum of the Vorderasiatisches Museum, Berlin) |
| WVDOG | Wissenschaftliche Veröffentlichungen der deutschen Orient-Gesellschaft (Wiesbaden) |
| YOS | Yale Oriental Series, Babylonian Texts (New Haven) |
| *ZA* | *Zeitschrift für Assyriologie* |
| *ZAR* | *Zeitschrift für Altorientalische und Biblische Rechtsgeschichte* |
| Zub. | texts from Tell Zubeidi published by Kessler 1985 |
| √ | checkmark |

## Dating of the Tablets

The tablets published in this volume are dated to the reigns of the following Kassite kings (absolute dates are BC and follow Brinkman 2017):

| | |
|---|---|
| Burna-Buriaš II | 1359–1333 |
| Nazi-Maruttaš | 1307–1282 |
| Kadašman-Turgu | 1281–1264 |
| Kadašman-Enlil II | 1263–1255 |
| Kudur-Enlil | 1254–1246 |
| Šagarakti-Šuriaš | 1245–1233 |

Dates are rendered according to the sequence day-month-year—e.g.,

2.VIII.16 Kadašman-Turgu = day 2, month VIII, year 16 of Kadašman-Turgu

Month names are attested in the following forms (references are given only for unusual variants, cf. Brinkman 1976, 398–400):

| | |
|---|---|
| I | $^{iti}$BÁR.ZAG.GAR |
| II | $^{iti}$GU$_4$.SI.SÁ, $^{iti}$GU$_4$ |
| III | $^{iti}$SIG$_4$.GA, $^{iti}$SIG$_4$.A.AN (**203**: 6, **308**: ix 30′) |
| IV | $^{iti}$ŠU.NUMUN.NA, $^{iti}$ŠU.X.NUMUN.NA (**64**: 8, **215**: 6), $^{iti}$<ŠU>.NUMUN.NA (**37**: 22) |
| V | $^{iti}$NE.NE.GAR, $^{iti}$NE.NE (**268**: 5), $^{iti}$NE.GAR (**237**: 10, **308**: ix 37′), $^{iti}$NE |
| VI | $^{iti}$KIN.$^{d}$INANNA, $^{iti}$KIN |
| VIa* | $^{iti}$KIN.$^{d}$INANNA.2.KAM.MA, $^{iti}$KIN.$^{d}$INANNA.2.KAM, $^{iti}$KIN.2.KAM, $^{iti}$DIRI (**68**: 1; **176**: 28) |
| VII | $^{iti}$DU$_6$.KÙ, $^{iti}$DU$_6$ |
| VIII | $^{iti}$APIN.DU$_8$.A, $^{iti}$APIN |
| IX | $^{iti}$GAN.GAN.È, $^{iti}$GAN.È, $^{iti}$GAN |
| X | $^{iti}$AB.È, $^{iti}$AB |
| XI | $^{iti}$ZÍZ.A.AN, $^{iti}$ZÍZ.AN (**308**: iv 10′), $^{iti}$ZÍZ |
| XII | $^{iti}$ŠE.KIN.KU$_5$, $^{iti}$ŠE.KIN, $^{iti}$ŠE |

* Month VIa is attested for the following years: NM 14, NM 23, KT 7, KT 8, KT 10, KT 13, and KaE 3.

## Capacity Measures

Capacity measures are rendered as follows:

1.2.3 4 (SÌLA) = 1 kor + 2 *pānu* + 3 *sūtu* + 4 *qû*

# Catalog

## 1. Administration of Agricultural Products

1.1 Accounts of Agricultural Revenues

1.1.1 Annual *tēlītu*-Accounts for One Town

*i. Barley Together with Other Cereals, Pulses, and Cress*

| Text no. | CUNES no. | Date | Measurements in mm[1] |
|---|---|---|---|
| 1 | 52-10-103 | NM 22 | 95×131×25★ |
| 2 | 52-12-003 | KT 1 | 126×178 |
| 3 | 52-10-041 | KT 5 | 116×142×30★ |
| 4 | 52-12-004 | KT 8? | 111×145×29 |
| 5 | 52-10-047 | KT 8 | 67×105×27 |
| 6 | 52-12-019 | KT 8 | 68×118×27 |
| 7 | 52-10-044 | KT 11 | 93×120×32 |
| 8 | 52-10-046 | KT 11 | 56×93×24 |
| 9 | 52-16-019 | KT 11 | 81×136×30 |
| 10 | 52-10-042 | KT 12 | 103×133×30★ |
| 11 | 52-10-061 | KT 12 | 68×113×34 |
| 12 | 52-10-045 | KT 13 | 88×138×36 |
| 13 | 52 10 051 | KT 13 | 61×92×24 |
| 14 | 52-10-048 | KT 14 | 64×125×28 |
| 15 | 52-10-049 | KT 14 | 59×120×25 |
| 16 | 52-00-091 | KT x | 52×47★×21 |

*ii. Sesame*

| | | | |
|---|---|---|---|
| 17 | 52-16-099 | (NM) 23 | 61×96×25 |
| 18 | 52-10-078 | KT 3 | 48×75×24 |
| 19 | 52-15-044 | KT 12 | 48×93×23 |
| 20 | 52-18-833 | n.d. | 68×56★×26 |
| 21 | 52-20-305 | n.d. | 58×48★×24★ |

1 height×width×thickness; ★ indicates that the tablet is not complete.

1.1.2 Annual *tēlītu*-Accounts for Several Towns

*i. Barley Together with Other Cereals, Pulses, and Cress*

| | | | |
|---|---|---|---|
| 22 | 52-10-052 | NM 19 | 65×108×29 |
| 23 | 52-12-015 | KT 10 | 71×151×27 |

*ii. Sesame*

| | | | |
|---|---|---|---|
| 24 | 52-10-106 | KT 15? | 46×68×24 |

*iii. Wheat*

| | | | |
|---|---|---|---|
| 25 | 52-10-060 | KT 1 | 49×69×21 |

1.1.3 Annual EDIN-Accounts for One Town

| | | | |
|---|---|---|---|
| 26 | 52-10-080 | NM 18 | 55×91×26 |
| 27 | 52-10-071 | NM 20 | 60×93★×28 |
| 28 | 52-10-073 | NM 24 | 58×82×23 |
| 29 | 52-19-148 | NM 24 | 59×96×25 |
| 30 | 52-14-076 | KT 4 | 58×73×19 |
| 31 | 52-10-082 | KT 5 | 62×95×26 |
| 32 | 52-10-062 | KT 11 | 81×107×30 |
| 33 | 52-12-006 | KT 12? | 80×109×27 |
| 34 | 52-14-070 | KT 12 | 78×159×30 |
| 35 | 52-10-043 | KT 13 | 83×116×27 |
| 36 | 52-10-050 | year 5 | 68×101★×30 |

1.1.4 Accounts of "Shares"

| | | | |
|---|---|---|---|
| 37 | 52-12-014 | KT 1 | 148×89×28 |
| 38 | 52-10-056 | KT 3 | 58×83×25 |
| 39 | 52-18-810 | KT 10 | 54×82×22 |

1.1.5 Other Accounts of Revenues

| | | | |
|---|---|---|---|
| 40 | 52-10-123 | NM 9+ | 63★×48★×31 |
| 41 | 52-20-301 | NM 18 | 70×104★×29 |

| | | | |
|---|---|---|---|
| 42 | 52-10-124 | NM 19 | 56×83×27 |
| 43 | 52-10-063 | KT 1 | 50×81×24 |
| 44 | 52-13-134 | KT 1 | 60×82×25 |
| 45 | 52-10-094 | KT 4 | 86×112×32 |
| 46 | 52-16-018 | KT x | 133×103×29 |

1.2 Stored Goods

1.2.1 "Stored Barley/Grain"

| | | | |
|---|---|---|---|
| 47 | 52-12-011 | NM 21 | 116×80×31 |
| 48 | 52-10-096 | NM 24 | 93×64×26 |
| 49 | 52-10-079 | KT 1 | 86×67×24 |
| 50 | 52-19-152 | KT 1 | 92×58×25 |
| 51 | 52-12-048 | KT 7 | 92×65×26 |
| 52 | 52-10-053 | KT 11 | 105×78×28 |
| 53 | 52-10-055 | KT 12 | 67×85×25 |
| 54 | 52-10-057 | KT 12 | 58×82×28 |
| 55 | 52-12-020 | KT 12 | 114×85×29 |
| 56 | 52-10-054 | KT 13 | 70×78×24 |
| 57 | 52-10-095 | KT x | 93×70×27 |

1.2.2 "Rest of the Stores"

| | | | |
|---|---|---|---|
| 58 | 52-14-074 | NM 18? | 75×129×33 |
| 59 | 52-16-017 | KT 4 | 70×134×25 |
| 60 | 52-18-860 | KT 12 | 65×87×24 |

1.2.3 Stored Flour

| | | | |
|---|---|---|---|
| 61 | 52-12-052 | n.d. | 50×65×22 |

1.3 Expenditures

1.3.1 Single Expenditures

| | | | |
|---|---|---|---|
| 62 | 52-18-776 | NM 7 | 28×31×16 |
| 63 | 52-16-084 | NM 8 | 39×53×20 |
| 64 | 52-12-044 | NM 18? | 44×50×19 |
| 65 | 52-12-050 | NM 18 | 34×33×19 |
| 66 | 52-18-799 | NM 20 | 27×43×18 |
| 67 | 52-19-114 | NM 24? | 36×43×20 |
| 68 | 52-16-075 | KT 7 | 37×40×18 |
| 69 | 52-12-025 | KT 9 | 33×45×16 |
| 70 | 52-16-076 | KT 9 | 38×43★×20 |
| 71 | 52-12-026 | KT 9 | 32×38×17 |
| 72 | 52-16-078 | KT 9 | 39×46×18 |
| 73 | 52-14-100 | KT 10 | 27×33×17 |
| 74 | 52-14-098 | KT 10 | 31×40×18 |
| 75 | 52-17-276 | KT 11 | 45×56×21 |
| 76 | 52-14-101 | KT 12 | 24×26×13 |
| 77 | 52-18-769 | KT 12 | 37×47×15 |
| 78 | 52-19-134 | KT 13 | 48×54×20 |
| 79 | 52-17-266 | KT 13 | 41×53×22 |
| 80 | 52-12-055 | KT 13+ | 42×45×21 |
| 81 | 52-16-090 | KT 14 | 30×35×15 |
| 82 | 52-13-165 | KT 14 | 47×52×23 |
| 83 | 52-14-045 | KT 14 | 44×56×23 |
| 84 | 52-14-032 | KT 14 | 43×53×16 |
| 85 | 53-01-128 | KT 14 | 41×49×22 |
| 86 | 53-01-116 | KT 15 | 27×38×15 |
| 87 | 52-19-117 | KT 15 | 44×63×20 |
| 88 | 52-14-025 | KT x | 41×48×22 |
| 89 | 52-14-102 | KT x | 32×35×16 |
| 90 | 52-18-800 | KT x | 34×40×17 |
| 91 | 52-16-108 | ŠŠ 1 | 34×36×20 |

1.3.2 Multiple Expenditures for One Purpose

*i. Rations*

| | | | |
|---|---|---|---|
| 92 | 52-12-058 | NM 19 | 56×78×25 |
| 93 | 52-20-320 | KT 2 | 87★×68×30 |
| 94 | 52-10-118 | KT 2 | 68★×48×25 |
| 95 | 52-10-116 | KT 6 | 158★×83×31 |
| 96 | 52-13-110 | KT 9 | 53×86×23 |
| 97 | 52-12-016 | KT 9 | 79×104×27 |
| 98 | 52-19-146 | KT 9 | 80×106×27 |
| 99 | 52-15-030 | KT 9 | 75×50×25 |
| 100 | 52-18-812 | KT 12 | 70×47×21 |
| 101 | 52-19-005 | KT 15 | 92×56×27 |
| 102 | 52-20-306 | KT 15 | 61★×50×25 |
| 103 | 52-00-072 | KT x | 55★×47★×24 |
| 104 | 52-16-071 | ŠŠ 2 | 39×45×17 |

*ii. Fodder*

| | | | |
|---|---|---|---|
| 105 | 52-16-110 | (NM) 22 | 56★×57×27 |
| 106 | 52-10-119 | NM 23 | 93×60×26 |
| 107 | 52-12-029 | KT 2 | 43×60×19 |

*iii. Seed*

| | | | |
|---|---|---|---|
| 108 | 52-10-072 | KT 3 | 56×69×24 |
| 109 | 52-13-078 | n.d. | 44×53×20 |

*iv. Production Supplies*

| | | | |
|---|---|---|---|
| 110 | 52-19-127 | NM 18 | 50×73×23 |
| 111 | 52-12-036 | NM $18^{?}$ | 38×44×17 |
| 112 | 52-12-008 | NM 19 | 81×145×31 |
| 113 | 52-10-090 | KT 3 | 59×99×25 |
| 114 | 52-10-092 | KT 4 | 58×105×26 |
| 115 | 52-10-067 | KT 6 | 56×69×24 |
| 116 | 52-12-007 | KT 9 | 53×94★×26 |
| 117 | 52-00-050 | n.d. | 25★×47★×23 |

*v. Allocations for Temples*

| | | | |
|---|---|---|---|
| 118 | 52-00-062 | KT 9 | 30★×94×22 |
| 119 | 52-12-010 | KT 9 | 65×120×28 |

*vi. Loan with Interest*

| | | | |
|---|---|---|---|
| 120 | 52-18-865 | NM $19^{?}$ | 138×73×30 |
| 121 | 52-13-153 | NM $13^{?}$–KT 3 | 46×61×19 |
| 122 | 52-13-132 | KT 14 | 50×69×31 |

*vii. "Delivery"*

| | | | |
|---|---|---|---|
| 123 | 52-00-049 | KT 9 | 57×31★×23 |

*viii. Gifts*

| | | | |
|---|---|---|---|
| 124 | 52-19-156 | NM [x]–21 | 78×138×33 |
| 125 | 52-10-074 | (NM) 21–23 | 53×64×22 |

*ix. "Exchange"*

| | | | |
|---|---|---|---|
| 126 | 52-14-047 | KT 13 | 30×38×17 |

### 1.3.3 Multiple Expenditures for Various Purposes

| | | | |
|---|---|---|---|
| 127 | 52-18-794 | NM $10^{+}$ | 30×37★×18 |
| 128 | 52-19-118 | NM $17^{?}$ | 42×58×20 |
| 129 | 52-13-139 | NM 17 | 45×51×19 |
| 130 | 52-12-041 | NM 18 | 37×45×13 |
| 131 | 52-12-046 | NM 18 | 60×77×22 |
| 132 | 53-01-174 | NM 19 | 72×98×22★ |
| 133 | 52-13-111 | NM 20 | 53×84×25 |
| 134 | 52-18-816 | NM 21 | 56★×78×23★ |
| 135 | 52-10-077 | (NM) $21^{+}$ | 57×86×23 |
| 136 | 52-19-151 | NM 23 | 99×75×24 |
| 137 | 52-20-303 | NM x | 53×72×23 |
| 138 | 52-16-038 | NM x | 73×91×25 |
| 139 | 52-10-102 | NM x | 150×90×32 |
| 140 | 52-20-319 | NM 21–KT 3 | 133★×80★×34 |
| 141 | 52-12-023 | NM 24–KT 3 | 72×47×20 |
| 142 | 52-13-074 | NM 24–KT 3 | 45×85×22 |
| 143 | 52-10-058 | KT 1 | 59×90×25 |
| 144 | 52-12-022 | KT 1 | 49×63×21 |
| 145 | 52-17-274 | KT 2 | 51×62×22 |
| 146 | 52-17-286 | KT 2 | 48×79×26 |
| 147 | 52-13-184 | KT 2 | 51×71×21 |
| 148 | 52-10-065 | KT 2 | 57×90×25 |
| 149 | 52-10-068 | KT 2 | 55×79×23 |
| 150 | 52-12-013 | KT 3 | 82×109×30 |
| 151 | 52-10-059 | KT 3 | 57×72×24 |
| 152 | 52-19-125 | KT 4 | 63×84×24 |
| 153 | 52-18-859 | KT 6 | 63×89×25 |
| 154 | 52-18-864 | KT $6^{?}$ | 77×103×27 |
| 155 | 53-01-114 | KT 8 | 41×44×20 |
| 156 | 52-10-093 | KT 8 | 118×82×28 |
| 157 | 52-10-066 | KT 8 | 48×72×22 |
| 158 | 52-18-824 | KT 9 | 52×62×22 |
| 159 | 52-12-009 | KT 9 | 139×91×27 |
| 160 | 52-12-040 | KT 9 | 41×52×18 |
| 161 | 52-12-024 | KT 9 | 42×43×20 |
| 162 | 52-12-045 | KT 9 | 79×57×24 |
| 163 | 52-12-031 | KT 9 | 48×66×23 |
| 164 | 52-12-005 | KT 9 | 100×68×28 |
| 165 | 52-14-037 | KT 10 | 37×46×15 |
| 166 | 52-14-091 | KT 10 | 50×70×22 |
| 167 | 52-00-063 | KT 11 | 46★×50★×24 |
| 168 | 52-18-791 | NM 19–20, KT 11–12 | 39×47×21 |
| 169 | 52-16-096 | KT 12 | 87★×63×28 |

| | | | |
|---|---|---|---|
| 170 | 52-14-082 | KT 12 | 107×82×28 |
| 171 | 52-19-145 | KT 12 | 55×90×23 |
| 172 | 52-14-038 | KT 12 | 39×47×18 |
| 173 | 52-18-792 | KT 12 | 37×48×19 |
| 174 | 52-19-123 | KT 13 | 65×88×27 |
| 175 | 52-18-841 | KT 13 | 60×88×25 |
| 176 | 52-12-017 | KT 13 | 110×80×26 |
| 177 | 52-14-077 | KT 15 | 42×48×20 |
| 178 | 52-16-097 | KT 15 | 81×56×25 |
| 179 | 52-13-192 | KT 15 | 98★×67×26 |
| 180 | 52-18-857 | KT 2–15? | 52×80×23 |
| 181 | 52-13-112 | KT 15–17 | 51×75×22 |
| 182 | 52-13-100 | KT x | 57×81×23 |
| 183 | 52-18-765 | KT x | 41×45×18 |
| 184 | 52-20-307 | KT x | 65×91×26 |
| 185 | 52-20-308 | KT x | 58×80★×26 |
| 186 | 52-12-047 | n.d. | 58×83×25 |
| 187 | 52-12-012 | KaE 3 | 111×60×26 |
| 188 | 52-16-113 | year 8 | 52×70×24 |
| 189 | 52-16-109 | year 8 | 53★×35★×21 |
| 190 | 52-16-027 | n.d. | 52×44★×20★ |

#### 1.3.4 *aklu*-Expenditures of Foodstuffs

##### *i. Single* aklu-*Expenditures*

| | | | |
|---|---|---|---|
| 191 | 53-01-113 | NM 5 | 35×36×21 |
| 192 | 52-17-256 | NM 9 | 37×42★×20 |
| 193 | 52-13-061 | NM 12 | 38×44×21 |
| 194 | 52-18-789 | NM 13 | 28×33×17 |
| 195 | 52-16-053 | NM 13 | 29×32×20 |
| 196 | 52-13-002 | NM 13 | 31×33×20 |
| 197 | 52-19-138 | NM 13 | 26×27×17 |
| 198 | 52-19-130 | NM 15 | 27×35×20 |
| 199 | 52-13-055 | NM 16 | 37×43×20 |
| 200 | 52-13-063 | NM 16 | 39×40×19★ |
| 201 | 52-13-005 | NM 16 | 39×41×23 |
| 202 | 52-13-007 | NM 18 | 30×37×15 |
| 203 | 52-16-058 | NM 21+ | 30×37×18 |
| 204 | 53-02-149 | NM x | 32×35×23 |
| 205 | 52-13-057 | KT 1 | 31×41×20 |
| 206 | 52-13-013 | KT 2 | 39×48×20 |
| 207 | 52-16-055 | KT 2 | 26×32×15 |
| 208 | 52-13-006 | KT 2 | 24×32×17 |
| 209 | 52-13-010 | KT 2+ | 32×34★×17 |
| 210 | 52-13-014 | KT 3 | 38×43★×20 |
| 211 | 53-01-110 | KT 4 | 38×43×22 |
| 212 | 52-15-025 | KT 5 | 49×53×20 |
| 213 | 52-16-051 | KT 7 | 32×40×16 |
| 214 | 52-16-045 | KT 7 | 42×45×21 |
| 215 | 52-15-024 | KT 8 | 40★×46×22 |
| 216 | 52-16-054 | KT 9 | 25×34×15 |
| 217 | 52-16-052 | KT 10 | 33×38×18 |
| 218 | 52-17-255 | KT 11 | 37×39×18 |
| 219 | 52-16-021 | KT 11 | 39×46×19 |
| 220 | 52-19-113 | KT 11 | 48×60×22 |
| 221 | 52-12-035 | KT 11 | 38×44×17 |
| 222 | 52-13-058 | KT 12 | 35×45×20 |
| 223 | 52-13-004 | KT 12 | 41×50×19 |
| 224 | 52-15-026 | KT 13 | 45×33★×20 |
| 225 | 52-13-011 | KT 13 | 35×40×15 |
| 226 | 52-13-001 | KT 14 | 39×48×18 |
| 227 | 52-12-034 | KT 14 | 40×47×18 |
| 228 | 52-16-047 | KT 14 | 41×45×18 |
| 229 | 52-18-160 | KT 14 | 43×42★×18 |
| 230 | 52-16-020 | KT 15 | 44×52×19 |
| 231 | 52-16-048 | KT 16 | 38×45×18 |
| 232 | 52-20-317 | KT x | 35×38★×17 |
| 233 | 52-16-059 | KT x | 52×54×22 |
| 234 | 52-13-012 | KT x | 37×43×18 |
| 235 | 53-01-096 | n.d. | 43×45×20 |

##### *ii. Summaries of* aklu-*Expenditures*

| | | | |
|---|---|---|---|
| 236 | 52-18-767 | NM 8 | 27×35×15 |
| 237 | 52-18-764 | NM 9 | 52×66×24 |
| 238 | 52-13-060 | NM 19 | 35×40×20 |
| 239 | 53-01-167 | NM 22 | 83×59×22 |
| 240 | 52-18-815 | KT 8 | 45×48×22 |
| 241 | 52-14-085 | KT 13? | 68×100×28 |
| 242 | 52-16-056 | KT 14 | 43×55★×20 |
| 243 | 52-19-141 | KT x | 43×51×19 |
| 244 | 52-13-079 | KuE 8 | 76×55×17 |
| 245 | 52-12-063 | KuE 9 | 26×33×17 |

## 2. Administration of Animal Husbandry

### 2.1 Sheep

| | | | |
|---|---|---|---|
| 246 | 53-01-132 | NM 14 | 36×35×20 |
| 247 | 52-18-771 | NM 19 | 30×33×21 |
| 248 | 52-16-070 | NM 21 | 46×36×18 |

| | | | |
|---|---|---|---|
| 249 | 53-01-160 | (NM) 24 | 40×40*×14 |
| 250 | 52-18-795 | KT 4? | 35×44×20 |
| 251 | 52-18-798 | KT 5 | 30×39×17 |
| 252 | 52-12-053 | KT 14 | 45×60×20 |
| 253 | 52-13-083 | ŠŠ 1 | 67×44×20 |

2.2 Goats

| | | | |
|---|---|---|---|
| 254 | 52-18-770 | NM 19 | 67×46×23 |

2.3 Sheep and Goats

| | | | |
|---|---|---|---|
| 255 | 52-10-122 | NM 4 | 51×42×20 |
| 256 | 52-16-068 | NM 9 | 45×52*×20 |
| 257 | 52-12-027 | NM 17 | 70×47×22 |
| 258 | 52-18-863 | NM 19 | 48×80×25 |
| 259 | 52-20-311 | NM 20 | 26*×65*×25* |
| 260 | 52-19-142 | NM x | 42×94×23 |
| 261 | 52-20-310 | n.d. | 83×135×34 |
| 262 | 52-16-112 | n.d. | 45*×52×24 |

2.4 Cattle

| | | | |
|---|---|---|---|
| 263 | 52-16-028 | NM 23 | 60×40×23 |
| 264 | 52-13-003 | KT 6 | 82×56×24 |
| 265 | 52-18-136 | KT 7 | 47*×47×24 |
| 266 | 52-16-111 | n.d. | 73*×62×28 |

## 3. Textile Production

3.1 Allocation of Wool as Work Material

| | | | |
|---|---|---|---|
| 267 | 52-13-109 | NM 16 | 63×97×25 |
| 268 | 52-16-091 | KT 1 | 32×42×13 |
| 269 | 52-17-270 | KT 8 | 36×37×18 |
| 270 | 52-12-033 | KT 9 | 41×51×20 |
| 271 | 52-18-152 | KT 13 | 35*×51×22 |
| 272 | 52-18-796 | KT 16 | 36×43×20 |

3.2 Garments and Textiles

| | | | |
|---|---|---|---|
| 273 | 52-12-043 | KT 1 | 54×43×20 |
| 274 | 52-13-056 | KT 2 | 34×39×21 |
| 275 | 52-16-066 | KT? 5 | 44×59×23 |
| 276 | 52-16-046 | KT 6 | 28×34×17 |
| 277 | 52-10-088 | KT 6? | 175*×80×30 |
| 278 | 52-16-050 | KT 7 | 39×47×19 |
| 279 | 52-13-059 | KT 7 | 33×43×17 |
| 280 | 52-16-081 | KT 9 | 37×40×17 |
| 281 | 52-14-029 | KT 15 | 36×38×18 |
| 282 | 52-14-099 | KT 15? | 26×31×14 |
| 283 | 52-12-062 | KT 15? | 28×31×17 |
| 284 | 52-16-092 | KT 16 | 31×36×15 |
| 285 | 52-12-061 | KT 16 | 28×40×15 |
| 286 | 52-15-028 | KT 16 | 41×47×20 |
| 287 | 52-13-107 | KT 17 | 37×43×20 |
| 288 | 52-14-043 | KT 17 | 30×35×17 |
| 289 | 52-12-057 | (KT) 17 | 27×28×15 |
| 290 | 52-15-027 | KT x | 40×48×22 |

## 4. Miscellaneous Administrative Texts

4.1 Personnel Lists

| | | | |
|---|---|---|---|
| 291 | 53-01-142 | KT 5–7 | 70×119×27 |
| 292 | 52-19-003 | n.d. | 75×48×20 |

4.2 Beer

| | | | |
|---|---|---|---|
| 293 | 53-02-148 | NM 5 | 28×32×20 |

4.3 Beer and Bread

| | | | |
|---|---|---|---|
| 294 | 52-12-051 | NM 19 | 45×52×23 |

4.4 Beer and Draff

| | | | |
|---|---|---|---|
| 295 | 52-19-120 | KT 9 | 52×66×24 |

4.5 Pig's Fat

| | | | |
|---|---|---|---|
| 296 | 52-10-105 | KT 12 | 44×61×19 |

4.6 Receipt of Aromatics and Disbursement of Cereal

| | | | |
|---|---|---|---|
| 297 | 52-13-194 | KT 6 | 92×59×25 |

4.7 Hides

| | | | |
|---|---|---|---|
| 298 | 52-16-026 | NM 22 | 42×59×21 |
| 299 | 52-13-088 | SS x | 47×51×21 |

4.8 Bricks

| | | | |
|---|---|---|---|
| 300 | 52-18-818 | KT 3 | 45×63×21 |

4.9 Paint

| | | | |
|---|---|---|---|
| 301 | 52-12-028 | KT 3 | 43×54×21★ |

4.10 Wood

| | | | |
|---|---|---|---|
| 302 | 53-01-111 | KT 10 | 35×46×18 |

4.11 Sickles

| | | | |
|---|---|---|---|
| 303 | 52-18-797 | NM 23 | 43×50×19 |

4.12 Sacks

| | | | |
|---|---|---|---|
| 304 | 52-13-077 | NM 15 | 33×45×17 |

4.13 Metal

| | | | |
|---|---|---|---|
| 305 | 52-13-196 | KT 11 | 34×45×20 |

4.14 Inventory of Precious Goods

| | | | |
|---|---|---|---|
| 306 | 52-12-038 | n.d. | 40×42×20 |

4.15 Uncertain

| | | | |
|---|---|---|---|
| 307 | 52-10-112 | (NM?) 21 | 51×61×24 |
| 308 | 52-18-867 | NM 18–22 | 165★×139×37 |
| 309 | 52-16-073 | KT 2 | 30×42×18 |
| 310 | 52-16-080 | KT 7 | 35×50×20 |
| 311 | 52-13-131 | KT 11 | 38×49×21 |
| 312 | 52-17-268 | KT 12 | 41★×60×17★ |
| 313 | 52-17-260 | KT 12 | 46×54×21 |
| 314 | 52-18-763 | KT 12 | 40×48×19★ |
| 315 | 52-18-814 | KT 13 | 49×70×23 |
| 316 | 52-18-842 | year 17 | 62×62★×23 |
| 317 | 52-13-084 | n.d. | 37×51×19 |
| 318 | 52-12-065 | n.d. | 24×31×15 |
| 319 | 52-13-082 | n.d. | 45×54×21 |
| 320 | 52-00-052 | n.d. | 50×59×22 |
| 321 | 52-00-054 | n.d. | 34★×23★×19 |
| 322 | 52-16-106 | n.d. | 58★×36★×23 |
| 323 | 53-01-124 | n.d. | 22★×32★×16★ |

## 5. Legal Texts

5.1 *Tuppi aḫūzati*

| | | | |
|---|---|---|---|
| 324 | 52-10-089 | BB 18 | 87×60×26 |

5.2 Contract of Exchange

| | | | |
|---|---|---|---|
| 325 | 52-13-101 | NM 14 | 64×48×22 |

5.3 Purchase of an Ox

| | | | |
|---|---|---|---|
| 326 | 52-14-030 | NM 22 | 83★×54★×26 |

5.4 Settlements of Disputes

| | | | |
|---|---|---|---|
| 327 | 52-16-105 | KT 5 | 64×43×17 |
| 328 | 52-16-069 | KT 17 | 60×42×22 |

5.5 Loans

| | | | |
|---|---|---|---|
| 329 | 52-16-088 | KT 5 | 39×46★×17 |
| 330 | 52-10-064 | KT 14 | 52×62×21 |
| 331 | 52-18-142 | KT x | 78×49×23 |

5.6 Uncertain

| | | | |
|---|---|---|---|
| 332 | 53-00-040 | NM 23 | 34×43×19 |
| 333 | 53-02-150 | NM x | 83×54×25 |
| 334 | 52-00-053 | n.d. | 35★×27★×18★ |

## 6. Letters

| | | | |
|---|---|---|---|
| 335 | 52-12-066 | n.d. | 58×43×21 |
| 336 | 52-12-030 | n.d. | 50×39×18 |
| 337 | 52-12-032 | n.d. | 67×47×21 |
| 338 | 52-12-039 | n.d. | 61×45×20 |

# CONCORDANCES

*Texts Arranged by CUNES Number*

| CUNES no. | Text no. | Date |
|---|---|---|
| 52-00-049 | 123 | KT 9 |
| 52-00-050 | 117 | n.d. |
| 52-00-052 | 320 | n.d. |
| 52-00-053 | 334 | n.d. |
| 52-00-054 | 321 | n.d. |
| 52-00-062 | 118 | KT 9 |
| 52-00-063 | 167 | KT 11 |
| 52-00-072 | 103 | KT x |
| 52-00-091 | 16 | KT x |
| 52-10-041 | 3 | KT 5 |
| 52-10-042 | 10 | KT 12 |
| 52-10-043 | 35 | KT 13 |
| 52-10-044 | 7 | KT 11 |
| 52-10-045 | 12 | KT 13 |
| 52-10-046 | 8 | KT 11 |
| 52-10-047 | 5 | KT 8 |
| 52-10-048 | 14 | KT 14 |
| 52-10-049 | 15 | KT 14 |
| 52-10-050 | 36 | year 5 |
| 52-10-051 | 13 | KT 13 |
| 52-10-052 | 22 | NM 19 |
| 52-10-053 | 52 | KT 11 |
| 52-10-054 | 56 | KT 13 |
| 52-10-055 | 53 | KT 12 |
| 52-10-056 | 38 | KT 3 |
| 52-10-057 | 54 | KT 12 |
| 52-10-058 | 143 | KT 1 |
| 52-10-059 | 151 | KT 3 |
| 52-10-060 | 25 | KT 1 |
| 52-10-061 | 11 | KT 12 |
| 52-10-062 | 32 | KT 11 |
| 52-10-063 | 43 | KT 1 |
| 52-10-064 | 330 | KT 14 |
| 52-10-065 | 148 | KT 2 |
| 52-10-066 | 157 | KT 8 |
| 52-10-067 | 115 | KT 6 |
| 52-10-068 | 149 | KT 2 |
| 52-10-071 | 27 | NM 20 |
| 52-10-072 | 108 | KT 3 |

| CUNES no. | Text no. | Date |
|---|---|---|
| 52-10-073 | 28 | NM 24 |
| 52-10-074 | 125 | (NM) 21–23 |
| 52-10-077 | 135 | (NM) 21$^{+}$ |
| 52-10-078 | 18 | KT 3 |
| 52-10-079 | 49 | KT 1 |
| 52-10-080 | 26 | NM 18 |
| 52-10-082 | 31 | KT 5 |
| 52-10-088 | 277 | KT 6$^{?}$ |
| 52-10-089 | 324 | BB 18 |
| 52-10-090 | 113 | KT 3 |
| 52-10-092 | 114 | KT 4 |
| 52-10-093 | 156 | KT 8 |
| 52-10-094 | 45 | KT 4 |
| 52-10-095 | 57 | KT x |
| 52-10-096 | 48 | NM 24 |
| 52-10-102 | 139 | NM x |
| 52-10-103 | 1 | NM 22 |
| 52-10-105 | 296 | KT 12 |
| 52-10-106 | 24 | KT 15$^{?}$ |
| 52-10-112 | 307 | (NM$^{?}$) 21 |
| 52-10-116 | 95 | KT 6 |
| 52-10-118 | 94 | KT 2 |
| 52-10-119 | 106 | NM 23 |
| 52-10-122 | 255 | NM 4 |
| 52-10-123 | 40 | NM 9$^{!}$ |
| 52-10-124 | 42 | NM 19 |
| 52-12-003 | 2 | KT 1 |
| 52-12-004 | 4 | KT 8$^{?}$ |
| 52-12-005 | 164 | KT 9 |
| 52-12-006 | 33 | KT 12$^{?}$ |
| 52-12-007 | 116 | KT 9 |
| 52-12-008 | 112 | NM 19 |
| 52-12-009 | 159 | KT 9 |
| 52-12-010 | 119 | KT 9 |
| 52-12-011 | 47 | NM 21 |
| 52-12-012 | 187 | KaE 3 |
| 52-12-013 | 150 | KT 3 |
| 52-12-014 | 37 | KT 1 |
| 52-12-015 | 23 | KT 10 |

| CUNES no. | Text no. | Date |
|---|---|---|
| 52-12-016 | 97 | KT 9 |
| 52-12-017 | 176 | KT 13 |
| 52-12-019 | 6 | KT 8 |
| 52-12-020 | 55 | KT 12 |
| 52-12-022 | 144 | KT 1 |
| 52-12-023 | 141 | NM 24–KT 3 |
| 52-12-024 | 161 | KT 9 |
| 52-12-025 | 69 | KT 9 |
| 52-12-026 | 71 | KT 9 |
| 52-12-027 | 257 | NM 17 |
| 52-12-028 | 301 | KT 3 |
| 52-12-029 | 107 | KT 2 |
| 52-12-030 | 336 | n.d. |
| 52-12-031 | 163 | KT 9 |
| 52-12-032 | 337 | n.d. |
| 52-12-033 | 270 | KT 9 |
| 52-12-034 | 227 | KT 14 |
| 52-12-035 | 221 | KT 11 |
| 52-12-036 | 111 | NM 18$^{?}$ |
| 52-12-038 | 306 | n.d. |
| 52-12-039 | 338 | n.d. |
| 52-12-040 | 160 | KT 9 |
| 52-12-041 | 130 | NM 18 |
| 52-12-043 | 273 | KT 1 |
| 52-12-044 | 64 | NM 18$^{?}$ |
| 52-12-045 | 162 | KT 9 |
| 52-12-046 | 131 | NM 18 |
| 52-12-047 | 186 | n.d. |
| 52-12-048 | 51 | KT 7 |
| 52-12-050 | 65 | NM 18 |
| 52-12-051 | 294 | NM 19 |
| 52-12-052 | 61 | n.d. |
| 52-12-053 | 252 | KT 14 |
| 52-12-055 | 80 | KT 13$^{+}$ |
| 52-12-057 | 289 | (KT) 17 |
| 52-12-058 | 92 | NM 19 |
| 52-12-061 | 285 | KT 16 |
| 52-12-062 | 283 | KT 15$^{?}$ |
| 52-12-063 | 245 | KuE 9 |
| 52-12-065 | 318 | n.d. |
| 52-12-066 | 335 | n.d. |
| 52-13-001 | 226 | KT 14 |
| 52-13-002 | 196 | NM 13 |
| 52-13-003 | 264 | KT 6 |

| CUNES no. | Text no. | Date |
|---|---|---|
| 52-13-004 | 223 | KT 12 |
| 52-13-005 | 201 | NM 16 |
| 52-13-006 | 208 | KT 2 |
| 52-13-007 | 202 | NM 18 |
| 52-13-010 | 209 | KT 2$^{+}$ |
| 52-13-011 | 225 | KT 13 |
| 52-13-012 | 234 | KT x |
| 52-13-013 | 206 | KT 2 |
| 52-13-014 | 210 | KT 3 |
| 52-13-055 | 199 | NM 16 |
| 52-13-056 | 274 | KT 2 |
| 52-13-057 | 205 | KT 1 |
| 52-13-058 | 222 | KT 12 |
| 52-13-059 | 279 | KT 7 |
| 52-13-060 | 238 | NM 19 |
| 52-13-061 | 193 | NM 12 |
| 52-13-063 | 200 | NM 16 |
| 52-13-074 | 142 | NM 24–KT 3 |
| 52-13-077 | 304 | NM 15 |
| 52-13-078 | 109 | n.d. |
| 52-13-079 | 244 | KuE 8 |
| 52-13-082 | 319 | n.d. |
| 52-13-083 | 253 | ŠŠ 1 |
| 52-13-084 | 317 | n.d. |
| 52-13-088 | 299 | SS x |
| 52-13-100 | 182 | KT x |
| 52-13-101 | 325 | NM 14 |
| 52-13-107 | 287 | KT 17 |
| 52-13-109 | 267 | NM 16 |
| 52-13-110 | 96 | KT 9 |
| 52-13-111 | 133 | NM 20 |
| 52-13-112 | 181 | KT 15–17 |
| 52-13-131 | 311 | KT 11 |
| 52-13-132 | 122 | KT 14 |
| 52-13-134 | 44 | KT 1 |
| 52-13-139 | 129 | NM 17 |
| 52-13-153 | 121 | NM 13$^{?}$–KT 3 |
| 52-13-165 | 82 | KT 14 |
| 52-13-184 | 147 | KT 2 |
| 52-13-192 | 179 | KT 15 |
| 52-13-194 | 297 | KT 6 |
| 52-13-196 | 305 | KT 11 |
| 52-14-025 | 88 | KT x |
| 52-14-029 | 281 | KT 15 |

| CUNES no. | Text no. | Date |
|---|---|---|
| 52-14-030 | 326 | NM 22 |
| 52-14-032 | 84 | KT 14 |
| 52-14-037 | 165 | KT 10 |
| 52-14-038 | 172 | KT 12 |
| 52-14-043 | 288 | KT 17 |
| 52-14-045 | 83 | KT 14 |
| 52-14-047 | 126 | KT 13 |
| 52-14-070 | 34 | KT 12 |
| 52-14-074 | 58 | NM 18[?] |
| 52-14-076 | 30 | KT 4 |
| 52-14-077 | 177 | KT 15 |
| 52-14-082 | 170 | KT 12 |
| 52-14-085 | 241 | KT 13[?] |
| 52-14-091 | 166 | KT 10 |
| 52-14-098 | 74 | KT 10 |
| 52-14-099 | 282 | KT 15[?] |
| 52-14-100 | 73 | KT 10 |
| 52-14-101 | 76 | KT 12 |
| 52-14-102 | 89 | KT x |
| 52-15-024 | 215 | KT 8 |
| 52-15-025 | 212 | KT 5 |
| 52-15-026 | 224 | KT 13 |
| 52-15-027 | 290 | KT x |
| 52-15-028 | 286 | KT 16 |
| 52-15-030 | 99 | KT 9 |
| 52-15-044 | 19 | KT 12 |
| 52-16-017 | 59 | KT 4 |
| 52-16-018 | 46 | KT x |
| 52-16-019 | 9 | KT 11 |
| 52-16-020 | 230 | KT 15 |
| 52-16-021 | 219 | KT 11 |
| 52-16-026 | 298 | NM 22 |
| 52-16-027 | 190 | n.d. |
| 52-16-028 | 263 | NM 23 |
| 52-16-038 | 138 | NM x |
| 52-16-045 | 214 | KT 7 |
| 52-16-046 | 276 | KT 6 |
| 52-16-047 | 228 | KT 14 |
| 52-16-048 | 231 | KT 16 |
| 52-16-050 | 278 | KT 7 |
| 52-16-051 | 213 | KT 7 |
| 52-16-052 | 217 | KT 10 |
| 52-16-053 | 195 | NM 13 |
| 52-16-054 | 216 | KT 9 |

| CUNES no. | Text no. | Date |
|---|---|---|
| 52-16-055 | 207 | KT 2 |
| 52-16-056 | 242 | KT 14 |
| 52-16-058 | 203 | NM 21[+] |
| 52-16-059 | 233 | KT x |
| 52-16-066 | 275 | KT[?] 5 |
| 52-16-068 | 256 | NM 9 |
| 52-16-069 | 328 | KT 17 |
| 52-16-070 | 248 | NM 21 |
| 52-16-071 | 104 | ŠŠ 2 |
| 52-16-073 | 309 | KT 2 |
| 52-16-075 | 68 | KT 7 |
| 52-16-076 | 70 | KT 9 |
| 52-16-078 | 72 | KT 9 |
| 52-16-080 | 310 | KT 7 |
| 52-16-081 | 280 | KT 9 |
| 52-16-084 | 63 | NM 8 |
| 52-16-088 | 329 | KT 5 |
| 52-16-090 | 81 | KT 14 |
| 52-16-091 | 268 | KT 1 |
| 52-16-092 | 284 | KT 16 |
| 52-16-096 | 169 | KT 12 |
| 52-16-097 | 178 | KT 15 |
| 52-16-099 | 17 | (NM) 23 |
| 52-16-105 | 327 | KT 5 |
| 52-16-106 | 322 | n.d. |
| 52-16-108 | 91 | ŠŠ 1 |
| 52-16-109 | 189 | year 8 |
| 52-16-110 | 105 | (NM) 22 |
| 52-16-111 | 266 | n.d. |
| 52-16-112 | 262 | n.d. |
| 52-16-113 | 188 | year 8 |
| 52-17-255 | 218 | KT 11 |
| 52-17-256 | 192 | NM 9 |
| 52-17-260 | 313 | KT 12 |
| 52-17-266 | 79 | KT 13 |
| 52-17-268 | 312 | KT 12 |
| 52-17-270 | 269 | KT 8 |
| 52-17-274 | 145 | KT 2 |
| 52-17-276 | 75 | KT 11 |
| 52-17-286 | 146 | KT 2 |
| 52-18-136 | 265 | KT 7 |
| 52-18-142 | 331 | KT x |
| 52-18-152 | 271 | KT 13 |
| 52-18-160 | 229 | KT 14 |

| CUNES no. | Text no. | Date |
|---|---|---|
| 52-18-763 | 314 | KT 12 |
| 52-18-764 | 237 | NM 9 |
| 52-18-765 | 183 | KT x |
| 52-18-767 | 236 | NM 8 |
| 52-18-769 | 77 | KT 12 |
| 52-18-770 | 254 | NM 19 |
| 52-18-771 | 247 | NM 19 |
| 52-18-776 | 62 | NM 7 |
| 52-18-789 | 194 | NM 13 |
| 52-18-791 | 168 | NM 19–20, KT 11–12 |
| 52-18-792 | 173 | KT 12 |
| 52-18-794 | 127 | NM 10$^{+}$ |
| 52-18-795 | 250 | KT 4$^{?}$ |
| 52-18-796 | 272 | KT 16 |
| 52-18-797 | 303 | NM 23 |
| 52-18-798 | 251 | KT 5 |
| 52-18-799 | 66 | NM 20 |
| 52-18-800 | 90 | KT x |
| 52-18-810 | 39 | KT 10 |
| 52-18-812 | 100 | KT 12 |
| 52-18-814 | 315 | KT 13 |
| 52-18-815 | 240 | KT 8 |
| 52-18-816 | 134 | NM 21 |
| 52-18-818 | 300 | KT 3 |
| 52-18-824 | 158 | KT 9 |
| 52-18-833 | 20 | n.d. |
| 52-18-841 | 175 | KT 13 |
| 52-18-842 | 316 | year 17 |
| 52-18-857 | 180 | KT 2–15$^{?}$ |
| 52-18-859 | 153 | KT 6 |
| 52-18-860 | 60 | KT 12 |
| 52-18-863 | 258 | NM 19 |
| 52-18-864 | 154 | KT 6$^{?}$ |
| 52-18-865 | 120 | NM 19$^{?}$ |
| 52-18-867 | 308 | NM 18–22 |
| 52-19-003 | 292 | n.d. |
| 52-19-005 | 101 | KT 15 |
| 52-19-113 | 220 | KT 11 |
| 52-19-114 | 67 | NM 24$^{?}$ |
| 52-19-117 | 87 | KT 15 |
| 52-19-118 | 128 | NM 17$^{?}$ |
| 52-19-120 | 295 | KT 9 |
| 52-19-123 | 174 | KT 13 |
| 52-19-125 | 152 | KT 4 |
| 52-19-127 | 110 | NM 18 |
| 52-19-130 | 198 | NM 15 |
| 52-19-134 | 78 | KT 13 |
| 52-19-138 | 197 | NM 13 |
| 52-19-141 | 243 | KT x |
| 52-19-142 | 260 | NM x |
| 52-19-145 | 171 | KT 12 |
| 52-19-146 | 98 | KT 9 |
| 52-19-148 | 29 | NM 24 |
| 52-19-151 | 136 | NM 23 |
| 52-19-152 | 50 | KT 1 |
| 52-19-156 | 124 | NM [x]–21 |
| 52-20-301 | 41 | NM 18 |
| 52-20-303 | 137 | NM x |
| 52-20-305 | 21 | n.d. |
| 52-20-306 | 102 | KT 15 |
| 52-20-307 | 184 | KT x |
| 52-20-308 | 185 | KT x |
| 52-20-310 | 261 | n.d. |
| 52-20-311 | 259 | NM 20 |
| 52-20-317 | 232 | KT x |
| 52-20-319 | 140 | NM 21–KT 3 |
| 52-20-320 | 93 | KT 2 |
| 53-00-040 | 332 | NM 23 |
| 53-01-096 | 235 | n.d. |
| 53-01-110 | 211 | KT 4 |
| 53-01-111 | 302 | KT 10 |
| 53-01-113 | 191 | NM 5 |
| 53-01-114 | 155 | KT 8 |
| 53-01-116 | 86 | KT 15 |
| 53-01-124 | 323 | n.d. |
| 53-01-128 | 85 | KT 14 |
| 53-01-132 | 246 | NM 14 |
| 53-01-142 | 291 | KT 5–7 |
| 53-01-160 | 249 | (NM) 24 |
| 53-01-167 | 239 | NM 22 |
| 53-01-174 | 132 | NM 19 |
| 53-02-148 | 293 | NM 5 |
| 53-02-149 | 204 | NM x |
| 53-02-150 | 333 | NM x |

## *Texts Arranged by Date*

| Date | Text no. | CUNES no. |
|---|---|---|
| BB 18 | 324 | 52-10-089 |
| NM 4 | 255 | 52-10-122 |
| NM 5 | 191 | 53-01-113 |
| NM 5 | 293 | 53-02-148 |
| NM 7 | 62 | 52-18-776 |
| NM 8 | 63 | 52-16-084 |
| NM 8 | 236 | 52-18-767 |
| NM 9 | 192 | 52-17-256 |
| NM 9 | 237 | 52-18-764 |
| NM 9 | 256 | 52-16-068 |
| NM 9$^{+}$ | 40 | 52-10-123 |
| NM 10$^{+}$ | 127 | 52-18-794 |
| NM 12 | 193 | 52-13-061 |
| NM 13 | 194 | 52-18-789 |
| NM 13 | 195 | 52-16-053 |
| NM 13 | 196 | 52-13-002 |
| NM 13 | 197 | 52-19-138 |
| NM 14 | 246 | 53-01-132 |
| NM 14 | 325 | 52-13-101 |
| NM 15 | 198 | 52-19-130 |
| NM 15 | 304 | 52-13-077 |
| NM 16 | 199 | 52-13-055 |
| NM 16 | 200 | 52-13-063 |
| NM 16 | 201 | 52-13-005 |
| NM 16 | 267 | 52-13-109 |
| NM 17 | 129 | 52-13-139 |
| NM 17 | 257 | 52-12-027 |
| NM 17$^{?}$ | 128 | 52-19-118 |
| NM 18 | 26 | 52-10-080 |
| NM 18 | 41 | 52-20-301 |
| NM 18 | 65 | 52-12-050 |
| NM 18 | 110 | 52-19-127 |
| NM 18 | 130 | 52-12-041 |
| NM 18 | 131 | 52-12-046 |
| NM 18 | 202 | 52-13-007 |
| NM 18$^{?}$ | 58 | 52-14-074 |
| NM 18$^{?}$ | 64 | 52-12-044 |
| NM 18$^{?}$ | 111 | 52-12-036 |
| NM 19 | 22 | 52-10-052 |
| NM 19 | 42 | 52-10-124 |
| NM 19 | 92 | 52-12-058 |
| NM 19 | 112 | 52-12-008 |

| Date | Text no. | CUNES no. |
|---|---|---|
| NM 19 | 132 | 53-01-174 |
| NM 19 | 238 | 52-13-060 |
| NM 19 | 247 | 52-18-771 |
| NM 19 | 254 | 52-18-770 |
| NM 19 | 258 | 52-18-863 |
| NM 19 | 294 | 52-12-051 |
| NM 19$^{?}$ | 120 | 52-18-865 |
| NM 20 | 27 | 52-10-071 |
| NM 20 | 66 | 52-18-799 |
| NM 20 | 133 | 52-13-111 |
| NM 20 | 259 | 52-20-311 |
| NM 21 | 47 | 52-12-011 |
| NM 21 | 134 | 52-18-816 |
| NM 21 | 248 | 52-16-070 |
| (NM$^{?}$) 21 | 307 | 52-10-112 |
| (NM) 21$^{+}$ | 135 | 52-10-077 |
| NM 21$^{+}$ | 203 | 52-16-058 |
| NM [x]–21 | 124 | 52-19-156 |
| NM 22 | 1 | 52-10-103 |
| (NM) 22 | 105 | 52-16-110 |
| NM 22 | 239 | 53-01-167 |
| NM 22 | 298 | 52-16-026 |
| NM 22 | 326 | 52-14-030 |
| NM 18–22 | 308 | 52-18-867 |
| (NM) 23 | 17 | 52-16-099 |
| NM 23 | 106 | 52-10-119 |
| NM 23 | 136 | 52-19-151 |
| NM 23 | 263 | 52-16-028 |
| NM 23 | 303 | 52-18-797 |
| NM 23 | 332 | 53-00-040 |
| (NM) 21–23 | 125 | 52-10-074 |
| NM 24 | 28 | 52-10-073 |
| NM 24 | 29 | 52-19-148 |
| NM 24 | 48 | 52-10-096 |
| (NM) 24 | 249 | 53-01-160 |
| NM 24$^{?}$ | 67 | 52-19-114 |
| NM x | 137 | 52-20-303 |
| NM x | 138 | 52-16-038 |
| NM x | 139 | 52-10-102 |
| NM x | 204 | 53-02-149 |
| NM x | 260 | 52-19-142 |
| NM x | 333 | 53-02-150 |

| Date | Text no. | CUNES no. |
|---|---|---|
| KT 1 | 2 | 52-12-003 |
| KT 1 | 25 | 52-10-060 |
| KT 1 | 37 | 52-12-014 |
| KT 1 | 43 | 52-10-063 |
| KT 1 | 44 | 52-13-134 |
| KT 1 | 49 | 52-10-079 |
| KT 1 | 50 | 52-19-152 |
| KT 1 | 143 | 52-10-058 |
| KT 1 | 144 | 52-12-022 |
| KT 1 | 205 | 52-13-057 |
| KT 1 | 268 | 52-16-091 |
| KT 1 | 273 | 52-12-043 |
| KT 2 | 93 | 52-20-320 |
| KT 2 | 94 | 52-10-118 |
| KT 2 | 107 | 52-12-029 |
| KT 2 | 145 | 52-17-274 |
| KT 2 | 146 | 52-17-286 |
| KT 2 | 147 | 52-13-184 |
| KT 2 | 148 | 52-10-065 |
| KT 2 | 149 | 52-10-068 |
| KT 2 | 206 | 52-13-013 |
| KT 2 | 207 | 52-16-055 |
| KT 2 | 208 | 52-13-006 |
| KT 2 | 274 | 52-13-056 |
| KT 2 | 309 | 52-16-073 |
| KT 2$^{+}$ | 209 | 52-13-010 |
| KT 3 | 18 | 52-10-078 |
| KT 3 | 38 | 52-10-056 |
| KT 3 | 108 | 52-10-072 |
| KT 3 | 113 | 52-10-090 |
| KT 3 | 150 | 52-12-013 |
| KT 3 | 151 | 52-10-059 |
| KT 3 | 210 | 52-13-014 |
| KT 3 | 300 | 52-18-818 |
| KT 3 | 301 | 52-12-028 |
| NM 13$^{?}$–KT 3 | 121 | 52-13-153 |
| NM 21–KT 3 | 140 | 52-20-319 |
| NM 24–KT 3 | 141 | 52-12-023 |
| NM 24–KT 3 | 142 | 52-13-074 |
| KT 4 | 30 | 52-14-076 |
| KT 4 | 45 | 52-10-094 |
| KT 4 | 59 | 52-16-017 |
| KT 4 | 114 | 52-10-092 |
| KT 4 | 152 | 52-19-125 |

| Date | Text no. | CUNES no. |
|---|---|---|
| KT 4 | 211 | 53-01-110 |
| KT 4$^{?}$ | 250 | 52-18-795 |
| KT 5 | 3 | 52-10-041 |
| KT 5 | 31 | 52-10-082 |
| KT 5 | 212 | 52-15-025 |
| KT 5 | 251 | 52-18-798 |
| KT 5 | 327 | 52-16-105 |
| KT 5 | 329 | 52-16-088 |
| KT 6 | 95 | 52-10-116 |
| KT 6 | 115 | 52-10-067 |
| KT 6 | 153 | 52-18-859 |
| KT 6 | 264 | 52-13-003 |
| KT 6 | 276 | 52-16-046 |
| KT 6 | 297 | 52-13-194 |
| KT 6$^{?}$ | 154 | 52-18-864 |
| KT 6$^{?}$ | 277 | 52-10-088 |
| KT 7 | 51 | 52-12-048 |
| KT 7 | 68 | 52-16-075 |
| KT 7 | 213 | 52-16-051 |
| KT 7 | 214 | 52-16-045 |
| KT 7 | 265 | 52-18-136 |
| KT 7 | 278 | 52-16-050 |
| KT 7 | 279 | 52-13-059 |
| KT 7 | 310 | 52-16-080 |
| KT 5–7 | 291 | 53-01-142 |
| KT 8 | 5 | 52-10-047 |
| KT 8 | 6 | 52-12-019 |
| KT 8 | 155 | 53-01-114 |
| KT 8 | 156 | 52-10-093 |
| KT 8 | 157 | 52-10-066 |
| KT 8 | 215 | 52-15-024 |
| KT 8 | 240 | 52-18-815 |
| KT 8 | 269 | 52-17-270 |
| KT 8$^{?}$ | 4 | 52-12-004 |
| KT 9 | 69 | 52-12-025 |
| KT 9 | 70 | 52-16-076 |
| KT 9 | 71 | 52-12-026 |
| KT 9 | 72 | 52-16-078 |
| KT 9 | 96 | 52-13-110 |
| KT 9 | 97 | 52-12-016 |
| KT 9 | 98 | 52-19-146 |
| KT 9 | 99 | 52-15-030 |
| KT 9 | 116 | 52-12-007 |
| KT 9 | 118 | 52-00-062 |

| Date | Text no. | CUNES no. |
|---|---|---|
| KT 9 | 119 | 52-12-010 |
| KT 9 | 123 | 52-00-049 |
| KT 9 | 158 | 52-18-824 |
| KT 9 | 159 | 52-12-009 |
| KT 9 | 160 | 52-12-040 |
| KT 9 | 161 | 52-12-024 |
| KT 9 | 162 | 52-12-045 |
| KT 9 | 163 | 52-12-031 |
| KT 9 | 164 | 52-12-005 |
| KT 9 | 216 | 52-16-054 |
| KT 9 | 270 | 52-12-033 |
| KT 9 | 280 | 52-16-081 |
| KT 9 | 295 | 52-19-120 |
| KT 10 | 23 | 52-12-015 |
| KT 10 | 39 | 52-18-810 |
| KT 10 | 73 | 52-14-100 |
| KT 10 | 74 | 52-14-098 |
| KT 10 | 165 | 52-14-037 |
| KT 10 | 166 | 52-14-091 |
| KT 10 | 217 | 52-16-052 |
| KT 10 | 302 | 53-01-111 |
| KT 11 | 7 | 52-10-044 |
| KT 11 | 8 | 52-10-046 |
| KT 11 | 9 | 52-16-019 |
| KT 11 | 32 | 52-10-062 |
| KT 11 | 52 | 52-10-053 |
| KT 11 | 75 | 52-17-276 |
| KT 11 | 167 | 52-00-063 |
| KT 11 | 218 | 52-17-255 |
| KT 11 | 219 | 52-16-021 |
| KT 11 | 220 | 52-19-113 |
| KT 11 | 221 | 52-12-035 |
| KT 11 | 305 | 52-13-196 |
| KT 11 | 311 | 52-13-131 |
| NM 19–20, KT 11–12 | 168 | 52-18-791 |
| KT 12 | 10 | 52-10-042 |
| KT 12 | 11 | 52-10-061 |
| KT 12 | 19 | 52-15-044 |
| KT 12 | 34 | 52-14-070 |
| KT 12 | 53 | 52-10-055 |
| KT 12 | 54 | 52-10-057 |
| KT 12 | 55 | 52-12-020 |
| KT 12 | 60 | 52-18-860 |
| KT 12 | 76 | 52-14-101 |
| KT 12 | 77 | 52-18-769 |
| KT 12 | 100 | 52-18-812 |
| KT 12 | 169 | 52-16-096 |
| KT 12 | 170 | 52-14-082 |
| KT 12 | 171 | 52-19-145 |
| KT 12 | 172 | 52-14-038 |
| KT 12 | 173 | 52-18-792 |
| KT 12 | 222 | 52-13-058 |
| KT 12 | 223 | 52-13-004 |
| KT 12 | 296 | 52-10-105 |
| KT 12 | 312 | 52-17-268 |
| KT 12 | 313 | 52-17-260 |
| KT 12 | 314 | 52-18-763 |
| KT 12? | 33 | 52-12-006 |
| KT 13 | 12 | 52-10-045 |
| KT 13 | 13 | 52-10-051 |
| KT 13 | 35 | 52-10-043 |
| KT 13 | 56 | 52-10-054 |
| KT 13 | 78 | 52-19-134 |
| KT 13 | 79 | 52-17-266 |
| KT 13 | 126 | 52-14-047 |
| KT 13 | 174 | 52-19-123 |
| KT 13 | 175 | 52-18-841 |
| KT 13 | 176 | 52-12-017 |
| KT 13 | 224 | 52-15-026 |
| KT 13 | 225 | 52-13-011 |
| KT 13 | 271 | 52-18-152 |
| KT 13 | 315 | 52-18-814 |
| KT 13? | 241 | 52-14-085 |
| KT 13+ | 80 | 52-12-055 |
| KT 14 | 14 | 52-10-048 |
| KT 14 | 15 | 52-10-049 |
| KT 14 | 81 | 52-16-090 |
| KT 14 | 82 | 52-13-165 |
| KT 14 | 83 | 52-14-045 |
| KT 14 | 84 | 52-14-032 |
| KT 14 | 85 | 53-01-128 |
| KT 14 | 122 | 52-13-132 |
| KT 14 | 226 | 52-13-001 |
| KT 14 | 227 | 52-12-034 |
| KT 14 | 228 | 52-16-047 |
| KT 14 | 229 | 52-18-160 |
| KT 14 | 242 | 52-16-056 |
| KT 14 | 252 | 52-12-053 |

| Date | Text no. | CUNES no. |
|---|---|---|
| KT 14 | 330 | 52-10-064 |
| KT 15 | 86 | 53-01-116 |
| KT 15 | 87 | 52-19-117 |
| KT 15 | 101 | 52-19-005 |
| KT 15 | 102 | 52-20-306 |
| KT 15 | 177 | 52-14-077 |
| KT 15 | 178 | 52-16-097 |
| KT 15 | 179 | 52-13-192 |
| KT 15 | 230 | 52-16-020 |
| KT 15 | 281 | 52-14-029 |
| KT 15$^{?}$ | 24 | 52-10-106 |
| KT 15$^{?}$ | 282 | 52-14-099 |
| KT 15$^{?}$ | 283 | 52-12-062 |
| KT 2–15$^{?}$ | 180 | 52-18-857 |
| KT 16 | 231 | 52-16-048 |
| KT 16 | 272 | 52-18-796 |
| KT 16 | 284 | 52-16-092 |
| KT 16 | 285 | 52-12-061 |
| KT 16 | 286 | 52-15-028 |
| KT 17 | 287 | 52-13-107 |
| KT 17 | 288 | 52-14-043 |
| (KT) 17 | 289 | 52-12-057 |
| KT 17 | 328 | 52-16-069 |
| KT 15–17 | 181 | 52-13-112 |
| KT x | 16 | 52-00-091 |
| KT x | 46 | 52-16-018 |
| KT x | 57 | 52-10-095 |
| KT x | 88 | 52-14-025 |
| KT x | 89 | 52-14-102 |
| KT x | 90 | 52-18-800 |
| KT x | 103 | 52-00-072 |
| KT x | 182 | 52-13-100 |
| KT x | 183 | 52-18-765 |
| KT x | 184 | 52-20-307 |
| KT x | 185 | 52-20-308 |
| KT x | 232 | 52-20-317 |
| KT x | 233 | 52-16-059 |
| KT x | 234 | 52-13-012 |
| KT x | 243 | 52-19-141 |

| Date | Text no. | CUNES no. |
|---|---|---|
| KT x | 290 | 52-15-027 |
| KT x | 331 | 52-18-142 |
| KT$^{?}$ 5 | 275 | 52-16-066 |
| KaE 3 | 187 | 52-12-012 |
| KuE 8 | 244 | 52-13-079 |
| KuE 9 | 245 | 52-12-063 |
| ŠŠ 1 | 91 | 52-16-108 |
| ŠŠ 1 | 253 | 52-13-083 |
| ŠŠ 2 | 104 | 52-16-071 |
| ŠŠ x | 299 | 52-13-088 |
| year 5 | 36 | 52-10-050 |
| year 8 | 188 | 52-16-113 |
| year 8 | 189 | 52-16-109 |
| year 17 | 316 | 52-18-842 |
| n.d. | 20 | 52-18-833 |
| n.d. | 21 | 52-20-305 |
| n.d. | 61 | 52-12-052 |
| n.d. | 109 | 52-13-078 |
| n.d. | 117 | 52-00-050 |
| n.d. | 186 | 52-12-047 |
| n.d. | 190 | 52-16-027 |
| n.d. | 235 | 53-01-096 |
| n.d. | 261 | 52-20-310 |
| n.d. | 262 | 52-16-112 |
| n.d. | 266 | 52-16-111 |
| n.d. | 292 | 52-19-003 |
| n.d. | 306 | 52-12-038 |
| n.d. | 317 | 52-13-084 |
| n.d. | 318 | 52-12-065 |
| n.d. | 319 | 52-13-082 |
| n.d. | 320 | 52-00-052 |
| n.d. | 321 | 52-00-054 |
| n.d. | 322 | 52-16-106 |
| n.d. | 323 | 53-01-124 |
| n.d. | 334 | 52-00-053 |
| n.d. | 335 | 52-12-066 |
| n.d. | 336 | 52-12-030 |
| n.d. | 337 | 52-12-032 |
| n.d. | 338 | 52-12-039 |

*Plates*

| Text no. | CUNES no. | Plate no. |
|---|---|---|
| 5 | 52-10-047 | 1. |
| 6 | 52-12-019 | 2. |
| 8 | 52-10-046 | 3. |
| 11 | 52-10-061 | 4. |
| 12 | 52-10-045 | 5. |
| 17 | 52-16-099 | 6. |
| 18 | 52-10-078 | 7. |
| 19 | 52-15-044 | 8. |
| 20 | 52-18-833 | 9. |
| 22 | 52-10-052 | 10. |
| 23 | 52-12-015 | 11. |
| 25 | 52-10-060 | 12. |
| 27 | 52-10-071 | 13. |
| 31 | 52-10-082 | 14. |
| 32 | 52-10-062 | 15. |
| 35 | 52-10-043 | 16. |
| 37 | 52-12-014 | 17. |
| 43 | 52-10-063 | 18. |
| 44 | 52-13-134 | 19. |
| 46 | 52-16-018 | 20. |
| 48 | 52-10-096 | 21. |
| 49 | 52-10-079 | 22. |
| 52 | 52-10-053 | 23. |
| 54 | 52-10-057 | 24. |
| 59 | 52-16-017 | 25. |
| 69 | 52-12-025 | 26. |
| 81 | 52-16-090 | 27. |
| 82 | 52-13-165 | 28. |
| 87 | 52-19-117 | 29. |
| 93 | 52-20-320 | 30. |
| 95 | 52-10-116 | 31. |
| 96 | 52-13-110 | 32. |
| 97 | 52-12-016 | 33. |
| 98 | 52-19-146 | 34. |
| 112 | 52-12-008 | 35. |
| 118 | 52-00-062 | 36. |
| 119 | 52-12-010 | 37. |
| 122 | 52-13-132 | 38. |

| Text no. | CUNES no. | Plate no. |
|---|---|---|
| 125 | 52-10-074 | 39. |
| 143 | 52-10-058 | 40. |
| 148 | 52-10-065 | 41. |
| 149 | 52-10-068 | 42. |
| 150 | 52-12-013 | 43. |
| 154 | 52-18-864 | 44. |
| 156 | 52-10-093 | 45. |
| 160 | 52-12-040 | 46. |
| 170 | 52-14-082 | 47. |
| 175 | 52-18-841 | 48. |
| 178 | 52-16-097 | 49. |
| 180 | 52-18-857 | 50. |
| 181 | 52-13-112 | 51. |
| 194 | 52-18-789 | 52. |
| 212 | 52-15-025 | 53. |
| 242 | 52-16-056 | 54. |
| 252 | 52-12-053 | 55. |
| 257 | 52-12-027 | 56. |
| 264 | 52-13-003 | 57. |
| 291 | 53-01-142 | 58. |
| 303 | 52-18-797 | 59. |
| 306 | 52-12-038 | 60. |
| 308 | 52-18-867 | 61. |
| 324 | 52-10-089 | 62. |
| 325 | 52-13-101 | 63. |
| 326 | 52-14-030 | 64. |
| 327 | 52-16-105 | 65. |
| 328 | 52-16-069 | 66. |
| 330 | 52-10-064 | 67. |
| 331 | 52-18-142 | 68. |
| 333 | 53-02-150 | 69. |
| 335 | 52-12-066 | 70. |
| 336 | 52-12-030 | 71. |
| 337 | 52-12-032 | 72. |
| 338 | 52-12-039 | 73. |

Photographs of the other texts will be made available on CDLI (https://cdli.ucla.edu/)

# INTRODUCTION

This volume concludes the publication of the tablets of the Rosen Collection dating to the Kassite period, which were formerly on loan at Cornell University. The publication of the Kassite period tablets was initiated by Wilfred van Soldt with an edition of the texts dating from Kadašman-Enlil II until the end of the Kassite dynasty (CUSAS 30; van Soldt 2015). The majority of texts in this volume come from the reigns of Nazi-Maruttaš and Kadašman-Turgu, but the group includes also one tablet dating to the reign of Burna-Buriaš II; a few remaining documents from the reigns of Kadašman-Enlil II, Kudur-Enlil, and Šagarakti-Šuriaš; and some undated ones.

The Kassite tablets published here are, for the most part, administrative records dealing mainly with the income, storage, and redistribution of agricultural products (mostly cereals but also sesame, pulses, and cress) and by-products (beer and flour); with animal husbandry; and with textile production. Smaller groups of texts include legal documents and letters.

Despite the lack of information about their original context, it can be assumed safely that these documents originated from the same administration—if not from the same archive—because of the typological, prosopographical, geographical, and chronological features they share, which make them an internally interrelated set of sources. While the texts do not provide any explicit indication about the authority or institution that supervised this administration, the scope and organization of the economic activities revealed by the written records suggest that it must have been an institutional household run by a secular authority. The administrative and economic system reflected in the texts—despite some local "variations"—invites close comparison with that of the provincial capital at Nippur, and indeed there was close interaction between the two. At the same time, the texts edited here supplement and broaden, typologically and chronologically, the earlier picture that depended exclusively on the Nippur material. Thus they provide substantial new data for several central aspects of Kassite administration and economy.

The following observations are based primarily on the tablets published in this volume and will only refer occasionally to the chronologically later texts published by W. van Soldt in CUSAS 30.

## 1. Origin of the Tablets

### 1.1 The Nippur Area

Wilfred van Soldt suggested that the Kassite tablets in the Rosen Collection might have come from a town whose ancient name was Dūr-Enlilē, described by him as "an important economic center that was to a certain degree dependent on Nippur and played an important role in the administration" (van Soldt 2015, 30), even though it was "considerably smaller than Nippur" (23).[1] Before discussing this hypothesis in light of the evidence provided by the texts published here, it might be useful to review the overall geographic horizon that emerges from the Kassite tablets in the Rosen Collection.

One can start by considering the presence of place names whose locations are certain: these are Babylon, Dūr-Kurigalzu, Ḫursagkalama, Isin, Nippur, and Uruk.[2] Among them, Nippur stands out definitely as the most frequently attested site, even though the frequency with which it is mentioned varies considerably between the earlier and later texts (see below).

The following additional place names, whose exact locations are not known but that occur often in the Nippur texts and therefore are thought to have been situated in the Nippur area, appear also in our texts:

---

[1] This latter assumption is based on differences in the documentation—e.g., the lack of large rosters of servile laborers and of accounts of cattle like those known from Nippur (van Soldt 2015, 23).

[2] This list does not include place names occurring only in personal names, such as Akkad or Larsa (cf. van Soldt 2015, 574, 576).

Āl-iššakkī, Āl-Mār-Bā'ili, Bīt-bēri, Bīt-i'irti, Dimat-Enlil, Dimtu, Dunni-Adad, Dūr-Bēl-mātāti, Dūr-Enlilē, Emūqāt-Marduk, Ḫamru, Irra-gāmil, Kār-Nuska, Pān-ṣēri, Parak-māri, and Tukultī-Ekur.[1]

Furthermore, a number of archival and prosopographical links between the Rosen texts and the documents from Nippur show that the administrations of the two centers worked together closely. This evidence points to the Nippur area as the origin of the Kassite texts in the Rosen Collection.[2] Nevertheless, it can be excluded that these tablets came from Nippur itself. In fact, van Soldt (2015, 30) noted that "Nippur is normally seen as a town to and from which one had to travel. A number of residents are said to come from Nippur and the brewers from Nippur are listed separately" in documents recording the distribution of cereals as production supplies. This pattern is confirmed generally also by the earlier texts published here. Furthermore, no illegal excavation was reported at Nippur until May 2003; after that date, looters caused only minor damage on the West Mound, while major looting took place on two small mounds at the northern end of the site, where there seems to have been no pre-Sasanian occupation.[3]

According to McGuire Gibson, the source for the Kassite-period tablets that made their appearance in private collections over the last decades could have been one of the several Kassite-period mounds that lay within a few kilometers from Nippur, especially to the east.[4] Among them, a possible candidate is Umm al-Hafriyat, a site located ca. 28 km to the east of Nippur that suffered major looting in the 1970s, 1990s, and after 2003. Umm al-Hafriyat is a cluster of low mounds, known especially as a pottery-making center during the Akkadian period and as the probable source of the so-called Šuilišu archive, part of which is also kept in the Rosen Collection.[5] The excavation carried out in 1977 revealed that the settlement shifted its location over time and that one of the mounds was occupied during the Kassite period. Furthermore, it was noted that there were remains of a major river and of a set of canals that surrounded the mounds: this would fit very well with the frequent mention of boats and boatmen in the Rosen texts, which led van Soldt (2015, 30) to conclude that the town was probably located on a river or a canal.

---

[1] See the entries in RGTC 5 and the list of "settlements around Nippur" in Nashef 1992, 154 n. 17; for Dūr-Enlilē, see esp. RGTC 5, 91 (quoting J. A. Brinkman): "Wegen der Häufigkeit von D. in den unveröffentlichten Texten aus Nippur erwartet man eine Lage in der Nähe von Nippur." Dimtu can be added to Nashef's list because of its vicinity to Kār-Nuska and Tukultī-Ekur, documented by the topographical map CBS 10434 published by Clay (1905) and by several occurrences of the three toponyms together in the Nippur texts as well as in the Rosen Collection Kassite tablets; for Ḫamru belonging to the Nippur province, see Paulus 2014a, 205; for Parak-māri, seat of a temple of Ninurta close to Nippur, see Streck 2004 and Paulus 2007, 14 n. 71. I prefer to maintain the traditional reading Kār-Nuska instead of the alternative Ēṭir-Nuska proposed by Paulus 2014a, 204 n. 553; comparison of the topographical map published by Clay (1905) with the one published by Finkelstein (1962; CBS 13885, recently discussed by Paulus 2014a, 202–5, and Tenney 2016, 158–59) suggests that there were two towns with this name, located close to different canals.

[2] This is also in line with the provenance of other groups of tablets belonging to the same collection, namely, the Sargonic texts of the so-called Šuilišu archive (see n. 5), the Ur III texts from Iri-Saĝrig/Āl-Šarrākī (Owen 2013 and Molina 2013 regard site no. 1056 of Adams 1981 as the likeliest location of Iri-Saĝrig, while Viano 2019 proposes its identification with Tell al-Wilaya: neither site appears to have Kassite levels and thus cannot be the place of origin of the Kassite tablets in the Rosen Collection), and the Old Babylonian texts from Dūr-Abiešuḫ (see recently van Lerberghe and Voet 2016, with reference to previous literature).

[3] Gibson 2004, 116–18; Gibson 2016, 128.

[4] Gibson 2004, 119; Gibson 2016, 128.

[5] See Milano and Westenholz 2015, 13–15, for the hypothesis that the Sargonic texts of the so-called Šuilišu archive came from Umm al-Hafriyat (site no. 1188 in Adams 1981), perhaps to be identified with ancient Maškan-ili-Akkade (see p. 19 n. 2). On the only season of excavation at Umm al-Hafriyat, see Gibson 1978, with updates on the site's condition in Gibson 1996, 1997, 1998, 2003, 2004, 2006; all but one of the excavated cuneiform texts remain unpublished, as does the final excavation report.

1.2 Dūr-Enlilē?

As for the ancient name of the administrative center that produced these tablets, van Soldt (2015, 29) proposed that it could have been Dūr-Enlilē because this is the town that occurs most frequently (after Nippur) in his texts.[1] In the documents published in this volume, Dūr-Enlilē is by far the most frequently attested toponym, while the presence of Nippur is much less evident, and in frequency, it is clearly surpassed by references to Dūr-Enlilē, Tukultī-Ekur, Kār-Nuska, and Āl-irrē. Thus Dūr-Enlilē certainly played a central role in the economic activities witnessed by the Rosen texts; but is the high number of attestations of a toponym a reliable indication of the place of origin of a group of tablets? The question arises because other cases show that the name of the ancient settlement from which a collection of tablets originated may be mentioned in only a few texts,[2] thus suggesting a cautious approach.

Van Soldt's proposal relies further on the observation that a number of persons associated with Dūr-Enlilē in the Nippur texts can be found also in the tablets he published in CUSAS 30 (van Soldt 2015, 29–30). In this regard, he stresses the importance of BE 14 118, a Nippur text listing wagons that delivered the revenues (*tēlītu*) of Dūr-Enlilē in the 5th year of Kudur-Enlil; since several persons associated with these wagons in BE 14 118 appear also in CUSAS 30, he came to the conclusion that "BE 14 118 provides evidence that the town must have had this name" (i.e., Dūr-Enlilē). In the earlier Kassite texts of the Rosen Collection, one finds additional individuals who are associated with Dūr-Enlilē in the Nippur texts but also people connected with other towns—e.g., Baṣātu and Āl-atḫē, who occur both at Nippur and in the Rosen texts (see below). Thus if one applies van Soldt's reasoning to these cases, Baṣātu and Āl-atḫē would be equally valid candidates along with Dūr-Enlilē for the place of origin of the tablets.

Aside from the high number of its attestations, Dūr-Enlilē appears to "behave" as other toponyms in this corpus; it is one of the towns that delivers revenues to the local administration, one of the towns where the distribution of goods takes place, and one of the towns attested as the origin[3] and destination of goods.

However, there is one feature that applies often to Dūr-Enlilē and perhaps might be regarded as a clue that the documents were written locally by officials working there: the ventive form of the verb *našû,* "to bring" (thus "to bring here"), is used almost exclusively in connection with the delivery of goods to this town, as, e.g., in following passage:[4]

0.1.3 *kibtu sūtu rabû ana Dūr-Enlilē mār Kubbuti iššâm-ma ana zēri nadna*

"9 *sūtu*: wheat, (measured by) the big *sūtu*. The son of Kubbutu brought (it) here to Dūr-Enlilē and it was disbursed as seed." (**no. 48**: 25)

It is also worth noting the absence of Dūr-Enlilē in texts that record the disbursement of rations to the "outside" (*bābānu*), where several other towns are mentioned (Āl-Arad-Bēlti, Āl-atḫē, Āl-irrē, Āl-Mār-Bā'ili,

---

[1] Van Soldt (2015, 29) noted that Dūr-Enlilē "is attested almost 40 times, considerably more than most other place names. The only name that occurs more frequently is Nippur itself (47 times). After Dūr-Enlilē the best-attested names are Tukultī-Ekur (in the *tamirtu* of the same name, 12 times), Bābili (10) and Āl-irrē (9)." Note that when counting the attestations of Babylon, van Soldt considered also the nisbe *bābilāyu* indicating the origin of some individuals; the town of Babylon itself is only attested twice (cf. van Soldt 2015, 574).

[2] See, e.g., the case of the Šuilišu archive: a single tablet that mentions a delegation of Gutian leaders who came to a place called Maškan-ili-Akkade may be the sole indication of the ancient name of the town where the texts were originally kept (Milano and Westenholz 2015, 15).

[3] Dūr-Enlilē occurs only twice as the origin of persons or goods: **no. 137**: 12 mentions a messenger from Dūr-Enlilē (*mār šipri ištu Dūr-Enlilē*), and a badly preserved line of **no. 308**: ix 29′ seems to record items brought from Dūr-Enlilē (*ištu Dūr-Enlilē* ir ⸢x x *iš*?⸣*ši*).

[4] See also **no. 135**: 3–4 ([*an*]*a Dūr-Enlilē našâm-ma*); **no. 159**: 20 (*ana Dūr-Enlil*[*ē*] *iššûni*); **no. 242**: 8–9 (*ana Dūr-E*[*nlilē*] *iššûni*); once, though, the delivery of goods to Dūr-Enlilē is not marked by the ventive: **no. 52**: 27 (*ana Dūr-Enlilē išši*). Note also the use of the ventive in connection to Namkar-ešēgi: "fodder for the oxen of Rabâ-ša-Bēlti that carried (*izbilūni*) the grain from Zarāt-Šarri to Namkar-ešēgi" (CUSAS 30 142: 27–29).

Āl-Mār-kāri, Āl-šerikki, Bīt-Bēlāni, Dimtu, Ḫurād-Kaššî, Sikila, and Tukultī-Ekur).[1] This might be a coincidence, but perhaps it is another element indicating that Dūr-Enlilē was "here," while the other towns were "outside."

In conclusion, the data gained from the study of the earlier tablets in the Rosen Collection provide additional elements supporting the possibility that Dūr-Enlilē was the ancient name of the town that produced the Kassite texts in the collection, but the picture is not as clear and straightforward as one might wish, and thus one must still regard this solution as a working hypothesis.

### 1.3 House of Enlil-Kidinnī or Bīt-Enlil-Kidinnī?

Several persons who held key positions in the local administration are descendants of a certain Enlil-kidinnī and are linked to the "House (É) of Enlil-kidinnī," which van Soldt understands as a designation for a family or household; he also considered the possibility that this Enlil-kidinnī might have been identical with the person who held the office of *šandabakku* at Nippur during the reign of Burna-Buriaš II.[2] The nature of the social, economic, and geographic entity hidden behind the expression "House of PN"—where "PN" stands for the eponymous ancestor who gave the name to the "House"—has been widely discussed in Kassite studies[3] and is often difficult to assess. The House of Enlil-kidinnī is not the only "House" mentioned in the Rosen texts, but it is the one that occurs most often, especially in the later texts.[4] Cereals are disbursed from the granary of the House of Enlil-kidinnī[5] or from amounts that belonged to the House of Enlil-kidinnī,[6] and the House of Enlil-kidinnī appears also as a recipient of rations (CUSAS 30 326). Finally, there are individuals associated explicitly with the House of Enlil-kidinnī: a brewer (CUSAS 30 362: 5–6), a *ša rēši* (LÚ.SAG, CUSAS 30 360: 15–16),[7] and a *ḫazannu* (**no. 337**: 7–8). The latter deserves special attention; the Arad-nubatti mentioned as *ḫazannu* of the House of Enlil-kidinnī in letter **no. 337** is probably identical with the homonymous *ḫazannu* whom van Soldt regarded as the *ḫazannu* of Dūr-Enlilē, attested in several texts from the Rosen Collection dating to the last years of Kudur-Enlil and the first years of Šagarakti-Šuriaš.[8] Since the office of *ḫazannu* is connected typically with a town or village, this might indicate that at this time, the "House of Enlil-kidinnī" not only represented a family estate with administrative functions in the surrounding area but also began to function as a toponym—i.e., Bīt-Enlil-kidinnī.[9] In any case, the fact that the *ḫazannu* Arad-nubatti appears in connection with the House of Enlil-kidinnī as well as with Dūr-Enlilē is a strong indication that they are connected closely or perhaps even identical. Note also that emmer belonging to the House of Enlil-kidinnī was disbursed in Dūr-Enlilē (see CUSAS 30 242 and CUSAS 30 319).

---

[1] See **no. 97**, **no. 98**, and CUSAS 30 231. On the *bābānu*, see §4.3.

[2] Van Soldt 2015, 24.

[3] See most recently Sassmannshausen 1998, 226–27; 2001, 144ff.; Paulus 2014a, 179ff. with references to previous literature.

[4] See the attestations given by van Soldt 2015, 543, s.v. Enlil-kidinnī. The House of Enlil-kidinnī appears only twice in the texts published here: **no. 81**: 3 and **no. 337**: 8.

[5] CUSAS 30 204: 1–2, CUSAS 30 206: 1–2 (read É [G]UR$_7$ instead of É ⌜IŠKUR$^{?}$⌝), and CUSAS 30 319: 2.

[6] CUSAS 30 76, 105, 207, 242.

[7] The name, which is only preserved partially, might have been [$^{m}$IBI]LA-$^{d}$UTU. On the role of the *ša rēši*, see Sassmannshausen 2001, 45–48, who does not mention any *ša rēši* of a "House"; see also §4.2.

[8] See van Soldt 2015, 25: Arad-nubatti appears as *ḫazannu* in texts that deal with Dūr-Enlilē; however, see §4.2 for the difficulty of establishing a secure link between a *ḫazannu* and a town. It is not certain whether Arad-nubatti occurs with the title of *ḫazannu* already in a text dated to KT 1 (**no. 146**: 7).

[9] For the toponym Bīt-Enlil-kidinnī, see a *kudurru* of Meli-Šipak (MŠ 4 in Paulus 2014a, 402–15) and a legal text dated to Nabû-šuma-libur (NŠL-RU 1 in Paulus 2014a, 613–17).

## 2. Remarks on Selected Text Groups

2.1 Accounts of Agricultural Revenues

The local administrators used mainly three text types in order to keep track of the collection and storage of agricultural revenues, respectively identified in the text headings by the operative words *tēlītu*, "revenues"; *ṣēru* (EDIN), "countryside"; and *še'u tabku*, "stored grain/barley." The remainder of each heading usually contains the name of a town and a regnal year, written in a form that varies rarely. Compare, e.g., the following:

*tēlītu sūtu rabû Āl-irrē* MU.12.KAM *Kadašman-Turgu šarri*

"Revenues, (measured by) the big *sūtu*, Āl-irrē, year 12 of King Kadašman-Turgu" (**no. 11**: 1)

*ṣēru sūtu rabû Baṣāti* MU.⌜12?⌝.KAM *Kadašman-Turgu šarri*

"Countryside, (measured by) the big *sūtu*; Baṣātu; year ⌜12?⌝ of King Kadašman-Turgu" (**no. 33**: 1)

*še'u tabku sūtu rabû Āl-irrē* MU.12.KAM *Kadašman-Turgu šarri*

"Stored grain, (measured by) the big *sūtu*; Āl-irrē; year 12 of King Kadašman-Turgu" (**no. 54**: 1–2)

The different operative words in the text headings correspond to different layouts and sets of information recorded by the different text types. However, wherever it is possible to compare different text types referring to the same town and the same year, it becomes apparent that their contents overlap partially and that they deal with the same data. Such intertextual links show that we are dealing with a documentary chain of interconnected bookkeeping tools developed in order to keep track of different phases of the collection and storage of agricultural revenues.

None of these texts provides figures concerning the area of land yielding the harvest,[1] thus hampering any attempt to calculate the yield ratio and the area yield and to reconstruct general trends in productivity levels.

### 2.1.1 *tēlītu*-Accounts (Nos. 1–25)

Accounts characterized by the key word *tēlītu* have been known since the first publications of the Nippur epigraphic material. However, the texts from the Rosen Collection provide important new evidence for the meaning and range of the use of *tēlītu*, which is used consistently here to indicate the sum of different types of agricultural revenue.[2] The *tēlītu*-accounts published in this volume can be divided into three different groups, all utilizing a tabular layout in landscape format.

*A. Annual* tēlītu-*Accounts of Barley Together with Other Crops Regarding a Single Town (Nos. 1–16)*

Even though no two texts are precisely parallel, the documents belonging to this group tend to present a very standardized structure.[3] Along the horizontal axis, the first two columns are always designated as *rēš makkūri* (SAG NÍG.GA) and *šibšu*, which represent, respectively, the taxable capital and a payment levied on agricultural products that was calculated at a fixed rate based on the taxable capital. Even though not explicitly stated in the texts, it can be safely assumed that the quantities recorded in the first two columns refer to barley, which traditionally represented the main agricultural product of Mesopotamia and thus the main object of taxation. The following columns, arranged according to a very strict sequence (table 1), may record quantities of other

---

1 Differently than, e.g., the contemporary Middle Assyrian texts from Dūr-Katlimmu and Kār-Tukultī-Ninurta (see Röllig 2008, 19ff. and Freydank 2009, respectively, and Reculeau 2011, 93ff.; Johnson 2013, 67; Dornauer 2016, 67).

2 See Devecchi, in press, for a study specifically devoted to the evidence for *tēlītu* in Kassite sources related to agricultural revenues.

3 Other *tēlītu*-accounts showing the same basic features are MUN 62 and MUN 64 from Nippur and CUSAS 30 34–35. The latter two tablets, published by van Soldt (2015), do not belong to the Rosen Collection at Cornell University but are "part of a mixed group of texts that were brought to the attention of David I. Owen" (van Soldt 2015, 77); however, intertextual and prosopographical links show that they are associated with texts **nos. 7** and **9** published in this volume (see comments there). See Devecchi, in press, for a detailed analysis of CUSAS 30 35, which can be applied also to most of the *tēlītu*-accounts published in this volume.

| Text no. | SAG NÍG.GA | *šibšu* | *kiṣru* | GIG | ŠE.MUŠ$_5$ | ZÍZ.AN.NA | GÚ.TUR | GÚ.GAL | GÚ.NÍG.ÀR.RA | ZAG.ḪI.LI | MU.BI.IM |
|---|---|---|---|---|---|---|---|---|---|---|---|
| **1** (Dūr-Enlilē, NM 22) | x | x | | x | | | | | | x | x |
| **2** (Dūr-Enlilē, KT 1) | x | x | | x | | x | | x | | x | x |
| **3** (Kār-Nuska, KT 5) | x | x | | x | x | x | [x] | [x] | | [x] | [x] |
| **4** (Kār-Nuska, KT 8?) | x | x | | x | | x | x | x | x | x | x |
| **5** (Dūr-Enlilē, KT 8) | x | x | | | | x | x | x | | x | x |
| **6** (Dūr-Enlilē, KT 8) | x | x | | | | x | x | x | | x | x |
| **7** (Dūr-Enlilē, KT 11) | x | x | | x | | | | | | x | x |
| **8** (Dūr-Amurru, KT 11) | x | x | x | | | | | | | | x |
| **9** (Āl-irrē, KT 11) | x | x | | x | | x | | | | | x |
| **10** (Dūr-Amurru, KT 12) | x | x | | x | | x | x | x | x | x | x |
| **11** (Āl-irrē, KT 12) | x | x | | x | | x | | | | | x |
| **12** (Āl-irrē, KT 13) | x | x | | x | | x | | | | | x |
| **13** (Dikirtu, KT 13) | x | x | | | | | | | | | x |
| **14** (Kār-Nuska, KT 14) | x | x | | x | | x | | x | | x | x |
| **15** (Tukultī-Ekur, KT 14) | x | x | | x | | x | | x | | x | x |
| **16** (Āl-atḫē, KT x) | | | | | [not preserved] | | | | | | x |

**Table 1.** Sequence of columns in the annual *tēlītu*-accounts for a single town

types of cereals (wheat, emmer, *šeguššu*/ŠE.MUŠ$_5$), pulses (GÚ.TUR, GÚ.GAL, GÚ.NÍG.ÀR.RA), and cress (ZAG.ḪI.LI) or, in one case, the impost called *kiṣru*;[1] the last column always bears the heading MU.BI.IM, "its entry," and determines the content of the text along its vertical axis. Since all amounts are "unrounded" figures, they probably represent the actual harvest of a given agricultural product rather than an assessment of the expected yield.

The amounts of *rēš makkūri* and *šibšu* in these texts show that the proportion *rēš makkūri* : *šibšu* is either exactly or roughly 2.5 : 1—i.e., the *šibšu*-payment on barley is usually set at roughly 2/5 (40 percent) of the taxable capital, while at Nippur, it is usually calculated at roughly 1/3.[2]

These ledgers are usually divided into two sections along their vertical axis, each corresponding to a subtotal.[3] The first section consists of different types of imposts, such as *miksu* (NÍG.KUD.DA); *abullu* (KÁ.GAL); ŠE *mākisi*, "grain of the tax collector";[4] *qarīt* (ÉSAG) *mākisi*, "granary of the tax collector"; *zittu* (ḪA.LA); *ludû*;[5] ŠE *liqtāti*, "grain of the gleaning"; and entries especially devoted to the deliveries of the "farmers" (ÉNSI$^{meš}$). The second section lists the names of the individuals who delivered the *šibšu*-payment, sometimes identified by

---

1 For which see below.

2 The proportion 2.5 : 1 can be found also in CUSAS 30 34, 35, 39, and 42. On the proportion *rēš makkūri* : *šibšu* at Nippur, see the remarks by Torczyner 1913, 15ff. and Ellis 1976, 114ff. based on the *tēlītu*-accounts published in BE 14, BE 15, and PBS 2/2; most of the *tēlītu*-accounts published by Sassmannshausen 2001 conform to the same ratio. BE 15 131 and MUN 64 are two Nippur texts that record the same *rēš makkūri* : *šibšu* proportion as in the Rosen texts (i.e., 2.5 : 1).

3 Exceptions are **nos. 14–15**, which do not have subtotals, and **no. 8** (see below).

4 Sassmannshausen (2001, 35) suggests that this was an amount that the tax collector could keep for himself.

5 A type of field on which probably specific work obligations had to be performed: see commentary to **no. 1**: 6.

their profession and associated with the formula *ana ṭēmišu*[1] or with *ḫaršû*;[2] also women can appear in these lists. The first individual named in a given line is repeated often as the first one in the following line(s), using ᵐKI.MIN. In such cases (e.g., **no. 2**: 14–18), the quantities associated with that individual are recorded in decreasing order of magnitude. The final grand total is the sum of the first and second subtotals and is identified in the last column as *tēlītu*, showing that this term indicated the sum of all annual revenues of a given town.

After the final grand total, some *tēlītu*-accounts indicate that certain individuals are exempted (*zakû*) from delivering the *šibšu* on barley and occasionally also on other crops.[3] Such exemptions are attested also in MUN 62 and MUN 64,[4] which, perhaps not accidentally, are two *tēlītu*-accounts from Nippur showing similar features as the *tēlītu*-accounts from the Rosen Collection.

*B. Annual* tēlītu*-Accounts of Sesame Regarding a Single Town (Nos. 17–21)*

These ledgers have a basic structure similar to those of the first group—i.e., the first two columns are devoted to the taxable capital (*rēš makkūri*/SAG NÍG.GA) and the *šibšu*, and the last one is labeled MU.BI.IM, "its entry." In these accounts, the proportion *rēš makkūri* : *šibšu* is either exactly or roughly 2 : 1 (i.e., *šibšu* is half of the taxable capital), as in the accounts regarding sesame revenues from Nippur. Further columns are devoted to amounts of other payments, such as *kiṣru*, *naḫḫuḫu*,[5] and *parṣu* (GARZA).

*C. Annual* tēlītu*-Accounts of Different Crops Regarding Several Towns (Nos. 22–25)*

These are summaries drawn up on the basis of the annual *tēlītu*-accounts of single towns.[6] They do not have a column for the taxable capital (*rēš makkūri*) but indicate only the actual amounts of crops delivered by the different towns; the last column lists several geographical names and can bear the heading URU$^{\text{didli}}$ instead of MU.BI.IM. Summaries devoted especially to sesame and wheat are recorded on separate tablets (see texts nos. 23–24).

### 2.1.2 EDIN-Accounts (Nos. 26–36)

The next group of texts concerned with revenues is of a type that appears to be peculiar to the texts in the Rosen Collection.[7] The texts have a tabular layout in landscape format and contain at least three columns: the taxable capital (*rēš makkūri*/SAG NÍG.GA), the *kiṣru*-payment, and MU.BI.IM, "its entry." As in the case of the *tēlītu*-accounts, it is assumed that the columns devoted to the taxable capital and to the *kiṣru*-payment referred to barley. Additional columns are inserted occasionally before the last one: these recorded quantities of other types of cereals (wheat, emmer, *šeguššu*/ŠE.MUŠ$_5$, *ennēnu*/*innin(n)u*/ŠE.IN.NU.ḪA), pulses (GÚ.GAL), and cress (ZAG.ḪI.LI) (see table 2).[8]

---

[1] "At his discretion" or "by (his own) authority"? See most recently van Soldt 2015, 33; Farber and Farber 2018, 217.

[2] A field-parcel or a type of land: see commentary to **no. 2**: 36.

[3] See texts **nos. 2**, **4**, **5**, **7**, **9**.

[4] Sassmannshausen (2001, 251) regards them as the first attestations of *zakû* in accounts of revenues from Nippur.

[5] On *naḫḫuḫu*, a term that might have indicated a portion of "soaked" sesame crop, which would be kept apart in order to use it as seed as soon as it sprouted, see Devecchi 2018; on *parṣu* (GARZA), see comments to text **no. 19**.

[6] This is nicely demonstrated by the correspondence between the total amounts of wheat delivered by Dūr-Enlilē in the 1st year of Kadašman-Turgu recorded by texts **no. 2** (annual *tēlītu*-account of a single town) and **no. 25** (annual *tēlītu*-summary of several towns).

[7] I can cite presently only one unpublished example of such a text from Nippur (UM 29-15-684): its heading on the upper edge reads *šu-ni-e* EDIN ᵍⁱˢB[ÁN . . .], and the first two columns bear the headings [*re-e*]*š* NÍG.GA and *ki-iṣ-rù*. Only the left half of the tablet is preserved; the date is not preserved. On *šunê ṣēri* (EDIN), see below.

[8] CUSAS 30 40, 43, 44, 45 have a similar structure but a different heading or no heading at all.

| Text no. | SAG NÍG.GA | *kiṣru* | ŠE.MUŠ$_5$ | *kiṣru* | GIG | ZÍZ.AN.NA | ŠE.IN.NU.ḪA | GÚ.GAL | ZAG.ḪI.LI | MU.BI.IM |
|---|---|---|---|---|---|---|---|---|---|---|
| **26** (Āl-atḫē, NM 18) | x | x | | | x | | | | | x |
| **27** (Dūr-Amurru, NM 20) | x | x | x | x | x | x | | | | x |
| **28** (Dikirtu, NM 24) | x | x | | | | | | | | x |
| **29** (Āl-atḫē, NM 24) | x | x | | | x | | | | | x |
| **30** (Kār-Nuska, KT 4) | x | x | | | | | | | | x |
| **31** (Dūr-Amurru, KT 5) | x | x | | | x | | | | x | x |
| **32** (Dūr-Enlilē, KT 11) | x | x | x | | x | | | | x | x |
| **33** (Baṣātu, KT 12$^?$) | x | x | | | x | | | | | x |
| **34** (Dimtu, KT 12) | x | x | x | | x | x | | x | x | x |
| **35** (Āl-irrē, KT 13) | x | x | x | | x | x | | | | x |
| **36** (Āl-atḫē, year 5) | x | x | | | x | | x | | | x |

**Table 2.** Sequence of columns in the EDIN-accounts

The entries in the MU.BI.IM-column largely correspond to those of the *tēlītu*-accounts, even though EDIN-accounts do not distinguish between two sections with corresponding subtotals, summed up by a final grand total, as in the *tēlītu*-accounts. They do, however, often list the total of the amounts recorded in the *kiṣru*-column, which may or may not be explicitly identified as *kiṣru* in the corresponding entry of the MU.BI.IM-column.[1]

A comparison between a *tēlītu*-account and an EDIN-account referring to the same town and the same year shows that these texts deliver in part the same categories of information. Compare, e.g., **no. 12** with **no. 35**, both concerned with the revenues of Āl-irrē in the 13$^{\text{th}}$ year of Kadašman-Turgu (corresponding parts are highlighted in gray):[2]

## Text No. 12

U.e. *te-li-tu*$_4$ $^{\text{giš}}$BÁN GAL MU.⸢13⸣.[KAM] ⸢$^{\text{d}}$⸣*Ka-dáš-man-Túr-gu* LUGAL.E

| Obv. | SAG NÍG.GA | *šib-šu*$_{14}$ | GIG | ZÍZ.⸢AN⸣.[NA] | MU.BI.[IM] |
|---|---|---|---|---|---|
| | | 7.1.3 | | | NÍG.KUD.DA EN 0.3.5 ⸢*ḫir*⸣-[*ga-le*]-⸢*e*⸣ |
| | | | | | KÁ.[GAL] |
| | | 0.2.3 | | | ŠE *ma-ki-*⸢*si*⸣ |
| PAP | | 7.4$^{\text{PI}}$.0 | | | NÍG.KUD.DA *ù* ŠE ⸢*ma*⸣-[*ki-si*] |
| | 17.2.4 | 7.0.1 | | | ⸢$^{\text{m}}$*Za-ki*⸣-*rù* $^{\text{m}}$*Bu-un-na-*[$^{\text{d}}$AMAR.UTU] |
| | 16.1$^{\text{PI}}$.0 | 6.2.3 | | 0.1.1 | $^{\text{m}}$*Eri-ba-*$^{\text{d}}$IŠKUR ⸢$^{\text{m}}$⸣[*Ú-sa-tu-ú-a*] |
| | 11.2$^{\text{pi}}$.0 | 4.2.5 | 0.0.1 2 SÌLA | | $^{\text{m}}$⸢*Iz-kùr*⸣-$^{\text{d}}$*Nin-urta* [$^{\text{md}}$*Nin-urta*]-⸢*ki-na-i-de*⸣ |

---

1 **Nos. 28, 33,** and **34**.

2 The same similarities can be found also by comparing **no. 7** and **no. 30**, respectively, a *tēlītu*-account and an EDIN-account concerned with the revenues of Dūr-Enlilē in the 11$^{\text{th}}$ year of Kadašman-Turgu.

| | | | | | |
|---|---|---|---|---|---|
| | 8.4$^{pi}$.0 | 3.2.4 | | | $^{m}$⸢ZÁLAG⸣-$^{d}$AMAR.UTU $^{m}$⸢*A-bi-ul-i*⸣*-de* |
| | 6.2.3 | 2.3$^{pi}$.0 | | | $^{m}$KI.MIN $^{m}$*Iz-kùr*-$^{d}$IŠKUR |
| | 3.4.3 | 1.2.5 | | | $^{m}$*Ri-iš*-$^{d}$IŠKUR |
| | 3.1$^{pi}$.0 | 1.1.2 | | | $^{m}$*Iz-kùr*-$^{d}$IŠKUR $^{lú}$DÙ |
| | 2.4.2 | 1.0.4 | | | $^{m}$NÍG.BA-$^{d}$AMAR.UTU |
| | 2.3.4 | 1.0.3 | | | $^{m}$*A-mi-lu-ú-ba-nu-ú* |
| | 2.2.3 | 1.0.0 | | | $^{m}$*In-[nu]-un-nu* $^{m}$*Iz-kùr*-$^{d}$⸢*Nin-urta*$^{?}$⸣ |
| Rev. | 1.3.3 | 0.3.3 | | | $^{m}$*Di-maḫ-di*-$^{d}$*Uraš* |
| | 1.0.2 | 0.2.1 | | | $^{md}$*Nin-urta-ki-na-i-de*<br>$^{m}$BA-*šá*-$^{d}$*Nin-urta* |
| | 1.0.0 | 0.2$^{pi}$.0 | | | $^{m}$*Ib-ni*-$^{d}$IŠKUR $^{lú}$NAGAR<br>$^{m}$*Iz-kùr*-$^{d}$30$^{?}$ |
| PAP | | 31.4.1 | 0.0.1 2 SÌLA | 0.1.1 | [*ši*]*-ib-šu* |
| ŠU.NIGIN | | 39./3.1 | 0.0.1 2 SÌLA | 0.1.1 | *te-li-tu*$_4$ URU-*ir-re*-⸢*e*⸣<br>⸢MU.13.KAM $^{d}$⸣*Ka-dáš-man-Túr-gu*<br>LUGAL.E |

## Text No. 35

U.e. EDIN $^{giš}$BÁN GAL URU-*ir-re-e* MU.13.KAM *Ka-dáš-man-Túr-gu* LUGAL.E

| Obv. | SAG NÍG.GA | *ki-iṣ-rù* | ŠE.MUŠ$_5$ | GIG | ZÍZ.AN.NA | MU.BI.I[M] |
|---|---|---|---|---|---|---|
| | 7.1.3 | 0.0.4 | | | | NÍG.KUD.DA EN 0.3.5 ⸢*ḫir-ga*⸣*-le-e* |
| | | | | | | KÁ.GAL *a-na* ÉRIN$^{hi.a}$ *dul-li* x<br>*ù* ŠUKU ANŠE.KUR.RA$^{meš}$ SUM-*at* |
| | 1.1$^{pi}$.0 | 0.0.1 | | | | ŠE *ma-ki-si* |
| | 17.2.4 | 0.1$^{pi}$.0 | | | | $^{m}$*Za-ki-rù* $^{m}$*Bu-un-na*-$^{d}$AMAR.UTU |
| | 16.1$^{pi}$.0 | 0.1$^{pi}$.0 | | | 0.2.4 | $^{m}$*Eri-ba*-$^{d}$IŠKUR $^{m}$*Ú-sa-tu-ú-a* |
| | 11.2$^{pi}$.0 | 0.0.5 | | 0.0.4 | | $^{m}$*Iz-kùr*-$^{d}$*Nin-urta* $^{md}$*Nin-urta-kí-na-i-de* |
| | 8.4$^{pi}$.0 | 0.0.5 | | | | $^{m}$ZÁLAG-$^{d}$AMAR.UTU $^{m}$*A-bi-u*[*l-i*]*-de* |
| | 6.2.3 | 0.0.4 | | | | $^{m}$KI.MIN $^{m}$*Iz-kùr*-$^{d}$IŠKUR |
| | 3.4.3 | 0.0.3 | | | | $^{m}$*Ri-iš*-$^{d}$IŠKUR |
| | 3.1$^{pi}$.0 | 0.0.2 | | | | $^{m}$*Iz-kùr*-$^{d}$IŠKUR *a-na ṭe-m*[*i-šu*] |
| | 2.4.2 | 0.0.2 | | | | $^{m}$NÍG.BA-$^{d}$AMAR.UTU |
| | ⸢2$^{?}$⸣.3.4 | 0.0.2 | | | | $^{m}$*A-mi-lu-ba-*[*nu-ú*] |
| Rev. | 2.2.3 | 0.0.2 | | | | $^{m}$*In-nu-u*[*n-nu*]<br>SIPA ANŠ[E] |
| 16 | | | 1.3.3 | | | $^{m}$*Di-maḫ-di*-⸢$^{d}$⸣[*Uraš*] |
| | | | 1.0.2<br>0.0.1 | | | $^{md}$*Nin-urta-ki-n*[*a-i-de*]<br>[$^{m}$B]A-*šá*-$^{d}$*Nin-u*[*rta*] |
| | 1.0.0 | 0.0.1 | | | | ⸢$^{m}$*Ib-ni*⸣-$^{d}$IŠKUR ⸢$^{l}$⸣[$^{ú}$NAGAR]<br>$^{m}$*Iz-kùr*-$^{d}$*Nin-urta* [ |
| | | 1.2.1 | 0.0.1 | | | |

Note the following shared features:

- The quantity booked as *šibšu* in no. 12: 3 becomes the taxable capital (*rēš makkūri*/SAG NÍG.GA) in no. 35: 3, where it forms the basis for the calculation of the *kiṣru*-payment. The corresponding entry in the MU.BI.IM-column is the same in both texts and mentions *miksu*/NÍG.KUD.DA together with a quantity of *ḫirgalû*.
- Neither text records quantities corresponding to the impost called *abullu*/KÁ.GAL, but no. 35: 4 provides an explanation for this: "(the amount of) the city-gate was given to the workmen of the *dullu*-service and as fodder for the horses"—i.e., it was probably disbursed before it could be collected.
- The quantities recorded as *rēš makkūri* in no. 12: 7–16, 19 correspond to those of no. 35: 6–15, 18. Also the corresponding entries in the MU.BI.IM-column match almost exactly.
- The quantities recorded as *šegušš u*/ŠE.MUŠ$_5$ of Dimaḫdi-Uraš and Ninurta-kīna-īde in no. 35: 16–17 are booked as *rēš makkūri* of the same persons in no. 12: 17–18.

This shows that the *tēlītu*-accounts and the EDIN-accounts deal with the same amounts of agricultural products, but the first accounts were focused on the calculation of the *šibšu*-payment, while the second accounts were mainly meant primarily to calculate the impost called *kiṣru*, a payment whose exact nature in the Kassite period remains to be determined.[1]

I cannot offer any convincing explanation for the reason why this type of revenue was identified by the operative word EDIN, "countryside."[2] Equally obscure is the meaning of the word *šunû*/*šunê*, which often precedes EDIN in the headings:[3] the lemmata listed by the dictionaries do not seem to fit this context,[4] and positing an unattested Š-stem of *enû*, "to change," does not suggest a feasible solution at present.[5]

In contrast to the annual *tēlītu*-accounts, we do not have EDIN-accounts about sesame (cf. 2.1.1.b), nor do we have EDIN-accounts that summarize the revenues of several towns (cf. 2.1.1.c).

### 2.1.3 Further Texts

Further texts connected to the management of revenues are **nos. 36–38**, characterized by the presence of the operative word "share," *zittu*/ḪA.LA, in their headings and **nos. 39–46**, a mixed group of documents that do not correspond to any of the major text types identified above. In some cases, a more precise classification is hindered by their poor state of preservation. Among them, **no. 45** is especially noteworthy because it is an account of wagons ($^{\text{giš}}$MAR.GÍD.DA$^{\text{meš}}$) delivered by several individuals who were connected to the towns of Tukultī-Ekur and Dimtu; comparable texts from Nippur are BE 14 118 and BE 15 91, which explicitly state in their headings that the wagons transported the revenues (*tēlītu*) of Dūr-Enlilē and Ekallātu, respectively.

### 2.1.4 *še'u* (ŠE) *tabku*, "Stored Barley/Grain" (Nos. 47–57)

This group of texts is explicitly linked to the storage of agricultural products through the operative word *še'u* (ŠE) *tabku*, "stored barley/grain," which appears in their headings followed by a place name and a year. They

---

1 The interpretations range from some kind of rental fee (Torczyner 1913, 119), perhaps linked to the use of granaries (CAD Š/2, *šibšu* c 2′, 384), to a generic "payment (in kind) for services or taxes" (CAD K, *kiṣru* 3b 2, 439), to "costs related to the transportation of goods" (CAD Z, *zittu* 1d 2′, 143); see Ellis 1976, 113 for an overview up to that date. Based on the new evidence of the First Sealand Dynasty, Boivin 2016, 56–57, recently argued for the interpretation of *kiṣru* as an impost related to packaging and transportation.

2 Note also CUSAS 30 12: 2, where EDIN$^{\text{ki}}$ might identify a quantity of barley received by Arad-nubatti in Mannu-nāṣiršu.

3 See *šunû ṣēri* (EDIN) in **no. 27**: 1 and *šunê ṣēri* (EDIN) in **no. 31**: 1, **no. 32**: 1, **no. 36**: 1, and UM 29-15-684: 1. The attestations of *šunû*/*šunê* are not restricted to the headings of the EDIN-accounts; see also **no. 43**: 1, 10; **no. 46**: 1; CUSAS 30 162: 2–3; CUSAS 30 274: 5, 11; and BE 14 88: 1. Also van Soldt 2015, 34, regards its meaning as unclear and leaves the word untranslated.

4 It can hardly be a shrub, perhaps to be identified with the chaste tree according to CAD Š/3, *šunû* A, 309–10 and AHw III, *šunû* II, 1277.

5 A Št-stem of *enû* is already attested with the meaning "to interchange, replace one another" (CAD E, *enû* 3, 176–77; AHw I, *enû* Št, 221).

usually have a portrait format.[1] I do not know any example of this text type from Nippur, where scribes used instead texts with the heading *še'u* (ŠE) *maḫru ša ina* GN *tabku* MU.X.KAM KN, "grain received, which is stored in GN; year x of KN."[2] Comparison with their Nippur "counterparts" suggests that in the Rosen texts, the name of the town indicated not only the origin of the crops but probably also their place of storage.

The features of this text group are less standardized than the previous ones, but one can identify some common traits. Along the horizontal axis, these texts are often divided into two columns without headings: the first records amounts, the second types of imposts and names of individuals; in such cases, it is assumed that the term *še'u* (ŠE) in the text heading refers to barley (rather than being a generic term for "grain, cereals") and that the first column records amounts of barley. When more than two columns are present, the first ones explicitly mention different types of cereals (barley, wheat, and emmer, but more often *arsuppu*/ŠE.EŠTUB and *šeguššu*/ŠE.MUŠ$_5$), and the last one bears the usual heading MU.BI.IM, "its entry." Along the vertical axis, the data are often grouped in two distinct sections corresponding to two subtotals: usually, the amount of the first subtotal is measured with the big *sūtu* ($^{giš}$BÁN GAL), while the second subtotal, which is sometimes identified as *zēru* (NUMUN) *esru*, "collected seed," is measured with the *sūtu* of 10 *qû* ($^{giš}$BÁN 10 SÌLA). The final grand total is then measured with the big *sūtu*, an operation that required the calculation of the *rubbû* (GAL).[3] The MU.BI.IM-column has entries already known from the documents that record the collection of revenues and may include different types of agricultural imposts, such as *miksu* (NÍG.KUD.DA), *abullu* (KÁ.GAL), ŠE *mākisi*, *qarīt* (ÉSAG) *mākisi*, *zittu* (ḪA.LA), *ludû*, *kiṣru*, *kiṣir ṣēri* (EDIN), and *kiṣir maḫri*, as well as the names of several individuals.

But there is an even deeper and less apparent connection between these texts and the *tēlītu*-accounts, which can be illustrated through text **no. 8**. This is an exceptional document that contains both text types on the same tablet: the *tēlītu*-account of Dūr-Amurru in the 11$^{th}$ year of Kadašman-Turgu on the obverse and the corresponding "stored grain" on the reverse (the corresponding elements are highlighted in gray).[4]

## Text No. 8

| | | | | |
|---|---|---|---|---|
| U.e. | *te-li-tu*$_4$ $^{giš}$BÁN GAL BÀD-$^{d}$KUR$^{ki}$ MU.11.KAM *Ka-dáš-man-Túr-gu* | | | |
| Obv. | SAG NÍG.GA | *ši-ib-šu*$_{14}$ | *ki-iṣ-rù* | MU.BI.IM |
| | | | | NÍG.KUD.⸢DA⸣ |
| | 26.0.3 | 10.2.1 | 0.1.3 5 SÌLA | $^{m}$⸢ÌR-$^{d}$AMAR.UTU $^{m}$*Ba-i*⸣*-rù* |
| | 9.2.3 | 3.4$^{pi}$.0 | 0.0.4 5 | $^{m}$KI.MIN $^{m}$⸢X X X X $^{d}$⸣KA.DI |
| | 0.1.5 | 0.0.5 | 0.0.1 | ⸢ŠE *ma-ki-si*⸣ |
| PAP | | 14.2$^{pi}$.0 | 0.2.3 | *ši-*˹*ib-šu*$_{14}$˺ |

---

[1] The only two in landscape format are **nos. 53** and **56**. Another text belonging to this group is CUSAS 30 46.

[2] Ellis 1976, 119–26 discussed the few examples of these texts known to her, to which one should add now further examples published by Sassmannshausen 2001.

[3] See nos. **8, 47–50, 52, 54, 55, 57** in this text group; *rubbû* occurs especially often in the expenditures; see **nos. 75, 86, 97, 112, 115, 132, 133, 136, 138, 139, 146–50, 153, 157, 162–64, 170, 171, 174–76, 184–86**. See van Soldt 2015, 31 for the occurrences in the later Kassite texts of the Rosen Collection. Among the meanings suggested by the dictionaries (CAD R, 394; AHw II, 991 s.v.), "increase" is perhaps preferable to "additional payment" because the calculation of the *rubbû* seems to be linked to the use of different measuring units (the big *sūtu* and the *sūtu* of 10 *qû*), but the several new attestations provided by the Rosen texts make it necessary to reevaluate thoroughly the meaning of *rubbû* in the Middle Babylonian sources.

[4] Scribes usually used two distinct tablets, each containing only one or the other type of text: cf. the pairs represented by MUN 64 (*tēlītu*) and text **no. 49** (*še'u tabku*), both concerned with Baṣātu in the 1$^{st}$ year of Kadašman-Turgu, and by text **no. 11** (*tēlītu*) with **no. 54** (*še'u tabku*), both concerned with Āl-irrē in the 11$^{th}$ year of Kadašman-Turgu; note also texts **no. 29** (EDIN) and **no. 48** (*še'u tabku*), both concerned with Āl-atḫē in the 24$^{th}$ year of Nazi-Maruttaš.

Rev. ŠE *tab-ku* $^{\text{giš}}$BÁN GAL MU.11.KAM
*Ka-dáš-man-Túr-gu* LUGAL
10.2.1 $^{\text{m}}$ÌR-$^{\text{d}}$AMAR.UTU $^{\text{m}}$*Ba-i-rù*
3.4$^{\text{pi}}$.0 $^{\text{m}}$KI.MIN $^{\text{m}}$*I-ku-na*
0.0.5 ŠE *ma-ki-si*
0.2.3 *ki-iṣ-rù*
0.2$^{\text{pi}}$.0 ŠUKU EN *pi-ḫa-ti*
PAP 15.1.3 $^{\text{giš}}$BÁN GAL
PAP 5.0.0 NUMUN *es-rù* $^{\text{m}}$*Ba-i-rù* $^{\text{lú}}$LUNGA
$^{\text{giš}}$BÁN 10 SÌLA EN 1 GUR *ki-mu* 2 GUR ZÍZ.⌜AN⌝.NA
ŠU.NIGIN 19.1.3 $^{\text{giš}}$BÁN GAL
TA 1 GUR GAL $^{\text{giš}}$BÁN 10 SÌLA *i-na* 1 GUR
0.1$^{\text{pi}}$.0 *šu-lu-ú*

Text no. 8 reveals the relationship between the content of the two types of texts: in fact, the entries about *šibšu* and *kiṣru* in the *tēlītu*-text correspond to the first lines of the "stored grain" on the reverse. This shows that, even though the texts about "stored grain" do not have a column explicitly designated as *šibšu*, at least in some cases, they do refer to the quantities acquired as *šibšu* and can be used as further evidence for the study of this levy.

Such texts could record also expenditures, as suggested by entries that explicitly mention quantities received by some individuals, once as production supplies (see, e.g., **no. 53**: 15–16 and **no. 54**: 26).

A further phase in the bookkeeping of stored goods is represented by accounts that record the *rīḫti* (ÍB.TAK$_4$) *tabki*, "rest of the stores" (**nos. 58–60**).

An account of different types of flour, summarized as *qēmu* (ZÌ.DA) *tabku*, "stored flour," is included here as well (**no. 61**).

## 2.2 Expenditures

The bulk of the documentation is represented by texts that witness activities supported by the administration through the disbursement of resources—i.e., mainly raw agricultural products but also beer, flour, and small cattle.

One can distinguish in general two main types of documents recording the allocation of goods: records of single expenditures and records of multiple expenditures.

**Records of single expenditures (nos. 62–91)** refer to allocations of commodities to one recipient on one occasion. They were written on small, usually unsealed tablets[1] whose text tends to conform to the following structure and formulary:

**1** **commodity (measured by) the *sūtu* xy**
1a source of the expenditure (*ina libbi* . . .)
1b purpose of the expenditure
1c place of the expenditure (*ina* GN)
1d from PN$_1$ (*ina qāt* PN$_1$)
1e in place/as representative of PN$_2$ (*kī qāt* PN$_2$)
**2** **PN$_3$**
**3** **received (*maḫir*/*maḫrātu*/*imḫur*/*imḫurū*)**[2]
**4** **date (month/**day**/year)**

[1] See **no. 88** for a sealed one.

[2] Only **nos. 64**, **69**, and **79** have *iddin*, "he gave," instead of a form of *maḫāru*.

The elements in bold are present in all records of single expenditures; the others (1a–1e) may or may not be included and their sequence can differ slightly from text to text.

**Records of multiple expenditures** are much more abundant and varied with regard to form and content. They are formatted often as multicolumn tables, usually unsealed.[1]

Records of multiple expenditures that deal with only one type of expenditures (**nos. 92–126**) have been organized in groups according to their purpose—i.e.,

- rations (ŠE.BA) and other barley allocations that were probably meant as rations to groups of persons, even though the text does not specify the purpose of the expenditure;
- fodder (ŠUKU) for animals;
- seed (NUMUN);
- production supplies (ÉŠ.GÀR) for millers and brewers, including also brewing ingredients (ZÌ.MUNU$_4$);
- allocations (ŠUKU) for temples;
- loans with interest (UR$_5$.RA);
- deliveries (*maššītu*);
- gifts (*rīmūtu*);
- exchange[2] (ŠE.BAL).

Most records of multiple expenditures are summaries of commodities disbursed for various purposes (**nos. 127–90**), which can include any of the previously listed items but also staples (*maššartu*),[2] rental fees of boats and wagons, payments for different goods, offerings for the cult of dead ancestors (*kispu*), *aklu*-expenditures (see below), compensation for cereals given as an interest-free loan, *nikis karê*,[3] and the still-elusive item of expenditure identified as "delivery" (*maššītu*).[4] Such texts summarize allocations that took place over several months or several years or that were associated with different places.[5]

Sometimes the purpose is not indicated and the document seems to focus more on recording the source of the expended commodities (see, e.g., **nos. 180** and **182**).

Within the records of multiple expenditures, one can recognize two distinct types of texts characterized by the presence of different "verbs of transmission" (either *nadānu*, "to give," or *maḫāru*, "to receive") in their headings, whose most basic formulations are respectively *še'u ša* ... *nadnu*, "grain/barley which ... was given," and *še'u ša* PN ... *maḫru*/*mitaḫḫuru*, "grain/barley that PN ... received/has been receiving." Thus the administration could record such transactions from the point of view of either the institution that disbursed the goods or the person who received them. With the caveat that no two texts are precisely parallel and each heading can provide additional different details, the following examples can be considered representative of the different phrasings of the two types of headings.

## *nadānu*, "to give"

*še'u ša ina libbi tēlīti ša Dūr-Enlilē ša* MU.19.KAM *Nazi-Maruttaš šarri ina Nisanni ša* MU.20.KAM *nadnu*

"Barley that was disbursed in month 1 of year 20 from the revenues of Dūr-Enlilē of year 19 of Nazi-Maruttaš"[6] (**no. 133**: 1–3)

---

[1] See **no. 158** for a sealed example.

[2] On this term, see p. 40 n. 4.

[3] See §4.2, s.v. *ḫazannu*.

[4] See comments to **no. 123**.

[5] For a case of expenditure handed down as a single record and as an entry in a summary, see **nos. 73** and **180**: 3.

[6] When indicated, the year of the expenditure usually follows the year when the revenues (*tēlītu*) were collected.

*še'u sūt 5 qâ ša ana zēri kurummat alpī u iprī [ikkarī] ina* MU.8.KAM *Kadašman-Turgu nadnu*

"Barley, (measured by) the *sūtu* of 5 *qû*, that was disbursed as seed, fodder for the oxen, and rations for the [plowmen] in year 8 of Kadašman-Turgu" (**no. 156**: 1–2)

### *maḫāru*, "to receive"

*še'u sūt 5 qâ ša ina qāt Mudammiq-Adad Meli-Šuqamuna mitaḫḫuru*

"Barley, (measured by) the *sūtu* of 5 *qû*, which Meli-Šuqamuna has been receiving from Mudammiq-Adad" (**no. 177**: 1–4)

*še'u sūtu rabû ša ina* MU.3.KAM *Kadašman-Turgu šarri ana iškari Ninurta-ašarēd mār Tarībat-ili mitaḫḫuru*

"Grain, (measured by) the big *sūtu*, which Ninurta-ašarēd, son of Tarībat-ili, has been receiving as production supplies in year 3 of King Kadašman-Turgu" (**no. 113**: 1–2)

Both single and multiple expenditures can indicate the source from which the expended commodities originated: these can be the annual revenues (*tēlītu*) of various towns, stocks acquired as different types of imposts (*zittu, šibšu, kiṣru, miksu, naḫḫuḫu*), the "delivery" (*maššītu*) of a person or a town, and amounts generically associated with a person, a town, or a storage facility.

A particular group of documents recording the issue of foodstuffs is represented by the ***aklu*-texts**. Here, again, one can distinguish between single *aklu*-expenditures and summaries of *aklu*-expenditures.[1]

**Single *aklu*-expenditures (nos. 191–235)** are recorded on small, usually sealed tablets. The following scheme applies to several *aklu*-expenditures in this volume, but it is difficult to define a type that would fit them all, especially because there is a significant degree of variation in the sequence of information conveyed by these documents:

1 commodity / commodities
1a purpose of the expenditure
2 *aklu* / *aklu ašābu* / *aklu lā ašābu* / *aklu ašābu u lā ašābu* / *aklu u ṣītu* (ZI.GA)
3 (ŠU) $PN_1$
4 geographic indication
5 month
6 day / from day x till day y (TA $U_4$.X.KAM EN $U_4$.Y.KAM)
7 year of reign
8 seal caption ($NA_4$.KIŠIB $PN_2$)

The first element is always the expended commodity or commodities, which can be cereals, flour, beer, jars, or small cattle, and it is sometimes accompanied by an indication of the expenditure's purpose.

This information is followed by the key term *aklu*, which is assumed to be a verbal adjective from the verb *akālu*, "to eat," thus literally meaning "consumed" and by extension "consumption." It is often specified further through the words *ašābu* and *lā ašābu*, which may appear separately (*aklu ašābu, aklu lā ašābu*) or together (*aklu ašābu u lā ašābu*) and whose exact meaning and function are still unclear; literally, they are both infinitives meaning "to stay" and "not to stay" but have been interpreted also as "resident" and "nonresident."[2] Similarly,

---

[1] Deheselle (1996, 216) draws a similar distinction in the *aklu*-texts from Nippur. A summary of the discussion on the *aklu*-texts from Nippur is provided by Murai 2018, 17–24.

[2] Thus Torczyner 1913, 112 and van Soldt 2015, 33; the dictionaries do not translate them (see CAD A/1, *aklu* B a, 281; CAD A/2, *ašābu* 3d, 904; AHw III, *(w)ašābu* 2d, 1481). See Murai 2018, 249–53, for an overview of the attestations of *ašābu* and *lā ašābu* at Nippur and in the texts published in CUSAS 30.

it remains to be determined why some texts refer to these allocations as *aklu u ṣītu* (ZI.GA), "consumption and expenditure."[1]

The next information recorded by these texts usually consists of a personal name, often preceded by the logogram ŠU, "hand," which probably should be rendered as "on charge to PN."[2] In a few places ŠU is missing,[3] but I do not see any clear reason for assuming that the presence or absence of ŠU implies a different role for the person in question.[4] Cf., e.g., the following two texts:

| **No. 205** | | **No. 206** | |
|---|---|---|---|
| Obv. | 2.4.⸢3⸣ 2 ½ SÌLA ZÌ.DA $^{giš}$BÁN 5 SÌLA | Obv. | 5.2$^{pi}$.0 1 ½ SÌLA ZÌ.DA $^{giš}$BÁN [x] SÌLA |
| | 0.1.4 ŠE $^{giš}$BÁN 5 SÌLA | | 1.2.2 ŠE $^{giš}$BÁN 5 SÌLA |
| | ⸢*ak*⸣-*lu*$_4$ $^{m}$*Ṭà-ab-ki-din-*$^{d}$*Gu-la* | | *ak-lu*$_4$ ŠU $^{m}$*Ṭà-ab-ki-din-*$^{d}$*Gu-la* |
| | *a-ša-bu ù la a-ša-b*[*u*] | | *a-ša-bu* |
| 5 | $^{iti}$DU$_6$.⸢KÙ⸣ | 5 | $^{iti}$ŠU.NUMUN.NA |
| L.e. | TA U$_4$.1.KAM EN U$_4$.30.K[AM] | L.e. | [T]A U$_4$.1.KAM EN U$_4$.29.KAM |
| Rev. | MU.1.KAM *Ka-dáš-man-Túr-*[*gu*] LUGAL.E | Rev. | MU.2.KAM *Ka-dáš-man-Túr-gu* LUGAL.E |
| 9 | NA$_4$.KIŠIB $^{md}$*Nin-urta-*MU-MU | | NA$_4$.KIŠIB $^{m⸢d}$*Nin*⸣-*urta-*MU-MU |

Despite the absence of ŠU in **no. 205**: 3, there is no significant difference between the two texts that suggests that Ṭāb-kidin-Gula was in one case the recipient and in the other case the person in charge of the expenditure.

The *aklu*-texts mention a relatively limited number of persons in this position. These individuals never correspond to those who seal the texts and only rarely bear a title or profession. However, in some instances, they are identified as brewers or shepherds, respectively associated with *aklu*-expenditures of beer and small cattle. Some of these persons (e.g., Ṭāb-kidin-Gula, Bītu-rabi, and the daughter of Ṣāḫitu) occur in other texts as recipients of cereals as production supplies, but their profession(s) is nowhere indicated.

The month and year of the expenditure are always indicated, in most cases also the day or a time span of several days.

The last element is always the seal caption. The persons who seal the *aklu*-texts are considered to be the officers authorizing or supervising the expenditures;[5] most of them are sealed by Ninurta-zākir-šumi (see §4.1). In some occasions, the tablet is sealed but the seal caption is missing.[6]

**Summaries of *aklu*-expenditures (nos. 236–45)** are usually tabular accounts that record allocations of different foodstuffs for several persons and/or for several purposes, sometimes over a time span of several months; recipients and/or purposes of the expenditures are indicated in the last column to the right, which bears the usual heading MU.BI.IM, "its entry."

---

1 Gurney 1983, 170, 173; Sassmannshausen 2001, 320 (comments to MUN 162): "*aklu u ṣītu* (ZI.GA) ist offensichtlich Hendiadyoin: Verbrauch und Ausgabe."

2 Following Gurney 1983, 170; Petschow 1974, 62 understands ŠU PN in these texts as "(received) from PN," but one would rather expect *ina qāt* (ŠU) PN to express the origin.

3 **Nos. 193, 198, 202–3, 205**.

4 Cf. the remarks by Del Monte (1994, 196) with regard to the *aklu*-texts from Nippur: "*aklu* NP «consumo di NP» o *aklu* šu NP «consumo sotto la responsabilità di NP»."

5 Clay 1906, 14; Matthews 1992, 58; Deheselle 1996, 216; Postgate 2013, 422–23.

6 **Nos. 191, 194, 196–98, 200, 201, 204**.

When indicated, the purposes of the *aklu*-expenditures include *naptanu*-meals,[1] offerings for the cult of dead ancestors (*kispu*), the "coming/going down of the king" (*arād šarri*), extispicy, sacrifice, travel provisions, greeting gifts, allocations to temples, and fodder for animals. This is in line with the wide semantic range of the term *aklu* noted by some authors with regard to the Nippur documentation (Del Monte 1994, 193; Deheselle 1996, 216).

### 2.3 Flock Records

The largest group of texts dealing with animal husbandry is formed by flock and herd records, among which one can distinguish two types: lists and ledgers.

Lists are attested for flocks of sheep, goats, sheep and goats together, and herds of cattle (see table 3). Even though the state of preservation of the texts does not always allow a full assessment of their formulation and content, they all seem to share some common features: the animals are listed according to age and sex, followed by the total number of animals, the names of the owner and of the shepherd or herdsman responsible for the animals, and the date. These lists can be further divided between sealed and unsealed ones. The first may be sealed by the owner (who used a cylinder seal) and/or by the shepherd (who used his fingernail); because of the presence of a seal impression, they can be regarded as formal bilateral agreements between livestock owners and shepherds. The unsealed ones, on the other hand, may rather be seen as memoranda without legal force.[2] While such unsealed lists do not explicitly express any liability of the shepherds, the very existence of a written record witnessing that a specific shepherd was in charge of a certain flock or herd would have been enough to hold him accountable for it.

Among the sealed lists, two contain a reference to the obligations of the shepherd toward the flock's owner. **No. 257**: 14–16 records that "he (i.e., the shepherd) gave 50 newborns every 100 (and) hide, sinew and fat every 10 (dead animals)." These lines recall the obligations of the persons responsible for herds and flocks at Nippur, as described in BE 14 137 and MUN 318–19, 321 (dealing with cattle), and MUN 329–30 (dealing with sheep and goats).[3] These texts establish that for every ten dead animals, the herdsmen and the *ḫazannu*s will have to deliver the hides, and they set the expected yield of a herd at fifty newborns per hundred animals (as in our text). However, there are also some interesting differences arising from a comparison of no. 257 with the published texts from Nippur. While the Nippur texts describe the future obligations of the shepherd, our

| | Text no. | Owner | Shepherd | Sealing(s) |
|---|---|---|---|---|
| Sheep | **249** | Ninurta-zākir-šumi | Rēš-aṣûšu | – |
| Goats | **254** | Ninurta-zākir-šumi | Sîn-aḫa-iddina | Fingernail impression of Sîn-aḫa-iddina + seal of Ninurta-zākir-šumi |
| Sheep and | **256** | Iqīša-Marduk | [Son of] Ṭābiḫu | Sealed by Iqīša-Marduk |
| goats | **257** | Ninurta-zākir-šumi | Apil-Nergal | Fingernail impression of Apil-Nergal |
| | **262** | Dimaḫdi-Uraš | [...] | Sealed by Dimaḫdi-Uraš |
| Cattle | **263** | Ninurta-zākir-šumi | Namru | – |
| | **264** | Ninurta-zākir-šumi | Namru | Sealed by Ninurta-zākir-šumi |
| | **265** | Ninurta-kīn-pīšu | Namru | – |

**Table 3.** Lists recording flocks and herds

[1] On *naptanu* being ritual banquets, see Sassmannshausen 2001, 327–28.

[2] Cf. the remarks by Postgate (2013, 295, 297) on the unsealed and unwitnessed Middle Assyrian flock lists from Tell Ali.

[3] See the discussion of these texts by Brinkman (2004, 290–91), who improves Sassmannshausen's readings and lists other similar unpublished texts from Nippur.

text states that such obligations have been fulfilled already;[1] this difference probably explains why the Nippur texts are sealed by the *šandabakku* (the livestock's owner), while our text is sealed by the shepherd. Finally, Brinkman noted that "all the texts in this group preserving a full year date come from either year 10 or 11 of Šagarakti-Šuriaš" (Brinkman 2004, 290 n. 36); our text indicates that the same regulations were already valid during the reign of Nazi-Maruttaš.

A description of the future obligation of a shepherd is contained in **no. 264**: 10–11: here, he is required to deliver ghee "according to (the requirements of) the offerings."

From these lists, Ninurta-zākir-šumi appears to have been the most important livestock owner at this time, who disposed of hundreds of animals.

A subset of these flock lists consists of smaller texts that record the allocation of only a few animals, belonging to different persons, to a shepherd (**nos. 246–47**).

The second type of flock record is represented by multicolumn ledgers that record flocks of sheep and goats together. They are not sealed and must have been secondary compilations drawn up to facilitate supervising several flocks at once. **Nos. 258–60** have a similar structure: the first set of columns records the numbers of different types of sheep, classified by age and sex, followed by a column listing the subtotal (PAP) of sheep; the second set of columns records goats classified by age and sex and the subtotal (PAP) of goats; the next column provides the grand total (ŠU.NÍGIN) of animals; and the last column, preserved only in one case (**no. 260**), bears the usual heading MU.BI.IM and lists names of individuals, who might have been either the owners or shepherds in charge of the flocks.[2] Note that the fragmentary heading of text **no. 258** refers to the content of the account as LA'U$_4$ "arrears." **No. 261** is a tabular account of adult sheep (UDU.NÍTA, U$_8$) and goats (MÁŠ, ÚZ), associated in the last column with personal names and subtotals for different towns (Dūr-Bēl-mātāti, Dūr-Enlilē, Kār-Nin-[Eanna?]); the small figures and the presence of the word *aklu*, even though in fragmentary context (l. 40), may suggest that it was an account of animals meant as *aklu*-expenditures.

There are no similar records for herds of donkeys or horses.[3]

## 3. Economic Activities

### 3.1 Primary Production

#### 3.1.1 Agriculture

A large part of the documentation deals with the centralized management of agricultural activities and concerns mainly the cultivation of the following products:

- cereals: barley (ŠE, ŠE.BAR), wheat (GIG), emmer (ZÍZ.AN.NA), *arsuppu* (ŠE.EŠTUB), *šeguššu* (ŠE.MUŠ$_5$),[4] and *ennēnu/innin(n)u* (ŠE.IN.NU.ḪA)
- sesame (ŠE.GIŠ.Ì)
- pulses (GÚ.TUR, GÚ.GAL, GÚ.NÍG.ÀR.RA)[5]
- cress (ZAG.ḪI.LI$^{(sar)}$)

---

[1] Cf. the use of durative verbal forms such as *inaddin*, *imaddin*, and *ušetteq* in MUN 329 and 330 with the preterite *iddin* in **no. 257**: 16.

[2] See also CUSAS 30 413, an undated multicolumn ledger about sheep and goats with a similar structure: here, however, the last column contains references to six month names. This ledger has also a column headed *kaniktu*: according to van Soldt (2015, 494), this column "lists how many of the sheep and goats have been recorded in a sealed document."

[3] See, however, CUSAS 30 412, an undated multicolumn ledger that lists horses and donkeys by age.

[4] *arsuppu* (ŠE.EŠTUB) and *šeguššu* (ŠE.MUŠ$_5$) might correspond to two varieties of millet, sown respectively in spring and in autumn (see most recently Dornauer 2018, 45–67).

[5] The corresponding Akkadian words and the identification with specific types of pulses are still debated: GÚ.TUR (Akk. *kakkû*?) might correspond to pea or lentil, GÚ.GAL (Akk. *ḫallūru*?) to chickpea or broad bean, and GÚ.NÍG.ÀR.RA (Akk. *kiššanu*?) to vetch; see Powell 2003, 21–22 and Dornauer 2018, 27 with previous literature.

Agricultural production took place at different locations, as witnessed, e.g., by the fact that agricultural revenues were delivered by several towns or villages (**nos. 1–46**). The accounts recording "stored grain" (**nos. 47–60**) suggest that the crops were stored locally and not necessarily physically sent to the administrative center, which oversaw production and kept the relevant written records. At least part of the crops remained *in loco*, as indicated by the evidence that agricultural goods were being disbursed at different locations (*ina* GN *nadānu*);[1] the distribution would have been much easier to organize if the resources were locally available.

The distribution of seed and rations for plowmen is often attested in the accounts of expenditures, either as distinct items or in combination with fodder for the oxen.[2] In some cases, the recipients are identified as farmers (ÉNSI; see, e.g., **no. 147**: 6–8 and **no. 176**: 3–5). A preliminary survey of a sample of recipients of seed highlighted also several correspondences with the individuals mentioned in the accounts of revenues, usually listed in pairs. See, e.g., the following:

| | Disbursement of seed | Collection of revenues |
|---|---|---|
| Ninurta-zākir-šumi + Banâ-ša-Marduk | **no. 162**: 6, **no. 156**: 6 | **no. 5**: 7, **no. 7**: 8, **no. 53**: 8 |
| Ninurta-zākir-šumi + Bunna-Marduk | **no. 108**: 3, **no. 164**: 6 | **no. 5**: 11 |
| Ninurta-zākir-šumi + Kalbu | **no. 108**: 4 | **no. 1**: 15, **no. 2**: 21 |
| Ninurta-zākir-šumi + Nūr-Ištar | **no. 156**: 9, **no. 164**: 10 | **no. 5**: 10, **no. 6**: 10, **no. 2**: 25, **no. 7**: 6 |
| Ninurta-zākir-šumi + Nuska-nābûšu | **no. 162**: 5 | **no. 53**: 6 |
| Ninurta-zākir-šumi + Rabâ-ša-Bēlti | **no. 108**: 5, **no. 156**: 5 | **no. 5**: 12, **no. 6**: 11, **no. 55**: 12, 18 |

The administration provided also copper sickles (**no. 303**) and sacks, probably meant for the transport of harvested crops (**no. 304**).[3]

Activities connected with the maintenance of the irrigation system are witnessed by the allocation of rations for workers employed in the excavation of canals (**no. 94, 97**: 14, **98**: 13, **184**: 4).

### 3.1.2 Animal Husbandry

Evidence for this sector of the economy can be garnered first and foremost from texts specifically devoted to the management of livestock such as the flock records seen above, which provide information about the composition of flocks and herds, and the livestock owners and the shepherds in charge of the animals (**nos. 244–64**, see above §2.3).

The composition of the flocks shows the usual preponderance of female animals.

Plucking took place in spring, as witnessed by an account of 96 sheep that "entered the plucking house" (*bīt buqūni*) in month II of Kadašman-Turgu's 14th year (**no. 250**).

Further evidence for livestock breeding and for the employment of animals in agricultural activities is provided also by other types of documents. Texts recording the disbursement of cereals often include fodder (ŠUKU) for sheep, oxen, donkeys, and horses, and once also bird seed (ŠUKU MUŠEN$^{ḫi.a}$, **no. 139**: 34). They used barley, emmer, flour, and draff as fodder for the animals.

The main use of oxen was as plow animals, and one often finds the distribution of fodder for oxen associated with the distribution of seed and rations for plowmen (see, e.g., **no. 156** and **no. 176**). In addition to

---

[1] For instance, in Dūr-Enlilē (**no. 108**, **no. 131**, and **no. 144**) as well as in Āl-irrē (**no. 161** and **no. 176**).

[2] Seed: see, e.g., **no. 108**, **no. 147**: 6–8, and **no. 162**: 5–11; rations for plowmen: see, e.g., **no. 159**: 15–16, **no. 134**: 2′, and **no. 171**: 8; rations for plowmen together with fodder for oxen: see, e.g., **no. 131** and **no. 179**; seed, rations for plowmen, and fodder for oxen: see, e.g., **no. 156** and **no. 176**: 4–6.

[3] The persons who receive the sickles and the sacks are the same, even though the two texts are dated to different years of the reign of Nazi-Maruttaš.

the generic term for ox (GU$_4$), one finds also GU$_4$.NIGA, "fattened ox" (**no. 136**: 20, **no. 150**: 11, 23, **no. 98**: 5);[1] GU$_4$.ŠÀ.GU$_4$, "plow-ox" (**no. 266**: 2′); GU$_4$ *ritti*, "plow$^{?}$-ox" (**no. 325**: 6); GU$_4$.NÍNDA DIRI, "extra bull-calf" used a as reserve in plow teams (**no. 325**: 1); and [GU$_4$].⸢Á$^{?}$⸣.ÚR.RA, "rear-[ox]" (**no. 326**: 1).

Oxen and donkeys were employed as draft animals for the transportation of agricultural products (see, e.g., **no. 159**: 19–21).

Sheep, lambs, and goats are among the items disbursed as *aklu*-expenditures. There are several attestations of UDU.NIGA, "fattened sheep,"[2] which in three cases belonged to a *ḫazannu* (**no. 150**: 22, **no. 153**: 9, **no. 162**: 12).

Among the texts published in this volume, there is no evidence for the distribution of carcasses and cuts of meat attested in the later Kassite texts of the Rosen Collection (see, e.g., CUSAS 30 383, 384, 387).

Shepherds appear among the recipients of barley expenditures, sometimes explicitly defined as rations (ŠE.BA). The usual term for shepherd in these texts is SIPA (*rē'û*), irrespective of the animals they took care of.[3] The term can be used in a generic way, but sometimes the texts specify that the herdsmen were in charge of cattle (SIPA ÁB.GU$_4$$^{\text{ḫi.a}}$, SIPA GU$_4$$^{\text{meš}}$), donkeys (SIPA ANŠE$^{\text{(meš)}}$), or horses (SIPA ANŠE.KUR.RA$^{\text{meš}}$). There are a few references to shepherds linked to the royal house (see §4.6).

Shepherds supplied the textile industry with goat hair (**no. 268**) and leather workers with hides (**no. 298**).

## 3.2 Secondary Production

### 3.2.1 Milling

Among the earlier Kassite texts in the Rosen Collection, there are considerably fewer attestations of millers than in the later ones.[4] Millers (KA.ZÌ.DA) are never explicitly indicated as recipients of rations, although female *ararratu*-millers (MUNUS.ÀR) do receive rations (**no. 96**, **no. 186**: 5–6). In contrast, production supplies are attested only for millers (**no. 111**, **no. 112**, **no. 139**: 18–20, **no. 150**: 4, **no. 153**: 6), not for female *ararratu*-millers.

Texts usually refer to millers as an anonymous group, sometimes associated with a toponym ("millers of Nippur" in **no. 139**: 20 and "millers of Dūr-[Enlil]ē$^{?}$" in **no. 153**: 6). On the millers from Nippur and the geographic range of the millers' activities, see the discussion in the section about brewing (§3.2.2).

The distribution of production supplies to millers was supervised by Ninurta-ašarēd (**no. 111** and **no. 139**: 18–20; see also §4.1).

Flour (ZÌ.DA) occurs often among the foodstuffs disbursed in the *aklu*-expenditures. Different types of flour are listed in **no. 61**. Bread occurs only once, together with beer, as a foodstuff for the *bītānu* (**no. 294**).

### 3.2.2 Brewing

Beer brewing is indicated by the frequent presence of brewers in the texts, where they mainly appear as recipients of cereals as production supplies (ÉŠ.GÀR).[5] Unlike the millers, brewers are mentioned usually by name (see attestations in the Index of Professions). Among the texts that provide the names of brewers, **no. 112** deserves special attention. The text is a tabular account of barley disbursed as production supplies for brewers and millers between month VII and month XII of Nazi-Maruttaš's 19$^{\text{th}}$ year and is noteworthy for several reasons. First of all, some names of the recipients, which appear as column headings along the horizontal axis of the table, correspond to the names of brewers and millers attested at Nippur during the reign

1 The fattened oxen of **no. 150** belonged to a *ḫazannu*. See Sassmannshausen 2001, 455 n. 3681 for attestations of fattened oxen in the Nippur texts.

2 See Sassmannshausen 2001, 455 n. 3681 for attestations of fattened sheep in the Nippur texts.

3 On shepherds in the Kassite period see Sassmannshausen 2001, 109–14.

4 See van Soldt 2015, 578–79, s.v. *ararratu*, *ararru*, and *kaṣṣidakku*.

5 **No. 110**, **no. 112**, **no. 114**, **no. 133**: 5–7, **no. 135**: 6–7, **no. 136**: 7, **no. 149**: 5, **no. 138**: 4, **no. 160**: 2, **no. 163**: 6. Note also the distribution of brewing ingredients (ZÌ.MUNU$_4$) in **no. 115**.

of Nazi-Maruttaš: these are the brewers Bā'eru and Rīmūtu and the millers Lā-qīpu, Sîn-muballiṭ, and Tarību (cf. Sassmannshausen 2001, 78 and 80). The presence of these workers at two locations not only represents an important link between Nippur and the administrative center that produced the Rosen tablets (see §4.6) but also supports Deheselle's (2004) picture of itinerant brewers and millers during the Kassite period[1] and provides a key to interpreting the entries of the MU.BI.IM-column of no. 112. These consist of geographical names, usually followed by the indication of a month, sometimes also by the name of the person who delivered the barley. Consider, for instance, the entries for the brewer Bā'eru:

| | Bā'eru | [Its] entry |
|---|---|---|
| l. 2 | | |
| l. 4 | 2.0.0 | Āl-irrē [ |
| l. 6 | 26.1.1 | Āl-Arad-Bīt-Kiš, mon[th |
| l. 7 | 2.0.0 | Dūr-Enlilē [<br>from Nuska-nābûšu. |
| l. 8 | 4.2.3 | Tukultī-Ekur, from Ki[. . . |
| l. 11 | 5.0.0 | Ḫamru, month XII. |
| l. 14 | 12.1.3<br>TA 1.2.4 | From that of Zarāt-šarri:<br>Āl-Arad-Bīt-Kiš, month X[II],<br>from Ninurta-zākir-šumi. |
| l. 15 | 15.0.0 | Tukultī-Ekur (eras.),<br>month VII. |

In light of the previous considerations, it is possible that these geographical names indicate the towns where Bā'eru carried out his "itinerant" job as brewer—i.e., Āl-irrē, Āl-Arad-Bīt-Kiš, Dūr-Enlilē, Tukultī-Ekur, and Ḫamru. The same scheme would apply also to the entries about the other brewers and millers mentioned in the text.

A different case is represented by **no. 110**, which records the production supplies for the brewer Agab-šenni. The text states that the barley came "fr[om the reven]ues of the towns" (*i[na libbi tēl]īti ša ālāni*, l. 1); more precisely, different amounts are said to originate from the revenues of Dūr-Enlilē, Ḫamru, and Dūr-Bēl-mātāti. Here it cannot be determined whether Agab-šenni worked as a brewer in the different towns that delivered the barley or whether the barley was available at a single location, where Agab-šenni worked and probably also where the tablet was written.

Sometimes the texts indicate the institutional or geographic affiliation of the brewers: hence, we meet Nannaya, brewer of the Ekur temple (**no. 66**: 2–3); Kidin-Gula, brewer of the Ešumeša temple (**no. 187**: 6; CUSAS 30 68: 11); and Kagiya, brewer from Parak-māri (**no. 171**: 10).

A "share of the brewing" (*zitti sibûti*) is mentioned in accounts of revenues (**no. 4**: 10–11) and as an amount delivered by a brewer for storage in the granary, for which he receives compensation (**no. 146**: 5); it is difficult to establish the exact nature of this "share" that, to my knowledge, was previously unattested.

Brewers appear among the recipients of loans (**no. 164**: 18–19, 21) and of gifts (**no. 171**: 10).

Beer of first and second quality (KAŠ.SAG and KAŠ.ÚS) occurs among the foodstuffs disbursed in the *aklu*-expenditures, for which brewers are sometimes explicitly designated as responsible (**no. 235**). Other allocations of beer are **nos. 293–95**.

Allocations of sourdough (BAPPIR) are only rarely attested (**no. 159**: 19, 23, 26; **no. 164**: 27; and **no. 179**: 23′).

Draff (DUḪ/*tuḫḫū*), a by-product of the brewing process, could be used as fodder for animals (**no. 149**: 10; **no. 156:** 14, 19, 34; and **no. 295**: 8).

1 Deheselle's reconstruction has been recently challenged by Paulus, in press, who regards it as unlikely that brewers and millers would have been traveling craftsmen who moved from town to town.

### 3.2.3 Textile Industry

Activities linked with textile production are witnessed mainly by allocations of wool (**nos. 267–72**) and various types of records dealing with garments and fabrics (**nos. 273–90**).

The allocations refer either generically to wool (SÍG, see **no. 267** and **no. 269**) or to wool dyed in different colors and to combed wool (see **nos. 270–72**); once, goat hair is mentioned (**no. 268**).

The term *mandattu* appears to be a key word in textile production. In most cases, it is further defined as the *mandattu* of a certain year. It occurs

- in connection with wool deliveries to textile workers and with an indication of the types of garments they had to produce;[1]
- in texts that record the allocations of garments to different persons, which sometimes specify that the garments came from the *mandattu* of a certain textile worker (*ina libbi mandatti ša* MU.X.KAM *ša* PN);[2]
- in memoranda that record the delivery of garments as "arrears of the *mandattu*" of a textile worker (*ribbat mandatti ša* MU.X.KAM *ša* PN).[3]

The evidence from the Rosen texts suggests that *mandattu* indicated the "work assignment" of textile workers[4] rather than the "work material" assigned to them[5] and referred likely to a system of centrally issued quantities of wool from which textile workers had to produce every year a fixed number of garments. Similar systems are known also from other regions and historical periods of the ancient Near East.[6] As for "work material" in the context of textile production, some texts from Nippur suggest that the term used was *iškaru* (ÉŠ.GÀR),[7] the same term that indicated cereals disbursed to millers and brewers as raw materials to produce flour and beer.

Unsurprisingly, most of the persons who received wool or delivered garments on completion of their work assignments were women. One of them, Bunna-Gula, had an important position within this system, since she not only produced garments but also was responsible for most of the expenditures.[8] A similar role was held by Sugir-bunni, a man who issued garments and also received the arrears of the work assignments delivered by other workers.[9]

The officials who authorized the expenditures by sealing them were Ninurta-zākir-šumi, who sealed most of the receipts; Ninurta-gāšir-ilāni; and Enlil-gešir?-ilāni.

---

1 **No. 267** and CUSAS 30 366; see also CUSAS 30 369, which, however, does not specify which garments had to be crafted. For Nippur, see MUN 350 and MUN 351.

2 **No. 279**, **no. 286**, **no. 287**, **no. 289**.

3 **No. 282**, **no. 284**, **no. 285**.

4 See also CAD M/1, *maddattu* 2 a, 15 "work assignment," and AHw II, *ma(d)dattu(m)*, *mandattu* 3 a, 572 "etwa Ablieferungspensum (v Web- und Näharbeiten)."

5 Sassmannshausen 2001, 299–300; Tenney 2011, 100.

6 Cf., e.g., the *iškāru*-system of work assignments to weavers known from the Middle Assyrian (Postgate 2014, 401–4) and Neo-Babylonian sources (Zawadzki 2006, 20–21; Joannès 2013, 401, 403).

7 See, e.g., MUN 345 (allocation of goat hair) and MUN 355 (allocation of wool).

8 Identified as (ZI.GA) ŠU *Bunna-Gula* "(expenditure), responsibility of Bunna-Gula" in **nos. 274–78** and CUSAS 30 372 (for which see also the following footnote).

9 Expenditures supervised by Sugir-bunni: **nos. 273, 281**, and **290**; deliveries of (arrears of) work assignments to Sugir-bunni: **nos. 282, 284**, and **286**. Sugir-bunni, who bears an Elamite name, has been discussed by van Soldt (2015, 27–28) as one of the "main actors" of the later texts. Van Soldt considered that CUSAS 30 371 and CUSAS 30 372, both accounts of garments respectively dated to year 15 and year 17+, could be assigned to the reign of Kadašman-Turgu and would therefore represent the earliest attestations of Sugir-bunni in the texts he published: this is now confirmed by the evidence provided by the earlier texts, where most of Sugir-bunni's activity is concentrated in years 15–16 of Kadašman-Turgu.

The purpose of the expenditures is not always specified, but one often finds garments listed as a "votive offering" (SISKUR).[1] Two texts connect the issuing of garments with the "ceremony for dedication" known as *tērubtu*[2] (**no. 277** and **no. 280**).

Outside this group of texts, textile workers are mentioned among the recipients of rations (see esp. **nos. 100–101**). While women are never explicitly identified as weavers, men are identified as weavers (*išparu*/UŠ.BAR), knotters (*kāṣiru*/KA.KÉŠ), and fullers (*ašlāku*/[lú]ÁZLAG); there is also one reference to a *māḫiṣu*-weaver in an account of revenues (**no. 3**: 16′).

## 4. Administrative Structure

In the earlier Kassite texts of the Rosen Collection, some individuals stand out because of the central role they played in the local administration. Among the "main actors," the most prominent is Ninurta-zākir-šumi, a member of the family of Enlil-kidinnī; his presence in the texts is ubiquitous, and he certainly had a central role in several branches of the administration. However, it is not clear whether he should be regarded also as the head of the whole administrative system. In fact, it is difficult to reconstruct a precise chain of command and to define the specific areas of responsibility and range of activities of each official. They rather seem to have shared responsibilities, as they were all involved in several types of transactions concerning different branches of resource management.

In this context, it seemed useful to review also the evidence about other officials, identified as such by their titles, who did not necessarily play a prominent role in the administrative structure witnessed by these texts. Their presence is nonetheless significant because it reveals the degree to which the local administration was modeled on the administrative and governmental apparatus of Nippur. Parallels between the administrative systems in these two locations partially compensate for the lack of any explicit information about the institution or higher authority for which the persons mentioned in the texts worked.

As part of a preliminary assessment of the administrative and economic reality reflected by these documents, the following discussion also considers the presence and role of administrative units, storage facilities, and temples mentioned in the texts and highlights additional features shared by the local administration and Nippur.

Finally, the discussion takes into account the degree of interaction between the royal and provincial government in order to evaluate how the local administrative center that produced the Rosen texts was embedded in the administrative structure of the kingdom and of the Nippur province.

### 4.1 The Main Actors

**Ninurta-zākir-šumi.** Ninurta-zākir-šumi is by far the personal name that occurs most often in the texts published in this volume.[3] It is never associated with a title and only rarely with a patronymic. In two legal texts, Ninurta-zākir-šumi is named as the son of Enlil-kidinnī (CUSAS 30 1: 4–5 and CUSAS 30 3: 3) and as the father of Aḫu-damqu (CUSAS 30 1: 6–7) and of Ninurta-kiššat-ilāni (CUSAS 30 3: 7); perhaps he was also the father of Bēlānu (CUSAS 30 358: 7). While Aḫu-damqu is otherwise almost absent from the

---

[1] Also at Nippur; see Sassmannshausen 2001, 166.

[2] See Sassmannshausen 2001, 171; CAD T, *tērubtu* 1b, 369.

[3] This name is fully spelled [md]*Nin-urta-za-kir-šu-mi* only once (CUSAS 30 1); otherwise, the second part of the name is always written logographically -MU-MU, which led to some uncertainty about its reading either as Ninurta-zākir-šumi or as Ninurta-nādin-šumi (cf. the entries on Ninurta-nādin-šumi and Ninurta-zākir-šumi in Hölscher 1996, 157, 159; van Soldt 2015, 558 leaves Ninurta-MU-MU unread). However, in this corpus, the PNs containing a form of the verb *nadānu* are usually written with the logogram SUM, rather than with MU: thus, it might be safely assumed that the logographic writing Ninurta-MU-MU corresponds to Ninurta-zākir-šumi. This assumption is supported by the use of two distinct spellings at Nippur for Ninurta-zākir-šumi ([md]*Nin-urta*-MU-MU) and for Ninurta-nādin-šumi ([md]*Nin-urta*-SUM-MU; Sassmannshausen 2001, 487).

sources and Bēlānu is too common a name to distinguish the son of Ninurta-zākir-šumi from possible namesakes, Ninurta-kiššat-ilāni becomes an important official in the later phase of the archive (van Soldt 2015, 24). As for the chronological framework, the first secure attestation of Ninurta-zākir-šumi dates to Nazi-Maruttaš 13 and the latest to Kadašman-Turgu 15, covering a time span of some thirty years.[1]

Assuming that all attestations refer to the same person,[2] Ninurta-zākir-šumi appears in a wide variety of functions. He is prominent in accounts of revenues delivered by different towns (passim), even though he is often exempted from paying the *šibšu* (**no. 2**: 47, **no. 4**: 36, **no. 5**: 18, **no. 7**: 25) and the *kiṣru* (**no. 32**: 8). He is the holder of "shares" of cereals (*zittu*/ḪA.LA), which are accounted for in records of revenues (**no. 38**: 1, **no. 39**: 1, **no. 52**: 14–15, **no. 55**: 12–13) but are also indicated as amounts from which cereals are disbursed for various purposes (**no. 135**, **no. 144**, **no. 84**, and **no. 168**).

From the flock and herd records, we learn also that he was an important livestock owner (**nos. 249, 254, 257, 263–64**).

But his key role in the administration is revealed especially by the fact that he supervises the distribution of all types of goods: cereals disbursed for different purposes, foodstuffs allocated as *aklu*-expenditures, and garments. In fact, he is the official who seals most of the documents from the reigns of Nazi-Maruttaš and Kadašman-Turgu. In doing so, he uses mainly a seal whose seven-line legend reads, "Uṣi-ana-nūr-Enlil, *nêšakku* of Enlil, son of Ninurta-muballiṭ, descendant of Erība-Marduk, descendant of the fourth generation of Nuska-nīšu, servant of Nuska and of Sadaranunna."[3] Since the *nêšakku* of Enlil was the highest religious dignitary of the Kassite kingdom and this title was often held by the *šandabakku*,[4] it reveals Ninurta-zākir-šumi's strong connections with Nippur. Uṣi-ana-nūr-Enlil, the original seal's owner, is otherwise unknown; thus it is difficult to reconstruct Ninurta-zākir-šumi's relationship to him, but this situation can be compared with a similar one at Nippur, where a number of *aklu*-texts were sealed by Ninurta-nādin-aḫḫē with a seal that actually belonged to the *šandabakku* Enlil-alsa.[5] While Enlil-alsa was *šandabakku* of Nippur during the reign of Kurigalzu II and at the beginning of Nazi-Maruttaš's reign,[6] the documents sealed by Ninurta-nādin-aḫḫē with Enlil-alsa's seal date to the reigns of Kadašman-Enlil II and Kudur-Enlil, some forty years after Enlil-alsa's "mandate" as *šandabakku*. This suggests that also Ninurta-zākir-šumi and Uṣi-ana-nūr-Enlil might have lived and worked in periods that were decades apart from each other and that the use of Uṣi-ana-nūr-Enlil's seal indicates that Ninurta-zākir-šumi worked for the Nippur administration, but it does not necessarily imply a direct, personal connection with the authority to which the seal belonged originally.

Ninurta-zākir-šumi's degree of responsibility for resource management is revealed also by texts such as **no. 58**, where he is identified as the official in charge of more than 700 kor of barley described as the "rest of the stores."

A legal document shows that Ninurta-zākir-šumi held some authority also in the administration of justice, since he could decide whether a person should be released from prison (CUSAS 30 17).

---

1 It is not certain whether the attestations in CUSAS 30 56 (KuE x) and CUSAS 30 358 (ŠŠ 3) refer to the same person.

2 The prosopography of this corpus presents the same difficulties known to those who work with the prosopography of other Kassite sources, especially with the Nippur texts—i.e., a relatively limited repertoire of names, coupled with sporadic information about filiation or title (cf. Hölscher 1996, 6–7; Brinkman 2003–4, 398).

3 The same seal could be used also by another official, Ninurta-gašir-ilāni (see **no. 231** and **no. 281**). This and the other seals used in this corpus, as well as the sealing practices, will be the subject of a separate study by the author.

4 Sassmannshausen 2001, 61–62.

5 See MUN 164–80 and 181–86 (Sassmannshausen 2001, 320ff.).

6 Enlil-alsa took over the office of *šandabakku* from his father Enlil-kidinnī, who held it during the reign of Burna-Buriaš (see Sassmannshausen 2001, 16ff.; Hölscher 1996, 66).

Unfortunately, the identity of the addressee of Ninurta-zākir-šumi's letter to "his lord" remains unknown (CUSAS 30 31).

Two *aklu*-texts from Nippur (BE 14 78 and MUN 159) mention a Ninurta-zākir-šumi in connection with Dūr-Enlilē; they date to the reign of Nazi-Maruttaš, which falls within the period of activity of the Ninurta-zākir-šumi attested in the Rosen texts, and thus these *aklu*-texts very likely refer to the same person.

**Ninurta-ašarēd**. Ninurta-ašarēd, who is once identified as a scribe (CUSAS 30 135: 5),[1] was the son of Tarībat-ili and brother of Rēš-aṣûšu.[2] His activity is attested from year 18 of Nazi-Maruttaš to year 13 of Kadašman-Turgu.

He stands out as someone who often receives considerable amounts of cereals as production supplies (ÉŠ.GÀR)[3] and as staples (*maššartu*).[4] In some cases, it is further specified that the production supplies were for millers (KA.ZÌ.DA$^{(meš)}$; see CUSAS 30 135, **no. 111**, and **no. 139**). In CUSAS 30 311, a text that records the allocation of barley (probably rations) to a group of women, Ninurta-ašarēd is the person who receives the total amount and was probably in charge of disbursing it. We know from **no. 96** that some of these women were *ararratu*-millers (MUNUS.ÀR$^{meš}$), providing further evidence for Ninurta-ašarēd's involvement in activities linked with the milling process.

However, this was not Ninurta-ašarēd's only area of responsibility. This is clearly revealed by texts such as **no. 174**, where he receives large amounts of barley as production supplies (ÉŠ.GÀR), as supplies for temples (ŠUKU É.DINGIR$^{didli}$), as offerings for the cult of dead ancestors (*kispu*), and also as rations for three women whose profession is not indicated. Elsewhere, he is indicated as the person in charge of barley assigned to workers of the House of Tarībat-ili (**no. 120**: 37).

**No. 170** and CUSAS 30 141 shed light on another aspect of Ninurta-ašarēd's activities. In both texts, he receives several amounts of barley as compensation for what he provided to different people: the expression used is *qāssu turrat* (lit. "his hand is turned"), which might imply that Ninurta-ašarēd was being reimbursed for quantities of barley he gave as an interest-free loan.[5]

---

[1] This text, dated to the 21st year of an unnamed king, can be assigned to the reign of Nazi-Maruttaš because of the presence of Ninurta-ašarēd and of Kidin-Enlil, son of Sāmu: the latter occurs also in **no. 134**: 5′, which dates to NM 21.

[2] See the entries for Ninurta-ašarēd and Rēš-aṣûšu in the Index of Personal Names, showing that they are both attested as sons of Tarībat-ili; conclusive proof that they were brothers is provided by CUSAS 30 144: 4–5 (collation shows that van Soldt's reading $^{m}$*It-ti*-DINGIR can be corrected to $^{m}$*Ta-ri-bat*-DINGIR). The texts mention also Izkur-Marduk as a son of Tarībat-ili (**no. 28**: 15 and CUSAS 30 64: 17), but it cannot be ascertained whether he is the same Tarībat-ili who is father of Ninurta-ašarēd and of Rēš-aṣûšu.

[3] **No. 111** (NM 18), **no. 133** (NM 20), CUSAS 30 135 (NM 21), **no. 138** (NM x), **no. 147** (KT 2), **no. 113** (KT 3), **no. 153** (KT 6), **no. 51** (KT 7), **no. 54** (KT 12), CUSAS 30 132 (year 13, perhaps KT).

[4] **No. 146** (KT 2), CUSAS 30 141 (n.d.), CUSAS 30 143 (n.d.; from the granary of Nippur), CUSAS 30 131: 6 (n.d.); I suspect that Ninurta-ašarēd might also have been the recipient of 25 kor of barley assigned as *maššartu* to the "son of Tarībat-ili" in **no. 128**: 6 (NM 17). The term *maššartu* has been variously interpreted: "Entnahme" (AHw II, 629; Petschow 1974: 108), "assignment" (Gurney 1983, 172), or "staples set aside in a household for specific periods to be processed by its craftsmen" (CAD M/1, 387); cf. also van Soldt 2015, 34: "the exact meaning of this word is still not clear, at least for the Middle Babylonian period." Sassmannshausen (2001, 309–10) reviewed the Nippur occurrences and noted that *maššartu* can indicate a quantity of cereals that is disbursed (often as production supplies to millers and brewers) but also a quantity from which other amounts are disbursed (*ina libbi maššarti*); he then leaves the word untranslated (501: *maššartu* "[eine Getreidelieferung]"). The fact that in our texts Ninurta-ašarēd is often attested as a recipient of production supplies reinforces the idea that *maššartu* referred to "staples set aside in a household for specific periods to be processed by its craftsmen," as suggested by CAD; even though this was probably the main purpose of *maššartu*, it did not prevent the administrators from withdrawing amounts of cereals from it and allocate them for different purposes, not necessarily only as production supplies.

[5] On the legal meaning of the expression *qāta turru* and its connection with interest-free loans, see Paulus, in press.

Notably, his activity is connected to different towns: Āl-atḫē, Āl-irrē, Āl-Mīnâ-ēpuš-ila, Baṣātu, Dūr-Amurru, Dūr-Enlilē, Dūr-Nuska, Kār-Nuska, Nippur, Pī-nāri, and Tamirtu. In this regard, it is worthwhile to discuss **no. 182**, because it provides an insight into the geographic range of Ninurta-ašarēd's activities and his interaction with his brother Rēš-aṣûšu. The text is a summary of amounts of cereals received by Rēš-aṣûšu from Mudammiq-Adad. Each entry indicates a town, the person who delivered a specific amount of cereals, and a month.

**No. 182: iv 2–9**

| (Cereals) that Rēš-aṣûš[u, son of] Tarībat-ili, received fr[om Muda]mmiq-Adad: |
|---|
| Dūr-Enlilē, **from Ninurta-ašarēd**; month VI. |
| Ditto (i.e., Dūr-Enlilē), from Iqīša-Marduk, son of Ṭābiḫu; month VI. |
| Dimtu, from Šēmû, the gardener; month VI. |
| Kār-Nuska, **from Ninurta-ašarēd**; month VI. |
| Āl-irrē, **from Ninurta-ašarēd**; month VII. |
| Nippur, from the delivery (*maššītu*) of Āl-irrē, **from Ninurta-ašarēd**; month IX. |
| Ditto (i.e., Nippur), **from ditto (i.e., Ninurta-ašarēd)**; month XII. |
| Dūr-Enlilē, from Lūṣi-ana-nūr-Adad; month XII. |

In the operational flow recorded by this text, Rēš-aṣûšu is the final recipient; Mudammiq-Adad acts as a middleman; and Ninurta-ašarēd, Iqīša-Marduk, Šēmû, and Lūṣi-ana-nūr-Adad are those who provide the cereals. It is clear that Ninurta-ašarēd disposed of amounts of crops associated with different locations (Dūr-Enlilē, Kār-Nuska, Āl-irrē, Nippur), even though the terseness of the formulation does not indicate whether the different towns represented the origin of the cereals or the location(s) where the disbursements took place. It may be noted that the three protagonists of this transaction (Rēš-aṣûšu, Mudammiq-Adad, and Ninurta-ašarēd) were all scribes.[1]

Ninurta-ašarēd seals three texts in which he appears as the recipient of quantities of cereals (**nos. 88, 111,** and **143**).

In view of his connections with Nippur, one should probably identify the Ninurta-ašarēd, son of Tarībat-ili, mentioned as recipient of an unknown quantity of barley in a Nippur document from the reign of Nazi-Maruttaš (MUN 138), with the individual of the same name in the Rosen texts.

**Mudammiq-Adad.** This personal name occurs very often in both the earlier as well as the later texts of the corpus. His patronymic is never indicated. Among the several attestations, one can cite a Mudammiq-Adad who played a central role in the distribution of cereals; the earlier texts often indicate that different individuals receive cereals "from the hand" (*ina qāt*) of Mudammiq-Adad. He might be the same person who appears with the title of scribe in several legal documents that date from year 23 of Nazi-Maruttaš to year 3 of Šagarakti-Šuriaš, indicating a period of activity of some forty years.[2] If all attestations from the later texts refer to the same person, it seems that at a certain point, Mudammiq-Adad stops acting as a person in charge of distributing goods and is henceforth attested only as the recipient of relatively small quantities of cereals.

There are no texts sealed by him.

---

1 Rēš-aṣûšu appears with the title of scribe as witness of the legal document **no. 325** (NM 14). On Mudammiq-Adad, see below.

2 CUSAS 30 17 ([NM] 23?), **no. 327** (KT 5), **no. 330** (KT 14), CUSAS 30 2 (KaE 8, where he also bears the title of [lú]ḪAL "diviner"), CUSAS 30 10 (KuE 1), CUSAS 30 11 (KuE 9), CUSAS 30 12 (KuE x), CUSAS 30 7 (ŠŠ acc.), CUSAS 30 8 (ŠŠ 3), CUSAS 30 9 (ŠŠ x), CUSAS 30 16 (year 2), **no. 334** (n.d.). CUSAS 30 17 can be assigned to the reign of Nazi-Maruttaš because of the presence of Ninurta-zākir-šumi and of Namru, who is probably the shepherd frequently mentioned in the earlier texts of the corpus. Very likely, he is also the same scribe who wrote the legal texts published in Levavi 2017.

**Sîn-balāṭa-īriš**. In the earlier Kassite texts of the Rosen Collection, Sîn-balāṭa-īriš is mentioned frequently in association with Mudammiq-Adad: he receives cereals from him (*ina qāt Mudammiq-Adad*) but may also act as his representative (*kī qāt Mudammiq-Adad*). That the two officials collaborated closely is clearly witnessed by **no. 158**: this text records amounts of barley that Mudammiq-Adad received at different times from Sîn-balāṭa-īriš; then states that over several years, Mudammiq-Adad "turned the hand of Sîn-balāṭa-īriš" with regard to certain amounts of barley; and finally indicates the amount of barley that is still at the disposal of Mudammiq-Adad. Sîn-balāṭa-īriš acknowledges this account by sealing the tablet. The expression *qāt* PN *turru*, "to turn the hand of PN," probably implies that the barley was given as an interest-free loan by Sîn-balāṭa-īriš to Mudammiq-Adad and that the latter was now paying back part of his debt.[1]

Sîn-balāṭa-īriš is also one of the persons who is most often in charge of *aklu*-expenditures, where he acts under the supervision of Ninurta-zākir-šumi.

He sealed texts **no. 158** and **no. 269**.

### 4.2 Further Officials

***āpil bābi*, "gatekeeper."** Three persons with this title occur in this group of texts: Ardu, Baḫû, and Ibni-Marduk. Gatekeepers appear at Nippur almost exclusively in personnel rosters and ration lists (Sassmannshausen 2001, 56–57). Similarly, Ardu and Baḫû appear in a text that records the disbursement of rations (**no. 95**), while Ibni-Marduk, who is identified either simply as "gatekeeper" or as "gatekeeper of (the palace of) Isin,"[2] disposes of large amounts of barley, from which he might disburse loans (CUSAS 30 1 and **no. 138**) and production supplies (**no. 113**); he also appears among the recipients of *aklu*-expenditures (CUSAS 30 277 and CUSAS 30 293) and on one occasion receives a significant quantity of paint (**no. 301**).

***bēl pīḫāti*, "provincial governor."** This official, whose position in the hierarchy of the Kassite kingdom is not entirely clear (Sassmannshausen 2001, 27–29), appears twice in texts that record small amounts of barley identified as *kurummat bēl pīḫāti* (**no. 8** and **no. 51**; see comments to no. 8).

***ḫazannu*, "mayor."** Several *ḫazannu*s are mentioned in the texts published here. With the exception of Arad-nubatti, who is clearly identified as *ḫazannu* of the House of Enlil-kidinnī in the letter **no. 337**,[3] the documents usually do not explicitly indicate which town or village was under the authority of a certain *ḫazannu*. Thus establishing a sure link between a *ḫazannu* and a town is difficult, as shown by the case of Āl-irrē. In a summary of cereals expended from the revenues of this town (**no. 150**), two *ḫazannu*s are mentioned among the recipients of barley and emmer: the *ḫazannu* Adāya receives barley as compensation for an amount that he delivered to the granary, while the *ḫazannu* Adad-ilu-ina-māti receives barley as staples (*maššartu*), as fodder for an ox, and as *nikis karê*; he also receives emmer as fodder for sheep and an ox. Was any of these *ḫazannu*s the *ḫazannu* of Āl-irrē? Adad-ilu-ina-māti is a good candidate, since he receives the amount indicated as *nikis karê*, which might indicate that he was responsible for the distribution of the cereals expended from the revenues of Āl-irrē (see below). However, Adāya appears again in connection with cereals from Āl-irrē also in **no. 153**, where he receives staples (*maššartu*) and fodder for a sheep. Does this repeated connection imply that he was the *ḫazannu* of Āl-irrē? It is possible also that Adāya is simply a hypocoristic of Adad-ilu-ina-māti and that we are dealing with the same person; however, it seems odd that two versions of the name would be used alternately in the same text.

---

[1] This is not the only occasion when Sîn-balāṭa-īriš receives compensation for barley that he gave to different persons; see also CUSAS 30 90, discussed by Paulus, in press.

[2] To the occurrences listed in the Index of Personal Names at the end of this volume, add also those given by van Soldt 2015, 546.

[3] See §1.3.

In addition, another *ḫazannu* linked to Āl-irrē is Nūr-Adad, who receives emmer as seed and fodder for a sheep expended from the revenues of this town (**no. 162**).

Āl-irrē appears also in connection with the *ḫazannu* Izkur-Ninurta. In **no. 176**, an account of cereals disbursed in Āl-irrē, he receives a quantity of emmer, whose purpose is not specified, and an amount of barley intended as supplies for the temple of Ninurta in Parak-māri, which may be an indication that he was the *ḫazannu* of this locality.

Two more *ḫazannu*s can be associated with towns. One may assume that Ḫunābu was the *ḫazannu* of Āl-atḫē since he appears among the persons who deliver the revenue of sesame from this town (**no. 19**). Similarly, one may assume that Nuska-nāṣir was the *ḫazannu* of Āl-Mār-Bā'ili because he is associated with this town in the parallel texts **no. 97**, **no. 98**, and CUSAS 30 231.

Among the tasks associated often with the *ḫazannu*, one finds the so-called *nikis karê* (lit. "cut of the granary"), which appears as an item of expenditure in several documents that record the disbursement of cereals.[1] The evidence provided by the Rosen texts supports Sassmannshausen's proposal, based on the Nippur material, that *nikis karê* was a share that the *ḫazannu* could keep for himself.[2] The term *nikis karê*, "cut of the granary," may refer to the division of the granary's content among several recipients—an operation that might have been supervised by the local *ḫazannu*, who would have received a share as a reward.

Another recurrent pattern is the delivery of fodder for fattened animals to the *ḫazannu*s, which may be connected with the role played by these officials in the activities linked to livestock breeding witnessed in the Nippur texts (Sassmannshausen 2001, 31–32).

Finally, two *ḫazannu*s appear as witnesses in legal documents (Tukultī-lū-dāri in **no. 324** and Bananû in **no. 327**).

***mākisu*, "tax collector."** This official appears regularly in the *tēlītu*-texts in the word compound ŠE *mākisi*, "grain of the tax collector," which perhaps indicates a share of the revenues that the tax collector could keep for himself (Sassmannshausen 2001, 35); the same texts sometimes mention the *qārit* (ÉSAG) *mākisi*, "granary of the tax collector," which probably also indicated a type of agricultural revenue intended for the tax collector. It is only associated rarely with a personal name: in the earlier texts, the only tax collector known by name is Aḫēdūtu, who is responsible for the disbursement of an amount of barley received as a loan by another person in Dūr-Enlilē (**no. 122**). Interestingly, two texts from the 2nd year of Šagarakti-Šuriaš attest to the presence of two different tax collectors simultaneously: one acts as a witness in a legal document (Sîn-ibni in CUSAS 30 15), while the other is mentioned in a *tēlītu*-account (Tarību in CUSAS 30 38).

***mandidu*, "measuring official."** Contrary to the later Kassite texts of the Rosen Collection,[3] the earlier ones contain only a few attestations of measuring officials who occur in an account of revenues (Innunnu in **no. 17**) and in legal documents among the witnesses (Zākiru in **no. 330** and CUSAS 30 17).[4]

---

1 Associated with a *ḫazannu*: **no. 133**, **no. 147**, **no. 150**, **no. 185**, **no. 164**; not associated with a *ḫazannu*: **no. 55**, **no. 154**, **no. 159**, **no. 184**. See van Soldt 2015, 34 for the occurrences of *nikis karê* in the later Kassite texts of the Rosen Collection (note the writing KUD $GUR_7$ in CUSAS 30 149: 11, instead of the usual spelling *ni-ki-is* $GUR_7$).

2 Sassmannshausen 2001, 175.

3 See the attestations for *mandidu* listed by van Soldt 2015, 480.

4 The name of the measuring official who appears as a witness in CUSAS 30 17: 16′ can be restored [m*Za*]-⸢*ki*⸣-*rù*; the text is dated to year 23 of a king whose name is not preserved but probably belongs to the reign of Nazi-Maruttaš on prosopographic grounds.

***mār bīti*, lit. "son of the house."** The earlier Rosen texts offer new evidence on individuals identified as *mār bīti*,[1] which seems to confirm the view expressed by Sassmannshausen on the basis of the few attestations from Nippur—namely, that these persons represented a special category of palace employees who enjoyed a relatively high status (Sassmannshausen 2001, 126). They appear in texts dealing with the storage of revenues (Mūrānu, **no. 48**); as recipients of barley disbursed as compensation (again Mūrānu, **no. 150**), as seed (Ḫunābu, **no. 150**), and as a loan (Lūṣi-ana-nūr-Marduk in **no. 164**); as owners? of amounts of barley (Lūṣi-ana-nūr-Marduk, **no. 144**);[2] and also among the recipients of garments (Bēlānu, **no. 281**).

***rab zarāti*, lit. "chief of the tents."** To my knowledge, this title was previously known only from the text UDBD 96, where a *rab zarāti* named Adad-bēla-uṣur is involved in certain agricultural activities.[3] The Rosen texts do not contribute much to clarify the functions of this official, but Rīmūtu *rab zarāti* is named as a recipient of a loan in Āl-irrē (**no. 176**) and of an *aklu*-expenditure (**no. 184**).

***ṣuḫurtu*, "(an official)."** In MB texts, *ṣuḫurtu* probably indicates "a class or profession" rather than an age designation;[4] the *ṣuḫurtu* and the *ṣuḫurti šarri* must have had a relatively high status, but their exact function has not yet been determined.[5] In the earlier Kassite texts of the Rosen Collection, individuals identified as *ṣuḫurtu* appear delivering revenues (Rīmūtu in **no. 4**: 31 and Rabâ-ša-Sîn in **no. 43**: 4, 8) and as recipients of barley as gifts and of *aklu*-expenditures (Erība-Šuqamuna in **no. 150** and **no. 239**). Note also the anonymous *ṣuḫurtu* of the king who occurs among the recipients of beer in a text from the reign of Kudur-Enlil (CUSAS 30 281) and Itti-Marduk-balāṭu, another *ṣuḫurtu* of the king who collects a delivery of garments in the 2nd year of Šagarakti-Šuriaš (CUSAS 30 367).

***šaknu*, "overseer."** According to the evidence from Nippur, the *šaknu* often acts as an overseer of groups of workers (Sassmannshausen 2001, 42–43). In the texts of the Rosen Collection, this function of the *šaknu* is attested in CUSAS 30 434: 25 (n.d.). The texts published in this volume record the names of two overseers, who are also involved in other types of administrative acts. Arad-Marduk appears in an account of revenues from Dūr-Amurru (**no. 51**: 7) and as a recipient of 2 kor of barley as a gift, which he receives in place of Ninurta-zākir-šumi (**no. 150**: 16); rations are disbursed from the "delivery" (*maššītu*) of Arad-Marduk (**no. 69**). The overseer Lūṣi-ana-nūr-Adad occurs as a recipient of cereals as production supplies (**no. 159**: 27), as seed (**no. 164**: 12), and for an unspecified purpose (**no. 163**: 6). He might be the same person who appears as a witness in two legal texts dated to the accession year of Šagarakti-Šuriaš (CUSAS 30 7 and BE 14 127; see also §4.6).

***ša rēši*, "attendant."**[6] The texts published in this volume mention only two persons acting as *ša rēši*: Aḫēdūtu, who appears among the individuals who delivered wagons, probably transporting agricultural revenue, from the town of Tukultī-Ekur (**no. 45**), and Šamaš-qarrād, who receives an unknown amount of barley as a loan in Āl-irrē (**no. 176**). A *ša rēši* of the king occurs as a recipient of beer in a text from the reign of Kudur-Enlil (CUSAS 30 281).

---

[1] See van Soldt 2015, 34, 480 for *mār* and *mārat bīti* in the later texts.

[2] See also CUSAS 30 142 and CUSAS 30 150.

[3] CAD Z, 66; Sassmannshausen (2001) does not discuss this official.

[4] CAD Ṣ, 237, followed by Sassmannshausen 2001, 122–23; cf. AHw III, 1109 "etwa Jugentliche(r)."

[5] Sassmannshausen 2001, 122; Tenney 2011, 126 n. 185.

[6] It is not certain whether in Kassite Babylonia, the official or courtier identified by the term *ša rēši* was a eunuch; see Sassmannshausen 2001, 45 with reference to previous literature.

***tupšarru*, "scribe."** The lists of witnesses in the legal documents published here provide the names of four scribes:[1] Mudammiq-Adad (**nos. 327, 330, 334**), Rēš-aṣûšu (**no. 325**), Arad-Bēlti (**no. 326**), and Nuska-nābûšu (**no. 333**).[2] Another scribe active in the same period was Ninurta-ašarēd, mentioned with this title in the account of expenditures CUSAS 30 135 (NM? 21). These scribes probably correspond to the homonymous individuals who appear in prominent positions in the administrative texts, even though they are not explicitly identified there as scribes.

Two summaries of expenditures record small amounts of cereals as "food allocation (ŠUKU) for the donkeys and the scribe," in both cases for a time span of two days (**no. 162**: 14 and **no. 170**: 19). Because of such cases, it seems likely that the Mudammiq-Adad, who received an allocation of "fodder for the donkeys, food supplies, and sourdough bread" for six days (**no. 179**: 24′) was the person known as a scribe from the legal documents.

4.3 Administrative Units

***bābānu*, "outside."** The *bābānu* appears only as a recipient of rations. A group of three tablets, which provide three subsequent versions of an account of rations disbursed for the *bābānu* during the 9th year of Kadašman-Turgu (**no. 97**, **no. 98**, and CUSAS 30 231), are particularly useful for assessing the meaning of *bābānu* in these sources. They list amounts of barley and emmer associated with different localities (Āl-Arad-Bēlti, Āl-atḫē, Āl-irrē, Āl-Mār-Bā'ili, Āl-Mār-Kāri, Āl-šerikki, Bīt-Bēlāni, Dimtu, Ḫurād-Kaššî, Sikila, and Tukultī-Ekur), and some entries specify that such amounts were intended, e.g., as "rations of the workmen who dug the Nār-Tukultī-Ekur" or as "rations of 15 workmen who carried out the *dullu*-service in Āl-Arad-Bēlti" but also as food allocations for a temple of Ninnisi, probably located in Tukultī-Ekur. The geographic and typological range of the expenditures that fall under the heading *bābānu* suggests that here this term did not indicate only the "outer area of the palace" as in the Nippur texts (Sassmannshausen 2001, 153, 155) or the "personnel stationed outside the palace" (CAD B, *bābānu* 2, 7) but was used to refer generally to different activities taking place "outside"—i.e., in the surrounding areas under the authority of the administrative center that produced these documents. The three texts indicate Iqīša-Adad as the person in charge of the rations for the *bābānu*, a function he held already during the reign of Nazi-Maruttaš (see **no. 138**: 8); the presence of an overseer favors an identification of the *bābānu* as an administrative unit. It is not clear whether the *bābānu* might have corresponded to a specific building or sector of a palace.

Rations for the *bābānu* are recorded also in **no. 133**: 10.

Among the data provided by the later Rosen texts, note the "rations for families (working) outside" (*ipir qinnāti bābānu*), a phrase that appears in CUSAS 30 301: 28 and CUSAS 30 321: 28 as a caption for entries that record amounts of barley for several individuals.

***bītānu*, "inside, inner quarter."** The Nippur evidence suggests that the *bītānu* represented the "inner quarter" of a palace (Sassmannshausen 2001, 153, 155–56); it cannot be ascertained whether this was the case also in the center that produced the Kassite tablets of the Rosen Collection or whether here it referred simply to an administrative unit. Individuals associated with the *bītānu* (**no. 22**: 5, 16 and **no. 33**: 13) and an entry identified as "share of/for the brewing of the *bītānu*" (**no. 4**: 11) are attested in the records of revenues. Officials associated with the delivery of foodstuffs for the *bitānu* are Ninurta-zākir-šumi (**no. 128**: 5) and Ninurta-nāṣir

[1] In the legal texts from this corpus, if a scribe appears as witness, he is always mentioned at the end of the list, and the title can either follow or precede the scribe's name: see also CUSAS 30 1–12, 15–17, 21?; see the remarks of Sassmannshausen (2001, 48 n. 732) on the conventions at Nippur and Ur.

[2] Actually, the formulation IGI *Nuska-nābûšu mār Ayari tupšarri* is ambiguous: the title could have referred either to Nuska-nābûšu or to his father, Ayaru. The first option seems more likely because of Nuska-nābûšu's position at the end of the list of witnesses and because he should probably be identified with an individual who often occurs in the administrative texts, while Ayaru is otherwise almost absent from the sources.

(**no. 294**: 5). Considerable quantities of barley are expended as rations for the *bītānu* (**no. 133**: 9 and **no. 138**: 9). Finally, the *bītānu* had its own stocks of barley, from which the administration could withdraw amounts to be disbursed as rations (**no. 92**: 4).

***ēkallu*, "palace."** A palace is mentioned as the source of a quantity of barley in a record of expenditure (**no. 74**: 4) and in a letter (**no. 338**: 13).

4.4 Storage Facilities

***bīt kunukki* (É NA$_4$.KIŠIB), "storehouse."** At Nippur, the *bīt kunukki* was a building that belonged to the palace, where copper, precious metals, wood, and tools were stored; Sassmannshausen (2001, 171) suggests that the small quantities of foodstuffs delivered to the *bīt kunukki* were disbursed to cover the needs of those who worked there. The texts published in this volume provide evidence for the *bīt kunukki* as a place of storage for agricultural tools (copper sickles, see **no. 303**: 6) but also for cereals, as shown by documents that record the disbursement of fairly sizeable amounts of barley taken "from the *bīt kunukki*" (*ina libbi ša bīt kunukki*, see **no. 115**: 1 and **no. 152**: 1). One text records the allocation of barley as rations of the *bīt kunukki* (**no. 150**: 13).

***karû* (GUR$_7$), "silo," and *bīt karê* (É GUR$_7$), "granary."** The earlier Rosen texts often refer to cereals and other crops that are stored in silos (*ana karê tabku/tubbuku*).[1] There is one attestation of the granary of a person (*bīt karê Sîn-aḫa-iddina*, **no. 180**: 4).

For *nikis karê*, see §4.2, s.v. *ḫazannu*.

***qarītu* (ÉSAG), "granary."** The Rosen texts add to the limited information concerning this storage facility in MB sources, which was previously attested only in two Nippur texts (Sassmannshausen 2001, 175). It occurs as "granary of the tax collector" (*qarīt mākisi*) in tablets that deal with the collection or storage of agricultural revenues (**no. 11**: 6, **no. 51**: 5, and **no. 54**: 7). The inventory of tablets CUSAS 30 428: 1 mentions "one tablet of the granaries (ÉSAG$^{meš}$) of Dūr-Enlilē," probably referring to an account of the stocks stored therein.

On the storage of crops, see also §2.1.

4.5 Temples

Temples appear almost exclusively as recipients of cereals as supplies (ŠUKU).

Two texts from the 9th year of Kadašman-Turgu are devoted specifically to recording the allocation of barley for temples in different locations (**no. 118** and **no. 119**), which partially correspond to those listed in the Nippur text MUN 307, dated to the 3rd year of the same king (Sassmannshausen 2001, 374–75). The list includes locations in the Nippur area (e.g., Parak-māri) as well as farther away (e.g., Ḫursagkalama, close to Kiš).[2] Notably, **no. 119** shows that different towns contributed to the maintenance of such temples (Āl-irrē, Āl-atḫē, Tukultī-Ekur, and Dūr-Enlilē).

---

1 **No. 37**: 40, **no. 146**: 3, **no. 150**: 6, **no. 175**: 3.

2 The connection with a temple of Ištar suggests an identification with the settlement of Ḫursagkalama (Tell Ingharra) east of Kiš, which housed a sacred precinct of this goddess, but note that other occurrences of the toponym Ḫursagkalama in the Rosen texts might refer to a small town not far from the center that produced these tablets (van Soldt 2015, 152).

| | no. 119 | no. 118 | MUN 307 |
|---|---|---|---|
| Temple of Ninurta in Parak-māri | x | | x |
| Temple of Ninurta in Burranu | x | x | |
| Temple of Ninurta in Bīt-Bēri | x | | |
| Temple of Ninurta in Āl-ṣalamti | x | | x |
| Temple of Ninurta in Dunni-Isin | x | x | |
| Temple of Ištar in Ḫursagkalama | x | | x |
| Temple of Gula in Dūr-Enlilē | x | | x |
| Temple of Šarrat-[Nippur?] | x | | |
| Temple of Ninnisi (in Tukultī-Ekur?) | x | | |

Food allocations for temples are recorded also in summaries of barley expended for different purposes: as recipients, we find again the temples of Ninurta in Bīt-Bēri and Āl-ṣalamti (**no. 138**) and in Parak-māri (**no. 176**: 27), but more often there are only generic references to temples, with no indication of the deities worshipped in them or their locations.[1]

The reverse of **no. 24** probably records allocations of sesame to different shrines of the Ekur (KI.GUB SAG É.KUR and KI.GUB ÚS É.KUR) and to the Eki'ur, the shrine of Ninlil in the Ekur at Nippur.

Ovids are twice allocated to a temple of Gula as *aklu*-expenditures and, in one case, explicitly described as an offering (**no. 219**: 1–2 and **no. 243**: 8).

4.6 Interactions with the Royal and Provincial Government

Neither the king nor a member of the royal family appears to be personally involved in our texts. There are only a few references to royal employees, who do not seem to have particularly prominent roles: besides the *ṣuḫurtu*s of the king and the *ša rēši* of the king mentioned earlier (see §4.2 s.v.), note also the presence of some royal shepherds as recipients of barley.[2] An *aklu*-expenditure is issued on the occasion of the *arād šarri*, the royal voyage that took place on the occasion of the New Year's celebrations.

Attestations of the *šandabakku* of Nippur and of officials connected to him are rare. A letter of Amīl-Marduk to Ninurta-kiššat-ilāni (**no. 335**), containing a reprimand and a request for barley, might have been sent by the homonymous *šandabakku* who held this position between the 6th year of Kadašman-Enlil II and the 1st year of Kaštiliaš IV to the local official who was very active during the reigns of Kadašman-Enlil II, Kudur-Enlil, and Šagarakti-Šuriaš.[3]

A summary of rations allocated to female millers is noteworthy because it mentions the "son of Enlil-alsa" as the person who provided the barley (**no. 96**: 1, 11); the text is dated to Kadašman-Turgu 9, and the son of Enlil-alsa might have been the son of the homonymous *šandabakku* who governed Nippur during the reigns of Kurigalzu II and Nazi-Maruttaš (see Redina-Thomas 2015, 97–98).

Finally, a Rašu'u, "shepherd of the *šandabakku*" (SIPA *ša* GÚ.EN.NA), appears in an account of small cattle dated to the first year of Šagarakti-Šuriaš (CUSAS 30 394).

Nonetheless, other elements in the texts suggest that interactions with Nippur were frequent.

An important link between the two centers is represented by Ninurta-zākir-šumi, who was discussed earlier among the central figures of the reigns of Nazi-Maruttaš and Kadašman-Turgu (§4.1).

---

1 **No. 110**: 7, **no. 139**: 35, **no. 157**: 6, **no. 163**: 10 (here for the "temples of Ḫursagkalama"), **no. 174**: 6, **no. 187**: 7, **no. 214**: 2.

2 Baba-īriš "shepherd of the king" (SIPA LUGAL, **no. 159**), an anonymous shepherd of the horse of the king (SIPA ANŠE.KUR.RA *ša* LUGAL, CUSAS 30 293), and Arad-Nergal "shepherd of the horses of the prince" (SIPA ANŠE.KUR.RA$^{meš}$ *ša* DUMU.LUGAL, **no. 239**).

3 On the office of Amīl-Marduk, see recently Redina-Thomas 2015, 15–16; on Ninurta-kiššat-ilāni, see van Soldt 2015, 24–25.

Another official who provides a link between the two administrations is Rīmūtu. Four *aklu*-expenditures and one account of sheep from the Rosen Collection, all dated to the second half of Nazi-Maruttaš's reign, are sealed by him. Among these documents, the *aklu*-text **no. 202** is particularly noteworthy because it mentions the *arād šarri*, "coming/going down of the king,"[1] as well as Nippur as the place of the expenditure. Likely, there is a correspondence between this Rīmūtu and the homonymous official who sealed several *aklu*-texts from Nippur between Nazi-Maruttaš 14 and Kadašman-Turgu 15.[2] It is impossible to reconstruct the design of Rīmūtu's seal impressed on the texts from the Rosen Collection because usually only impressions of its cap are preserved, and so it cannot be compared with Rīmūtu's seal from Nippur.[3] It is remarkable, however, that in both cases, the cap was decorated with a triangular pattern. The number of shared features (text type, chronology, the cap of the seal, and the reference to Nippur in **no. 202**) makes it likely that we are dealing with the same official using the same seal.

The Rosen texts mention several brewers and millers as recipients of cereals as production supplies (ÉŠ.GÀR). Among them, the brewers Bā'eru and Rīmūtu and the millers Lā-qīpu, Sîn-muballiṭ, and Tarību probably correspond to the homonymous brewers and millers attested in texts from Nippur dating in the reign of Nazi-Maruttaš (see Sassmannshausen 2001, 78, 80). Here, one should recall also the presence of Nannaya, brewer of the Ekur, who occurs once as recipient of a quantity of wheat (**no. 66**), and of Kidin-Gula, brewer of the Ešumeša (**no. 187**: 6; CUSAS 30 68: 11).

Furthermore, it is certainly not a coincidence that the overseer (*šaknu*) Arad-Marduk and a certain Erība-Šuqamuna appear together in BE 14 81 (NM 23) and also in **no. 150** (KT 3). While Arad-Marduk is well known at Nippur as well as in the texts of the Rosen Collection, Erība-Šuqamuna is attested presently only once at Nippur but occurs frequently in the Rosen texts, where he bears the title of *ṣuḫurtu* and often receives amounts of barley as gifts (*rīmūtu*).[4]

In addition, the overseer (*šaknu*) Lūṣi-ana-nūr-Adad, who appears in three Rosen texts dated to the 9th year of Kadašman-Turgu (**nos. 159, 163, 164**), should probably be identified with the homonymous official who acts as a witness in two legal texts dated in the accession year of Šagarakti-Šuriaš, from the Rosen Collection (CUSAS 30 7) and from Nippur (BE 14 127). Interestingly, the Nippur text deals with the displacement of some people to Dūr-Enlilē and mentions the *ḫazannu* Arad-nubatti, who is well known from the later Kassite texts in the Rosen Collection (van Soldt 2015, 25).

The *ḫazannu* Tukultī-lū-dāri, who acts as a witness in a legal document dated to the 18th year of Burna-Buriaš (**no. 324**: 22), might be the same official mentioned in BE 15 199: 2, an account of livestock from Nippur that refers to year 15 of an unnamed king.

There are also some archival links between the Rosen tablets and those from Nippur, showing that the two administrations may have shared the same sphere of influence.

The most striking example is represented by the pair formed by text **no. 49** together with MUN 64. Text no. 49 deals with the "stored grain" of the town of Baṣātu from the 1st year of Kadašman-Turgu. The amounts and the personal names recorded in the first half of this tablet match almost exactly the amounts and personal names listed in the *šibšu*-column and the MU.BI.IM-column of MUN 64, from Nippur, which is an account of revenues from Baṣātu of the 1st year of Kadašman-Turgu (Sassmannshausen 2001, 252).

---

[1] The translation depends on the points of departure and arrival of the king; see Brinkman 1976, 411–14; Sassmannshausen 2001, 10, 302, 324, 335.

[2] See Sassmannshausen 2001, 317 for a list of the *aklu*-texts from Nippur sealed by Rīmūtu.

[3] Seal no. 148 in Matthews 1992, 111–13; Matthews provides a list of all Nippur documents sealed with this seal. Note that not all of them bear the indication "seal of Rīmūtu"—i.e., theoretically, the same seal could have been used by different officials.

[4] For Nippur, see the respective entries in Hölscher 1996, 36, 72; see also the Index of Personal Names at the end of this volume as well as CUSAS 30 134: 6 (because of the frequent allocation of "gifts" to Erība-Šuqamuna in the earlier texts, I presume that this tablet dates to Nazi-Maruttaš and that l. 6 can be restored ᵐ*Eri-ba-*ᵈ*Šu-qa-mu-na ṣú-ḫu*[*r-tu₄ ri-mu-t*]*u₄*).

Compare text **no. 49**: 1–12 with MUN 64 (the corresponding elements are highlighted in gray; see also comments to text no. 49):

### Text No. 49: 1–12

| | | |
|---|---|---|
| Obv. | ŠE *tab-ku* $^{giš}$BÁN GAL *Ba-ṣa-a-t*[*i*$^{ki}$] | |
| | MU.1.KAM *Ka-dáš-man-Túr-gu* ⸢LUGAL.E⸣ | |
| | 38.1.2 | NÍG.KUD.DA |
| | 6.3.3 | KÁ.GAL |
| | 10.3.4 | $^{m}$*Ri*-⸢*mu-tu*$_4$ $^{m}$KAR-$^{d}$⸣[AMA]⸢R.UTU⸣ |
| | ⸢9.3.2⸣ | $^{m}$ŠEŠ-⸢TUR⸣ $^{m}$*Tukul-ti*-[$^{d}$IŠKU]R |
| | x.[x.x] | $^{m}$*Ṭà-ab-k*[*i*]*-din-*$^{d}$*N*[*in-urta* $^{m}$]*Ri-iš-Á-ki-tu*$_4$ |
| | x.[x.x] | $^{m}$⸢ZÁLAG-GAŠAN-*Ak-ka-di* $^{m}$*Ḫu-za-lu*$_4$⸣ |
| | 5.⸢1.1⸣ | $^{m}$ZÁLAG-$^{d}$AMAR.UTU $^{m}$KI-DINGIR-*ia-aḫ-b*[*u-u*]*t* |
| | ⸢3?⸣.[x].2 | $^{m}$*Ki*-[*din*]-$^{d}$30 $^{md}$*Nin-urta-re-man-ni* |
| | [x.x].5? | $^{m}$DÙ-⸢*šá*-$^{d}$UTU $^{m}$*Ú-sa*⸣*-tu-ú-a* |
| | ⸢2.3⸣.2 | $^{m}$GAL-*šá*-[GAŠAN $^{m}$*Mul-te*]-⸢*e*⸣-*a* |

### MUN 64

| | | | | |
|---|---|---|---|---|
| U.e. | [*te-l*]*i-tu*$_4$ $^{giš}$BÁN GAL *Ba-ṣa-a-ti*$^{ki}$ MU.1.KAM $^{d}$*Ka-dáš-man-Túr-gu* | | | |
| | LUGAL.E | | | |
| Obv. | ⸢*re*⸣*-eš* NÍG.GA | *ši-ib-šu* | *ki-ib-šu* | MU.BI.IM |
| | | 37.1.2 | 0.1.0 | NÍG.KUD.DA *a-di* 1 GUR *ḫír-gal-lu-ú* |
| | | 6.3.3 | | KÁ.GAL |
| | PAP | 43.4.5 | | NÍG.KUD.DA |
| | 26.4.⸢3?⸣ | 10.3.5 | 0.1.3 | $^{m}$*Ri-mu-tu*$_4$ $^{m}$KAR-$^{d}$AMAR.UTU |
| | 25$^{+}$.[x.x] | 9.3.2 | 0.1⸢$^{pi}$⸣.0 | $^{m}$ŠEŠ-TUR $^{m}$*Tukul-ti*-$^{d}$IŠKUR |
| | [ ] | 7.3.0 | 0.0.5 | $^{m}$*Ri-iš-Á-ki-tu*$_4$ $^{m}$*Ṭà-ab-ki-din*-$^{d}$*Nin-urta* |
| | [ ] | 6.4.0 | 0.0.5 | $^{m}$ZÁLAG-GAŠAN-*Ak-ka-di* $^{m}$*Ḫu-za-lu*$_4$ |
| | [ ] | 5.1.1 | 0.0.4 | $^{m}$ZÁLAG-$^{d}$AMAR.UTU $^{m}$KI-DINGIR-*aḫ-bu-ut* |
| | [ ] | [ ] | | $^{md}$*Nin-urta-re-man-ni* |
| | ⸢8?⸣[x.x] | ⸢3.2.3⸣ | 0.0.⸢x⸣ | $^{m}$BA-*šá*-$^{d}$30 |
| | 8.2.4 | 3.⸢2.1⸣ | [ ] | ⸢$^{m}$⸣DÙ-*šá*-$^{d}$UTU $^{m}$*Ú-sa-tu-šu* |
| | 6.3.2 | 2.3.2 | 0.0.2 | [$^{m}$GAL]-*šá*-GAŠAN $^{m}$*Mul-te-e-a* |
| | 3.0.0 | 1.1$^{pi}$.0 | [ ] | [x $^{giš}$M]AR.GÍD.DA$^{meš}$ |
| | PAP 127.0.1 ŠU.NÍGIN36.4.⸢3?⸣ | 50.4.⸢2⸣9⸢4⸣.4.0 | 1.3.10.4.1 GIG | *t*[*e-li*]*-tu*$_4$$^{m}$*I*[*a*]*-ú-ba-ni za-ku* |

Even though the information recorded in the two texts does not correspond exactly, it is clear that they deal with the same lot of barley acquired by the central administration as revenues from the same town in the same year. Note also that the proportion of *rēš makkūri* to *šibšu* in MUN 64 is 2.5 : 1 (i.e., *šibšu* corresponded to 2/5 of the taxable capital): this is the usual proportion in the accounts of revenues from the Rosen Collection, while at Nippur, the *šibšu* is normally calculated at roughly 1/3 of the taxable capital.[1]

[1] See above and Devecchi, in press.

Furthermore, the two towns seem to have been responsible for provisioning the same temples. Texts **nos. 118–19** record the delivery of barley as allocations (ŠUKU) for several temples located in different towns, disbursed in the 9th year of Kadašman-Turgu. Some of the same temples are listed in the same order also in the fragmentary Nippur text MUN 307, which dates to the 3rd year of Kadašman-Turgu (Sassmannshausen 2001, 374–75).

Finally, some individuals mentioned in two tablets that deal with revenues from the town of Āl-atḫē from the 24th year of Nazi-Maruttaš (**no. 28** and **no. 48**) appear also in MUN 121, a text from Nippur that records the delivery of seed and fodder for oxen to several individuals in Āl-atḫē in the 2nd year of Nazi-Maruttaš (Sassmannshausen 2001, 300–301).

Thorough and systematic prosopographic studies of both text groups will certainly reveal further connections between Nippur and the source of the Kassite texts of the Rosen Collection. However, even preliminary observations make it clear that the close ties posited by van Soldt on the basis of the later Kassite texts in the Rosen Collection existed already during the reigns of Nazi-Maruttaš and Kadašman-Turgu.

# 1. ADMINISTRATION OF AGRICULTURAL PRODUCTS

## 1.1 Accounts of Agricultural Revenues

### 1.1.1 Annual *tēlītu*-Accounts for One Town

i. Barley Together with Other Cereals, Pulses, and Cress

#### 1. CUNES 52-10-103

-.-.22 Nazi-Maruttaš

U.e. *te-li-*⸢*tu*$_4$ $^{giš}$BÁN GAL⸣ BÀD-$^{d+}$*En-líl*$^{ḫi.a.ki}$ MU.22.KAM *Na-zi-M*[*a-*

| | [*r*]*e-eš* NÍG.GA | *ši-ib-šu*$_{14}$ | GIG | ZAG.ḪI.LI | MU.BI.IM |
|---|---|---|---|---|---|
| Obv. | | 80.0.5 | | | NÍG.KUD.DA EN 6.3.3 *ḫí*[*r-ga-le-e*] *ù* 3.2.5 *ak-li š*[*a* |
| | | 12.1.5 | | | ŠE KÁ.GAL EN 2.4.3 *ak-*[*li*] |
| | | 1$^?$.0.2 | | | ŠE *ma-ki-s*[*i*] |
| | | 20.2.3 | | | *lu-du-*[*ú*] |
| | | 71.4.3 | 0.4.⸢5⸣ | | DUMU $^{m}$*A-*⸢*ga*⸣*-mu-za* É[NSI] |
| | | 32.2.⸢1$^?$⸣ | ⸢0.2.2⸣ | | DUMU $^{m}$DUB.SA[R KI.MIN] |
| | | 27.⸢1$^+$.4⸣ | 0.0.3 | | DUMU $^{m}$*A-na-*$^{d}$30*-tak-*[*la-ku* KI.MIN] |
| | | 25$^+$.[x].⸢4⸣ | 0.0.5 | | DUMU $^{m}$*Ì-lí-re-man-n*[*i* KI.MIN] |
| | | ⸢20$^+$⸣.[x].⸢4⸣ | 0.2.0 | | DUMU $^{mf}$*In-na-ni-*⸢*bu*⸣*-*[*ti* KI.MIN] |
| | | ⸢24$^+$⸣.[x].⸢5⸣ | 0.1.2 | | DUMU $^{m}$*Ku-ub-bu-ti* KI.MIN |
| PAP | | 3 ME ⸢22$^?$⸣.4.0 | 2.1.5 | | NÍG.KUD.DA *lu-du-ú ù* ÉNSI$^{meš}$ |
| | 79.1.2 | ⸢30$^+$.3$^?$⸣.3 | | | $^{m}$MU-*líb-ši* $^{m}$*Bi-i'-šu*$_{14}$ |
| | 59.0.5 | 23.3.2 | | | $^{md}$*Nin-urta-*MU-MU $^{m}$*Kal-bu* |
| | 44.0.4 | 17.3.2 | | | $^{md}$*Nin-urta-qar-rad* $^{m}$ZÁLAG-$^{d}$*Ištar* |
| | 39.4.4 | 15.4.5 | | | $^{m}$ÌR-GAŠAN DUMU.MUNUS $^{m}$*Li-ba-šu* |
| | 32.1.0 | 12.4.2 | | | $^{m}$DÙ-*šá-*$^{d}$UTU DUMU $^{m}$*Ki-rib-ti-*$^{d+}$*En-líl* |
| | 21.2.3 | 8.3.0 | | | $^{md}$*Nin-urta-*MU-MU |
| Rev. | 25.0.0 | | [ ] | [ ] | [. . .] ⸢x x x⸣ |
| | 26.⸢2$^?$.4$^?$⸣ | ⸢10$^+$.4⸣.[x] | [ ] | [ ] | [. . .] ⸢DUMU $^{md}$*Nin*$^?$⸣-[ |
| | ⸢5$^{?+}$⸣.4.[x] | [ ] | [ ] | [ ] | [. . .] ⸢*ḫar-šu-ú*⸣ |
| | ⸢6.2$^+$⸣.[x] | [ ] | [ ] | [ ] | [. . .] ⸢x x x⸣ |
| | 5.[x.x] | [ ] | [ ] | [ ] | [. . .] ⸢x x⸣ |
| | ⸢x⸣.[x.x] | [ ] | [ ] | [ ] | [. . .] ⸢x-x⸣*-ti* |
| | [ ] | [ ] | [ ] | [ ] | [. . .] ⸢x x x⸣ |
| | [ ] | [ ] | [ ] | [ ] | [. . .] ⸢x⸣*-ti* |
| PAP | | [ ] | [ ] | [ ] | [. . .] |
| [ŠU.NIGIN$^?$] | | ⸢x⸣.[x.x] | [ ] | [ ] | [BÀD-$^{d+}$*En-líl*]$^{ḫi.a}$ [( . . . )] |

The reverse is badly damaged and encrusted, thus it cannot be ascertained whether the text continued after the last line transliterated here. However, the layout of the preserved text suggests that it did end with l. 28, which probably recorded the grand total of the revenues delivered by Dūr-Enlilē in the 22nd year of Nazi-Maruttaš.

Commentary

1. "Revenues, (measured by) the big *sūtu*; Dūr-Enlilē; year 22 of Nazi-M[aruttaš]."

2. Wherever it is possible to verify it (ll. 15–19), the proportion *rēš makkūri* : *šibšu* is almost exactly 2.5 : 1 (i.e., *šibšu* is 40 percent of *rēš makkūri*).

3. In these texts, *miksu*/NÍG.KUD.DA is often associated with a quantity of *ḫirgalû*; the latter is always spelled either ḪAR-*ga-le-e* or ḪAR-*ga-lu-ú* and is usually read *ḫír-ga-le-e* and *ḫír-ga-lu-ú* because of the spellings *ḫi-ir-ga-lu-u* in the Practical Dictionary of Assur and *ḫi-ri-ga-lu-ú* in a NB text (CAD Ḫ, 197; AHw I, 347 s.v.), but the spelling *ḫa-ar-ga-lu-ú* in a text from the First Sealand Dynasty would now support also the readings *ḫar-ga-le-e* and *ḫar-ga-lu-ú* (Dalley 2009, 192). *ḫirgalû* has been interpreted as a category of grain as well as the flour made from it, but possibly also as a type of allocation (see most recently Sassmannshausen 2001, 251; Dalley 2009, 192; Boivin 2018, 137, 169–74).

6. The term *ludû* indicates a type of field (AHw I, 561 s.v.; Sassmannshausen 2001, 251; van Soldt 2015, 87), "probably a field on which specific work obligations have to be performed" (see CAD L, 238 s.v.; Paulus 2014b, 166, 203–5).

13. Even though only the *miksu* (NÍG.KUD.DA), *ludû*, and the "farmers" (ÉNSI[meš]) are mentioned in the MU.BI.IM-column, the sum of the *šibšu*-column includes also the quantities of the "barley of the city-gate" (ŠE KÁ.GAL) and the "barley of the tax collector" (ŠE *mākisi*) recorded in ll. 4–5. The "farmers" (ÉNSI[meš]) are the individuals listed in ll. 7–12.

17. The presence of a woman (the daughter of Libāšu) is unusual in this type of text, but see also **no. 9**: 12, **no. 46**: 38, and CUSAS 30 35: 21.

## 2. CUNES 52-12-003

-.-.1 Kadašman-Turgu

U.e. [*te-li*]-*tu*$_{4}$ $^{giš}$BÁN GAL BÀD-$^{d+}$*En-líl*$^{ki.a.ki}$ MU.1.KAM *Ka-dáš-man-Túr-gu* LUGAL.E

| | [SAG NÍG.GA] | [*šib*]-*šu*$_{14}$ | GIG | ZÍZ.AN.NA | GÚ.GAL | ZAG.ḪI.LI$^{sar}$ | MU.BI.I[M] | |
|---|---|---|---|---|---|---|---|---|
| Obv. | | 1 ME 9⸢6⸣.4.0 | | | | | NÍG.KUD.DA EN 6.4.3 *ḫír-ga-le-*⸢*e*⸣ | |
| | | 19.⸢3.1⸣ | | | | | ŠE KÁ.G[AL] | |
| | | 6.0.3 | | | | | ŠE *liq-ta-ti* | |
| | | 2.1.4 | | | | | ŠE *ma-ki-si* | |
| | | 85.3.5 | | | | | $^{m}$*A-na-*$^{d}$*Nin-urta-tak-la-ku* ÉNSI | |
| | | 81.0.2 | | | | | DUMU $^{mf}$*In-na-ni-bu-ti* | KI.MIN |
| | | 74.2.5 | | | | | DUMU $^{m}$*Ku-ub-bu-ti* | KI.MIN |
| | | 1-*šu* 8.4$^{pi}$.0 | | | | | DUMU $^{m}$DUB.SAR | KI.MIN |
| | | 1-*šu* 0.1.4 | | | | | DUMU $^{m}$*Šu-ri-ḫa*-DINGIR | KI.MIN |
| | | 76.1.2 | 26.0.0 | | | | *lu-du-ú* | |
| PAP | | 6 ME 71.3.2 | 26.0.0 | | | | NÍG.KUD.DA KÁ.GAL ŠE *liq-ta-ti* ŠE *ma-ki-si* ÉNSI$^{meš}$ *ù lu-du-ú* | |
| | 1 ME 30.3.0 | 47.4.3 *i-na* 1.1.5 *ša-bi-iš* | | | | | $^{m}$*Ḫu-za-lu*$_{4}$ | $^{m}$ZÁLAG-$^{d}$AMAR.UTU |
| | 1 ME 20.3.5 | 44.1.2 KI.MIN | | | | | $^{m}$KI.MIN | $^{m}$DINGIR-SUM-⸢*na*⸣ |
| | ⸢16$^{+}$⸣.3.2 | 42.4.2 KI.MIN | | | | | $^{m}$KI.MIN | $^{m}$MU-*líb-ši* |
| | ⸢10$^{+}$⸣.0.5 | 40.2.[x] KI.MIN | | | | | $^{m}$KI.MIN | $^{m}$DÙ-*a-šá-*$^{d+}$*En-líl* |
| | ⸢5$^{+}$⸣.2.5 | 36.0.5 KI.MIN | | | | | $^{m}$KI.MIN | $^{m}$*A-ḫe-du-tu*$_{4}$ |
| | [x.x].1 | 40.0.1 | | | | 0.2.1 | $^{md}$*Nin-urta*-MU-MU | |
| | [x.x].⸢1⸣ | 33.⸢3.1⸣ | 0.⸢3⸣.3 | | | | $^{m}$KI.MIN | $^{md}$*Nuska-ib-ni* |
| | [ ] | 23$^{+}$.[x.x] | | | | | ⸢$^{m}$⸣KI.MIN | $^{m}$*Kal-bu* |
| | [ ] | [ ] | | | | | ⸢$^{m}$⸣KI.MIN | $^{m}$ÌR-GAŠAN-*ti* |
| | [ ] | [ ] | | | | | ⸢$^{m}$⸣MU-*líb-ši* | $^{m}$*Bi-i'-šu*$_{14}$ |
| | [ ] | [ ] | | | | | [$^{m}$]KI.MIN | $^{m}$IBILA-$^{d}$IŠKUR |
| | [ ] | [ ] | | | 0.0.⸢2$^{?}$ x⸣ | 0.⸢x⸣.2 ⸢4⸣ [SÌLA] | [$^{m}$]KI.MIN | $^{m}$ZÁLAG-$^{d}$*Iš-tar* |
| | [ ] | [ ] | | | | | [$^{m}$]KI.MIN | $^{m}$ZÁLAG-$^{d}$INANNA-*A-ga-dè* |
| Rev. | [ ] | [x.x].2 | | | | | [$^{m}$*Ri*]-*mu-tu*$_{4}$ | $^{m}$*Tu-ša*-TI.LA |
| | [ ] | [ ] | 0.3.1 6 SÌLA | | | | $^{m}$[*Ḫu-u*]*n-zu-ú* | $^{m}$*Ta-ri-bu* |
| | [ ] | [x.x].5 | 0.1.1 | | | | $^{m}$[$^{d}$*Nu*]*ska-ib-ni* | $^{m}$ZÁLAG-$^{d}$*Iš-tar* |
| | [ ] | ⸢4$^{+}$⸣.1.5 | | | | | $^{m}$*K*[*i-ri*]*b-tu*$_{4}$ | $^{m}$ÌR-GAŠAN-*ti* |
| | [ ] | 14.4.0 | 0.2$^{pi}$.0 | 4.2.2 | | | $^{m}$*Ì-lí-re-man-ni* | $^{m}$*Ì-lí-ma*-DINGIR |

| | | | | | | | | | |
|---|---|---|---|---|---|---|---|---|---|
| | [ ] | ⌜17⌝.3.5 | | | | | $^{m}$*Ḫu-un-nu-bu* | $^{m}$*Ia-ù'-um* | |
| | [ ] | 12.2.0 | | | | 0.3.1 8 SÌLA | $^{m⌜}$*Ša-an-na⌝-bu* | $^{m}$*Za-ki-rù* $^{lú}$NAGAR | |
| | [ ] | 2.3.3 | | | | 0.2.3 5 SÌLA | $^{m⌜}$KI.MIN⌝ | $^{m}$*Bu-un-na*-$^{d}$AMAR.UTU | |
| | [ ] | 12.1.1 | | | | | $^{m}$NÍ[G.B]A-$^{d}$*Gu-la* | $^{m}$*Tu-ša*-TI.LA | |
| | ⌜x⌝.0.0 | 10.4.0 | | | | | $^{m⌜}$*Ú-ri-a*-$^{d}$AMAR⌝.UTU $^{m}$ZÁLAG-$^{d}$AMAR.UTU *ḫar-šu-ú* | | |
| | [ ] | 1.3.0 | | | | 0.0.3 4 SÌLA | $^{m}$NÍG.⌜BA-$^{d}$U.GUR | DUMU $^{mf}$*In-na-ni-bu⌝-ti* | KI.MIN |
| | ⌜4⌝.0.0 | 1.3.0 | | | | | $^{m⌜}$*Ba-bi-la⌝-a-a-ú* | $^{md}$<30>-EN-NUMUN | KI.MIN |
| | 3.3.2 | 1.2.2 | | 0.3.0 | | | $^{m⌜}$*Il-lul⌝-lu$_4$* | DUMU $^{m⌜}$*Šu-ri⌝-ḫa*-DINGIR | KI.MIN |
| | 2.0.4 | 0.4.2 | | | | | $^{m}$*A-na*-$^{d}$*Nin-urta-tak-la-ku* | | KI.MIN |
| | 0.3.2 | 0.1.2 | | | | | $^{m}$*Bi-⌜it⌝-ta-a* | | KI.MIN |
| | [x.x].5 | 0.1.1 | | 0.0.5 | | 0.1.1 ⌜4 SÌLA⌝ | $^{md}$*Nin-urta*-MU-MU | DUMU $^{m}$*Ku-ub-bu-ti* | KI.MIN |
| | | | | ⌜14$^{+}$⌝.[x.x] | ⌜x.x.x x SÌLA⌝ | | $^{m}$KI.MIN | $^{m}$MU-*líb-ši* | KI.MIN |
| | | | | | | 0.0.1 | $^{m}$*Ṭà-ab-ṣíl-lu$_4$* | $^{m}$KI.MIN | KI.MIN |
| [PAP] | | 6 ME 31./3.4 | 1.4.5 6 SÌLA | ⌜22.4.3⌝ | ⌜0.0.4 5$^{?}$ SÌLA⌝ | ⌜2.1.2 5 SÌLA⌝ | *ši-ib-šu* | | |
| ŠU.NIGIN | | 1 LIM 3 ME 3./2$^{pi}$.0 | 27./4.5 6 SÌLA | 22.4.3 | 0.0.4 ⌜5$^{?}$ SÌLA⌝ | ⌜2.1.2 5 SÌLA⌝ | *te-li-tu$_4$* BÀD-$^{d+}$*En-líl*$^{ki.a.ki}$ | | |
| | 1 ME 0.0.1 | | 14.2.2 | | | | $^{md}$*Nin-urta*-MU-MU *za-ku* | | |

Commentary

1. "[Reve]nues, (measured by) the big *sūtu*; Dūr-Enlilē; year 1 of King Kadašman-Turgu."

2. The proportion *rēš makkūri* : *šibšu* is exactly 2.5 : 1 in ll. 38–39, 41 (i.e., *šibšu* is 40 percent of *rēš makkūri*), while it is 2.46 : 1 in l. 40 and 2.72 : 1 in ll. 14–15.

5. The entry ŠE *liqtāti* "barley from the gleanings" (CAD L, *liqtu* 3, 207) is unusual in this type of ledger, but see also **no. 37**: 10, 26 and CUSAS 30 40: 11.

12. On *ludû*, see above, **no. 1**: 6.

14–18. In this context, *ša-bi-iš* ("it is collected," 3 sg. masc. stative G of *šabāšu*) seems more likely than *ša* BÁPPIR, which would be another possible reading of the same signs.

27. This previously unattested PN could be read Tuša-iballuṭ—i.e., "Will he stay alive?" (see CAD T, *tuša*, 495: "the most likely function of *tuša(ma)* is that of an interrogative particle, usually introducing rhetorical questions to which a negative answer is expected"); cf. Minde-iballuṭ "Perhaps he will stay alive" (Hölscher 1996, 142).

36. Following CAD Ḫ, 116 s.v. and Sassmannshausen 2001, 238, *ḫaršû* is more likely a field-parcel or a type of land rather than a roller (AHw I, 328 s.v. translates "Ackerwalze"); see also van Soldt 2015, 34. In this type of entry, it can either precede or follow a PN.

38. I cannot see any sign between DINGIR and EN, but the emendation suggests itself because Sîn is the only god attested in the combination DN-bēl-zēri (cf. Clay 1912b, 163–64; Hölscher 1996, 264).

46. The same amount of wheat is recorded also in **no. 25**: 3, a summary of revenues delivered by Dūr-Enlilē and other towns in the 1st year of Kadašman-Turgu.

47. Ninurta-zākir-šumi is exempted (*zakû*) from delivering the amounts of barley and wheat recorded respectively in col. i and col. iii. According to Sassmannshausen 2001, 251, the only attestations of *zakû* in accounts of revenues from Nippur are MUN 62: 20 and MUN 64: 19.

## 3. CUNES 52-10-041

-.-.5 Kadašman-Turgu

U.e. ⸢*te*⸣-*li-tu*$_4$ $^{giš}$BÁN GAL *Kar*-$^{d}$*Nuska*$^{ki}$ MU.5.KAM *Ka-dáš-man-Túr-gu* LUGAL.E

| Obv. | [*r*]*e-eš* ⸢NÍG⸣.GA | *ši-ib-šu*$_{14}$ | ⸢GIG⸣ | ⸢ŠE.MUŠ$_5$⸣ | ⸢ZÍZ.AN.NA⸣ | [GÚ.TUR] | [GÚ.GAL] | [ZAG.ḪI.LI] | [MU.BI.IM] |
|---|---|---|---|---|---|---|---|---|---|
| | | ⸢60$^{+}$⸣.[x].⸢1⸣ | [ ] | [ ] | [ ] | [ ] | [ ] | [ ] | [ ] |
| | | ⸢1$^{?}$⸣.[x.x] | [ ] | [ ] | [ ] | [ ] | [ ] | [ ] | [ ] |
| | | ⸢x⸣.[x.x] | [ ] | [ ] | [ ] | [ ] | [ ] | [ ] | [ ] |
| | | [ ] | [ ] | [ ] | [ ] | [ ] | [ ] | [ ] | [ ] |
| | | [ ] | [ ] | [ ] | [ ] | [ ] | [ ] | [ ] | [ ] |

The rest of the obverse is lost, but after ca. 14 missing lines one can read a few traces at the beginning of the last two lines:

| | | | | | | | | | |
|---|---|---|---|---|---|---|---|---|---|
| 7′ | 60$^{+}$.[x.x] | ⸢20$^{+}$⸣.[x.x] | [ ] | [ ] | [ ] | [ ] | [ ] | [ ] | [ ] |
| | ⸢63$^{?}$.1$^{?}$.3$^{?}$⸣ | ⸢25$^{+}$⸣.[x.x] | [ ] | [ ] | [ ] | [ ] | [ ] | [ ] | [ ] |
| Rev. | 59.3.3 | 23.4.3 | 0.1.1 8 | 0.1.1 | 1.0.3 | 3 SÌLA | | | $^{m}$⸢KI.MIN$^{?}$⸣ $^{md}$IŠKUR-LUGAL-K[UR$^{?}$] |
| | 57.2.0 | 22.4.5 | 0.0.1 | | 3.2.4 | 5 SÌLA | | | $^{m}$KI.MIN DUMU $^{m}$*Ia-a-a*-⸢*i*$^{?}$⸣-[ |
| | 1 ME 13.2.3 | 45.2.0 | | | 6.0.1 | | | 0.0.2 | $^{m}$*Sar-ri-qu* $^{m}$*Ḫu-na-bu* |
| | 71.1.5 | 28.2.5 | | | 11.1.0 | | | | $^{m}$KI.MIN $^{md}$IŠKUR-LU[GAL$^{?}$-KUR$^{?}$] |
| | 77.3.0 | 31.0.1 | | | | | | | $^{md}$*Nin-urta*-MU-MU $^{md}$⸢x⸣[ |
| | 55.3.5 | 22.1.3 | 0.4.2 | | 6.4.1 | 8 SÌLA | 0.1.2 4 | | $^{m}$*È-a-na*-ZÁLAG-$^{d}$AMAR.UTU DUM[U$^{?}$ |
| | 37.2.0 | 14.4.5 | | | | | | 0.0.3 | $^{md}$IGI.DU-ÙRU $^{m}$*Bi-in-na-nu* |
| | 16.0.0 | 6.2.0 | | | | | | | $^{m}$*Ši-ri-iš-tu*$_4$ *ma-ḫi-ṣu* $^{m}$*Iz-kur*-$^{d}$[ |
| | 13.2.3 | 5.2.0 | 1.2.2 8 | 0.1.4 | 16.2.4 | 0.0.1 1 SÌLA | | | $^{md}$30-*iš-man-ni* $^{m}$*Eri-ba*-$^{d}$IŠKUR |
| | | | | | 2.1.4 | | 0.0.5 2 SÌLA | 0.0.3 1 SÌLA | $^{m}$BA-*šá*-$^{d}$*Nin-imma* $^{m}$*Tukul-ti*-$^{d}$AMAR.UTU |
| | 1.4.3 | 0.3.5 | | | | | | | *ḫar-šu-ú* DUMU $^{m}$*E-ri-bu* |
| | 1.3.2 | 0.3.2 | | | | | 0.0.2 6 | | KI.MIN $^{m}$*Iz-kur*-$^{d}$UTU |
| | 1.0.2 | 0.2.1 | | | | | | | KI.MIN $^{m}$*Gu-ub-bu-ḫu* |
| | 1.0.2 | 0.2.1 | | | | | | | KI.MIN $^{md}$*Nin-urta-qar-rad* $^{m}$BA-*šá*-$^{d}$[ |
| | 1.0.0 | 0.2.0 | | | | | | | KI.MIN $^{m}$*Ri-iš-ik-kil-la-šu* |
| | 0.⸢4⸣.0 | 0.1.3 | | | | | | | KI.MIN DUMU $^{md}$30-*ma*-DINGIR ÉNSI |
| | | | | | | | | | |
| PAP | | 3 ME 7./1.5 | 5./3.1 5 | 0.2.5 | 51./1.4 | 0.0.3 7 SÌLA | 0.2.4 2 SÌLA | 0.1.2 1 SÌLA | *ši-ib-šu*$_{14}$ |
| ŠU.NIGIN | | 6 ME 33./0.2 5 | 9./4.4 6 SÌLA | 0.⸢3⸣.4 | 71.2.2 5 SÌLA | 0.0.4 6 SÌLA | 0.2.4 2 SÌLA | 0.1.2 1 SÌLA | *te-li-tu*$_4$ *Kar*-$^{d}$*Nuska*$^{k}$[$^{i}$] |

COMMENTARY

1. "Revenues, (measured by) the big *sūtu*; Kār-Nuska; year 5 of King Kadašman-Turgu."

2. Wherever it is possible to verify it, the proportion *rēš makkūri : šibšu* is 2.5 : 1 (i.e., *šibšu* is 40 percent of *rēš makkūri*).

16. A Širištu *māḫiṣu* occurs at Nippur in an *aklu*-text from the 2nd year of Kudur-Enlil (MUN 173).

23′. Rīš-ikkillašu "Exulted is his (i.e., of Adad) thunder"; for *ikkillu* "rumor, clamor, loud cry, uproar" as a designation of Adad's thunder in a neo-Assyrian treaty, see CAD I/J, *ikkillu* f, 59.

# 4. CUNES 52-12-004

-.-.8? Kadašman-Turgu

U.e. [*te-l*]*i-tu*$_4$ ⸢$^{giš}$BÁN GAL⸣ *Kar-*$^{d}$*Nuska*$^{ki}$ MU.⸢8?⸣.KAM *Ka-dáš-man-*[*Túr-gu*] LUGAL.E

| | [SAG NÍG].GA | *ši-ib-šu*$_{14}$ | GIG | ZÍZ.AN.NA | ⸢GÚ.TUR⸣ | ⸢GÚ. GAL⸣ | ⸢GÚ. NÍG. ÀR.RA⸣ | ZAG. ḪI.LI$^{sar}$ | MU.BI.IM |
|---|---|---|---|---|---|---|---|---|---|
| Obv. | | ⸢1 ME⸣ 15.⸢x⸣.4 | | 14.0.5 | | | | | NÍG.KUD.DA EN 1.2.4 *ḫír-ga-le-e* |
| | | 18.0.0 4 SÌLA | | | | | | | KÁ.GAL |
| | | 4.⸢x.x⸣ | | | | | | | ŠE *ma-ki-si* |
| | | 21.0.0 1 SÌLA | | 1.2.2 | 1 SÌLA | | | | ḪA.LA $^{md}$*Nin-urta*-GI-KA-*šu* KI ⸢$^{m}$*Ša-muḫ*⸣-*ri-gim-šu* |
| | | 20.4.1 5 | | | | | | | ḪA.LA $^{m}$KI.MIN KI $^{m}$*Ku-du-*⸢*ra*⸣*-nu* |
| | | 9.4.3 | | 1.2.5 5 | | | | | ḪA.LA $^{m}$KI.MIN KI $^{m}$DINGIR-*ip-pa-aš-ra* |
| | | 8.2.2 5 | | | | | | | ḪA.LA DUMU $^{m}$*Tar-za-me* KI $^{m}$*Nap-ši-*[*ra*]-⸢$^{d}$UTU⸣ |
| | | 4.2.5 5 | | | | | | | ḪA.LA *si-bu-ti* DUMU $^{m}$KI.MIN |
| | | 6.4.5 | | | | | | | ḪA.LA KI.MIN É-*a-nu* ⸢KI $^{m}$x-$^{d?}$x-x DUMU $^{md}$U.GUR-ÙRU⸣ |
| | | ⸢0.4⸣.[x] | [ ] | 10.4.0 5 | | | | 0.0.2 | ḪA.LA $^{md}$*Nin-urta*-GI-KA-*šu* KI $^{m}$È-*a-na*-ZÁLAG-$^{d}$AMAR.UTU |
| [PAP] | | 2 ME 10.4.3 | [ ] | 28.0.1 | 1 SÌLA | | | 0.0.2 | NÍG.KUD.DA KÁ.GAL ŠE *ma-ki-si ù* ḪA.LA$^{meš}$ |
| | 1 ME ⸢10$^{+}$.3⸣.0 | ⸢34?.x.x⸣ | [ ] | [ ] | | | | 0.0.1 ⸢5⸣ | $^{m}$BA-*šá*-$^{d}$*Nin-ìmma* $^{md}$AMAR.UTU-*mu-bal-liṭ* |
| | ⸢70$^{+}$.x.x⸣ | ⸢20$^{+}$.x.x⸣ | [ ] | ⸢x.x.4?⸣ | 2 SÌLA | | | | $^{md}$*Nin-urta*-GI-KA-*šu* $^{m}$*Ša-muḫ-*⸢*ri-gim-šu*⸣ |
| | 1-*šu* ⸢4$^{+}$.x.x⸣ | [ ] | [ ] | [ ] | | | | | $^{m}$KI.MIN $^{m}$*Ku-du-*[*ra*]*-nu* |
| | ⸢30$^{+}$.x.x⸣ | ⸢10$^{+}$.x.x⸣ | [ ] | [ ] | | | | | $^{m}$KI.MIN $^{m}$DINGIR-*ip-pa-aš-ra* |
| | [ ] | [ ] | [ ] | [ ] | | | | | ⸢$^{m}$KI.MIN⸣ $^{m}$È-*a-na*-ZÁLAG-$^{d}$AMAR.UTU |
| | ⸢30?$^{+}$.x.x⸣ | [ ] | [ ] | [ ] | [9 SÌLA] | ⸢0.1.2 2⸣ | ⸢0.0.1 2⸣ | ⸢0.1.3 7⸣ | ⸢$^{md}$*Nin-urta*⸣-MU-MU $^{m}$*Ḫu-na-bu* |

| | | | | | | | | | | |
|---|---|---|---|---|---|---|---|---|---|---|
| | [ ] | [ ] | [ ] | [ ] | | | | | $^{m}$KI.MIN | $^{m}$KI.MIN $^{md}$AMAR.UTU-*mu-bal-liṭ* |
| | [ ] | | | [ ] | | | | | $^{m}$KI.MIN | $^{m}$KI.MIN $^{m}$*E-mi-du* |
| Rev. | [x.x].2 | 20.0.3$^{?}$ | | | 0.0.3 5 | 8 SÌLA | | | $^{md}$30-*iš-man-ni* | $^{m}$DINGIR-*ip-pa-aš-ra* |
| | | | | | | 0.0.3 6 SÌLA | | 3 S[ÌLA] | $^{m}$KI.MIN | $^{md}$30-SUM-*na* |
| | [2]⌜8⌝.2.0 | 11.1.5 | | | | | | | $^{m}$⌜*Ú*⌝*-su-ub-Ši-pak* | $^{m}$*Nap-ši-ra-*$^{d}$UTU |
| | 27.3.1 | 11.0.5 | | 3.0.5 | 7 SÌLA | | | | $^{m}$NÍG.BA-$^{d}$U.GUR NAGAR | $^{md}$IŠKUR-*qar-rad* |
| | 6.0.0 | 2.2.0 | | | | | | | $^{m}$KI.MIN | $^{md+}$*En-ki*-MU.PÀD.DA |
| | 20.0.5 | 8.0.2 | | | | | | | $^{m}$*Ḫu-na-bu* | $^{m}$NÍG.BA-$^{d}$*Pap-sukkal* |
| | 16.1.3 | 6.2.4 | | 1.1.5 | | | | | $^{m}$KAR-*ni*-$^{d}$AMAR.UTU | $^{m}$*E-zi-ù-pa-ši-ir* |
| | ⌜10⌝.1$^{pi}$.0 | 4.0.2 | | | | | | | $^{m}$*Ki-din*-$^{d}$AMAR.UTU | $^{m}$*Aš-ri-qu* |
| | [x].3.4 | 1.4.3 | | | | | | | $^{m}$*Eri-ba-a-*[*tu*$_4$] | $^{m}$*Iz-kùr*-$^{d}$GÌR |
| | [x].⌜x⌝.4 | 1.3.4 | | | | | | | $^{m}$*Ri-mu-tu*$_4$ | *ṣú-ḫur-tu*$_4$ |
| | ⌜3⌝.2.3 | 1.2.0 | | | | | | | $^{m}$*Tukul-ti*-$^{d}$U.GUR | $^{m}$*Bu-gur-ra-nu* |
| | ⌜3⌝.0.3 | 1.1.1 | | | | | | | $^{m}$*I-na-kit-ti-e-le* DUMU $^{m}$*Ia-nu-kit-tu*$_4$ | |
| [PAP] | | 2 ME 12./4.2 | 1.4.3 | 30.!/1.4 | 0.0.5 3 SÌLA | 0.2.1 6 SÌLA | 0.0.1 2 SÌLA | 0.1.5 5 SÌLA | *ši-ib-šu* | |
| [ŠU.NIGIN] | | 4 ME 23./4⌜$^{pi}$⌝.0 | 1./4.3 | 58.!/1.5 | 0.0.5 4 SÌLA | 0.2.1 6 SÌLA | 0.0.1 2 SÌLA | 0.2.1 5 SÌLA | *te-li-tu*$_4$ *Kar*-$^{d}$*Nuska*$^{ki}$ | |
| 36 | 74.1.4 | *za-ku* | | | | | | | $^{md}$*Nin-urta*-MU-MU $^{m}$*Ḫu-na-bu* | |

COMMENTARY

1. "[Rev]enues, (measured by) the big *sūtu*; Kār-Nuska; year ⸢8?⸣ of King Kadašman-[Turgu]."

2. The proportion *rēš makkūri* : *šibšu* is 2.5 : 1 (i.e., *šibšu* is 40 percent of *rēš makkūri*).

6–8. The same individuals appear in the same order also in ll. 15–17.

10. ḪA.LA *sibûti* "share of/for the brewing"; cf. the "barley of/for the brewing" in **no. 37**: 27.

19. The restoration 9 SÌLA in col. v (GÚ.TUR) is required by the sum in l. 34.

36. Ninurta-zākir-šumi and Ḫunābu are exempted (*zakû*) from paying the *šibšu* on the amount of barley indicated in col. i; these two persons are mentioned together also in l. 19.

## 5. CUNES 52-10-047 (Plate No. 1)

-.-.8 Kadašman-Turgu

Restorations are based on **no. 6**. The content of the two texts matches almost exactly, even though some of the entries are listed in a different order. The main difference lies in the fact that, according to no. 5: 18, Ninurta-zākir-šumi and Illūriya are exempted (*zakû*) from paying the *šibšu*, while no. 6: 6 indicates the amount of *šibšu* they had to pay. It is difficult to decide which of the two texts was drafted later and thus records the final calculation.

U.e. *te-li-tu*$_4$ $^{giš}$BÁN GAL BÀD-$^{d+}$*En-líl*$^{ḫi.a.ki}$ MU.8.KAM *Ka-dáš-man-Túr-gu*

| | SAG NÍG.GA | ⸢*ši-ib-šu*$_{14}$⸣ | ⸢ZÍZ.AN.NA⸣ | ⸢GÚ.TUR⸣ | ⸢GÚ.GAL⸣ | ⸢ZAG.HI.LI⸣ | MU.BI.IM |
|---|---|---|---|---|---|---|---|
| Obv. | | | | | | | |
| | | ⸢6.2.5⸣ | | | | | NÍG.KUD.DA EN 2.0.0 *ḫír-ga-le-e* |
| | | 1.1.2 | | | | | KÁ.GAL |
| ⸢PAP⸣ | | ⸢7⸣.4.1 | | | | | NÍG.KUD.DA *ù* KÁ.GAL |
| | 24.⸢4.2⸣ | 9./4.5 | | | | 0.0.5 8 | $^{m}$MU-*líb-ši* ⸢$^{m}$*Bi-i'-šu*$_{14}$⸣ |
| | 24.3.5 | 9./4.3 | 0.4.3 | 0.0.1 6 | 0.0.5 6 | 0.2.3 4 | $^{md}$*Nin-urta*-MU-MU $^{m}$DÙ-*šá*-$^{d}$AMAR.UTU |
| | 3.3.3 | 1.2.3 | 2.1$^{pi}$.0 | 0.0.3 2 | 0.0.5 2 | 0.3.1 2 | $^{m}$KI.MIN $^{m}$MU-*líb-ši* |
| | 2.0.3 | 0.2.1 | 0.4.4 | | | 0.4.1 | $^{m}$KI.MIN $^{md}$*Nin-nisi-mu*-SIG$_5$-*iq* |
| | 0.4.1 | 0.1.4 | 1.0.0 | | | 0.3.4 3 SÌLA | $^{m}$KI.MIN $^{m}$ZÁLAG-$^{d}$*Iš*-[*tar*] |
| Rev. | | | | | | 0.3.1 | $^{m}$KI.MIN $^{m}$*Bu-un-na*-$^{d}$[ |
| | | | 0.2.5 | 0.0.4 3 | 8 SÌLA | 0.1.1 7 | $^{m}$KI.MIN $^{m}$GAL-*šá*-GAŠAN [ |
| | 10.1$^{pi}$.0 | 4.0.2 | | | | | $^{m}$*In-nu-un-nu* DUMU $^{md}$*É-a*-⸢x-x⸣-[ |
| | | 1.0.0 | 0.4.3 | | | 0.0.1 7 SÌLA | $^{m}$MU-*líb-ši* $^{m}$KAR-*ub*-$^{d}$AMAR.UTU |
| | | | | | | 0.0.1 5 | $^{m}$*Ba-na-nu-ú* $^{m}$KI.MIN |
| PAP | | 27./1$^{pi}$.0 | 6./2.3 | 0.1.3 1 SÌLA | 0.1.5 6 SÌLA | 3.4.[3] 6 SÌLA | *ši-ib-šu*$_{14}$ |
| ŠU.NIGIN | | 35.0.1 | 6./2.3 | 0.1.3 1 SÌLA | 0.1.5 6 SÌLA | 3.4.3 6 SÌLA | *te-li-tu*$_4$ |
| | ⸢35⸣./1$^{pi}$.0 | *za-ku* | | | | | $^{md}$*Nin-urta*-MU-MU $^{m}$*Il-lu-ri-ia* |

Commentary

1. "[R]evenues, (measured by) the big *sūtu*; Dūr-Enlilē; year 8 of Kadašman-Turgu."

2. The proportion *rēš makkūri* : *šibšu* is exactly 2.5 : 1 in ll. 6–8, 10, 13, while it is 4.8 : 1 in l. 9.

18. Ninurta-zākir-šumi and Illūriya are exempted (*zakû*) from paying the *šibšu* on an amount of *rēš makkūri* that corresponds to the quantity of *rēš makkūri* associated with these two persons in **no. 6**: 6 (35.1$^{pi}$.0); there, the text indicates the amount of *šibšu* they had to pay (14.0.2), which corresponds to 40 percent of the *rēš makkūri*. Note that the sum of *šibšu* indicated in **no. 5**: 16 (27.1.0) corresponds to the total of *šibšu* in **no. 6**: 17 (41.1.2) minus the amount of *šibšu* that Ninurta-zākir-šumi and Illūriya would have had to pay according to **no. 6**: 6 (14.0.2).

## 6. CUNES 52-12-019 (Plate No. 2)

-.-.8 Kadašman-Turgu

Restorations are based on **no. 5**. See there for comments on the intertextual links between the two documents.

U.e. *te-li-tu*$_4$ $^{giš}$BÁN GAL BÀD-$^{d+}$*En-líl*$^{meš.ki}$ MU.8.KAM *Ka-dáš-man-Túr-gu* LUGAL.E

| | SAG NÍG.GA | *ši-ib-šu*$_{14}$ | ZÍZ.AN.NA | GÚ.TUR | GÚ.GAL | ZAG.⸢ḪI.LI⸣ | MU.BI.IM |
|---|---|---|---|---|---|---|---|
| Obv. | | 6.2.5 | | | | | NÍG.KUD.DA EN 2.0.0 *ḫír-ga-le-e* |
| | | 1.1.2 | | | | | KÁ.GAL |
| PAP | | 7.4.1 | | | | | NÍG.KUD.DA *ù* KÁ.GAL |
| | 35.1$^{pi}$.0 | 14.0.2 | | | | | $^{md}$*Nin-urta*-MU-MU $^{m}$*Il-lu-ri-i*[*a*] |
| | 24.3.5 | 9.4.3 | 0.4.3 | 0.0.1 6 | 0.0.5 6 | 0.2.3 4 | $^{m}$KI.MIN $^{m}$DÙ-*šá*-$^{d}$AMAR.UTU |
| | 3.3.3 | 1.2.3 | 2.1$^{pi}$.0 | 0.0.3 2 | 0.0.5 2 | 0.3.1 2 | $^{m}$KI.MIN $^{m}$MU-*líb-ši* |
| | 2.0.3 | 0.2.1 | [0.4].4 | | | 0.4.1 | $^{m}$KI.MIN $^{md}$*Nin-nisi-mu*-SIG$_5$-*iq* |
| | [0.4].⸢1⸣ | 0.⸢1⸣.4 | [1.0.0] | | | 0.3.4 3 | $^{m}$KI.MIN $^{m}$ZÁLAG-$^{d}$*Iš-tar* |
| | [ ] | | 0.2.[5] | 0.0.4 3 | 8 SÌLA | 0.1.1 7 | $^{m}$KI.MIN $^{m}$GAL-*šá*-GAŠAN |
| Rev. | [ ] | | | | | ⸢0.3.1⸣ | ⸢$^{m}$KI.MIN $^{m}$*Bu-un-na*⸣-[ |
| | [x.x].⸢x⸣ | [9.4.5] | | | | [0.0.5 8] | ⸢$^{m}$MU-*líb-ši*⸣ [$^{m}$*Bi-i'-šu*$_{14}$] |
| | [2].⸢2⸣.3 | 1.0.0 | 0.4.3 | | | ⸢0.0.1 7?⸣ | ⸢$^{m}$KI.MIN $^{m}$KAR⸣-[*ub*-$^{d}$AMAR.UTU] |
| | ⸢10.1⸣$^{pi}$.0 | 4.0.2 | | | | | $^{m}$⸢*In-nu*⸣-[*un-nu* |
| | | | | | | ⸢0.0.1 5⸣ | ⸢$^{m}$*Ba-na-nu-ú*⸣ [ |
| PAP | | 41.1.2 | 6.2.3 | 0.1.3<br>1 SÌLA | 0.1.5<br>⸢6⸣ | 3.⸢4.3⸣<br>⸢6⸣ SÌLA | *ši-i*[*b-šu*$_{14}$] |
| ŠU.NIGIN | | 49./0.3 | 6./2.3 | 0.1.3<br>1 SÌLA | ⸢0.1.5⸣<br>6 | ⸢3⸣.4.3<br>⸢6⸣ SÌLA | *t*[*e-li-tu*$_4$] |

Commentary

1. "Revenues, (measured by) the big *sūtu*; Dūr-Enlilē; year 8 of King Kadašman-Turgu."

2. The proportion *rēš makkūri* : *šibšu* is 2.5 : 1 (i.e., *šibšu* is 40 percent of *rēš makkūri*), while it is 4.8 : 1 in l. 9.

11–12. Based on the parallel text **no. 5**: 11–12, I do not expect any amount in the gaps in col. i.

14. The quantity of *rēš makkūri* (col. i) is restored assuming that the proportion *rēš makkūri* : *šibšu* is 2.5 : 1 also in this line.

## 7. CUNES 52-10-044

-.-.11 Kadašman-Turgu

This text is a virtual duplicate of the tablet FFA 02, published as CUSAS 30 34, which does not belong to the Rosen Collection but is "part of a mixed group of texts that were brought to the attention of David Owen" (van Soldt 2015, 77; see there, Plate VI, for a photograph of the tablet). Beside some minor divergences in spelling, the only significant differences between the two texts occur in ll. 20–24 (see below).

**No. 7** and CUSAS 30 34 show several correspondences also with **no. 32**, which records the EDIN-revenues from Dūr-Enlilē in the 11th year of Kadašman-Turgu and lists the same individuals in the same order as no. 7 and CUSAS 30 34.

It can therefore be suggested that FFA 02 originally belonged to the same archive as the texts published here and in CUSAS 30.

Restorations are based on CUSAS 30 34 and no. 32.

U.e. [*t*]*e-li-tu*$_4$ $^{giš}$BÁN GAL BÀD-$^{d+}$*En-líl*$^{meš.ki}$ MU.11.KAM *Ka-dáš-man-Túr-gu* LUGA[L.E]

| | | | | | |
|---|---|---|---|---|---|
| Obv. | SAG NÍG.GA | *ši-ib-*⸢*šu*$_{14}$⸣ | GIG | ZAG.ḪI.LI$^{sar}$ | MU.BI.I[M] |
| | | 97.1.2 | | | NÍG.KUD.DA EN 4.3.2 *ḫír-ga-l*[*e*]*-e* |
| | | 18.2.4 | | | KÁ.GAL |
| PAP | | 1 ME 15.4$^{pi}$.0 | | | NÍG.KUD.DA *ù* KÁ.GAL |
| | 95.2.3 | 38.1$^{pi}$.0 | 3.3.5 | 0.0.2 5 | $^{md}$*Nin-urta*-MU-MU $^{m}$ZÁLAG-$^{d}$*Iš-tar* |
| | 57.2.3 | 23.0.0 | | | $^{m}$KI.MIN $^{md}$*Nin-nisi-mu*-SIG$_5$-*iq* |
| | ⸢55⸣.0.0 | 22.0.0 | | | $^{m}$KI.MIN $^{m}$DÙ-*a-šá*-$^{d}$AMAR.UTU |
| | 49.3.0 | 19.4.1 | | | $^{m}$KI.MIN $^{m}$*Mar-tu-ku* |
| | ⸢46⸣.2.4 | 18.3.1 | 0.2.5 6 | | $^{m}$KI.MIN $^{m}$*Eri-ba*-$^{d}$AMAR.UTU |
| | 36.3.2 | 14.3.2 | | | $^{m}$KI.MIN DUMU $^{m}$*Ba-aq-ni* |
| | 35.1.2 | 14.0.3 | | | $^{m}$KI.MIN $^{m}$*Il-lu-ri-ia* |
| | 91.1.3 | 36.2.4 | | | $^{m}$MU-*líb-ši* $^{m}$*Bi-i'-šu*$_{14}$ |
| | [7]7.0.5 | 30.4.2 | 0.0.4 2 | | $^{m}$KI.MIN DUMU $^{m}$*Ka-ak-k*[*i-ia*] |
| | [9].2.3 | 3.4.0 | | | $^{m}$KI.MIN $^{m}$*Ša-*[*ga-rak-ti*] |
| | [3.4.2] | 1.2.5 | | | $^{m}$KI.MIN $^{m}$[UD-*ni-bi*] |
| Rev. | [37.0.0] | ⸢14⸣.4.0 | | | $^{m}$È-[*a-na*-ZÁLAG-$^{d}$IŠKUR $^{m}$ÌR-*nu-bat-ti*] |
| | 23.0.3 | 9.1.1 | | | ⸢$^{md}$⸣[*Nuska-na-bu-šu* $^{m}$*Ab-bu-dan-nu*] |
| | 15.2.3 | 6.⸢1$^{pi}$.0⸣ | 0.0.⸢3⸣ 8 SÌLA | | $^{m}$*Ib-*[*nu-tu*$_4$ $^{m}$KI.MIN] |
| | 5.0.0 | 2.0.0 | | | *ḫar-šu-ú* $^{m}$*M*[*ar-tu-ku a-na ṭe-mi-šu*] |
| | 2.0.0 | 0.4.0 | | | KI.MIN $^{m}$KI.MIN DUMU $^{m}$*Na-b*[*u-na-a*]*-tu*$_4$ |
| | 2.0.0 | 0.4.0 | | | KI.MIN $^{md}$30-TI-URU$_4$ $^{m}$*E-mi-du* |
| PAP | | 2 ME 57./0.1 | 4.3.0 6 SÌLA | 0.0.2 5 SÌLA | *ši-ib-šu* |
| ŠU.NIGIN | | 3 ME 72./4.1 | 4.3.0 6 SÌLA | 0.0.2 5 SÌLA | *te-li-tu*$_4$ |
| | 1 ME 93.2.2 | *za-ku* | | | $^{md}$*Nin-urta*-MU-MU |

COMMENTARY

1. "[R]evenues, (measured by) the big *sūtu*; Dūr-Enlilē; year 11 of Kin[g] Kadašman-Turgu."

2. The proportion *rēš makkūri* : *šibšu* is 2.5 : 1 (*šibšu* corresponds to 40 percent of *rēš makkūri*).

6. Collation of the photograph of CUSAS 30 34: 6 shows that there too the first PN in the MU.BI.IM-column can be read $^{md}$*Nin-urta*-MU-MU (instead of $^{md}$*Nin-urta*-ŠEŠ-MU as suggested in van Soldt's edition).

16. On the PN $^{m}$UD-*ni-bi*, see commentary to **no. 32**: 15.

18. The restoration [m]*Ab-bu-dan-nu*, based on **no. 32**: 17, is confirmed also by CUSAS 30 34: 18, where one finds [m]*A-bu-dan-nu* (read [m]*A-pu*[?]*-pa-a-nu* by van Soldt; see also Apupānu(?) in his index of PNs). The proposed reading Abbū-dannū ("the parents are strong") is currently unattested in MB onomastic repertoires, but cf. Abbū-ṭābū (Hölscher 1996, 15) and see also Aḫḫū-dannū in later texts (Nielsen 2015, 16). Alternatively one could read also [m]*Ab-bu-tan-nu* and regard it as a variant spelling of Abbuttānu, which, however, is usually written differently (see Hölscher 1996, 15; van Soldt 2015, 533).

20–22. The corresponding lines in **no. 32**: 19–21 also label these entries as *ḫaršû*, while CUSAS 30 34: 20–22 has only the PNs.

20. [*a-na ṭe-mi-šu*] is restored after **no. 32**: 19, but note that it is absent in CUSAS 30 34: 20.

21. Van Soldt (2015, 556) regards Nabûnātu in CUSAS 30 34: 21 as the father of Martuku, but the presence of two PNs without family ties in the following line suggests that here too we are dealing with two individuals, the second one indicated with the patronymic "son of Nabûnātu."

23–24. The total and grand total in col. ii do not correspond to those of CUSAS 30 34, which has respectively 2 ME 55.2.0 and 3 ME 71.1[pi].0. The respective grand totals of both tablets are correct—i.e., they give the correct sum of the amounts recorded in no. 7: 15 + no. 7: 23 and in CUSAS 30 34: 15 + CUSAS 30 34: 23. The problems lie in the amounts of no. 7: 23 and of CUSAS 30 34: 23, since neither one represents the correct sum of the quantities listed in ll. 16–22 of both tablets. These lines feature also further differences:

- no. 7 repeats the total of the GIG- and ZAG.ḪI.LI-columns also in the grand total, while CUSAS 30 34 mentions them only in the total;
- the grand total of no. 7 is explicitly identified as *tēlītu* in the MU.BI.IM-column, while CUSAS 30 34 has no label.

25. Again, Ninurta-zākir-šumi is exempted (*zakû*) from paying the *šibšu* on an amount of barley recorded as *rēš makkūri* in col. i. He is exempted from paying the same amount also in **no. 32**: 23.

## 8. CUNES 52-10-046 (Plate No. 3)

-.-.11 Kadašman-Turgu

To my knowledge, this tablet is thus far a unique case among the published Kassite administrative texts: it presents an account of revenues (*tēlītu*) from Dūr-Amurru in the 11th year of Kadašman-Turgu on the obverse and of stored barley (*še'u tabku*) in the 11th year of Kadašman-Turgu on the reverse. The correspondence between the entries on the obverse and reverse suggests that the stored barley also concerned Dūr-Amurru. Usually, scribes recorded these data on two distinct tablets, each containing either one or the other type of information (see Introduction §2.1).

The obverse is arranged as a horizontal ledger, while the reverse has a vertical layout with rulings; another example of such a mise-en-page is BE 15 59, from Nippur, whose content is, however, different.

U.e. *te-li-tu*$_4$ $^{giš}$BÁN GAL BÀD-$^{d}$KUR$^{ki}$ MU.11.KAM *Ka-dáš-man-Túr-gu*

| | | | | |
|---|---|---|---|---|
| Obv. | SAG NÍG.GA | *ši-ib-šu*$_{14}$ | *ki-iṣ-rù* | MU.BI.IM |
| | | | | NÍG.KUD.⸢DA⸣ |
| | 26.0.3 | 10.2.1 | 0.1.3 5 SÌLA | $^{m}$⸢ÌR-$^{d}$AMAR.UTU $^{m}$*Ba-i*⸣*-rù* |
| | 9.2.3 | 3.4$^{pi}$.0 | 0.0.4 5 | $^{m}$KI.MIN $^{m}$⸢x x x x $^{d}$⸣KA.DI |
| | 0.1.5 | 0.0.5 | 0.0.1 | ⸢ŠE *ma-ki-si*⸣ |
| PAP | | 14.2$^{pi}$.0 | 0.2.3 | *ši-*⸢*ib-šu*$_{14}$⸣ |

Rev. ŠE *tab-ku* $^{giš}$BÁN GAL MU.11.KAM
*Ka-dáš-man-Túr-gu* LUGAL

10.2.1 $^{m}$ÌR-$^{d}$AMAR.UTU $^{m}$*Ba-i-rù*
3.4$^{pi}$.0 $^{m}$KI.MIN $^{m}$*I-ku-na*
0.0.5 ŠE *ma-ki-si*
0.2.3 *ki-iṣ-rù*
0.2$^{pi}$.0 ŠUKU EN *pi-ḫa-ti*
PAP 15.1.3 $^{giš}$BÁN GAL
PAP 5.0.0 NUMUN *es-rù* $^{m}$*Ba-i-rù* $^{lú}$LUNGA
$^{giš}$BÁN 10 SÌLA EN 1 GUR *ki-mu* 2 GUR ZÍZ.⸢AN⸣.NA
ŠU.NIGIN 19.1.3 $^{giš}$BÁN GAL
TA 1 GUR GAL $^{giš}$BÁN 10 SÌLA *i-na* 1 GUR
0.1$^{pi}$.0 *šu-lu-ú*

### Commentary

1. "[R]evenues, (measured by) the big *sūtu*; Dūr-Amurru; year 11 of Kadašman-Turgu."

2. The proportion *rēš makkūri* : *šibšu* is 2.5 : 1 (i.e., *šibšu* corresponds to 40 percent of *rēš makkūri*) in ll. 4–5, while it is 2.2 : 1 in l. 6.

3. There is a line for the *miksu*-payment, even though no amounts are assigned to it.

5. For the second PN, one might expect Ikūna as in l. 10, but the signs at the end of the line are clearly $^{d}$KA.DI.

6. In other *tēlītu*-accounts, ŠE *mākisi* is usually not associated with a quantity of *rēš makkūri*; however, see **no. 44**: 15.

8–9. "Stored barley, (measured by) the big *sūtu*; year 11 of King Kadašman-Turgu."

14. In the Neo-Babylonian period, *kurummat bēl pīḫāti* was the designation for a tax payed by the temple to the crown (Jursa 2011, 169–70). As far as I know, this payment was hitherto not attested in the MB documentation (but see here also **no. 51**: 16) and its function within the taxation system remains to be assessed. For the *bēl pīḫāti* as one of the officials in charge of the collection of revenues, see Sassmannshausen 2001, 28.

## 9. CUNES 52-16-019

-.-.11 Kadašman-Turgu

Some of the individuals mentioned in this text (e.g., the daughter of Ilī-rabi, Dimaḫdi-Uraš, and Aṣûšu-namir) are probably identical with the homonymous individuals who appear in CUSAS 30 35, a *tēlītu*-account concerning the revenues of Āl-irrē in the 14th year of Kadašman-Turgu. Thus the two tablets might have had the same origin, even though CUSAS 30 35 does not belong to the Rosen Collection (van Soldt 2015, 77).

U.e. *te-li-tu*$_4$ $^{giš}$BÁN GAL URU-*ir-re-e* MU.11.KAM $^{d}$*Kad-<aš>-man-Túr-gu* LUGAL.E

| | SAG NÍG.GA | *šib-šu*$_{14}$ | GIG | ZÍZ.AN.NA | MU.BI.IM | |
|---|---|---|---|---|---|---|
| Obv. | | | | | | |
| | | 40.0.4 | | | NÍG.KUD.DA EN 1.0.3 *ḫír-ga-lu-ú* | |
| | | 28.3.0 | | | *lu-du-ú* | |
| | | 9.4.4 5 | | | ḪA.LA $^{md}$*Nin-urta*-GI-KA-*šu* KI $^{m}$KAR-*ub*-$^{d}$AMAR.UTU | |
| | | 1.3.0 | | | ŠE *ma-ki-si* | |
| PAP | | 80.3.0 5 SÌLA | | | NÍG.KUD.DA *lu-du-ú* ḪA.LA *ù* ŠE *ma-ki-si* | |
| | 33.0.4 | 13.1.1 | | 0.3.4 | $^{md}$*Nin-urta*-GI-KA-*šu* | $^{m}$KAR-*ub*-$^{d}$AMAR.UTU |
| | 29.0.3 | 11.3.1 | | 0.4.0 | $^{md}$*Nin-urta*-MU-MU | $^{m}$ZÁLAG-$^{d}$AMAR.UTU |
| | 20.0.3 | 8.0.1 | | | $^{m}$KI.MIN | $^{m}$SUM-$^{d}$AMAR.UTU $^{lú}$⸢MUḪALDIM$^{?}$⸣ |
| | 29.3.0 | 11.4.1 | 0.0.5 | 0.1.1 | $^{m}$KI-$^{d}$AMAR.UTU | *a-na ṭe-mi-*⸢*šu*⸣ |
| | 22.0.5 | 8.4.2 | | | DUMU.MUNUS $^{m}$DINGIR-GAL | $^{m}$⸢ÌR$^{?}$⸣-$^{d}$IŠKUR |
| | 21.4.2 | 8.3.4 | | | $^{m}$SUM-$^{d}$U.GUR | $^{md}$*Nin-urta-mu-ter*-ŠU |
| | 1.0.1 | 0.2.1 | | | $^{m}$KI.MIN | $^{m}$LÚ-$^{d}$AMAR.UTU NAGAR |
| | 23.0.3 | 9.1.1 | | 0.1.5 | $^{m}$*Ib*$^{!}$*-ba-ši-ma-ru-uq* | $^{m}$*Bi-in-na-nu* |
| | 19.2.4 | 7.4.1 | | 1.1$^{pi}$.0 | $^{m}$*Di-maḫ-di-*$^{d}$*Uraš* | $^{m}$*Za-ki-rù* |
| | 13.2.1 | 5.1.5 | | | $^{m}$*In-nu-un-«un»-nu* | $^{m}$LÚ-*ba-nu-ú* |
| | 11.2.2 | 4.3.0 | | | $^{m}$*Iz-kùr*-$^{d}$IŠKUR | $^{md}$*Nin-urta-ki-na-i-de* |
| Rev. | 9.3.2 | 3.4.2 | | | $^{m}$*Ki-rib-ti*-$^{d}$AMAR.UTU $^{m}$*Ib-ni*-$^{d}$[ | |
| | 8.2.3 | 3.2.0 | | | $^{m}$*Iz-kùr*-$^{d}$IŠKUR | ⸢$^{lú}$x⸣ |
| | 3.2.0 | 1.1.5 | | | $^{m}$SU-$^{d}$AMAR.UTU | *ḫar-šu-ú* |
| | 3.1.0 | 1.1.2 | | | $^{m}$LÚ-$^{d}$AMAR.UTU DU[MU] $^{md}$30-KUR-*ni* KI.MIN | |
| | 1.4.0 ŠE GE$_6$ | 0.3.4 | | | $^{m}$*Di-maḫ-di-*$^{d}$*Uraš* | KI.MIN |
| | 1.2.5 | 0.3.1 | | | $^{m}$KI.MIN | $^{m}$*Tu-nam-is-Saḫ* Ì.SUR KI.MIN |
| | 1.0.1 | 0.2.1 | | | $^{m}$*Tu-nam-is-Saḫ a-na* [*ṭ*]*e-mi-šu* KI.MIN | |
| | | | | 0.3.5 | $^{m}$UD-*šú*-ZÁLAG-*ir* ÉNSI $^{md}$*Nin-urta-ki-na-i-de* | |
| PAP | | 1 ME 1.2.3 | 0.0.5 | 4.0.3 | *ši-ib-šu*$_{14}$ | |
| ŠU.NIGIN | | 1 ME 81./3.5 5 SÌLA | 0.0.5 | 4.0.3 | *te-li-tu*$_4$ URU-*ir-re-e* | |
| | 46.1.3 | *za-ku* | 1.1$^{pi}$.0 | 2.4.1 | $^{m}$*Di-maḫ-di-*$^{d}$*Uraš* $^{m}$*Iz-kùr*-$^{d}$*Nin-u*[*rta*] | |
| | 8.1.3 | *za-ku* | | | $^{m}$KI.MIN ŠE KÁ.GAL | |

Commentary

1. "Revenues, (measured by) the big *sūtu*; Āl-irrē; year 11 of King Kadašman-Turgu." For the unusual spelling $^{d}$*Kad-<aš>-man-* in the names of Kadašman-Turgu and Kadašman-Enlil, see Brinkman 1976, 141 with nn. 20–21, 164.

2. The proportion *rēš makkūri* : *šibšu* is always 2.5 : 1 (i.e., *šibšu* corresponds to 40 percent of *rēš makkūri*) with the exception of l. 14, where it is 2.38 : 1.

5. The same persons are mentioned again in l. 8.

12. The presence of women in this type of text is unusual, but see also **no. 1**: 17, **no. 46**: 38, and CUSAS 30 35: 21.

15. Even though the first sign looks more like UR, the PN is probably to be understood as Ibbaši-ma-rūq ("He came into existence but is distant").

23. The dictionaries quote only one attestation of ŠE GE$_6$ (Akk. *še'u ṣalmu*) "black barley," in a Sum.-Akk. incantation (AHw III, 1078; CAD Š/2, 345 s.v.).

29. Even though *zakû* "free, exempted" is in col. ii (*šibšu*), it might refer also to the amounts of wheat and emmer recorded in cols. iii–iv.

# 10. CUNES 52-10-042

-.-.12 Kadašman-Turgu

U.e. *te-li-tu*$_{4}$ $^{giš}$BÁN GAL BÀD-$^{d}$KUR$^{ki}$ MU.12.KAM *Ka-dáš-man-Túr-gu* LUGAL.E

| | *re-eš* NÍG.GA | *šib-šu*$_{14}$ | GIG | ZÍZ.AN.NA | GÚ.TUR | GÚ.GAL | GÚ.NÍG.ÀR.RA | ZAG.ḪI.<LI>$^{sar}$ | MU.BI.IM |
|---|---|---|---|---|---|---|---|---|---|
| Obv. | | 83.1.2 | | 4.4.5 | | | | | NÍG.KUD.DA EN 0.4.3 *ḫír-ga-le-e* |
| | | 13.0.4 | | | | | | | KÁ.GAL |
| | | 1.3.0 | | | | | | | *šib-šu*$_{14}$ $^{giš}$MAR.GÍD.DA$^{meš}$ *ša ma-ki-si* |
| | | 37./1.2 5 | 0.0.2 7 | | 0.0.2 | | | | ḪA.LA DUMU $^{md}$30-*tak-la-ku* ÉNSI KI $^{m}$ÌR-$^{d}$AMAR.UTU |
| | | 8.2.2 5 | | | | | | | ḪA.LA $^{m}$È-*a-ri-iš*-URU KI.MIN KI KI.MIN |
| | | 2.2.5 5 | | | | | | | ḪA.LA $^{m}$*Ri-iš*-$^{d}$U.GUR KI.MIN KI $^{m}$*Ri-iš*-⸢UD-*šú*⸣ |
| PAP | | 1 ME 46. 1.4 5 SÌLA | 0.0.2 7 | 4.4./5 | 0.0.2 | | | | NÍG.KUD.DA KÁ.GAL *ù* ŠE *ma-ki-si* |
| | 1 ME 24.1.3 | 49./4.4 | 0.0.3 6 | | 0.0.4 | | | | DUMU $^{md}$30-*tak-la-ku* ÉNSI $^{m}$ÌR-$^{d}$AMAR.UTU |
| | 28.1.2 | 11.1.3 | | | | | | | $^{m}$È-*a-ri-iš*-URU KI.MIN $^{m}$⸢KI.MIN⸣ |
| | 8.3.0 | 3.2.1 | | | | | | | $^{m}$*Ri-iš*-$^{d}$U.GUR $^{m}$*Ri-iš*-⸢UD-*šú*⸣ |
| | 53.2.3 | 21.2$^{pi}$.0 | 6.4.3 | | | | | 0.1.1 | $^{m}$ÌR-$^{d}$AMAR.UTU $^{m}$*Ḫa-an-na-bu* |
| | 13.0.2 | 5.1.1 | | | | | | | $^{m}$KI.MIN $^{m}$*Ba-e-*[*rù*] |
| | 2.0.0 | 0.4$^{pi}$.0 | | 10.3.5 | | 0.0.2 | 7 SÌLA | 0.1.4 | $^{m}$KI.MIN *a-na* ⸢*ṭe*⸣-[*mi-šu*] |
| | 4.4.2 | 1.4.4 | | | | | | | $^{m}$KI.MI $^{m}$*Lu*-⸢*ud*?⸣-*mi-i*[*q*] |
| | 37.1$^{pi}$.0 | 14.4.2 | | | | | | | $^{md}$*Nin-urta*-MU-MU $^{m}$[ |
| Rev. | ⸢25?⸣.4.2 | 10?.3.[x] | [ ] | | | | | | $^{m}$KI.MIN $^{m}$ZÁLAG-$^{d}$[ |
| | 24.1.5 | ⸢x.x.x⸣ | [ ] | | | | | | $^{m}$KI.MIN $^{md}$*Nu*[*ska*?- |
| | 34.0.0 | 13.⸢2+⸣.[x] | [ ] | | | | | | ⸢$^{m}$*Ḫu*?⸣-[*un*]-⸢*nu*?-*bu*?⸣ [x x] ⸢x x⸣ mu l[i? |
| | 23.3.2 | ⸢x⸣.2+.[x] | [ ] | [ ] | | | | ⸢5? SÌLA?⸣ | ⸢$^{m}$⸣[x-x-(x)] -⸢x⸣-$^{d}$*Nin-nisi* ⸢x x⸣ $^{m}$EN-*šu-nu* |
| | 22.4.⸢1?⸣ | ⸢x.x⸣.4 | [ ] | [ ] | | | | [ ] | [$^{md}$x-x-*m*]*u-tak-kil* $^{md}$30-EN-IBI[LA] |
| | 18.⸢2?.5?⸣ | [x].2.0 | [ ] | [ ] | | | | [ ] | [x x DU]MU? $^{m}$*Ṭà-ab*-$^{giš}$MI-⸢*Ul*⸣-*maš* |
| | 2.⸢2+⸣.[x] | 1.0.1 | [ ] | [ ] | | | | [ ] | [x x] ⸢$^{md}$*Nuska*-x-x-x⸣ [x x $^{m}$Ì]R?-$^{d}$[ |
| | 1.0.0 | [x].⸢4?.2?⸣ | [ ] | [ ] | [ ] | [ ] | [ ] | [ ] | [x x]⸢x⸣ la? [$^{m}$*Ḫu*?-*u*]*n*?-*nu-bi* |
| | [ ] | [x].⸢2?⸣.[x] | [ ] | [ ] | [ ] | [ ] | [ ] | [ ] | KI.MIN $^{m}$⸢*Ki-di-nu-ú*⸣ |
| | [ ] | [ ] | [ ] | [ ] | [ ] | [ ] | [ ] | [ ] | [KI.MIN?] ⸢$^{m}$EN-*šu-nu* $^{m}$ÌR-$^{d}$AMAR.UTU⸣ |
| | [ ] | [ ] | [ ] | [ ] | [ ] | [ ] | [ ] | [ ] | [KI.MIN?] ⸢$^{m}$*E-ṭi-rù*⸣ [ |
| | [ ] | [ ] | [ ] | [ ] | [ ] | [ ] | [ ] | [ ] | $^{m}$NÍG.BA-$^{d}$U.GU[R |
| PAP | [ ] | [ ] | [ ] | [ ] | [ ] | [ ] | ⸢x.x.1?⸣ | ⸢0.3.1⸣ 3 [SÌLA] | ⸢*ši-ib-šu*⸣ |
| ŠU.⸢NIGIN⸣ | [ ] | [ ] | [ ] | [ ] | [ ] | [ ] | [x.x].⸢x⸣ | ⸢x x x⸣ | ⸢*te-li-tu*$_{4}$ $^{giš}$BÁN GAL⸣ BÀD-$^{d}$KUR$^{ki}$ |

COMMENTARY

1. "Revenues, (measured by) the big *sūtu*; Dūr-Amurru; year 12 of King Kadašman-Turgu."

2. The proportion *rēš makkūri* : *šibšu* is 2.5 : 1 (i.e., *šibšu* corresponds to 40 percent of *rēš makkūri*) where the condition of the tablet permits verification.

5. "*šibšu* of the wagons of the tax collector"; this quantity is identified in the first subtotal simply as "barley of the tax collector." Cf. "barley of the tax collector of the wagons" in **no. 11**: 5 and **no. 54**: 6. Perhaps it is not a coincidence that in both cases the *šibšu*-quantity amounts to 48 *sūtu*.

6–8. The persons mentioned in these lines occur again in ll. 10–12.

7. Even though it occurs without the personal determinative, the last KI.MIN must refer to Arad-Marduk in l. 6.

9. Only NÍG.KUD.DA, KÁ.GAL, and ŠE *mākisi* are mentioned in the MU.BI.IM-column, but the sum 1 ME 46.1.4 5 SÌLA actually includes also the amounts designated as ḪA.LA of different persons in ll. 6–8.

15. *ana ṭēmīšu* "at his disposal/discretion(?)"; see most recently van Soldt 2015, 33.

25. In the MU.BI.IM-column, one would expect *ḫar-šu-ú* at the beginning of the line because of KI.MIN without the personal determinative in the following line, but the traces do not seem to support this reading.

## 11. CUNES 52-10-061 (Plate No. 4)

-.-.12 Kadašman-Turgu

This text is complementary to **no. 54**, which records the "stored grain" (*še'û tabku*) of Āl-irrē in the 12th year of Kadašman-Turgu.

The content of the MU.BI.IM-column of no. 11: 3–15 matches almost perfectly that of no. 54: 4–15 (no. 54 has one line less because it does not have an entry corresponding to the first subtotal recorded by no. 11: 7). The quantities of *šibšu* in no. 11: 3–15 correspond to those recorded in the ŠE-column of no. 54: 4–15. Both tablets record also the same quantities of emmer (ZÍZ.AN.NA) and wheat (GIG), even though the latter appears in no. 54: 26 as production supplies (ÉŠ.GÀR) received by Ninurta-ašarēd.

The handwritings seem to be different (cf., in addition to the general appearance of the tablets, the forms for KÁ and ÉSAG).

| | SAG NÍG.GA | *ši-ib-šu*$_{14}$ | GIG | ZÍZ.AN.NA | MU.BI.IM |
|---|---|---|---|---|---|
| U.e. | *te-li-tu*$_{4}$ $^{giš}$BÁN GAL URU-*ir-re-e*$^{ki}$ MU.12.KAM $^{d}$*Ka-dáš-man-Túr-gu* LUGAL | | | | |
| Obv. | | 4.3.2 | | | NÍG.KUD.DA |
| | | 1.0.2 | | | KÁ.GAL |
| | | 1.3.0 | | | ŠE *ma-ki-si ša* $^{giš}$MAR.GÍD.DA$^{meš}$ |
| | | 1.4.4 | | | ÉSAG KI.MIN |
| PAP | | 9.1.2 | | | NÍG.KUD.DA KÁ.GAL *ù* ŠE *ma-ki-si* |
| | 22.4.4 | 9.0.5 | | | $^{m}$*Di-maḫ-di-*$^{d}$*Uraš* $^{m}$*Iz-kùr-*$^{d}$*Nin-urta* |
| | 9.1.2 | 3.3.3 | 0.1$^{pi}$.0 | | $^{m}$KI.MIN $^{md}$*Nin-urta-ki-na-i-de* |
| | 5.4.1 | 2.1.4 | 0.1$^{pi}$.0 | 1.0.5 | $^{m}$KI.MIN $^{m}$*Za-ki-rù* |
| | 2.4.4 | 1.0.5 | | 0.1.4 | $^{m}$KI.MIN $^{m}$EN-BA-*šá* |
| | 1.2.3 | 0.3.0 | 0.1$^{pi}$.0 | | $^{m}$KI.MIN $^{m}$*Qu-*[*nu*]*-nu* |
| | 3.3.5 | 1.2.3 | | | $^{m}$KI.MIN <$^{m}$>*Ša*-DI-*mi* |
| Rev. | ⸢x⸣.[x.x] | ⸢3.1.1⸣ | | | $^{m}$*In-nu-nu La-ar-su-ú* |
| | [x.x].⸢4$^{?}$⸣ | [0.3.3] | | | $^{m}$*La-ar-su-*⸢*ú*⸣ $^{m}$*I-re-man-ni-*DINGIR |
| [PAP] | [ ] | ⸢22.2.0⸣ | 0.3$^{p}$[$^{i}$.0] | 1.2.3 | *ši-ib-šu*$_{14}$ |
| [ŠU.NIGIN] | [ ] | ⸢31./3.2⸣ | 0.3$^{p}$[$^{i}$.0] | 1.2.3 | *te-li-tu*$_{4}$ URU-*ir-re-e*$^{ki}$ MU.12.KAM $^{d}$*Ka-dáš-man-Túr-gu* |

COMMENTARY

1. "Revenues, (measured by) the big *sūtu*; Āl-irrē; year 12 of King Kadašman-Turgu."

2. The proportion *rēš makkūri* : *šibšu* is 2.5 : 1 (i.e., *šibšu* corresponds to 40 percent of *rēš makkūri*).

5. "Barley of the tax collector of the wagons." Cf. **no. 10**: 5, which records the same quantity of *šibšu* and describes it as "*šibšu* of the wagons of the tax collector." Both texts are dated to the 12th year of Kadašman-Turgu, but they record the revenues from two different towns (Āl-irrē and Dūr-Amurru).

6. "Granary of ditto (i.e., the tax collector)." The granary (ÉSAG) of the tax collector is mentioned also in **no. 51**: 5, **no. 54**: 7, PBS 2/2 112: 2, and MUN 68: 29′.

7. Even though it is not mentioned in the MU.BI.IM-column, this sum includes the quantity of the "granary of the tax collector" recorded in l. 6.

13. Cf. $^{m}$*Ša*-DI-*mi* with the personal determinative in **no. 54**: 13, perhaps to be read *Ša-šùl-mi*. This PN, however, is currently unattested and the phonetic value *šùl* for DI is not used in MB texts (von Soden and Röllig 1991, 51–52). Another possibility would be to read *ša ṭe-mi* (cf. **no. 53**: 6): in this case, the personal determinative in **no. 54**: 13 might be a mistake.

14. *La-ar-su-ú* is probably a PN (as suggested by its occurrence with the personal determinative in the following line and in **no. 54**: 14–15), but potentially it could also be a nisba for "Innunnu, the one from Larsa."
15. The figure [0.3.3] in col. ii (*šibšu*) is restored after **no. 54**: 15.
16–17. According to the usual structure of these texts, no quantities are expected in the gaps in col. i.

## 12. CUNES 52-10-045 (Plate No. 5)

-.-.13 Kadašman-Turgu

Restorations are based on **no. 35**, which records the EDIN-revenues of Āl-irrē in the 13th year of Kadašman-Turgu and lists the same individuals in the same order as no. 12. There are correspondences also in the quantities recorded by the two texts (see commentary below).

| | | | | | |
|---|---|---|---|---|---|
| U.e. | *te-li-tu*$_{4}$ $^{giš}$BÁN GAL MU.⸢13⸣.[KAM] ⸢$^{d}$⸣*Ka-dáš-man-Túr-gu* LUGAL.E | | | | |
| Obv. | SAG NÍG.GA | *šib-šu*$_{14}$ | GIG | ZÍZ.⸢AN⸣.[NA] | MU.BI.[IM] |
| | | 7.1.3 | | | NÍG.KUD.DA EN 0.3.5 ⸢*ḫír*⸣-[*ga-le*]-⸢*e*⸣ |
| | | | | | KÁ.[GAL] |
| | | 0.2.3 | | | ŠE *ma-ki*-⸢*si*⸣ |
| PAP | | 7.4$^{pi}$.0 | | | NÍG.KUD.DA *ù* ŠE ⸢*ma*⸣-[*ki-si*] |
| | 17.2.4 | 7.0.1 | | | ⸢$^{m}$*Za-ki*⸣-*rù* $^{m}$*Bu-un-na*-[$^{d}$AMAR.UTU] |
| | 16.1$^{pi}$.0 | 6.2.3 | | 0.1.1 | $^{m}$*Eri-ba*-$^{d}$IŠKUR ⸢$^{m}$⸣[*Ú-sa-tu-ú-a*] |
| | 11.2$^{pi}$.0 | 4.2.5 | 0.0.1 2 SÌLA | | $^{m}$⸢*Iz-kùr*⸣-$^{d}$*Nin-urta* [$^{md}$*Nin-urta*]-⸢*ki-na-i-de*⸣ |
| | 8.4$^{pi}$.0 | 3.2.4 | | | $^{m}$⸢ZÁLAG⸣-$^{d}$AMAR.UTU $^{m}$⸢*A-bi-ul-i*⸣-*de* |
| | 6.2.3 | 2.3$^{pi}$.0 | | | $^{m}$KI.MIN $^{m}$*Iz-kùr*-$^{d}$IŠKUR |
| | 3.4.3 | 1.2.5 | | | $^{m}$*Ri-iš*-$^{d}$IŠKUR |
| | 3.1$^{pi}$.0 | 1.1.2 | | | $^{m}$*Iz-kùr*-$^{d}$IŠKUR $^{lú}$DÙ |
| | 2.4.2 | 1.0.4 | | | $^{m}$NÍG.BA-$^{d}$AMAR.UTU |
| | 2.3.4 | 1.0.3 | | | $^{m}$*A-mi-lu-ú-ba-nu-ú* |
| | 2.2.3 | 1.0.0 | | | $^{m}$*In*-[*nu*]-*un-nu* $^{m}$*Iz-kùr*-$^{d}$⸢*Nin-urta*$^{?}$⸣ |
| Rev. | 1.3.3 | 0.3.3 | | | $^{m}$*Di-maḫ-di*-$^{d}$*Uraš* |
| | 1.0.2 | 0.2.1 | | | $^{md}$*Nin-urta-ki-na-i-de* $^{m}$BA-*šá*-$^{d}$*Nin-urta* |
| | 1.0.0 | 0.2$^{pi}$.0 | | | $^{m}$*Ib-ni*-$^{d}$IŠKUR $^{lú}$NAGAR $^{m}$*Iz-kùr*-$^{d}$30$^{?}$ |
| PAP | | 31.4.1 | 0.0.1 2 SÌLA | 0.1.1 | [*ši*]-*ib-šu* |
| ŠU.NIGIN | | 39./3.1 | 0.0.1 2 SÌLA | 0.1.1 | *te-li-tu*$_{4}$ URU-*ir-re*-⸢*e*⸣ ⸢MU.13.KAM $^{d}$⸣*Ka-dáš-man-Túr-gu* LUGAL.E |

COMMENTARY

1. "[R]evenues, (measured by) the big *sūtu*; year 13 of King Kadašman-Turgu."
2. The proportion *rēš makkūri* : *šibšu* is roughly 2.5 : 1 (i.e., *šibšu* corresponds to ca. 40 percent of *rēš makkūri*).
3. 7.1.3 in the *šibšu*-column is the same amount that **no. 35**: 3 records as *rēš makkūri*.
4. The absence of quantities in the entry for the "city-gate" (KÁ.[GAL]) can probably be explained by comparing this line with no. 35: 4, where it is stated that "(the amount of) the city-gate was given to the workmen of the *dullu*-service and as fodder for the horses"; i.e., it was apparently disbursed even before being collected by the administration.

7–16. The quantities recorded as *rēš makkūri* in these lines correspond to those of **no. 35**: 6–15.
16. The corresponding entry in **no. 35**: 15 has instead $^{m}$*In-nu-u*[*n-nu*] SIPA ANŠ[E].
17–18. The quantities recorded as *rēš makkūri* of Dimaḫdi-Uraš and Ninurta-kīna-īde are booked as *šeguššu* (ŠE. MUŠ$_{5}$) of the same persons in **no. 35**: 16–17.
19. The corresponding entry in **no. 35**: 18 has $^{m}$*Iz-kùr-*$^{d}$*Nin-urta* instead of $^{m}$*Iz-kùr-*$^{d}$30$^{?}$.

## 13. CUNES 52-10-051

-.-.13 Kadašman-Turgu

U.e. *te-li-*⸢*tu*$_{4}$⸣ $^{giš}$BÁN GAL *Di-kir-tu*$_{4}$$^{ki}$ MU.13.KAM
*Ka-dáš-man-Túr-gu* LUGAL

| | SAG NÍG.GA | *šib-šu*$_{14}$ | MU.BI.IM |
|---|---|---|---|
| Obv. | | 3.0.5 | NÍG.KUD.DA |
| | | ⸢1.0.0⸣$^{?}$ | KÁ.GAL |
| 5 | | 3.0.5 | ḪA.[LA $^{m}$*Ḫa*]*-an-bu* ÉNSI KI ⸢DUMU $^{m}$⸣[*R*]*i-šu-ti* |
| PAP | | 6.4.5 | NÍG.KUD.DA KÁ.GAL *ù* ḪA.LA |
| | 10.2.5 | 4.1.1 | $^{m}$*Ḫa-an-bu* ÉNSI DUMU $^{m}$*Ri-šu-ti* |
| | 13.1.4 | 5.1.4 | $^{m}$*I-na-ṣíl-lí-*$^{d}$*É-a-lu-ub-lu-uṭ* $^{m}$*Si-bu-tu*$_{4}$ |
| 9 | 2.[0.0] | 0.4$^{pi}$.0 | $^{m}$LÚ-$^{d}$AMAR.UTU $^{m}$*Ta-qí-šu* |
| Rev. | 1.2.4 | 0.2.1 | $^{m}$*Eri-ba-*$^{d}$IŠKUR DUMU $^{m}$*Ri-šu-ti* |
| | 0.3.3 | 0.1.3 | $^{m}$*A-na-*$^{d}$*Nin-urta-tak-la-ku* $^{m}$*I-na-ṣíl-lí-*$^{d}$*É-a-lu-ub-lu-uṭ* |
| | 0.3.3 | 0.1.3 | $^{m}$*Muš-te-šim-*DINGIR $^{m}$*Ḫu-un-nu-bu* |
| PAP | | 11.3.0 | *ši-ib-šu*$_{14}$ |
| ŠU.NIGIN | | 18.2.5 | *te-li-tu*$_{4}$ $^{giš}$BÁN GAL *Di-kir-tu*$_{4}$$^{ki}$ |

COMMENTARY
1. "Revenues, (measured by) the big *sūtu*; Dikirtu; year 13 of King Kadašman-Turgu."
2. The proportion *rēš makkūri* : *šibšu* is almost exactly 2.5 : 1 (i.e., *šibšu* corresponds to 40 percent of *rēš makkūri*) in ll. 7–9, while it is 3.5 : 1 in l. 10 and 2.3 : 1 in ll. 11–12.
5. The same persons are mentioned again in l. 7.
6. The figures in this text show several inconsistencies: this total would be correct if the quantity in l. 4 (KÁ. GAL) were 0.3.1, but the traces suggest instead a GUR-quantity.
13. The correct sum of the quantities in ll. 7–12 would be 11.2.0.

## 14. CUNES 52-10-048

-.-.14 Kadašman-Turgu

U.e. [*t*]*e-li-tu*$_{4}$ $^{giš}$BÁN GAL *Kar-*$^{d}$*Nuska*$^{ki}$ MU.14.KAM *Ka-dáš-man-Túr-gu* LUGAL.E

| Obv. | SA[G NÍG].GA | *šib-šu*$_{14}$ | GIG | ZÍZ.AN.NA | GÚ.GAL | ZAG.ḪI.LI | MU.BI.IM |
|---|---|---|---|---|---|---|---|
| | | | | 6.2.4 | | | NÍG.KUD.DA |
| | 3.0.3 | 1.1.1 | | 2.4.4 | | | $^{m}$*Aš-ri-qu* $^{md+}$*En-ki*-MU.PÀ.DA |
| | 2.3.2 | 1.0.2 | | 1.3.3 | | 7 ½ SÌLA | $^{md}$AMAR.UTU-*mu-bal-liṭ* $^{m}$*Ša-muḫ-ri-gim-šu* |
| | 1.1.2 | 0.2.3 | | 1.1.2 | | | $^{m}$KI.MIN $^{m}$*Ta-qí-šu* |
| | | | 0.1.5 | 1.4.3 | 0.0.1 | 0.0.1 3 SÌLA | $^{m}$KI.MIN $^{m}$*E-zi-ù-pa-ši-ir* |
| | | | | 0.4.3 | | | $^{m}$KI.MIN *a-na ṭe-mi-šu* |
| | 1.1.2 | 0.⌜2⌝.3 | | 1.1.2 | | | $^{m}$*Iz-kùr-*$^{d}$IŠKUR DUMU $^{m}$*E-ri-bi a-na ṭe-mi-šu* |
| [P]AP | | 3.1.3 | 0.1.5 | 16./2.3 | 0.0.1 | 0.0.2 ½ SÌLA | *te-li-tu*$_{4}$ *Kar-*$^{d}$*Nuska* |

The reverse is blank.

Commentary

1. "[R]evenues, (measured by) the big *sūtu*; Kār-Nuska; year 14 of King Kadašman-Turgu."
2. The proportion *rēš makkūri* : *šibšu* is 2.5 : 1 (i.e., *šibšu* corresponds to 40 percent of *rēš makkūri*).

## 15. CUNES 52-10-049

-.-.14 Kadašman-Turgu

U.e. [*te*]-⌜*li-tu*$_{4}$⌝ *Tukul-ti*-É.KUR$^{ki}$ MU.14.KAM *Ka-dáš-man-Túr-gu* LUGAL.E

| Obv. | [SAG NÍ]G.GA | *šib-šu*$_{14}$ | GIG | ZÍZ.AN.NA | GÚ.GAL | ZAG.ḪI.LI | MU.BI.IM |
|---|---|---|---|---|---|---|---|
| | | 5.4.4 | | | | | NÍG.KUD.DA |
| | | 0.3.2 | | | | | KÁ.GAL |
| | | 21.3.3 | 0.0.3 | 7./3.0 | 0.0.2 | 0.0.1 6 SÌLA | $^{m}$*Ḫa-ni-bu* ÉNSI |
| | | 8.4.0 | | 8./2$^{pi}$.0 | | 0.0.5 | $^{m}$*At-ta*-DINGIR-*ma* KI.MIN |
| | 0.2.2 ŠE.MUŠ$_{5}$ | 0.1$^{pi}$.0 | | 1.1.3 | | | $^{m}$*A-ḫe-du-tu*$_{4}$ $^{m}$NÍG.BA-$^{d}$*Pap-sukkal* |
| PAP | | 37./1.3 | 0.0.3 | 17./1.3 | 0.0.2 | 0.1$^{pi}$.0 6 SÌLA | *te-li-tu*$_{4}$ *Tukul-ti*-É.KUR$^{ki}$ |

The reverse is blank, with the exception of a "4" written in the middle of the tablet's surface.

Commentary

1. "[Re]⌜venues⌝; Tukultī-Ekur; year 14 of King Kadašman-Turgu." Note the absence of $^{giš}$BÁN GAL ("[measured by] the big *sūtu*") after *tēlītu*.
2. The proportion *rēš makkūri* : *šibšu* is attested only in l. 7, where it is 2.33 : 1. Note that the amount of *rēš makkūri* in l. 7 represents a quantity of *šeguššu* (ŠE.MUŠ$_{5}$).

## 16. CUNES 52-00-091

-.-.[ . . . ] Kadašman-Turgu

Only the right half of the tablet, which contains the MU.BI.IM-column, is preserved. The reverse is almost completely lost; the number of lines is uncertain.

The tablet is tentatively assigned here because it might have ended with a total identified as *šibšu* (l. 15) and a grand total identified as *tēlītu* (l. 16), which are typical features of this group of texts.

| | |
|---|---|
| U.e. | [ $^{giš}$BÁN G]AL URU-*at-ḫe-e*$^{ki}$ |
| | [MU.X.KAM] *Ka-dáš-man-Túr-gu* LUGAL |
| Obv. | MU.BI.IM |
| | [Ḫ]A.LA $^{md}$*Nin-urta*-GI-KA-*šu* KI $^{m}$*Pa-a-a-ni-i* |
| | [Ḫ]A.LA $^{m}$KI.MIN KI $^{m}$È-*a-na*-ZÁLAG-$^{d}$AMAR.UTU |
| | [Ḫ]A.LA $^{m}$KI.MIN KI $^{md}$*Šu-qa-mu-na*-URU$_4$-*iš* |
| | [$^{m}$]*Ri-šu-tu* É $^{m}$*Ḫaš-mar* |
| | ] *es-rù* |
| | [ḪA.LA]$^{meš\ md}$*Nin-urta*-G[I-KA-*šu* |
| Rev. | [ ] |
| | [ ] |
| | [ ] |
| | [ ] |
| | [ ]⸢ x igi$^?$⸣ |
| | [*šib*$^?$]-⸢*šu*$_{14}$$^?$⸣ |
| | [*te*$^?$-*li*$^?$]-*tu*$_4$ |

ii. Sesame

## 17. CUNES 52-16-099 (Plate No. 6)

-.-.23 (Nazi-Maruttaš)

Even though the king's name is not mentioned, the text can be assigned to Nazi-Maruttaš because he is the only king attested in the Kassite texts of this corpus whose reign is long enough to accommodate a date in the 23rd year. Furthermore, some of the individuals listed in this text are often attested in tablets from his reign.

The tablet is a pastiche: the reverse has been plastered with clay by the sellers and the original text on the upper edge is partially disturbed by fake signs incised in the modern clay.

U.e. ŠE.GIŠ.Ì *te-li-tu*$_4$ ⸢X X BÀD⸣-$^{d+}$*En-líl*$^{hi.a}$ MU.23.KAM

| Obv. | SAG NÍG.GA | *ši-ib-šu*$_{14}$ | *na-ḫu-ḫu* | MU.BI.IM |
|---|---|---|---|---|
| PAP | | 0.4.5 | 0.0.1 | 3 ÉNSI⸢meš⸣ |
| | 1.1.5 2 SÌLA | 0.3.2 6 SÌLA | 0.0.1 | $^{md}$*Nin-urta*-MU-MU $^{m}$MU-*líb-ši* |
| | 1.1.0 | 0.3.0 | 0.0.1 | $^{m}$KI.MIN $^{m}$ÌR-GAŠAN |
| | ⸢0.2$^?$.4⸣ | 0.1.2 | 5 SÌLA | $^{m}$*In-nu-un-nu man-di-du* |
| | ⸢X.X.X X⸣ SÌLA | 0.1.1 6 SÌLA | 0.0.1 | $^{m}$*Ki-rib-tu*$_4$ $^{m}$ÌR-*nu-bat-ti* |
| | 1.⸢X.X X⸣ SÌLA | 0.0.4 6 SÌLA | ⸢5⸣ | $^{m}$MU-*líb-ši* $^{m}$⸢X X X⸣ |
| | 0.0.3 | 0.0.4 5 | 5 | $^{m}$KI.MIN $^{m}$⸢X X X⸣ |
| | ⸢0.1.3⸣ 1 SÌLA | 0.0.4 5 SÌLA | [5$^?$] | [$^{m}$]⸢X X X X $^{m}$ZÁLAG$^?$-$^{d}$AMAR.UTU$^?$⸣ |

The reverse is not preserved.

COMMENTARY

1. "Sesame, revenues, ⸢. . .⸣; Dūr-Enlilē; year 23."

2. The proportion *rēš makkūri* : *šibšu* is either exactly or roughly 2 : 1 (i.e., *šibšu* is half of *rēš makkūri*) in ll. 4–5 and 10; in l. 9 the quantity of *šibšu* is exceptionally higher than the quantity of *rēš makkūri*. On *naḫḫuḫu* (usually spelled *na-aḫ-ḫu-ḫu*), a term that might have indicated a portion of "soaked" sesame crop, which would be kept apart in order to use it as seed as soon as it sprouted, see Devecchi 2018.

## 18. CUNES 52-10-078 (Plate No. 7)

-.-.3 Kadašman-Turgu

| | | | |
|---|---|---|---|
| U.e. | ⸢X X⸣ [X] ⸢ŠE.GIŠ.Ì $^{\text{giš}}$BÁN GAL BÀD-$^{\text{d+}}$*En-líl*$^{\text{meš.ki}}$⸣ | | |
| | [MU].3.KAM *Ka-dáš-man-Túr-gu* LUGAL.E | | |
| Obv. | [SA]G N[ÍG.GA] | *šib-šu*$_{14}$ | M[U].BI.IM |
| | 0.3.⸢1 6⸣ | ⸢0.1⸣.3 8 SÌLA | $^{\text{md}}$⸢*Nin*⸣-*urta*-MU-MU ⸢*a-na ṭe-mi*⸣-*šu* |
| | 0.1.5 6 | [0.0].5 8 SÌLA | $^{\text{m}}$KI.MIN $^{\text{m}}$MU-⸢*líb-ši*⸣ |
| ⸢PAP⸣ | | 0.2.3 6 SÌLA | *te-li-t*[*u*$_4$] |
| Rev. | 0.1.3 8 SÌLA ḪA.LA *ša* $^{\text{m}}$*Bu-un-na*-$^{\text{d}}$[ | | |
| | 0.0.2 9 SÌLA ḪA.LA KI $^{\text{m}}$MU-*líb-ši* | | |
| | 8 SÌLA NUMUN *ša* $^{\text{m}}$MU-*líb-ši* | | |
| | P[AP 0.2].⸢1 5⸣ SÌLA $^{\text{giš}}$BÁN GAL | | |

COMMENTARY

1–2. ". . . [ . . . ] sesame, (measured by) the big *sūtu*; Dūr-Enlilē; [year] 3 of King Kadašman-Turgu."

3. The proportion *rēš makkūri* : *šibšu* is 2 : 1 (i.e., *šibšu* is half of *rēš makkūri*).

10. This is the expected total based on the quantities recorded in ll. 6–8.

## 19. CUNES 52-15-044 (Plate No. 8)

-.-.12 Kadašman-Turgu

| | | | | | |
|---|---|---|---|---|---|
| U.e. | ŠE.GIŠ.Ì $^{giš}$BÁN GAL *te-li-tu*$_4$ URU-*at-ḫe-e*$^{k}$[$^{i}$]<br>MU.12.KAM $^{d}$*Ka-dáš-man-Túr-gu* L[UGAL] | | | | |
| Obv. | SAG NÍG.<br>GA | *šib-šu*$_{14}$ | GARZA<br>⸢$^{m?}$⸣*Qù-ru-un-ni* | *ki-iṣ-*<br>*ru* | MU.B[I.IM] |
| 5 | | 2.4.4 | 0.0.1 | 5 SÌLA | ⸢$^{m?}$⸣[x x] É[NSI] |
| | [1.0].2 | 0.2.4 | 0.0.1 | 2 SÌLA | [$^{m}$*M*]*u*-⸢*ra*⸣-*nu* |
| | 0.4.1 6 | 0.2.0 8 | 0.0.1 | 2 SÌLA | $^{m}$*Ri-mu-tu*$_4$<br>[*š*]*a ṭe-mi-šu* |
| | 1.0.0 | 0.⸢2⸣.3 | 0.0.1 | [ ] | $^{m}$*Ḫu-na-bi*<br>[*ḫ*]*a-za-an-nu* |
| Rev. | | | | | |
| | | 4.1.5<br>8 SÌLA | 0.0.4 | 0.0.1 ⸢2$^{?}$ SÌLA⸣ | $^{giš?}$[BÁN$^{?}$ GAL$^{?}$] ⸢x⸣ |
| 9 | | ŠU.NIGIN 4.2.3 8 SÌLA | 4$^{?}$ | | ⸢*te-li-tu*$_4$ $^{giš}$BÁN GAL⸣<br>MU.12.[KAM]<br>*Ka-dáš-man-T*[*úr-gu*]<br>LUGAL.[(E)] |
| L.e. | | | | 8 | |

Commentary

1–2. "Sesame, (measured by) the big *sūtu*; revenues; Āl-atḫē; year 12 of K[ing] Kadašman-Turgu."

3. The proportion *rēš makkūri* : *šibšu* is 2 : 1 (i.e., *šibšu* is half of *rēš makkūri*). In the heading of col. iii I tentatively understand PA-AN as GARZA—i.e., Akk. *parṣu*—a term that occurs often in MB documents in connection with the disbursement of oil (Sassmannshausen 2001, 170). This fits well with the fact that our text deals with sesame, the main raw material used for the production of oil. Furthermore, in MB documents *parṣu* is often attested in the bound form with personal names (Sassmannshausen 2001, 170), thus we may have here the *parṣu* of Qurunnu (note, however, that according to the occurrences of this PN in Hölscher 1996, 172 and Sassmannshausen 2001, 489 one would expect the spelling *Qu-ru-un-ni*). This use of *parṣu* could be connected with its meaning "temple office, prebend, income for a prebend" and "Kultsteuer(?)," attested by the dictionaries (see respectively CAD P, *parṣu* 2c, 199–200, which lists here other MB occurrences, and AHw II, *parṣu* B 12, 836). Otherwise, perhaps we have here the Akk. word *q/gurunnu* "heap, mound," which, however, is not used in reference to heaps of agricultural goods (AHw II, *q/gurunnu*, 822; CAD G, *gurunnu*, 142) and is not attested in relation to *parṣu*.

8. Even though not explicitly indicated by a PAP, the amounts in col. ii and col. iii are the sums of the amounts listed in the previous lines.

9. The grand total corresponds to the sum of cols. ii–iii.

10. This "4" and the "8" on the edge must have been calculations or doodles.

## 20. CUNES 52-18-833 (Plate No. 9)

Date not preserved.

| | | | | |
|---|---|---|---|---|
| U.e. | [ŠE.GIŠ.Ì *t*]*e-li-tu*$_4$ ⸢$^{giš}$B⸣[ÁN GAL | | | |
| Obv. | [SAG NÍG].⸢GA⸣ | *ši-ib-šu*$_{14}$ | ⸢*na-aḫ-*⸣ *ḫu-ḫu* | [MU.BI.IM] |
| | | 1.4.2 | 0.0.1 | DUM[U |
| | | 1.1.3 | 0.0.1 | DUM[U |
| | | 1.0.0 | | DUM[U |
| | | 0.0.3 | | DUM[U |
| PAP | | 4.1.2 | 0.0.2 | É[NSI$^{meš?}$ |
| | 4.0.4 | 2.0.2 | 0.0.1 | $^{m}$x[ |
| | 2.0.2 5 SÌLA | 1.0.1 2 SÌLA | 0.0.1 | $^{m}$x[ |
| | 0.2.5 | 0.1.2 5 SÌLA | 0.0.1 | $^{m}$x[ |
| PAP | | 3.1.5 7 SÌLA | 0.0.3 | [ |
| PAP | | 7.3.1 7 SÌLA | 0.0.5 | x[ |
| Rev. | | 0.3.4 | | DUM[U |
| | | 0.3.0 | | DUM[U |
| | | 0.1.0 | | DUM[U |
| | | 0.0.2 2 SÌLA | | [ |
| | | 1.2.2 4 SÌLA | | [ |
| | | 0.2.3 | | [ |
| | | 0.2.2 ⸢6?⸣ [SÌLA] | | [ |
| | | ⸢0.3.3 x SÌLA⸣ | | [ |
| [PAP] | | 4.3.5 4 SÌLA | [ ] | [ |
| [ŠU.NIGIN] | | 12.2.1 1 SÌLA | [ ] | [ |

COMMENTARY

1. "[Sesame, r]evenues, (measured by) the [big] *sū*[*tu* . . .]." The restoration [ŠE.GIŠ.Ì *t*]*e-li-tu*$_4$ suggests itself because the heading of col. iii reads *naḫḫuḫu*, a term that appears only in texts recording revenues of sesame (see comments to **no. 17** and Devecchi 2018).
2. The proportion *rēš makkūri* : *šibšu* is exactly 2 : 1 (i.e., *šibšu* is half of *rēš makkūri*) in ll. 8–10.
7. PA before the break is clear. The restoration is supported also by the fact that usually no quantities of *rēš makkūri* are associated with the entries about farmers (see also **nos. 1, 2, 15**, and **17**).

## 21. CUNES 52-20-305

Date not preserved.

Only the right half of the tablet is preserved.

| | | |
|---|---|---|
| Obv. | [*n*]*a-aḫ-* [*ḫ*]*u-ḫu* | MU.BI.IM |
| | [ ] | ÉNSI$^{meš}$ |
| | [ ] | *ša iš-tu* URU$^{ki}$ *šu-lu-ni* |
| | [ ] | |
| 5 | [ ] | $^{m}$ÌR-GAŠAN DUMU $^{md}$[KUR].GAL-ÙRU |
| | [ ] | [$^{m}$*In*]-*ni-bu* |
| | [ ] | [$^{m}$x]-*ḫi-rù* |
| | ⸢x⸣ | $^{m}$*I-din-*$^{d}$IŠKUR |
| 9 | [ ] | $^{md}$UTU-EN-*ú-kit-ti* |
| Rev. | [ ] | [*šib*$^{?}$]-*šu*$_{14}$ |
| | [ ] | [x].⸢x⸣.5 5 SÌLA $^{giš}$BÁN GAL |
| | | [ ] ⸢*ša*$^{?}$⸣ ŠE.GIŠ.Ì |
| | | [ ] ⸢x x e⸣ |

COMMENTARY

7. Perhaps [Nā]ḫiru (see **no. 26**: 7) or [Bu]ḫiru (see **no. 94**: 11).

9. One would rather expect $^{md}$UTU-EN-*kit-ti* (see Hölscher 1996, 202 and Sassmannshausen 2001, 493).

### 1.1.2 Annual *tēlītu*-Accounts for Several Towns

#### i. Barley Together with Other Cereals, Pulses, and Cress

## **22. CUNES 52-10-052 (Plate No. 10)**

-.-.19 Nazi-Maruttaš

This ledger has mixed features: it records the revenues of several towns but also mentions the names of individuals associated with each town; the fact that the heading does not refer to a specific town suggests that the text was regarded as a summary. See MUN 46, MUN 69, and MUN 463 for Nippur texts with a similar structure.

| | | | | | |
|---|---|---|---|---|---|
| U.e. | | [*t*]*e-li-*$tu_4$ $^{giš}$BÁN GAL MU.19.KAM *Na-zi-Ma-ru-ut-taš* LU[GAL.(E)] | | | |
| Obv. | | ŠE | GIG | ZAG.ḪI.LI | MU.[B]I.[IM] |
| | | 76.⸢0.2⸣ | 1.1.4 | 0.3.5 | $^{md}$MAŠ-MU-M[U] |
| | | 1-⸢*šu*⸣ [x.x.x] | | | $^{m}$KI.MIN [DU]MU $^{m}$⸢x-x-*ti*⸣ |
| | | 20.0.0 | | | $^{m}$*Aḫ-*[*la*]-⸢*mu*⸣-*ú* É-*nu* |
| | | 50.0.0 | | | $^{m}$*E*[*ri*]-⸢*bu-ni*⸣ DUMU $^{m}$*Ša-i-li* |
| | | 22.0.0 | | | $^{m}$KI.MIN ⸢$^{m}$ZÁLAG-GAŠAN⸣-*Ak-ka*-⸢*de*⸣ |
| | | [x.x].⸢x⸣ | | | $^{m}$DÙ-*a-šá*-$^{d}$UTU *ša* $^{giš}$MAR.GÍD.DA$^{meš}$ |
| | | ⸢20.3.2⸣ | | | $^{m}$KI.MIN TA 20.3.2 $^{m}$*Ap-lu-*$tu_4$ *šu-ta-ap-šu šab-šu* |
| | PAP | 2 ME 59./⸢x.1$^{?}$⸣ | [1.1].⸢4⸣ | 0.3.5 | BÀD-$^{d+}$*En-líl*$^{meš}$ |
| | | ⸢18⸣.[x].⸢5⸣ | | | $^{m}$*Ḫu-un-zu-ú* *Kar*-$^{d}$*Nin-É-an-na* |
| L.e. | | [X X X T]A$^{?}$ 19.0.5 *šu-ta-ap-šu šab-šu* | | | |
| Rev. | | 58$^{+}$.[x.x][1] | 1.2.3 | | $^{m}$È-*a-na*-ZÁLAG-$^{d}$AMAR.UTU |
| | | 55$^{+}$.[x.x] | [2] | | $^{md+}$*En-líl-mu-tak-kil* DUMU $^{m}$TI-*su*-$^{d}$AMAR.UTU |
| | PAP | 1 ME 16.4.⸢3$^{+}$⸣ | 1.2.3 | | *Ḫu-uṣ-ṣu*$^{ki}$ |
| | | ⸢50⸣.2.3 | | | $^{m}$*At-kal-šu* É-*nu* *Ḫa-am-ri*$^{ki}$ |
| | | 20.0.5 | | | $^{m}$KI.MIN BÀD-$^{d}$MAR.TU |
| | | 28.3.0 | 0.2.2 | 0.0.2 6 SÌLA | $^{m}$KI.MIN URU-*ir-re-e* |
| | | 51.2.2 | | | $^{m}$*Ap-lu-*$tu_4$ URU-*ir-re-e* |
| | PAP | 1 ME 50.3.4 | 0.2.2 | 0.0.2 6 | *Ḫa-am-ri*$^{ki}$ BÀD-$^{d}$MAR.TU ⸢*ù*⸣ URU-*ir-re-e* |
| ŠU.NIGIN | | ⸢5 ME 46⸣./2.1 | 3.1.3 | 0.4.1 6 SÌLA | *ḫar-bu za-ku-tu* |

### Commentary

1. "Revenues, (measured by) the big *sūtu*; year 19 of K[ing] Nazi-Maruttaš."

9. "Ditto (i.e., Banâ-ša-Šamaš); after Aplūtu, his partner, collected 620 *sūtu*." For *šutāpu* as "partner" in agricultural activities during the Kassite period, see Sassmannshausen 2001, 106–7. In the texts from the Rosen Collection, *šutāpu* is attested also in **no. 316**: 13, CUSAS 30 36: 19, CUSAS 30 92: 8, 11, and CUSAS 30 428: 8, while CUSAS 30 4: 4 provides a new occurrence of *šutāpūtu* "partnership."

---

1 A small fragment has been wrongly glued here.

2 A small fragment has been wrongly glued here.

12. "[. . . afte]r[?] his partner collected 575 *sūtu*."

21. *ḫar-bu* is written on an erasure. *ḫarbu* is a kind of plow, but in this context it is probably used with its transferred meaning indicating a field or land plowed with the *ḫarbu*-plow (cf. CAD Ḫ, *ḫarbu* A 2, 98; for attestations in MB texts, see Aro 1957, 35–37 and Sassmannshausen 2001, 104). *ḫarbu*-fields were subject to a special fiscal regime: see most recently Paulus 2014b, 169–75. In other texts recording revenues, *zakû* indicates that a person was exempted from paying certain taxes (usually the *šibšu*-tax); if *zakû* is used with the same meaning here too, *ḫarbū zakûtu* might indicate that the *ḫarbu*-fields were exempted from delivering the amounts of barley, wheat and cress recorded by the text (cf. BE 17 39: 12–14 *ḫarbu ša Burruti ša ina tāmirti Ḫamri zakû dulla ul īpuš* "the *ḫarbu*-field of Burrutu, which is in the district/region of Ḫamru, is exempted: he has not done any *dullu*-service": see Paulus 2014b, 174).

## 23. CUNES 52-12-015 (Plate No. 11)

-.-.10 Kadašman-Turgu

U.e. *te-li-tu*$_4$ $^{giš}$BÁN GAL MU.10.[KAM] *Ka-dáš-man-Túr-gu* LUGAL.E

| | ŠE | ⸢GIG⸣ | ⸢ZÍZ⸣.AN.NA | GÚ.TUR | GÚ.GAL | GÚ.NÍG.ÀR.RA | ZAG.ḪI.LI | ŠE.IN.NU.ḪA | ⸢URU⸣$^{didli}$ |
|---|---|---|---|---|---|---|---|---|---|
| Obv. | 8 ME 1-*šu*<br>5./0.5<br>5 SÌLA | 9./4.4<br>4 SÌLA | 73./4.5 | 0.2.3<br>8 SÌLA | 1.1$^{pi}$.0<br>5 SÌLA | 4 SÌLA | 0.⸢4?⸣.3<br>⸢2⸣ ½ SÌLA | | AN.ZA.GÀR$^{ki}$ |
| | 4 [ME]<br>55./0.3<br>5 SÌLA | 25./2.0<br>1 SÌLA | 2 ME<br>21./4.⸢4⸣ | 0.2.4<br>1 ½ SÌLA | ⸢3.3.0⸣ | ⸢1⸣.[2.2]<br>3 SÌLA | ⸢3.0/.5⸣<br>1 SÌLA | ⸢0.0.4⸣<br>⸢4⸣ [SÌL]A | *Tukul-ti*-É.KUR$^{ki}$ |
| | 1 ME<br>74./2.3 | 0.1$^{pi}$.0<br>2 SÌLA | 1 ME<br>20./3.4 5 | 0.1.5 | 0.2.⸢5⸣ 3 | | [x.x.x]<br>⸢6⸣ S[ÌLA] | ⸢0.0.1 3⸣ | *Kar*-$^{d}$⸢*Nuska*⸣$^{ki}$ |
| | 1 ME<br>3.4.3 | 5./3.5 2 | 97./1$^{pi}$.0 | 0.0.⸢1 2⸣<br>SÌLA | 0.2.5 ⸢2⸣<br>SÌLA | | ⸢2?.0.0⸣<br>⸢2⸣ ½ SÌLA | | BÀD-$^{d+}$*En-líl*$^{meš.ki}$ |
| | ⸢38?⸣.4.2<br>5 SÌLA | | | | | | | | URU-*ir-re-e*$^{ki}$ |
| Rev. | ⸢x.x⸣.2 | | | | | | | [ ] | ⸢*Ta mir tu*$_4$$^{ki}$⸣ |
| | ⸢10?⸣ 2 5 | | | | | | | [ ] | ⸢URU-*a*⸣*t-ḫe-e*$^{ki}$ |
| | | | | | | | | [ ] | *Di-kir-tu*$_4$$^{ki}$ |
| PAP | 1 LIM<br>6 ME<br>73./3.0<br>5 SÌLA | 42./1.3<br>9 SÌLA | 5 ME<br>12./4.1<br>5 SÌLA | 1.2.2<br>1 ½ SÌLA | 5./4.5 | 1.2.2<br>7 SÌLA | 6./1.4<br>2 SÌLA | 0.1.2 | *te-li-tu*$_4$<br>*pu-ḫur-tu*$_4$<br>MU.10.KAM<br>*Ka-dáš-man-Túr-gu*<br>LUGAL.E |

COMMENTARY

1. "Revenues, (measured by) the big *sūtu*; year 10 of King Kadašman-Turgu."

2. Since the column headings in this type of text usually refer to raw agricultural products, it seems more likely that ŠE.IN.NU.ḪA (Akk. *ennēnu/innin(n)u*) indicates a type of barley (as suggested by CAD I, 151 s.v.), rather than a type of groat(s) (as suggested by AHw I, 219 s.v.). The only MB attestation mentioned by the dictionaries comes from a literary text (SEM 117 iii 23), but see now also **no. 36**: 2, **no. 130**: 4 and CUSAS 30 64: 26–27, 36 for further occurrences in administrative context. ŠE.IN.NU.ḪA is not mentioned by Ellis 1976, 112 nor by Sassmannshausen 2001, 229 among the agricultural goods listed in texts recording revenues from Nippur.

11. "Assembled revenues; year 10 of King Kadašman-Turgu."

ii. Sesame

## 24. CUNES 52-10-106

-.-.15$^{?}$ Kadašman-Turgu

The obverse of the text is a summary of the revenues (*tēlītu*) of sesame delivered by several towns in the 15$^{th?}$ year of Kadašman-Turgu, while the reverse seems to have recorded allocations, probably of sesame, to different shrines of the Ekur and to the Eki'ur, the temple of Ninlil. Note that the amounts on the reverse are much higher than the incoming quantities on the obverse.

| | | |
|---|---|---|
| U.e. | [ŠE.GIŠ.Ì $^{\text{giš}}$]BÁN GAL *te-li-*[*tu*$_{4}$ x x] ⸢x$^{?}$⸣ MU.15$^{?}$.KAM $^{\text{d}}$*Ka*⸣-[ | |
| Obv. | [ŠE.GI]Š.Ì $^{\text{giš}}$BÁN GAL MU.BI.IM | |
| | ⸢4⸣.2.2 8$^{?}$ SÌLA | URU-*at-ḫ̮e-e*$^{\text{ki}}$ |
| 5 | 1.2.4 8 SÌLA | $^{\text{uru}}$BÀD-$^{\text{d}}$KUR$^{\text{ki}}$ |
| | 0.2.1 6 SÌLA | *Ta-mi-ir-tu*$_{4}$$^{\text{ki}}$ |
| [PAP$^{?}$] | ⸢6⸣.2.⸢3 4$^{?}$ SÌLA⸣ ŠE.GIŠ.⸢Ì $^{\text{giš}}$⸣[BÁN GAL] | ŠU $^{\text{m}}$BA-*šá*-[$^{\text{d}}$ |
| L.e. | $^{\text{iti}}$ZÍZ.A.AN | |
| Rev. | MU.⸢15$^{?}$⸣.KAM $^{\text{d}}$*Ka-daš-man-Túr-gu* | |
| 11 | 32.1.1 KI.GUB SAG É.KUR | |
| | 33.0.5 KI.GUB ÚS É.KUR ⸢x x x x⸣ | |
| | ⸢10$^{+}$.3⸣.4 | KI.ÙR ⸢*ak*$^{?}$-*lu*$_{4}$$^{?}$ *i*$^{?}$-*din*$^{?}$⸣ |
| | 7 | 4$^{?}$ |

COMMENTARY

1–2. "[Sesame], (measured by) the big *sūtu*; reven[ues . . .]; year 15$^{?}$ of Ka[dašman-Turgu]." [ŠE.GIŠ.Ì] at the beginning of the line is restored after l. 3 and l. 7.

7. If the reading 8 SÌLA in l. 4 were correct, the sum expected here would be 6.2.3 2 SÌLA, but the traces suggest a higher SÌLA-figure. PAP at the beginning of the line is a logical assumption, but remains hypothetical. The amount is at the disposal or under the responsibility (ŠU) of Iqīša-[DN].

11. The quantity 32.1.1 is written over an erasure. For KI.GUB SAG É.KUR, cf. É.KUR KI.GUB SAG as a recipient of barley flour in MUN 187: 13 (read KI-DU-SAG by Sassmannshausen 2001, 325); KI.GUB ÚS É.KUR is, to my knowledge, otherwise unattested. The meaning of KI.GUB (Akk. *mazzāzu*) in this context is not clear (respectively "first position/location" and "second position/location" of the Ekur?). MUN 187: 14–15 attests also the KI.GUB SAG of the temple of Nuska and of another building—probably a sanctuary—whose name is unclear, suggesting that it was not a peculiar feature of the Ekur.

12. The quantity 33.0.5 is written over an erasure. É.KUR is followed by signs written in a smaller script, which continue on the edge (perhaps x ra/um/dub ḫi).

13. The signs following KI.ÙR are written in a smaller script; their reading is very tentative. KI.ÙR is probably written over an erasure. On the (É.)KI.ÙR "leveled place," a shrine of Ninlil in the Ekur at Nippur, see George 1993, 112 no. 636. The Eki'ur is mentioned, among other Nippur temples, as a recipient of sesame also in BE 14 148: 3.

14. The "7" and the "4" at the end of the reverse must have been calculations or doodles.

iii. Wheat

## 25. CUNES 52-10-060 (Plate No. 12)

-.-.1 Kadašman-Turgu

Obv. ⸢GIG⸣ $^{\text{giš}}$BÁN GAL *te-li-tu*$_4$

MU.1.KAM *Ka-dáš-man-Túr-gu*

| | | |
|---|---|---|
| | ⸢27.4⸣.5<br>⸢6⸣ SÌLA | BÀD-$^{\text{d+}}$*En-líl*$^{\text{ḫi.a.ki}}$ |
| | [x.x].5 ⸢6 SÌLA⸣ | BÀD-EN-KUR.KUR$^{\text{ki}}$ |
| | 0.3.2 4 SÌLA | *Ḫu-uṣ-ṣu*$^{\text{ki}}$ |
| | 0.2.3 6 SÌLA | URU-*ir-re-e*$^{\text{⸢ki⸣}}$ |
| | 1.4.2 4 SÌLA | ⸢*Ta-mi-ir-tu*$_4$⸣$^{\text{ki}}$ |
| Rev. | 4.0.4 | BÀD-$^{\text{d}}$⸢KUR⸣$^{\text{ki}}$ |
| PAP | ⸢35$^{?}$⸣.2.5 6 SÌLA | ⸢$^{\text{giš}}$BÁN GAL⸣ |

COMMENTARY

1–2. "Wheat, (measured by) the big *sūtu*; revenues; year 1 of Kadašman-Turgu."

3. Note that the amount of wheat associated with Dūr-Enlilē corresponds to that recorded by **no. 2**: 46 as revenues of wheat from the same town in the same year.

### 1.1.3 ANNUAL EDIN-ACCOUNTS FOR ONE TOWN

## 26. CUNES 52-10-080

-.-.18 Nazi-Maruttaš

U.e. [EDIN M]U.18.KAM ⸢*Na-zi-Ma-ru-ut-ta*⸣*-aš* URU-*at-ḫe-e*$^{\text{ki}}$

| | | | | |
|---|---|---|---|---|
| Obv. | [*re*]-*eš* NÍG.GA | *ki-iṣ-rù* | GIG | MU.BI.IM |
| | 55.0.0 | 0.1.5 | | DUMU $^{\text{m}}$*Ku-up-pí-ta-ti* ÉNSI |
| | 41.3.2 | ⸢0.1$^{?}$.x⸣ | | [DUMU $^{\text{mf?}}$]⸢*Baq*⸣-*ni-ti* KI.MIN |
| | 1-*šu* ⸢5$^{?}$.x.x⸣ | ⸢0.1.1⸣ | | ⸢NÍG.KUD.DA⸣ EN 8.0.1 ⸢x (x) x⸣<br>⸢EN⸣ 0.4$^{\text{pi}}$.0 *ḫír-ga-le-e* |
| | 1.2.⸢x⸣ | [ ] | | ⸢ŠE *ma*⸣-*ki-si* |
| | ⸢90$^{+}$.x.x⸣ | 0.⸢1$^{?}$.2$^{?}$⸣ | ⸢x.3.1$^{?}$⸣ | ⸢$^{\text{m}}$ÌR⸣-GAŠAN-*ti* $^{\text{m}}$*Na-ḫi-rù* |
| | 1-*šu* ⸢2$^{?}$⸣.0.0 | 0.⸢3$^{?}$⸣.1 | | $^{\text{m}}$KI.MIN $^{\text{m}}$*Ḫa-ni-bu* |
| | ⸢6$^{+}$⸣.1.2 | 0.2.2 | | $^{\text{m}}$*E-tel*-KA-$^{\text{d}}$MAŠ $^{\text{m}}$GAL-*šá*-$^{\text{d}}$*Gu-la* |
| | ⸢2$^{+}$⸣.4.3 | 0.1.5 | 0.1.2 | $^{\text{m}}$*Gu-bu-ḫu* $^{\text{m}}$*Bur-ra-Saḫ* |
| Rev. | [x].3.4 | 0.1.4 | [ ] | $^{\text{m}}$KI.MIN $^{\text{m}}$*Man-nu-ba-lu*-$^{\text{d}}$⸢UTU$^{?}$⸣ |
| | 6.⸢1$^{?}$.5$^{?}$⸣ | [ ] | [ ] | $^{\text{m}}$KI.MIN $^{\text{md}}$MAŠ-*qar-rad* |

The rest of the reverse is blank.

COMMENTARY

1. "[Countryside; y]ear 18 of Nazi-Maruttaš; Āl-atḫē." The space at the beginning of the upper edge allows for only one sign; the restoration EDIN is suggested by the content and the sequence of the columns, which is common in this type of text (see Introduction §2.1, Table 2).

4. For the restoration, cf. DUMU $^{mf}$*Baq-ni-tu*$_4$ ÉNSI in CUSAS 30 150: 41′ (n.d.).

## 27. CUNES 52-10-071 (Plate No. 13)

-.-.20 Nazi-Maruttaš

U.e. *šu-nu-ú* EDIN $^{giš}$BÁN GAL ⸢BÀD⸣-$^{d}$KUR$^{ki}$ MU.20.KAM
*Na-zi-Ma-ru-ut-taš* LUGAL.E

| | SAG NÍG.GA | *ki-iṣ-rù* | ŠE.MUŠ$_5$ | *ki-iṣ-rù* | GIG | ZÍZ.AN.NA | MU.BI.IM |
|---|---|---|---|---|---|---|---|
| Obv. | ⸢21+⸣.4$^{pi}$.0 | 0.1.2 | ⸢1.1.x⸣ | ⸢0.0.1⸣ | | | ⸢DUMU $^{m}$*Ku-up*⸣*-pi-ta-t*[*i* É]NSI |
| | ⸢8+⸣.1.4 | 0.0.5 | | | | | N[ÍG.KUD.D]A EN 1.4$^{pi}$.0 [*hír-ga*]-⸢*le*⸣*-e* |
| | ⸢12+⸣.2.3 | | 4.⸢3?⸣.1⸢?⸣ | | | | $^{m}$⸢*Ḫa-am-bu*⸣ $^{m}$*Gu-*⸢*ra-aš*⸣ |
| | ⸢4+⸣.2.4 | 0.0.3 5 | 2.1.5 | 0.0.1 | | | $^{m}$ŠEŠ-⸢SIG$_5$?⸣ $^{m}$DÙ-⸢*šá*-$^{d}$AMAR.UTU⸣ |
| | | | 2.0.0 | 0.0.2 | 0.0.3 5 | 0.4.1 | $^{m}$⸢*Bu-ga-áš*?⸣*-Ḫa*[*r*?*-be*?] $^{m}$*Re-eš*-$^{d}$U.[GUR] |
| Rev. | [ ] | [0].⸢2⸣.4 5 | | 0.0.4 | | | *ki-iṣ-r*[*ù*] |
| | [ ] | [x].1.0 2 | | | | | *ki-ṣir ma*[*ḫ-ri*] |

The rest of the reverse is blank.

COMMENTARY

1–2. "*šunû*, countryside, (measured by) the big *sūtu*; Dūr-Amurru; year 20 of King Nazi-Maruttaš."

7. The Kassite PN Bugaš-Ḫarbe is to my knowledge not attested, but see Bugaš-Enlil (van Soldt 2015, 540) for another name of the type Bugaš-DN.

9. The amounts in col. ii and col. iv correspond to the sums of the amounts entered in the previous lines.

## 28. CUNES 52-10-073

-.-.24 Nazi-Maruttaš

The reverse of the tablet is very worn.

Some of the PNs (Damu-nāṣir, Siyātu) are attested also in CUSAS 30 67, a tablet that probably recorded revenues from Dikirtu (see CUSAS 30 67: 22), and in **no. 44**, an account regarding the same town dated to the 1$^{st}$ year of Kadašman-Turgu.

| | | | |
|---|---|---|---|
| U.e. | [EDI]N *Di-*⌜*kir-tu*$_4$⌝[$^{ki}$ M]U.24.KAM $^{d}$*Na-zi-Múru-taš* LUGAL.E | | |
| Obv. | ⌜*re-eš* NÍG.GA⌝ | ⌜*ki-iṣ-ru*⌝ | ⌜MU⌝.BI.IM |
| | 2.3.2 | 0.0.2 | NÍG.KUD.DA |
| | 16.0.1 | 0.0.4 | $^{md}$*La-ta-ra-ak-ba-ni* ⌜ÉNSI⌝<br>*it-ti* DUMU $^{m}$*Ri-šu-ti* |
| | 3.0.0 | 0.0.1 5 SÌLA | DUMU $^{md}$30-*re-mì-ni* |
| | 1.2.2 | 5 SÌLA | DUMU $^{m}$*Ba-qí-li* |
| | 1.1.⌜1⌝ | [ ] | $^{md}$*Da-mu*-ÙRU DUMU $^{m}$*A-gi-ia* |
| | 1.2.3 | ⌜2$^{+}$⌝ [SÌLA] | $^{md}$*Da-mu*-ÙRU DUMU $^{m}$⌜*E*$^{?}$*-la*$^{?}$*-mi*$^{?}$*-i*$^{?}$⌝ |
| | 1.0.1 | 5 SÌLA | $^{m}$*Muš-te-ši-ir*-$^{d}$IŠKUR |
| | [x.x]$^{pi}$.0 | 2 SÌLA | $^{m}$DÙ-*a-šá*-$^{d}$⌜*Pap*⌝*-sukkal* |
| Rev. | [ ] | [ ] | $^{m}$⌜*A-na*⌝-$^{d}$UTU-⌜*tak-la*⌝*-ku* |
| | ⌜x⌝ | [ ] | $^{md}$30-[TI]-⌜URU$_4$⌝ |
| | ⌜x⌝ | [ ] | $^{m}$[x]-⌜x-x-at$^{?}$-x⌝ |
| | ⌜x⌝ | [ ] | $^{m}$⌜*Si-ia*⌝*-tu*$_4$ |
| | [ ] | ⌜x⌝ | ⌜$^{m}$*Iz-kùr*-$^{d}$AMAR.UTU⌝ DUMU $^{m}$*Ta-ri-bat*-DINGIR<br>⌜*il-te-qé*⌝ |

COMMENTARY

1. "[Countrysi]de; Dikirtu; [ye]ar 24 of King Nazi-Maruttaš." The restoration [EDI]N is suggested by the headings of the columns, which are common in this type of text, and it fits the traces after the break.

5. With the 2 sg. imperative *rēmīni*, one would expect a female deity as the theophoric element in the name. Perhaps it is a misspelling of Sîn-rēmni (see AHw II, *rêmu* 1 a, 970; CAD R, *rêmu* 1 b 3′, 264–65). Neither PN, however, is attested in MB texts (see *rêmu* in Hölscher 1996, 258–59).

6–7. I assume that here too the text records only one person, as in the previous and following lines; the presence of the patronymics is probably due to the homonymy between the two persons, both called Damu-nāṣir.

## 29. CUNES 52-19-148

-.-.24 Nazi-Maruttaš

Restorations of the PNs are based on the complementary text **no. 48**, which records the stored barley (*še'u tabku*) of Āl-atḫē in the 24$^{th}$ year of Nazi-Maruttaš. See commentary there.

| | | | | |
|---|---|---|---|---|
| U.e. | ⸢x x x⸣ URU-*at-ḫe-e*$^{ki}$ MU.24.KAM *Na-*⸢*zi*⸣-[ | | | |
| Obv. | [SAG] NÍG.GA | *ki-iṣ-rù* | GIG | MU.BI.IM |
| | [2]⸢7⸣.3.0 | 0.2.0 | | DUMU $^{m}$*Šu-ri-ḫa*-DINGIR *ù* DUMU [$^{mf}$*Ku-up-pi-ta-ti*] ÉNSI$^{meš}$ |
| | 15.⸢1$^{pi}$⸣.0 | 0.1.2 | | NÍG.KUD.DA EN 0.4$^{pi}$.0 [*ḫír-g*]*a-le-e* |
| | 3.3.0 | 0.0.3 | | ŠE KÁ.GAL |
| | 0.4.1 | 5 SÌLA | | ŠE *ma-ki-si* |
| | 44.0.3 | 0.2.3 4 SÌLA | | $^{m}$*Mu-ra-nu* $^{m}$*I-re-man-ni-*$^{d}$IŠKUR |
| | ⸢23$^{?}$⸣.0.0 | 0.2.3 | | $^{m}$ÌR-GAŠAN $^{m}$*Gu-ub-bu-ḫu* |
| | ⸢22$^{?}$⸣.3.4 | 0.2.3 | 0.1.3 | $^{m}$KI.MIN $^{md}$*Šu-qa-mu-na*-URU$_4$-*iš* |
| | 28.1.5 | 0.2.3 | | $^{m}$SU-$^{d}$*Šu-qa-mu-na* DUMU $^{m}$*Kit-tu-*⸢x⸣-[x] |
| Rev. | ⸢5⸣.3.3 | 0.0.2 | | $^{m}$ÌR-GAŠAN $^{md}$*Nin-urta-qar-r*[*ad*] |
| | 1.0.0 | 0.0.1 | | $^{m}$*Re-eš-*$^{d}$U.GUR $^{m}$È-*a*-[*na*-ZÁLAG-$^{d}$AMAR.UTU] |
| | 0.2.2 | 5 SÌLA | | DUMU $^{m}$*Šu-ri-ḫa*-DINGIR |

COMMENTARY

1. "⸢ . . . ⸣; Āl-atḫē; year 24 of Nazi-[Maruttaš]." Because of the column headings, one would expect at the beginning of this line either (*šu-nu-ú/šu-ni-e*) EDIN (cf. headings of other texts in this group) or SAG NÍG.GA (cf. CUSAS 30 40 and CUSAS 30 45), but the remaining traces are not clear.

3–5. The data in the first and last columns correspond to those of **no. 48**: 3–5.

7–13. The individuals listed in the last column correspond to those in the last column of **no. 48**: 7–13.

10. If the restoration in **no. 48**: 10 is correct, the second PN should be Kittu-lîšir, but the traces after TU can hardly be the beginning of a LI, or of a SI, if the verbal form was written with the logogram SI.SÁ for *ešēru*. The traces could perhaps be interpreted as the beginning of an IŠ (thus *i*[*š-šir*]?), but *ešēru* G is attested in PNs only in the precative form (see Stamm 1968, 152; Hölscher 1996, 250).

### 30. CUNES 52-14-076

-.-.4 Kadašman-Turgu

U.e. EDIN $^{giš}$BÁN GAL ⸢*Kar-*$^{d}$*Nuska*⸣ MU.4.KAM *Ka-dáš-m*[*an-Túr-gu*]

| | SAG NÍG.GA | *ki-iṣ-rù* | MU.BI.IM |
|---|---|---|---|
| Obv. | 7.4.2 | 0.0.4 | NÍG.KUD.DA |
| | 35.1$^{pi}$.0 | 0.2.2 | $^{md}$AMAR.UTU-*mu-bal-liṭ* $^{m}$*Ri-*⸢*mu*$^{?}$*-ti*$^{?}$⸣ |
| 5 | 7.1.4 | 0.0.4 | $^{m}$KI.MIN $^{m}$*Ša-muḫ-ri-gim-*⸢*šu*⸣ |
| | 4.1.1 | 0.0.2 ⸢5⸣ | ⸢$^{m}$KI.MIN $^{md}$30⸣*-iš-man-ni* |
| | 7.2.5 | 0.0.4 | $^{m}$ZÁLAG-$^{d}$AMAR.UTU ⸢$^{m}$x-x⸣ [ |
| | ⸢6$^{?}$⸣.2.3 | 0.0.5 | $^{m}$*Ku-du-ra-nu* $^{m}$⸢$^{d}$U⸣[TU$^{?}$/IŠKUR$^{?}$ |
| 9 | ⸢x⸣.[x.x] | 0.0.⸢4⸣ | ⸢$^{m}$x-x⸣[ |
| Rev. | ⸢4.x.2⸣ | 0.0.⸢2⸣ 5 | ⸢$^{m}$*Eri-ba-*$^{d}$AMAR.UTU x⸣ [ |
| | 3.1.4 | 0.0.2 5 | $^{m}$*Iz-kùr-*$^{d}$IŠKUR $^{m}$[ |
| | 2$^{?}$.1.4 | 0.0.⸢1⸣ 5 | ⸢$^{m}$*Ši*$^{?}$*-ri*$^{?}$*-iš*$^{?}$*-ti*$^{?}$⸣ [ |
| | 2 20 | 1.2.2 | |

Commentary

1. "Countryside, (measured by) the big *sūtu*; Kār-Nuska; year 4 of Kadašm[an-Turgu]."

13. The figure 1.2.2 corresponds to the total of the quantities in col. ii (*kiṣru*).

14. Probably calculations, written smaller than the rest.

### 31. CUNES 52-10-082 (Plate No. 14)

-.-.5 Kadašman-Turgu

Some of the individuals mentioned in this text appear also in **no. 51**, which records the "stored barley" (*še'u tabku*) of Dūr-Amurru in the 7th year of Kadašman-Turgu (see Enlil-mutakkil, Šamaš-muballiṭ, Kidin-Enlil, Arad-Marduk, and Ṭāb-ṣilli-Eulmaš).

U.e. *šu-ni-e* EDIN $^{giš}$BÁN GAL BÀD-$^{d}$KUR$^{ki}$ MU.5.KAM *Ka-dáš-man-Túr-gu* ⸢LUGAL⸣

| | *re-eš* NÍG.GA | *ki-iṣ-rù* | GIG | ZAG.ḪI.LI | MU.BI.IM |
|---|---|---|---|---|---|
| Obv. | 20.2.3 | 0.1$^{pi}$.0 | | | NÍG.KUD.DA EN 1.1.3 *ḫír-ga-le-e* |
| | ⸢4$^{?}$⸣.3.1 | 0.0.2 | | | KÁ.[G]AL |
| 5 | ⸢1.3$^{?}$.0$^{?}$⸣ | | | | ŠE *ma-ki-s*[*i*] |
| | 81.2.0 | 0.3.5 | 1.2.1 | | $^{md+}$*En-líl-*⸢*mu-tak-kil* $^{m}$⸣[$^{d}$UTU]-⸢*mu-bal-liṭ*⸣ |
| | 76.4.1 | 0.3.3 4 | 5 SÌLA | | $^{m}$*Ki-din-*$^{d+}$*En-líl* $^{m}$*A-ḫu-na* |
| | ⸢70$^{+}$.3$^{+}$⸣.4 | 0.3.3 | | 0.0.1 2 SÌLA | $^{m}$ÌR-$^{d}$AMAR.UTU $^{m}$*Ṭà-ab-*⸢*ṣíl-lí*-É.UL.MAŠ⸣ |
| 9 | [x].3.0 | 0.3.4 | | | $^{m}$*Ṭà-ab*-IM-$^{d}$IŠKUR $^{m}$*Ta-ri-bu* |
| Rev. | ⸢70$^{+}$.3$^{+}$⸣.4 | 0.3.2 | 4 SÌLA | | $^{m}$*E-tel-pu* $^{m}$*Tab-ni-i-bu-li-ṭi* |
| | 11.0.5 ŠE.MUŠ$_{5}$ | 0.0.4 | | | *ḫír-ga-lu-ú* DUMU $^{m}$*Ḫu-di-ia* |

The rest of the reverse is blank.

Commentary

1. "*šunû* (of' the) countryside, (measured by) the big *sūtu*; Dūr-Amurru; year 5 of King Kadašman-Turgu."

6. The reading of the two PNs is supported by **no. 51**: 11.

10. Tabnî-bulliṭī "You created, (now) keep alive!" (cf. Sîn-tabni-šuklil in Hölscher 1996, 192); the feminine verbal forms indicate that the name invoked a goddess.

## 32. CUNES 52-10-062 (Plate No. 15)

-.-.11 Kadašman-Turgu

This text can be linked to **no. 7** and CUSAS 30 34, two ledgers that record the revenues (*tēlītu*) of Dūr-Enlilē in the 11th year of Kadašman-Turgu. Note that no. 32 has a column for ŠE.MUŠ$_5$, which is absent in no. 7 and CUSAS 30 34, and that it sometimes records under this heading quantities that the other two texts register under SAG NÍG.GA (see below).

There is no correspondence between the quantities of wheat (GIG) and cress (ZAG.ḪI.LI) recorded by this text and those recorded by no. 7 and CUSAS 30 34.

U.e. [*š*]*u-ni-e* EDIN $^{giš}$BÁN GAL BÀD-$^{d+}$*En-líl*$^{meš.ki}$ MU.11.KAM *Ka-dáš-man-Túr-g*⌜*u* LUGAL⌝

| | | | | | | |
|---|---|---|---|---|---|---|
| Obv. | [SA]G NÍG.GA | *ki-iṣ-rù* | ŠE.MUŠ$_5$ | GIG | ZAG.ḪI.LI | MU.BI.IM |
| | ⌜97⌝?.1.2 | 0.4.1 5 | | | | NÍG.KUD.DA EN 4.3.2 *ḫír-ga-le-e* |
| | 18.2.4 | 0.1.2 | | | | KÁ.GAL |
| | 83.2.0 | 0.3.5 | 12.0.3<br>0.0.5 | 9./2.1 | 0.0.5 | $^{md}$*Nin-urta*-MU-MU $^{m}$ZÁLAG-$^{d}$*Iš-tar* |
| | 57.2.3 | 0.3.0 | | | | $^{m}$KI.MIN $^{md}$*Nin-nisi-mu*-SIG$_5$-*iq* |
| | 55.0.0 | 0.2.5 | | | | $^{m}$KI.MIN $^{m}$DÙ-*a-šá*-$^{d}$A[MAR.UT]U |
| | 49.3.0 | 0.2.4 *za-ku* | | | | $^{m}$KI.MIN $^{m}$*Mar-tu-k*[*u*] |
| | 46.2.4 | 0.2.3 | | 1.2.2 | | $^{m}$KI.MIN $^{m}$*Eri-ba*-$^{d}$A[MAR.UT]U |
| | 36.3.2 | 0.2.1 | | | | $^{m}$KI.MIN DUMU $^{m}$*Ba-aq-ni* |
| | 35.1.2 | 0.2.1 | | | | $^{m}$KI.MIN $^{m}$*Il-lu-ri*-⌜*ia*⌝ |
| | 81.3.3 | 0.3.5 *za-ku* | 9.3$^{pi}$.0<br>0.0.5 | | | $^{m}$MU-*líb-ši* $^{m}$*Bi-i'*-⌜*šu*$_{14}$⌝ |
| | 73.0.0 | 0.3.3<br>*za-ku* | 4.0.5<br>0.0.3 | 0.1.4 5 | | $^{m}$KI.MIN DUMU $^{m}$*Ka-ak-ki-i*[*a*] |
| Rev. | 9.2.3 | 0.0.5 | | | | $^{m}$KI.MIN $^{m}$*Ša-ga-rak-t*[*i*] |
| | | | 3.4.2<br>0.0.3 | | | $^{m}$KI.MIN $^{m}$UD-*ni-bi* |
| | ⌜37⌝?.0.0 | 0.3.1 | | | | $^{m}$È-*a-na*-ZÁLAG-$^{d}$IŠKUR $^{m}$ÌR-*nu-bat-t*[*i*] |
| | 23.0.3 | 0.1.2 | | | | $^{md}$*Nuska-na-bu-šu* $^{m}$*Ab-bu-dan-nu* |
| | | | 15.2.3<br>0.1$^{pi}$.0 | 0.1.3 5 | | [$^{m}$]*Ib-nu-tu*$_4$ $^{m}$KI.MIN |
| | 5.0.0 | 0.0.2 *za-ku* | | | | *ḫar-šu-ú* $^{m}$*Mar-tu-ku a-na ṭe-mi-šu* |
| | 2.0.0 | 0.0.1 *za-ku* | | | | KI.MIN $^{m}$KI.MIN DUMU $^{m}$*Na-bu-na-a-tu*$_4$ |
| | 2.0.0 | 0.0.2 | | | | KI.MIN $^{md}$30-TI-URU$_4$ $^{m}$*E-mi-du* |
| | | | | | | |
| | 1 ME 93.2.2 | | | | | $^{md}$*Nin-urta*-MU-MU *za-ku* |

COMMENTARY

1. "*šunû* (of? the) countryside, (measured by) the big *sūtu*; Dūr-Enlilē; year 11 of King Kadašman-Turgu."

3–4. The quantities recorded here under SAG NÍG.GA appear in **no. 7**: 3–4 in the *šibšu*-column.

5. The sum of 83.2.0 (SAG NÍG.GA) + 12.0.3 (ŠE.MUŠ$_5$) corresponds to 95.2.3, the amount recorded for the SAG NÍG.GA of Ninurta-zākir-šūmi and Nūr-Ištar in **no. 7**: 6. In col. iii (ŠE.MUŠ$_5$), the figure 0.0.5 entered in the second line of the text box might represent the *kiṣru* calculated on the figure 12.0.3; see also ll. 12, 13, 15,

and 18 in the same column. For the same accounting technique, see also **nos. 33–34**. Cf. **no. 27**, which has a separate column for the *kiṣru* levied on quantities of *šeguššu*.

8. The annotation *zakû* next to quantities of *kiṣru* (here and also in ll. 12, 13, 19, and 20) likely indicates that the persons associated with this entry in the MU.BI.IM-columns were exempted from delivering this payment.

12. The sum of 81.3.3 (SAG NÍG.GA) + 9.3.0 (ŠE.MUŠ$_5$) corresponds to 91.1.3, which is the amount recorded as SAG NÍG.GA of Šumu-libši and Bi'šu in **no. 7**: 13.

13. The sum of 73.0.0 (SAG NÍG.GA) + 4.0.5 (ŠE.MUŠ$_5$) corresponds to [7]7.0.5, which is the amount recorded as SAG NÍG.GA of Šumu-libši and the son of Kakkiya in **no. 7**: 14.

15. The amount 3.4.2 in col. iii (ŠE.MUŠ$_5$) corresponds to the amount recorded for the SAG NÍG.GA of Šumu-libši and UD-nibi in CUSAS 30 34: 16. I am not aware of any other attestation of a PN $^{m}$UD-*ni-bi*, which might be Kassite: in fact, *nibi* occurs as the second element also in Urpa-nibi and K/Qunanibi (see Hölscher 1996, 127, 230) and perhaps also in Uzub-nibu (**no. 169**: 22). I cannot offer an interpretation of the first element, but note that UD is used with the phonetic value *tam* in Kassite PNs of the type Tamda/i-DN (Balkan 1954, 183, 213).

18. The amount 15.2.3 in col. iii (ŠE.MUŠ$_5$) corresponds to the amount recorded as the SAG NÍG.GA of Ibnûtu and Abbū-dannū in **no. 7**: 19.

23. According to this line, Ninurta-zākir-šumi is exempt (*zakû*) from paying the *kiṣru* on the amount of taxable capital indicated in col. i. See also **no. 7**: 25.

## 33. CUNES 52-12-006

-.-.12$^{?}$ Kadašman-Turgu

U.e. EDIN $^{giš}$BÁN GAL *Ba-ṣa-a-ti*$^{ki}$ MU.⸢12$^{?}$⸣.KAM *Ka-dáš-man-Túr-gu* LUGAL.E

| | *re-eš* NÍG.GA | *ki-iṣ-rù* | GIG | MU.BI.IM |
|---|---|---|---|---|
| Obv. | ⸢1 ME 2$^{?}$.3.1⸣ | 1.0.0 | | NÍG.KUD.DA EN 1.3.1 *ḫír-ga-le-e* |
| | ⸢15$^{?}$⸣.2.2 | 0.1.2 | | KÁ.GAL |
| | ⸢x.0.4⸣ | 0.0.4 | | ŠE *ma-ki-si* |
| | ⸢85$^{?}$⸣.4.4 | 0.3.4 | 0.4.1 | $^{m}$*A-na*-$^{d}$*Nin-urta-tak-la-ku* ÉNSI $^{m}$MU-*líb-ši* |
| | 1-*šu* 8.3.0 | 0.3.2 | 0.2.1 | DUMU $^{m}$*Ì-lí-re-man-ni* ÉNSI DUMU $^{m}$*Ḫa-na-na-a-a* |
| | 1-*šu* 5.2.3 | 0.3.1 | 0.4.3 | DUMU $^{m}$*Šu-ri-ḫa*-DINGIR KI.MIN $^{m}$*Ik k*[*a rù*] |
| | 1-*šu* 4.4.1 | 0.3.1 | 0.2.4 | $^{m}$UD-*šú*-ZÁLAG-*ir* KI.MIN $^{md}$[x-x-x-*ma*]*n-ni* |
| | 1-*šu* 2.2.3 | 0.3.1 | 0.1.4 | DUMU $^{m}$*Ku-ub-bu-ti* KI.MIN $^{md}$*Pap-sukkal*-MU-MU |
| | 1-*šu* 1.0.2 | 0.3.0 | 0.3.1 | DUMU $^{md}$30-*ma*-DINGIR KI.MIN $^{m}$*Ṭà-ab*-IM-$^{d}$IŠKUR |
| | ⸢59$^{?}$⸣.3.5 | 0.3.0 | | $^{m}$*Ṭà-ab-ki-din*-$^{d}$*Nin-urta* $^{md}$*Gu-la*-URU$_4$ |
| | ⸢x.x.3$^{?}$⸣ | 0.3.0 | | $^{m}$MU-*líb-ši* É-*a-nu* $^{m}$*Ik-ka-rù* |
| | ⸢50$^{+}$.x.x⸣ | ⸢0.1$^{?}$.5$^{?}$⸣ | 0.2$^{pi}$.0 | $^{m}$KAR-*ub*-$^{m}$AMAR.UTU $^{m}$*Im-bu*-⸢*ub*$^{?}$⸣-*bu* |
| Rev. | 53.3.4 | ⸢x.x.5⸣ | | ⸢$^{md}$*Nin*⸣-*urta-re-man-ni* $^{m}$*Eri-ba*-$^{d}$⸢MAŠ$^{?}$⸣ |
| | 50.4.3 | 0.2.5 | 0.2.2 | $^{m}$*Ri-mu-tu*$_4$ $^{m}$GAL-*š*[*á*]-GAŠAN |
| | 43.1.1 | 0.2.3 | | ⸢$^{m}$BA-*šá*-$^{d}$*Nin-ìmma*⸣ $^{md}$30-*iš-man-ni* |
| | ⸢6$^{+}$⸣.4.5 | 0.0.3 5 SÌLA | | *ḫar-šu-ú* $^{m}$*Muš-te-ši-ir*-$^{d}$AMAR.UTU |
| | ⸢5$^{+}$⸣.2.0 | 0.0.3 | | KI.MIN $^{m}$*Na-aḫ-zu-tu*$_4$ $^{md}$UTU-*qar-rad* |

COMMENTARY

1. "Countryside, (measured by) the big *sūtu*; Baṣātu; year ⸢12$^{?}$⸣ of King Kadašman-Turgu."

13. On the *bītānu*, see Introduction §4.3.

## 34. CUNES 52-14-070

-.-.12 Kadašman-Turgu

U.e. [(x) EDIN$^{?}$ $^{giš}$BÁN GA]L AN.ZA.GÀR$^{ki}$ MU.12.KAM *Ka-dáš-man-Túr-gu* LUGAL.E

| | [SAG NÍG.GA$^{?}$] | [*ki-iṣ-r*]*ù*$^{?}$ | ŠE.MUŠ$_5$ | GIG | ZÍZ.AN.NA | GÚ.GAL | ZAG.ḪI.LI | MU.BI.IM |
|---|---|---|---|---|---|---|---|---|
| Obv. | ⸢x⸣.1.5 | 1.0.3 | | | 6.2$^{pi}$./4 | | | NÍG.KUD.DA EN 2.1⸢$^{pi}$⸣.0 *ḫír-ga-le-e* |
| | ⸢x⸣.1$^{pi}$.0 | 1.0.4 | | | 1.2$^{pi}$./2 | | | KÁ.GAL |
| | ⸢5$^{+}$⸣.0.0 | 0.0.3 | | | | | | ŠE *ma-ki-si* |
| | ⸢47$^{?}$⸣.0.0 | ⸢4$^{?}$.1⸣$^{pi}$.0 | | | | | | *lu-du-*⸢*ú*⸣ |
| | ⸢22$^{+}$⸣.4.4 | 1.3.0 | | 6.0.3 | 12.3.1<br>0.1$^{pi}$.0 | 0.0.4 | 0.2$^{pi}$.0 | $^{m}$*Bu-un-na-*$^{d}$IŠKUR É[NS]I<br>$^{m}$*È-a-na-*ZÁLAG-$^{d}$AMAR.UTU |
| | [x].⸢x⸣.1 | 0.3.3 | 2.0.4<br>0.0.2 | 5.2.4 | | | | $^{md}$AMAR.UTU-MU-MU [KI.MIN$^{?}$]<br>$^{m}$*Eri-ba-*$^{d}$IŠKUR ⸢2$^{?}$ *ḫar*$^{?}$⸣-*b*[*u*$^{?}$] |
| | [ ] | 0.2.1 | | 1.2.3 | | | | $^{m}$*I-ri-bu* ⸢KI⸣.[MIN D]UMU $^{m}$*Ṣíl-*⸢*li*$^{?}$⸣-[ |
| | [ ] | ⸢0.2$^{?}$.1$^{?}$⸣ | | 0.4.1 | | | | $^{m}$*Ki-din-*$^{d}$MAR.TU K[I.MIN |
| | [ ] | ⸢0.3$^{?}$.0$^{?}$⸣ | 3.2.4<br>0.0.2 | ⸢1.2.5⸣ | 2.0.5<br>0.0.2 | | 8 SÌLA | $^{m}$*Ri-mu-tu*$_4$ $^{m}$[ |
| | [ ] | [ ] | [ ] | [ ] | ⸢x.x.x⸣ | ⸢0.0.2 5 SÌLA⸣ | ⸢0.0.2 8 SÌLA⸣ | $^{m}$KI.MIN $^{m}$[ |
| Text breaks off (1–2 lines missing) | | | | | | | | |
| Rev. | [ ] | [ ] | [ ] | [ ] | [ ] | | | [ |
| | [ ] | [ ] | [ ] | ⸢x.x.x⸣ | | | | $^{m}$*Ṭa-bi-ia* DUMU $^{m}$*A-ḫ*[*e*$^{?}$ |
| | [ ] | [ ] | | 1.0.1 | | | 0.0.1 2 SÌLA | $^{m}$*Eri-ba-*$^{d}$AMAR.UTU $^{m}$*Nam-*[ |
| | [ ] | [ ] | | | 1.3.2<br>0.0.2 | | | ⸢*ḫar-šu-ú*⸣ $^{m}$*Ša-ba-a-a-ú-t*[*u*$_4$] |
| | [x.x].⸢4$^{?}$⸣ | 0.0.2 | | | | | | KI.MIN $^{md}$*Nin-urta-mu-ba*[*l-liṭ*] |
| | [x].⸢x⸣.1 | | | | | | | KI.MIN $^{m⸢d}$IŠKUR$^{?}$⸣-[x-x] ⸢*ša*$^{?}$⸣ [ |
| | | | | | 1.1$^{pi}$.0<br>0.0.1 | | | KI.MIN $^{m}$*Bu-un-na-*$^{d⸢}$IŠKUR⸣ [ |
| | | | 2.0.0<br>0.0.2 | | 2.2$^{pi}$.0<br>0.0.2 | | | KI.MIN $^{m}$*Nam-rù* $^{m}$*Ṣíl-lu-t*[*u*$_4$ |

COMMENTARY

1. "[. . . countryside?, (measured by) the bi]g [*sūtu*]; Dimtu; year 12 of King Kadašman-Turgu."

7. In col. v (ZÍZ.AN.NA), the annotation 0.1$^{pi}$.0 in the second line of the text box might represent the *kiṣru* calculated on the figure 12.3.1; the same applies probably also to the figures recorded in ll. 11, 16′, 19′, and 20′ in the same column.

8. In col. iii (ŠE.MUŠ$_5$), the annotation 0.0.2 in the second line of the text box might represent the *kiṣru* calculated on the figure 2.0.4; the same applies probably also to the figures recorded in ll. 11 and 20′ in the same column. The sign I tentatively read as *ḫar* in col. viii is now gone but was visible on a photograph taken before the tablet was baked.

16′. For the PN cf. DUMU $^{m}$⸢*Ša*?⸣-*ba-a-a-ú-ti* in BE 14 166: 10 (Clay 1912b, 127).

## 35. CUNES 52-10-043 (Plate No. 16)

-.-.13 Kadašman-Turgu

Restorations are based on **no. 12**, which records the revenues (*tēlītu*) from Āl-irrē in the 13th year of Kadašman-Turgu and lists the same individuals in the same order as no. 35. There are correspondences also in the quantities recorded by the two texts (see below). Note that no. 35 has a column for *šeguššu*/ŠE.MUŠ$_5$, absent in no. 12.

U.e. EDIN $^{giš}$BÁN GAL URU-*ir-re-e* MU.13.KAM *Ka-dáš-man-Túr-gu* LUGAL.E

| Obv. | SAG NÍG.GA | *ki-iṣ-rù* | ŠE.MUŠ$_5$ | GIG | ZÍZ.AN.NA | MU.BI.I[M] |
|---|---|---|---|---|---|---|
| | 7.1.3 | 0.0.4 | | | | NÍG.KUD.DA EN 0.3.5 ⸢*ḫir-ga*⸣*-le-e* |
| | | | | | | KÁ.GAL *a-na* ÉRIN$^{ḫi.a}$ *dul-li* x<br>*ù* ŠUKU ANŠE.KUR.RA$^{meš}$ SUM-*at* |
| | 1.1$^{pi}$.0 | 0.0.1 | | | | ŠE *ma-ki-si* |
| | 17.2.4 | 0.1$^{pi}$.0 | | | | $^{m}$*Za-ki-rù* $^{m}$*Bu-un-na-*$^{d}$AMAR.UTU |
| | 16.1$^{pi}$.0 | 0.1$^{pi}$.0 | | | 0.2.4 | $^{m}$*Eri-ba-*$^{d}$IŠKUR $^{m}$*Ú-sa-tu-ú-a* |
| | 11.2$^{pi}$.0 | 0.0.5 | | 0.0.4 | | $^{m}$*Iz-kùr-*$^{d}$*Nin-urta* $^{md}$*Nin-urta-kí-na-i-de* |
| | 8.4$^{pi}$.0 | 0.0.5 | | | | $^{m}$ZÁLAG-$^{d}$AMAR.UTU $^{m}$*A-bi-u*[*l-i*]*-de* |
| | 6.2.3 | 0.0.4 | | | | $^{m}$KI.MIN $^{m}$*Iz-kùr-*$^{d}$IŠKUR |
| | 3.4.3 | 0.0.3 | | | | $^{m}$*Ri-iš-*$^{d}$IŠKUR |
| | 3.1$^{pi}$.0 | 0.0.2 | | | | $^{m}$*Iz-kùr-*$^{d}$IŠKUR *a-na ṭe-m*[*i-šu*] |
| | 2.4.2 | 0.0.2 | | | | $^{m}$NÍG.BA-$^{d}$AMAR.UTU |
| | ⸢2$^{?}$⸣.3.4 | 0.0.2 | | | | $^{m}$*A-mi-lu-ba-*[*nu-ú*] |
| Rev. | 2.2.3 | 0.0.2 | | | | $^{m}$*In-nu-u*[*n-nu*]<br>SIPA ANŠ[E] |
| 16 | | | 1.3.3 | | | $^{m}$*Di-maḫ-di-*⸢d⸣[*Uraš*] |
| | | | 1.0.2<br>0.0.1 | | | $^{md}$*Nin-urta-ki-n*[*a-i-de*]<br>[$^{m}$B]A-*šá-*$^{d}$*Nin-u*[*rta*] |
| | 1.0.0 | 0.0.1 | | | | ⸢$^{m}$*Ib-ni*⸣-$^{d}$IŠKUR $^{l}$⸢$^{ú}$NAGAR] <br>$^{m}$*Iz-kùr-*$^{d}$*Nin-urta* [ |
| | | 1.2.1 | 0.0.1 | | | |

Commentary

1. "Countryside, (measured by) the big *sūtu*; Āl-irrē; year 13 of King Kadašman-Turgu."

3. 7.1.3 in col. i (SAG NÍG.GA) is the same amount that **no. 12**: 3 records in the *šibšu*-column.

4. "(the amount of) the city-gate was given to the workmen of the *dullu*-service and as fodder for the horses." The fact that the barley levied as (the amount of) the city-gate was disbursed probably explains the lack of quantities in this line. On the *dullu*-service, see most recently Paulus 2014b, 174. Cf. **no. 97** and related texts for documents recording the disbursement of rations to workmen who carried out the *dullu*-service.

6–15. The quantities recorded in col. i (SAG NÍG.GA) correspond to those in col. i (sag níg.ga) of **no. 12**: 7–16.

14. ⸢2$^{?}$⸣.3.4 is the expected figure according to **no. 12**: 15.

15. For the restoration Innunnu SIPA ANŠ[E], see **no. 46**: 12, another text recording revenues from Āl-irrē.

16–17. The quantities recorded here as the *šegušš̌u* (ŠE.MUŠ$_5$) of Dimaḫdi-Uraš and Ninurta-kīna-īde are listed as the *rēš makkūri* (SAG NÍG.GA) of the same persons in **no. 12**: 17–18.

17. In col. iii (ŠE.MUŠ$_5$), the annotation 0.0.1 in the second line of the text box might represent the *kiṣru* calculated on the figure 1.0.2.

19. The figure 1.2.1 in col. ii is the sum of all quantities recorded in the *kiṣru*-column, while the figure 0.0.1 in col. iii corresponds to the *kiṣru* calculated on the 1.0.2 of *šeguššu*/ŠE.MUŠ$_5$ in l. 17. The figures in this line are written in a smaller script and are lightly impressed, as if they were written when the tablet was already partially dry.

## 36. CUNES 52-10-050

-.-.5 [. . .]

| | | | | | |
|---|---|---|---|---|---|
| U.e. | *šu*-⸢*ni-e*⸣ EDIN $^{giš}$⸢BÁN⸣ [GAL] URU-*at-ḫe-e* MU.5.K[AM | | | | |
| Obv. | SAG NÍ[G.GA] | ⸢*ki-iṣ-rù*⸣ | ⸢GIG$^{?}$⸣ | [Š]E.IN.NU.ḪA | MU.BI.I[M] |
| | 1-*šu*$^{?}$ 9.3$^{?}$.5 | ⸢x.x.2$^{?}$⸣ | | | NÍG.KUD.DA EN 1.[x.x *ḫír-ga-le-e*] |
| | 4.0.0 | [ ] | | | NÍG.KUD.⸢DA *ša*⸣ $^{uru}$[ |
| | 13.1$^{pi}$.0 | ⸢x.x.5$^{?}$⸣ | | | KÁ.GA[L] |
| | ⸢2$^{?}$⸣.2.0 | 0.0.2 | | | ŠE *ma-ki-si* |
| | ⸢8⸣4.4.2 | 0.⸢3⸣.5 | 1.0.4 | 0.0.5 | $^{md}$*Nin-urta-ki-in-pi-šu*<br>$^{m}$*Ki*-⸢*rib-tu*$_4$$^{?}$⸣ |
| | ⸢1-*šu*⸣ 1.1.4 | 0.3.0 | 1.3.0 | 0.0.4 | $^{m}$KI.MIN $^{md}$*Nin-urta*-ŠEŠ-[ |
| | ⸢82$^{?}$⸣.2.5 | 0.3.4 | | | $^{m}$SU-$^{d}$*Šú-qa-mu-na* [ |
| | 1-*šu* 5.1.4 | 0.3.1 | 0.4.1 5 | | $^{m}$ŠEŠ-⸢*ṣi*⸣-*nu* DUMU $^{m}$⸢*Mu*$^{?}$⸣-[ |
| | ⸢35$^{?}$⸣.2.0 | 0.2.2 | 0.4.1 | | $^{m}$KI.MIN $^{m}$⸢*E-ez-ù-pa*⸣-[*ši-ir*] |
| | ⸢35$^{?}$⸣.1.4 | 0.2.4 | 1.0.1 8 | | $^{md}$*Nin-urta*-ÁG-*kit*-[*ti*]<br>$^{m}$*Iz-kùr*-$^{d}$*Dil*-[*bat*] |
| | ⸢19⸣.4.0 | 0.1.2 | | | $^{m}$*I-qí-ša*-$^{d}$[<br>$^{md}$KUR-⸢x⸣[ |
| | [x].⸢2$^{+}$⸣.4 | 0.0.2 6 | | | $^{md}$*Šú-qa*-[<br>$^{m}$*Iz-kù*[*r*- |
| Rev. | 3.0.3 | 0.0.2 6 SÌLA | | | $^{m}$[<br>$^{m}$[ |
| | 3.0.2 | 0.0.2 | | | $^{m⸢d?⸣}$[<br>$^{m}$*K*[*i*$^{?}$- |
| | 2.2.0 | 0.0.2 | | | DUMU $^{m}$[<br>$^{md}$[ |
| | 1.3.3 | 0.0.1 | | | $^{m}$*A*-⸢*gab*$^{?}$-x⸣[<br>$^{m}$*A-ḫe*-⸢*du-t*⸣[*u*$_4$ |
| | | 4.1.1 2 SÌLA | | | *ki-ṣir* EDI[N] |

Commentary

1. "*šunû* (of? the) countryside, (measured by) the [big] *sūtu*; Āl-atḫē; year 5 [of. . .]."

10. For the PN Aḫu-ṣīnu "The brother is help," cf. Adad-ṣīnū'a (Hölscher 1996, 18; Sassmannshausen 2001, 466) and Sîn-ṣīn (van Soldt 2015, 564).

19. Even though it is not possible to verify all the figures in col. ii (*kiṣru*), this amount likely corresponds to the sum of the amounts recorded in the previous lines.

### 1.1.4 Accounts of "Shares"

## 37. CUNES 52-12-014 (Plate No. 17)

-.-.1 Kadašman-Turgu

The structure, content, and function of this document are difficult to describe due to its complexity and poor state of preservation. According to its heading, it was a summary of the "shares" and of the *kiṣru*-payments associated with a person whose name must have been mentioned at the end of l. 1, but is now unfortunately lost (perhaps Ninurta-zākir-šumi? Cf. **nos. 38–39**). According to the column headings, the goods collected were [barley$^{?}$], wheat, and emmer. The entries of the MU.BI.IM-column mention, besides the "shares" and *kiṣru*-payments, items known also from other texts recording revenues, such as the "barley of the gleaning" (ŠE *liqtāt*[*i*], ll. 10, 26), the "collected seed" (*zēru esru*, l. 12), the "barley of the brewing" (ŠE [*s*]*ibûti*, l. 27), and the *kiṣir ṣēri* and *kiṣir maḫri* (ll. 35–36). Several entries are then summed up together, and each sum (PAP) is associated with the name of a town in the MU.BI.IM-column: Dūr-Enlilē (ll. 14, 29), Zarāt-šarri (l. 20), Āl-irrē (l. 23), Dūr-Bēl-mātāti (l. 38), and Dūr-Amurru (l. 39). The text indicates through the expression *qāt* (ŠU) PN the names of different individuals who are in charge of larger or smaller amounts of the collected goods: Sîn-išmanni (l. 23), Ilī-remanni (l. 25), Ninurta-ašarēd (l. 39), and Mudammiq-Adad (l. 42).

Obv. [x x x] ⸢ḪA.LA⸣$^{meš}$ *ù ki-iṣ-rù ša* $^{md}$[

MU.1.[KAM] *Ka-dáš-man-Túr-gu* ⸢LUGAL.E⸣

| | [ŠE$^{?}$] | GIG | ZÍZ.AN.NA | MU.BI.IM |
|---|---|---|---|---|
| | [x].⸢x.5⸣ | ⸢10$^{+}$.2⸣.2 | | $^{m}$*Bu-un-na-*$^{d}$AMAR.UTU |
| | ⸢12$^{?}$⸣.0.4 ⸢x SÌLA⸣ | | | $^{m}$*Ba-bi-la-a-a-ú* |
| | ⸢2⸣8.2.1 ⸢4⸣ | ⸢x.x.1⸣ 6 SÌLA | | ḪA.LA KI $^{md}$*Nuska-ib-ni* |
| | 26.1.5 5<br>EN 4 GUR *ša i-na la šab-ši le-qú-ú* | | | ḪA.LA KI $^{m}$*Kal-bu* |
| | 20$^{+}$.[x.x x] ⸢SÌLA⸣ | | | ḪA.LA ⸢KI $^{m}$ÌR⸣-GAŠAN |
| | 10$^{+}$.[x.x] | | | ḪA.LA $^{m}$*Ì-lí-re-m*[*an-ni*] |
| | ⸢12⸣.[x.x] | [ ] | [ ] | ŠE *li-iq-ta-t*[*i*] |
| | | [ ] | [ ] | ḪA.LA KI $^{m}$MU-*líb-ši* |
| | | [ ] | [ ] | ⸢NUMUN⸣ *es-rù* |
| | | [ ] | [ ] | ⸢*ki*⸣-*iṣ-rù* |
| PAP | 1 [ME$^{?}$ x.x.x] | [ ] | [ ] | ⸢x x x BÀD-$^{d+}$*En-líl*$^{ḫi.a.ki}$⸣<br>[ |
| PAP | 30$^{+}$.[x.x] | [ ] | [ ] | ⸢x x⸣ [x x x] ⸢x ni/ir⸣<br>[ |
| | 17.[x.x] | [ ] | [ ] | [x x x x] ⸢x⸣ GAŠAN |
| | 16.[x.x] | [ ] | [ ] | [x x x x]⸢$^{d}$KUR$^{?}$⸣ |
| | 10.0.0 | [ ] | [ ] | [x x] ⸢x⸣ *a* ⸢x⸣ *ú-a* |
| | 14.[x.x] | [ ] | [ ] | ⸢NUMUN *es-rù*⸣ |
| P[AP$^{?}$] | [ ] | [ ] | | ⸢*Za-rat*-LUGAL$^{ki}$⸣ |
| PAP | 20$^{+}$.[x.x] | 0.3.[x] ⸢x⸣<br>⸢x x⸣ | | ḪA.LA ⸢x⸣[x x $^{m}$*T*]⸢*a*$^{?}$⸣-*qí-šu* DUMU<br>$^{m}$EN-SUM-⸢*na*⸣<br>⸢x mi$^{?}$⸣ [x $^{m}$*Ta*$^{?}$]-⸢*qí-šu* x⸣ |

| | | | | |
|---|---|---|---|---|
| | ⌜x.x.x⌝ | | | [ḪA].⌜LA KI⌝ [<br>⌜$^{iti}$<ŠU>.NUMUN.NA 4?⌝ [<br>⌜ŠU $^{m}$⌝ [ |
| Rev. | 22.0.4 | 0.1.3 EN 0.0.2<br>*ki-iṣ-rù*<br>ŠU $^{md}$30-*iš-man-ni* | 0.4.5 EN 0.0.5<br>*ki-iṣ-rù*<br>ŠU $^{m}$KI.MIN | ḪA.LA KI $^{m}$[<br>URU-*ir-re-*[*e* |
| 24 | | | | |
| ŠU.NIGIN | 4 ME 34./[x.x] | ⌜16?. x.x⌝ | 25./⌜x.x⌝ 5 SÌLA | $^{giš}$BÁN [GA]L<br>ŠU $^{m}$*Ì-l*[*í-r*]*e-man-ni* |
| | 40+.[x.x] | | | ŠE *li-iq-ta-ti* |
| | ⌜4+⌝.[x.x] | | | ŠE [*s*]*i-bu-ti* KI $^{m}$ZÁLAG-$^{d}$U.GUR |
| | ⌜14+⌝.[x.x] | | | ⌜*ki*⌝-[*iṣ*]-*rù* |
| PAP | 1-*šu* 6+.[x.x]<br>⌜1+⌝ [SÌLA?] | | | B[ÀD-$^{d+}$*En-l*]*íl*$^{hi.a.ki}$ |
| 30 | ⌜10+⌝.[x.x][1] | | | ḪA.LA KI $^{m}$*Ib-ni-*⌜*ia*⌝ |
| | 14.[x.x] ⌜5⌝ | | | ḪA.LA KI $^{m}$*In-n*[*u-un*]-*nu* |
| | 13.2.0 5 | 0.0.1 5 SÌLA | | ⌜ḪA.LA KI $^{m}$⌝[x-x]-$^{d}$A[MAR.UT]U? |
| | 11.1.5 5 | | | ḪA.LA KI $^{m}$KI.MIN $^{m}$*Ib-ni-ia* |
| | 11.2.0 | | | ḪA.LA KI $^{m}$ÌR-*nu-bat-ti* |
| 35 | 8.2.2 | | | *ki-ṣir* EDIN |
| | 1.1.1 | | | *ki-ṣir maḫ-ri* |
| | 1.3.4 5 | | | *si-ir-ri-im-du* |
| PAP | 80.2.5 | 0.0.1 5 SÌLA | | BÀD-EN-KUR.KUR$^{ki}$ |
| PAP | 10.3.4 | 0.0.3 8 SÌLA ŠU $^{md}$*Nin-urta*-SAG | | *ki-iṣ-rù* BÀD-$^{d}$KUR$^{ki}$ |
| 40 | | | | |
| [Š]U.NIGIN | 1 ME 1-*šu* 0.3.0 | 0.0.5 3 SÌLA | | *ša a-na* ŠÀ GUR$_7$ *tu-u*[*b-bu*]-⌜*ku*⌝ |
| [ŠU.NIGIN] | ⌜5?⌝ ME 94.0.0<br>4 SÌLA | 16.3.3<br>ŠU $^{m}$*Mu-da-mi-iq-*$^{d}$IŠKUR | 25./2.0 5 SÌLA | $^{giš}$BÁN GAL |

COMMENTARY

1–2. "[ . . . ] shares and *kiṣru* of [PN]; year 1 of King Kadašman-Turgu." The amounts are measured by the big *sūtu* (ll. 25, 42).

7. "Including 120 *sūtu* which are taken from? what was not collected."

10. For the "barley of the gleanings," see also l. 26, **no. 2**: 5 and CUSAS 30 40: 11.

27. Cf. the "share (ḪA.LA) of/for the brewing" in **no. 4**: 10.

37. The meaning of this entry is unclear; the closest lemmata in the dictionaries are *sirimtu, sirendu* ("a cutting tool" according to CAD S, 31 s.v., "ein Gegenstand" according to AHw II, 1050 s.v.), and *serremtu* ("female wild ass, onager," AHw II, 1038 s.v.), none of which fit this context. Cf. *si-ir-im-du* in **no. 317**: 1 (also measured in units of volume). Perhaps it is the same word that is spelled *ṣi-rim-ti* in MUN 31: 56 but was tentatively read *ṣi-bit*!?*-ti* by Sassmannshausen 2001, 233.

41. This grand total, which refers to the quantities of ll. 26–39, is described in the MU.BI.IM-column as an amount "which is stored in the granary" (see *tubbuku* in CAD T, 445–46; AHw III, 1365).

42. Even though it is not possible to verify all of the entries, this line must have recorded the final grand total of all the amounts recorded by the text.

---

1 A little fragment has been wrongly glued here.

## 38. CUNES 52-10-056

-.-.3 Kadašman-Turgu

| | | | | |
|---|---|---|---|---|
| Obv. | ŠE $^{giš}$BÁN GAL ḪA.LA$^{⸢meš}$ *ša*⸣ $^{md}$*Nin-urta*-MU-MU | | | |
| | BÀD-$^{d+}$*En-líl*$^{ḫi.a.ki}$ MU.3.KAM *Ka-dáš-man-Túr-gu* LUGAL.E | | | |
| | ŠE.EŠTUB | ŠE.MUŠ$_5$ | ZÍZ.AN.NA | MU.BI.IM |
| | 5.0.0 | 3.1.4<br>5 SÌLA | 5.3.5<br>5 SÌLA | ḪA.LA KI $^m$ÌR-GAŠAN |
| | | 3.1.4 5 | | ḪA.LA $^m$ÌR-GAŠAN |
| | 5.1.3 | | | ḪA.LA KI $^m$*Ḫu-za-*[*l*]*u*$_4$ |
| | 0.4.4 | 0.0.1 | 0.4.2<br>5 SÌLA | ḪA.LA KI $^m$[Š]EŠ$^?$-DÙ |
| | 0.1.3 5 SÌLA | | | ḪA.LA KI $^m$ZÁLAG-$^d$*Ištar* |
| Rev. | 0.4.4 5 SÌLA | | 1.0.2 5<br>SÌLA | *ki-ṣir* EDIN |
| | 0.1.2 5 SÌLA | | 0.1.4 5<br>SÌLA | *ki-ṣir maḫ-ri* |
| PAP | 12.3.5<br>5 SÌLA | 6.3.4 | 8.0.3 | $^{giš}$BÁN GAL |

COMMENTARY

1–2. "Grain, (measured by) the big *sūtu*; shares of Ninurta-zākir-šumi; Dūr-Enlilē; year 3 of King Kadašman-Turgu."

## 39. CUNES 52-18-810

-.-.10 Kadašman-Turgu

| | | | | | | | |
|---|---|---|---|---|---|---|---|
| Obv. | [ḪA.L]A$^{?meš}$ $^{giš}$BÁN GAL *ša* $^{md}$*Nin-urta*-MU-MU | | | | | | |
| | MU.10.⸢KAM *Ka*⸣-*dáš-man-Túr-gu* LUGAL.E | | | | | | |
| | ŠE.EŠTUB | ŠE.MUŠ$_5$ | GIG | ZÍZ.AN.NA | [G]Ú$^?$.⸢GAL$^?$⸣ | ZAG.ḪI.<br>LI | MU.BI.IM |
| | 20.1.4 | 0.0.4 | | | | | *Man-nu*-ÙRU-[*šu*]<br>KI $^m$*Ḫu*-⸢*za*⸣-[*li*$^?$] |
| | | | 11.4.3 | | | | BÀD-$^{d+}$*En*-[*líl*$^{ḫi.a/meš.ki}$]<br>*ša ki-iṣ-*[*ri*] |
| | | | 0.2.4 TA 2.0.0 ⸢*ša*$^?$ $^m$⸣*Ta-ri-bat*-DINGIR<br>*ù* 0.0.4 $^m$*Šim-di-*$^d$*Šu-qa-mu-na* | | | | KI.⸢MIN⸣ KI $^m$⸢x⸣[ |
| Rev. | | | | | [ ] | | URU-ÉNS[I$^{meš}$]<br>KI $^m$ZÁLAG-$^d$[ |
| | | 2.1.3<br>6 SÌLA<br>EN 1.2.2 ÉŠ.GÀR$^?$ *ša* 3.⸢1.1 1⸣ | | 0.4.0 ⸢5$^?$⸣ | ⸢x x⸣ | ⸢*ki*$^?$-*i*$^?$⸣ | ⸢*lu-du-ú*⸣<br>$^m$[<br>[ |

COMMENTARY

1–2. "[Shar]es$^{?}$, (measured by) the big *sūtu*, of Ninurta-zākir-šumi; year 10 of King Kadašman-Turgu."

4. The town of Mannu-nāṣiršu occurs in connection with Ḫuzālu also in **no. 160**: 1.

8. EN 1.2.2 ÉŠ.GÀR$^{?}$ *ša* 3.⸢1.1 1⸣ "including 44 *sūtu* as production supplies$^{?}$ (out?) of 97 *sūtu* and 1 *qû*." If the interpretation of the last signs as a quantity is correct, then the production supplies were taken from that quantity; however, the usual formulation in such cases would be *ina libbi* (ŠÀ) "from."

### 1.1.5 Other Accounts of Revenues

## 40. CUNES 52-10-123

-.-.9$^{+}$ Nazi-Maruttaš

The text was a multicolumn table, but only part of the last column is preserved. I assign it to the texts recording revenues because of the entries mentioning *ludû* (l. 7) and *miksu* (NÍG.KUD.DA) together with a quantity of *ḫirgalû* (l. 8), which are typical of this group of documents, but in the absence of the heading and of the first columns a more precise classification is not possible. Note that *esirtu* "collected payment" (l. 5) usually occurs in MB texts with regard to sheep and precious metals (CAD I, *isirtu* A, 197–98), but see also CUSAS 30 53: 1 for another attestation in connection with cereals.

| | |
|---|---|
| U.e. | MU].⸢9$^{+}$⸣.KAM *Na-*[ |
| Obv. | M]U.BI.[IM |
| | D]UMU $^{m}$*Ì-lí-r*[*e-man-ni*] |
| | D]UMU $^{m}$*A-na-*$^{d}$30-⸢*tak-la-k*⸣[*u*] |
| | D]UMU $^{m}$KI.MIN *e-si-ir-t*[*u*$_{4}$ |
| | L]A'U$_{4}$$^{?}$ ÉNSI $^{m}$*Bu-un-na-*⸢$^{d}$⸣[ |
| | *l*]*u-du-ú* |
| | N]ÍG.KUD.DA EN 2.3.0 *ḫír-ga-l*[*e-e*] |
| | $^{m}$]*Ba-ḫu-ú* ÉNSI $^{m}$*Ša-gi-*⸢x⸣[ |
| | $^{m}$]*Bu-un-na-*$^{d}$GÌR $^{m}$*Tu-ni-*⸢x⸣[ |
| | $^{m}$]⸢$^{d?}$⸣MAŠ-MU-MU $^{m}$*Ib-ni-*[ |
| | ] ⸢x x x x x⸣ [ |
| Text breaks off | |
| Rev. | x x x] ⸢ki$^{?}$ x⸣ [ |
| | DUMU$^{?}$ $^{m}$*A-na-*$^{d}$]30-*tak-l*[*a-ku* |
| | DUMU$^{?}$ $^{m}$]⸢*Ì*⸣-*lí-re-man-*[*ni* |
| | $^{m}$*Mar*$^{?}$]-*tu-ku* $^{m}$TI-*su-*⸢$^{d}$⸣[ |
| | ]-⸢*ti*$^{?}$⸣ *maḫ-ra*[*t* |
| | *k*]*i-iṣ-r*[*ù* |
| | $^{m}$]⸢È⸣-*a-na-*ZÁLAG-$^{d}$A[MAR$^{?}$.UTU$^{?}$] |
| | ] ⸢x⸣-$^{d+}$*En-líl* ⸢m[u$^{?}$ |

## 41. CUNES 52-20-301

-.-.18 Nazi-Maruttaš

This ledger is assigned to this category because it mentions *miksu* (l. 3, NÍG.KUD.DA), *šibšu* (ll. 6, 9–10), and *zittu* (l. 11, ḪA.LA), but its structure and content are otherwise different from the other texts recording revenues. Tukultī-Ekur and Kār-Nuska seem to have been the towns responsible for the delivery (see the subtotals in ll. 7 and 12, and the entries in ll. 15–16).

The right edge of the tablet is unnaturally flat, as if it had been cut or smoothened.

| | | | | | | | |
|---|---|---|---|---|---|---|---|
| U.e. | | MU.18.KAM *Na-zi-Mu-ru-ut-ta-aš* | | | | | |
| Obv. | ⸢ŠE x x x⸣ | ⸢ŠE.MUŠ$_5$?⸣ | ⸢GIG⸣ | ⸢ZÍZ.AN.NA⸣ | GÚ.[TUR] | GÚ.GAL | MU.BI.I[M] |
| | ⸢x.x.x⸣ | | | | | | NÍG.KUD.DA *ša* ⸢ka ḫi x⸣ [ |
| | ⸢x.x.x⸣ | | | | | | ⸢*ḫír-ga-lu-ú*⸣ |
| | ⸢x.x.x⸣ | | | | | | NUMUN [x] x e aš [ |
| | | ⸢0.1.x⸣ | | | 0.0.3 2 | 0.0.1 6 | *ši-⸢ib⸣-šu*$_{14}$ |
| [PAP] | ⸢x.x.x⸣ | ⸢0.1.x⸣ | | | 0.0.3 2 | 0.0.1 6 | *Tu-kul-ti-*⸢É⸣.[KUR$^{ki}$] |
| | | | | | | | *ḫír-ga-lu-ú* |
| | | | | | 0.0.4 3 | | *ši-ib-šu*$_{14}$ |
| | | | | | 0.0.5 5 | | KI.MIN *ša* DUMU $^{m}$ŠEŠ-SUM-[*na*] |
| | | | | | 0.0.2 | | ḪA.LA $^{md}$MAŠ-MU-M[U] |
| [PAP] | ⸢1+⸣.1.3 | | | | 0.1.5 8 SÌLA | | *Kar-*$^{d}$*Nuska* |
| Rev. | 0.0.1 1 x | | | | | | ⸢*ḫír*?-*ga*?-*lu-ú*⸣ |
| [ŠU].NIGIN | 16.4.3 | 0.1.2 5 | | | 0.2.3 | 0.0.1 6 | ŠU $^{m}$*Iz-kur-*[ |
| | | | 0.0.2 | | | | *Tu-kul-ti-*⸢É⸣.[KUR$^{ki}$] |
| | | | 1/.2.4 | 3.4.0 | | | *Kar-*$^{d}$*Nuska* |
| PAP | | | ⸢1⸣.3.0 | 3.4.0 | | | $^{m}$*Ta-ri-bu* LÚ.SA[G? |

## 42. CUNES 52-10-124

-.-.19 Nazi-Maruttaš

According to its heading, this text was a memorandum listing quantities "not collected" (*lā esru*) associated with the town of Āl-Arad-Bēlti. The nature of the delivery was indicated at the beginning of l. 1, which is now lost. It may have been seed, which is elsewhere often recorded as *esru* "collected."

| | | |
|---|---|---|
| Obv. | [x x] $^{giš}$BÁN 10 SÌLA *ša* MU.19.KAM $^{d}$*Na-zi-Ma-*⸢*ru-ut-ta*?-*aš*?⸣ | |
| | | *la es-*⸢*ru*⸣ URU-ÌR-GAŠAN$^{ki}$ |
| | 1.0.0 | $^{md}$*Nuska*-MU-SIG$_5$ |
| | 0.2.2 | $^{md}$*Nin-urta*-ÙRU |
| | 1.0.0 | *lu-du-ú* |
| | [x.x].2 | $^{m}$*Kal-bu* DUMU $^{md}$UTU-ÙRU |
| | [x.x].3 | $^{m}$GAL-*a-šá-*$^{d}$*Gu-la* |
| | [x].⸢x⸣.4 5 SÌLA | ⸢$^{m}$*Iz-kùr*⸣-$^{d}$AMAR.UTU DUMU $^{md}$⸢U.GUR⸣-ÙRU |
| | ⸢1+⸣.0.1 | $^{m}$⸢*E*⸣-*ri-b*[*u*] DUMU $^{md}$UTU-ÙRU |
| | ⸢4+.2⸣.3 | $^{m}$KI.MIN *ba-ru-*⸢x⸣[ |
| Rev. | [ ] | $^{m}$*Ú-bal-liṭ-su-*$^{d}$A[MAR.UTU?] |
| | ⸢3⸣.0.0 | $^{md}$AMAR.UTU-*re-ú-*[ |
| | 0.2.3 | $^{m}$*Ap-li-id-en-ši-*⸢*iš*?⸣-*t*[*u*$_4$] |
| | PAP 18.1.5 5 SÌLA | |

Commentary

1–2. "[ . . . ], (measured by) the *sūtu* of 10 *qû* of year 19 of Nazi-Maruttaš; not collected; Āl-Arad-Bēlti."

12. Cf. PNs like DN-rē'û'a and DN-rē'ûni "DN is my/our shepherd" (Hölscher 1996, 259).

13. Aplī-id-enši-ištu must be a case of hypercorrection for Aplī-id-enši-iltu "Answer for the weak, O goddess" (for which see Clay 1912b, 56; Stamm 1968, 75, 171; Hölscher 1996, 34; CAD A/2, *apālu* A 1f 2′).

## 43. CUNES 52-10-063 (Plate No. 18)

-.-.1 Kadašman-Turgu

| | | | |
|---|---|---|---|
| Obv. | ŠE $^{giš}$BÁN GAL QA ⸢*šu-ni-e* URU⸣$^{ki}$ | | MU.BI.IM |
| | SAG NÍG.GA | *šib-*⸢*šu*$_{14}$⸣ | |
| | 0.2.0 | 0.1$^{p}$[$^{i}$].0 | $^{md}$30-*eri-ba* |
| | 0.0.4 | 0.0.3 | $^{m}$*Ki-di-nu-ú a-mur-ru-ú* |
| 5 | 0.1$^{pi}$.0 | 0.0.3 | $^{m}$GAL-*a-šá-*$^{d}$30 *ṣú-ḫur-tu*$_{4}$ |
| | 0.0.4 5 SÌLA | 0.0.3 | $^{m}$*Tak-la-ku-a-na-*$^{d}$*Nin-urta* |
| | 0.0.4 | 0.0.3 | $^{m}$*Aḫ-la-mu-*⸢*ú*⸣ |
| | 0.0.3 | 0.0.3 | $^{m}$IBILA-$^{d}$*Nin-urta* |
| 9 | 5.0.0 | 1.0.0 | $^{m}$GAL-*a-šá-*$^{d}$30$^{!?}$ ⸢*ṣú*$^{?}$*-ḫur*$^{?}$*-tu*$_{4}$⸣ |
| Rev. PAP | | 1.3.3 | ⸢*šu-ni-e* URU⸣ |
| PAP | 8.0.3 | ŠE NÍG.KUD.DA | |
| PAP | 1.1$^{pi}$.0 | ŠE KÁ.GAL | |
| | MU.1.[KA]M [*K*]*a-dáš-man-*⸢*Du-ur-gu*⸣ | | |

Commentary

1. "Barley, (measured by) the big *sūtu*, . . . *šunê* of the town." I do not know how to explain QA. *šunê āli* (URU$^{ki}$) "*šunê* of the town" (see also l. 10) is probably to be understood in opposition to *šunê ṣēri* (EDIN) "*šunê* of the countryside," which often occurs in the heading of the EDIN-accounts.

2. The proportion between *rēš makkūri* and *šibšu* in this text is not consistent: twice it is 2 : 1 (ll. 2, 5), but it can be also 5 : 1 (l. 9) or even 1 : 1 (l. 8).

4. "Kidinnû the Amorite." See Sassmannshausen 2001, 131 and Brinkman 2004, 296 for the few attestations of Amorites in Nippur texts; van Soldt 2015 does not add any new occurrences.

9. The traces rather suggest a reading $^{m}$GAL-*a-šá-*$^{d}$GAŠAN, but if it is correct to read *ṣú-ḫur-tu*$_{4}$ in the following line, it is likely that the person mentioned here is the same one who occurs in l. 5 (Rabâ-ša-Sîn); the emendation is suggested also by the fact that GAŠAN is usually not preceded by the divine determinative (cf. the attestations of the name Rabâ-ša-Bēlti in the Index of Personal Names, as well as other names containing the element *bēltu* in Hölscher 1996, 248).

10. The sum of *šibšu* is identified in the last column as *šunê āli* (URU).

12. The spelling *-Du-ur-gu* is unusual: the only other attestation known to me comes from the MA text VAT 15420: 2′, 14′, 15′, where the royal name is spelled $^{m}$*Ka-ta-áš-ma-Du-ur-gu* (see most recently Frahm 2009, 127–28).

## 44. CUNES 52-13-134 (Plate No. 19)

-.-.1 Kadašman-Turgu

Despite the probable mention of EDIN "countryside" in the heading, the first two columns are devoted to *rēš makkūri* and *šibšu* as in the *tēlītu*-accounts, rather than recording *rēš makkūri* and *kiṣru* as in the EDIN-accounts (see Introduction §2.1, Tables 1 and 2).

Many of the PNs and some of the quantities in the *šibšu*-column correspond to those of CUSAS 30 67, an undated tablet that probably recorded revenues from Dikirtu (CUSAS 30 67: 22). Some of the PNs listed here (Damu-nāṣir, Siyātu) are associated with Dikirtu also in **no. 28** (NM 24).

U.e. [x x E]DIN $^{uru}$*Di-ki-ir-tu*$_4$ $^{giš}$BÁN GAL

MU.1.KAM $^{m}$*Ka-da-áš-man-Du-gu*

| | | | | |
|---|---|---|---|---|
| Obv. | *r*[*e-eš*] ⌜NÍG.GA⌝ | *ši-ib-šu*$_{14}$ | *ki-iṣ-rù* | MU.BI.IM |
| | | 16.1.3 | 0.1.1 | NÍG.KUD.DA |
| | | 3.2.4 | 0.0.1 | KÁ.GAL |
| | 23.3.2 | 9.2.2 | 0.1.2 | $^{m}$*È-a-na*-ZÁLAG-$^{d}$30<br>$^{md}$*Nin-urta-ki-pi-šu* |
| | 11.1.2 | 4.2.2 | 0.0.4 | $^{m}$KI.MIN $^{m}$*I-še-em-mi-i-na*-É.SAG.ÍLA |
| | 20.1.3 | 8.0.3 | [x.x.x] 4 SÌLA | $^{md}$*Da-mu*-ÙRU<br>$^{m}$*Ba-na-nu-ú* |
| | 12.2.0 | 4.4.5 | 0.0.4 | $^{md}$*Da-mu*-ÙRU<br>$^{m}$*Ta-qí-šu* |
| | 3.1$^{pi}$.0 | 1.1.2 | 0.0.1 4 SÌLA | $^{m}$*Mu-u*[*l-te-šim*-DINGIR]<br>$^{m}$*A-ḫe-d*[*u-tu*$_4$] |
| Rev. | 2.0.4 | 0.4.2 | 0.0.1 2 | $^{m}$*A-ḫe-d*[*u-tu*$_4$]<br>$^{m}$*I-qí-*[ |
| | 0.4.0 | 0.1.⌜x⌝ | 0.0.1 | $^{md}$*Da-mu*-Ù[RU]<br>$^{m}$*Ta-qí-šu* |
| | 0.2.0 | ⌜x.x.x 8?⌝ | [ ] | $^{m}$*Si-ia-a-tu*$_4$<br>$^{lú}$MÁ.LAḪ$_5$ |
| | 0.1.1 | 0.0.2 8 | ⌜2 SÌLA⌝ | $^{md}$U.GUR-ŠEŠ-SUM-*na* |
| | 1.0.0 | 0.2.0 | ⌜2 SÌLA⌝ | ŠE *ma-ki-si* |

COMMENTARY

1–2. "[ . . . ], countryside, (measured by) the big *sūtu*; Dikirtu; year 1 of King Kadašman-Turgu." The use of the masculine personal determinative before the royal name, which is attested also in **no. 83**: 8 and **no. 87**: 8, is unusual in texts of Kadašman-Turgu (Brinkman 1976, 404; see also Hölscher 1996, 117). This particular spelling of the royal name is otherwise unattested (see Brinkman 1976, 163–64; Hölscher 1996, 117; date formulae in Sassmannshausen 2001; van Soldt 2015, 551). The indented line with the reignal year seems to have been added by a different hand when the clay was already partially dry.

10. Restoration of the PNs after CUSAS 30 67: 12.

## 45. CUNES 52-10-094

-.-.4 Kadašman-Turgu

The text is an account of wagons ({giš}MAR.GÍD.DA{meš}, l. 45) delivered by several individuals associated with two towns: Tukultī-Ekur (l. 28) and Dimtu (l. 36).

Other texts recording the delivery of wagons are, e.g., BE 14 118 and BE 15 91, which explicitly state in their headings that the wagons transported the revenues (*tēlītu*) of Dūr-Enlilē and Ekallātu respectively. BE 15 91 makes it possible to estimate the average load of a wagon as ca. one-half of a kor (see Torczyner 1913, 32–33): thus, the 2,244 wagonloads of our text would have corresponded ca. 1,122 kor of cereals.

U.e. [ ] ⸢URU{hi.a} x x⸣

Obv. [ MU].⸢4.KAM {d}⸣*Ka-dáš-man-Túr-gu*

| | | | | | |
|---|---|---|---|---|---|
| | [ ] | [ ] | [ ] | [ŠU.NÍGIN] | MU.BI.IM |
| | [ ] | [ ] | 7 | ⸢x x x⸣ | {m}SUD-{d}IŠKUR {m}*Ṭa-bi-ia* |
| | ⸢30?+⸣ | ⸢40?⸣ | 4 | [ ] | {md}KUR-ŠEŠ-SUM-*na* {m}KI.MIN |
| | ⸢80+⸣ | ⸢x x⸣ | 2 | [ ] | ⸢{m}*Ša-muḫ*⸣-{d}U.GUR {m}*Ri-mu-*⸢*tu4*⸣ |
| | 84 | ⸢10?⸣ | | 1 ME 24 | {m}SU-{d}IŠKUR {m}⸢x-x-x⸣ |
| | 1 ME 5 | ⸢15?⸣ | ⸢8⸣ | 1 ME 28 | {m}*E-mi-du* {m}*Be-la-nu* |
| | 1 ME 35 | ⸢10⸣ | 7 | 1 ME 52 | {m}*È-a-na*-ZÁLAG-{d}AMAR.UTU |
| | 1 ME ⸢10?⸣ | ⸢30?⸣ | 3 | 1 ME ⸢33?⸣ | {md}⸢AMAR.UTU?⸣-*mu-bal-liṭ* {m}ŠU-{d}IŠKUR {lú}ÉNSI |
| | ⸢24?⸣ | ⸢x x⸣ | | [ ] | {m}⸢*È-a-na*-ZÁLAG⸣-{d}*Gu-la* |
| | ⸢30?⸣ | | ⸢2⸣ | [ ] | {m}⸢*Ki-din?*-x-x⸣ {md}*Nin-urta*-MU-MU |
| | ⸢1 ME 30?⸣ | | ⸢2⸣ | [ ] | {m}[x-x-(x)]-DINGIR-*ma* {lú}ÉNSI{meš} |
| | [ ] | [ ] | 1 | 1 ME 21 | {m}[x-x]-⸢x⸣ KI.MIN |
| | [ ] | [ ] | ⸢3⸣ | 1 ME 13 | {m}⸢*Na?-aḫ?*⸣-*zi*-{d}AMAR.UTU {m}SUD-*ik-ki-*⸢*la*⸣-[*šu*] |
| | ⸢x x⸣ | [ ] | | 1 ME 10 | {m}⸢SU?⸣-{d}⸢*Nin?*-x⸣ {m}*Ṭa-bi-ia* |
| | [50] | 2 | 3 | 55 | {m}SU-{d}AMAR.UTU {m}*Ri-mu-tu4* |
| | [40] | | | 40 | *ḫar-šu-ú* {md}*Nanna*-LÚ-SA6 {m}ŠEŠ-SUM-*na*-{d}AMAR.UTU |
| | [12] | | | 12 | KI.MIN {m}*A-da-gal*-IGI-DINGIR {m}*I-la-nu-ú-a* |
| | [20] | | | 20 | KI.MIN {m}NÍG.BA-{d}*Pap-sukkal* |
| | [18] | | | 18 | KI.MIN {m}*Il-lu-ul-lu4* |
| | [14] | | | 14 | KI.MIN {m}*Ri-mu-tu4* DUMU {m}ŠE[Š- |
| Rev. | | 12 | | [1]⸢2⸣ | KI.MIN {md}MAŠ-*re-ṣu-ú-šu* |
| | 8 | | | ⸢8⸣ | KI.MIN {m}NÍG.BA-{d}*Gu-la* |
| | 8 | | | ⸢8⸣ | KI.MIN {m}*Ṭà-ab*-{giš}MI {lú}NU.{giš}KIRI6 |
| | 7 | | | 7 | KI.MIN {m}NÍG.BA-{d}U.GUR {lú}NAGAR |
| | 6 | | | 6 | KI.MIN {m}ŠEŠ-*du-tu4* LÚ.SAG |
| PAP | ⸢1 LIM x x x x⸣ | ⸢x x x⸣ | 42 | 1 LIM 6 ME 15 | {uru}*Tukul-ti*-É.KUR{⸢ki⸣} |
| | 80 | | [15] | 95 | {m}*Ri-mu-tu4* {m}*Nam-rù* |
| | 85 | | ⸢10⸣ | 95 | {m}SU-{d}IŠKUR {md+}*En-líl-ṣú-lu-li* |
| | ⸢73⸣ | | | ⸢73⸣ | {m}ÌR-{d}IMIN.KAM {m}SU-{d}AMAR.UTU |
| | 1-*šu* | | 1 | 1-*šu* 1 | {m}*Ri-mu-tu4* {m}*Šu-muḫ*-{d⸢}U?⸣.[GUR?] |
| | 70 | | 1 | 71 | {md}30-ŠEŠ-SUM-*na* {m}*Mu-*⸢*ra?*⸣*-nu* |
| | 70 | | 3 | 73 | {m}*È-a-na*-ZÁLAG-{d⸢}AMAR?.UTU?⸣ |
| | 31 | | | 31 | *ḫar-šu-ú* {lú}NAGAR |
| PAP | 4 ME 1-*šu* 9 | | 30 | 4 ME 99 | {⸢uru⸣}AN.ZA.GÀR{ki} |

| | | | | |
|---|---|---|---|---|
| | 40 | ⸢ZÍZ⸣.AN.NA 10 | 50 | $^{m}$*Ṭa-bi-ia* $^{m}$SUD-$^{d⸢}$IŠKUR⸣ |
| | 24 | | 24 | $^{m}$*Be-la-nu* |
| | 24 | | 24 | $^{m}$*Iš-ri-qu* |
| | ⸢4⸣ | 3 | 7 | $^{m}$*Šu-nu-ḫu* |
| | ⸢5⸣ | | 5 | $^{m}$*Iz-kùr*-$^{d}$IŠKUR |
| | 10 | | 10 | $^{m}$*E-zu-ú-pa-ši-ir* |
| | 1⸢4?⸣ | | 1⸢4?⸣ | $^{md}$IŠKUR-*ṣíl-lí* [$^{m}$]ZÁLAG-$^{d}$GAŠAN |
| [ ] | [ ] | [ ] | [ ] | $^{m}$*Šu-muḫ-r*[*i-gim*]-*šú* |

Left e. ŠU.NIGIN 2 LIM 2 ME 44 $^{giš}$MA[R].GÍ[D.DA$^{meš}$]
2 URU$^{didli}$

COMMENTARY

13. There does not seem to be enough space in the gap to allow two PNs, which would justify the plural determinative in $^{lú}$ÉNSI$^{meš}$.

28. The calculated total in col. i would be 1,573.

40. Šūnuḫu "weary, miserable": for the use of the word as a PN in Kassite texts, cf. the feminine version Šūnuḫtu (attestations in Clay 1912b, 134; Tenney 2011, 263).

## 46. CUNES 52-16-018 (Plate No. 20)

-.III.[ . . . ] Kadašman-Turgu

The exact nature of this text is uncertain: it is assigned to the revenues because of the terms *rēš makkūri* ([SA]G NÍG.GA) *šunê* in the heading, but could also be an account of disbursed goods (see commentary below).

U.e. [SA]G NÍG.GA *šu-ni-e* URU-*ir-re-e* $^{iti}$SIG$_4$.GA MU.[X.KAM]
*Ka-dáš-man-Túr-g*[*u*]

| Obv. | ⸢ŠE.EŠTUB⸣ | ⸢ŠE.MUŠ$_5$⸣ | GIG | ZÍZ.AN.NA | NÍG.ÀR.RA | ⸢MUNU$_4$⸣ | ⸢DUG⸣ | MU.B[I.IM] |
|---|---|---|---|---|---|---|---|---|
| | 1.0.1 | | | | 0.0.4 | | | $^{m}$*Iz-kùr*-$^{⸢d⸣}$[ |
| | 1.0.2 | | | | | | | $^{m}$*Za-ki-⸢rù?* x-x⸣-*la-tu*$_4$ |
| | 2.3.2 | | | | | | | $^{m}$*Qu-nu-nu* |
| | 4.1.4 | | | | 0.0.1 | | 4 | $^{m}$*Di-maḫ-di*-$^{d}$*Uraš ša* $^{lú}$KÚRUN.NA |
| | 0.1.4 5 | | | | 0.1.2 | | | $^{md}$*Nin-urta-ki-na-i-de* |
| | 1.0.4 | | | | | | | $^{m}$*Iz-kùr*-$^{d}$IŠKUR |
| | | 1.0.2 | | | | | | $^{m}$EN-BA-*šá* |
| | 1.0.0 5 SÌLA | | | | | | | $^{m}$KAR-*an-ni*-$^{d}$UTU |
| | 0.0.3 | 0.0.4 | | | | | | $^{m}$*In-nu-un-nu* SIPA ANŠE |
| | 0.0.3 | | | | | | | $^{m}$*In-nu-un-nu*-«*nu*» ÉNSI |
| | 0.2.1 | | | | | | | $^{m⸢}$*Bu?*⸣-*šar-šu* KI.MIN |
| | 0.1.3 | | | | | | | $^{md}$30-KUR-*ni* $^{lú}$NAGAR |
| | 0.2.4 5 | | | | | | | $^{md}$AG-ÙRU $^{uru}$*Ḫu-ra-du* |
| | | 0.1.2 | | 0.1.4 | | | | $^{m}$*Tu-nam-is-Saḫ* $^{lú}$Ì.SUR |
| | 0.4.2 | | | | | | | $^{m}$*Mi-na-e-gu-a-na*-DINGIR |
| | 0.4$^{pi}$.0 | | | | | | | $^{md}$AMAR.UTU-*re-man-ni* |
| | 0.4.3 | | | 0.0.2 | | | | $^{m}$*Eri-ba*-$^{d}$IŠKUR |

| | | | | | | | | |
|---|---|---|---|---|---|---|---|---|
| PAP | 14./4.1 5 | 0.3.2 | | 0.2.0 | 0.2.1 | | 4 | *a-šib* URU-*ir-re-*⸢*e*⸣ |
| | 1.2.1 | | 0.1.2 5 | | | [ ] | [ ] | $^{m}$*Ta-rib-ti-*$^{d}$IŠKU[R] |
| | 0.1.4 | | | | | [ ] | | DUMU $^{m}$*Ḫu-mur-bi-i*[*a-Saḫ*?] |
| | 0.0.4 | | 0.1$^{pi}$.0 | | | | | DUMU $^{m}$*Ša-ru-ku*?-⸢x⸣ [ |
| Rev. | [ ] | 0.0.3 | | [ ] | [ ] | | | $^{lú}$*ka-ṣi-rù* [ |
| | | | | 0.1.⸢1⸣ | | | | $^{m}$ZÁLAG-$^{d}$AMAR.UTU ⸢DUMU $^{m}$*Za*-x⸣-[ |
| | 0.1.4 | | | | | | | $^{m}$*Muš-te-ši-*⸢*ir*⸣-[ |
| | 0.1.4 | | | | | | | DUMU $^{m}$*I-din-*$^{d}$IŠKUR |
| | 0.3.5 | | | 0.1.1 | | | | $^{md}$AMAR.[UTU]-*lí-su* |
| | 0.3.5 | | | | | | | $^{md}$IŠKUR-LUGAL-DINGIR$^{meš}$ |
| | 0.2.0 | | | | | | | $^{m}$*Mar-tu-ku* |
| | 0.4.2 | | | | | | | $^{m}$*Ba-na-tu-ú-a* |
| | ⸢2.4?.x⸣ | | | | | | | $^{m}$IGI-$^{d}$AMAR.UTU-*lu-mur* DUMU $^{m}$*Za-nin-ni* |
| | 0.1.1 | | | | | | | $^{m}$*A-da-a-a-ú-tu*$_{4}$ |
| | 1.0.0 | | | | | | | DUMU $^{m}$*Ba-ri-i*[*a*] |
| | ⸢x.x.2⸣ | | | | | | | $^{m}$*Ri-mu-tu*$_{4}$ |
| | [x.x].2 | | | | | | | $^{m}$*Gu-ub-bu-ḫu* |
| | [x.x].4 | | | | | | | DUMU.MUNUS $^{m}$DINGIR-*ri-gim*?-⸢x⸣ |
| | 0.2.3 | | | | | | | $^{md}$*Nin-urta*-ŠEŠ-SUM-*na* |
| PAP | 10.1.2 | 0.0.3 | 0.2.2 5 | 0.2.2 | | | | *né-re-eb-ti* URU-*ir-re-e* |

Commentary

1–2. "[Tax]able capital, *šunê*; Āl-irrē; month III, year [x] of Kadašman-Turgu."

3. Cf. PBS 2/2 91, MUN 72, and MUN 73 for other ledgers recording quantities of groats? (NÍG.ÀR.RA), malt (MUNU$_{4}$), and jars (DUG); there, however, these goods are associated with different items (barley, flour, sourdough, and garlic?). Sassmannshausen published MUN 72 and MUN 73 among the revenues ("Abgabelisten") because of the mention of *miksu* and *abullu* in MUN 72, but noted that the presence of processed products actually speaks against this interpretation, since revenue accounts usually record only quantities of raw agricultural goods (Sassmannshausen 2001, 256). Note that the column devoted to malt is actually left empty. The term "jar" (DUG) could indicate, depending on the context, either an actual container or its content (see Sassmannshausen 2001, 257; Del Monte 1994).

16. After the PN one would expect a profession rather than a GN, but the determinative $^{uru}$ is clear. To my knowledge, a town named Ḫurādu or Āl-ḫurādu is thus far not attested.

21. *ašib Āl-irrē* "resident of Āl-irrē." The totals refer to the quantities in ll. 4–20. Several persons listed in this section of the text are associated with Āl-irrē also in other texts (see, e.g., **nos. 11** and **54**).

23. I restore Ḫumurbiya-Saḫ because it is the only attested PN beginning with the element Ḫumurbiya (Hölscher 1996, 84).

38. The presence of a woman is unusual in this type of text, but cf. also **no. 1**: 17, **no. 9**: 12, and CUSAS 30 35: 21.

40. *nērebti Āl-irrē*: "entrance of Āl-irrē"—i.e., perhaps people who entered Āl-irrē in opposition to those already living in Āl-irrē (cf. *ašib Āl-irrē* in l. 20)? The total is the sum of the quantities in ll. 22–39.

# 1.2 Stored Goods

1.2.1 "Stored Barley/Grain"

Here belongs also **no. 8**, which is a "hybrid" since it records a *tēlītu*-account on the obverse and the corresponding "stored barley" on the reverse.

## 47. CUNES 52-12-011

-.-.21 Nazi-Maruttaš

Obv. ŠE *tab-ku* $^{giš}$⸢BÁN GAL DUMU$^{?}$ $^{m}$*Aš-šur-a-a-ú*$^{ki}$⸣

MU.⸢21.KAM *Na-zi-Ma-ru-ut-ta*⸣-*aš* LUGAL.E

| | ŠE.⸢EŠTUB$^{?}$⸣ | [x (x)] | ⸢GIG⸣ | MU.BI.IM |
|---|---|---|---|---|
| | ⸢10$^{+}$.1$^{?}$.0⸣ | | 4.1.0 | *lu-du-ú* |
| | ⸢11$^{?}$⸣.0.1 | | | NÍG.KUD.DA EN 1.1.0 *ḫír-ga-le-e* |
| | 0.2.3 | | | ŠE KÁ.GAL |
| | 2.⸢3$^{?}$⸣.5 | | | ŠE *ma-ki-si* |
| | 11.4.2 | | 0.0.5 6 | ḪA.LA $^{m}$*Di-maḫ-di-*$^{d}$*Uraš*<br>⸢KI⸣ $^{m}$KAR-*ub-*$^{d}$AMAR.UTU |
| | 5.3.2 5 | | | ḪA.LA $^{m}$*Ṣú-up-pu-ri* KI $^{m}$*Za-ki-rù* NAGAR |
| PAP | ⸢5⸣[5$^{?}$.1.1]<br>⸢5⸣ [SÌLA] | | 4.1.5 6<br>SÌLA | NÍG.KUD.DA *lu-du-ú*<br>*ù* ḪA.LA$^{meš}$ |
| | ⸢15$^{?}$.3$^{?}$⸣.1 | | 0.1.1 5 | $^{m}$*Di-maḫ-di-*$^{d}$*Uraš* $^{m}$KAR-*ub-*$^{d}$AMAR.UTU |
| | 20.4.2 | | 0.1.2 8 | $^{m}$*La-qí-pu* $^{md}$30-*muš-te-šìr* |
| | 11.3.0 | | 0.0.4 7 | $^{m}$SUM-$^{d}$IŠKUR $^{m}$DINGIR-*ma-*$^{d}$IŠKUR |
| | 9.⸢0.4$^{?}$⸣ | 0.2.3 | 0.0.5 6 | $^{m}$*Ṣú-up-pu-rù* $^{m}$*Ṣi-*⸢*is-su*$^{!}$⸣*-nam-rat* |
| | 7.4.0 | | ⸢0.0.3 4⸣ | [$^{m}$]⸢KI.MIN⸣ $^{m}$*Za-ki-rù* ⸢NAGAR⸣ |
| | [x.x].⸢4⸣ | | | $^{m}$*I-*⸢*la*$^{?}$⸣*-nu-ú-*[*a*$^{?}$] |
| | [ ] | 0.2.⸢5⸣ | [ ] | ⸢$^{m}$SUM⸣-⸢$^{d}$IŠKUR⸣ |
| Rev. | | 0.2.⸢2⸣ | | [$^{m}$KI.MI]N$^{?}$ $^{m}$*Ṣú-u*[*p-pu-rù*] |
| | 2.2.5 | 0.0.3 | 0.0.3 | *ki-ṣir* EDIN |
| | 1.0.1 | | | *ki-ṣir maḫ-ri* |
| PAP | 76./0.5 | 1.3.1 | 5.⸢2⸣.3 | ⸢*ši*⸣*-ib-šu*$_{14}$ |
| PAP | 1 ME 31./2.0 5 | 1.3.1 | 5.2.3 | $^{giš}$BÁN GAL |
| | 5.2.3 | | | $^{m}$KAR-*ub-*$^{d}$AMAR.UTU |
| | 3.2.⸢3⸣ | | | $^{m}$*Ṣi-is-su-nam-rat* |
| | 3.2.3 | [ ] | | $^{m}$*Ṣú-up-pu-rù* |
| | 4.0.0 | | | $^{m}$*Za-ki-rù* NAGAR |
| | 4.0.0 | | | $^{m}$DINGIR-*ma-*$^{d}$IŠKUR $^{m}$SUM-$^{d}$IŠKUR |
| | 4.0.0 | | | $^{m}$*La-qí-pu* |
| PAP | 24.2.3 | 1.3.3 | | NUMUN *es-ru* $^{giš}$BÁN 10 SÌLA |
| ŠU.NIGIN | 1 ME 51.0.0<br>5 SÌLA<br>⸢TA 4⸣.4.3 | 2.4.5<br>TA 0.1.5 | 5.2.3 | $^{giš}$BÁN GAL<br>GAL $^{giš}$BÁN 10 SÌLA<br>*i-na* 1.0.0 0.1$^{pi}$.0 *šu-lu-ú* |

Commentary

1–2. "Stored grain, ⸢(measured by) the big *sūtu*; the son$^{?}$ of Aššurāyu⸣; year ⸢21⸣ of King Nazi-Maruttaš." For the use of the place determinative $^{ki}$ in PNs formed as a nisba, see, e.g., $^{m}$*La-ar-si-i*$^{ki}$ in CUSAS 30 139: 10 and $^{m}$NIBRU$^{ki}$-*ú* in CUSAS 30 256: 14. However, one would expect here a town rather than a person (cf. the headings of the following texts in this group); perhaps one should assume a toponym of the type URU-DUMU-PN (see examples in RGTC 5, 16–17)? A town called Āl-Mār-Aššurāyu is not attested, though.

21. While the figures in col. i–ii correspond to the sums of the respective amounts in ll. 11–20, the figure in col. iii already gives the sum of the first subtotal in l. 10 (4.1.5 6 SÌLA) together with the amounts in the following lines (ll. 11–20).
22. The figures in col. i and col. ii correspond to the sum of the subtotals in l. 10 and l. 21; for the figure in col. iii, see the comment on l. 21.
30. The amounts that follow TA in col. i–ii (⌜TA 4⌝.4.3, TA 0.1.5) represent the increase (GAL/*rubbû*) deducted for each item.

## 48. CUNES 52-10-096 (Plate No. 21)

-.-.24 Nazi-Maruttaš

This text has several features in common with **no. 29**, which is an EDIN-account about Āl-atḫē in the 24th year of Nazi-Maruttaš (see commentary below).

Some of the same persons are mentioned also in MUN 121 (the son of Kuppitātu, Erība-Šuqamuna, and the son of Kittu-līšir), which dates to the 2nd year of Nazi-Maruttaš and records the delivery of seed and fodder for oxen to several individuals in Āl-atḫē.

Obv. ŠE *tab-ku* $^{giš}$BÁN GAL URU-*at-ḫe-e*

MU.24.KAM *Na-zi-Ma-ru-ut-ta-aš*

| | | |
|---|---|---|
| | 27.3.0 | DUMU $^{mf}$*Ku-up-pi-ta-ti*<br>*ù* DUMU $^{m}$*Šu-ri-ḫa*-DINGIR ÉNSI$^{meš}$ |
| | 15.1$^{pi}$.0 | NÍG.KUD.DA EN 0.4.0 *ḫír-ga-[le]-e* |
| | 3.3.0 | ŠE KÁ.GAL |
| | 0.1.4 | ŠE *ma-ki-[s]i* |
| | 8.4.1 | $^{m}$*Mu-ra-nu* $^{m}$⌜*I-re*⌝*-man-ni*-$^{d}$IŠKUR |
| | 17.1.0 | $^{m}$ÌR-GAŠAN $^{m}$*Gu-ub-bu-ḫu* |
| | 17.0.5 | $^{m}$KI.MIN $^{md}$*Šu-qa-mu-na*-URU$_4$ |
| | 15.1.5 | $^{m}$*Eri-ba*-$^{d}$*Šu-qa-mu-na*<br>DUMU $^{m}$*Kit-tu$_4$-[li-š]ìr* |
| | 2.1.3 | $^{m}$ÌR-GAŠAN $^{md}$*N[in-urt]a-qar-rad* |
| | 0.2.0 | $^{m}$*Ri-iš*-$^{d}$U.G[UR $^{m}$È]-⌜*a*⌝*-na*-ZÁLAG-$^{d}$AMAR.UTU |
| | 0.0.5 | ⌜DUMU $^{m}$*Šu-ri*⌝*-[ḫa*-DINGIR] |
| | 2.2.0 | *ki-*⌜*iṣ-rù*⌝ |
| ⌜PAP⌝ | ⌜1 ME 10.2.5⌝ | ⌜$^{giš}$BÁN GAL⌝ |
| Rev. | [2.0.0] | $^{m}$*Mu-ra-nu* DUMU É |
| | 3.1.5 | $^{m}$ÌR-GAŠAN DUMU $^{md}$KUR.GAL-ÙRU |
| | 0.1.4 | $^{md}$*Nin-urta-qar-rad* |
| | 0.1.4 | $^{m}$*Gu-ub-<bu>-ḫu* $^{lú}$AŠGAB |
| | 0.1.4 | $^{m}$*E-tel*-KA-$^{d}$*Nin-urta* |
| | 1.1.4 | $^{m}$KI.MIN *ša* ŠU $^{m}$*Il-li-ia* |
| PAP | 7.3.3 | ŠE.NUMUN *es-ru* $^{giš}$BÁN 10 SÌLA |
| ŠU.NIGIN | 1 ME 16.3.4 | $^{giš}$BÁN GAL<br>TA 1.2.4 GAL $^{giš}$BÁN 10 SÌLA<br>*i-na* 1.0.0 0.1$^{pi}$.0 *šu-lu-ú* |
| | 0.0.3 6 SÌLA | *ši-ib-šu* $^{m}$ÌR-GAŠAN |
| | 0.0.5 4 SÌLA | ḪA.LA $^{m}$KI.MIN ŠE ŠU-*su tur-rat* |
| PAP | 0.1.3 | GIG $^{giš}$BÁN GAL<br>*a-na* BÀD-$^{d+}$*En-líl*$^{ḫi.a.ki}$<br>DUMU $^{m}$*Ku-*⌜*ub-bu*⌝*-ti iš-ša-am-ma*<br>*a-na* NUMUN *na-ad-na* |

COMMENTARY

1–2. "Stored barley, (measured by) the big *sūtu*; Āl-atḫē; year 24 of Nazi-Maruttaš."

3. See **no. 29**: 3 for the same PNs. The son of Kuppitātu and the son of Šurīḫa-ilī appear together also in CUSAS 30 257: 11 (collation shows that a reading DUMU $^{mf?}$*Ku-up-pi-ta*$^{?}$*-ti* is possible instead of van Soldt's DUMU $^{m}$x-x-UB-*pi-*⸢*il*$^{?}$⸣*-ti*).

4–6. The quantities in col. i and the entries in the MU.BI.IM-column correspond to those in the columns about *rēš makkūri* and MU.BI.IM in **no. 29**: 4–6.

7–13. The PNs are the same as in **no. 29**: 6–12, but there is no correspondence between the quantities in these sections of the texts.

16. The restored quantity is required by the subtotal in l. 22.

25. "5 *sūtu* and 4 *qû*: share of ditto (i.e., Arad-Bēlti); barley; his hand is turned."

26. "Total: 9 *sūtu*. Wheat (measured by) the big *sūtu*. The son of Kubbutu brought (it) here to Dūr-Enlilē and it was disbursed as seed." The total refers to the quantities in ll. 24–25.

## 49. CUNES 52-10-079 (Plate No. 22)

-.-.1 Kadašman-Turgu

This text is complementary to MUN 64, from Nippur, which records the revenues (*tēlītu*) of Baṣātu from the 1st year of Kadašman-Turgu (see Introduction §4.6 and comments below).

Restorations are based on MUN 64.

Obv. ŠE *tab-ku* $^{giš}$BÁN GAL *Ba-ṣa-a-t*[*i*$^{ki}$]

MU.1.KAM *Ka-dáš-man-Túr-gu* ⸢LUGAL.E⸣

| | | |
|---|---|---|
| | 38.1.2 | NÍG.KUD.DA |
| | 6.3.3 | KÁ.GAL |
| | 10.3.4 | $^{m}$*Ri-*⸢*mu-tu*$_4$ $^{m}$KAR-$^{d}$[AMA]⸢R.UTU⸣ |
| | ⸢9.3.2⸣ | $^{m}$ŠEŠ-⸢TUR⸣ $^{m}$*Tukul-ti-*[$^{d}$IŠKU]R |
| | x.[x.x] | $^{m}$*Ṭà-ab-k*[*i*]*-din-*$^{d}$*N*[*in-urta* $^{m}$]*Ri-iš-á-ki-tu*$_4$ |
| | x.[x.x] | $^{m}$⸢ZÁLAG-GAŠAN-*Ak-ka-de* $^{m}$*Ḫu-za-lu*$_4$⸣ |
| | 5.⸢1.1⸣ | $^{m}$ZÁLAG-$^{d}$AMAR.UTU $^{m}$KI-DINGIR-*ia-aḫ-b*[*u-u*]*t* |
| | ⸢3$^{?}$⸣.[x].2 | $^{m}$*Ki-*[*din*]-$^{d}$30 $^{md}$*Nin-urta-re-man-ni* |
| | [x.x].5$^{?}$ | $^{m}$DÙ-⸢*šá*-$^{d}$UTU $^{m}$*Ú-sa*⸣*-tu-ú-a* |
| | ⸢2.3⸣.2 | $^{m}$GAL-*šá*-[GAŠAN $^{m}$*Mul-te*]-⸢*e*⸣*-a* |
| | 1.1.⸢1$^{?}$⸣ | ŠE ⸢*ma-ki-si*⸣ |
| Rev. | 1.3.4 | *ki-iṣ-rù* |
| PAP | 97.2.5 $^{giš}$BÁN GAL | |
| | 0.3.4 5 SÌLA | $^{m}$KAR-*ub*-$^{d}$AMAR.UTU DUMU $^{m}$*Ur-*$^{d}$*Asar-alim-ma* |
| | 1.1.1 5 SÌLA | $^{m}$*Ú-sa-tu-ú-a* DUMU $^{m}$*Ka-ra-am-da-ri-*⸢x⸣ |
| | ⸢1.2⸣.3 | $^{m}$⸢*Ri-iš*⸣-UD-*šú* DUMU $^{m}$*Ta-ri-bat*-DINGIR |

[PAP] 3.2.3 NUMUN *es-rù* $^{giš}$BÁN 10 SÌLA

ŠU.NIGIN 1 ME 0.2.2 5 SÌLA $^{giš}$BÁN GAL

TA 0.2.5 5 SÌLA GAL $^{giš}$BÁN 10 SÌLA 3$^{?}$

*i-na* 1.0.0 0.0.5 *šu-lu-ú* 4 34

Commentary

1–2. "Stored barley, (measured by) the big *sūtu*; Baṣāt[u]; year 1 of King Kadašman-Turgu."

3. The figure 38.1.2 corresponds to 37.1.2 of *miksu* together with 1 kor of *ḫirgalû* recorded by MUN 64: 4 (NÍG.KUD.DA *a-di* 1 GUR *ḫír-gal-lu-ú*).

5. In MUN 64: 7 the amount of *šibšu* associated with these two persons is 10.3.5.

7. In MUN 64: 9 the two PNs are listed in inverted order.

8. $^{m}$*Ḫu-za-lu*$_4$ is what one would expect according to MUN 64: 10, and the traces seem to support it.

10. MUN 64: 12 has only Ninurta-rēmanni.

11. According to Sassmannshausen's copy, MUN 64: 14 reads Usātušu instead of Usātū'a. The corresponding quantity of *šibšu* in MUN 64 seems to be 3.⸢2.1⸣, while here one can clearly see the final *Winkelhaken* of BÁNIA (i.e., 5 *sūtu*).

13. The quantity recorded in col. i may correspond to that recorded by MUN 64: 16 in the *šibšu*-column (1.1.[x]). There it is associated with [x $^{giš}$M]AR.GÍD.DA$^{meš}$, while here it is associated with the barley of the tax collector. Note that the two items are sometimes attested together: see **nos. 11**: 5 and **54**: 6 for the "barley of the tax collector of the wagons" and **no. 10**: 5 for "*šibšu* of the wagons of the tax collector."

14. This amount of *kiṣru* (1.3.4) is slightly higher than the total of *kiṣru* recorded by MUN 64: 17 (1.3.1).

21–22. The numbers written at the end of these lines (3$^{?}$, 4, 34) must have been calculations or doodles.

## 50. CUNES 52-19-152

-.-.1 Kadašman-Turgu

| | | | |
|---|---|---|---|
| Obv. | [ŠE.MU]$Š_5$ *tab-ku* BÀD-$^{d+}$*En-líl*$^{ki.}$[$^{a.(ki)}$] | | |
| | MU.1.KAM *Ka-dáš-man-Túr-gu* | | |
| | ⸢9⸣.1.5 | √ | $^{m}$MU-*líb-ši* $^{m}$ZÁLAG-$^{d⸢}$*Ištar*⸣ |
| | 2.3.3 | √ | $^{m}$*Bu-na-*$^{d}$AMAR.UTU $^{m}$*Ša-na-bu* |
| | ⸢0.4.0⸣ | √ | $^{m⸢}$*Ì-lí*⸣*-re-man-ni* |
| | 0.1.1 | √ | ⸢DUMU⸣ $^{m}$*Ku-ub-bu-ti* |
| | 1.2.2 | √ | $^{m⸢}$*Il*⸣*-lul-lu*$_4$ DUMU $^{m}$*Ḫal*$^{?}$*-di-ia* |
| | 0.⸢1.2$^{?}$⸣ | √ | $^{m⸢}$*Bi-it*⸣*-ta-a* |
| | 0.1.4 | √ | ⸢*ki*⸣*-iṣ-rù* |
| ⸢PAP⸣ | 15.0.5 | | $^{giš}$BÁN GAL |
| | ⸢5$^{?}$.0.5⸣ | | $^{m}$MU-*líb-ši* |
| | ⸢x⸣.1.2 | | $^{m}$*Ša-an-na-b*[*u*] |
| | 2.0.0 | | $^{m}$*Bu-un-na-*[$^{d}$]AMAR.UTU |
| | 1.2.⸢x⸣ | | ⸢$^{m}$*Il-lul-lu*$_4$ DUMU $^{m}$⸣[*Ḫal-di-ia*] |
| | 1.2.3 5 | | [DUMU $^{m}$*Š*]*u-ri-ḫa*-DINGIR |
| Rev. | [ ] | | DUMU $^{m}$*Ku-ub-bu-*[*ti*] |
| | [ ] | | $^{m}$*Bi-it-*[*ta-a*] |
| | 0.1.2 | | $^{md}$30-ŠE[Š$^{?}$ |
| PAP | 9.4$^{pi}$.0 $^{giš}$BÁN 10 [SÌLA] | | |
| ⸢ŠU.NIGIN⸣ | 23.1.4 ŠE.MUŠ$_5$ $^{giš}$BÁN GAL | | |
| | ⸢TA⸣ 1.3.1 GAL $^{giš}$BÁN 10 SÌLA | | |
| | ⸢*i-na*⸣ 1.0.0 0.0.5 *šu-lu-ú* | | |

Commentary

1–2. "Stored [*šeguš*]*šu*; Dūr-Enlilē; year 1 of Kadašman-Turgu."

3–8. Most of the persons who appear in ll. 3–8 occur again in ll. 11–17 (Šumu-libši, Šannabu, Bunna-Marduk, the son of Kubbutu, Illullu the son of Ḫaldiya$^{?}$, and Bittā).

7. "Illullu, son of Ḫaldiya$^{?}$" is attested also in l. 14 and in **no. 147**: 10 and may be the same person named in CUSAS 30 228: 2, whose patronymic was read by van Soldt as $^{m}$⸢ÌR$^{?}$⸣-*di-ia*—i.e., Ardiya. These would be the first attestations of the PN Ḫaldiya. A reading ÌR for the first sign is unlikely, although not impossible: here as well as in **no. 147** one can see a very faint trace of the head of the vertical of ÌR, but not its continuation. In CUSAS 30 228: 2 a reading *Ḫal-* cannot be completely excluded but the sign is very eroded.
20–22. "Grand total: 700 *sūtu of šegušsu*, (measured by) the big *sūtu*, after 49 *sūtu* have been deducted, the increase of the *sūtu* of 10 *qû* being at a rate of 5 *sūtu* per kor."

## 51. CUNES 52-12-048

-.-.7 Kadašman-Turgu

Some of the individuals mentioned in this text appear also in **no. 31**, which is an EDIN-account regarding Dūr-Amurru dated in the 5$^{th}$ year of Kadašman-Turgu (see Enlil-mutakkil, Šamaš-muballiṭ, Kidin-Enlil, Arad-Marduk, and Ṭāb-ṣilli-Eulmaš).

| | | |
|---|---|---|
| Obv. | ŠE *tab-ku* BÀD-$^{d}$⸢MAR.TU⸣$^{ki}$ | |
| | MU.7.KAM *Ka-d[áš-man-Túr-g]u* LUGAL.E | |
| | ⸢50⸣.0.2 | NÍG.⸢KUD.DA⸣ [EN] 1.1.1 *ḫír-ga-le-e* |
| | 3.3.0 | KÁ.⸢GAL⸣ |
| | ⸢2$^{?}$⸣.3.4 | ŠE *ma-ki-si* EN 1.0.3 ÉSAG *ma-ki-si* |
| | 1-*šu* 0.1$^{pi}$.0 | DUMU $^{m}$ÌR-$^{d}$KUR ÉNSI |
| | 16.⸢3$^{?}$⸣.⸢x⸣ | HA.LA $^{m}$ÌR-$^{d}$AMAR.UTU GAR-*ni* |
| | 16.⸢4$^{?}$⸣.[x] ⸢x⸣ | ⸢KI$^{?}$.MIN$^{?}$ $^{m}$⸣[*Ri*]-⸢*mu-tu*$_4$ DUMU $^{m}$ŠEŠ⸣-*ba-ni* |
| | 22.2.5 | ⸢$^{m}$*Ri-mu-tu*$_4$⸣ $^{md}$UTU-*mu-bal-liṭ* |
| | 22.2.1 | $^{m}$ÌR-$^{d}$AMAR.UTU $^{m}$*Ṭà-ab-ṣíl-lí*-É.UL.MAŠ |
| | 2⸢2⸣.0.1 | $^{md+}$*En-líl-mu-tak-kil* $^{md}$UTU-*mu-bal-liṭ* |
| | 17.2.1 | $^{m}$*Ki-din-*⸢$^{d+}$*En-líl*⸣ DUMU $^{m}$*Sa-niq*-KA-$^{d}$*Ištar* |
| | 3.1.2 | [$^{m}$]*Mar-tu-ku* [*ḫa*]-⸢*za*⸣-*nu* |
| Rev. | 3.2.5 | *ki-ṣir* ⸢EDIN⸣ |
| | 0.3.1 | *ki-ṣir maḫ-ri* |
| | 0.1.3 | ÍB.TAK$_4$ ŠUKU EN *pi-ḫa-ti* |
| | 0.0.5 | ⸢$^{lú}$⸣ÁZLAG |
| PAP | 2 ME 33.0.4 5 SÌLA $^{giš}$BÁN GAL | |
| | ⸢1$^{?}$.1$^{pi?}$.0 GIG⸣ $^{giš}$BÁN GAL ÉŠ.GÀR | |
| | $^{md}$*Nin-urta*-SAG | |

COMMENTARY

1–2. "Stored grain, (measured by) the big *sūtu*; Dūr-Amurru; year 7 of King Kad[ašman-Turg]u."
5. "Grain of the tax collector together with 33 *sūtu* of the granary of the tax collector."
7. "Share of Arad-Marduk, the overseer." On the overseer (*šaknu*) Arad-Marduk, see Introduction §4.2.
16. See **no. 8**: 14 for another attestation of *kurummat* (ŠUKU) *bēl pīḫāti*.
19–20. "36$^{?}$ *sūtu* of wheat, (measured by) the big *sūtu*, (as) production supplies: Ninurta-ašarēd." Even though the text does not specify it, Ninurta-ašarēd must have been the person who received this amount (cf. **no. 54**: 26).

## 52. CUNES 52-10-053 (Plate No. 23)

-.-.11 Kadašman-Turgu

The text contains two different accounts. The first one (ll. 1–25), which bears the heading "stored grain," concerns *arsuppu* (ŠE.EŠTUB), *šegušša* (ŠE.MUŠ$_5$), and emmer (ZÍZ.AN.NA) and has the usual structure of this type of text. The second one (ll. 26–29) records various administrative acts that involve quantities of wheat (GIG), pulses (GÚ.TUR, GÚ.GAL, GÚ.NÍG.ÀR.RA), and cress (ZAG.ḪI.LI).

Obv. ŠE *tab-ku* $^{giš}$BÁN GAL *Kar-*$^{d}$*Nuska*$^{ki}$

MU.11.KAM *Ka-dáš-man-Túr-gu* LUGAL.E

| | ŠE.EŠTUB | ŠE.MUŠ$_5$ | ZÍZ.AN.NA | MU.BI.IM |
|---|---|---|---|---|
| | 14.0.5 | | 2.2.4 | NÍG.KUD.DA |
| | 2.2.5 | | | KÁ.GAL |
| | 6.2.2 | 2.3.3 | 3.2.4 | $^{md}$*Nin-urta*-MU-MU $^{md}$*Nin-u*[*rta-r*]*e-ṣú-šu* |
| | | 0.4.2 | 2.1.5 | $^{m}$KI.MIN [$^{md}$]AMAR.UTU-*mu-bal-liṭ* |
| | | 1.4.0 | 3.3.[0] | $^{⸢m⸣}$[*Š*]*a-muḫ-ri-gim-šu* $^{m}$KI.MIN |
| | | 0.3.5 | 2.0.⸢3⸣ | [$^{m}$]$^{⸢d⸣}$AMAR.UTU-*mu-bal-liṭ* $^{m}$*Ta-qí-šu* |
| | 0.2.1 | 0.2.0 | | $^{m}$*E-ṭi-rù* $^{m}$*Ri-iš*-É.KUR |
| | 0.1.1 | | 0.⸢1.5⸣ | $^{m}$*Aš-ri-qu* $^{m}$*Iz-kùr*-$^{d}$IŠKUR |
| | 0.3$^{pi}$.0 | 0.2.3 | 0.3.4 | *ki-iṣ-rù* |
| | 0.0.5 | | | *ki-ṣir maḫ-ri* |
| | 4.4.1 ⸢5⸣ | ⸢2⸣.0.1 | 2.3.1 5 SÌLA | ḪA.LA $^{md}$*Nin-urta*-MU-MU KI $^{md}$*Nin-urta-re-ṣú-šu* |
| | | 0.3.1 5 | 1.3.4 5 | ḪA.LA $^{m}$KI.MIN KI $^{md}$AMAR.UTU-*mu-bal-liṭ* |
| PAP | ⸢29⸣.2.2 5 SÌLA | 9./3.3 5 | 19./3.1 | $^{giš}$BÁN GAL |
| Rev. | | 2.0.0 | 3.0.0 | $^{m}$*Ša-muḫ-ri-g*[*im-š*]*u* $^{md}$AMAR.UTU-*mu-bal-liṭ* |
| | | 1.0.0 | 3.0.0 | $^{md}$AMAR.UTU-*mu-bal-liṭ* $^{m}$*Ta-qí-šu* |
| | | 0.4.5 | 3.2.3 | $^{m}$KI.MIN $^{md}$*Nin-urta*-MU-MU |
| | 1.0.0 | 1.0.0 | 2.2.3 | $^{md}$*Nin-urta*-MU-MU $^{md}$*Nin-urta-re-*⸢*ṣú-šu*⸣ |
| | 1.0.0 | 1.0.0 | | $^{m}$*E-ṭi-rù* $^{m}$*Ri-iš*-É.KUR |
| | 0.2.2 | | 0.⸢3.4⸣ | $^{m}$*Aš-ri-qu* $^{m}$*Iz-kùr*-$^{d}$IŠKUR |
| | 0.0.3 | 0.1$^{pi}$.0 | 0.2$^{⸢pi⸣}$.0 | *ki-ṣir maḫ-*[*ri*] |
| PAP | 2.2.5 | 6.0.5 | 13.0.4 | NUMUN *es-rù* $^{giš}$BÁN 10 SÌLA |
| ŠU.NIGIN | 31./2.4 ⸢TA⸣ 0.⸢2⸣.3 5 | 14./3.1 5 TA 1.1.1 | 30./0.4 TA 2.2.0 6 SÌLA | $^{giš}$BÁN GAL TA GAL $^{giš}$BÁN 10 SÌLA *i-na* 1.0.0 0.1$^{pi}$.0 *šu-*[*lu*]*-ú* |

| | GIG | GÚ.TUR | GÚ.GAL | GÚ.NÍG.ÀR.RA | ZAG.ḪI.LI | MU.BI.IM |
|---|---|---|---|---|---|---|
| 26 | | | | | | |
| | 0.1$^{pi}$.0 5 SÌLA | 0.1.3 9 ⸢SÌLA⸣ | 0.2.5 | | | *i-na* $^{giš}$BÁN 10 SÌLA *šu-un-na-ma a-na* $^{m}$*I-la-nu-ú-a paq-da* EN ḪA.LA$^{meš}$ *ša* $^{md}$*Nin-urta*-MU-M[U] |
| | | | | 0.0.2 | | $^{m}$*Ṭà-ab-ki-din-*$^{d}$*Gu-la im-ḫur-ma a-na* BÀD-$^{d+}$*En-líl*$^{meš.ki}$ *iš-ši* |
| | | | | | 0.0.1 | $^{md}$*Nin-urta-re-ṣú-šu ma-ḫi-ir* |

COMMENTARY

1–2. "Stored grain, (measured by) the big *sūtu*; Kār-Nuska; year 11 of King Kadašman-Turgu."

25. The amounts that follow TA in col. i–iii (⸢TA⸣ 0.⸢2⸣.3 5, TA 1.1.1, TA 2.2.0 6 SÌLA) represent the increase (GAL/*rubbû*) deducted for each item.

27. The amounts recorded in col. i–iii "have been remeasured with the *sūtu* of 10 *qû* and entrusted to Ilānū'a, including the shares of Ninurta-zākir-šumi."

28. "Ṭāb-kidin-Gula has received and brought to Dūr-Enlilē."

## 53. CUNES 52-10-055

-.-.12 Kadašman-Turgu

Obv. ŠE.MUŠ$_{5}$ *tab-ku* $^{giš}$BÁN GAL BÀD-$^{d+}$*En-líl*$^{meš.ki}$

MU.12.KAM *Ka-dáš-man-Túr-gu* LUGAL.E

| | |
|---|---|
| 9.2.3 | NÍG.KUD.DA |
| 2.2.0 | KÁ.GAL |
| 0.2.1 | ŠE *ma-ki-si* |
| 16.⸢4⸣.4 | $^{md}$*Nin-urta*-MU-MU *ša ṭe-mi* |
| 13.0.2 | $^{m}$KI.MIN $^{md}$*Nuska-na-bu-šu* |
| 11.1.4 | $^{m}$KI.MIN $^{m}$ZÁLAG-$^{d}$*Iš-tar* |
| 1.1.1 | $^{m}$KI.MIN $^{m}$DÙ-*a-šá*-$^{d}$AMAR.UTU |
| 15.3.0 | $^{m}$MU-*líb-ši* $^{m}$*Bi*-⸢*i*⸣-[*šu*$_{14}$] |
| Rev. 1.3.3 | $^{m}$KI.MIN $^{md}$*Nin-urta*-M[U-MU] |
| 1.2.3 | $^{m}$KI.MIN $^{m}$ÌR-*nu-bat-ti* |
| 3.3.0 | $^{m}$*Ab-bu-dan-nu* $^{md}$IŠKUR-URU$_{4}$ |
| ŠU.NIGIN 77.1.3 $^{giš}$BÁN GAL | |
| | *ki-iṣ-rù ù* NUMUN *es-rù* |
| | *a-na* ŠÀ ḪA.LA$^{meš}$ *ta-bi-ik* |
| 0.3.4 GIG $^{giš}$BÁN GAL $^{m}$*Mu*-SIG$_{5}$-$^{d}$IŠKUR *ma-ḫi-ir* | |
| 0.2.0 4 SÌLA ZAG.ḪI.LI $^{giš}$BÁN GAL $^{m}$KI.MIN *ma-ḫi-ir* | |

COMMENTARY

1–2. "Stored *šegušš̌u*, (measured by) the big *sūtu*; Dūr-Enlilē; year 12 of King Kadašman-Turgu."

14. "Grand total: 2319 *sūtu*, (measured by) the big *sūtu*: *kiṣru* and collected seed, stored with the shares."

15. "22 *sūtu* of wheat, (measured by) the big *sūtu*: Mudammiq-Adad received."

16. "12 *sūtu* and 4 *qû* of cress, (measured by) the big *sūtu*: ditto (i.e., Mudammiq-Adad) received."

## 54. CUNES 52-10-057 (Plate No. 24)

-.-.12 Kadašman-Turgu

This text is complementary to **no. 11**, which records the revenues (*tēlītu*) of Āl-irrē in the 12th year of Kadašman-Turgu. See commentary there.

Obv. ŠE *tab-ku* $^{giš}$BÁN GAL URU-*ir-re-e*

MU.12.KAM *Ka-dáš-man-Túr-gu* LUGAL.E

| | ŠE | ZÍZ.AN.NA | MU.BI.IM |
|---|---|---|---|
| | ⸢4.3.2⸣ | | NÍG.KUD.DA |
| | 1.0.2 | | KÁ.GAL |
| | 1.3.0 | | ŠE *ma-ki-si ša* $^{giš}$MAR.GÍD.DA$^{meš}$ |
| | 1.4.4 | | ÉSAG KI.MIN |
| | 9.0.5 | | $^{m}$*Di-maḫ-di-*$^{d}$*Uraš* $^{m}$*Iz-kùr-*$^{d}$*Nin-urta* |
| | 3.3.3 | | $^{m}$KI.MIN $^{md}$*Nin-urta-*⸢*ki*⸣*-na-i-de* |
| | 2.1.4 | 1.0.5 | $^{m}$KI.MIN $^{m}$*Za-ki-rù* |
| | 1.0.5 | 0.1.4 | $^{m}$KI.MIN $^{m}$EN-BA-*šá* |
| | 0.3.0 | | $^{m}$KI.MIN $^{m}$*Qu-nu-nu* |
| | 1.2.3 | | $^{m}$KI.MIN $^{m}$*Ša*-DI-*mi* |
| | 3.1.1 | | $^{m}$*In-nu-un-nu* $^{m}$*La-ar-su-ú* |
| | 0.3.3 | | $^{m}$*La-ar-su-ú* $^{m}$*I-re-man-ni*-DINGIR |
| | 17.0.0 | 4.0.1<br>5 SÌLA | NUMUN *es-rù* $^{m}$*Di-maḫ-di-*$^{d}$*Uraš*<br>$^{m}$*Ku-du-ra-nu* DUMU $^{m}$DINGIR-GAL *im-du-ud*<br>SAR-*šu ša-ki-in* |
| L.e. | | 4 10 | |
| Rev. | 0.⸢2⸣.2 | | *ki-ṣir* EDIN |
| | 0.2.5 | | *ki-ṣir maḫ-ri* |
| PAP | 49./3.3 | 5./2.4 5 SÌLA | $^{giš}$BÁN GAL |
| | 0.2.3 | | $^{m}$*Tu-nam-is-Saḫ* $^{lú}$Ì.SUR<br>*ki-mu* 1 GUR ZÍZ.AN.NA |
| | 0.1.3 5 SÌLA | | $^{md}$*Nin-urta-ki-na-i-de*<br>*ki-mu* 0.3.1 ZÍZ.AN.NA |
| | 0.0.1 5 SÌLA | | *ki-ṣir maḫ-ri* |
| PAP | 0.4.2 | | $^{giš}$BÁN 10 SÌLA |
| ŠU.NIGIN | 50./2$^{pi}$.0<br>TA 0.0.5 | 5.2.4<br>5 SÌLA | $^{giš}$BÁN GAL<br>TA GAL $^{giš}$BÁN 10 SÌLA *šu-lu-ú* |

0.3$^{pi}$.0 GIG $^{giš}$BÁN GAL ÉŠ.GÀR $^{md}$*Nin-urta*-SAG

*ma-ḫi-ir*

COMMENTARY

1–2. "Stored grain, (measured by) the big *sūtu*; Āl-irrē; year 12 of King Kadašman-Turgu."

13. On $^{m}$*Ša*-DI-*mi*, see commentary to **no. 11**: 13.

16. "Collected seed: Dimaḫdi-Uraš; Kudurrānu, son of Ilī-rabi, weighed (it); his document is deposited."

17. The numbers written on the lower edge seem to be calculations or doodles.

18. "14 sūtu (of barley): *kiṣru* of the countryside."

19. "17 *sūtu* (of barley): *kiṣru* of what has been received."

21. "15 *sūtu* (of barley): Tunami-Saḫ, oil-presser, instead of 30 *sūtu* of emmer."

22. "9 *sūtu* and 5 *qû* (of barley): Ninurta-kīna-īde, instead of 19 *sūtu* of emmer."

25. The grand total expected from the sum of l. 20 and l. 24 (49.3.3 + 0.4.2) would have been 50.2.5, thus 50.2$^{pi}$.0 TA 0.0.5 indicates that 5 *sūtu* have been deducted from the grand total. This amount probably corresponds to the increase (GAL/*rubbû*), mentioned on the same line in the last column.

26. "18 *sūtu* of wheat, (measured by) the big *sūtu*, (as) production supplies: Ninurta-ašarēd received."

## 55. CUNES 52-12-020

-.-.12 Kadašman-Turgu

Obv. [ŠE *ta*]*b-ku* $^{giš}$BÁN GAL *Tukul-*⸢*ti*-É.KUR$^{ki}$⸣ MU.12.KAM *K*[*a-dáš-man*]-*Túr-gu* LUGAL

| | ŠE.EŠTUB | ŠE.MUŠ$_{5}$ | ZÍZ.A[N.NA] | MU.BI.IM |
|---|---|---|---|---|
| | 1-*šu* 3.3.5 | | 2.4$^{pi}$.0 | NÍG.KUD.DA EN 0.4.3 *ḫír-*⸢*ga*⸣*-le-e* |
| | 11.3.3 | | 0.3.1 | KÁ.GAL |
| | 1.0.2 | | | ŠE *ma-ki-si* |
| | 1 ME 2.3.4 | 1.4.1 | 9.2.2 | $^{m}$BA-*šá*-$^{d}$KUR ⸢ÉNSI⸣ |
| | 80.4.1 | | | $^{m}$*Ḫa-ni-*⸢*bu* KI.MIN⸣ |
| | 22.3.0 | 1.1.4 | 2.2.1 | $^{md}$*Nin-urta*-MU-MU $^{m⸢}$MU⸣-*líb-ši* |
| | 15.⸢2⸣.0 | | 3.0.2 | $^{md}$*Nanna*-LÚ-S[A$_{6}$] $^{m}$*Ba-at-ti-ia-ú-tu*$_{4}$ |
| | | 0.2.4 | 3.0.0 | $^{m}$KI.MIN $^{m}$*Muš-ta-lu*$_{4}$ SIPA *su-u'-rù* |
| | | | 0.2.2 | *ḫar-šu-ú* $^{m}$*Iz-kùr*-$^{d}$AMAR.UTU |
| | | 0.3.3 5 | 0.1.5 | ḪA.LA $^{md}$*Ni*[*n-urta*-MU-M]U ⸢KI⸣ $^{m}$GAL-*šá*-GAŠAN |
| | | 0.1.2 | 0.1.2 | ḪA.LA $^{m}$KI.MIN KI $^{m}$MU-*líb-ši* |
| | | | 1.0.3 | *ki-ṣir* EDIN |
| | | | 0.0.3 5 SÌLA | *ki-ṣir maḫ-ri* |
| P[AP] | ⸢2 ME 9⸣[8]./[0].3 | 4.3.2 5 SÌLA | 23./3.3 5 SÌLA | $^{giš}$BÁN GAL |
| Rev. | ⸢6$^{?}$⸣.2.3 | 1.0.0 | 3.0.0 | $^{md}$*Nanna*-LÚ-SA$_{6}$ $^{m}$*Ba-at-ti-ia-ú-tu*$_{4}$ |
| | | 2.0.0 | 4.0.0 | $^{md}$*Nin-urta*-MU-MU $^{m}$GAL-*šá*-GAŠAN |
| | | 2.0.0 | 4.0.0 | $^{m}$KI.MIN $^{m}$MU-*líb-ši* |
| | | 1.0.0 | | $^{m}$GAL-*šá*-GAŠAN *a-na ṭe-mi-šu* |
| | | 0.4.1 | 1.2.1 *ki-mu* ŠE | $^{m}$*E-ṭi-rù* DUMU $^{m}$*Sar-ri-qu* $^{m}$LÚ-*ba-nu-ú* ŠEŠ.A.NI |
| | 0.2.3 | | | $^{md}$*Nin-nisi-*⸢*mu*-SIG$_{5}$*-iq*⸣ *ša sa-ar-ti* |
| | 0.0.5 | | | *ni-ki-is* GUR$_{7}$ $^{m}$NÍG.BA-$^{d}$*Pap-Sukkal i-si-ru-ni* |
| | 0.1$^{pi}$.0 5 SÌLA | 0.1.1 | 0.2$^{pi}$.0 | *ki-ṣir maḫ-ri* |
| PAP | 7.1.5 5 | 7.0./2 | 12.4.1 | $^{giš}$BÁN 10 SÌLA NUMUN *es-rù* |
| ŠU.NIGIN | 3 ME 4.0.0 TA 1.2.2 ⸢5⸣ SÌLA | 10.1.4 5 SÌLA ⸢TA⸣ 1.2$^{pi}$.0 | 34.0.0 TA 2.2.5 | $^{giš}$BÁN GAL TA GAL $^{giš}$BÁN 10 SÌLA *i-na* 1.0.0 0.1$^{pi}$.0 *š*[*u-lu-ú*] |

| | GIG | ⸢GÚ⸣.TUR | GÚ.GAL | ZAG.ḪI.LI | MU.BI.IM |
|---|---|---|---|---|---|
| | ⸢9$^{?}$⸣.2$^{pi}$.0 | 0.0.1 5 ½ SÌLA | 0.0.3 1 SÌLA | 0.0.1 4 SÌLA | *te-li-tu*$_{4}$ |
| L.e. | [ ] 9 (SÌLA) | 0.0.1 ⸢8 ½⸣ SÌLA | 0.2$^{pi}$./⸢2$^{?}$⸣ 4 | 0.0.5 4 SÌLA | *ši-ib-šu ša* $^{m}$GAL-*šá*-GAŠAN ḪA.LA$^{meš}$ *ki-iṣ-rù ù* NUMUN *es-rù ša* $^{md}$*Nin-urta*-MU-MU |

COMMENTARY

1. "[Sto]red [grain], (measured by) the big *sūtu*; Tukultī-Ekur; year 12 of King K[adašman]-Turgu."

22. The meaning of *ša sarti* ("of the falsehood$^?$/fraud$^?$") in this context is difficult to explain.

23. "They collected the *nikis karê* of Qīšat-Papsukkal." Note that the amounts identified as *nikis karê* usually refer to items disbursed rather than collected (Sassmannshausen 2001, 175; Introduction §4.2, s.v. *ḫazannu*).

29. "*šibšu* of Rabâ-ša-Bēlti; shares, *kiṣru*, and collected seed of Ninurta-zākir-šumi."

## 56. CUNES 52-10-054

-.-.13 Kadašman-Turgu

Obv. ŠE *tab-ku* $^{giš}$BÁN GAL BÀD-$^{d+}$*En-líl*$^{meš.ki}$

MU.13.KAM *Ka-dáš-man-Túr-gu* LUGAL.E

| | ŠE | ZÍZ.AN.NA | MU.BI.IM |
|---|---|---|---|
| | 6.3.1 | | NÍG.KUD.DA |
| | 0.4$^{pi}$.0 | | KÁ.GAL |
| | 0.1.5 | | ŠE *ma-ki-si* |
| | 8.0.1 | | $^{md}$*Nin-urta*-MU-MU *a-na ṭe-mi-šu* |
| | 7.1.5 | 0.1.2 | $^{m}$KI.MIN $^{m}$MU-*líb-ši* |
| | 6.4.2 | | $^{m}$KI.MIN $^{m}$È-*a-na*-ZÁLAG-$^{d}$IŠKUR |
| | 5.1.5 | | $^{m}$KI.MIN $^{m}$*I-lu-lu-tu*$_4$ |
| | 5.1.3 | | $^{m}$KI.MIN $^{md}$*Nin-nisi-m*[*u*-SIG$_5$-*i*]*q* |
| | 2.1.2 | | $^{m}$KI.MIN $^{md+}$*En-ki*-M[U.PÀ.DA] |
| Rev. | 2.1$^{pi}$.0 | 0.0.4 | $^{m}$MU-*líb-ši* $^{m}$*Bi*-⸢*i*'⸣-[*šu*$_{14}$] |
| | | 2.0.4 | $^{md}$*Nuska-na-bu-šu* |
| | | 0.1.5 | $^{m}$KI.MIN $^{md}$*Nin-urta*-M[U-MU] |
| PAP | 45./1$^{pi}$.0 | 2.4.3 | $^{giš}$BÁN GAL |

0.0.1 5 SÌLA ZAG.ḪI.LI $^{giš}$BÁN GAL *te-li-tu*$_4$

$^{m}$*Mu*-SIG$_5$-$^{d}$IŠKUR *im-ḫur*

COMMENTARY

1–2. "Stored grain (measured by) the big *sūtu*; Dūr-Enlilē; year 13 of King Kadašman-Turgu."

17–18. "1 *sūtu* and 5 *qû* of cress, (measured by) the big *sūtu*, revenues: Mudammiq-Adad has received."

## 57. CUNES 52-10-095

-.-.[ . . . ] Kadašman-Turgu

Obv. ⸢ŠE *tab-ku* $^{giš}$⸣[BÁN GAL] ⸢x x⸣$^{ki}$

⸢MU⸣.[x.KAM *Ka-dáš-man-Tú*]*r-gu* LUGAL.E

| | |
|---|---|
| 8.2.⸢3$^{+}$⸣ | [NÍG.KUD].DA |
| 1.4.2 | K[Á].GAL |
| 0.2.1 | Š[E *ma-ki*]-*si* |
| 4.⸢4$^?$.2⸣ | ⸢$^{md}$⸣[*Nin-urta*-MU]-MU $^{md}$⸢*La*⸣-*ta-rak-še-mi* |
| 1.3.1 | $^{m}$⸢KI.MIN⸣ ⸢$^{md}$⸣30-*nap*-⸢*ši-ra*⸣ |

| | | | |
|---|---|---|---|
| | | 3.4.3 | $^{m}$⸢*I-ri-bu*⸣*-ni* ⸢DUMU⸣ $^{m}$*Lu-da-[ri-be]-lí* |
| | | 3.3.4 | $^{m}$⸢*I-din-*$^{d}$⸣U.GUR $^{m}$*Be-*⸢*la-nu*⸣ |
| | | 3.0.1 | $^{m}$K[I.M]IN $^{m}$*Bu-un-na-*$^{d}$*Gu-la* |
| | | 3.1.3 | $^{m}$*Ḫu-na-bu* $^{md}$*La-ta-rak-še-mi* |
| | | 2.3$^{?}$.2 | $^{m}$*Ri-mu-tu*$_4$ $^{m}$BA-*šá-*$^{d}$*Pap-sukkal* |
| | | ⸢2$^{?}$⸣.3.2 | $^{m}$KI.MIN $^{m}$*Si-ia-tu*$_4$ |
| | | 1.3.4 | $^{m}$KI.MIN $^{m}$*Ri-iš-*DINGIR$^{meš}$ |
| | | 2.1.5 | $^{m}$*Ì-lí-*BA-*šá* $^{m}$*Be-lu*$_4$*-mu-šal-lim* |
| Rev. | | 2.0.2 | $^{m}$*Ba-na-na-a-a* $^{md}$⸢UTU⸣-SUM-ŠEŠ⸢$^{meš}$⸣ |
| | | 1.2.2 | $^{m}$*Ḫu-un-nu-bu* $^{m}$BA-*šá-*$^{d}$KUR |
| | | 0.4.4 | $^{m}$*Id-di-nu* $^{m}$*Ib-nu-tu*$_4$ NAGAR |
| | | 0.3.5 | $^{m}$*Tukul-ti-*$^{d+}$*En-líl ḫar-šu-ú* |
| | | 0.1$^{pi}$.0 | $^{m}$*Si-ia-tu*$_4$ KI.MIN |
| | | 2.0.4 | ḪA.LA $^{m}$*Ri-*<*mu*>*-ti* KI $^{m}$BA-*šá-*$^{d}$*Pap-sukkal*<br>*ki-mu šib-ši ša Ba-ṣa-a-ti*$^{ki}$<br>*ša il-lu-ú i-din* |
| | | 2.0.0 5 SÌLA | ḪA.LA $^{m}$KI.MIN KI $^{m}$*Si-ia-ti*<br>*ki-mu* KI.MIN |
| | | 1.1.3 | ḪA.LA $^{m}$KI.MIN KI $^{m}$*Ri-iš-*DINGIR$^{meš}$<br>*ki-mu* KI.MIN |
| | PAP | 51.3.5 5 SÌLA | $^{giš}$BÁN GAL |
| | PAP | 2.2.3 | NUMUN *es-rù* $^{giš}$BÁN 10 SÌLA $^{m}$*I-din-*$^{d}$U.GUR |
| | ŠU.NIGIN | 53.3.5 5 SÌLA $^{giš}$BÁN GAL | |
| | | | TA 0.2.3$^{?}$ GAL $^{giš}$BÁN 10 SÌLA *i-na* 1.0.0 0.1$^{pi}$.0<br>*šu-lu-ú* |

COMMENTARY

1–2. "Stored barley, [(measured by) the big *sūtu*]; ⸢ . . . ⸣; year [x of] King [Kadašman-Tu]rgu."

6. The restoration, which fits the space in the break, suggests itself because Ninurta-zākir-šumi is very often the first PN in these lists.

21. "Share of Rīmūtu together with Iqīša-Papsukkal; he delivered (it) in place of the *šibšu* of Baṣātu which *will go up* (to the administration)." The emendation of the first PN is suggested by the parallels between the PNs in ll. 12–15 and those in ll. 21–23. For the use of *elû* with reference to revenues, cf. the NB and LB examples given by CAD E, *elû* 1c 3′, 120 ("referring to *tēlītu*-tax (going up to the administration)") and AHw I, *elû* IV 6f, 209.

22. "Share of ditto (i.e., Rīmūtu) together with Siyātu, in place of ditto (i.e., the *šibšu* of Baṣātu which *will go up*)."

23. "Share of ditto (i.e., Rīmūtu) together with Riš-ilāni, in place of ditto (i.e., the *šibšu* of Baṣātu which *will go up*)."

1.2.2 "Rest of the Stores"

## 58. CUNES 52-14-074

-.-.18? Nazi-Maruttaš

The text records the *rīḫti* (ÍB.TAK$_4$) *tabki* "rest of the stores" (l. 8) of different crops. Ninurta-zākir-šumi appears twice (ll. 6, 8) as the person in charge of the available goods.

| | | | | | | | | |
|---|---|---|---|---|---|---|---|---|
| Obv. | [ | M]U.⸢18?⸣.KAM *Na⸣-zi-Ma-ru-ut-ta-a[š* | | | | | | |
| | [ ] | [ ]⸢x⸣ | [ ]⸢x⸣ | ZÍZ.AN.N[A] | GÚ.GAL | ⸢ZAG.ḪI.LI⸣ | ŠE.GIŠ.Ì | MU.B[I.IM] |
| | ⸢x x x⸣<br>⸢x x x ŠE.GIŠ.Ì *ša* ᵐ*Ip?-pu-t*⸣[*u$_4$*? | | [ ] | ⸢x.x.x⸣ | [ ] | [ ] | | ⸢*te-li*⸣-[*tu$_4$*]<br>⸢x x⸣ [ |
| | 1 LIM 6 ME 1-*šu* 2./1.3 5 SÌLA | | | | | | [ ] | ⸢x x x⸣ |
| 5 | 20.0.0 | | | | | | | ⸢x x x *ša?* *te?-li?*⸣-[*ti?*<br>⸢x x x⸣ |
| PAP | 3 LIM 1 ME 44./3.3<br>5 SÌLA | 4.4.0<br>5 SÌLA | 1 ME<br>31./3.1 | ⸢x.1.2⸣<br>4 SÌLA | ⸢2./2.2⸣<br>3 SÌLA | 1./1.1<br>⸢x x⸣ | | ⸢ŠU ᵐᵈMAŠ⸣-MU-M[U] |
| Rev. | 1 LIM 4 ME 23./2.1 | 5.0.3 | 42./1.2 | 0.1.2<br>⸢4⸣ SÌLA | 0.4.0<br>⸢x x⸣ | [ ] | | ⸢*ak?*⸣-[*lu$_4$*? |
| 8 | 7 ME 21.1.2<br>5 SÌLA | | 90.1.5 | | 1.⸢1+⸣.[x]<br>4 ⸢SÌLA?⸣ | [ ]<br>⸢2? SÌLA?⸣ | | ÍB.TAK$_4$ *tab*-⸢*ki*⸣<br>ŠU ᵐᵈMAŠ-MU-MU |

## 59. CUNES 52-16-017 (Plate No. 25)

8.XII.4 Kadašman-Turgu

This ledger is assigned to this category because of the "rest of the stores" in the heading of col. vi, but a complete understanding of its content and function is hindered by the poor state of preservation.

U.e. [x x x x $^{\text{md}}$*Nin-urta*]-MU-MU $^{\text{iti}}$ŠE.KIN.KU$_5$ U$_4$.⸢8⸣.KAM M[U].⸢4⸣.KAM $^{\text{d}}$*Ka-dáš-man-Tú*[*r-gu* LUGAL].⸢E⸣

| | | | | | | | |
|---|---|---|---|---|---|---|---|
| Obv. | [x x] ⸢x⸣ | [x x] ⸢x⸣ | ŠE *šub-*⸢*ti*⸣ | ŠU.NIGIN | *ak-lu ša i-na* ŠÀ<br>*tab-ku-ú* | ÍB.TAK$_4$<br>*tab-ki* | MU.[BI.I]M |
| 3 | [x 1]⸢-*šu*⸣,30<br>[x.x].⸢3⸣ | 1 LIM 5 ME<br>34./3.3 | 78./3.3 | 3 LIM 1 ME 5./1.5 | [1$^?$] LIM 6 ME 36./2.3 | 1 LIM 4 ME 1-*šu*<br>8.4.2 | ŠE [*t*]*ab-ku*<br>TA ⸢1 LIM x ME 30$^+$⸣[x.x] |
| | [TA$^?$] ⸢1 ME 20.3.1⸣ LA'U$_4$ *šu-lu-ú-ma* NA$_4$.KIŠIB $^{\text{md}}$⸢*Nin-urta*⸣-MU-MU *ṣa-ab-tu*$_4$ | | | | | | LA'⸢U$_4$⸣ [ |
| 4 | [x.x]$^{\text{pi}}$.0<br>⸢TA$^?$⸣ 34.2.5<br>LA'U$_4$ *šu-lu-ú* | 7.4$^{\text{pi}}$.0 | | 11.0.0<br>NA$_4$.KIŠIB $^{\text{m}}$⸢KI.MIN⸣ | 5.4.4 | 3.0.2<br>TA 34.2.⸢5$^?$⸣ | GI[G<br>[LA']⸢U$_4$⸣ *šu-*⸢*lu-ú*⸣ |
| 5 | 38.4.3<br>⸢TA$^?$ 1 ME$^?$⸣ 82/4.4<br>LA'⸢U$_4$ *šu*⸣*-lu-ú* | 1 ME 88.0.0 | | 1[x],26.<br>[x] ⸢x x⸣<br>NA$_4$.[KIŠIB $^{\text{m}}$KI.MIN] | 1⸢ME$^?$⸣ [x].4.4 | 1 ME 22./4.5<br>TA ⸢1 ME 81⸣.4.4 | ⸢ZÍZ.AN.NA⸣ [<br>LA'U$_4$ *šu-*[*lu-ú*] |
| 6 | | 1.3.5<br>2 SÌLA | | 1.3.⸢5 2 SÌLA⸣<br>NA$_4$.KIŠIB [$^{\text{m}}$KI].MIN | 0.2.3 8 SÌLA | [ ] | GÚ.TUR ⸢*ù* GÚ$^?$.G⸣[AL$^?$]<br>TA 6.1.⸢3$^?$⸣ LA'U$_4$<br>$^{\text{m}}$KI.MIN *šu-lu-ú* |
| Rev. | | 3.4.4<br>3 ½ SÌLA | | 3.4.4<br>3 ½ SÌLA<br>NA$_4$.KIŠIB $^{\text{m}}$[KI.MI]N | 2.0.1 | 1.0.3 3 ½ SÌLA<br>TA 5.0.3 | ⸢ZAG.ḪI⸣.LI$^{\text{sar}}$<br>L[A']U$_4$ $^{\text{m}}$KI.MIN *šu-lu-ú* |
| PAP<br>10 | | | | | | | $^{\text{giš}}$BÁN GAL<br>⸢*ša*⸣ ŠE *šub-tu*$_4$<br>*ša* $^{\text{md}}$*Nin-urta*-MU-[MU]<br>$^{\text{iti}}$ŠE.KIN.KU$_5$<br>⸢U$_4$.8⸣.KAM<br>MU.4.K[AM]<br>$^{\text{d}}$*Ka-dáš-man-Túr-*[*gu*]<br>LUGAL.E |

COMMENTARY

2. ŠE *šub-ti* "barley of the residence$^?$/settlement$^?$" occurs also in **no. 68**: 1, **no. 151**: 11 and probably also in CUSAS 30 161: 12 (read *i-na* ŠÀ ŠE *šub-ti* instead of *i-na* ŠÀ ŠE *qa*$^?$*-ti*); cf. ŠE *šub-tu*$_4$ in l. 9 and CUSAS 30 141: 1.

## 60. CUNES 52-18-860

-.-.12 Kadašman-Turgu

Summary of the "rest of the (barley) stores of the towns" (*rīḫti tabki ša alāni*) from the 12$^{th}$ year of King Kadašman-Turgu.

The preserved names of towns include Baṣāti, Āl-atḫē, Dimtu, Kār-Nuska, Tukultī-Ekur, and Āl-irrē.

| | | |
|---|---|---|
| Obv. | [ŠE $^{giš}$BÁN] GAL ÍB.TAK$_4$ *tab-ki ša* URU$^{didli}$ | |
| | [M]U.12.KAM *Ka-dáš-man-Túr-gu* LUGAL.E | |
| | [x.x].4 5 SÌLA | *Ba-ṣa-*⸢*a*⸣*-ti*$^{ki}$ |
| | [x x]⸢5$^+$⸣.3.3 | URU-*at-ḫe-e*$^{ki}$ |
| 5 | [x x x] 9$^+$.4.1 5 SÌLA | AN.ZA.GÀR$^{ki}$ |
| | [x].⸢x⸣.4 | ⸢*Kar*-$^{d}$⸣*Nuska*$^{ki}$ |
| | 1 ME 45.1.4 | *Tukul-*⸢*ti*⸣-É.KUR$^{ki}$ |
| | | EN 30.0.0 ḪA.LA $^{m⸢d}$*Nin*$^?$*-urta*$^{?⸣}$-[ |
| | ⸢7$^+$⸣.2.1 5 SÌLA | URU-*ir-re-e*$^{k}$[$^{i}$] |
| | [ | ] ⸢x x x ḫi$^?$ x⸣ [ |
| Rev. | [ | ] ⸢x x x te$^{?⸣}$ |
| 11 | PAP 1 LIM 5 ME 36.2$^{pi}$.0 ⸢5$^{?⸣}$ [ | |
| | [x x x] ⸢4$^+$⸣ ME 54.2.5 5 SÌLA ÍB.⸢TAK$_4$⸣ | |
| | [$^{giš}$]BÁN GA[L] | |

1.2.3 STORED FLOUR

## 61. CUNES 52-12-052

Not dated.

This text is included here because the amounts of different types of flour, listed on the obverse, are summed up under the label *qēmu* (ZÌ.DA) *tabku* "stored flour" (l. 5).

The reverse is an account of "large jars" (DUG.GAL$^{meš}$, l. 9).

| | | |
|---|---|---|
| Obv. | 8.2.3 | ZÌ.DA *ri-du* |
| | 1.2.4 | ZÌ *ar-sa-*⸢*nu*⸣ |
| | 1.0.0 | ZÌ ⸢*pa-ḫi*⸣*-du* |
| | 0.3.0 | ZÌ *ṣe-eḫ-ḫe-ru* |
| 5 | PAP 11.3.1 | ZÌ.DA *tab-ku* |
| Rev. | 20 | DUG.GAL zu áš ⸢na⸣[ |
| | 40 | KI.MIN ÚS |
| | 8 | *ša* $^{f}$*Ub-bu-*⸢*ti*⸣ |
| 9 | PAP 1-*šu* 8 DUG.GAL$^{meš}$ | |

COMMENTARY

1–4. On the different types of flour attested in MB documents, see Sassmannshausen 2001, 451–52. For similar accounts of flour in the Rosen Collection, see CUSAS 30 263, CUSAS 30 267, CUSAS 30 269, and CUSAS 30 274.

6. The last sign could also be t[i]; the interpretation of these signs is uncertain. On DUG.GAL "large jar" (with the variants DUG.GAL SAG "large jar of first quality" and DUG.GAL ÚS "large jar of second quality"), see Del Monte 1994 and Sassmannshausen 2001, 257, both suggesting that it could have been used to indicate either actual containers or their content.

## 1.3 Expenditures

### 1.3.1 Single Expenditures

#### 62. CUNES 52-18-776

26.XI–6.[XII$^{?}$].7 Nazi-Maruttaš

Expenditure of flour as fodder for sheep.

Obv. 0.1.5 ZÌ.DA
ŠUKU 5 UDU $^{m}$*Ḫu-ur-ti*
TA U$_4$.26 *ša* $^{iti}$ZÍZ.A.AN
4 EN U$_4$.6 *ša* [$^{iti}$ŠE.KIN.K]U$_5^{?}$
L.e. ⸢x⸣ KAŠ 1 ½ SÌLA ⸢x⸣[
Rev. MU.7.KAM
*Na-zi-Ma-ru-ut-taš*

A "5" is written in smaller script at the end of the reverse.

Translation

Obv. 11 *sūtu* of flour:
fodder for 5 sheep of Ḫurtu,
from day 26 of month XI
4 till day 6 of [month XI]I$^{?}$.
L.e. ⸢. . .⸣ beer, 1 ½ *qû* ⸢. . .⸣[
Rev. Year 7 of
Nazi-Maruttaš.

#### 63. CUNES 52-16-084

-.VII–I.8 Nazi-Maruttaš

Expenditure of barley as flour and brewing ingredients received by Ninnisiš-tikal from Nuska-nābûšu.

Obv. 18.0.0 ŠE $^{giš}$BÁN GAL ZÌ.D[A (*ù*)]
[ZÌ$^{?}$].MUNU$_4$ ŠU $^{md}$MAŠ-*di*-[
TA $^{iti}$DU$_6$.KÙ EN $^{iti}$BÁR.⸢ZAG.GAR⸣
$^{md}$*Nin-nisi-iš-ti-kal*
5 *i-na* ŠU $^{md}$*Nuska-na-bu-šu*
Rev. *ma-ḫi-ir*
________________
MU.8.KAM
*Na-zi-Ma-*⸢*ru-ut*⸣*-taš*

Translation

Obv. 540 *sūtu* of grain, (measured by) the big *sūtu*, (as) flou[r (and)]
brewing ingredients, under the responsibility of Ninurta-dī[nanni$^{?}$],
from month VII till month I:
6 Ninnisiš-tikal

received
from Nuska-nābûšu.

---

Year 8 of
Nazi-Maruttaš.

Commentary

3. The expression of time should probably be understood as "from month VII (of year 7) till month I (of year 8)" (see also **nos. 107**: 2–3 and **294**: 7–8). J. A. Brinkman kindly brought to my attention some Nippur texts that express a span of time in a similar way—e.g., TA U$_4$.6.KAM *ša* $^{iti}$ŠE.KIN.KU$_5$ EN U$_4$.6.KAM *ša* $^{iti}$BÁR.ZAG.GAR MU.3.KAM (MUN 177: 6–8)—where one should assume that month XII refers to the previous year (for other examples, see MUN 240: 6–7, Ni. 5920: 9–11, and Ni. 2221: 7–9).

## 64. CUNES 52-12-044

-.IV.18$^?$ Nazi-Maruttaš

Obv. 20.0.0 ŠE $^{giš}$BÁN GAL
ŠE.BAL *ša* $^{m}$LÚ-$^{d}$AMAR.UTU
DUMU $^{m}$*Il-li-ia*
*ša ta-an-ti*
*i-na* NIBRU$^{ki}$
*a-na* $^{md}$MAŠ-SAG DUMU $^{m}$*Ta-ri-bat*-DINGIR
*i-di-in*
Rev. $^{iti}$ŠU.X.NUMUN.NA
MU.⌜18$^?$⌝.KAM
[*Na-z*]*i-Ma-ru-ut-taš*
[L]UGAL.E

Translation

Obv. 600 *sūtu* of barley, (measured by) the big *sūtu*:
exchange$^?$ of Amīl-Marduk.
The son of Illīya,
of the Sea(land)$^?$,
7 gave
5 in Nippur
6 to Ninurta-ašarēd, son of Tarībat-ili.
Rev. Month IV,
year 18$^?$ of
King [Naz]i-Maruttaš.

Commentary

1–7. An alternative translation of these lines could be: "600 *sūtu* of barley, (measured by) the big *sūtu*: exchange$^?$ of Amīl-Marduk, son of Illīya, of the Sea(land)$^?$. He gave (it) in Nippur to Ninurta-ašarēd, son of Tarībat-ili."

2. For the interpretation of ŠE.BAL as Akk. *šupêltu* "exchange," I follow here MesZL no. 579 and the dictionaries (CAD Š/III, 319–21; AHw III, 1279 s.v.); see also van Soldt 2015, 222. Sassmannshausen 2001, 307 (MUN 134: 7, 9) favors the interpretation of ŠE.BAL as the logogram for Akk. *ḫirgalû* (AHw I, 347 s.v.), which, however, relies on a fragmentary passage of Ḫḫ XXIV 155 (see remarks by Powell 1984, 65). For other attestations of ŠE.BAL in this corpus, see **no. 77**: 2, **no. 126**: 4, **no. 150**: 4, and CUSAS 30 150: 28′. It remains unclear what this "exchange" actually implied.

4. *ša ta-an-ti* is tentatively understood as *ša tâmti* "from the Sea(land)," even though this region is usually indicated with the writings (KUR/NAM) A.AB.BA or KUR *tam-tim* (RGTC 5, 193).
8. The sign between ŠU and NUMUN in the month name looks like SI or LAGAB. I know only another attestation of this spelling: **no. 215**: 6.

## 65. CUNES 52-12-050

-.XI.18 Nazi-Maruttaš

Allocation of wheat to a "brewer of the Ekur."

Obv. 0.0.5 GIG $^{\text{giš}}$BÁN 10 SÌLA
$^{\text{m}}$*Na-an-na-a-a*
$^{\text{lú}}$LUNGA ⸢*ša*⸣ É.KUR
*i-na* ŠU $^{\text{m}}$*Ḫu-na-bi im-ḫu-ur*
$^{\text{iti}}$ZÍZ.A.AN
Rev. MU.18.KAM
*Na-zi-Ma-ru-ut-taš*
⸢LUGAL.E⸣

Translation

Obv. 5 *sūtu* of wheat, (measured by) the *sūtu* of 10 *qû*:
Nannaya,
brewer of the Ekur,
received from Ḫunābu.
Month XI,
Rev. year 18
of King Nazi-Maruttaš.

## 66. CUNES 52-18-799

-.X.20 Nazi-Maruttaš

Obv. 0.2.3 ŠE.GIŠ.Ì $^{\text{giš}}$BÁN GAL
*i-na* ŠÀ *na-aḫ*$^{!}$*-ḫu-ḫ*[*i*]
*ša* $^{\text{m}}$É.SAG.ÍLA-*l*[*i-d*]*i-iš*
4 $^{\text{m}}$*Ḫa-am-bu ma-ḫi-ir*
Rev. ⸢$^{\text{iti}}$AB⸣.È
MU.20.KAM
*Na-zi-Ma-ru-ut-ta-aš*
LUGAL.E

Translation

Obv. 15 *sūtu* of sesame, (measured by) the big *sūtu*,
from the *naḫḫuḫu*
of Esagil-l[īd]iš:
4 Ḫambu received (it).
Rev. Month X,
year 20 of
King Nazi-Maruttaš.

COMMENTARY

2. On *naḫḫuḫu*, see also texts **nos. 17, 20–21** and Devecchi 2018.
4. A certain Ḫambu receives sesame also in the Nippur text MUN 140, dated to the 18$^{th}$ year of Nazi-Maruttaš.

### 67. CUNES 52-19-114

1–12.VIII.24$^{?}$ Nazi-Maruttaš

Allocation of barley received by Pungulu as fodder for the horses.

Obv. 2 GUR ŠE $^{giš}$BÁN 5 SÌLA
ŠUKU A[N]ŠE.KUR.RA$^{meš}$
TA U$_4$.1.KAM EN U$_4$.12.KAM
[$^{m}$]⸢*Pú*⸣-*un-gu-lu*$_4$
⸢*ma-ḫi-ir*⸣
Rev. $^{iti}$APIN.DU$_8$.A
MU.⸢24$^{?}$⸣.KAM
*Na-zi-Ma-ru-ut-taš*

Translation

Obv. 60 *sūtu* of barley, (measured by) the *sūtu* of 5 *qû*,
fodder for the horses
from day 1 till day 12:
Pungulu
received (it).
Rev. Month VIII,
year 24$^{?}$ of
Nazi-Maruttaš.

### 68. CUNES 52-16-075

6.V.7 Kadašman-Turgu

Obv. 16.1$^{pi}$.0 ŠE *šub*-⸢*ti*⸣ EN *ša*⸣ $^{iti}$DIRI
*ša* $^{md}$*Nin-urta*-MU-MU
$^{giš}$BÁN K[IN$^{?}$.SI]G$^{?}$ *ša* DINGIR
36.[X.X *i*$^{?}$-*na*$^{?}$ $^{giš}$BÁN$^{?}$] ⸢5⸣ SÌLA
*šu-un-n*[*a*
*i-na* ŠU $^{m}$X[
$^{m}$*É-ra-bi*
Rev. *ma-ḫi-ir*
$^{iti}$NE.NE.GAR
U$_4$.6.KAM
MU.7.KAM *Ka-dáš-man-Túr-gu*
LUGAL.E

COMMENTARY

1. "486 *sūtu*, barley of the residence$^{?}$/settlement$^{?}$, including that of month VIa." For ŠE *šub-ti* "barley of the residence$^{?}$/settlement$^{?}$," see comments to **no. 59**: 2. For $^{iti}$DIRI as writing of month VIa, see **no. 176**: 28.

3. "(measured by) the *sūtu n[aptan]u*? of the god"; for the *sūtu naptanu*, see van Soldt 2015, 32, with previous literature.

4–5. If it is correct to assume a form of *šunnû* "to remeasure" in l. 5, l. 4 could have contained an indication that the barley was remeasured "[by the *sūtu*] of 5 *qû*"; cf. the formulation of **no. 52**: 27.

## 69. CUNES 52-12-025 (Plate No. 26)

-.-.9 Kadašman-Turgu

| | |
|---|---|
| Obv. | 0.3.2 ŠE $^{giš}$BÁN 10 SÌLA |
| | *i-na* ŠÀ *maš-ši-ti* |
| | *ša* $^{m}$ÌR-$^{d}$AMAR.⌜UTU⌝ GAR-*ni* |
| | *i-na* AN.AN.MAR.TU$^{ki}$ |
| | ŠE.BA MUNUS *i-na* ⌜É *ša*⌝ |
| | EN MAR.ZA ÍB.T[AK$_4$?] |
| Rev. | *a-na ka-ni-ik-t[i]* |
| | *i-le-eq-qu-ú* |
| | $^{m}$ÌR-$^{d}$AMAR.UTU *i-din* |
| | MU.9.KAM *Ka-dáš-man-Túr-gu* |
| | LUGAL.E |

Translation

| | |
|---|---|
| Obv. | 20 *sūtu* of barley, (measured by) the *sūtu* of 10 *qû*, |
| | from the delivery |
| | of Arad-Marduk, the overseer, |
| | in AN.AN.MAR.TU$^{ki}$: |
| | ration for the woman in the house of |
| 6–8 | the *bēl parṣi*. They will take the re[st?] to/for the sealed document?/bag?. |
| | Arad-Marduk disbursed (it). |
| | Year 9 of King Kadašman-Turgu. |

Commentary

3. The overseer Arad-Marduk must correspond to the homonymous person associated with the delivery (*maššītu*) of AN.AN.MAR.TU$^{ki}$ in **no. 97**: 7 (KT 9).

4. For AN.AN.MAR.TU$^{ki}$, see also **no. 97**: 7. The GN is to my knowledge not attested in MB sources, but the OB document VS 13 13: 14 contains the toponym $^{uru!}$*Ma-ar-ti*$^{!ki}$ with the gloss AN.AN.MAR.TU (see RGTC 3, 16; Edzard 1957, 23 with n. 94). In the Kassite documentation the writing AN.AN.MAR.TU as a god's name is attested, e.g., in the legends of some seals (see nos. 2.4 and 8.15 in Limet 1971, 57 and 107). It has been proposed to read AN.AN.MAR.TU either $^{d}$DINGIR-MAR.TU (Richter 1998, followed by Beaulieu 2005) or AN-$^{d}$MAR.TU (Selz 2008, 22).

6. MAR.ZA, one of the logographic writings of Akk. *parṣu* (CAD P, 195), has not previously been attested in the combination EN MAR.ZA. This is also the first MB attestation of *bēl parṣi* "an administrator of or participant in rites" (CAD P, 202 s.v.; AHw I, *bēlu(m)* I D 17, 120).

## 70. CUNES 52-16-076

-.-.9 Kadašman-Turgu

The tablet is a pastiche with a fake piece still attached to it. The transliteration renders the text as if the fake part had been removed.

The text lists quantities of crops identified as *kiṣru*, the remnant of the granary, and collected seed; it is placed in this category because of the presence of the verbal form [*ma*]*ḫir* (l. 8).

Obv. [x x] ⸢x⸣ *ki-iṣ-rù*
[x].3.1 ÍB.TAK$_4$ GUR$_7$
[(x x)] *ša* $^{m}$*Ḫu-na-bi*
[x x] ⸢x⸣ NUMUN *es-rù*
[PAP$^{?}$ x.x.x] $^{\text{giš}}$BÁN GAL
Rev. [x x x x] ki
[x x *ma*]-*ḫi-ir*
[x x] ⸢x⸣ MU.9.KAM
[*Ka-dáš-ma*]*n-Túr-gu*
[LUGAL].E
L.e. [x x] $^{m}$KAR$^{?}$-$^{d}$UTU$^{?}$ *ki-iṣ-rù*
[x x] ⸢x x x⸣

## 71. CUNES 52-12-026

-.I.9 Kadašman-Turgu

Allocation of barley taken from the stocks of Kār-Nuska and used to pay the ransom for the shepherd Namru.

Obv. ⸢2$^{?}$.0.0⸣ ŠE ⸢$^{\text{giš}}$BÁN⸣ 5 SÌLA *ša* ŠE.BA
*i-na* ŠÀ *ša Kar-*$^{d}$*Nuska*$^{ki}$
*i-na* É NA$_4$.KIŠIB
*a-na ip-ṭi-ri*
*ša* $^{m}$*Nam-ri* SIPA
$^{m}$EN-*kit-ti*
Rev. DUMU $^{m}$*Qí-il-ti*
*ma-ḫi-ir*
$^{\text{iti}}$BÁR.ZAG.GAR
MU.9.KAM *Ka-dáš-man-Túr-gu*
LUGAL.E

Translation

Obv. ⸢60$^{?}$⸣ *sūtu* of barley, (measured by) the *sūtu* of 5 *qû* of the ration,
from that of Kār-Nuska,
(which is) in the storehouse:
6 Bēl-kitti,
7 son of Qiltu,
8 received (it)
4 as ransom (money)
5 of Namru, the shepherd.
Month I,
10 year 9 of King Kadašman-Turgu.

COMMENTARY

4. A disbursement of barley "as ransom (money)" is attested also in PBS 2/2 103: 17 (*ana ipṭiri*) and CUSAS 30 27: 7 (*kīmū ipṭiri*).

## 72. CUNES 52-16-078

[x].VII.9 Kadašman-Turgu

Allocation of barley taken from the stocks of Kār-Nuska of the 8th year of Kadašman-Turgu and received by Bunna-Marduk as seed for the town of Mannu-nāṣiršu in the 9th year of Kadašman-Turgu. One month later, Bunna-Marduk received another amount of seed from the barley of Kār-Nuska of year 8 (see **no. 160**: 4).

Obv. 1.0.0 ŠE $^{\text{giš}}$BÁN 10 SÌLA
*i-na* ŠÀ *ša Kar-*$^{\text{d}}$*Nuska*$^{\text{k}}$[$^{\text{i}}$]
*ša* MU.8.KAM
⸢*a*⸣*-na* NUMUN *ša Man-nu-*[ÙRU*-šu*]
[$^{\text{m}}$*Bu*]*-un-na-*$^{\text{d}}$AMAR.UTU *m*[*a*$^{?}$*-ḫir*$^{?}$]
Rev. [$^{\text{iti}}$DU$_6$].KÙ
[U$_4$].⸢X⸣.KAM
[M]U.⸢9⸣.KAM *Ka-dá*[*š-man-Túr-gu*]
LUGAL.⸢E⸣

Translation

Obv. 30 *sūtu* of barley, (measured by) the *sūtu* of 10 *qû*,
from that of Kār-Nuska
of year 8:
5 [B]unna-Marduk r[eceived$^{?}$ (it)]
4 as seed for Mannu-[nāṣiršu].
Rev. [Month V]II,
[day] ⸢. . .⸣,
[ye]ar 9 of King Kada[šman-Turgu].

## 73. CUNES 52-14-100

-.II.10 Kadašman-Turgu

The content of this text corresponds to the entry of **no. 180**: 3, a summary of various amounts of cereals received by Riš-aṣûšu from Mudammiq-Adad.

Obv. ⸢0.3.2 ŠE $^{\text{giš}}$BÁN 10 SÌLA⸣
⸢*i-na* ŠÀ *maš-ši-ti ša Tukul*⸣*-ti-*É.KUR
*ki-i* ŠU $^{\text{m}}$*Mu-*SIG$_5$-$^{\text{d}}$IŠKUR
*i-na* ŠU $^{\text{md}}$30*-nap-ši-ra*
$^{\text{md}}$30-TI-URU$_4$ *ma-ḫi-ir*
[$^{\text{it}}$]$^{\text{i}}$GU$_4$.⸢SI.SÁ⸣
Rev. MU.10.KAM
$^{\text{d}}$*Ka-dáš-man-*⸢*Túr-gu*⸣

Translation

| | |
|---|---|
| Obv. | 20 *sūtu* of barley, (measured by) the *sūtu* of 10 *qû*, |
| | from the delivery of Tukultī-Ekur: |
| 5 | Sîn-balāṭa-īriš received |
| 4 | from Sîn-napšira |
| 3 | in place of Mudammiq-Adad. |
| | Month II, |
| Rev. | year 10 of |
| | Kadašman-Turgu. |

COMMENTARY

3. While Sîn-balāṭa-īriš receives here barley "in place of" (*kī qāt*) Mudammiq-Adad, according to **no. 180**: 1 he received it "from" (*ina qāt*) Mudammiq-Adad.

## 74. CUNES 52-14-098

-.VIII.10 Kadašman-Turgu

| | |
|---|---|
| Obv. | 1.0.0 ŠE $^{giš}$BÁN 10 SÌLA |
| | *i-na* ŠÀ *ša* $^{md}$30-EN-IBILA |
| | *i-na* ŠU $^{md}$*Nin-urta*-MU-MU |
| | *i-na* ŠÀ É.GAL |
| | *ki-i* ŠU $^{m}$*Mu*-SIG$_5$-$^{d}$IŠKUR |
| L.e. | $^{md}$30-TI-URU$_4$ |
| | *ma-ḫi-ir* |
| Rev. | $^{iti}$APIN.DU$_8$.A |
| | MU.10.KAM $^{d}$*Ka-dáš-man-Túr-gu* |
| | LUGAL.E |

Translation

| | |
|---|---|
| Obv. | 30 *sūtu* of barley, (measured by) the *sūtu* of 10 *qû*, |
| | from that of Sîn-bēl-apli: |
| 6 | Sîn-balāṭa-īriš |
| 7 | received (it) |
| 3 | from Ninurta-zākir-šumi |
| 4 | from that of the palace, |
| 5 | in place of Mudammiq-Adad. |
| Rev. | Month VIII, |
| | year 10 of King Kadašman-Turgu. |

### 75. CUNES 52-17-276

-.II.11 Kadašman-Turgu

Obv. 45.1.3 4 SÌLA ŠE $^{giš}$BÁN
*ša* DINGIR *ša i-na* BÀD-$^{d}$*Pa*$_4$*-nig*$_6$*-gar-ra*$^{ki}$
*maḫ-ra-tu*$_4$
TA 2.3.3 6 SÌLA GAL $^{giš}$BÁN *ša* DINGIR
*i-na* 1 GUR 0.0.1 7 SÌLA *šu-lu-ú*

---

Rev. $^{iti}$GU$_4$.SI.SÁ
MU.11.[KAM *Ka-dá*]*š-man-Túr-gu*
[LUGAL].E

Translation

Obv. 1,359 *sūtu* and 4 *qû* of barley, (measured by) the *sūtu*
2-3 of the god, which were received in Dūr-Pa(p)-niĝara,
after 81 *sūtu* and 6 *qû* have been deducted, the increase of the *sūtu* of the god
being at a rate of 1 *sūtu* and 7 *qû* per kor.
Rev. Month II,
year 11 [of Kin]g [Kada]šman-Turgu.

COMMENTARY

1–2, 4. For the "*sūtu* of the god," see also PBS 13 70: 1 ($^{giš}$BÁN DINGIR) and BE 14 16: 1 ($^{giš}$BÁN GAL *ša* DINGIR); cf. $^{giš}$BÁN K[IN$^?$.SI]G$^?$ *ša* DINGIR "the *sūtu n*[*aptan*]*u*$^?$ of the god" in **no. 68**: 3.

2. The GN Dūr-Pa(p)-niĝara has not previously been attested in MB texts (cf., however, the difficult GN in BE 17 40: 3, for which van Soldt 1988, 112 proposed the reading BÀD-$^{d}$pà.ni$_x^?$.gar.ra$^{ki}$, while RGTC 5, 97 has BÀD-$^{d?}$*Pap*-$^{šuk}$SUKKAL$^{?ki}$ and Sassmannshausen 2001, 41 n. 617 reads BÀD-$^{d}$*Pa*$_4$-U.GAR.RA$^{ki}$).

### 76. CUNES 52-14-101

-.V.12 Kadašman-Turgu

Obv. 0.0.4 ŠE $^{giš}$BÁN 10 SÌLA
*i-na* ŠÀ *ši-ib-ši*
*ù* ḪA.LA
*ša* KI $^{m}$ZÁLAG-$^{d}$*Iš-tar*
*i-na* ŠU $^{m}$*Mu*-SIG$_5$-$^{d}$IŠKUR
L.e. $^{md}$30-TI-URU$_4$
*ma-ḫi-ir*
Rev. $^{iti}$NE.NE.GAR
MU.12.KAM
⸢$^{d}$⸣*Ka-dáš-man-Túr-gu*
LUGAL.E

Translation

Obv. 4 *sūtu* of barley, (measured by) the *sūtu* of 10 *qû*,
from the *šibšu*
and the share
which are with Nūr-Ištar:
6 Sîn-balāṭa-īriš
7 received (it)
5 from Mudammiq-Adad.
Rev. Month V,
year 12 of
King Kadašman-Turgu.

## 77. CUNES 52-18-769

-.VIII.12 Kadašman-Turgu

Obv. 1 GUR ZÍZ.AN.NA $^{\text{giš}}$BÁN 10 SÌLA
*i-na* ŠÀ ŠE.⸢BAL⸣
*ša* $^{\text{m}}$*E-re-e*[*m*]*-še-e-a*
$^{\text{m}}$*Ḫu-sa-rak-ku*
5 *ma-ḫi-ir*
Rev. [$^{\text{iti}}$APIN].⸢DU$_{8}$⸣.A
MU.12.KAM
*Ka-dáš-man-Túr-gu* LUGAL.E

Translation

Obv. 30 *sūtu* of emmer, (measured by) the *sūtu* of 10 *qû*,
from the exchange$^{?}$
of Erēmšē'a:
Ḫusarakku
5 received (it).
Rev. [Month V]III,
year 12 of
King Kadašman-Turgu.

COMMENTARY

2. On ŠE.BAL "exchange$^{?}$," see comments to **no. 64**: 2.

## 78. CUNES 52-19-134

16.III.13 Kadašman-Turgu

Obv. 5.0.0 ŠE $^{giš}$BÁN 10 SÌLA
*i-na* ŠÀ *maš-ši-ti*
*ša Kar-$^{d}$Nuska$^{ki}$*
*a-na* ÉŠ.GÀR
DUMU.MUNUS $^{lú}$Ì.SUR
*ma-aḫ-rat*
$^{iti}$SIG$_4$.GA
Rev. U$_4$.16.KAM
MU.13.KAM
*Ka-dáš-man-Túr-gu* LUGAL.E

Translation

Obv. 150 *sūtu* of barley, (measured by) the *sūtu* of 10 *qû*,
from the delivery
of Kār-Nuska:
5 the daughter of Ṣāḫitu
6 received (it)
4 as production supplies.
Month III,
Rev. day 16,
year 13
10 of King Kadašman-Turgu.

## 79. CUNES 52-17-266

[x].VI.13 Kadašman-Turgu

Obv. ⸢5⸣.0.4 5 SÌLA ŠE $^{giš}$BÁN 10 SÌLA
*i-na* ŠÀ ⸢*te-li*⸣*-ti ša* $^{m}$*Bu-un-na-*$^{d}$AMAR.UTU
ÉŠ.GÀR ⸢DUMU.MUNUS⸣ $^{lú}$Ì.SUR
$^{md}$30-⸢*nap*⸣*-ši-ra*
*ip-te-ma i-din*
Rev. $^{iti}$KIN.$^{d}$INANNA
U$_4$.[x].KAM
MU.13.KAM
*Ka-dáš-man-Túr-gu*
LUGAL.E

Translation

Obv. 154 *sūtu* of barley, (measured by) the *sūtu* of 10 *qû*,
from the revenues of Bunna-Marduk:
production supplies for the daughter of Ṣāḫitu.
Sîn-napšira
5 opened and disbursed (it).
Rev. Month VI,
day [x],
year 13
9-10 of King Kadašman-Turgu.

Commentary

5. For other MB references to the administrative practice of "opening (a container)" before distributing goods, see, e.g., CUSAS 30 162: 6–7, 8–9 (referring to barley), CUSAS 30 309: 1–2 (referring to emmer), CUSAS 30 362: 10–14 (referring to wool), and PBS 2/2 58: 5–7 (referring to barley).

### 80. CUNES 52-12-055

$13^{+}$.IV.$13^{+}$ Kadašman-Turgu

Despite the statement in l. 12, no seal impression is detectable on the tablet, whose surface is very worn.

Obv. ⸢x⸣ 20.0.0 ⸢ŠE $^{giš}$BÁN GAL⸣
⸢10$^{?}$.x.1$^{?}$ GIG⸣
⸢x x x ZÍZ⸣.AN.NA
_____
4 ⸢x⸣ 37.0.1 ⸢*im*$^{?}$-*ḫur*⸣
L.e. ⸢$^{giš}$⸣BÁN ⸢GAL$^{?}$⸣
Rev. $^{m}$*Ṭà-ab*-IM-⸢$^{d}$IŠKUR$^{?}$⸣
$^{md}$*Nin*-[*urta*$^{?}$]-⸢x⸣-[
*ù* $^{m}$BA-⸢*šá*⸣-$^{d}$*Dil-bat* ⸢$^{lú}$NAGAR⸣
*im-ḫu-rù*
10 $^{iti}$ŠU.NUMUN.NA U$_{4}$.⸢$13^{+}$⸣.KAM
MU.⸢$13^{+}$⸣.KAM ⸢$^{d}$*Ka-dáš-man-Túr-gu*⸣
⸢NA$_{4}$.KIŠIB $^{md}$*Nin*$^{?}$-*urta*$^{?}$⸣-[

## 81. CUNES 52-16-090 (Plate No. 27)

-.I.14 Kadašman-Turgu

The same individuals occur together and with the same functions also in **no. 84**.

Obv. 0.3.2 ŠE $^{\text{giš}}$BÁN 10 SÌLA
*i-na nap-ṭar-ti*
*ša* É $^{\text{md+}}$*En-líl-ki-di-ni*
*ki-*[*i*] ŠU $^{\text{m}}$*Mu-*SIG$_5$-$^{\text{d}}$IŠKUR
$^{\text{md}}$30-TI-URU$_4$ *im-ḫur*
$^{\text{md}}$30-ŠEŠ-SUM-*na*
L.e. *im-du-ud*
Rev. $^{\text{iti}}$BÁR.ZAG.GAR
MU.14.KAM
$^{\text{d}}$*Ka-dáš-man-Túr-gu*
LUGAL.E

Translation

Obv. 20 *sūtu* of barley, (measured by) the *sūtu* of 10 *qû*,
in the guest quarter?
of the House of Enlil-kidinnī:
Sîn-balāṭa-īriš received (it)
4 in place of Mudammiq-Adad.
Sîn-aḫa-iddina
L.e. weighed (it).
Rev. Month I,
year 14
of King Kadašman-Turgu.

COMMENTARY

2. While none of the meanings of *napṭartu* listed by the dictionaries fit the context ("a part of a lock," "desertion," "a class of women"; see CAD N/1, 324 and AHw II, 742 s.v.), a more suitable parallel is provided by the *bīt napṭarti* mentioned in a MA text from Tell Chuera, where it probably indicated a guest house or hostel (see text no. 12: 15 in Jakob 2009, 52–53); see also **no. 180**: 12. A town Napṭartu is mentioned in MUN 134: 17 ($^{\text{uru}}$*Nap-ṭa-ar-tu*$_4^{\text{ki}}$) but the context and the lack of geographic determinatives makes it a less likely solution.

## 82. CUNES 52-13-165 (Plate No. 28)

11.I.14 Kadašman-Turgu

Obv. 8 GUR Š[E x x]
$^{giš}$BÁN ⸢GAL⸣
NÍG.GÀR $^{m}$*Ṭà-ab-ki-din-*$^{d}$*Gu-la*
$^{iti}$BÁR.ZAG.GAR
⸢U$_4$⸣.11.KAM
L.e. [M]U.14.KAM
Rev. [$^{(d)}$*K*]*a-dáš-man-Túr-gu* LUGAL
⸢*ša*?⸣ 2 GUR EŠ$^{?!}$.DÉ.A
[*a-n*]*a* ŠÀ-*bi la qer-bu*
[$^{m}$*Ṭà-a*]*b-ki-din-*$^{d}$*Gu-la*
[*i*]*l*?-*ṭú-ur*

Translation

Obv. 240 *sūtu* of bar[ley . . .],
(measured by) the big *sūtu*:
. . . of Ṭāb-kidin-Gula.
Month I,
day 11,
L.e. [ye]ar 14
Rev. of King Kadašman-Turgu.
As for the 60 *sūtu* of the interest-free loan?,
they are not included in it.
[Ṭā]b-kidin-Gula
[wr]ote (it).

COMMENTARY

3. For NÍG.GÀR, see also **no. 87**: 2. I do not know any other attestations of this Sumerogramm: the first element NÍG would link it with NÍG.GA "property," while the second element GÀR reminds one of ÉŠ.GÀR "production supplies." Note that Ṭāb-kidin-Gula often appears as recipient of production supplies.

8. The first sign in EŠ$^{?!}$.DÉ.A looks more like KUR. For EŠ.DÉ.A (Akk. *ḫubuttatu*) in MB texts, see Paulus, in press.

9. For *lā qerbu* "not included," see Aro 1970, 21 (no. 6); Kessler 1982, 66–68 (Iml. 4) and 91–92 (Iml. 20); Gurney 1983, 165 (MBTU 65); and Sassmannshausen 2001, 280 (MUN 98) and 295 (MUN 118).

## 83. CUNES 52-14-045

19.I.14 Kadašman-Turgu

| | |
|---|---|
| Obv. | 2.1.1 ŠE $^{\text{giš}}$BÁN 5 SÌLA |
| | *i-na* $^{\text{m}}$*Mu*-SIG$_5$-$^{\text{d}}$IŠKUR |
| | $^{\text{md}}$30-*nap-ši-ra ma-ḫi-ir* |
| | *ul-tu*$_4$ 0.0.1 ŠE *ša* $^{\text{m}}$*Ta-qu-li* |
| | *ma-aḫ-ru šu-lu-ú* |
| | $^{\text{iti}}$BÁR.ZAG.GAR U$_4$.19.KAM |
| L.e. | MU.14.KAM |
| Rev | $^{\text{m}}$*Ka-dáš-man-Túr-gu* |

Translation

| | |
|---|---|
| Obv. | 67 *sūtu* of barley, (measured by) the *sūtu* of 5 *qû*: |
| 3 | Sîn-napšira received (it) |
| 2 | from Mudammiq-Adad, |
| | after 1 *sūtu* of barley, which Taqulu |
| 5 | received, had been deducted. |
| | Month I, day 19, |
| L.e. | year 14 |
| Rev. | of Kadašman-Turgu. |

Commentary

2. See MUN 140: 4 for another attestation of *ina* PN meaning "from PN," instead of the more common *ina qāt* (ŠU) PN.
3. I take *ša* as a relative pronoun and $^{\text{m}}$*Ta-qu-li* as the subject of the relative sentence, even though the ending in –*i* might suggest *ša* + genitive.
8. The name of Kadašman-Turgu is rarely preceded by the masculine personal determinative, but see also **no. 44**: 2 and **no. 87**: 8.

## 84. CUNES 52-14-032

2.VIII.14 Kadašman-Turgu

The same individuals occur together and with the same functions also in **no. 81**.

Obv. 0.1.4 ŠE $^{\text{giš}}$BÁN 10 SÌLA
*i-na* ŠÀ ḪA.LA
*ša* $^{\text{md}}$*Nin-urta*-MU-MU
*i-na* É GUR$_7$
5 $^{\text{md}}$30-TI-URU$_4$
*ki-i* ŠU $^{\text{m}}$*Mu*-SIG$_5$-$^{\text{d}}$IŠKUR
*im-ḫu-ur*
$^{\text{md}}$30-ŠEŠ-SUM-*na* $^{\text{lú}}$KÚRUN.NA
9 ⸢*im*⸣-*du-ud*
Rev. $^{\text{iti}}$APIN.DU$_8$.A
U$_4$.2.KAM
MU.14.KAM $^{\text{d}}$*Ka-dáš-man-Túr-gu*
LUGAL.E

Translation

Obv. 10 *sūtu* of barley, (measured by) the *sūtu* of 10 *qû*,
from the share
of Ninurta-zākir-šumi
(which is) in the granary:
5 Sîn-balāṭa-īriš
7 received (it)
6 in place of Mudammiq-Adad.
Sîn-aḫa-iddina, the innkeeper,
weighed (it).
Rev. Month VIII,
day 2,
year 14 of King Kadašman-Turgu.

Commentary

4. For the storage of "shares" (ḪA.LA) in the granary, see also CUSAS 30 150: 17′.

## 85. CUNES 53-01-128

23.X.14 Kadašman-Turgu

There are textile impressions on the surface of the tablet, which has a rather irregular shape.

Obv. 0.0.1 ŠE $^{giš}$BÁN 4 SÌLA<br>
$^{m}$*Ta-ri-bu*<br>
*ki-i* ŠU $^{m}$*Qu-un-nu-ni*<br>
*ma-ḫi-ir*<br>
5 $^{iti}$AB.È<br>
L.e. $U_4$.23.KAM<br>
Rev. MU.14.KAM<br>
$^{d}$*Ka-dáš-man-Túr-gu*<br>
LUGAL.E

Translation

Obv. 1 *sūtu* of barley, (measured by) the *sūtu* of 4 *qû*:<br>
Tarību<br>
4 received (it)<br>
3 in place of Qunnunu.<br>
5 Month X,<br>
L.e. day 23,<br>
Rev. year 14 of<br>
King Kadašman-Turgu.

COMMENTARY

2. BU is written on an erasure. The scribe perhaps wrote first $^{m}$*Ta-ri-bi*, then corrected it.

7. DINGIR is written on an erasure.

## 86. CUNES 53-01-116

5.I.15 Kadašman-Turgu

Obv. [x.x.x Š]E $^{giš}$BÁN 5 SÌLA<br>
[*ki-i* / *i-na*] ŠU $^{m}$È-*ana*-ZÁLAG-$^{d}$IŠKUR<br>
[$^{m}$Q]*u-nu-nu*<br>
4 [*ma*]-*ḫi-ir*<br>
Rev. $^{iti}$BÁR.ZAG.GAR<br>
$U_4$.5.KAM<br>
MU.15.KAM<br>
8 $^{d}$*Ka-dáš-man-Túr-gu*<br>
LUGAL.E

Translation

Obv. [. . . *sūtu* of bar]ley, (measured by) the *sūtu* of 5 *qû*:
3 [Q]unnunu
4 [re]ceived (it)
2 [in place of/from] Lūṣi-ana-nūr-Adad.
Rev. Month I,
day 5,
year 15
of King Kadašman-Turgu.

COMMENTARY
2. Both restorations seem possible based on the context and the space in the break.

## 87. CUNES 52-19-117 (Plate No. 29)

2.II.15 Kadašman-Turgu

Obv. 5.0.0 ŠE $^{giš}$BÁN 10 SÌLA
NÍG.GÀR DUMU.MUNUS $^{m}$LÚ-INANNA
EN 0.2.3 *ša* $^{m}$*Ṭà-ab-ki-din-*$^{d}$*Gu-la*
*im-ḫu-ru-ú-ma*
⸢Á$^{?}$⸣-*ša i-di-na-áš-ši*
[$^{it}$]$^{i}$GU$_4$.SI.SÁ U$_4$.2.KAM
Rev. MU.15.KAM
$^{m}$*Ka-dáš-man-Túr-gu* LUGAL.E

Translation

Obv. 150 *sūtu* of barley, (measured by) the *sūtu* of 10 *qû*,
. . . of the daughter of Amīl-Ištar
together with 15 *sūtu*, which Ṭāb-kidin-Gula
received and
gave her (as) ⸢her salary$^{?}$⸣.
Month II, day 2,
Rev. year 15 of
King Kadašman-Turgu.

COMMENTARY
2. For NÍG.GÀR, see commentary to **no. 82**: 3.

## 88. CUNES 52-14-025

24.I.[ . . . ] Kadašman-Turgu
Sealed by Ninurta-ašarēd.

Obv. ⸢1$^{+}$⸣.0.3 ZÍZ.AN.NA $^{giš}$BÁN [
*i-na* ŠU $^{m}$SIG$_{5}$-*iq*-$^{d}$[IŠKUR]
*i-na* BÀD-$^{d+}$*En-líl*$^{hi.a.ki}$
$^{md}$*Nin-urta*-SAG *im-ḫur*
$^{iti}$BÁR.ZAG.GAR U$_{4}$.24.KAM
Rev. [MU.x].KAM
⸢$^{d}$*Ka-dáš*$^{?}$⸣-[*man*]-*Túr-gu* LUGAL.E
⸢NA$_{4}$.KIŠIB $^{md}$*Nin*$^{?}$-*urta*$^{?}$-SAG$^{?}$⸣

Translation

Obv. ⸢33$^{+}$ *sūtu*⸣ of emmer, (measured by) the *sūtu* [ . . . ]:
4 Ninurta-ašarēd received (it)
2 from Mudammiq-[Adad]
3 in Dūr-Enlilē.
5 Month I, day 24,
Rev. [year x] of
King Kadaš[man]-Turgu.
Seal of Ninurta-ašarēd$^{?}$.

## 89. CUNES 52-14-102

-.IV.[. . .] Kadašman-Turgu

Obv. ⸢0.2.1 ŠE⸣ $^{giš}$BÁN ⸢5$^{?}$⸣ [SÌLA]
⸢*ša*$^{?}$⸣ $^{m}$*Ur*$^{?}$-[x-x-x]-⸢x⸣
⸢*ki-i* ŠU⸣ [$^{m}$x-x-x-$^{d}$IŠK]UR$^{?}$
$^{m}$BA-*ša*-$^{d}$[AMAR.UTU DUMU $^{m}$*Ṭa*]*b-bi-ḫi*
*a-na* $^{m}$*Lu-d*[*a*$^{?}$-
$^{m}$*Tak-la-ku* DUMU.A.NI EN 0.1.1 *ar-ki-ti*
*im-ḫur*
Rev. $^{i}$[$^{ti}$ŠU.NU]MUN.NA
[MU.x].KAM
[*K*]*a-dáš-man-Túr-gu*
LUGAL.E

Commentary

4. The PN can be restored after **no. 182**: 3.

6–7. "Taklāku, his son (i.e., of Lū-d[a$^{?}$- . . .], cf. l. 5), received it together with 7 *sūtu* of a later delivery$^{?}$." AHw III, (*w*)*arkītu*(*m*) A 5, 1470 proposes the meaning "Rückstand" and quotes only one attestation from PBS 1/2 54: 20; the Nippur text MUN 269: 8 contains another occurrence, translated "Späteres" by Sassmannshausen 2001, 353. Since the adjective *arkû* is well attested in MB administrative texts with the meaning "later" in reference to deliveries of goods (CAD A/2, *arkû* 1 b 7′), it seems more likely that *arkītu* refers here to a later delivery rather than to a "remainder."

## 90. CUNES 52-18-800

-.VIII.[ . . . ] Kadašman-Turgu

Obv. 0.2.3 ŠE $^{giš}$BÁN 10 SÌLA
*ki-i* ŠU $^{md}$30-TI-URU$_4$
$^{m}$*Ki-din-*$^{d}$*Gu-la ka-ṣi-rù*
*i-na* ŠU $^{m}$*Mu*-SIG$_5$-$^{d}$IŠKUR *i-na* NIBRU$^{ki}$ *ma-ḫi-ir*
[$^{it}$]$^{i}$APIN.DU$_8$.A
[MU.X.KA]M
L.e. [*Ka-dáš-man-T*]*úr-gu*
[ LUGAL].E

The reverse is blank.

Translation

Obv. 15 *sūtu* of barley, (measured by) the *sūtu* of 10 *qû*:
3 Kidin-Gula, the knotter,
4 received in Nippur from Mudammiq-Adad,
2 in place of Sîn-balāṭa-īriš.
5 Month VIII,
[year x] of
[Kin]g [Kadašman-T]urgu.

## 91. CUNES 52-16-108

-.I.[ . . . ] Šagarakti-Šuriaš

Obv. 0.0.1 GÚ.TUR $^{giš}$BÁN 5 SÌLA
*a-na* KIN.SIG
$^{md}$*Gu-la*-TI-URU$_4$
[*m*]*a-ḫi-ir*
[$^{iti}$BÁR].ZAG.GAR
L.e. [MU].⌜X.KAM⌝
Rev. [*Šagarakti*]-*Šu-ri-aš*
⌜LUGAL.E⌝

Translation

Obv. 1 *sūtu* of peas?, (measured by) the *sūtu* of 5 *qû*:
3 Gula-balāṭa-īriš
4 received
2 for a *naptanu*-meal.
5 Month I,
L.e. [year] ⌜. . .⌝ of
Rev. King [Šagarakti]-Šuriaš.

COMMENTARY

3. Gula-balāṭa-īriš appears also in CUSAS 30 400 (ŠŠ 2?) and CUSAS 30 427 (year 2?).

1.3.2 MULTIPLE EXPENDITURES FOR ONE PURPOSE

i. Rations

### 92. CUNES 52-12-058

-.-.19 Nazi-Maruttaš

The text records an allocation of barley as rations, but instead of giving details about the recipients, it indicates the sources from which the barley was taken.

Obv. ŠE ${}^{giš}$BÁN 5 SÌLA ˹*ša*˺ *a-na* ŠE.BA ˹*na-ad*˺-[*nu*]
10.2.5 *i-na* ŠÀ *ša a*[*r*?-
10.3.0 *i-na* ŠÀ *ša* ${}^{m}$MU-˹*líb-ši*˺ [x x x (x)] na
9.4.3 *i-na* ŠÀ *ša* É-*nu* ˹${}^{iti}$NE.NE˺.GAR
PAP 31.0.2 MU.19.KAM
*Na-zi-Ma-ru-ut-ta-aš* LUG[AL.E]

The reverse is blank.

COMMENTARY

1. "Barley, (measured by) the *sūtu* of 5 *qû*, which was disburs[ed] as rations."

3. A possible restoration of the end of the line is [${}^{iti}$ŠU.NUMUN].NA.

## 93. CUNES 52-20-320 (Plate No. 30)

-.-.2 Kadašman-Turgu

This tablet records an inspection of workers identified either as GURUŠ "(adult) man" or as GURUŠ.TUR "male adolescent," apparently listed together in groups according to their family relations (see the notations DUMU.A.NI "his son" and ŠEŠ.A.NI "his brother" next to some individuals). The main goal of the inspection seems to have been estimating or recording the amounts of barley necessary for each worker, as shown by the introductory lines of the text ("Bar[ley], (measured by) the *sūtu* of 5 *qû*") and by the indication of an amount of barley corresponding to each individual. The text seems therefore to have had a different structure and function than the inspections of workers from Nippur described by Tenney 2011, 15–18; Tenney 2017, 211 n. 12.

The quantities largely correspond to those attested as monthly rations for servile workers in the Nippur texts (for which see Del Monte 1988; Paulus 2014a): 60 *qû* of barley for a GURUŠ (but only 25 *qû* in one case, see l. 7) and 30 *qû* for a GURUŠ.TUR (but only 20 *qû* in two cases, see ll. 23′ and 25′).

It is hard to recognize the column dividers and reconstruct the exact layout of the tablet because some parts of its surface are very worn, while others have been plastered with new clay and incised with fake signs, here indicated through asterisks.

| | | |
|---|---|---|
| Obv. | Š[E] ⸢$^{giš}$BÁN 5 SÌLA x⸣ [ | |
| | ⸢x x x⸣ [ | |
| | *ša* ⸢MU.2.KAM *Ka-dáš-man-Túr-gu* LUGAL.E⸣ | |
| | *re-e-ša* *iš-šu-ú* | |
| | ⸢GURUŠ⸣ $^{md}$AMAR.UTU-MU-MU$^?$ DUMU $^{mf}$*In-na-ni-bu-ti* 0.2.0 | |
| | ⸢GURUŠ.TUR $^{md}$x-ŠEŠ⸣-URU$_4$ | DUMU.A.NI 0.1.0 |
| | ⸢GURUŠ $^{m}$⸣*Qu-nu-nu* | DUMU.A.NI 0.0.5 |
| | ⸢GURUŠ $^{m}$*I-ši-im-me-i-na*⸣-É.SAG.ÍLA 0.2.0 | |
| | PAP ⸢4⸣ 1.0.5 | |
| | ⸢x $^{m}$x x x x x x x x x 0.2.0⸣ | |
| | ⸢x $^{m}$x x x x x x x x ni 0.2.0⸣ | |
| | ⸢x $^{m}$x x x x x x x x x⸣ | |
| | ⸢x $^{m}$⸣[x] ⸢x x x DUMU$^?$ $^{md}$30-*ma*$^?$-DINGIR⸣ | |
| | [PAP$^?$ 4$^?$] ⸢x x x⸣ | |
| | [...] ⸢x x x⸣ [ | |
| | [...] x [ | |
| | [...] * * * [ | |
| Text breaks off | | |
| Rev. | [...] ⸢x x⸣ [ | |
| | [...] * * * * [ | |
| | [...] [ | |
| | 31 6 ⸢*ṭà*⸣-*bu* | |
| | ⸢GURUŠ $^{m}$*Ri-iš*-$^{d}$⸣U.GUR DUMU ⸢$^{md+}$*En-líl-tukul*⸣-*ti* 0.2.0 | |
| | ⸢GURUŠ.TUR $^{m}$BA-*ša*-$^{d}$U.GUR | DUMU.A.NI 0.0.4 |
| | GURUŠ $^{m}$EN-*qa-li* | ⸢ŠEŠ⸣.A.NI 0.2.0 |
| | ⸢GURUŠ.TUR⸣ $^{m}$È-*a-ri*-<*iš*>-URU DUMU.A.NI 0.0.4 | |
| | PAP ⸢4⸣ | 1.0.2 |
| | GURUŠ ⸢$^{m}$UD$^?$-*šú*-ZÁLAG⸣-*ir* DUMU $^{m}$*Ba-ḫe-e* | 0.2.0 |
| | GURUŠ.TUR $^{m}$*Ta-ri-ba*-$^{d}$*Gu-la* DUMU.A.NI | 0.1.0 |
| | GURUŠ $^{m}$*Ta-rib-tu*$_4$ DUMU $^{m}$*E-še-mu-ti* | 0.2.0 |
| | GURUŠ.TUR $^{m}$*Il-qa-šu*-DINGIR ŠEŠ.A.NI | 0.1.0 |
| | PAP ⸢4⸣ | 1.1.0 |
| | PAP 8 2 *ṭà-bu* | 2.1.2 |
| | ⸢ŠU.NIGIN 10 *ṭà-bu*⸣ | 15.1.⸢5$^?$⸣ |

COMMENTARY

4. *rēša iššû* "they have inspected/verified": cf. *rēša našû* "to check on quality or quantity of fields, materials, staples, animals" in CAD N/2, *našû* A 6, 107; for other MB attestations, see, e.g., MUN 395: 3 and CUSAS 30 371: 2.

21′. The same word, always spelled ḪI-*bu/pu*, appears also in ll. 32′–33′; I am not aware of other attestations in MB texts. The term *ḫīpu* "break(age)" (CAD Ḫ, 196; AHw I, 347 s.v.) does not seem to fit the context. The proposed reading *ṭà-bu* could perhaps refer to "good (i.e., healthy?)" workers, but is very tentative.

32′. The amount of this subtotal (2.1.2) gives the sum of the quantities in ll. 26′ and 31′, which in turn sum up the quantities disbursed to two groups of four workers each.

## 94. CUNES 52-10-118

28.II.2 Kadašman-Turgu

| | | |
|---|---|---|
| U.e. | ŠE $^{giš}$BÁN 5 SÌLA *ša i-na* ŠÀ | |
| | *maš-ši-ti ša* $^{m}$*Ṭà-ab*-IM-$^{d}$IŠKUR | |
| | SUM-*nu* | |
| Obv. | ÉRIN$^{ḫi.a}$ *ša a-na* ÍD-*ḫa-aḫ-ḫi šap-rù* | |
| | 0.3.0 | √ $^{m}$NÍG.BA-$^{d}$U.GUR |
| | 0.3.0 | √ $^{m}$*Kal-bu* |
| | 0.3.0 | √ $^{md}$*Dil-bat-*[*ba*]*-ni* |
| | 0.3.0 | √ $^{md}$⸢*Nin-urta*⸣-SUM-*na* |
| | 0.3.0 | √ $^{m}$⸢*Ri*⸣-[*iš*]-$^{d}$AMAR.UTU |
| | 0.3.0 | √ $^{m}$Ì[R]-⸢$^{d}$*Ku-bi*⸣ |
| | 0.3.0 | √ $^{md}$⸢*Dil-bat*⸣*-ba-ni* DUMU $^{m}$*Bu-ḫi-ri* |
| | 0.3.0 | $^{m}$⸢x⸣ ḫu dag/kal ÀR$^{?}$ |
| | 0.3.0 | √ $^{md}$UTU-LÚ-TI.LA |
| | 0.3.0 | √ $^{m}$*Ta-qí-š*[*u*] |
| | PAP 6.0.0 ⸢10 ÌR$^{?}$ x x⸣ | |
| Text breaks off (1–2 lines missing) | | |
| Rev. | 0.3.0 | √ $^{m}$⸢*Ki-di*⸣[*n-* |
| | 0.3.0 | √ $^{m}$⸢*Ki-rib-ti*⸣-[ |
| | 0.3.0 | √ $^{m}$*Ba-nu-ú* |
| | 0.3.0 | √ $^{m}$GAL-*šá*-$^{d}$*Nin-urta* $^{l}$[$^{ú}$EN]GAR$^{?}$ |
| | 0.3.0 | √ $^{m}$*Ri-iš*-É.KUR KI.MIN |
| | 1.2.4 $^{md}$*Nin-urta*-KIŠ-DINGIR$^{meš}$ | |
| | PAP 3.3.0 6 *um-ma-nu* | |
| | ŠU.NIGIN 9.3.0 | |
| | $^{iti}$GU$_{4}$.SI.SÁ U$_{4}$.28.KAM | |
| | MU.2.KAM *Ka-dáš-man-Túr-gu* | |
| | LUGAL.E | |

COMMENTARY

The checkmarks are placed on the personal determinatives.

1–3. "Barley, (measured by) the *sūtu* of 5 *qû*, that was disbursed from the delivery of Ṭab-šār-Adad."

4. "Workers who were sent to the Nār-ḫaḫḫi." The canal Nār-ḫaḫḫi is attested here for the first time; *ḫaḫḫu* is a type of tree, perhaps the plum tree (CAD Ḫ, *ḫaḫḫu* B, 29; AHw I, *ḫaḫḫu*, 308); for a similar canal name, cf. Nār-bīni "Tamarisk-canal" (RGTC 5, 309).

12. Although there is no checkmark in this entry, the quantity given to this individual is included in the subtotal of l. 15.

22′. "In total 108 *sūtu* (for) 6 workmen." The quantity associated with Ninurta-kiššat-ilāni (l. 21′) is not included in this sum, nor in the grand total of l. 23′.

## 95. CUNES 52-10-116 (Plate No. 31)

-.-.6 Kadašman-Turgu

Summary of rations disbursed in Dūr-Ištar during the 6th year of Kadašman-Turgu.

Sex-age designations are used in this text only for individuals who do not belong to the category "(adult) man" or the category "(adult) woman"—i.e., only for those who are identified as GURUŠ.TUR "male adolescent," GURUŠ.TUR.TUR "male child," MUNUS.TUR.TUR "female child," DUMU.GABA "male infant," and DUMU.MUNUS.GABA "female infant." Family relations among some of the individuals are indicated as well.

The amounts in col. i largely correspond to the monthly rations attested for servile laborers in Nippur (cf. Del Monte 1988; Paulus 2014a). Comparison of the amounts in col. i with those in col. ii shows that col. ii summarized the rations disbursed over a span of eight months; this allows the restoration of the missing column headings in the first two columns. Col. iii recorded the sum of the rations allocated to some workers over a span of twelve months. As far as one can tell from the preserved text, the entries in col ii and col. iii are mutually exclusive—i.e., workers received rations for either eight or twelve months.

Cf. PBS 2/2 53 for a Nippur text recording rations and indicating the amount for one month and the sum for eight months.

| | | | | |
|---|---|---|---|---|
| U.e. | [ŠE.BA $^{giš}$BÁN] ⸢5⸣ SÌLA BÀD-$^{d}$INANNA MU.⸢6⸣.KAM *Ka-dáš-man-Túr-[gu* | | | |
| Obv. | [ŠE.BA 1 ITI] | [ŠE.BA 8 ITI] | [ŠE].⸢BA⸣ [1]⸢2 ITI⸣ | ⸢MU.BI.IM⸣ |
| | [ ] | [ ] | ⸢16+⸣.0.0 | $^{m}$*Tak-[l]a-k[u* |
| | [ ] | [ ] | ⸢4+⸣.0.0 | $^{md+}$*En-líl*-ŠEŠ-SUM-*na* DUMU [ |
| | [ ] | [ ] | ⸢6+⸣.0.0 | $^{f}$*A-am-tu*$_4$ DUMU.MUNUS $^{md}$*Nin*?-*u[rta*?- |
| | [ ] | [ ] | 3.1.0 | $^{f}$*Ša-ma-ša-li-tu*$_4$ |
| | [0.0.5] | ⸢1⸣.1.4 | | $^{f}$*Ri-im-tu*$_4$ DUMU.MUNUS $^{m}$*Ab-bu-ú-ṭa-bu* |
| | 0.0.5 | 1.1.4 | | $^{fd}$*Iš-tar-i-da-a-a-al-ki* DUMU.MUNUS *Baq-ni-t[i]* |
| | | | | $^{md}$⸢UTU⸣-DI.KU$_5$ DUMU.A.NI |
| | 0.0.5 | 1.1.4 | | $^{⸢f⸣}$[x-x-x]-⸢x⸣ [x x] ⸢x⸣ |
| | 0.0.5 | 1.1.4 | | $^{f}$*Mi-na-a-e*-⸢*gu*?⸣-[ |
| | | | | ZÁḪ $^{f}$*I-na*-É.KUR-⸢*dan*?⸣-[ |
| | 0.0.5 | 1.1.4 | | $^{f}$GAŠAN-*te-re-m[an*?-*ni*? |
| | 0.0.3 | 0.4.0 | | GURUŠ.TUR $^{md+}$*En-líl-m[u*?- |
| | | | | GURUŠ.TUR $^{m}$DINGIR-⸢ŠEŠ⸣-[ |
| | 0.0.3 | 0.4.0 | | GURUŠ.TUR $^{md+}$*En-líl*-[ |
| | [ ] | ⸢0.4.0⸣ | | DUMU.GABA $^{m}$*Šu-zi-ib-a[n-ni*-$^{d}$ |
| | 0.0.1 | 0.1.2 | | ⸢DUMU.GABA $^{m}$x-$^{d}$x⸣-[ |
| | 0.0.1 | 0.1.2 | | DUMU.MUNUS.GABA ⸢*A-na*⸣-$^{d}$*Namma-tak-la-k[u]* |
| | [ ] | [ ] | | $^{⸢f}$*I-na*⸣-KUR-*ša-[al*?]-⸢*si*?⸣-[*iš*? |
| | [ ] | [ ] | | $^{fd⸢}$x⸣-[x]-*a*?-*bíl-ti* ⸢ta? x⸣ [ |
| | [ ] | | | [$^{⸢f}$x-x]-*su-nu* NIN $^{md+}$*En-líl*-[x]-⸢x-x⸣ |
| | | | | [$^{m}$x]-$^{d}$UTU ⸢DUMU.A.NI KASKAL⸣ |
| | 0.0.2 | 2.0.4 | | $^{m}$*Gi-mil-lu*$_4$ ⸢ŠEŠ?⸣.A.NI UŠ.BAR |
| | 0.0.4 | 1.0.2 | | GURUŠ.TUR $^{m}$*Iz-kùr*-$^{d}$UTU ⸢DUMU⸣.A.NI UŠ.BAR |
| | 0.0.3 | 0.4.0 | | ⸢GURUŠ.TUR $^{m}$*Ki-din*⸣-$^{d}$*La-ta*-⸢*ra*⸣-*ak* DUMU.A.NI |
| | 0.0.5 | 1.1.4 | | $^{f}$*Tu-ša*-TI.L[A x x] ⸢DUMU.MUNUS.A.NI⸣ |
| | | | | $^{⸢f}$*Di*?-x-x⸣ [x x x] DUMU.MUNUS.A.NI |
| | 0.0.2 | 0.⸢2⸣.4 | | GURUŠ.TUR.TUR $^{m}$*Ša-m[uḫ*?]-⸢$^{d}$*Nin-urta*⸣ DUMU.A.NI |
| | [ ] | [x].⸢2⸣.4 | | $^{f}$*Ba-ḫu-tu*$_4$ É.GI$_4$.A |
| | [ ] | [x.x].⸢2⸣ | | $^{f}$*I-na-ni-ip-ḫi-ša-al-si-iš* DUMU.MUNUS.A.NI |
| | [ ] | [ ] | | $^{f}$*Daq-qá-tu*$_4$ NIN $^{md}$IŠKUR-DINGIR-*i-na*-KUR |
| | [0.0.5] | [1.1].⸢4⸣ | | $^{f}$GAL-*šá*-$^{d}$*Še-em-me*-⸢*i-u*⸣ DUMU.⸢MUNUS.A⸣.NI |

| | | | | |
|---|---|---|---|---|
| | [ ] | [ ] | | GURUŠ.TUR.TUR $^{md}$*Nin-urta*-DÙ DUMU[ |
| | [ ] | [ ] | | DUMU.GABA *It-ti-ša*-⸢*ah-bu-ut*⸣ [ |
| Text breaks off | | | | |
| Rev. | [ ] | [ ] | [ ] | [ |
| | [ ] | | 1.0.0 | ⸢x⸣[ |
| | [ ] | ⸢x.x.x⸣ | | GURUŠ.⸢TUR⸣ $^{md+}$*En-líl*-⸢x⸣[ |
| | [ ] | 0.0.4 | | GURUŠ.TUR.TUR $^{m}$*I-ma-a'-da* ⸢x⸣ [ |
| | 0.0.5 | | 2.0.0 | MUNUS.TUR *Ba-ni-tu*$_4$ ⸢NIN$^?$.A.NI⸣ |
| | 0.0.5 | | 2.0.0 | $^{m}$*Ba-hu-ú* ⸢*a*⸣-*pil* KÁ |
| | 0.1.0 | 1.3.0 | | $^{m}$*Ar-du* ⸢KI.MIN⸣ |
| | 0.0.3 | | 1.1.0 | MUNUS.TUR.TUR ⸢*Lu*⸣-*da-an-né-me-di* |
| | 0.0.5 | | 2.0.0 | MUNUS É $^{d}$SUKKAL$^?$ DUMU.MUNUS $^{m}$*Ba-ti-ia-ú-ti* |
| | | | | ZÁH GURUŠ.TUR $^{m}$*Bu-un-na*-$^{d}$*Gu-la ša* DUMU.MUNUS $^{m}$*Ì*$^?$-*din*-$^{d}$AMAR.UTU |
| | [ ] | | | MUNUS.TUR *Lul-ta-mar-zi-kir-ša* |
| | [ ] | [ ] | | ⸢$^{md}$*Nin-urta*⸣-EN-*uṣ-ri* $^{m}$ÌR-$^{d}$AMAR.UTU |
| | [ ] | [ ] | [ ] | [ŠU].NIGIN 95.1$^{pi}$.0 ŠE.BA $^{m}$*Tak-la-ku* |
| | [ ] | [ ] | | [$^{f}$*I*]-*na*-É.GA[L.MAH]-*šar-rat* DUMU.⸢MUNUS$^?$ x⸣ da ⸢x x⸣ |
| | ⸢0.1.0⸣ | [ ] | | ⸢GURUŠ$^?$.TUR⸣ $^{m}$*Ṣíl-li*-$^{d}$IGI.DU |
| | 0.1.0 | 1.[x.x] | | $^{m}$*Ki-di-ia* *e-la-mu-ú* |
| | 0.0.5 | 1.1.⸢4$^?$⸣ | | $^{m}$*Eri-ba*-$^{d}$UTU KI.MIN |
| | 0.0.5 | 1.1.4 | | $^{f}$*Ši-me-e-su-up-pa*-⸢*a-a*⸣ *lul-lu-bi-tu*$_4$ |
| | 0.0.3 | 0.4$^{pi}$.0 | | GURUŠ.TUR.TUR $^{m}$*Ri-iš*-⸢*Á*⸣-*ki-tu*$_4$ DUMU.A.NI |
| PAP | | 8.0.0 | | ⸢6⸣ *a-mi-lu-tu*$_4$ É $^{md}$*Nin-urta-ib-ni* ŠU $^{m}$*Tak-la-ku* |
| ŠU.NIGIN | | 36./3.[0] | 1-*šu* 6./3$^{pi}$.0 | ŠU.NIGIN 1 ME 3.1$^{pi}$.0 ŠE.BA $^{giš}$BÁN 5 SÌLA |

COMMENTARY

1. "[Rations, (measured by) the *sūtu*] of 5 *qû*; Dūr-Ištar; year 6 of Kadašman-Tur[gu]."

8. This reading is preferable to DUMU $^{f}$*Baq-ni-ti* because Ištar-idāya-alkī is a feminine name and one expects her to be identified as the "daughter" rather than the "son" of Baqnītu.

12. The PN may have been Ina-Ekur-dannat (for attestations, see Sassmannshausen 2001, 478). The persons listed here and in l. 45′ are identified as "escapee" (ZÁH) and therefore did not receive any rations; on the phenomenon of flight among servile laborers, see Tenney 2011, 104–21.

22. The first PN may have been Bēlessunu.

23. KASKAL at the end of the line may have indicated that this man was either "(on the) road"—i.e., traveling (Tenney 2011, 62–63)—or on a military campaign (Paulus 2014a, 223–24). Because he was absent, no ration was allocated to him.

30. On the status of *kallātu* (É.GI$_4$.A), see Tenney 2011, 74–75, who regards these women as "unrelated females brought into the household upon the agreement that they will wed the head or one of the other males in the household."

33. To my knowledge, the only previously known PN containing the theophoric element Šēmû is Ana-Šēmî-atkal (Hölscher 1996, 271; Krebernik 2009).

46′. Cf. $^{f}$*Lu-ul-ta-mar-zi-kir-ša* in CBS 12635, quoted by Clay 1912b, 103.

55′. The six servile laborers (*amīlūtu*) of the House of Ninurta-ibni are the persons listed in ll. 49′–54′. On the term *amīlūtu* applied to servile personnel, see Sassmannshausen 2001, 117–19; Tenney 2011, 129–32.

## 96. CUNES 52-13-110 (Plate No. 32)

-.-.9 Kadašman-Turgu

This summary of rations disbursed to female millers is noteworthy because it mentions the "son of Enlil-alsa" (ll. 1, 11): the latter may have been the homonymous *šandabakku*, who governed Nippur during the reigns of Kurigalzu II and Nazi-Maruttaš (see Redina-Thomas 2015, 97–98).

Col. i indicates the monthly amount ("rations for one month"), while col. ii gives the total disbursed over one year ("rations for the year").

Some of the same women appear as recipients of barley also in CUSAS 30 311 (Ina-Isin-bā'ilat, Ērišti-Adad, Baba-šarrat, Ina-Sagila-bāltī, and Ina-Sagila-kabtat); this text, which is dated to year 3 without a royal name, should probably be assigned to the reign of Kadašman-Turgu.

U.e. ŠE.BA $^{giš}$BÁN 10 SÌLA *i-na* ŠÀ ŠE.BAR *ša* DUMU $^{md+}$*En-líl*-AL.SA$_6$ *i-na* K[A-ÍD.DA$^?$]
MU.9.KAM $^{d}$*Ka-dáš-man-Túr-gu i-na* NIBRU$^{k}$[$^{i}$]

| | | | | | |
|---|---|---|---|---|---|
| Obv. | ŠE.BA 1 ITI | ŠE.BA MU.AN.NA | | MU.BI.IM | |
| | 0.1$^{pi}$.0 | 2.2.0 | √ | $^{f}$*I-na-Ì-si-in-ba-'i-lat* | DUMU.MUNUS $^{m⌈}$x-x⌉-[ |
| 5 | 0.1$^{pi}$.0 | ⌈2⌉.[2.0] | √ | $^{⌈f⌉}$*E-riš-ti*-$^{d}$IŠKUR | DUMU.MUNUS $^{m}$*Ku-ub-bu-ti* |
| | 0.1$^{pi}$.0 | ⌈2⌉.[2.0] | √ | $^{⌈fd}$*Ba-ba*$_6$*-šar-rat*⌉ | DUMU.MUNUS $^{m}$[ |
| | [ ] | [ ] | √ | $^{⌈f}$GAŠAN⌉-*iri*-[*š*]*a* | DUMU.MUNUS $^{m}$*Pa-ḫa-ri* |
| | 0.0.2 ⌈5$^?$⌉ | [ ] | √ | $^{⌈f}$*Ì$^?$-na$^?$*⌉-SAG.ÍLA-*ba*[*l-t*]*i* | DUMU.MUNUS $^{m}$*Ik-ka-ri* |
| 9 | 0.0.3 5 | 1.2.0 | √ | $^{f}$*Šar-ra-tu*$_4$ | DUMU.MUNUS $^{m}$*Qa-diš-ti* |
| Rev. | 0.0.4 | 1.3.0 | √ | $^{f⌈}$*I-na*⌉-SAG.ÍLA-DUGUD-*at* | DUMU.MUNUS $^{f}$*Ḫu-un-bi-⌈i-na*-UNUG$^?$⌉[$^{ki}$] |
| ⌈PAP⌉ | | 14.0.0 | | ŠE.BA 7 MUNUS.⌈ÀR$^{meš}$ MU.9.KAM⌉ $^{d}$*Ka-daš-man-Túr-gu* <br> *i-na* ŠU DUMU $^{m⌈d+}$*En-líl*-AL⌉.SA$_6$ <br> ⌈*i-na* KA⌉-ÍD.DA $^{m⌉}$ÌR-$^{d}$AMAR.UTU <br> *im-ḫur-ma i-na-di-in* | |

COMMENTARY

1–2. "Rations, (measured by) the *sūtu* of 10 *qû*, from the barley of the son of Enlil-alsa in P[ī-nāri$^?$]. Year 9 of Kadašman-Turgu, in Nippur."

8. Even though the traces and the space do not fully support a reading $^{⌈f}$*Ì$^?$-na$^?$*⌉ at the beginning of the PN, Ina-Sagila-bāltī seems the most likely solution.

11. "Total: 420 *sūtu*. Rations for seven *ararratu*-millers, year 9 of Kadašman-Turgu. Arad-Marduk received in Pī-nāri from the son of Enlil-alsa and will disburse (it)."

## 97. CUNES 52-12-016 (Plate No. 33)

-.-.9 Kadašman-Turgu

The content of this text is duplicated in **no. 98** and CUSAS 30 231, but these tablets include further entries, which suggests that they represent later stages in the bookkeeping process necessary to keep track of the amounts of barley and emmer received by Iqīša-Adad as rations for the *bābānu* during the 9$^{th}$ year of Kadašman-Turgu.

On the *bābānu*, see Introduction §4.3.

Obv. ŠE $^{giš}$BÁN 10 SÌLA *ša a-na* ŠE.BA KÁ-*a-nu i-na* MU.9.KAM *Ka-dáš-man-Túr-gu* LUGAL.E
$^{m}$BA-*šá*-$^{d}$IŠKUR DUMU $^{m}$*Ḫa-am-bu mi-taḫ-ḫu-rù*

| | ŠE | ZÍZ.AN.NA | MU.BI.IM |
|---|---|---|---|
| | 27.4.0 | | *i-na* ŠÀ NÍG.KUD.DA *ša* AN.ZA.GÀR$^{ki}$ TA *i-du šu-la-a* |
| | 18.1.4 5 | | *i-*[*na* Š]À *maš-ši-ti-šu* $^{uru}$*Si-ki-la* |
| | 4.0.0 | | *i-na* [ŠÀ KI.MI]N *ša* $^{m}$*Ṭà-ab*-IM-$^{d}$IŠKUR KI.MIN<br>ŠUKU G[U$_4$.NIGA] $^{m}$ÌR-AMAR.UTU |
| | 7.0.0 | | *i-na* ŠÀ KI.MIN [*ša* $^{m}$Ì]R-$^{d}$AMAR.UTU AN.AN.MAR.TU$^{ki}$<br>EN 3.1.4 ŠE.[BA] ⸢GÉME$^{?meš}$⸣ *ša* DUMU ⸢$^{md}$IŠKUR-ÙRU⸣ |
| | 1.0.0 | | *i-na Tukul-ti*-É.KUR$^{ki}$ ŠE.BA KI.MIN [<br>$^{m}$BA-*šá*-$^{d}$AM[AR].UTU DUMU $^{m}$*Kun$_8$-zu-b*[*i*] |
| | 35.2.4<br>5 SÌLA | | URU-*ir-re-e*$^{ki}$ $^{iti}$NE.N[E.GAR] |
| | 1 ME 6.2.2 | 35./1.1 | AN.ZA.GÀR$^{ki}$ $^{iti}$KIN.⸢$^{d}$⸣I[NANNA] |
| Rev. | ⸢23$^{?}$⸣.1$^{pi}$.0 | | KI.MIN *i-na* ŠÀ ŠE *ša* $^{m}$*Ri-mu-tu$_4$* |
| | 75.0.0 | | *Tukul-ti*-É.KUR$^{ki}$ EN 5.0.0 $^{md}$UTU-ŠEŠ-x[<br>$^{iti}$KIN.$^{d}$INANNA |
| | 1 ME 50.1.1 | | URU-*at-ḫe-e* $^{iti}$DU$_6$.KÙ |
| | 1.0.0 | | URU-*ir-re-e*$^{ki}$ *a-na* ŠE.BA ÉRIN$^{ḫi.a}$ *š*[*a*<br>*iḫ-ru-ú* $^{m}$BA-*šá*-$^{d}$*Nin-urta* DUMU $^{m}$[ |
| | 2.3.4 5 | | *Tukul-ti*-É.⸢KUR$^{ki}$⸣ [*a-na*] ŠE.BA ⸢KI.MIN *š*⸣*a* ⸢x⸣ [ |
| | 10.2.1 5 | | KI.MIN ŠE.BA ⸢*a-mi-lu-ti*⸣ *ša š*[*u-lu*]-⸢*ti* $^{iti}$⸣[ |
| | 7.2.3 | | KI.MIN ŠE.BA 15 ⸢ÉRIN⸣[$^{ḫi}$]$^{.a}$ *ša i-na* URU-ÌR-GAŠAN$^{ki}$<br>*dul-la i-pu-*[*šu*] $^{iti}$GAN |
| | 1.1.1 5 SÌLA | | KI.MIN ŠUKU É $^{d}$⸢*Nin*⸣*-nisi* TA U$_4$.10.KAM *ša* $^{iti}$APIN.DU$_8$.A<br>EN U$_4$.10.KAM ⸢*ša*⸣ $^{iti}$BÁR.ZAG.GAR *ša* MU.10.KAM |
| | 3.0.0 | | KI.MIN *ri-mu-ut* 3 UŠ.BAR$^{meš}$ $^{iti}$GAN |
| | 43.1.4 | | URU-DUMU-*Ba-ʾi-li i-na* ŠÀ *ša* $^{md}$*Nuska*-ÙRU *ḫa-za-nu* $^{iti}$ZÍZ.A.AN<br>TA 6.3.2 GAL $^{giš}$BÁN <10 SÌLA> *i-na* 1.0.0 0.0.4 *šu-lu-ú* |
| PAP | 5 ME 3/7.4.2 5 | 35./1.1 | ŠU.NIGIN 5 ME 55.2.3 $^{giš}$BÁN 10 SÌLA<br>ŠE.BA KÁ-*a-nu* $^{m}$BA-*šá*-$^{d}$IŠKUR |

Translation

Obv. Grain, (measured by) the *sūtu* of 10 *qû*, which Iqīša-Adad, son of Ḫambu, has been receiving as rations of the *bābānu* in year 9 of King Kadašman-Turgu.

| | Barley | Emmer | Its entry |
|---|---|---|---|
| | 834 *sūtu* | | From the *miksu* of Dimtu, after the wages have been deducted. |
| | 550 *sūtu*, 5 *qû* | | Fr[om] his delivery; Sikila. |
| | 120 *sūtu* | | Fr[om ditt]o (i.e., the delivery) of Ṭāb-šār-Adad; ditto (i.e., Sikila[?]); (as) fodder for a [fattened] ox (of) Arad-Marduk. |
| | 210 *sūtu* | | From ditto (i.e., the delivery) [of Ar]ad-Marduk; AN.AN.MAR.TU[ki]; together with 100 *sūtu* (as) rat[ions] for the female servants[?] of the son of Adad-nāṣir. |
| | 30 *sūtu* | | In Tukultī-Ekur, rations, ditto [ . . . ]; Iqīša-M[ar]duk, son of Kunzubu. |
| | 1,066 *sūtu*, 5 *qû* | | Āl-irrē, month V. |
| | 3,194 *sūtu* | 1,057 *sūtu* | Dimtu, month VI. |
| Rev. | 696[?] *sūtu* | | Ditto (i.e., Dimtu), from the barley of Rīmūtu. |
| | 2,250 *sūtu* | | Tukultī-Ekur together with 150 *sūtu* of Šamaš-aḫa-[ . . . ]; month VI. |
| | 4,507 *sūtu* | | Āl-atḫē, month VII. |
| | 30 *sūtu* | | Āl-irrē, rations of the workmen w[ho] dug [ . . . ]; Iqīša-Ninurta, son of [ . . . ]. |
| | 82 *sūtu*, 5 *qû* | | Tukultī-Ekur, rations of ditto (i.e., workmen) who x[ . . . ]. |
| | 313 *sūtu*, 5 *qû* | | Ditto (i.e., Tukultī-Ekur), rations of the personnel who have been summoned; month [ . . . ]. |
| | 225 *sūtu* | | Ditto (i.e., Tukultī-Ekur), rations of 15 workmen who carried out the *dullu*-service in Āl-Arad-Bēlti; month IX. |
| | 37 *sūtu*, 5 *qû* | | Ditto (i.e., Tukultī-Ekur), supplies for the temple of Ninnisi from day 10 of month VIII till day 10 of month I of year 10. |
| | 90 *sūtu* | | Ditto (i.e., Tukultī-Ekur), gift for 3 weavers; month IX. |
| | 1,300 *sūtu* | | Āl-Mār-Bā'ili from that of Nuska-nāṣir, *ḫazannu*, month XI, after 200 *sūtu* have been deducted, the increase of the *sūtu* <of 10 *qû*> being at a rate of 4 *sūtu* per kor. |
| Total | 16,136 *sūtu*, 5 *qû* | 1,057 *sūtu* | Grand total: 16,665 *sūtu*, (measured by) the *sūtu* of 10 *qû*, rations of the *bābānu*, Iqīša-Adad. |

Commentary

1–2. Iqīša-Adad is in charge of the rations of the *bābānu* also in **no. 138**: 8.

6. It is not clear what the second KI.MIN in this line refers to; it is absent in the parallel passages of **no. 98**: 6 and CUSAS 30 231: 6.

7. This Arad-Marduk must correspond to the homonymous person identified as an overseer (*šaknu*) and associated with the delivery (*maššītu*) of AN.AN.MAR.TU[ki] in **no. 69**. On the GN, see comments on no. 69: 4.

8. The corresponding line in CUSAS 30 231: 8 has a different amount. It is not clear what KI.MIN refers to.

13–14. These two entries, here kept separate, are accounted for together in **no. 98**: 13 and CUSAS 30 231: 13–15.

20. The emendation [giš]BÁN <10 SÌLA> is suggested by the parallels in **no. 98**: 18 and CUSAS 30 231: 21.

## 98. CUNES 52-19-146 (Plate No. 34)

-.-.9 Kadašman-Turgu

This text is complementary to **no. 97** and CUSAS 30 231. See comments to no. 97.

Obv. [Š]E $^{giš}$BÁN 10 SÌLA *ša a-n*[*a* Š]E.BA KÁ-*a-nu* $^{m}$BA-*šá*-$^{d}$[IŠKUR]
MU.9.KAM *Ka-dáš-man-Túr-gu* LUGAL [

| | ŠE | ZÍZ.AN.NA | MU.BI.⸢IM⸣ |
|---|---|---|---|
| | 27.4.0 | | *i-na* ŠÀ NÍG.KUD.DA *ša* AN.ZA.GÀR$^{ki}$ TA 2 GUR *i-du šu-la-a* |
| | 18.1.4 5 | | *i-na* ŠÀ *maš-ši-ti-šu i-na* $^{uru}$*Si-ki-la* |
| | ⸢4⸣.0.0 | | *i-na* ŠÀ KI.MIN *ša* $^{m}$*Ṭà-ab*-IM-$^{d}$IŠKUR ŠUKU GU$_4$.NIGA $^{m}$ÌR-$^{d}$AMAR.UTU *im-ḫur* |
| | [ ] | | *i-na* ŠÀ KI.MIN *ša* $^{m}$ÌR-$^{d}$AMAR.UTU EN 3.1.4 ŠE.B[A ... DUMU $^{md}$I]ŠKUR-ÙRU |
| | [ ] | [ ] | ⸢*Tukul-ti*-É.KUR$^{ki}$⸣ EN 1.0.0 KI.MIN |
| | [ ] | [ ] | URU-*ir-re-e* ⸢$^{iti}$NE.NE.GAR⸣ |
| | [ ] | [ ] | ⸢AN⸣.ZA.GAR$^{ki}$ $^{iti}$KIN.⸢$^{d}$⸣I[NANNA] |
| | ⸢40$^{+}$⸣.[x.x] | [ ] | KI.MIN *i-na* ⸢ŠÀ⸣ ŠE *ša* $^{m}$*Ri-mu-ti* $^{iti}$KIN |
| | 1 ME [50.1].1 | [ ] | ⸢URU-*at*⸣-*ḫe-e*$^{⸢ki⸣}$ $^{iti}$DU$_6$.KÙ |
| | ⸢3$^{?}$.3.4 5⸣ | [ ] | ⸢*Tukul-ti*⸣-É.KUR$^{ki}$ ⸢EN 1.0.0⸣ URU-*ir-re-e* |
| L.e. | | | *a-na* ŠE.BA ÉRIN$^{ḫi.a}$ *š*[*a*] ⸢ÍD-*Tukul-ti*-É.KUR$^{ki}$⸣ *iḫ-ru-ú n*[*a*]-*ad-nu* $^{iti}$⸢APIN$^{?}$⸣ |
| Rev. | [ ] | | KI.MIN ŠE.BA *a-mi-lu-ti ša šu-lu-ti* $^{iti}$[GAN] |
| | ⸢7⸣.2.3 | | KI.MIN ŠE.BA 15 ÉRIN$^{ḫi.a}$ ⸢*ša dul-la*⸣ *i-na* URU-ÌR-[GAŠAN$^{ki}$] ⸢*i-pu-šu*⸣ |
| | 1.1.1 5 | | KI.MIN TA U$_4$.10.KAM *ša* $^{iti}$APIN.DU$_8$.A ⸢EN⸣ [U$_4$.10].KAM *ša* $^{iti}$BÁR.ZAG.GAR ⸢É $^{d}$⸣[*Nin-nisi*] |
| | 3.0.0 | | KI.MIN *ri-mu-ut* ⸢3 UŠ.BAR⸣[$^{meš}$ $^{iti}$GAN] |
| | ⸢43.1.4⸣ | | ⸢URU-DUMU-*Ba*⸣-*'i-li i-na* ŠÀ ⸢ŠE *ša* $^{m}$⸣[$^{d}$*Nuska*-ÙRU *ḫa-z*]*a-nu* TA 6.3.2 GAL $^{giš}$BÁN 10 SÌLA ⸢*i-na* 1⸣.[0.0 0.0.4 *šu-lu-ú*] |
| | ⸢8$^{+}$⸣.4.5 | | URU-DUMU-*Ka-a-ri i-na* ŠÀ ŠE *ša* DUMU ⸢x⸣ [ |

Translation

Obv. [Gr]ain, (measured by) the *sūtu* of 10 *qû*, which Iqīša-Adad [disbursed$^{?}$] as rations of the *bābānu*; year 9 of King Kadašman-Turgu.

| | Barley | Emmer | Its entry |
|---|---|---|---|
| | 834 *sūtu* | | From the *miksu* of Dimtu, after 60 *sūtu* of wages have been deducted. |
| | 550 *sūtu*, 5 *qû* | | From his delivery in Sikila. |
| | 120 *sūtu* | | From ditto (i.e., the delivery) of Ṭāb-šār-Adad: Arad-Marduk received (as) fodder for a fattened ox. |
| | [ ] | | From ditto (i.e., the delivery) of Arad-Marduk, together with 100 *sūtu* (as) ratio[ns for the female servants$^{?}$ of the son of A]dad-nāṣir. |
| | [ ] | [ ] | Tukultī-Ekur, together with 30 *sūtu*, ditto. |
| | [ ] | [ ] | Āl-irrē; month V. |
| | [ ] | [ ] | Dimtu; month VI. |
| | ⌜1,200$^{+}$⌝ *sūtu* | [ ] | Ditto (i.e., Dimtu), from the barley of Rīmūtu; month VI. |
| | 4,507 *sūtu* | [ ] | Āl-atḫē; month VII. |
| L.e. | ⌜40$^{+}$⌝ *sūtu*, 5 *qû* | [ ] | Tukultī-Ekur; given together with 30 *sūtu* (of/in) Āl-irrē as rations of the workmen w[ho] dug the (canal) Nār-Tukultī-Ekur; month ⌜VIII$^{?}$⌝. |
| Rev. | [ ] | | Ditto (i.e., Tukultī-Ekur), rations of the personnel who have been summoned; month [IX]. |
| | 225 *sūtu* | | Ditto (i.e., Tukultī-Ekur), rations of 15 workmen who carried out the *dullu*-service in Āl-Arad-[Bēlti]. |
| | 37 *sūtu*, 5 *qû* | | Ditto (i.e., Tukultī-Ekur); from day 10 of month VIII till 10 day of month I, temple of [Ninnisi]. |
| | 90 *sūtu* | | Ditto (i.e., Tukultī-Ekur); gift for 3 weavers; [month IX]. |
| | 1,300 *sūtu* | | Āl-Mār-Bā'ili; from the barley of [Nuska-nāṣir, *ḫazan*]*nu*, after 200 *sūtu* have been [deducted], the increase of the *sūtu* of 10 *qû* being at a rate of [4 *sūtu*] per kor. |
| | ⌜269$^{+}$⌝ *sūtu* | | Āl-Mār-Kāri; from the barley of the son of ⌜. . .⌝[ |

Commentary

1–2. The relative pronoun *ša* suggests that there was a verbal form at the end of the heading, but there does not seem to be enough space for *mitaḫḫuru*, which is what one would expect based on the parallel text **no. 97**. Iqīša-Adad is in charge of the rations of the *bābānu* also in **no. 138**: 8.

4. The 3 pl. fem. stative *šūlâ* must refer to *idu*; for the rare use of *idu* as fem. pl., see AHw I, *idu* 9a, 365.

7. The restoration is based on **no. 97**: 7.

12. The Nār-Tukultī-Ekur was in the area of Nippur, as suggested by the several attestations in the Nippur texts and especially on the topographical map published by Clay 1905.

15. The spelling *i-pu-šu* here and in **no. 97**: 17 suggests that this verbal form should be understood as a 3 pl. preterite (*īpušū*), while CUSAS 30 231: 17 has *ip-pu-šu*$_{14}$, a 3 pl. durative (*ippušū*). Collation of CUSAS 30 231: 17 shows that van Soldt's reading ŠE.BA ŠUKU ÉRIN$^{meš}$ can be corrected to ŠE.BA 15 ÉRIN$^{meš}$.

15–18. These lines are restored after **no. 97**: 17–19.

## 99. CUNES 52-15-030

-.IX–X.9 Kadašman-Turgu

This text gives a detailed account of the rations assigned to 15 workers in Tukultī-Ekur over a span of two months during the 9th year of Kadašman-Turgu (ll. 19ff.); the workers are divided into two groups, each of which is assigned to a supervisor (see l. 12 and l. 18).

This allocation is recorded also in three summaries of rations given to the *bābānu* during the 9th year of Kadašman-Turgu, which include "225 *sūtu* (of barley): ditto (i.e., Tukultī-Ekur), rations of 15 workmen who carried out the *dullu*-service in Āl-Arad-Bēlti; month IX" (**no. 97**: 17, **no. 98**: 15, and CUSAS 30 231: 13). Combining the information provided by all texts, the following conclusions may be drawn:

- the workers were organized into two squads of 10 and 5 men each;
- each squad had a different supervisor;
- the workmen received rations while they carried out the *dullu*-service in Āl-Arad-Bēlti (the nature of the *dullu*-service is not further specified);
- the monthly ration amounted to 75 *qû* per person (measured by the *sūtu* of 10 *qû*);
- the disbursement took place in Tukultī-Ekur;
- they were regarded as personnel of the *bābānu*.

| | | |
|---|---|---|
| Obv. | ŠE.BA $^{giš}$BÁN 10 SÌLA MU.BI.⸢IM⸣ | |
| | 0.2.3 | $^{m}$GAL-*šá*-$^{d}$*Gu-la* |
| | 0.2.3 | $^{m}$*Bur-ru-qu* |
| | 0.2.3 | $^{m}$*Ki-din*-$^{d}$*Gu-la* |
| | 0.2.3 | $^{m}$*Nu-ur-za-nu* |
| | 0.2.3 | $^{m}$*Ri-ḫe-tu-ša* |
| | 0.2.3 | $^{md}$IŠKUR-*šub-ši* |
| | 0.2.3 | $^{m}$*Zi-ik-ri*-$^{d}$IŠKUR |
| | 0.2.3 | $^{m}$*Sa-mi-du* |
| | 0.2.3 | $^{m}$*Tukul-ti*-$^{d+}$*En-líl* |
| | 0.2.3 | $^{md}$IŠKUR-⸢*za*?⸣-*k*[*i*?-*ir*?] |
| | PAP 5.0.0 | 10 ŠU [ |
| Rev. | 0.2.3 | $^{m}$*Ta-r*[*i*?-*bu*?] |
| | 0.2.3 | $^{m}$*Bi-l*[*i-ia*] |
| | 0.2.3 | $^{md}$U.GUR-*mu-š*[*al*?-*lim*?] |
| | 0.2.3 | $^{m}$*Il-lu-ul*-[*lu*$_{4}$] |
| | 0.2.3 | $^{m}$*Re-eš*-È-*šu* ⸢$^{lú?}$ x a x⸣ |
| | PAP 2.⸢2⸣.3 | 5 ŠU $^{m}$*Bur*-$^{d}$30 |
| | ŠU.NIGIN 7.2.3 15 ÉRIN$^{meš}$ | |
| | | $^{iti}$GAN.GAN.È |
| | | *ù* $^{iti}$AB.È |
| | | MU.9.KAM |
| | | $^{d}$*Ka-dáš-man-Túr-gu* |
| | | ⸢*i-na*⸣ *Tukul-ti*-⸢É⸣.[KUR$^{ki}$] |
| L.e. | | *ma-ḫi-ir* |

COMMENTARY

19–25. "Grand total: 225 *sūtu* (for) 15 workmen, month IX and X, year 9 of Kadašman-Turgu; received in Tukultī-E[kur]."

## 100. CUNES 52-18-812

21.VIII.12 Kadašman-Turgu

Small amounts of barley for a group of women who appear as recipients of rations in **no. 101** (see comments there).

Obv. ⸢x x x ŠE⸣ [$^{giš}$]BÁN 5 SÌLA
0.0.1 $^{f}$⸢*Ki*⸣-[*di*]-*ni-tu*$_4$
0.0.1 $^{f}$⸢*Ri-ša-tu*$_4$⸣
0.0.1 $^{f}$⸢*Bu*⸣-*un-na*-$^{d}$*Gu-la*
0.0.1 $^{f}$*Ni-ip-pu*-⸢*ri-tu*$_4$⸣
3 SÌLA $^{f}$*A-ta-mar*-ŠU-*sa*
3 SÌLA $^{f}$*Ma-lu-uk-tu*$_4$
3 SÌLA $^{f}$*D*[*a*]-⸢*a*⸣-*a-an-du*
3 SÌLA $^{fd}$*Ba-ba*$_6$-*šar-rat*
[PAP 0].⸢1⸣$^{pi}$.0 $^{giš}$⸢BÁN⸣ 5 SÌLA
Rev. $^{iti}$APIN.DU$_8$.A
U$_4$.21.KAM
MU.12.KAM
*Ka-dáš-man-Túr-gu*
LUGAL.E

COMMENTARY

10. 2 *qû* are missing from the written total.

## 101. CUNES 52-19-005

-.[ . . . ].15 Kadašman-Turgu

Several of the persons listed in this text were involved in textile production: besides the three men qualified here as a *kāṣiru* "knotter" (Mandidaya, Rīš-Marduk, and Eulmaš-iqīša), Dayyandu appears among some recipients of wool in **no. 267**, Bunna-Gula and Ekūtu may be identified with the homonymous women who produced some garments according to **no. 287** and **no. 289**, and Arad-U$_4$.9.KAM may be the same person identified as a weaver (UŠ.BAR) in **no. 271**.

Obv. [ŠE$^?$.B]A$^?$ $^{giš}$BÁN 5 SÌLA $^{iti}$[
MU.15.KAM *Ka-dáš-man-T*[*úr-gu*]
0.2.3 √ $^{f}$*Ki-di-ni-t*[*u*$_4$]
0.2$^{pi}$.0 √ $^{f}$*Ri-ša-t*[*u*$_4$]
0.1.4 √ $^{f}$*Ni-ip-pu-ri*-⸢*tu*$_4$⸣
0.1.4 √ $^{f}$*Bu-un-na*-$^{d}$*Gu-la*
0.1.3 √ $^{f}$*A-ta-mar*-ŠU-*sa*
0.1.3 √ $^{f}$*Ma-lu-uk-tu*$_4$
0.1.3 √ $^{f}$*Da-a-a-an-du*

| | | | |
|---|---|---|---|
| | 0.1.3 | √ | $^{fd}$*Ba-ba*$_6$*-šar-rat* |
| | 0.1$^{pi}$.0 | | $^{f}$*E-ku-tu*$_4$ |
| | 0.1.2 | √ | $^{f}$*Ba-ni-tu*$_4$ EN 0.0.2 *ša [ra*$^?$*-ma*$^?$*]-ni-ša* |
| | 0.0.5 | √ | $^{m}$*Man-di-i-da-a-a ka-⸢ṣi⸣-rù* |
| | 0.1.1 | √ | $^{m}$ÌR-U$_4$.9.KAM TA 0.0.1 |
| | 0.1.1 | √ | $^{m}$*Eri-ba-*$^{d}$AMAR.UTU TA 0.0.1 |
| | 0.1$^{pi}$.0 | √ | $^{m}$*Ri-iš-*$^{d}$AMAR.UTU *ka-ṣi-rù* |
| | 0.0.5 | √ | $^{m}$É.UL.MAŠ-BA-*šá ka-⸢ṣi⸣-rù* |
| L.e. | 0.1$^{pi}$.0 TA 0.0.1 *ša* $^{m}$*Ur-*$^{d}$30$^?$ | | |
| | 0.1$^{pi}$.0 NIN $^{m}$*Pa-ḫal-la-ni* | | |
| Rev. | [ ] ⸢$^{f}$*Ṣú*⸣*-ḫar-tu*$_4$ | | |
| | 0.0.5 $^{fd}$*Ba-ba*$_6$*-a-sa-at* | | |
| | 0.0.5 $^{f}$*U-bar-tu*$_4$ | | |
| | PAP 5.0.4 $^{giš}$BÁN 5 SÌLA | | |

COMMENTARY

3–10. The same women appear as recipients of barley in text **no. 100**.

11. There does not seem to have been a checkmark in this entry.

## 102. CUNES 52-20-306

1.VIII.15 Kadašman-Turgu

The upper half of the tablet is lost.

| | | |
|---|---|---|
| Obv. | [ ] | [x x x] ⸢x⸣ [x] |
| | [ ] | [x x (x) *b]u-ša* |
| | [ ] | $^{m}$*Ki-din-*$^{d}$*G[u-la]* |
| | ⸢0.1⸣$^{pi}$.0 | $^{m}$*I-din-*É.U[L.MAŠ] |
| | 0.1$^{pi}$.0 | $^{m}$*Na-na-a-a* [ |
| | 0.1.1 | $^{m}$*I-na-kit-ti-e-l[e* |
| | 0.⸢2$^?$⸣.1 | $^{m}$ZÁLAG-$^{d}$AMA[R.UTU |
| | 0.1.4 | $^{m}$*É-ra-b[i* |
| | 0.4$^{pi}$.0 | DUMU.MUNUS $^{m}$*Is-ḫu-un-⸢ni⸣* |
| | 0.1$^{pi}$.0 | $^{m}$*Ṭà-ab-ki-din-*$^{d}$[ |
| Rev. | [ ] | [$^{m}$]⸢$^{d}$*Nin*⸣*-urta-a-⸢pil-Á-ia⸣* |
| PAP | 4.2.4 ŠE.BA $^{giš}$BÁN [5 SÌLA] | |

$^{iti}$APIN.DU$_8$.⸢A⸣

U$_4$.1.KAM

MU.15.KAM

$^{d}$*Kad-aš-man-Túr-[gu]*

[L]UGAL.⸢E⸣

[x (x) $^{md}$*Ni]n-urta-ga-š[i-ir-*DINGIR$^{meš}$]

COMMENTARY

4′. Iddin-Eulmaš was thus far not attested, but cf. Izkur-Eulmaš for another PN with the temple Eulmaš as subject.

## 103. CUNES 52-00-072

-.-.[ . . . ] Kadašman-Turgu

Only the right half of the tablet is preserved. The text probably recorded rations for different groups of workers; for each group, the text indicates the name of the person who received a given amount.

Obv. MU.X.KA]M ⌜*Ka-dáš-man-Túr*?⌝-[*gu*

] MU.BI.I[M]

]⌜X⌝ UGULA ÉRIN$^{ḫi.a}$ *ša qin-na-a-t*[*i*]

] $^{m}$BA-*šá*-$^{d}$*Nin-urta im-ḫur*

] 10 SIPA$^{meš}$ $^{m}$*Ri-iš*-UD-*šú*

D]UMU $^{m}$*Ta-ri-bat*-DINGIR *im-ḫur*

] *um-ma-nu* $^{m}$*Ib-ni*-$^{d}$IŠKUR $^{lú}$[NAGAR]

] *im-ḫur*

Rev. ] EDIN

]-⌜$^{d}$⌝IŠKUR «$^{m}$»ÌR.É.GAL *im-ḫur*

*š*]*a*? *ru-ku-bi* $^{m}$*Bu-un-na*-$^{d}$*G*[*u-l*]*a*

D]UMU $^{m}$ZÁLAG-GAŠAN-*Ak-ka-de im-ḫur*

$^{m}$*Ta*?-*ri*?]-*ba*-$^{d}$*Gu-la* DUMU $^{m}$ŠEŠ-*ba-ni*

$^{m}$]*Ri-iš*-UD-*šú* DUMU $^{m}$*Ta-ri*-⌜*bat*-DINGIR⌝

] $^{giš}$BÁN [

COMMENTARY

3. "(For) the overseer of the work gangs of the 'families'; Iqīša-Ninurta received (it)." The word order suggests that "the overseer of the work gangs of the 'families'" and Iqīša-Ninurta were two different persons, but one cannot exclude that he held that function.

5. "(For) 10 shepherds; Rīš-aṣûšu, son of Tarībat-ili, received (it)."

6. "(For) the workers; Ibni-Adad, the [carpenter] (received it)."

9. The personal determinative in front of ÌR.É.GAL "palace servant" seems to be redundant; this must have been the profession of [ . . . ]-Adad, the person who received the amount recorded by this line.

10. "(For) the boatman of a cargo boat; Bunna-Gula, son of Nūr-Bēlet-Akkade, received (it)." For other MB attestations of *ša rukūbi*, see CAD R, 411.

### 104. CUNES 52-16-071

12.XII.12 Šagarakti-Šuriaš

Textile impressions are visible on the lower edge of the tablet.

Obv. ZÍZ.AN.NA $^{\text{giš}}$BÁN [10 SÌLA]
0.2.3 DUMU.MUNUS ⸢$^{\text{m}}$*Me*⸣-[
0.1.3 DUMU.MUNUS *Ša-il-ti* [
0.1$^{\text{pi}}$.0 $^{\text{f}}$*Bu-un-na-*$^{\text{d}}$*Gu-la*
PAP 1.0.0 $^{\text{giš}}$BÁN 10 SÌLA
L.e. *i-na* ŠÀ
*ša Ì-lí-ia*
*ù ša* $^{\text{md}}$50-IBILA-[BA]-*šá*
Rev. *na-ad-*[*nu*]
$^{\text{iti}}$KIN.$^{\text{d}}$INANNA
U$_4$.12.KAM
MU.2.KAM $^{\text{d}}$*Ša-garak-ti-Šu-*[*ri-i*]*a-aš*
LUGAL.E

COMMENTARY

2. Probably to be restored DUMU.MUNUS ⸢$^{\text{m}}$*Me*⸣-[*li-*$^{\text{d}}$*Šu-qa-mu-na*]: she is mentioned together with the daughter of Šā'iltu and with Bunna-Gula in CUSAS 30 317, CUSAS 30 318, and CUSAS 30 366.

5–9. "Total: 30 *sūtu*, (measured by) the *sūtu* of 10 *qû*, disburs[ed] from that of Ilīya and Enlil-apla-[iqī]ša."

ii. Fodder

### 105. CUNES 52-16-110

-.-.22 (Nazi-Maruttaš)

Account of daily expenditures disbursed over several months. I assign this text to this category because it mentions horses at the end of the reverse (l. 14′) and because it seems to have a structure and layout similar to **no. 106**, which records the disbursement of fodder (ŠUKU) for horses.

The upper half of the tablet is missing. The column dividers are clearly visible only on the reverse of the tablet.

| | | | | | |
|---|---|---|---|---|---|
| Obv. | PAP | | 1.4.3 | 0.2.0 5 | $^{\text{iti}}$ZÍZ.A.AN MU.⸢22$^{?}$⸣.[KAM] |
| | | 5 ½ | 0.1.5 | 0.0.2 2 | U$_4$.1.KAM |
| | | 6 ½ | 0.2.1 | 0.0.2 4 | U$_4$.2.KAM |
| | | 6 ½ | 0.2.1 | 0.0.2 4 | U$_4$.3.KAM |
| 5′ | | 6 ½ | 0.2.1 | 0.0.2 4 | U$_4$.4.KAM |
| | | 6 ½ | 0.2.1 | 0.0.2 4 | U$_4$.5.KAM |
| | | 6 ½ | 0.2.1 | 0.0.2 4 | U$_4$.6.KAM |
| | | 6 ½ | 0.2.1 | 0.0.2 4 | U$_4$.7.KAM |
| 9′ | | ⸢6⸣ ½ | 0.2.1 | 0.0.2 4 | U$_4$.8.KAM |
| Rev. | | 6 ½ | 0.2.1 | ⸢0.0.2 4⸣ | U$_4$.9.KAM |
| | | | 0.0.2 | | U$_4$.10.KAM |
| | PAP | | 3.4.3 | 0.3.5<br>4 SÌLA | $^{\text{iti}}$ŠE.KIN.KU$_5$ |

14′ [ ] ⸢x x⸣ [x x AN]ŠE.KUR.RA$^{\text{meš}}$

COMMENTARY

12′. The figure 3.4.3 in col. ii is the correct total of the amounts in ll. 2′–11′; the correct total in col. iii would be 0.3.3 4 SÌLA.

## 106. CUNES 52-10-119

-.X.23 Nazi-Maruttaš

Account of daily expenditures disbursed as fodder for horses. For similar Nippur texts, see BE 14 43 and MUN 97.

| | | | |
|---|---|---|---|
| Obv. | [x x] ⸢x $^{giš}$BÁN 5$^?$ SÌLA⸣ ŠUKU ANŠE.KUR | | |
| | [ ] | 0.2.0 | ⸢U$_4$.13⸣.KAM U$_4$.14.KAM |
| | [ ] | ⸢0.0.2⸣ | ⸢ŠUKU *ù* BAPPIR$_x$ $^m$*Ki*$^?$⸣-[ U$_4$.13 U$_4$.14.KAM |
| | [ ] | ⸢0.0.2$^?$⸣ | KI.MIN 3 SIPA U$_4$.13 U$_4$.14.⸢KAM⸣ |
| ⸢PAP⸣ | ⸢x x x⸣ | ⸢x x x⸣ | [x x x] ⸢x x x⸣ *a-na* ⸢x⸣ ⸢x⸣ [x x x] ⸢x⸣ |
| | 5 | 0.1.3 | U$_4$.⸢15⸣.KAM |
| | 5 | 0.1.3 | U$_4$.⸢16.KAM⸣ |
| | [5] | ⸢0.1.3⸣ | U$_4$.⸢17.KAM⸣ |
| | [5] | 0.1.3 | ⸢U$_4$⸣.[18].KAM |
| | ⸢5⸣ | 0.1.3 | ⸢U$_4$⸣.[19].KAM |
| | 5 | 0.1.3 | ⸢U$_4$⸣.[20].KAM |
| | 5 | 0.1.3 | ⸢U$_4$.21⸣.KAM |
| | 5 | 0.1.3 | U$_4$.22.KAM |
| | 5 | 0.1.3 | U$_4$.23.KAM |
| | [5] | 0.1.3 | ⸢U$_4$.24⸣.[KAM] |
| Rev. | [5] | 0.1.3 | ⸢U$_4$.25⸣.[KAM] |
| | ⸢5⸣ | 0.1.3 | U$_4$.26.KAM |
| | ⸢5⸣ | 0.1.3 | U$_4$.27.KAM |
| | ⸢5⸣ | 0.1.3 | U$_4$.28.KAM |
| PAP | | 4.1⸢pi⸣.0 ŠUKU ANŠE.⸢KUR.RA⸣$^{meš}$ | |
| | | 0.3.5 2 ⸢SÌLA⸣ ŠUKU 5 [ANŠE.KUR].RA$^{meš}$ *ša* ⸢U$_4^?$.x⸣[ | |
| | | 0.1.2 ŠUKU ⸢x x⸣ [ ⸢x⸣ [x x] ⸢x⸣ [ | |
| PAP | | 1.1.1 2 SÌLA ŠUKU É$^?$ *ù* ⸢x x x⸣ | |
| PAP | | 5.2.1 2 ⸢SÌLA⸣ $^m$*Ḫa-ni-bu ú-ša-ki-il* | |
| ŠU.NIGIN | | 5.4.5 2 SÌLA ⸢ANŠE.KUR⸣.RA$^{meš}$ ⸢$^{giš}$BÁN 5 SÌLA⸣ $^{iti}$AB.È MU.23.KAM ⸢x$^?$⸣ ⸢*Na-zi*⸣-[ | |

COMMENTARY

3. Here and in all other instances (**no. 159**: 19, 23, 26; **no. 164**: 27; **no. 179**: 23′; CUSAS 30 138: 21; CUSAS 30 342: 17), BAPPIR is written šim×e, a variant that does not appear to be attested outside of this corpus.

5. The sign(s) at the end of the line, after *a-na,* have been obliterated by the signs of l. 26.

6–19. In my opinion, the figures in col. i, which are not summed in l. 20, are more likely to refer to items rather than units of capacity; perhaps they refer to teams of horses, as in col. ii of BE 14 43? Cf. also col. i in **no. 105**.
24. "In total: 163 *sūtu* and 2 *qû*, Ḫānibu gave as feed." This total sums up the subtotals of l. 20 and l. 23. Ḫānibu might be the same person who receives fodder for a horse in **no. 107**: 4.

## 107. CUNES 52-12-029

7.XI.2 Kadašman-Turgu

Obv. [x x] ⸢$^{\text{giš}}$BÁN⸣ 5 SÌL[A] MU.BI.IM

| | |
|---|---|
| [0.1.2] | $^{\text{md}}$UTU-LUGAL TA U$_4$.17.KAM EN U$_4$.7.KAM $^{\text{iti}}$ZÍZ.A.AN |
| 0.0.⸢4⸣ | ŠUKU ANŠE.KUR.RA TA U$_4$.11.KAM EN U$_4$.7.KAM KI.MIN |
| 0.0.4 | ŠUKU ANŠE.KUR.RA $^{\text{m}}$*Ḫa-ni-bu* U$_4$.15.KAM *ma-ḫi-ir* |
| 0.0.4 | ŠUKU 2 SIPA TA U$_4$.6.KAM EN U$_4$.10.KAM |

PAP 0.3.2 $^{\text{iti}}$ZÍZ.A.AN U$_4$.7.KAM
MU.2.KAM *Ka-dáš-man-Túr-gu*

The reverse is blank.

COMMENTARY

2. The restored quantity is required by the total in l. 6.
2–3. The expression of time should probably be understood as "from day 17 (of month X) till day 7 of month XI" and "from day 11 (of month X) till day 7 of ditto (i.e., month XI)." See also **nos. 63**: 3 (NM 8) and **294**: 7–8 (NM 19).
4. Ḫānibu might be the same person who is in charge of disbursing fodder for several horses in **no. 106**: 24.

### iii. Seed

## 108. CUNES 52-10-072

-.V.3 Kadašman-Turgu

Allocation of sesame as seed in Dūr-Enlilē.

Obv. ⸢ŠE⸣.GIŠ.Ì $^{giš}$BÁN 5 SÌLA *ša a-na* NUMUN
⸢*i-na*⸣ [BÀ]D-$^{d+}$*En-líl*$^{hi.a.ki}$ *i-na* $^{iti}$NE.NE.GAR
M[U].⸢3⸣.KAM *Ka-dáš-man-Túr-gu* LUGAL.E *na-ad-nu*

| | | | |
|---|---|---|---|
| | 0.1.2 | $^{m}$MU-*líb-ši* | |
| | 0.0.3 3 SÌLA | $^{md}$*Nin-urta*-MU-MU | $^{m}$*Bu-un-na*-$^{d}$⸢AMAR.UTU⸣ |
| | 0.0.4 | $^{m}$KI.MIN | $^{m}$*Kal-bu* |
| | 0.0.3 | $^{m}$KI.MIN | $^{m}$GAL-*šá*-GAŠAN |
| | [x.x].⸢2⸣ 3 SÌLA | $^{m}$KI.MIN | $^{m}$*Ì-lí-re-m*[*an-n*]*i* |
| | [x.x.x] ⸢3⸣ SÌLA | $^{m}$KI.MIN | $^{m}$ŠEŠ-[ |
| Rev. | [0.0].⸢4⸣ 3 SÌLA | $^{m}$KI.MIN | $^{m}$⸢ZÁLAG⸣-[ |
| | [x.x.x] 3 SÌLA | $^{m}$KI.MIN | $^{m}$*Ri-i*[*š*- |
| | [x.x.x] | ⸢$^{m}$KI.MIN | $^{m}$ÌR$^{?}$⸣-[ |
| P[AP] | ⸢I$^{?}$⸣.[x.x] | ⸢NUMUN$^{?}$⸣ SUM-*nu* | |

COMMENTARY

1–3. "Sesame, (measured by) the *sūtu* of 5 *qû*, that was disbursed as seed in [Dū]r-Enlilē in month V of ye[ar] 3 of King Kadašman-Turgu."

## 109. CUNES 52-13-078

Not dated.

Obv. ŠE.⸢NUMUN$^{?}$ *ša*⸣ *i-na* ŠÀ 0.3.4 $^{giš}$BÁN 10 SÌLA
⸢*i-na*⸣ $^{giš}$BÁN 5 SÌLA SUM-*nu*

| | |
|---|---|
| [x.x] 3 | $^{m}$*Ba-bi-la-a-a-ú i-na ma-a-a-ri* |
| [x.x.x] | $^{m}$⸢*Ki*-x-x-*tu*$_4$⸣ |
| [x.x].4 | $^{md}$30-EN-NUMUN *ù* ⸢x⸣[ |
| 0.0.2 | $^{m}$*Bu-na*-$^{d}$*Gu*-[*la*] |
| [PAP$^{?}$] 1.2.2 $^{giš}$BÁN 5 SÌLA | |

The reverse is blank.

COMMENTARY

1–2. "Seed which was disbursed by the *sūtu* of 5 *qû* out of 22 *sūtu*, (measured by) the *sūtu* of 10 *qû*." Cf. l. 6, where the total is indeed measured by the *sūtu* of 5 *qû*.

3. *i-na ma-a-a-ri* "in the *ma(y)yāru*-plowed field": for *ma(y)yāru* "plow (without seeder), land plowed with the *m.*-plow," see CAD M/1, *majāru*, 120ff.

## iv. Production Supplies

### 110. CUNES 52-19-127

-.-.18 Nazi-Maruttaš

Barley from the revenues (*tēlītu*) of Dūr-Enlilē, Ḫamru, and Dūr-bēl-mātāti, allocated as production supplies (ÉŠ.GÀR) and temple supplies (ŠUKU) to the brewer Agab-šenni.

| | | |
|---|---|---|
| Obv. | [ŠE $^{giš}$BÁN GAL *š*]*a i-na* MU.18.KAM ⸢*Na-zi-Múru-taš* LUGAL⸣.E | |
| | ⸢*i*⸣-[*na* ŠÀ *te-l*]*i-ti ša* URU$^{didli}$ | |
| | *a-na* ÉŠ.[GÀR $^{m}$]*A-gab-še-en-ni* $^{lú}$LUNGA *mi-taḫ-ḫu-rù* | |
| | 2.3.0 | *i-na* ⸢ŠÀ *te-li*⸣*-ti ša* BÀD-$^{d+}$*En-líl*$^{hi.a.ki}$ $^{iti}$KIN.$^{d}$INANNA |
| 5 | 2.0.0 | *i-na* ŠÀ KI.MIN *ša Ḫa-*⸢*am*⸣*-ri*$^{ki}$ $^{iti}$DU$_6$.KÙ |
| | 13.0.0 | ⸢*i-na* ŠÀ KI.MIN⸣ *ša* BÀD-EN-KUR.KUR$^{ki}$ $^{iti}$DU$_6$.KÙ |
| | 2.2$^{pi}$.0 | *i-na* ŠÀ KI.MIN *ša* KI.MIN *a-na* ŠUKU É.DINGIR$^{didli}$ *im-ḫur* |
| L.e. | PAP 20 GUR $^{giš}$BÁN GAL | |
| 9 | SUM-*nu ki-i* ŠU $^{md}$*Nin-urta*-MU-MU | |

The reverse is blank.

Translation

| | | |
|---|---|---|
| Obv. | [Barley, (measured by) the big *sūtu*, wh]ich Agab-šenni, the brewer, has been receiving fr[om the rev]enues of the towns as production [supplies] in year 18 of King Nazi-Maruttaš. | |
| | 78 *sūtu* | from the revenues of Dūr-Enlilē; month VI. |
| 5 | 60 *sūtu* | from ditto (i.e., the revenues) of Ḫamru; month VII. |
| | 390 *sūtu* | from ditto (i.e., the revenues) of Dūr-bēl-mātāti; month VII. |
| | 72 *sūtu* | from ditto of ditto (i.e., from the revenues of Dūr-bēl-mātāti); he received as supplies for the temples. |
| L.e. | Total: 600 *sūtu*, (measured by) the big *sūtu*, | |
| 9 | disbursed; on behalf of Ninurta-zākir-šumi. | |

## 111. CUNES 52-12-036

-.VII.18 Nazi-Maruttaš

Allocation of wheat, emmer, and cress as production supplies (ÉŠ.GÀR) for millers, in Āl-irrē. Despite the lack of a seal caption, the text is sealed.

| | |
|---|---|
| Obv. | ⸢7$^{?}$⸣.0.3 5 SÌLA GIG |
| | 1.2.3 ZÍZ.AN.NA |
| | 0.0.1 2 SÌLA ZAG.ḪI.LI |
| | *i-na* URU-*ir-re-e*$^{ki}$ |
| | ⸢*a*⸣-*na* ÉŠ.GÀR $^{lú}$KA.ZÌ.DA$^{meš}$ |
| | ⸢$^{m}$⸣$^{d}$MAŠ-SAG |
| Rev. | *i-na* ŠU $^{md}$MAŠ-MU-MU |
| | *maḫ-rù* |
| | ⸢TA$^{?}$ 0.0.5$^{?}$⸣ 5 SÌLA *ki-iṣ-ri* GIG |
| | *ù* 0.2$^{pi}$.0 KI.MIN ZÍZ.AN.NA |
| | *ša im-ḫu-ru šu-lu-ú* |
| | $^{iti}$DU$_{6}$.KÙ |
| | MU.18.KAM |
| L.e. | *Na-zi-Ma-ru-ut-taš* |

Translation

| | |
|---|---|
| Obv. | ⸢213$^{?}$ *sūtu*⸣ 5 *qû* wheat |
| | 45 *sūtu* emmer |
| | 1 *sūtu* 2 *qû* cress |
| 4 | in Āl-irrē |
| 6 | Ninurta-ašarēd |
| 8 | received |
| 7 | from Ninurta-zākir-šumi |
| 5 | as production supplies for the millers, |
| | after$^{?}$ 5$^{?}$ *sūtu* and 5 *qû* of *kiṣru* of wheat |
| 10 | and 12 *sūtu* of ditto (i.e., *kiṣru*) of emmer, |
| | which he received, have been deducted. |
| | Month VII, |
| | year 18 |
| L.e. | of Nazi-Maruttaš. |

## 112. CUNES 52-12-008 (Plate No. 35)

-.VII–XII.19 Nazi-Maruttaš

Summary of barley disbursed as production supplies (ÉŠ.GÀR) for brewers and millers (l. 16) in different towns, over several months.

The brewers are Ṣuḫḫutu, Bā'eru, Ana-nūr-Šamaš-lūṣi, and Rīmūtu; they are mentioned together also in **no. 114**, which records the production supplies disbursed for them and for another brewer in the 4th year of Kadašman-Turgu.

Lā-qīpu and Sîn-muballiṭ appear together as recipients of production supplies also in CUSAS 30 144: 6–7 (n.d.), where they are both identified as lúGAZ.ZÌ.DA—i.e., millers. CUSAS 30 144 is not dated, but perhaps it is not a coincidence that in both texts the two millers receive 5 kor of barley each. Lā-qīpu, Īriš-Ea, and Sîn-muballiṭ are mentioned together as recipients of production supplies in CUSAS 30 143: 12–14 (n.d.): here, only Lā-qīpu is identified by his profession, which can be restored GA[Z.ZÌ.DA] "mi[ller]" (rather than UŠ.[BAR?] "wea[ver?]," as in van Soldt 2015, 210).

The brewers Bā'eru and Rīmūtu and the millers Lā-qīpu, Sîn-muballiṭ, and Tarību are probably the same persons attested in Nippur texts dated in the reign of Nazi-Maruttaš (Sassmannshausen 2001, 78, 80 and Introduction §4.6).

| | ŠE ÉŠ.GÀR $^{giš}$BÁN GAL TA $^{iti}$DU$_{6}$.KÙ EN $^{iti}$ŠE.KIN.KU$_{5}$ *ša* MU.19.KAM *Na-zi-*⸢*Ma-r*⸣[*u-* | | | | | | | | |
|---|---|---|---|---|---|---|---|---|---|
| Obv. | $^{m}$*Ṣú-ḫu-tu*$_{4}$ | $^{m}$*Ba-i-rù* | $^{m}$URU$_{4}$-$^{d}$*É-a* | $^{m}$*A-na-*ZÁLAG-$^{d}$UTU-È | $^{m}$*Ri-mu-tu*$_{4}$ | $^{md}$30-*mu-bal-liṭ* | $^{m}$*La-qí-pu* | $^{m}$*Ta-*⸢*ri*⸣*-bu* | MU.B[I.IM] |
| | | | | | 15.0.0 | | | | *Tukul-ti-*É.K[UR$^{ki}$ |
| | | 2.0.0 | | | | | | | URU-*ir-re-e* [ |
| | | | | | | 5.0.0 | 5.0.0 | | BÀD-$^{d+}$*En-líl*$^{ḫi.a\ it}$[$^{i}$ |
| | 31.0.0 | 26.1.1 | 13.0.0 | | | 21.3.4 | 22.2.3 | | URU-ÌR-É-*Kiš*$^{ki\ it}$[$^{i}$ |
| | | 2.0.0 | | | | | | | BÀD-$^{d+}$*En-líl*$^{ḫi.a.ki}$ [<br>*i-na* ŠU $^{md}$*Nuska-na-bu-šu* |
| | | 4.2.3 | | | | | | | *Tukul-ti-*É.KUR$^{ki}$ *i-na* ŠU $^{m}$*Ki-*[ |
| | | | | 10.0.0 | | | | | *Ḫa-am-ri*$^{ki\ iti}$DU$_{6}$.KÙ |
| | | | | | | | | 3.1.4 *Kar-*$^{d}$*Nuska*$^{ki\ iti}$GAN.GAN.È<br>TA 0.3.2 GAL $^{giš}$BÁN 10 SÌLA *šu-lu-ú* | |
| | 5.0.0 | 5.0.0 | | | | | | | *Ḫa-am-ri*$^{ki\ iti}$ŠE.KIN.KU$_{5}$ |
| | | | 2.0.0 | | | | | | *Tukul-ti-*É.KUR$^{ki}$ *a-n*[*a* |
| | | | | 6.0.0 | | | | | *Kar-*$^{d}$*Nin-É-a*[*n-na*]<br>$^{iti}$DU$_{6}$.K[Ù] |
| Rev. | 12.0.1<br>TA 2.0.0 | 12.1.3<br>TA 1.2.4 | | | | ⸢3⸣.0.0 | 3.0.0 | | *i-na* ŠÀ *ša Za-rat-*LUGAL⸢$^{ki}$⸣<br>URU-ÌR-É-*Kiš*$^{ki\ iti}$ŠE.[KIN.KU$_{5}$]<br>*i-na* ŠÀ *ša* $^{md}$*Nin-urta-*M[U$^{?}$-MU$^{?}$] |
| | ⸢14$^{?}$⸣.0.0 | 15.0.0 | | | | | | 10.0.0 | *Tukul-ti-*É.KUR$^{ki}$ (eras.)<br>$^{iti}$DU$_{6}$.KÙ |
| PAP | 48.0./1 | 52.0./1 | 15.0.0 | 16.0.0 | 15.0.0 | 29./3.4 | 30.2.3 | 13.1.4 | ÉŠ.GÀR $^{lú}$LUNGA *ù* K[A.ZÌ.DA] |
| | | | | | | 13.0.0 | 13.0.0 | [ ] | BÀD-$^{d+}$*En-líl*$^{ḫi.a}$ [ |
| | | | | | | 16.0.4<br>5 | 16.0.⸢4⸣<br>5 | [ ] | BÀD-EN-KUR-KUR[$^{(ki)}$ |
| | | | | | | | | ⸢x⸣[ ] | *Tukul-ti-*[É.KUR$^{ki}$ |
| PAP | | | | | | 29./0.4 5 | 19./0.4 5 | ⸢4$^{+}$⸣.[x.x] | [ |

COMMENTARY

1. "Barley, production supplies, (measured by) the big *sūtu*, from month VII till month XII of year 19 of Nazi-Mar[uttaš]."

6. The GN is thus far not attested, but cf. Bīt-Arad-bīt-Kiš (RGTC 5, 54).

15. After Tukultī-Ekur, one can still see the traces of $^{iti}$DU$_6$.KÙ, which has been then erased and rewritten in the following line. Also, a faint trace of a horizontal line, originally dividing this row into two, is still visible.

16. The written totals in Ṣuḫḫutu's and Bā'eru's columns do not seem to include the respective quantities in l. 15. The restoration K[A.ZÌ.DA] is suggested by the fact that Lā-qīpu and Sîn-muballiṭ are identified as millers ($^{lú}$GAZ.ZÌ.DA) in CUSAS 30 144: 6, where they are mentioned as recipients of production supplies.

20. The expected total in Lā-qīpu's column should be 29.0.4 5; the written total (19.0.4 5) could be a scribal slip.

## 113. CUNES 52-10-090

-.-.3 Kadašman-Turgu

Account of cereals, pulses, and cress received by Ninurta-ašarēd as production supplies (ÉŠ.GÀR) in or from different towns.

Obv. ŠE $^{giš}$BÁN GAL *ša i-na* MU.3.KAM *Ka-dáš-man-Túr-gu* LUGAL.E
*a-na* ÉŠ.GÀR $^{md}$*Nin-⸢urta*-SAG⸣ DUMU $^{m}$*Ta-ri-bat*-DINGIR *mi-taḫ-ḫu-rù*

| | ŠE | ⸢GIG⸣ | ⸢ZÍZ.AN.NA⸣ | ⸢GÚ?.TUR?⸣ | GÚ.GAL | ZAG.ḪI.LI | MU.BI.IM |
|---|---|---|---|---|---|---|---|
| | 33.0.0 | 2.0.1<br>5 SÌLA | | | | | URU-*ir-re-e* $^{iti}$NE.NE.GAR |
| | 2.0.0 | | | | | | BÀD-$^{d}$*Nuska*$^{ki}$ $^{iti}$DU$_6$.KÙ |
| | 1.0.0 | 1.4.3<br>⸢TA 1.4.0 ŠE.NUMUN 2.0.0 ŠE $^{giš}$BÁN 10 SÌLA⸣<br>⸢*ša* MU.2.KAM⸣ *i-na* URU-DUMU-*Ba-'i-li šu-lu-ú* | | | | | BÀD-$^{d+}$*En-líl*$^{meš.ki}$ TA $^{iti}$BÁR.ZAG.[GAR]<br>EN $^{iti}$ŠU.NUMUN.NA |
| | | | | 0.0.3 | 0.1.4 | | KI.MIN $^{iti}$DU$_6$.KÙ |
| | | | 10.0.0 | | | | KI.MIN $^{iti}$APIN.DU$_8$.A |
| Rev. | | 1.3.0 | | | | | KI.MIN $^{iti}$GAN.GAN.È |
| | | 1.4$^{pi}$./⸢1⸣<br>⸢5⸣ [SÌLA] | | | | 0.4.1<br>8 SÌLA | KI.MIN $^{iti}$ZÍZ.A.AN |
| | 4.1.2 | | | | | | URU-*Mi-na*-DÙ-DINGIR$^{ki}$<br>*i-na* ŠÀ 20.0.0 *ša* $^{m}$*Ib*-[*n*]*i*-$^{d}$AMAR.UTU<br>*a-píl* KÁ *ša Ì-si-in*$^{ki}$<br>$^{iti}$ZÍZ.A.AN |
| | 15.0.0 | | | | | | *i-na* ŠÀ ŠE *ša* DUMU $^{m}$LÚ-$^{d}$30<br>$^{iti}$ŠE.KIN.KU$_5$ |
| PAP | 54./1.2 | 7./2$^{pi}$.0 | 10.0.0 | 0.0.3 | 0.1.4 | 0.4.1<br>8 SÌLA | ÉŠ.GÀR $^{giš}$BÁN GAL<br>$^{md}$*Nin-urta*-SAG |

COMMENTARY

1–2. "Grain, (measured by) the big *sūtu*, which Ninurta-ašarēd, son of Tarībat-ili, has been receiving as production supplies in year 3 of King Kadašman-Turgu."

6. Col. ii (GIG): "57 *sūtu*, after 54 *sūtu* of seed (and) 60 *sūtu* of barley, (measured by) the *sūtu* of 10 *qû*, of year 2 have been deducted in Āl-Mār-Bā'ili."

13. The expected total of barley in col. i would be 55.1.2.

## 114. CUNES 52-10-092

-.-.4 Kadašman-Turgu

Annual summary of barley disbursed as production supplies (ÉŠ.GÀR) for brewers.

On the brewers Ṣuḫḫutu, Bā'eru, Ana-nūr-Šamaš-lūṣi, and Rīmūtu, see comments to **no. 112**.

The surface of the obverse is too damaged to assess the exact number of lines.

Obv. ŠE $^{\text{giš}}$BÁN GAL ÉŠ.GÀR $^{\text{lú}}$LUNGA$^{\text{meš}}$ *ša* MU.4.KAM *Ka-dáš-man-⸢Túr-gu* LUGAL⸣

| | | | | | | |
|---|---|---|---|---|---|---|
| | $^{\text{m}}$*Ṣú-ḫu-⸢tu$_4$⸣* | $^{\text{m}}$*Ba-i-rù* | $^{\text{m.lú⸢}}$DUB⸣.⸢SAR⸣ | $^{\text{m⸢}}$*A-na*⸣-ZÁLAG-$^{\text{d}}$UT⸢U-È⸣ | $^{\text{m}}$*Ri-[mu-tu$_4$]* | [MU.BI].IM |
| | ⸢7$^{+}$⸣.[x.x] | ⸢3$^{+}$⸣.[x.x] | [ ] | [ ] | [ ] | [ |
| | [ ] | [ ] | [ ] | [ ] | [ ] | [ |
| 5 | [ ] | [ ] | ⸢2$^{+}$⸣.[x.x] | ⸢14$^{+}$⸣.[x.x] | [ ] | [ |
| ⸢PAP$^{?}$⸣ | ⸢40$^{+}$⸣.[x.x] | [ ] | [ ] | [ ] | [ ] | [ ] $^{\text{giš}}$BÁN GAL |

The reverse is blank.

COMMENTARY

1. "Barley, (measured by) the big *sūtu*, production supplies for the brewers of year 4 of King Kadašman-Turgu."

## 115. CUNES 52-10-067

-.II.6 Kadašman-Turgu

Barley from the storehouse (*bīt kunukki*), allocated as brewing ingredients (ZÌ.MUNU$_4$). For a similar text from the Rosen Collection, see CUSAS 30 280 (KuE 8).

Obv. ŠE $^{\text{giš}}$BÁN 10 SÌLA *ša i-na* ŠÀ *ša* É NA$_4$.KIŠIB
⸢*a*⸣*-na* ZÌ.MUNU$_4$ *ša si-bi-e-ti*
*i-na* $^{\text{iti}}$GU$_4$.SI.SÀ MU.6.KAM *Ka-dáš-man-Túr-gu na-ad-nu*

| | | |
|---|---|---|
| | 2.0.0 | ZÌ.MUNU$_4$ $^{\text{md}}$*Nin-urta*-MU-MU $^{\text{m}}$ZÁLAG-$^{\text{d}}$*Ištar* DUMU.MUNUS $^{\text{lú}}$NU.$^{\text{giš}}$KIRI$_6$ |
| 5 | 2.0.0 | ZÌ.MUNU$_4$ $^{\text{m}}$KI.MIN $^{\text{m}}$DÙ-*šá*-$^{\text{d}}$AMAR.UTU $^{\text{f}}$*Ra-ba-⸢tu⸣-tu ù* $^{\text{mfd}}$[x x x x-m]*an$^{?}$-ni* |
| | 4.0.0 | ZÌ.MUNU$_4$ $^{\text{m}}$KI.MIN $^{\text{m}}$GAL-*šá*-GA[ŠAN x x x x]-*tu$_4$* $^{\text{md}}$*Nin-urta*-ŠEŠ-SUM-*n*[*a* |
| Rev. | 4.0.0 | ZÌ.MUNU$_4$ $^{\text{m}}$KI.MIN $^{\text{m⸢}}$x⸣[ $^{\text{m}}$IBILA-$^{\text{d}}$IŠKUR ⸢*ù*$^{?}$ $^{\text{md}}$⸣[ |

8 PAP 12.0.0 $^{\text{giš}}$BÁN 10 SÌLA
ŠU.NIGIN 9.3$^{\text{pi}}$.0 $^{\text{giš}}$BÁN [GA]L
TA 2.2$^{\text{pi}}$.0 GAL $^{\text{giš}}$[BÁN] 10 SÌLA
*i-na* 1.0.0 0.1$^{\text{pi}}$.0 *šu-lu-ú*

Translation

| | | |
|---|---|---|
| Obv. | Barley, (measured by) the *sūtu* of 10 *qû*, that was disbursed from that of the storehouse as brewing ingredients of the female brewers$^{?}$ in month II, year 6 of Kadašman-Turgu: | |
| | 60 *sūtu* | brewing ingredients; Ninurta-zākir-šumi; Nūr-Ištar;<br>the daughter of Nukarribu. |
| 5 | 60 *sūtu* | brewing ingredients; ditto; Banâ-ša-Marduk;<br>Rabâtūtu and [. . . ma]nni$^{?}$. |
| | 120 *sūtu* | brewing ingredients; ditto; Rabâ-ša-bēlti [ . . . ] . . . ,<br>Ninurta-aḫa-iddina [ . . . ]. |
| Rev. | 120 *sūtu* | brewing ingredients; ditto; [PN];<br>Apil-Adad ⸢and$^{?}$⸣ [PN$^{?}$]. |
| 8 | Total: 360 *sūtu* (measured by) the *sūtu* of 10 *qû*.<br>Grand total: 288 *sūtu* (measured by) the [bi]g *sūtu*,<br>after 72 *sūtu* have been deducted, the increase of<br>the [*sūtu*] of 10 *qû* being at a rate of 1 *pānu* per kor. | |

Commentary

4. The daughter of Nukarribu appears together with Rabâtūtu also in CUSAS 30 313, an undated text about the dying of wool.

5. Or just $^{fd}$[ . . . ], with $^{f}$ written over an erased $^{m}$.

## 116. CUNES 52-12-007

-.-.9 Kadašman-Turgu

Allocation of different types of cereals (barley, wheat, and emmer), pulses, and cress as production supplies (ÉŠ.GÀR).

Obv. [ŠE $^{giš}$BÁN GAL] ÉŠ.GÀR *ša i-na* MU.9.KAM *Ka-dáš-man-Túr-gu* L[UGAL]
[$^{m}$*I*]*-la-nu-ú-a* DUMU $^{m}$*Lu-da-ri-be-lí ma*[*ḫ-rù*]

| | [Š]E | GIG | ZÍZ.AN.NA | GÚ.TUR | GÚ.GAL | GÚ.NÍG.ÀR.RA | ZAG.ḪI.LI | MU.BI.[IM] |
|---|---|---|---|---|---|---|---|---|
| | 70.0.0 | 5.3.5 | 20.0.0 | 0.1$^{pi}$.0 3 | 0.2.1 2 | 0.0.5 1 | 0.1.4<br>2 SÌLA | *ša* $^{it}$[$^{i?}$<br>*šu-nu* ⸢x⸣ [<br>$^{iti}$K[IN |
| 5 | 12.0.0 | | | | | | | *Tukul-ti-*[É.KUR$^{ki}$]<br>ŠUKU$^{?}$ AN[ŠE$^{?}$<br>*ša* ⸢x⸣ [<br>$^{iti}$[ |
| Rev. | 10.0.0 | | | | | | | *Tukul-t*[*i-*É.KUR$^{ki}$]<br>$^{iti}$⸢x⸣[<br>MU.10.K[AM |
| PAP | 92.0.0 | 5./3.5 | 20.0.0 | 0.1$^{pi}$.0<br>3 SÌLA | 0.2.1<br>2 SÌLA | 0.0.5<br>1 SÌLA | 0.1.4<br>2 SÌLA | ÉŠ.GÀR $^{giš}$BÁ[N GAL]<br>$^{m}$*I-la-nu-*[*ú-a* |

Commentary

1–2. "[Grain, (measured by) the big *sūtu*], which [I]lānū'a, son of Lū-dari-bēlī, rec[eived] as production supplies in year 9 of K[ing] Kadašman-Turgu."

### 117. CUNES 52-00-050

Date not preserved.

Allocation of barley, wheat, and emmer as production supplies (ÉŠ.GÀR).

(Beginning broken, ca. half of the tablet is missing)

| | | | | |
|---|---|---|---|---|
| Obv. | ⸢ŠE$^{?}$⸣ $^{giš}$BÁN 10 SÌLA ÉŠ.GÀR ⸢*ša*$^{?}$ x⸣ [ | | | |
| | ŠE | ⸢GIG⸣ | ZÍZ.AN.NA | M[U.BI.IM] |
| 3′ | [ ] | [ ] | | *i-n*[*a*<br>⸢x⸣ [ |
| Rev. | [x x] ⸢x$^{?}$⸣<br>2.1.4 | [ ] | [ ] | [ |
| 5′ | ⸢1.1.x⸣ | [ ] | [ ] | [ |

Text breaks off.

v. Supplies for Temples

### 118. CUNES 52-00-062 (Plate No. 36)

5.VII.9 Kadašman-Turgu

Barley disbursed by the town of Āl-atḫē as supplies (ŠUKU) for several temples; see also **no. 119** and comments there. The barley is qualified as "new" (GIBIL) and "old" (LIBIR.RA).

| Obv. | ŠE $^{giš}$BÁN GAL GIBIL | ŠE $^{giš}$BÁN 10 SÌLA GIBIL | ŠE $^{giš}$BÁN 10 SÌLA LIBIR.RA | | SUM-*nu* URU-*at-ḫe-e* ⸢MU$^{?}$⸣[ |
|---|---|---|---|---|---|
| | 14.2.0 | | | √ | ŠUKU É $^{d}$*Nin-urta* ⸢*ša*⸣ $^{uru}$*Bur-r*[*a-nu*$^{ki}$] |
| | 6.0.0 | | | √ | KI.MIN $^{u}$[$^{ru}$]⸢*Du-un-n*⸣[*i-Ì-si-in*$^{ki}$] |
| 4 | ⸢x.x.x⸣ | | ⸢x⸣ | | [ |

Text breaks off

| | | | | |
|---|---|---|---|---|
| Rev. | ⸢1 ME<br>40$^{+}$⸣./3.1 | ⸢10$^{+}$⸣./3.3 | ⸢x.x./5⸣ | ⸢x⸣ [<br>$^{iti}$DU$_{6}$.KÙ ⸢U$_{4}$.5$^{?}$⸣.KAM<br>MU.9.KAM<br>$^{d}$*Ka-dáš-man-Túr-gu* LUGAL [ |

Commentary

2–3. The GNs are restored after **no. 119**: 4, 7.

## 119. CUNES 52-12-010 (Plate No. 37)

-.-.9 Kadašman-Turgu

Annual summary of barley provided by the towns of Āl-irrē, Āl-atḫē, Tukultī-Ekur, and Dūr-Enlilē as supplies (ŠUKU) for several temples, mainly located in other towns. Cf. **no. 118**, which records the same quantities disbursed in the 9$^{th}$ year of Kadašman-Turgu by the town of Āl-atḫē for the temples of Ninurta in Burrānu and Dunni-Isin.

Note also that MUN 307 (KT 3) lists some of the same temples: the temples of Ninurta in Parak-māri and in Āl-ṣalamti, the temple of Ištar in Ḫursagkalama, and probably also the temple of Gula in Dūr-Enlilē (see below).

Obv. ŠE $^{\text{giš}}$BÁN GAL ŠUKU É.DINGIR$^{\text{didli}}$ MU.9.KAM *Ka-dáš-man-Túr-gu* LUGAL.E

| | URU-*ir-re-e* | URU-*at-ḫe-e* | *Tukul-ti-*É.KUR$^{\text{ki}}$ | BÀD-$^{\text{d+}}$*En-líl*$^{\text{meš}}$ | ŠU.NIGIN | MU.BI.IM |
|---|---|---|---|---|---|---|
| | 15.2.3 | | | | 15.2.3 | ŠUKU É $^{\text{d}}$*Nin-urta ša* BÁRA.DUMU$^{\text{ki}}$ EN 0.1$^{\text{pi}}$.0 Á $^{\text{giš}}$MÁ |
| | | 14.2.0 | | | 14.2.0 | ŠUKU É $^{\text{d}}$*Nin-urta ša* $^{\text{uru}}$*Bur-ra-nu*$^{\text{ki}}$ |
| | | | | | 6.0.0 | ŠUKU É $^{\text{d}}$*Nin-urta ša* É.DANNA$^{\text{ki}}$ |
| | 6.0.0 | | | | 6.0.0 | ŠUKU É $^{\text{d}}$*Nin-urta ša* URU-*ṣa-lam-ti*$^{\text{ki}}$ |
| | | 6.0.0 | | | 6.0.0 | ŠUKU É $^{\text{d}}$*Nin-urta ša* $^{\text{uru}}$*Du-un-ni-Ì-si-in*$^{\text{ki}}$ |
| | | 12.4.0 | | 1.3.0 | 14.2.0 | ŠUKU É $^{\text{d}}$*Iš-tar ša* ḪUR.SAG.K[ALAM.MA$^{\text{(ki)}}$] |
| | | 2.2.3 | | 0.2.3 | 3.0.0 | ŠUKU É $^{\text{d}}$*Gu-la ša* BÀ[D-$^{\text{d+}}$*En-líl*$^{\text{ḫi.a/meš.ki}}$] |
| | | 3.0.0 | | | 3.0.0 | ŠUKU É $^{\text{d}}$*Šar-ra*[*t*-NIBRU$^{\text{ki?}}$] |
| Rev. | | | 2.0.0 AN.ZA.GÀR | | 2.0.0 | ŠUKU É $^{\text{d}}$*Nin-nisi* $^{\text{m}}$KAR-*ub*-$^{\text{d}}$AMAR.UTU DUMU $^{\text{m}}$*Ur*-$^{\text{d}}$*A*[*sar-alim-ma*] |
| PAP | | | | | ⌜1⌝,10.1.3 | ŠUKU É.DINGIR$^{\text{didli}}$ |

COMMENTARY

1. "Barley, (measured by) the big *sūtu*: supplies of the temples, year 9 of King Kadašman-Turgu."
3. "Supplies of the temple of Ninurta in Parak-māri, including 6 *sūtu* for the rent of a boat." The temple of Ninurta in Parak-māri appears as a recipient of supplies also in **no. 176**: 28. See Sassmannshausen 2001, 375 for other attestations of payments for the rent of boats.
4. Probably to be distinguished from the GN Būrānu, which is usually written $^{\text{uru}}$PÚ$^{\text{meš}}$ (RGTC 5, 75).
5. Supplies for the temple of Ninurta in Bīt-bēri are mentioned also in **no. 138**: 3. Even though a total is indicated in col. v, there are no quantities in the previous columns.
6. Supplies for the temple of Ninurta in Āl-ṣalamti are mentioned also in **no. 138**: 2.
7. Supplies for the temple of Ninurta in Dunni-Isin are mentioned also in CUSAS 30 139: 5 (n.d.).
9. For the restoration of the GN, cf. MUN 307: 6, where Sassmannshausen read ]X-ID *ša* BÀD-$^{\text{d+}}$*En-líl*$^{\text{meš.ki}}$. After collation, a reading *G*]*u*-⌜*la*⌝ for the first signs after the break also seems possible. Note that this hypothesis is supported also by the sequence of temples in the two texts, since in both cases this entry is preceded by the temple of Ištar in Ḫursagkalama.
10. Šarrat-[Nippur] seems a reasonable restoration, but note that, beginning with the MB period, this local hypostasis of Ištar is usually identified as $^{\text{d}}$UN.GAL-NIBRU$^{\text{ki}}$ (Sassmannshausen 2001, 157ff.; Krebernik 2009).
11. This temple of Ninnisi might have been in Tukultī-Ekur, the town that provides its supplies; a connection between Tukultī-Ekur and a temple of Ninnisi is provided also by **no. 97**: 17. The restoration of Šūzub-Marduk's patronymic is based on **no. 325** (NM 14) and **no. 330** (KT 14).

### vi. Loan with Interest

## 120. CUNES 52-18-865

-.XI.19$^?$ Nazi-Maruttaš

Obv. ⌜ŠE UR$_5$⌝.RA $^{giš}$BÁN 10 SÌLA ⌜*ša i-na* ŠÀ *te-li-ti*⌝
*ša* MU.⌜19$^?$⌝.KAM ⌜*Na-zi-Ma*⌝*-ru-*[*ut-ta-aš* LUGAL].E
*i-na* $^{iti}$ZÍZ.[A.AN] ⌜SUM⌝-[*nu*]

| | | | | |
|---|---|---|---|---|
| | BÀD-EN-KUR.KUR | *Ḫu-u*[*ṣ*]-*ṣu*$^{k}$[$^{i}$] | | [MU.BI].I[M] |
| | 0.2.3 | | | [$^{m}$X-X]-*ir*-$^{d}$IŠKUR |
| | 0.2.3 | | | [$^{m}$X-X]-⌜X-$^{d}$*Dil*$^?$-*bat*$^?$⌝ |
| | 0.2.3 | | | $^{m⌜d}$*Dil*⌝-*bat*-⌜*ba*$^?$⌝-[*ni*$^?$] |
| | 1.0.0 | | | DUMU $^{md}$IŠKUR-*di*-⌜X-X⌝ |
| | 0.2.3 | | | [$^{m}$*Ri*]-*iš*-$^{d}$IŠK[UR] |
| | 0.2.3 | | | ⌜$^{m}$X-X-X⌝-$^{d}$IŠKUR |
| | | 1.0.0 | | ⌜$^{m}$X-X-*na*$^?$⌝ |
| | | ⌜0.X⌝.[X] | | $^{m}$*Li-ši*-⌜*ra-an-ni*⌝-$^{d}$UTU |
| | | [ ] | | ⌜$^{m}$X-X-X-$^{d}$U.GUR$^?$⌝ |
| PAP | ⌜3.2⌝.[3] | [ ] | | ⌜*Ḫu*⌝-*uṣ*-[*ṣu*$^{ki}$] |
| | | [ ] | | [ |
| | | [ ] | | [ |
| | | [ ] | | [ |
| | | [ ] | | [ |
| | | [ ] | | [ ]⌜X⌝ |
| | | [ ] | | [ ]⌜X⌝ |
| | | [ ] | | [ |
| | | [ ] | | [ |
| | | [ ] | | [ |
| Rev. | | 0.2.3 | √ | $^{m⌜d⌝}$[ |
| | | 0.2.3 | √ | $^{md}$IŠKU[R- |
| | | 0.2.3 | √ | $^{m}$*Ḫa-ni-*[*bu*] |
| | | 0.2.3 | √ | $^{m}$⌜*Aḫ*$^?$⌝-*ḫu-dan-*[*nu*] |
| | | 0.2.3 | √ | ⌜$^{md}$⌝MAŠ-*di-na-an-ni* |
| | | 0.2.3 | √ | ⌜$^{m}$*Kal*⌝-*bu* |
| | | 0.2.3 | √$^?$ | $^{m}$ZÁLAG-$^{d}$UTU |
| | | 0.2.3 | √ | $^{m}$*Ri-iš*-$^{d}$IŠKUR |
| | | 0.2.3 | √$^?$ | $^{m}$LÚ-*Ì-si-in*$^{ki}$ |
| PAP | | 5.2.3 | | ÌR.É.GAL$^{meš}$ |
| PAP | 4.0.0 | 17.2.3 | | ŠU $^{m}$*Ḫa-am-bi*<br>*i-na* ŠÀ ŠE.BA *i-kal-la*<br>(erasure) |
| | | 0.2.3 | √ | $^{m}$*I-re-man-ni*-DINGIR |
| | | 0.2.3 | √$^?$ | $^{m}$*E-mi-du* DUMU $^{m}$*E-la-mi-i* |

| | | | |
|---|---|---|---|
| PAP | | 1.0.0 | ÉRIN$^{\text{ḫi.a}}$ *ša* É $^{\text{m}}$*Ta-ri-bat*-DINGIR ŠU $^{\text{md}}$MAŠ-SAG |
| | | 0.2.3 √ | $^{\text{m}}$*Iz-kùr*-$^{\text{d}}$IŠKUR |
| | | 0.2.3 √ | $^{\text{m}}$*Ki-din*-$^{\text{d}}$*Dil-bat* |
| | | 0.2.3 √ | $^{\text{m}}$*Ú-sa-tu-ú-a* |
| PAP | | 1.2.3 | ÌR.É.GAL$^{\text{meš}}$ *Tukul-ti*-É.KUR$^{\text{ki}}$ *i-na* ŠE.BA *ik-kal-la* |
| PAP | | 0.1.3 √ | $^{\text{m}}$*Ta-ri-ba*-$^{\text{d}}$*Gu-la* DUMU $^{\text{m}}$*Ḫal-di-ia* BÀD-$^{\text{d+}}$*En-líl*$^{\text{meš}}$ *i-na* ŠE.BA KI.MIN |
| L.e.[ŠU.NI]GIN | 4.0.0 | 20.2.3 | |

COMMENTARY

1–3. "Barley as loan, (measured by) the *sūtu* of 10 *qû*, which was disbursed in month XI from the revenues of year 19$^{?}$ of [Kin]g Nazi-Maru[ttaš]."

33. This total corresponds to 0.2.3 (15 *sūtu*) for 11 persons.

34. "Under the responsibility of Ḫambu; he (i.e., Ḫambu$^{?}$) will withhold (it) from the rations." 4.0.0 in col. i would be the sum of 3.2.3 (l. 14) + 0.2.3, but I cannot see a "0.2.3" in the previous lines.

41. "Palace servants (of/in) Tukultī-Ekur; he will withhold (it) from the rations"; the subject is not clear. See also the following line.

42. *Gu-la* is written on an erasure.

## 121. CUNES 52-13-153

-.-.23$^{?}$ Nazi-Maruttaš, 3 Kadašman-Turgu

Allocations of *arsuppu* (ŠE.EŠTUB) and *šeguššu* (ŠE.MUŠ$_5$) as a loan with interest (UR$_5$.RA) in Dūr-Enlilē; the first was disbursed in the 23$^{\text{rd?}}$ year of Nazi-Maruttaš, the second in the 3$^{\text{rd}}$ year of Kadašman-Turgu.

Obv. ŠE $^{\text{giš}}$BÁN 10 SÌLA MU.BI.IM
2 2.2.3 ŠE.EŠTUB ⸢BÀD⸣-$^{\text{d+}}$*En-líl*$^{\text{meš.ki}}$
MU.⸢23$^{?}$⸣.KAM *Na-*[*z*]*i-Ma-ru-ut-taš* LUGAL
4 ⸢2.0.0 ŠE.MUŠ$_5$ KI⸣.MIN ⸢MU.3⸣.KAM
⸢$^{\text{d}}$⸣*Ka-dáš-man*-⸢*Túr*⸣-*g*[*u*] LUGAL.E
6 ⸢PAP⸣ 4.2.3 ŠE UR$_5$.RA ⸢$^{\text{giš}}$BÁN 10 SÌLA⸣
$^{\text{m}}$*Bu*-⸢*un-na*⸣-$^{\text{d}}$⸢*Gu*⸣-*la*
L.e. DUMU $^{\text{m}}$*In-ni-bu*
Rev. $^{\text{md+}}$*En-líl-tak-la-ku* DUMU.A.NI
*im-ḫu-ur*

Translation

Obv. Grain, (measured by) the *sūtu* of 10 *qû*; its entry:
2 75 *sūtu arsuppu*, Dūr-Enlilē
year ⸢23$^{?}$⸣ of King Nazi-Maruttaš.
4 60 *sūtu šeguššu*, ditto (i.e., Dūr-Enlilē) year 3$^{?}$
of King Kadašman-Turgu.
6 Total: 135 *sūtu*, grain as loan, (measured by) the *sūtu* of 10 *qû*,
L.e. (of) Bunna-Gula,
Rev. son of Innibu.
Enlil-taklāku, his son,
received (it).

## 122. CUNES 52-13-132 (Plate No. 38)

-.-.14 Kadašman-Turgu

| | |
|---|---|
| Obv. | ⸢ŠE⸣ $^{giš}$BÁN 10 [SÌLA UR$_5$].RA |
| | ⸢*ša*?⸣ *i*?*-na*?⸣ BÀD-$^{d+}$*En-líl*$^{meš.ki}$ |
| | [$^m$]*Ur-ra-a-a* DUMU $^m$ŠEŠ-SUM-*na*-$^d$AMAR.UTU *maḫ-rù* |
| 4 | [x.x.x] *i-na* ŠÀ *man-de-e i-na* ŠÀ *ši-ib-ši* |
| | *ša* $^m$*Ri-mu-ti* |
| 6 | [x.x].3 *i-na* ŠU $^m$*A-ḫe-du-ti ma-ki-si* |
| | *im-*⸢*ḫur*⸣*-ma* ŠU $^m$*A-ḫe-du-ti* |
| 8 | [x.x.x *i-na* Š]À *ši-ib-ši* |
| | *ša* [NÍG.KU]D.DA$^{meš}$ ŠU |
| L.e. | *tur-rat* |
| Rev. | 3.0.0 *i-na* ŠÀ *ki-iṣ-ri ša* NÍG.KU⸢D.DA⸣ |
| 12 | *i-na* ŠU $^m$*Mu*-SIG$_5$-$^d$IŠKUR |
| | *ma-ḫi-ir* |
| | PAP 11.2.3 UR$_5$.RA $^{giš}$BÁN 10 SÌLA |
| 15 | $^m$*Ur-ra-a-*⸢*a*⸣ DUMU $^m$ŠEŠ-SUM-*na*- |
| | $^d$AMAR.UTU |
| | *a-na* UGU NA$_4$.KIŠIB-*šu ú-rad-du-ma* |
| | *i-ṣa-ab-tu*$_4$ |
| U.e. | MU.14.KAM *Ka-dáš-man-Túr-gu* LUGAL |

Translation

| | |
|---|---|
| Obv. | Barley, (measured by) the *sūtu* of 10 [*qû*, lo]an |
| | which Urrāya, son of Aḫa-iddina-Marduk, |
| | received in Dūr-Enlilē. |
| 4 | [ . . . ] from the *mandê*(-field?), from the *šibšu* |
| | of Rīmūtu. |
| 6 | 3$^+$ *sūtu* he received from Aḫēdutu, the tax collector, |
| | and (it) is under the responsibility of Aḫēdutu. |
| 8 | [. . . from] the *šibšu* |
| | of the [*mik*]*su*-payments; the hand |
| L.e. | is turned. |
| Rev. | 90 *sūtu* from the *kiṣru* of the *miksu*-payment: |
| | he received (it) from Mudammiq-Adad. |
| | Total: 345 *sūtu*, loan, (measured by) the *sūtu* of 10 *qû*, |
| 15 | of Urrāya, son of Aḫa-iddina- |
| | Marduk. |
| | They added (it) to his sealed document |
| | and drew? it up. |
| U.e. | Year 14 of King Kadašman-Turgu. |

Commentary

4. For *i-na* ŠÀ *man-de-e* "from the *mandê*(-field?)," cf. *i-na man-de-e* (**no. 181**: 6) and TA *man-de-e* (CUSAS 30 240: 8 and CUSAS 30 247: 12). The word is left untranslated by van Soldt, who comments: "neither *mandû* 'base,' nor *minde* makes much sense. The word *mindu*, 'measured amount,' is attested only in Late Babylonian" (van Soldt 2015, 313). I wonder whether it could be somehow related to the verb *nandû* in the meaning "to be left fallow, uncared for (said of fields, orchards)" (CAD N/1, *nadû* II c, 98) and refer to some type of fields, perhaps fallow fields.

17. I take the sealed document mentioned in the previous line as the object of *iṣṣabtū*; for the expression NA$_4$.KIŠIB *ṣabātu*, meaning "to seize, to deposit into custody a sealed document" or "to draw up a sealed document," see comments to **no. 158**: 9.

## vii. "Delivery"

### 123. CUNES 52-00-049

-.-.9 Kadašman-Turgu

This poorly preserved tablet seems to have recorded "deliveries" (*maššātu*, l. 8′) of different towns. I assign it to this category because *maššītu* appears always in the context of expenditures, either as an item of expenditure or as a quantity from which other amounts are disbursed. While the literary meaning of *maššītu* as "delivery" might be clear (see AHw II, *maššītu* 2, 629, CAD M/1, *maššītu* 1, 389, and the translations in van Soldt 2015, passim), the nature and circumstances of this delivery still have to be investigated.

The left part of the tablet and ca. 2 lines at the beginning of the obverse are missing.

When it was acquired, it was attached to **no. 322**, with new clay used to fill the gap between the two fragments; it cannot be completely excluded that the two fragments did not originally belong to the same tablet.

Obv. ] MU.⸢BI.IM⸣
(1-2 empty lines)
2′ ] ⸢x⸣ *maš-ši-tu*$_4$ URU-ÌR-⸢GAŠAN⸣[$^{ki}$]
] ⸢$^{m}$⸣ZÁLAG-$^{d}$AMAR.UTU DUMU $^{m}$*Ì-lí-i-da-an-ni*
*i*]*š-ši*
5′ *maš-š*]*i-tu*$_4$ BÀD-*Ku-ri-gal-zu*
$^{m}$]*Ri-mu-tu*$_4$
[DUMU $^{m}$]⸢*Im*⸣-*gu-ri iš-ši*
8′ ] *maš-ša-a-tu*$_4$
L.e. M]U.9.KAM
*K*]*a-dáš-man-Túr-gu* LUGAL

The reverse is blank.

COMMENTARY

2′–4′. Nūr-Marduk, son of Ilī-īdânni, is mentioned in connection with the delivery (*maššītu*) of the town Āl-Arad-Bēlti also in **no. 157**: 5.

## 124. CUNES 52-19-156

-.-.[x]–21 Nazi-Maruttaš

Summary of expenditures given as a "gift" (*rīmūtu*, l. 12) over several years of Nazi-Maruttaš's reign. The tablet, which is too fragile to be baked, is still partially encrusted with dirt.

Obv. [x x (x)] ⸢x⸣ *iš-tu* ⸢MU⸣.[x.KAM] ⸢EN⸣ MU.2?.KA[M] *Na-zi-Múru-taš* ⸢*Di*-x-x⸣$^{ki}$[$^{i?}$

| | | | | | | |
|---|---|---|---|---|---|---|
| [ ] | [ ] | ⸢MU⸣.[x.KAM] | ⸢MU⸣.[x].⸢KAM⸣ | ⸢MU.21.KAM⸣ | ŠU.NÍGIN | MU.BI.I[M] |
| [ ] | [ ] | 15.⸢0.0⸣ | ⸢5.0.0⸣ | | ⸢1⸣-*šu* | $^{m}$ZÁLAG-*li-m*[*ur*$^{?}$ |
| [ ] | [ ] | 10.0.0 | 10.0.0 | | 40.0.0 | $^{md}$30-*mu*-⸢*šal*⸣-*l*[*im* |
| [ ] | ⸢x.0.0⸣ | 15.0.0 | 15.0.0 | 15.0.0 | ⸢7⸣5.0.0 | $^{m}$GAL-*šá*-$^{d}$AMAR.[UTU<br>⸢EN⸣ 2.0.0 *ša* ŠU $^{m}$[ |
| [ ] | ⸢10.0.0⸣ | 10.0.0 | ⸢5.0.0⸣ | | ⸢25⸣.0.0 | $^{m}$⸢x-x⸣-$^{d}$IŠKUR ⸢x⸣ [<br>*ša* ru/šub ba$^{?}$ ⸢x x⸣ [ |
| [ ] | | 5.0.4 | ⸢15.0.0⸣ | 17.1.2<br>⸢*a*$^{?}$⸣-[x-x] | ⸢37⸣.2.0 | $^{m}$SU-$^{d}$*Šu*-⸢*qa-mu*⸣-*n*[*a* |
| [ ] | | | 10.0.0 | | [ ] | $^{m}$*Bíl*-⸢*lu*⸣-*u*[*l*$^{?}$-*lu*$_{4}$$^{?}$] DUMU $^{md}$⸢UTU-*ki*⸣-*na-i-de* |
| [ ] | | | 2.2.3 | | ⸢2.2⸣.3 | $^{m}$ÌR-$^{d}$AMAR.[UTU DU]MU $^{md+}$*En-líl*-ÙRU *a-ši-pu* |
| [ ] | | | | ⸢3$^{+}$.1$^{+}$.3⸣<br>URU-*ir-re-e*[$^{(ki)}$] | [x.x].3 | *ki-mu* 5.0.0 ZÍZ.AN.NA *ša* ŠÀ ŠE ⸢LIBIR$^{?}$⸣.RA<br>$^{md}$*Sukkal*-ŠEŠ-SUM-*na* SU[M$^{?}$-*nu*$^{?}$] |
| [ ] | | | | | [x.x].⸢x⸣ | $^{m}$TI-*su*-$^{d}$AMAR.UTU DUMU $^{m}$*Ak-ni*-⸢*ša*$^{?}$⸣-KÁ$^{?}$-$^{d?}$x-x⸣ |
| [ ] | 50.0.0 | 55.0./4 | 72./2.3 | ⸢24$^{?}$./x.x⸣<br>⸢x x x⸣ | [ ] | *ri-mu-tu*$_{4}$ |

The reverse is blank.

COMMENTARY

7. See also **no. 125**, a summary of barley received as a "gift" by Erība-Šuqamuna from year 21 till year 23 of Nazi-Maruttaš.

### 125. CUNES 52-10-074 (Plate No. 39)

-.-.21–23 (Nazi-Maruttaš)

Summary of barley$^{?}$ received as a "gift" by Erība-Šuqamuna in Āl-atḫē and Mê-Zurud, over three years. Even though the king's name is not mentioned, the text must refer to years 21–23 of Nazi-Maruttaš, because Erība-Šuqamuna is often attested in texts from the last years of his reign (see esp. **no. 124**: 7, where Erība-Šuqamuna appears again as the recipient of a "gift"); he must also be identical with the homonymous *ṣuḫurtu* mentioned as a recipient of barley as a "gift" in **no. 150**: 14 (KT 3).

Obv. [ŠE$^{?}$] $^{\text{giš}}$BÁN 10 SÌLA ŠA TA MU.21.KAM EN MU.23.KAM
$^{\text{m}}$*Eri-ba-*$^{\text{d}}$*Šu-qa-mu-na mi-taḫ-ḫu-rù*

| | |
|---|---|
| (eras.) | URU-*at-ḫe-e* $^{\text{iti}}$APIN.DU$_8$.A MU.21.KAM |
| 0.2.3 | KI.MIN $^{\text{iti}}$ZÍZ.A.AN MU.22.KAM |
| 6.0.0 | *Me-e-Zu-ru-ud*$^{\text{ki}}$ $^{\text{iti}}$KIN.2.KAM MU.23.KAM |

PAP 6.2.3 *ri-mu-tu*$_4$ $^{\text{m}}$*Eri-ba-*$^{\text{d}}$*Šu-qa-mu-na*

The reverse is blank.

Translation

Obv. [Barley$^{?}$], (measured by) the *sūtu* of 10 *qû*,
which Erība-Šuqamuna has been receiving from year 21 till year 23:

| | |
|---|---|
| (eras.) | Āl-atḫē, month VIII, year 21. |
| 15 *sūtu* | Ditto (i.e., Āl-atḫē), month XI, year 22. |
| 180 *sūtu* | Mê-Zurud, month VIa, |
| year 23. | |

Total: 195 *sūtu*, gift of Erība-Šuqamuna.

The reverse is blank.

COMMENTARY

3. The scribe seems to have written and then erased the amount associated with this entry; one can still see some traces of cuneiform signs. As a matter of fact, the total in l. 6 is the correct sum of the amounts indicated in ll. 4–5.
5. I am aware of only one other attestation of the GN Mê-Zurud in MB texts (BE 15 110: 2).

## ix. "Exchange"

### 126. CUNES 52-14-047

-.XI.13 Kadašman-Turgu

Obv. 0.1.4 ŠE $^{\text{giš}}$BÁN 10 SÌLA *i-na* ⸢ŠÀ UR$_5$⸣.RA
⸢*ša*⸣ $^{\text{m}}$MU-*líb-ši i-na Tukul-ti*-É.KUR$^{\text{ki}}$
*im-ḫu-ru-ma*
*a-na* ŠE.BAL *a-na* $^{\text{m}}$*Ḫu-na-bi*
5 *ú-ter-ru*
*i-na* munus-*bi i-na* ŠU $^{\text{m}}$*Mu*-SI[G$_5$-$^{\text{d}}$IŠ]KUR
$^{\text{md}}$30-TI-URU$_4$ *im-ḫur*
L.e. $^{\text{md}}$30-ŠEŠ-ŠUM-*na*
9 *a-na pa-a-ni im-ḫur*
Rev. $^{\text{iti}}$ZÍZ.A.AN
MU.13.KAM
$^{\text{d}}$*Ka-dáš-man-Túr-gu*
LUGAL.E

Translation

Obv. 10 *sūtu* of barley, (measured by) the *sūtu* of 10 *qû*, (taken) from the loan
2–3 that Šumu-libši received in Tukultī-Ekur and
4–5 gave back to Ḫunābu as exchange?.
7 Sîn-balāṭa-īriš received
6 in . . . from Mud[ammiq-A]dad.
L.e. Sîn-aḫa-iddina
9 had received (it) before?.
Rev. Month XI,
year 13 of
King Kadašman-Turgu.

COMMENTARY

4. For ŠE.BAL "exchange?," see comments to **no. 64**: 2.

6. The reading of the signs munus-*bi*, which occur also in **no. 180**: 9, is uncertain; *rak-bi* is possible, but it can hardly be a form of *rakbû* "messenger, envoy," which is usually rendered logographically $^{\text{(lú)}}$RA/RÁ.GABA or spelled syllabically, stressing the final long vowel with an extra vowel (CAD R, 105–7 s.v.). Perhaps a toponym or geographical indication?

9. The interpretation of the prepositional phrase *ana pāni* as a temporal indication is tentative.

### 1.3.3 Multiple Expenditures for Various Purposes

## 127. CUNES 52-18-794

-.VII.10$^{+}$ Nazi-Maruttaš

Obv. ŠE *ša* $^{md}$MAŠ-MU-M[U

*i-na* $^{uru}$*Ḫa-am-r*[*i*

*a-na* $^{m}$*Ḫu-na-bi* ⸢$^{lú?}$⸣[

⸢13$^{+}$.4⸣.3 $^{giš}$[BÁN

Rev. [ ] ⸢bi$^{?}$⸣ [

$^{iti}$DU$_{6}$.KÙ MU.⸢10$^{+}$⸣.[KAM]

*Na-zi-Mu-ru-ut-*[

## 128. CUNES 52-19-118

-.VII.17 Nazi-Maruttaš

Obv. 0.2.3 ZAG.ḪI.LI $^{giš}$BÁN ⸢GAL⸣

0.2$^{pi}$.0 GÚ.GAL KI.MIN

0.0.4 GÚ.TUR ⸢KI.MIN⸣

PAP 1.0.1 $^{giš}$BÁN GAL *ša* $^{md}$MAŠ-MU-MU

É-*ta-nu*

25.0.0 *maš-šar-tu*$_{4}$ DUMU $^{m}$*Ta-ri-bat*-DINGIR

L.e. ⸢x$^{?}$ 3.0.1 x x (x) $^{giš}$BÁN$^{?}$ GAL$^{?}$⸣

Rev. [x.x].3 ZAG.⸢ḪI.LI⸣

⸢0.0.5⸣ 7 SÌLA GÚ.GAL

0.0.4 GÚ.GAL

PAP 0.4$^{pi}$.0 7 SÌLA $^{giš}$BÁN 10 SÌLA *a-na ta-kul-ti* DUMU $^{m}$*Ta-ri-bat*-DINGIR

$^{iti}$DU$_{6}$.KÙ

M[U].17$^{?}$.KAM *Na-zi-Ma-ru-ut-*[

Commentary

11. Sassmannshausen 2001, 170 and CAD T, 90–91 s.v. record only three MB attestations of *tākultu*, which may indicate a ceremonial or cultic meal, but also a festive meal or banquet, depending on the context.

## 129. CUNES 52-13-139

18.X.17 Nazi-Maruttaš

Allocation of barley as production supplies, seed, and fodder.

| | | |
|---|---|---|
| Obv. | ŠE $^{\text{giš}}$BÁN 5 SÌLA *ša i-na* $^{\text{iti}}$AB.È | |
| | *ša* MU.17.KAM *Na-zi-Ma-ru-ut-taš* LUGAL | |
| | 1.0.0 | ÉŠ.GÀR ⸢⸢X-X-X⸣ |
| | 1.0.0 NUMUN | ⸢DUMU$^{?}$⸣ $^{\text{m}}$*Šu-*⸢*ri-i*⸣ |
| | 0.2.3 | ŠUKU ⸢X X X⸣ |
| | | ŠU $^{\text{md}}$IŠKUR-[ |
| Rev. | [P]AP 2.2.3 | |
| | $^{\text{iti}}$AB.È U$_4$.18.KAM | |
| | MU.17.KAM | |

Translation

| | | |
|---|---|---|
| Obv. | Barley, (measured by) the *sūtu* of 5 *qû*, which (was disbursed) in month X of year 17 of King Nazi-Maruttaš: | |
| | 30 *sūtu* | Production supplies of ⸢ . . . ⸣ |
| | 30 *sūtu*, seed | ⸢Son$^{?}$ of⸣ Šuri |
| | 15 *sūtu* | Fodder ⸢ . . . ⸣ |
| | | at the disposal of Adad-[ . . . ] |
| Rev. | [To]tal: 75 *sūtu*. | |
| | Month X, day 18, | |
| | Year 17. | |

Commentary

1–2. The relative pronoun *ša* in l. 1 implies a verbal form such as *nadnu* at the end of l. 2.

## 130. CUNES 52-12-041

-.VII.18 Nazi-Maruttaš

| | |
|---|---|
| Obv. | 0.1.2 GÚ.GAL $^{\text{giš}}$BÁN GAL |
| | *ša* BÀD-EN-KUR.KUR$^{\text{ki}}$ |
| 3 | ŠU $^{\text{md}}$IŠKUR-*ša-gim* |
| | 0.0.2 2 SÌLA ŠE.IN.<NU>.ḪA |
| | É-*ta-nu* |
| Rev. | $^{\text{iti}}$DU$_6$.KÙ |
| | MU.18.KAM |
| | *Na-zi-Ma-ru-ut-taš* LUGAL |

## 131. CUNES 52-12-046

-.XII.18 Nazi-Maruttaš

Barley disbursed in Dūr-Enlilē as fodder for oxen and food for plowmen.

See BE 14 57 for a Nippur text dated to the 12th year of Nazi-Maruttaš and showing similar content and layout.

Obv. ŠE $^{giš}$BÁN 10 SÌLA *i-na* ŠÀ *maš-ši-ti ša ul-tu*$_4$ ⸢x⸣[
*na-ša-ta-am-ma i-na* BÀD-$^{d+}$*En-líl*$^{ḫi.a}$ *i-na* $^{iti}$⸢ŠE.KIN.KU$_5$⸣
*ša* MU.18.KAM *Na-zi-Ma-ru-ut-taš na-ad-na-tu*$_4$

| | ŠUKU GU$_4$ | ŠUKU $^{lú}$ENGAR | ŠU.NÍGIN | MU.BI.I[M] |
|---|---|---|---|---|
| | 1.0.0 | 1.4.4 | 2.4.4 | DUMU $^{m}$ÌR-$^{d}$[ |
| | 1.0.0 | 1.4.3 | 2.4.3 | DUMU $^{m}$*In-na-ni-bu-ti* |
| | | 0.2.5 | 0.2.5 | $^{md}$UTU-⸢x⸣[ |
| | [1.0.0] | 0.2.3 | 1.2.3 | $^{m}$*Ba-ḫu-*[ |
| | [1.0.0] | 1.⸢3.2⸣ | 2.3.2 | DUMU $^{m}$*A-n*[*a-* |
| | [1.0.0] | [0.4].⸢5⸣ | 1.4.5 | ⸢x x⸣ [ |
| Rev. | [ ] | 0.⸢1.4⸣ | 0.1.4 | [<br>[ |
| | 1.0.0 | 0.2$^{pi}$.0 | 1.2.0 | $^{m}$[ |
| | | 0.3.⸢4⸣ | 0.3.4 | $^{m}$*Ta-qí-šu*$_{14}$<br>DUMU $^{m}$*Be-lí-ia-a-tu*$_4$ |
| | | 1.0.[1] | 1.0.1 | DUMU $^{m}$*Ḫi-il-di-ia* |
| | | 0.3.0 | 0.3.0 | $^{f}$*Bì-il-ti-mar-ṣa-at*<br>DUMU $^{m}$*Ṣíl-lí-*$^{d}$*É-a*-LUGAL |
| | | 0.2.0 | 0.2.0 | $^{m}$ZÁLAG-$^{d}$AMAR.UTU *da-lu-ú* |
| | | 0.2.0 | 0.2.0 | DUMU $^{m}$ŠEŠ-*ni* KI.MIN |
| [PAP] | 6.0.0 | 11.2.1 | 17.2.1 | |

Commentary

1–3. "Barley, (measured by) the *sūtu* of 10 *qû*, from the delivery that was brought here from [GN] and disbursed in Dūr-Enlilē in month XII of year 18 of Nazi-Maruttaš." For verbal forms like *našâtam-ma* (3 pl. fem. stative of *našû* with ventive) in these texts, see van Soldt 2015, 34–35.

11. No quantity is expected in the gap in col. i, since the total recorded in col. iii corresponds to the amount of col. ii.

15. Unless DUMU is a mistake for DUMU.MUNUS, the fact that this feminine PN is followed by DUMU Ṣillī-Ea-šarru suggests that this entry refers to two different persons.

## 132. CUNES 53-01-174

-.-.19 Nazi-Maruttaš

Nothing of the obverse is preserved except for part of the heading and traces of a few signs on the right edge.

The presence of the *rubbû* formula at the end of the text and the landscape format suggest that the tablet might have recorded expenditures.

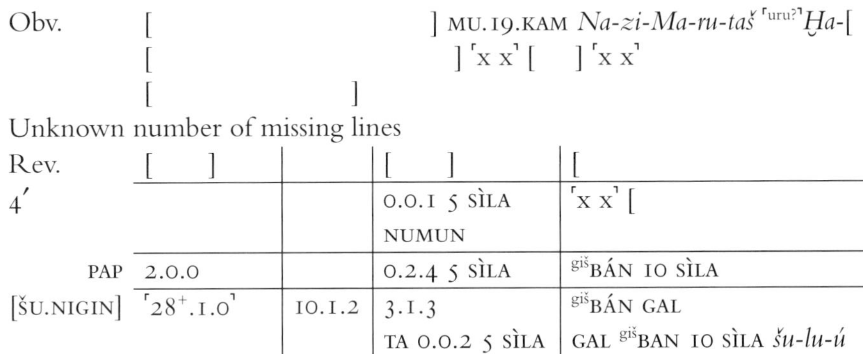

Obv. [ ] MU.19.KAM *Na-zi-Ma-ru-taš* $^{⸢uru?⸣}$*Ḫa-*[

[ ]⸢x x⸣ [ ]⸢x x⸣

[ ]

Unknown number of missing lines

| | | | | |
|---|---|---|---|---|
| Rev. | [ ] | | [ ] | [ |
| 4′ | | | 0.0.1 5 SÌLA<br>NUMUN | ⸢x x⸣ [ |
| PAP | 2.0.0 | | 0.2.4 5 SÌLA | $^{giš}$BÁN 10 SÌLA |
| [ŠU.NIGIN] | ⸢28$^{+}$.1.0⸣ | 10.1.2 | 3.1.3<br>TA 0.0.2 5 SÌLA | $^{giš}$BÁN GAL<br>GAL $^{giš}$BAN 10 SÌLA *šu-lu-ú* |

## 133. CUNES 52-13-111

-.I.20 Nazi-Maruttaš

Allocation of barley as production supplies and rations.

Obv. ŠE *ša i-na* ŠÀ *te-li-ti ša* BÀD-$^{d+}$*En-líl*$^{hi.a.ki}$

*ša* MU.19.KAM *Na-zi-Ma-ru-ut-ta-aš* ⸢LUGAL.E⸣

*i-na* $^{iti}$BÁR.ZAG.GAR *ša* MU.20.KAM *na-ad-nu*

| | ŠE $^{giš}$BÁN GAL | ŠE $^{giš}$BÁN 10 SÌLA | MU.BI.IM |
|---|---|---|---|
| | 20.0.0 | | ÉŠ.GÀR $^{m}$*Sú-uḫ-ḫu-tu₄* $^{lú}$LUNGA |
| | 20.0.0 | | ÉŠ.GÀR $^{m}$*Ba-i-rù* KI.MIN |
| | 20.0.0 | | ÉŠ.GÀR $^{m}$*Eri-ba-*$^{d}$*Nin-urta* KI.MIN |
| | 40.0.0 | | ÉŠ.GÀR [x x x $^{md}$*Nin-ur*]*ta-*SAG |
| | 10.0.0 | | ÉŠ.GÀR [ |
| | | 15.0.0 | ÉŠ.GÀR $^{m}$*Ṭà-ab-ki-*[*din-*$^{d}$*Gu-la*] |
| Rev. | | 30.0.0 | ŠE.BA É-*a-nu* DUB [<br>*ki-i ṭ*[*e-mi-ša*] |
| | | 25.0.0 | ŠE.BA KÁ-⸢*a*⸣-[*nu* |
| | | 6.0.0 | $^{m}$[<br>⸢x⸣ [x] ⸢x⸣ [<br>⸢x⸣ [x] $^{m}$*Šu-*[<br>⸢x⸣ [x] ⸢ur?⸣ [ |
| PAP | 1 ME 10.0.0 | 76.0.0 | ŠU.NIGIN 1 ME 70.4$^{pi}$.0 $^{giš}$BÁN GAL<br>TA ⸢1⸣5.1$^{pi}$.0 GAL $^{giš}$BÁN 10 SÌLA<br>*i-na* ⸢1⸣.0.0 0.1$^{pi}$.0 *šu-lu-ú* |
| | 0.3.0 | [ ] | *ni-ki-is* GUR₇ $^{m}$[x x x (x)]⸢x⸣ *ḫa-za-nu* |

Translation

Obv. Barley from the revenues of Dūr-Enlilē
of year 19 of King Nazi-Maruttaš,
which was disbursed in month I of year 20.

| | Barley (meas. by) the big *sūtu* | Barley (meas. by) the *sūtu* of 10 *qû* | Its entry |
|---|---|---|---|
| | 600 *sūtu* | | Production supplies (for) Ṣuḫḫutu, brewer. |
| | 600 *sūtu* | | Production supplies (for) Bā'eru, ditto. |
| | 600 *sūtu* | | Production supplies (for) Erība-Ninurta, ditto. |
| | 1,200 *sūtu* | | Production supplies (for) [. . . Ninur]ta-ašarēd. |
| | 300 *sūtu* | | Production supplies (for) [ |
| | | 450 *sūtu* | Production supplies (for) Ṭāb-ki[din-Gula]. |
| Rev. | | 900 *sūtu* | Rations of the inner quarter, the list [of names] is in accordance with [its] inst[ructions]. |
| | | 750 *sūtu* | Rations of the *bābā*[*nu*]. |
| | | 180 *sūtu* | [PN . . .<br>⸢. . .⸣ [<br>⸢. . .⸣ Šu[. . .<br>⸢. . .⸣ [ |
| Total | 3,300 *sūtu* | 2,280 *sūtu* | Grand total: 5,124 *sūtu* (meas. by) the big *sūtu* after 456 *sūtu* have been deducted, the increase of the *sūtu* of 10 *qû* being at a rate of 1 *pānu* per kor. |
| | 18 *sūtu* | [( . . .)] | *nikis karê* (of) [PN], *ḫazannu*. |

Commentary

10. For the restoration of the PN, cf. **nos. 136**: 9, **149**: 6, and **152**: 5.

11. For the restorations cf. **no. 150**: 8. On the expression *tuppi šumāti kī ṭēmiša* "the list of names is in accordance with its instruction (i.e., with the instructions for drafting this kind of list)," see van Soldt 2015, 33. Cf. also ŠE.BA É-*a-nu* DUB *šu-ma-a-ti* GAR-*at* "rations of the inner quarter, the list of names has been deposited" in CUSAS 30 89: 6.

11–12. On the *bītānu* and *bābānu*, see Introduction §4.3.

## 134. CUNES 52-18-816

-.XII.21 Nazi-Maruttaš

The upper part of the obverse is lost. The remaining portion of the text mentions rations and a loan with interest as purposes of the disbursement.

(Beginning broken)

| | |
|---|---|
| Obv. | ⸢x x⸣ [ x x x x x ] ⸢x x⸣ |
| 2′ | 1.⸢2.3⸣ ŠE.BA 2 $^{\text{lú}}$ENGAR$^{\text{meš}}$ 4 ITI $^{\text{md}}$30-SUM-*na* |
| Rev. | 1.0.0 UR$_5$.RA $^{\text{md}}$30-*šar-rù* |
| 5′ | 0.1.4 ŠE.BA $^{\text{m}}$*Ki-din-*$^{\text{d+}}$*En-líl* DUMU $^{\text{m}}$*Sa-a-mi* $^{\text{m}}$KI.MIN *im-ḫur* |
| | PAP 8.2.5 SUM-*nu* $^{\text{iti}}$ŠE.KIN.KU$_5$ MU.21.KAM *Na-zi-Ma-ru-ut-ta-aš* |

Translation

| | |
|---|---|
| Obv. | ⸢. . .⸣ [. . .] ⸢. . .⸣ |
| 2′ | 45 *sūtu* rations (for) 2 plowmen, for 4 months; Sîn-iddina. |
| Rev. | 30 *sūtu* loan (for) Sîn-šarru. |
| 5′ | 10 *sūtu* rations (for) Kidin-Enlil, son of Sāmu; ditto has received. |
| | Total: 257 *sūtu*, disbursed. Month XII, year 21 of Nazi-Maruttaš. |

Commentary

5′. Kidin-Enlil, son of Sāmu, appears as a recipient of barley also in CUSAS 30 131: 16 and CUSAS 30 135: 6; the latter is dated to year 21, which should be understood as NM 21 because of our text.

## 135. CUNES 52-10-077

-.XI.21$^{+}$ (Nazi-Maruttaš)

Allocation of barley as production supplies and fodder, and for other purposes not preserved.

Even though the king's name is not mentioned, the tablet must date in the reign of Nazi-Maruttaš, as suggested by the presence of Agab-šenni, Erība-Ninurta, and Arad-Bēlti, son of Iškun-līssu, who appear also in other texts from his reign (see below and Index of Personal Names).

Obv. ŠE *ša i-na* ŠÀ 11.⸢1⸣.3 $^{\text{giš}}$BÁN 10 SÌLA ⸢*ša i-na*⸣ ŠÀ ḪA.⸢LA$^{\text{meš}}$⸣
*ù ki-iṣ-ri ša* $^{\text{md}}$*Nin-urta*-MU-MU *ša Kar-*$^{\text{d}}$*Nuska*$^{\text{ki}}$
*i-na* $^{\text{iti}}$ZÍZ.A.AN MU.⸢21$^{+}$⸣.[KAM *a-n*]*a* BÀD-$^{\text{d+}}$*En-líl*$^{\text{ḫi.a.ki}}$
*na-ša-am-ma* SUM-*nu*

| | | | |
|---|---|---|---|
| | ŠE $^{\text{giš}}$BÁN GAL | ŠE $^{\text{giš}}$BÁN 10 SÌLA | [M]U.BI.IM |
| | 2.0.0 | | ÉŠ.GÀR $^{\text{m}}$*A-gab-še-en-ni* |
| | 1.0.0 | | ÉŠ.GÀR $^{\text{m}}$*Eri-ba-*$^{\text{d}}$*Nin-urta* |
| | | 2.0.0 | ŠUKU GU$_4$ [x] ⸢$^{\text{m}}$ÌR⸣-GAŠAN DUMU $^{\text{m}}$*Iš-*⸢*kun*$_8$*-lí-su*⸣ |
| | | 0.4.4 | ⸢ŠUKU$^?$⸣ [x x (x)] ⸢$^{\text{m}}$⸣*Ki-din-*$^{\text{d}}$*Gu-la* |
| | | 0.4.⸢1⸣ | [x x x] $^{\text{m}}$*Mu*-SIG$_5$-$^{\text{d}}$IŠKUR |
| Rev. | | ⸢0.2.x⸣ | [x x x x x (x) *b*]*u*$^?$-⸢x⸣ |
| | | 2.⸢1$^?$.x⸣ | [ |
| | | 0.1.3 5 SÌLA | [x x x x x] ⸢$^{\text{m}}$ŠEŠ$^?$⸣-[ |
| | | 0.1.1 | [x x x] ⸢x $^{\text{m}}$*Bu*⸣-*un-n*[*a*- |
| PAP | 3.0.0 | 7.⸢x.x 5⸣ | [ŠU.NI]GIN$^?$ 11.1.3 [$^{\text{gi}}$]$^{\text{š}}$BÁN 10 SÌLA |

Translation

Obv. Barley from 339 *sūtu*, (measured by) the *sūtu* of 10 *qû*, which are from the shares
and the *kiṣru*-tax of Ninurta-zākir-šumi of Kār-Nuska,
which was brought here [t]o Dūr-Enlilē in month XI of year ⸢21$^{+}$⸣ and disbursed.

| | | | |
|---|---|---|---|
| | Barley (meas. by) the big *sūtu* | Barley (meas. by) the *sūtu* of 10 *qû* | Its entry |
| | 60 *sūtu* | | Production supplies (for) Agab-šenni. |
| | 30 *sūtu* | | Production supplies (for) Erība-Ninurta. |
| | | 60 *sūtu* | Fodder for an ox [ . . . ] Arad-Bēlti, son of Iškun-līssu. |
| | | 28 *sūtu* | ⸢Fodder$^?$⸣ [ . . . ] Kidin-Gula. |
| | | 25 *sūtu* | [ . . . ] Mudammiq-Adad. |
| Rev. | | 12$^{+}$ *sūtu* | [. . . . . .]⸢ . . . ⸣ |
| | | 66$^{+}$ *sūtu* | [. . . . . .] |
| | | 9 *sūtu*, 5 *qû* | [ . . . ] ⸢Aḫu$^?$⸣-[ |
| | | 7 *sūtu* | [ . . . ] ⸢ . . . ⸣ Bunn[a- |
| Total | 90 *sūtu* | 210$^{+}$ ⸢*sūtu*, 5 *qû*⸣ | [Grand$^?$ to]tal$^?$: 339 *sūtu*, (meas. by) the *sūtu* of 10 *qû*. |

Commentary

6–7. Agab-šenni and Erība-Ninurta are brewers (cf., e.g., **nos. 133**: 7 and **136**: 7).

## 136. CUNES 52-19-151

-.XII.23 Nazi-Maruttaš

Allocation of barley$^?$ as production supplies, rent for a boat, rations, fodder, and for other purposes not preserved.

The first lines of the text (ll. 2–5) probably described the sources of the expended barley—i.e., the amounts of Enlil-mutakkil and Nuska-muballiṭ.

| | | | | |
|---|---|---|---|---|
| U.e. | | [x $^{iti}$ŠE.KI]N.KU$_5$ [MU].⸢23⸣.KAM *Na-zi-Múru-ta*[*š*] | | |
| Obv. | | [x $^{giš}$]BÁN GAL MU.[BI].IM | | |
| | | [x.x.x] *ša* $^{md+}$*En-líl-mu-tak-kil* | | |
| | | [x.x.x] *ša* $^{md}$*Nuska-mu-bal-li*[*ṭ*] | | |
| | [PAP$^?$] | ⸢8$^+$⸣.0.0 $^{giš}$BÁN GAL | | |
| | | [$^{giš}$]BÁN GAL | $^{giš}$BÁN 10 SÌLA | *ša i-na* ŠÀ SUM-⸢*nu*⸣ |
| | | ⸢1$^+$⸣.0.0 | | ÉŠ.GÀR $^m$*A-gab-še-en-ni* $^{lú}$LUNGA |
| | | [x.x].⸢4⸣ | | Á $^{giš}$MÁ |
| | | | 5.0.5 | ÉŠ.GÀR $^m$*Ṭà-ab-ki-din-*$^d$*Gu-la* |
| | | | 5.4.2 | ŠE.BA É |
| | | | 0.2.2 | ŠE.[B]A $^{lú}$ENGAR$^{meš}$ DUMU.MUNUS $^m$*I*[*n*$^?$*-nu*$^?$]-⸢*a*$^?$*-ti*$^?$⸣ |
| | | | 0.0.5 | ŠE.BA DUMU.MUNUS $^m$*Ri-iš-na-pa-aḫ-šu* |
| | | | 0.1.4 | ŠE.BA $^m$*Lul-ta-mar-*$^d$30 $^{lú}$⸢x⸣ |
| | | | 0.1.4 | ŠE.BA $^{md}$30-EN-NUMUN |
| | | | 0.2.3 | Š[E.BA] ⸢$^m$*Ba*⸣*-bi-la-a-a-ú* |
| | | | 0.1$^{pi}$.0 5 SÌLA | Š[E.BA $^m$x-x]-⸢$^d$AMAR.UTU x⸣ [ |
| Rev. | | | 0.1$^{pi}$.0 | ŠE.BA $^m$*Mu-un-*[ |
| | | | 0.0.4 5 SÌLA | ŠE.BA $^{md}$*Nin-nisi-*[<br>DUMU $^{mf}$*Ub-bu-*⸢*ut-ti*⸣ |
| | | | 0.1.1 5 SÌLA | ŠE.BA $^f$*Ap-par-ri-tu*$_4$ ⸢x x⸣ |
| | | | 0.1.3 | ŠUKU GU$_4$.NIGA DUMU.⸢MUNUS$^?$⸣ *In-nu-ú-a-ti* |
| | | | 0.0.4 ⸢5 SÌLA⸣ | ⸢*it*$^?$*-ti*$^?$⸣ GA.RAŠ$^{sar}$ $^m$*Ṭà-ab-ṣíl-lu*$_4$ ⸢NU⸣.$^{giš}$KIRI$_6$<br>$^{md}$30-TI.LA-URU$_4$ ⸢x x⸣ [ |
| | | | 0.0.3 | ⸢x x⸣ $^m$KI.MIN [ |
| | | [ ] | ⸢0.0.1 5⸣ | [$^m$*E*]-⸢*muq*-$^d$IŠKUR NU.$^{giš}$KIRI$_6$⸣ |
| | | [ ] | ⸢0.1.1 5⸣ | [x x x] ⸢x x DUMU $^m$⸣*Ì-lí-a-a-ba-aš* |
| | | [ ] | ⸢0.0.1 5⸣ | [x x x x x] ⸢$^m$*Še*$^?$*-mi-i*⸣<br>[x x x x x x ]⸢A.NI⸣ *im-ḫur* |
| | | [ ] | 0.2.3 | $^m$[x x x]-⸢*re-man*⸣*-ni* |
| | | [ ] | ⸢0.1.3 UR$_5$$^?$.RA$^?$⸣ | $^m$[$^d$30$^?$]-⸢*nap*⸣*-ši-*⸢*ra*$^?$⸣ |
| | | [ ] | ⸢x.x.x⸣ KI.MIN | ⸢$^m$*Bu-un*⸣*-na-*$^d$AMAR.UTU DUMU ⸢$^{mf}$*Ub*⸣*-bu-ut-ti* |
| | [PAP$^?$] | [ ] | ⸢15.4$^?$.x⸣<br>5 SÌLA | ⸢ŠU.NIGIN⸣ 18.1.2 5 SÌLA $^{giš}$BÁN GA[L]<br>⸢TA 3$^?$.3$^?$.0 GAL⸣ $^{giš}$BÁN 10 SÌLA<br>⸢*i-na* 1⸣.0.0 0.1$^{pi}$.0⸣ *šu-lu-ú* |

Translation

| | | | |
|---|---|---|---|
| U.e. | [. . . month X]II, [year] 23 of Nazi-Maruttaš | | |
| Obv. | [. . .] (measured by) the big *sūtu*; its entry: | | |
| | [. . .] of Enlil-mutakkil | | |
| | [. . .] of Nuska-muballiṭ | | |
| [Total?] | [x] ˹2400+˺ *sūtu* (measured by) the big *sūtu* | | |
| | (meas. by) the big *sūtu* | (meas. by) the *sūtu* of 10 *qû* | From which it is disbursed: |
| | ˹30+˺ *sūtu* | | Production supplies (for) Agab-šenni, brewer. |
| | ˹4+ *sūtu*˺ | | Rent (for) a boat. |
| | | 155 *sūtu* | Production supplies (for) Ṭāb-kidin-Gula. |
| | | 176 *sūtu* | Rations (for) the house. |
| | | 14 *sūtu* | Rations (for) the plowmen; the daughter of I[nnū]'atu?. |
| | | 5 *sūtu* | Rations (for) the daughter of Rīš-napāḫšu. |
| | | 10 *sūtu* | Rations (for) Lultamar-Sîn, ˹. . .˺. |
| | | 10 *sūtu* | Rations (for) Sîn-bēl-zēri. |
| | | 15 *sūtu* | Ra[tions] (for) Bābilāyu. |
| | | 6 *sūtu*, 5 *qû* | Ra[tions (for) . . .]-Marduk [ |
| Rev. | | 6 *sūtu* | Rations (for) Mun[ |
| | | 4 *sūtu*, 5 *qû* | Rations (for) Ninnisi-[ . . . ],<br>son of Ubbuttu. |
| | | 7 *sūtu*, 5 *qû* | Rations (for) Apparrītu, ˹. . .˺. |
| | | 9 *sūtu* | Fodder (for) a fattened ox, the daughter of Innū'atu. |
| | | 4 *sūtu*, 5 *qû* | ˹With?˺ leek (for) Ṭāb-ṣillu, gardener;<br>Sîn-balāṭa-īriš ˹. . .˺ [ |
| | | 3 *sūtu* | ˹. . .˺ ditto [ |
| | [ ] | 1 *sūtu*, 5 *qû* | [E]˹mūq?-Adad, gardener˺. |
| | [ ] | 7 *sūtu*, 5 *qû* | [. . .]˹. . .˺, son of Ilī-ayabaš. |
| | [ ] | 1 *sūtu*, 5 *qû* | [. . .] ˹Šēmû?˺<br>[. . .] ˹. . .˺ received. |
| | [ ] | 15 *sūtu* | [. . .]-rēmanni. |
| | [ ] | ˹9 *sūtu* loan?˺ | [Sîn?]-napšira?. |
| | [ ] | ˹. . . *sūtu*˺, ditto | Bunna-Marduk, son of Ubbuttu. |
| [Total?] | [ ] | ˹474? *sūtu*˺,<br>5 *qû* | ˹Grand total˺: 548 *sūtu*, 5 *qû* (meas. by) the big *sūtu*<br>˹after 98? *sūtu* have been deducted, the increase of the *sūtu* of 10 *qû* being at a rate of 1 *pānu* per kor. |

COMMENTARY

3–4. I expect a quantity in the gap at the beginning of both lines; the amounts of Enlil-mutakkil and Nuska-muballiṭ were then probably summed in l. 5. This total must have been the amount from which the different expenditures listed by the text originated.

21. The first sign after the PN Sîn-balāṭa-īriš could be KA or IŠ.

24. Other contemporary texts mention Marduk-zākir-šumi (mdAMAR.UTU-MU-MU) as son of Ilī-ayabaš (see Index of Personal Names), but the traces do not support the restoration.

## 137. CUNES 52-20-303

-.VI–[ . . . ].[ . . . ] Nazi-Maruttaš

The tablet is badly damaged, especially on the obverse. Different expended items are summed together in two subtotals (ll. 6, 13) and were allocated over a time span of several months (see l. 14, "from month VI till month [ . . . ]").

Obv. [x x x MU].⸢BI⸣.IM
[x.x.x x x x] DUMU $^{m}$*Ur-*⸢*ḫa*⸣*-bu*
[x.x.x] ⸢$^{m}$*Bu*$^{?}$*-na*⸣-[x x x] nu
⸢1$^{?}$⸣.0.0 ⸢DUMU $^{m}$*Ṭà*⸣-[*ab-* x x (x)] ⸢x⸣
1.0.0 DUMU $^{m}$⸢*Šu*$^{?}$⸣-[
PAP 3.0.5 ÌR.⸢É$^{?}$⸣.[GAL$^{?}$]
0.1.4 BÁRA.DUM[U$^{ki}$
0.⸢2$^{?}$⸣$^{pi}$.0 BÀD$^{?}$ t[a$^{?}$
Rev. 0.2.4 ŠUKU ANŠ[E
0.0.2 $^{m}$*Tu-na-mi-Saḫ* DUMU $^{m}$*Iš-*⸢x⸣[
0.0.2 DUMU *šip-ri ša im-*[
0.0.1 DUMU *šip-ri* TA BÀD-$^{d+}$*En-líl*⸢$^{hi.a}$⸣
[PA]P 1.2.1 ⸢x⸣ [x] ⸢x⸣ $^{md}$*Nin-urta-*⸢x⸣-[
[x x] ⸢TA⸣ [$^{iti}$KIN].$^{d}$INANNA EN $^{iti}$x[
[x x MU].⸢x⸣.KAM *Na-zi-Múru-t*[*aš*]

COMMENTARY

6. "Total: 95 *sūtu* (for) the pala[ce$^{?}$] servant(s)." On the *arad ēkalli* possibly being a construction worker, rather than an actual "palace servant," see Brinkman 2004, 294–95 and comments to **no. 300**.

12. "1 *sūtu* (for) the messenger from Dūr-Enlilē."

## 138. CUNES 52-16-038

-.VI.[ . . . ] Nazi-Maruttaš

Allocation of barley disbursed as supplies for temples, production supplies, rations, a loan, and to pay back an amount given by Ibni-Marduk.

Even though the date is missing, the text probably stems from the reign of Nazi-Maruttaš (see l. 11).

| Obv. | ŠE $^{giš}$BÁN GAL | ŠE [$^{giš}$BÁN 10 SÌLA] | [<br>[<br>*ša* ⸢x⸣ [x x (x)] ⸢x x x x x x⸣<br>*i-na* $^{iti}$KIN.$^{d}$INANNA *na-ad-n*[*u*] |
|---|---|---|---|
| | 6.0.0 | | ŠUKU É $^{d}$*Nin-urta ša* URU-*ṣa-lam-ti*⸢$^{ki}$⸣ |
| | 6.0.0 | | ŠUKU É $^{d}$*Nin-urta ša* É.DANNA$^{ki}$ |
| | 20.0.0 | | ÉŠ.GÀR $^{m}$*Ṣú-u*[*ḫ*]*-ḫu-tu*$_{4}$ $^{lú}$LUNGA |
| | 30.4.1 | 2.3.0 ⸢4$^{?}$⸣ SÌLA | ÉŠ.GÀR $^{md}$*Nin-urta*-SAG DUMU $^{m}$*Ta-ri-bat*-DINGIR |
| | 2.0.0 | | ÉŠ.GÀR A.GEŠTIN.NA DUMU $^{m}$*A-gab-ta-ḫi* |
| | 4⸢5$^{?}$⸣.4$^{pi}$.0 | | *ši-ib-šu*$_{14}$ *ša* 2 GUR$_{7}^{meš}$<br>$^{m}$*Ni-ip-pu-ru-ú* DUMU $^{m}$ÌR-*nu-bat-ti* |
| | | 1 ME 1-*šu* 6.0.0 | ŠE.BA KÁ-*a-nu* $^{m}$BA-*ša*-$^{d}$IŠKUR DUMU $^{m}$[*Ḫa-am-bu*] |
| | | 2 ME 1-*šu* 5./2.3 | ŠE.BA É-*a-nu* TA $^{iti}$BÁR.[ZAG.GAR]<br>EN $^{iti}$ŠE.KIN |
| | | 15.0.0 | [<br>[ |
| Rev. | | 1 ME | [$^{m}$*Ib-ni*-$^{d}$AMAR].UTU *a-píl* KÁ *ša Ì-s*[*i-in*$^{ki}$]<br>[*ki-mu* x x x *i*]*-na* MU.14.KAM<br>⸢$^{d}$⸣[*Na-zi-Ma-ru*]*-taš* LUGAL.E<br>⸢*id-di-nu* ŠU-*su*⸣ *tur-rat* |
| | | 33.1.4 | ⸢x x⸣ UR$_{5}$.RA *ša* ⸢x⸣ *i-na* 1.2$^{pi}$.[x<br>⸢x x⸣ *i-na* 1.⸢0.1$^{?}$⸣ *ki-iṣ-rù*<br>$^{m}$*Ib-ni*-$^{d}$AMAR.UTU ⸢*a-píl*⸣ KÁ<br>⸢*ša* $^{uru?}$⸣*Ì-si-in*$^{ki}$ *im-ḫur-šu*$^{?}$⸣ |
| PAP | 90.3.1 | 5 ME ⸢92⸣./1.1 4 SÌLA | [ŠU.NIGIN] ⸢5$^{?}$ ME⸣ 94.2.1 $^{giš}$BÁN [GAL]<br>[T]⸢A⸣ 18.2.1 4 SÌLA<br>[$^{giš}$]⸢BÁN⸣ 10 SÌLA *i-na* 1.0.0 0.1$^{pi}$.0 *šu*-⸢*lu-ú*⸣ |

Translation

| Obv. | Barley (meas. by) the big *sūtu* | Barley [(meas. by) the *sūtu* of 10 *qû*] | [<br>[<br>which [ . . . ] ⸢ . . . ⸣<br>was disbursed in month VI: |
|---|---|---|---|
| | 180 *sūtu* | | Supplies for the temple of Ninurta of Āl-ṣalamti. |
| | 180 *sūtu* | | Supplies for the temple of Ninurta of Bīt-bēri. |
| | 600 *sūtu* | | Production supplies for Ṣuḫ[ḫ]utu, brewer. |
| | 925 *sūtu* | 78 *sūtu*, ⸢4$^{?}$⸣ *qû* | Production supplies for Ninurta-ašarēd, son of Tarībat-ili. |
| | 60 *sūtu* | | Production supplies (for making) vinegar for the son of Agab-taḫi. |

| | | | |
|---|---|---|---|
| | 1,374$^{?}$ *sūtu* | | *šibšu* of two silos;<br>Nippurû (and$^{?}$) the son of Arad-nubatti. |
| | | 4,980 *sūtu* | Rations for the *bābānu*, Iqīša-Adad, son of [ |
| | | 8,400 *sūtu* | Rations for the inner quarter, from month I<br>till month XII. |
| | | 450 *sūtu* | [<br>[ |
| Rev. | | 3,000 *sūtu* | [(For) Ibni-Mar]duk, gate keeper of I[sin],<br>[in place of . . . which] he gave in year 14<br>of King [Nazi-Maru]ttaš;<br>his hand is turned. |
| | | 1,000 *sūtu* | ⸢. . .⸣ loan, which at 42$^{+}$ *sūtu* [<br>⸢. . .⸣ from$^{?}$ 31$^{?}$ *sūtu*$^{?}$ of *kiṣru*-payment;<br>Ibni-Marduk, gate keeper<br>of Isin, has received it. |
| Total | 2,719 *sūtu* | 17,767 *sūtu*,<br>4 *qû* | [Grand total:] 17,828$^{?}$ *sūtu*, (measured by) the [big] *sūtu*<br>[aft]er 553 *sūtu*, 4 *qû*<br>(measured by) the *sūtu* of 10 *qû* have been deducted,<br>at a rate of 1 *pānu* per kor. |

Commentary

2–3. Supplies for the temples of Ninurta in Āl-ṣalamti and Bīt-bēri are attested also in **no. 119**: 5–6.

6. The disbursement of barley as "production supplies (for making) vinegar" is rare; for similar entries, see also CUSAS 30 138: 20 (collation shows that *a-na* 2 GEŠTIN.NA can be read *a-na* A.GEŠTIN.NA) and CUSAS 30 165: 3–4 (*a-na ṭa-ba-a-ti*). According to CAD Ṭ, *ṭābātu*, 4, only two other attestations of vinegar were previously known from MB administrative texts (see the *aklu*-expenditure PBS 2/2 34 and its duplicate BE 14 167).

7. Since the entry mentions two silos, it is possible that Nippurû and the son of Arad-nubatti were the two persons in charge of them. Otherwise, we might be dealing with only one person ("Nippurû, son of Arad-nubatti").

8. This is probably the same Iqīša-Adad who is in charge of the rations of the *bābānu* in **no. 97** (where he is identified as son of Ḫambu), **no. 98**, and CUSAS 30 231.

12. The first two lines of this entry are not clear to me; it is possible that the signs which I tentatively read 1.⸢0.1$^{?}$⸣ are not to be interpreted as an amount expressed with a unit of capacity.

## 139. CUNES 52-10-102

-.-.[ . . . ] Nazi-Maruttaš

The text was divided into at least two sections, corresponding respectively to ll. 3–14 and ll. 16–38. The poor state of preservation of the first section makes it difficult to assess its content, but probably it was further divided into subsections with subtotals at l. 8 and l. 13. The second section is a summary of barley expended from the delivery (*maššitu*) of Arad-nubatti as production supplies, rations, gifts, fodder, and supplies for temples.

The presence of check marks in col. ii of the second section is not always certain, due to the poor state of preservation of the surface and to the fact that sometimes they were very faintly impressed in the clay.

| | | | | |
|---|---|---|---|---|
| Obv. | [ | | | *Na-zi-M*]*a-ru-taš* |
| | [ ] | [ ] | | [MU.BI.I]M |
| | [ ] | [ ] | | [$^{iti}$SIG$_4$].GA |
| | [ ] | [ ] | | [$^{iti}$NE.N]E.GAR |
| | [ ] | [ ] | | [$^{iti}$NE.N]E.GAR LA'U$_4$ *es-ru*<br>[BÀD-E]N-KUR.KUR$^{ki}$ |
| | [ ] | [ ] | | [$^{iti}$DU$_6$].KÙ |
| | [ ] | [ ] | | [$^{iti}$G]AN.GAN.È |
| | [ ] | [ ] | | [$^{giš}$B]ÁN GAL |
| | [ ] | [ ] | | [x-x]-*tu*$_4$ $^{md}$*Nin-urta*-SAG |
| | [ ] | [ ] | | [x x] ⌜x⌝ IŠ$^?$ $^{md}$*É-a*-ŠEŠ-SUM |
| | [ ] | [ ] | | [$^{md}$AMA]R.UTU-MU-MU DUMU $^{m}$*Ì-lí-a-ba-aš* |
| | [ ] | [ ] | | [$^{gi}$]$^{š}$BÁN 10 SÌLA |
| | [ ] | [ ] | | [$^{giš}$B]ÁN GAL |
| | [ ] | [ ] | | [L]A'U$_4$ $^{m}$ÌR-*nu-bat-ti* |
| | [ ] | [ ] | | |
| | ⌜ŠE⌝ *ša* ⌜*i*⌝-[*na* Š]À *maš-ši-t*[*i š*]*a* $^{m}$ÌR-*nu-bat-ti* SUM-*nu* | | | |
| | ŠE ⌜x x⌝ | [x x] ⌜x⌝ | | MU.B[I].IM |
| | [ ] | [ ] | | ÍB.TAK$_4$ ÉŠ.GÀR KA.ZÌ.D[A]$^{meš}$ $^{md}$*Nin*-⌜*urta*-SAG⌝ $^{iti}$NE |
| | [ ] | | | ÉŠ.GÀR KA.ZÌ.DA$^{meš}$ $^{m}$KI.MIN $^{iti}$GAN |
| | [ ] | ⌜1$^?$⌝.1.4 | √ | KI.MIN NIBRU$^{ki}$ $^{m}$KI.MIN $^{iti}$GAN |
| | [ ] | 21.1.0 | √ | ŠE.BA DUMU.MUNUS $^{m}$*A-a-rù* $^{m}$ÌR-U$_4$.9.KAM *im-ḫur*<br>NIBRU$^{ki}$ |
| Rev. | | 14.0.0 | √ | ŠE.BA ⌜$^{m}$⌝[x x] ⌜x⌝ TA 1 GUR<br>URU-*ir-re-e*$^{ki}$ |
| | | 12.0.0 | √ | ŠE.⌜BA $^{md}$⌝*Nin-urta*-AM-DINGIR$^{meš}$<br>EN 1 GUR NIBRU$^{ki}$ |
| | | 8.2.3 | √ | ⌜ŠE.BA MÁ$^?$.LAḪ$_5$$^?$⌝ [x x x $^{it}$]$^{i}$NE $^{iti}$KIN |
| | | ⌜1.4.5⌝ | √ | ŠE.BA ⌜KI.MIN $^{iti}$ŠU$^?$.NUMUN$^?$⌝ [x x x] x x$^{ki}$ |
| | | 6.2.3 | √ | Š[E.BA x x] DUMU$^?$ $^{m?}$[x x]⌜x⌝-$^{d}$IŠKUR |
| | | 1.1.3 | √ | Š[E].BA $^{lú}$Ì.ŠUR$^{meš}$ $^{m}$KI.MIN |
| | | 0.⌜3.4⌝ 5 SÌLA | √ | ŠE.BA 2 AD.KID$^{meš}$ *ù* $^{m}$*Pa-qa-a-a-i* $^{m}$KI.MIN |
| | | 0.2.3 | √ | ŠE.BA 2 UŠ.BAR$^{meš}$ $^{m}$KI.MIN *im-ḫur* |
| | | 0.3.4 5 SÌLA | √ | ŠE.BA 3 KA.KÉŠ$^{meš}$ $^{m}$KI.MIN |
| | | 0.2.3 | √ | ŠE.BA 2 $^{lú}$ÁZLAG$^{meš}$ $^{m}$KI.MIN |
| | | 5.0.0 | √ | *ri-mu-tu*$_4$ $^{md+}$*En-líl*-MU.PÀ.DA<br>$^{md}$*Nanna*-LUGAL-DI ŠEŠ.A.NI *im-ḫur* |
| | | 5.0.0 | √ | ŠUKU $^{m}$GAL-*šá*-$^{d}$AMAR.UTU ŠU $^{md}$*Nin-urta*-SAG |
| | | 3.0.0 | √ | ŠUKU MUŠEN$^{ḫi.a}$ DUMU $^{md}$*Nin-urta-ki*-KA-*šu*<br>ŠU $^{m}$*Ḫa-am-bi* |
| | | 2.0.0 | √ | ŠUKU É.DINGIR$^{didli}$ $^{m}$KI.MIN $^{m}$*Si-ia-tu*$_4$ *im-ḫur* |
| | 14.⌜4$^?$⌝.4 | 93.1.3 | | ŠU.NÍGIN 89.3.2 $^{giš}$BÁN GAL<br>TA 18.3.3 GAL $^{giš}$BÁN 10 SÌLA<br>*i-na* 1.0.0 0.1$^{pi}$.0 *šu-lu-ú* |

Translation

| | | | |
|---|---|---|---|
| Obv. | [ | | Nazi-M]aruttaš |
| | [ ] | [ ] | [Its entr]y: |
| | [ ] | [ ] | [month] III. |
| | [ ] | [ ] | [month] IV. |
| | [ ] | [ ] | [month] IV, collected arrears; [Dūr-Bē]l-mātāti. |
| | [ ] | [ ] | [month] VII. |
| | [ ] | [ ] | [month] IX. |
| | [ ] | [ ] | (measured by) the big [*sū*]*tu*. |
| | [ ] | [ ] | ⸢. . .⸣ Ninurta-ašarēd. |
| | [ ] | [ ] | ⸢. . .⸣ Ea-aḫa-iddina. |
| | [ ] | [ ] | [Mar]duk-zākir-šumi, son of Ilī-ayabaš. |
| | [ ] | [ ] | (measured by) the *sūtu* of 10 *qû*. |
| | [ ] | [ ] | (measured by) the big [*sū*]*tu*. |
| | [ ] | [ ] | [Arr]ears of Arad-nubatti. |
| | [ ] | [ ] | |
| | ⸢Barley⸣ that was disbursed [fro]m the deliver[y o]f Arad-nubatti: | | |
| | Barley ⸢. . .⸣ | [. . .] ⸢. . .⸣ | Its en[tr]y |
| | [ ] | [ ] | Rest of the production supplies of the millers; Ninurta-ašarēd; month V. |
| | [ ] | | Production supplies of the millers; ditto (i.e., Ninurta-ašarēd), month IX. |
| | [ ] | ⸢40? *sūtu*⸣ √ | Ditto (i.e., production supplies of the millers), Nippur; ditto (i.e., Ninurta-ašarēd); month IX. |
| | [ ] | 636 *sūtu* √ | Rations of the daughter of Ayaru; Arad-$U_4$.9.KAM has received (it); Nippur. |
| Rev. | | 420 *sūtu* √ | Rations [PN], minus 1 kor (of?) Āl-irrē. |
| | | 360 *sūtu* √ | Rations of Ninurta-rīm-ilāni, including 1 kor (of?) Nippur. |
| | | 255 *sūtu* √ | ⸢Rations for a boatman?⸣ [. . .] month V, month VI. |
| | | ⸢59 *sūtu*⸣ √ | Rations for ditto, ⸢month IV?⸣ [. . .] . . . |
| | | 195 *sūtu* √ | Ra[tions for . . .] son? [. . .]-Adad. |
| | | 39 *sūtu* √ | Rations for the oil-pressers, ditto. |
| | | 22 *sūtu*, 5 *qû* √ | Rations for two reed-weavers and for Paqqāyu, ditto. |
| | | 15 *sūtu* √ | Rations for two weavers, ditto has received (it). |
| | | 22 *sūtu*, 5 *qû* √ | Rations for three knotters, ditto. |
| | | 15 *sūtu* √ | Rations for two fullers, ditto. |
| | | 150 *sūtu* √ | Gift for Enlil-MU.PÀ.DA; Nanna-šar-dīni, his brother, has received (it). |
| | | 150 *sūtu* √ | Fodder of Rabâ-ša-Marduk, under the responsibility of Ninurta-ašarēd. |
| | | 90 *sūtu* √ | Fodder for the birds of the son of Ninurta-kīn-pīšu; under the responsibility of Ḫambu. |
| | | 60 *sūtu* √ | Supplies for the temples, ditto; Siyātu has received (it). |
| | 448? *sūtu* | 2,799 *sūtu* | Grand total: 2,690 *sūtu* (measured by) the big *sūtu* after 561 *sūtu* have been deducted, the increase of the *sūtu* of 10 *qû* being at a rate of 1 *pānu* per kor. |

## 140. CUNES 52-20-319

-.-.21 Nazi-Maruttaš–3 Kadašman-Turgu

The complete understanding of this text, of which only the central part is preserved, is hindered by its poor state of preservation.

On the obverse one can recognize at least two sections, corresponding respectively to the 21$^{st}$ (ll. 2′–10′) and 22$^{nd}$ year (ll. 11′–18′). The years must belong to the reign of Nazi-Maruttaš, since the reverse mentions the 3$^{rd}$ year of Kadašman-Turgu, his successor. The entries within each section refer to monthly amounts associated with the towns of Tukultī-Ekur and Kār-Nuska.

After a gap and some poorly preserved lines, the text resumes on the reverse with a summary of amounts disbursed as loans (UR$_{5}$.RA) by a certain Sarriqu to various persons over several years (ll. 22′–32′); the "rest" (ÍB.TAK$_{4}$), which is still at his disposal, is indicated as well (l. 33′).

The following and final section of the reverse lists various items in different towns, including the staples of Kār-Nuska (*maššartu*, l. 34′), the "old barley" of Tukultī-Ekur (ŠE LIBIR.RA, l. 37′), and the "rest of the (grain) stores" (ÍB.TAK$_{4}$ *tabki*, l. 38′), which remain in Kār-Nuska after certain amounts have been allocated as loan and as fodder; the nature of the other entries mentioning Āl-šēlebi and Kār-Nuska (ll. 35′–36′) is unclear.

(Beginning broken)

| | | | |
|---|---|---|---|
| Obv. | [ ] | ⸢2$^{+}$⸣.[x.x] | |
| | [ ] | | *Ka*[*r*-$^{d}$*Nuska*$^{ki}$ |
| | [ ] | | KI.MIN [MU$^{?}$.x].⸢KAM$^{?}$⸣ *ša* $^{m}$[*Sar*]-⸢*ri*⸣-*qu*<br>⸢*il-qú*$^{?}$-*ú*$^{?}$⸣ $^{iti}$APIN.DU$_{8}$.A KI $^{m}$x[ |
| | [ ] | | *Tukul-ti*-É.KUR$^{ki}$ $^{iti}$APIN.DU$_{8}$.A KI $^{m}$[ |
| 5′ | [ ] | 3.0.0 | *Kar*-$^{d}$*Nuska*$^{ki}$ $^{iti}$AB.È KI $^{m}$[ |
| | [ ] | | *Tukul-ti*-⸢É.KUR⸣$^{ki}$ $^{iti}$AB.È KI $^{m}$[ |
| | [ ] | 3.0.0 | *Kar*-$^{d}$*N*[*usk*]*a*$^{ki}$ $^{iti}$AB.È KI [ |
| | [ ] | 3.0.0 | KI.MIN $^{iti}$AB.È KI [ |
| | [ ] | | ⸢*Tukul-ti*⸣-É.KUR$^{ki}$ $^{iti}$ZÍZ.A.AN $^{m}$x[ |
| [PAP$^{?}$] | [x.x].5 | 9.0.0 | MU.21 |
| 11′ | [ ] | | *Kar*-$^{d}$*Nuska*$^{ki}$ $^{iti}$⸢ZÍZ⸣.[A.AN |
| | [ ] | | KI.MIN UR$_{5}$.RA ⸢*ša*⸣ $^{md}$*Nin-urta*-x[<br>*i-na ra-ma-ni*-⸢*šu* x x x⸣ [ |
| | [ ] | | KI.MIN UR$_{5}$.RA *ša* $^{m}$⸢IBILA$^{?}$-$^{d}$AMAR.UTU⸣ [<br>$^{m}$*Sar-ri-qu* ⸢*i-na*⸣ *ra-ma-ni*-⸢*šu*$^{?}$⸣ x[ |
| | [ ] | 0.2.3 | KI.MIN $^{iti}$ZÍZ.A.AN *a-na ṭe-mi* [ |
| 15′ | [ ] | 1.0.0 | KI.MIN $^{iti}$ZÍZ.A.AN KI $^{m}$IBILA-[ |
| | [x.x].5 | | KI.MIN $^{iti}$ZÍZ.A.AN KI $^{md}$x[ |
| | [ ] | 1.0.0 | KI.MIN $^{iti}$ZÍZ.A.AN KI ⸢$^{m}$⸣[<br>$^{md}$AMAR.UTU-*mu-bal-l*[*iṭ* |
| [PAP$^{?}$] | [ ] | [2].2.3 | MU.22 |
| | [ ] | [ ] | [x] ⸢x meš$^{?}$⸣ [ |

Text breaks off

| | | | |
|---|---|---|---|
| Rev. | [ ] | ⸢1$^{?}$⸣.0.0 | ⸢KI$^{?}$⸣.MIN KI $^{m}$x[ |
| 21′ | [ ] | ⸢3$^{?}$⸣.0.0 | MU.3 |
| | [ ] | ⸢22$^{?}$⸣.0.0 | UR$_{5}$.RA *ša* $^{m}$*Sar-ri*-⸢*qu*$^{?}$⸣[ |
| | [ ] | | MU.⸢12$^{?}$⸣.KAM KI $^{m}$*I-ri-b*[*u*$^{?}$ |

| | | |
|---|---|---|
| [ ] | ⸢2⸣.0.0 | ⸢MU.20$^{?}$⸣.KAM KI $^{m}$*Ib-ni*-x[ |
| [ ] | | ⸢MU⸣.22.KAM KI $^{m}$*Si-kil-t*[*i*$^{?}$ |
| [ ] | 3.0.0 | ⸢MU⸣.22$^{?}$.KAM KI $^{md}$IŠKUR-x[ |
| [ ] | 3.0.0 | ⸢MU⸣.22.⸢KAM KI⸣ $^{m}$ZÁLAG-$^{d}$AMAR.[UTU |
| [ ] | 1.⸢2.3⸣ | ⸢MU.22$^{?}$.KAM KI⸣ $^{m}$*Sar*$^{?}$*-ri-qu ša* x[ |
| [ ] | 0.2.3 | ⸢MU.23$^{?}$.KAM KI⸣ $^{md}$AMAR.UTU-*mu-bal-liṭ* [ |
| [ ] | 1.0.0 | ⸢MU.23$^{?}$.KAM KI⸣ $^{m}$IBILA-$^{d}$U.⸢GUR⸣ [ |
| [x.x].⸢x⸣ | | MU.3$^{?}$.KAM *Ka-dáš-man-Túr-gu* LUGAL $^{md}$AM[AR.UTU- |
| [x.x].⸢5⸣ | 11.0.0 | *ša* $^{m}$*Sar-ri-qu* ⸢*id-di*⸣-[*nu* |
| [x.x].⸢4$^{?}$⸣ | 11.0.0 | ÍB.TAK$_4$ ŠU $^{m}$*Sar-ri-*[*qí* |
| [ ] | | *maš-šar-tu*$_4$ *Kar-*$^{d}$*Nuska*$^{ki}$ ⸢x⸣ [ |
| [ ] | | URU-*še-le-bi* $^{iti}$BÁR.ZAG.GAR [ |
| [ ] | | *Kar-*$^{d}$*Nuska*$^{ki}$ $^{iti}$DU$_6$ |
| [ ] | ⸢x.2$^{?}$.4⸣ | ŠE LIBIR.RA *Tukul-ti-*É.KUR$^{ki}$ [ |
| [ ] | ⸢x.x.x⸣ | ÍB.TAK$_4$ *tab-ki ša Kar-*$^{d}$*Nuska*[$^{ki}$<br>TA 2 GUR $^{giš}$BÁN 10 SÌLA UR$_5$.RA $^{m}$x[<br>TA 2 PI ⸢$^{giš}$BÁN⸣ 10 SÌLA UR$_5$.RA $^{m}$[<br>TA 0.1.1 $^{giš}$BÁN 10 SÌLA ŠUKU x[ |
| [ ] | [ ] | [x x]-⸢*tu*$_4$$^{?}$⸣ $^{giš}$BÁN 10 SÌLA M[U$^{?}$.X.KAM$^{?}$<br>⸢x x⸣ [ |

(Rest broken)

Commentary

12′–13′. *ina ramānišu* "from his own (funds/possessions), at his own expenses."

32′. "[ . . . ], 330 *sūtu* which Sarriqu disburs[ed]."

33′. "[ . . . ], 330 *sūtu*: rest (still) at the disposal of Sarri[qu]."

38′. "[ . . . ], ⸢ . . . ⸣: rest of the (grain) stores of Kār-Nuska, after 60 *sūtu* (measured by) the *sūtu* of 10 *qû* [(have been disbursed)] as a loan of [ . . . ], 12 *sūtu* (measured by) the *sūtu* of 10 *qû* as a loan of [ . . . ], 7 *sūtu* (measured by) the *sūtu* of 10 *qû* as fodder [ . . . ]."

## 141. CUNES 52-12-023

-.-.24 Nazi-Maruttaš–3 Kadašman-Turgu

This text is complementary to **no. 142**, which has basically the same content but a tabular layout and identifies the total as "stored grain" (*še'u tabku*, see **no. 142**: 6).

| | | |
|---|---|---|
| Obv. | 5.2.0 | ŠE ⸢$^{giš}$BÁN⸣ GAL |
| | 0.4$^{pi}$.0 | GIG $^{giš}$BÁN ⸢5 SÌLA⸣ |
| | PAP 14.1.3 | $^{m}$MU-*líb-ši* $^{giš}$BÁN 5 SÌLA |
| | 4.0.0 | ZÍZ.AN.NA $^{giš}$BÁN 5 SÌLA |
| | 0.0.3 | ZAG.ḪI.LI $^{giš}$BÁN 5 SÌLA |
| | 0.1$^{pi}$.0 | GÚ.GAL $^{giš}$BÁN 5 SÌLA |
| | PAP ⸢4$^{?}$⸣.1.3 | $^{m}$*Bu-na*-$^{d}$AMAR.UTU |
| | 3.0.0 | ŠE $^{giš}$BÁN 5 SÌLA |
| | 5.0.0 | ZÍZ $^{giš}$BÁN 5 SÌLA |
| | ⸢PAP$^{?}$ 8$^{?}$⸣.2.3 | $^{md}$*Nuska-na-bu-šu* |
| | ⸢3$^{?}$⸣.0.0 | ŠE $^{giš}$BÁN 5 SÌLA |
| | 0.[1$^{?}$].4 | GIG $^{giš}$BÁN 5 SÌLA |
| | 1.0.0 | ZÍZ.AN $^{giš}$BÁN GAL |
| L.e. | 2.0.0 | ZÍZ.AN.NA $^{giš}$BÁN 5 SÌLA |
| Rev. | PAP 5.2.5 | $^{m}$*Mu*-SIG$_5$-$^{d}$IŠKUR |

ŠU.NIGIN 27.3.2 $^{giš}$BÁN 5 SÌLA
*ša i-na* ŠU $^{md}$*Nuska-ib-n*[*i*]
$^{md}$*Nin-urta*-MU-MU *mi-taḫ-ḫu-ru*
TA MU.24.KAM $^{d}$*Na-zi-Múru-taš* LUGAL
EN MU.3.KAM $^{d}$*Ka-dáš-man-túr-gu* LUGAL

Commentary

1. The corresponding entry in **no. 142** col. i 2 has instead 5.1.0, followed by some unclear signs.

10. The calculated total would be 8.0.0.

11–12. ⸢3$^{?}$⸣.0.0 and 0.[1$^{?}$].4 are the amounts one would expect according to the corresponding entries in **no. 142** cols. ii–iii 5.

16–20. "Grand total: 830 *sūtu* measured by the *sūtu* of 5 *qû*, which Ninurta-zākir-šumi has been receiving from Nuska-ibni, from year 24 of King Nazi-Maruttaš till year 3 of King Kadašman-Turgu."

## 142. CUNES 52-13-074

-.-.24 Nazi-Maruttaš–3 Kadašman-Turgu

This text has the same content as **no. 141**, but is organized as a table.

| | ⸢ŠE *tab-ku* $^{giš}$BÁN⸣ GAL | ⸢ŠE *tab*?⸣-[*ku*] ⸢$^{giš}$BÁN 5 SÌLA⸣ | ⸢GIG $^{giš}$BÁN 5 SÌLA⸣ | ⸢ZÍZ.AN.NA $^{giš}$BÁN GAL⸣ | ⸢ZÍZ.AN.NA $^{giš}$BÁN 5 SÌLA⸣ | ⸢GÚ.GAL⸣ $^{giš}$BÁN 5 SÌLA | ⸢ZAG.ḪI.LI⸣ $^{giš}$BÁN 5 SÌLA | MU.BI.IM |
|---|---|---|---|---|---|---|---|---|
| Obv. | 5.1.0 ⸢x x⸣ | | 0.4$^{pi}$.0 | | | | | $^{m}$MU-*líb-ši im-ḫur* |
| | | | | | 4.0.0 | 0.⸢1$^{pi}$.0⸣ | ⸢0.0⸣.3 | $^{m}$*Bu-un-na*-$^{d}$AMAR.UTU |
| | | 3.0.0 | | | 5.0.0 | | | $^{md}$*Nuska-na-bu-<šu> im-ḫur* |
| | | 3.0.0 | 0.1.4 | 1.0.0 | 2.0.0 | | | $^{m}$*Mu*-SIG$_{5}$-$^{d}$IŠKUR KI.MIN |
| [PAP] | [5.1.0] | [6.0.0] | 1.0.4 | 1.0.0 | 11.0.0 | 0.1$^{pi}$.0 | 0.0.3 | ŠU.NIGIN 27.3.2 ŠE *tab-ku* $^{giš}$BÁN 5 SÌLA |

Rev. [x x x] ⸢x⸣ [*š*]*a i-na* ŠU $^{md}$*Nuska-ib-ni* $^{md}$*Nin-urta*-MU-MU
[T]A MU.⸢24⸣.KAM *Na-zi-Múru-taš*
EN MU.3.KAM $^{d}$*Ka-dáš-man-Túr-gu*
*mi-taḫ-ḫu-rù*

COMMENTARY

4. For the PN cf. **no. 141**: 10.

7–10. "[ . . . ] . . . which Ninurta-zākir-šumi has been receiving from Nuska-ibni, from year 24 of Nazi-Maruttaš till year 3 of Kadašman-Turgu."

### 143. CUNES 52-10-058 (Plate No. 40)

-.-.1 Kadašman-Turgu

Sealed by Ninurta-ašarēd.

Summary of amounts of barley, wheat, and emmer received by Ninurta-ašarēd in or from different towns.

Obv. ⸢ŠE $^{giš}$BÁN 10 SÌLA *ša* $^{md}$⸣*Nin-urta*-SAG DUMU $^{m}$*Ta-ri-bat*-DINGIR
TA $^{iti}$BÁR.⸢ZAG⸣.GAR *ša* MU.1.KAM *Ka-dáš-man-Túr-gu mi-taḫ-*[*ḫu-rù*]

| | ŠE | GIG | ZÍZ.AN.NA | MU.BI.IM |
|---|---|---|---|---|
| | 21.2.3 | | | KA-ÍD.DA$^{ki}$ $^{iti}$BÁR.ZA[G.GAR] |
| 5 | 83.3.4 | 3.0.0 5 SÌLA | | *Ta-mi-ir-*⸢*tu*$_{4}$⸣[$^{ki}$ |
| | 51.3.0 5 SÌLA | 5.0.3 | | BÀD-$^{d}$KUR$^{ki}$ [ |
| | 48.2.1 5 | 1.4.2 5 SÌLA | 4.0.0 | BÀD-[$^{d+}$*En-líl*$^{lì}$]$^{i.a.ki}$ $^{iti}$⸢x⸣[ |
| | 7.3.3 | | | KI.MIN [x x] ⸢x *ḫír*⸣*-ga-lu* |
| Rev. | [ ] | | | [ |
| ⸢PAP⸣ | ⸢1 ME$^{?}$⸣ [ ] | [x.x].⸢x$^{?}$⸣ | 4.[0.0] | [ |

11 [ *i*$^{?}$*-n*]*a*$^{?}$ ŠU $^{md}$⸢*Nin*$^{?}$*-urta*$^{?}$⸣-[

$^{md}$⸢*Nin-urta*⸣-[SAG]

MU.1.KAM *Ka-dáš-ma*[*n-Túr-gu*]

NA$_{4}$.KIŠIB $^{md}$*Nin-urta*-⸢SAG⸣

COMMENTARY

1–2. "Grain, (measured by) the *sūtu* of 10 *qû*, which Ninurta-ašarēd, son of Tarībat-ili, has been [receiving] since month I of year 1 of Kadašman-Turgu."

### 144. CUNES 52-12-022

21.VIII.1 Kadašman-Turgu

Textile impression on the right side of the obverse.

Obv. ⸢ŠE.MUŠ$_{5}$ *ša*⸣ *i-na* ŠÀ ḪA.LA$^{meš}$
*ša* $^{md}$*Nin-urta*-MU-MU
*i-na* BÀD-$^{d+}$*En-líl*$^{meš.ki}$
[*i-n*]*a* $^{iti}$[API]N.DU$_{8}$.A U$_{4}$.⸢21⸣.KAM SUM-*nu*
5 ⸢MU⸣.1.[KAM] *Ka-dáš-man-Túr-gu* LUGAL.E

⸢x x x⸣ [$^{giš}$]BÁN 10 SÌLA ŠUKU GU$_{4}$$^{meš}$
$^{m}$*Mi-na*-DÙ-*uš*-DINGIR
$^{m}$MU-*líb-ši ú-šam-ḫi-ir*

9 2.0.0 $^{giš}$BÁN 5 SÌLA $^{m}$È-*a-na*-ZÁLAG-$^{d}$AMAR.UTU DUMU É
L.e. $^{md}$*Nin-urta*-EN-IBILA
*im-ḫur-ma a-na* ḪUR.SAG.KALAM.MA⸢$^{ki}$⸣
*ir-ku-us*

Rev. ŠU.NIGIN 0.4.4 5 SÌLA $^{giš}$BÁN GAL

Translation

| | |
|---|---|
| Obv. | ⌜*šegušsu*⌝ from the shares |
| | of Ninurta-zākir-šumi |
| | ⌜which⌝ was disbursed in Dūr-Enlilē |
| | in month VIII, day 21; |
| 5 | year 1 of King Kadašman-Turgu. |
| | ⌜. . . *sūtu*⌝, (meas. by) the *sūtu* of 10 *qû*, fodder for the oxen: |
| | Mīnâ-ēpuš-ila |
| | handed (it) over to Šumu-libši. |
| 9 | 60 *sūtu*, (meas. by) the *sūtu* of 5 *qû*, (of) Lūṣi-ana-nūr-Adad, *mār bīti*: |
| L.e. | Ninurta-bēl-apli |
| | received and assigned to Ḫursagkalama. |
| Rev. | Grand total: 28 *sūtu* and 5 *qû*, (measured by) the big *sūtu*. |

## 145. CUNES 52-17-274

-.VI.2 Kadašman-Turgu

Despite the statement in ll. 14–15, no traces of a seal impression are visible on the surface of the tablet.

| | | |
|---|---|---|
| Obv. | ŠE $^{giš}$BÁN 5 SÌLA MU.BI.IM | |
| | 2.0.0 | $^{m}$ŠEŠ-⌜*dam*⌝-*qu* $^{lú}$ENGAR |
| | 0.0.4 | ŠUKU ANŠE$^{meš}$ U$_4$.12.KAM U$_4$.13.KAM $^{m}$*Ì-lí-re-man-ni* |
| 5 | 0.0.3 | ŠUKU ANŠE$^{meš}$ U$_4$.12.KAM U$_4$.13.KAM $^{md}$*Nin-urta*-MU-MU |
| | 0.0.2 | ZÌ.DA $^{m}$*E-ri-bu* U$_4$.13.KAM |
| | PAP 2.1.3 ŠE $^{giš}$BÁN 5 SÌLA | |
| Rev. | | r[i?] ⌜x⌝ [x] |
| 10 | | $^{md}$*Nin-urta*-MU-MU |
| | | $^{iti}$KIN.$^{d}$INANNA |
| | | MU.2.KAM |
| | | ⌜$^{d}$⌝*Ka-dáš-man-Túr-g*[*u*] |
| | | [N]A$_4$.KIŠIB |
| 15 | | $^{m}$⌜*Ì*⌝-*lí-re-man-*[*ni*] |

Translation

| | | |
|---|---|---|
| Obv. | Barley, (measured by) the *sūtu* of 5 *qû*. Its entry: | |
| | 60 *sūtu* | (For) Aḫu-damqu, plowman. |
| | 4 *sūtu* | Fodder for donkeys, day 12 (and) day 13; Ilī-rēmanni. |
| 5 | 3 *sūtu* | Fodder for donkeys, day 12 (and) day 13; Ninurta-zākir-šumi. |
| | 2 *sūtu* | Flour, Erību, day 13. |
| | Total: 69 *sūtu* of barley, (meas. by) the *sūtu* of 5 *qû*. | |

Rev. ⸢. . .⸣

Ninurta-zākir-šumi.
Month VI,
year 2
of Kadašman-Turg[u].
[S]eal of
Ilī-rēman[ni].

## 146. CUNES 52-17-286

-.VII.2 Kadašman-Turgu

There are textile impressions on the reverse of the tablet.

Obv. [ŠE] $^{giš}$BÁN 10 SÌLA *ša i-na* ŠÀ *te-li-ti š*[*a* . . .]
*ša* MU.1.KAM *Ka-dáš-man-Túr-gu* LUGAL.⸢E$^{?!}$⸣
*i-na* $^{iti}$DU$_6$.KÙ *ša* MU.2.KAM *na-ad-nu*

| | | |
|---|---|---|
| | 25.0.0 | *maš-šar-tu*$_4$ $^{md}$*Nin-urta*-SAG |
| | 1.4.5 | $^{m}$*Ri-mu-tu*$_4$ $^{lú}$LUNGA *ki-mu* ḪA.LA-[*šu*] *ša si-bu-ti ša a-na* GUR$_7$ *tab-*[*ku*] ŠU-*su tur-rat* |
| | 2.0.0 UR$_5$.RA | $^{m}$GAL-*a-šá*-GAŠAN ⸢x⸣[ |
| | [x.x.x] KI.MIN | $^{m}$ÌR-*nu-bat-ti ḫa-*[*za-an-nu*] |
| Rev. | 0.0.3 | ŠE.BA $^{md}$UTU-LU[GAL$^?$] |
| | 0.0.3 | ŠUKU ANŠE $^{m}$*Ši-ri-iš-*⸢*ti*$^?$⸣ [ *il-*⸢*li*⸣*-*[*ik*$^?$] |
| PAP | 30.0.5 | $^{giš}$BÁN 10 SÌLA |
| [Š]U.NIGIN | 25.0.4 | $^{giš}$BÁN ⸢GAL TA 5.0.1⸣ [GAL $^{giš}$BÁN 10 SÌLA] *i-na* 1 GUR 0.0.5 *šu-l*[*u-ú*] |

Translation

Obv. [Barley], (measured by) the *sūtu* of 10 *qû*, from the revenues o[f GN]
of year 1 of King Kadašman-Turgu,
which was disbursed in month VII of year 2.

| | | |
|---|---|---|
| | 750 *sūtu* | staples (of/for) Ninurta-ašarēd. |
| | 59 *sūtu* | (For) Rīmūtu, the brewer, in place of [his] share of the brewing, which was stored in the silo; his hand is turned. |
| | 60 *sūtu*, loan | (For) Rabâ-ša-Bēlti ⸢. . .⸣[ |
| | [. . .], ditto | (For) Arad-nubatti, *ḫa*[*zannu*$^?$]. |
| Rev. | 3 *sūtu* | Rations (for) Šamaš-ša[rru$^?$]. |
| | 3 *sūtu* | Fodder (for) a donkey of Širištu [. . .] he wen[t$^?$] |
| Total | 905 *sūtu* | (measured by) the *sūtu* of 10 *qû* |
| [Gr]and total | 754 *sūtu* | (measured by) the big *sūtu*, after 151 *sūtu* have been deducted, [the increase of the *sūtu* of 10 *qû*] being at a rate of 5 *sūtu* per kor. |

Commentary

5. On the brewer Rīmūtu, see comments to **no. 112**.

7. The traces allow the restoration *ḫa*[*zannu*] at the end of the line, but note that most attestations of a *ḫazannu* called Arad-nubatti are later and date to the end of Kudur-Enlil's reign and the beginning of Šagarakti-Šuriaš's reign (see van Soldt 2015, 25).

8. The increase (151 *sūtu*) corresponds to the difference between the total and the grand total.

## 147. CUNES 52-13-184

-.IX.2 Kadašman-Turgu

Obv. ZÍZ.AN.NA *ša i-na* [Š]À *te-li-*⸢*ti ša*⸣ BÀD-$^{d+}$*En-líl*$^{meš.ki}$
*ša* MU.2.KAM [*K*]*a-dáš-man-Túr-gu* LUGAL.E
*i-na* $^{iti}$GAN.⸢GAN.È⸣ *na-ad-nu*

| | $^{giš}$BÁN GAL | $^{giš}$BÁN 10 SÌLA | ⸢MU⸣.BI.IM |
|---|---|---|---|
| 5 | 12.0.0 | | ÉŠ.GÀR $^{md}$*Nin-urta*-SAG DUMU $^{m}$*Ta-ri-bat*-DINGIR |
| | | 2.2.3 | NUMUN ⸢DUMU $^{m}$*Ku-ub-bu-ti*⸣ ÉNSI |
| | | 2.2.⸢3$^{?}$⸣ | NUMUN DUMU $^{m}$ÌR-$^{d}$K[UR] KI.MIN |
| | | 3.0.0 | NUMUN DUMU $^{m}$*Bu-un-n*[*a-* |
| 9 | | ⸢3.1.5⸣ | $^{md}$*Nuska-*⸢*ib-ni*⸣ |
| | | *ki-mu* ZÍZ.AN.NA-*šu ša i-na* MU.⸢21$^{+}$⸣.[KAM *Na-zi-Ma*]-⸢*ru*$^{?}$-*taš*$^{?}$⸣<br>*id-di-nu* ŠU-*su tur-rat* ⸢EN 0.1.5⸣ [<br>⸢GAL$^{?}$ x x x⸣ $^{m}$ZÁLAG-$^{d}$U.GUR *im-ḫur* | |
| Rev. | | ⸢1$^{?}$.0.0⸣ | *ni-ki-is* GUR$_{7}$<br>$^{m}$*Il-lul-lu* DUMU $^{m}$*Ḫal-di-ia* |
| [PAP] | 12.0.0 | 11.2.5 | ŠU.⸢NIGIN⸣ 21.1.2<br>$^{giš}$BÁN GAL<br>TA 2.0.3 GAL $^{giš}$BÁN 10 [SÌLA]<br>*i-na* 1.0.0 0.1$^{pi}$.0 *šu-lu-ú* |

Translation

Obv. Emmer from the revenues of Dūr-Enlilē
of year 2 of King [K]adašman-Turgu,
which was disbursed in month IX:

| | (meas. by) the big *sūtu* | (meas. by) the *sūtu* of 10 *qû* | Its entry |
|---|---|---|---|
| 5 | 360 *sūtu* | | Production supplies (for) Ninurta-ašarēd, son of Tarībat-ili. |
| | | 75 *sūtu* | Seed (for) the son of Kubbutu, farmer. |
| | | 75$^{?}$ *sūtu* | Seed (for) the son of Arad-Š[amaš$^{?}$], ditto. |
| | | 90 *sūtu* | Seed (for) the son of Bunn[a- . . .]. |
| 9 | | 101 *sūtu* | (For) Nuska-ibni |
| | | in place of his emmer, which he gave in the 21$^{+}$ year of [Nazi-Ma]ruttaš$^{?}$;<br>his hand is turned; including 11 *sūtu* [ . . . ]<br>⸢increase$^{?}$ . . .⸣; Nūr-Nergal received (it). | |
| Rev. | | ⸢30$^{?}$⸣ *sūtu* | *nikis karê* (of)<br>Illullu, son of Ḫaldīya$^{?}$. |
| [Total] | 360 *sūtu* | 347 *sūtu* | Grand total: 638 *sūtu*<br>(measured by) the big *sūtu*,<br>after 63 *sūtu* have been deducted, the increase<br>of the *sūtu* of 10 *qû* being at a rate of 1 *pānu* per kor. |

Commentary

10. On the reading of the PN $^{m}$*Ḫal-di-ia*, see comments to **no. 50**: 7. This Illullu might be the homonymous *ḫazannu* mentioned as recipient of the *nikis karê* in **no. 164**: 32 (KT 9).

## 148. CUNES 52-10-065 (Plate No. 41)

-.IX.2 Kadašman-Turgu

Obv. ŠE *ša i-na* ŠÀ *te-li-ti ša* BÀD-EN-KUR.KUR$^{ki}$
*ša* MU.1.KAM *Ka-dáš-man-Túr-gu* LUGAL.E *i-na* MU.2.KAM
*i-na* $^{iti}$GAN.GAN.È *na-ad-nu*

| | ŠE $^{giš}$BÁN GAL | ŠE $^{giš}$BÁN 10 SÌLA | MU.BI.IM |
|---|---|---|---|
| | 1.0.⸢5⸣ 5 SÌLA | | $^{m}$*Ki-rib-tu*$_4$ DUMU $^{m}$*Ḫa-an-bu ki-mu* LA'U$_4$ $^{giš}$MAR.GÍD.DA$^{meš}$ *ša i-na* URU-*ir-re-e le-qu-ú* ŠU-*su tur-rat* |
| | 7.2.4 | | $^{m}$KI.MIN ⸢*ki-mu*⸣ LA'U$_4$ *ši-ib-ši-šu ša* URU-*ir-re-e* *ša i-na* 1.0.0 0.1$^{pi}$.0 *šab-šu šu-lu-ú* |
| | | 1.0.0 | $^{m}$KI.MIN UR$_5$.RA |
| | | 0.2.3 UR$_5$.RA | $^{m⸢}$BA-*ša*⸣-$^{d⸢}$AMAR.UTU⸣ DUMU $^{mf}$*Qa-diš-ti* |
| 9 | | 0.2.3 KI.MIN | [$^{m}$]*Ib-ni-ia* |
| Rev. | | 0.2.3 | ŠE.BA $^{m}$GAL-*šá*-$^{d}$U.GUR $^{lú}$ENGAR $^{iti}$AB.È ⸢*ù*⸣ $^{iti}$ZÍZ.A.AN |
| PAP | 8.3.3 5 SÌLA | 2.2.3 | ŠU.NÍGIN 10 GUR 4 PI $^{giš}$BÁN GAL TA 0.2.0 5 SÌLA GAL $^{giš}$BÁN 10 SÌLA *i-na* 1.0.0 0.0.5 *šu-lu-ú* |

Translation

Obv. Barley from the revenues of Dūr-Bēl-mātāti
of year 1 of King Kadašman-Turgu,
which was disbursed in year 2 in month IX.

| | Barley (meas. by) the big *sūtu* | Barley (meas. by) the *sūtu* of 10 *qû* | Its entry |
|---|---|---|---|
| | 35 *sūtu*, 5 *qû* | | (For) Kiribtu, son of Ḫanbu, in place of the arrears of the wagons, which were taken in Āl-irrē; his hand is turned. |
| | 226 *sūtu* | | (For) ditto (i.e., Kiribtu), in place of the arrears of his *šibšu* of Āl-irrē, which was collected (and) deducted at a rate of 1 *pānu* per kor. |
| | | 30 *sūtu* | (For) ditto (i.e., Kiribtu), loan. |
| | | 15 *sūtu*, loan | (For) Iqīša-Marduk, son of Qadištu. |
| 9 | | 15 *sūtu*, ditto | (For) Ibnīya. |
| Rev. | | 15 *sūtu* | Ration (of) Rabâ-ša-Nergal, plowman; month X and XI. |
| Total | 261 *sūtu* 5 *qû* | 75 *sūtu* | Grand total: 324 *sūtu* (measured by) the big *sūtu*, after 12 *sūtu* (and) 5 *qû* have been deducted, the increase of the *sūtu* of 10 *qû* being at a rate of 5 *sūtu* per kor. |

Commentary

5. For a similar phrasing, see CUSAS 30 139: 7–8, which van Soldt read $^{m?}$*a-da-a-a ša ki-mu* LÁL.DÙ ŠE *ša* $^{giš}$MAR.GÍD.DA *im-ḫur le-qu-ú* ŠU-*su tur-rat* and translated "Adāya received 78 *sūtu* in place of the arrears of grain of the wagons. His hand is turned (concerning what) has been taken(?)," noting that "I take *leqû* as a verbal adjective, but other interpretations are possible." Collation shows that van Soldt's reading $^{giš}$MAR.

GÍD.DA *im-ḫur* can be corrected to $^{giš}$MAR.GÍD.DA$^{meš}$, so there too *leqû* is a 3 pl. stative referring to the wagons or to the arrears.

### 149. CUNES 52-10-068 (Plate No. 42)

-.X.2 Kadašman-Turgu

Obv. ŠE *ša i-na* ŠÀ ḪA.LA$^{meš}$ *ša* $^{md}$*Nin-*[*urt*]*a-*MU-MU
⌜*ša*⌝ BÀD-EN-KUR.KUR$^{ki}$ *i-na* $^{iti}$AB.⌜È⌝
MU.2.KAM *Ka-dáš-man-Túr-gu na-ad-nu*

| | ŠE $^{giš}$BÁN GAL | ŠE $^{giš}$BÁN 10 SÌLA | MU.BI.[I]M |
|---|---|---|---|
| | 10.0.0 | | ÉŠ.GÀR $^{m}$*A-gab-*⌜*še-en*⌝*-ni* |
| | | 10.0.0 | ÉŠ.GÀR $^{m}$*Ṭà-ab-ki-din-*$^{d}$*Gu-la* |
| L.e. | | 7.0.1 | ŠÁM [x x] 2 GÍN 15 ŠE KÙ.GI<br>EN ⌜x⌝ [(x)] ⌜Á⌝ $^{giš}$MAR.GÍD.DA$^{meš}$<br>$^{md}$NA[NNA-L]UGAL-DI DUMU $^{md}$AMAR.U[TU-K]AR-*an-n*[*i*]<br>TA 1 ⌜GUR⌝ *ša i-na* ⌜ŠU⌝ $^{md}$IŠKUR-⌜x-x⌝<br>*i-na* NIBRU$^{ki}$ *maḫ-rù*<br>*šu-lu-ú* |
| Rev. | | 2.0.0 | *ri-mu-tu*$_4$ $^{m}$⌜*Tur*$^{?}$*-rat*$^{?}$⌝-[x]$^{meš?}$ |
| | | 1.0.0 | ŠÁM 2 $^{túg}$GÚ.⌜È⌝$^{meš}$<br>$^{m}$*Ši-ri-iš-tu*$_4$ DUMU $^{m}$[x-(x)]-⌜$^{d+}$*En-líl*⌝<br>TA 0.2.3 *ša i-na* BÀD-⌜$^{d+}$*En-líl*$^{lí}$⌝$^{.a.ki}$<br>⌜*maḫ*⌝*-rù* |
| | | 1.0.0 3 ITI | ŠUKU GU$_4$ $^{m}$*Ib-ni-ia* ⌜TA$^{?}$⌝ DUḪ *ša* 1.0.0 ŠE.GUR<br>*ša si-*⌜*bi-e*⌝*-ti ša l*[*a š*]*u-lu-ú* |
| | | 1.0.0 | ŠE.BA $^{lú}$ENGAR $^{m}$KI.MIN NÍG[ |
| | | 0.1.1 ⌜4⌝ SÌLA | ÍB.TAK$_4$ ŠE.NUMUN $^{m}$KI.[MIN] |
| PAP<br><br>U.e. | 10.0.0 | 22.1.2 ⌜4⌝ SÌLA | ŠU.NIGIN 28.⌜4$^{?}$⌝.[x $^{gi}$]$^{š}$BÁN GAL<br>TA 3.0.1 GA[L$^{?}$ $^{giš}$]BÁN 10 SÌLA<br>⌜GAL$^{?}$⌝ $^{giš}$BÁN 10 SÌLA *i-na* ⌜1.0.0 0.1$^{pi}$.0⌝<br>*šu-l*[*u-ú*] |

Translation

Obv. Barley from the shares of Nin[urt]a-zākir-šumi
of Dūr-Bēl-mātāti, which was disbursed in month X
of year 2 of Kadašman-Turgu:

| | Barley (meas. by) the big *sūtu* | Barley (meas. by) the *sūtu* of 10 *qû* | Its entry |
|---|---|---|---|
| | 300 *sūtu* | | Production supplies (for) Agab-šenni. |
| | | 300 *sūtu* | Production supplies (for) Ṭāb-kidin-Gula. |
| L.e. | | 211 *sūtu* | Price [ . . . ] 2 shekels and 15 grains of gold including ⌜ . . . as rent⌝ for the wagons (of) Nan[na-š]ar-dīni, son of Mard[uk-šū]zibanni, after 30 *sūtu*, which he had received in Nippur from Adad-⌜ . . . ⌝, have been deducted. |
| Rev. | | 60 *sūtu* | Gift of Turrat$^{?}$- . . . |
| | | 30 *sūtu* | Price of 2 cloaks (of) Širištu, son of [ . . . ]-⌜Enlil⌝, after 15 *sūtu*, which he had received in Dūr-Enlilē, (have been deducted). |

| | | | |
|---|---|---|---|
| | | 30 *sūtu*, 3 months | Fodder for an ox (of) Ibnīya from? the draff of 30 *sūtu* of barley of the bre[wi]ng, which was no[t de]ducted. |
| | | 30 *sūtu* | Ration (for) the plowman (of) ditto (i.e., Ibnīya) . . . [ |
| | | 7 *sūtu*, 4 *qû* | Rest of the seed (of) ditto (i.e., Ibnīya) [ |
| Total | 300 *sūtu* | 668 *sūtu*, 4 *qû* | Grand total: 864$^{+}$ *sūtu* (measured by) the big *sūtu*, after 91 *sūtu* have been de[ducted], the incre[ase] of the *sūtu* of 10 *qû* being at a rate of 1 *pānu* per kor. |

COMMENTARY

5. Agab-šenni is known as a brewer from other texts that record the disbursement of barley as production supplies (see, e.g., **no. 110**: 3 and **no. 136**: 7).

9. It is assumed that this entry was phrased like the previous one and that *šu-lu-ú* was implied at the end of it.

13. The scribe erroneously wrote twice the formula GAL $^{giš}$BÁN 10 SÌLA "increase of the *sūtu* of 10 *qû*."

## 150. CUNES 52-12-013 (Plate No. 43)

-.VIII.3 Kadašman-Turgu

Obv. ŠE *ša i-na* ŠÀ *te-li-t*[*i ša* URU-*i*]*r-re-e*$^{ki}$ *i-*[*n*]*a* $^{iti}$APIN.DU$_8$.A

MU.3.KAM *Ka-dáš-man-Túr-gu* *na-ad-nu*

| | | ŠE $^{giš}$BÁN GAL | ŠE $^{giš}$BÁN [10] SÌLA | MU.BI.IM |
|---|---|---|---|---|
| | | 37.1.5 | | *a-na* ŠE.BAL $^{m}$*Bu-un-*[*n*]*a-nu* DUMU $^{md}$*Nuska-*⸢x-*šu*?⸣ $^{md}$30-*iš-man-ni* DUMU $^{m}$*Bu-su-ut ù be-e*[*l*] ⸢x x x x⸣ *im-ḫur* *i-na* BÀD-$^{d}$*Nuska*$^{ki}$ šu? gur? ma? *a-na* EŠ.GÀR $^{lú}$KA.ZÌ.DA |
| | | 4.0.0 | | $^{m}$*Ri-mu-tu*$_4$ DUMU $^{m}$ŠEŠ-[*b*]*a-ni* $^{m}$*Be-la-nu* DUMU $^{m}$⸢*In-ni-bu*⸣ |
| | | 3.0.0 | | $^{m}$*A-da-a-a ḫa-za-nu ki-mu* ŠE-*šu ša a-na* GUR$_7$ *tab-ku* ŠU-*su tur-rat* |
| | | 1.0.0 | | $^{m}$*Mu-ra-nu* DUMU É *ki-mu šib-ši-šu ša* URU-*at-ḫe-e*$^{ki}$ ŠU-*su tur-rat* |
| | | [ ] | 31.2.1 5 SÌLA | ŠE.BA ⸢É?⸣-*nu tup-pi*⸣ *šu-ma-ti ki-i ṭe-mi-ša* |
| | | | 12.0.0 √? | $^{m}$*Ḫu-na-bu* DUMU É *a-na* ŠE.NUMUN *ša* $^{uru}$*E-mu-qat-*$^{d}$AMAR.UTU$^{ki}$ *ki-i* ŠU $^{m}$*Ri-mu-ti* DUMU $^{m}$[ŠE]Š-*ba-ni im-ḫur* |
| | | [ ] | 5.0.0 | *maš-šar-tu*$_4$ $^{md}$IŠKUR-DINGIR-*i-*[*na*-KUR *ḫ*]*a-za-nu* |
| | | | 2.1.5 √ | ŠUKU GU$_4$.NIGA $^{m}$KI.MIN |
| | | | 0.3.2 √ | ŠE.BA $^{m}$*Bu-un-na-*$^{d}$*Gu-la* DUMU ⸢$^{m}$ÌR⸣-U$_4$.9.KA[M] ⸢SIPA⸣ ANŠE$^{meš}$ |
| | | | 0.2.3 √ | *a-na* ⸢ŠE.BA *ša* É NA$_4$.KIŠIB⸣ $^{m}$ÌR-$^{d}$U.GUR ⸢*im-ḫur*⸣ |
| Rev. | | | 2.0.0 *ri-mu-tu*$_4$ | $^{m}$SU-$^{d}$*Šu-qa-mu-na* ⸢*ṣú*⸣-*ḫur-tu*$_4$ |
| | | | 1.2.3 KI.MIN | $^{m}$GAL-[*a-š*]*a-*$^{d}$AMAR.UTU A.ZU |
| | | | 2.0.0 | $^{m}$ÌR-$^{d}$AMAR.UTU *šak-nu ki-i* ŠU $^{md}$*Nin-urta*-MU-MU |
| | | [ ] | 1.0.0 | $^{m}$*Ši-ri-iš-tu*$_4$ DUMU $^{m}$*Šu-da-aḫ*-x-[(x)] *ki-i* ŠU $^{m}$⸢KI.MIN⸣ |
| | | | 0.2.3 | $^{m}$NÍG.BA-$^{d}$AMAR.UTU DUMU $^{m}$*Ba-na-ni-i ki-i* ŠU $^{m}$⸢KI.MIN⸣ |
| | | | 0.1.5 | *ni-ki-is* GUR$_7$ $^{md}$IŠKUR-DINGIR-*i-na*-KUR *ḫa-za-nu* |
| | PAP | 45.1.5 | 59.1.4 5 SÌLA | ŠU.NIGIN 92.2.[x] 5 SÌLA $^{giš}$BÁN GA[L] TA 11$^{gur}$.4.⸢2? GAL⸣ [$^{giš}$BÁN] 10 SÌLA *i-n*[*a* 1.0.0 0.1$^{pi}$.0] *šu-lu-ú* |

| | ZÍZ.AN.NA $^{giš}$BÁN 10 SÌLA | MU.BI.IM |
|---|---|---|
| | 2.2.0 √ | ŠUKU UDU.NÍTA.NIGA$^{meš}$ $^{md}$IŠKUR-DINGIR-*i-na*-KUR *ḫa-za-nu* |
| | 1.1.2 √ | ŠUKU 1 GU$_4$.NIGA $^{m}$KI.MIN |
| PAP | 3.3.2 | ZÍZ.AN.NA $^{giš}$BÁN [10] SÌLA *na-ad-nu* |

Translation

Obv. Barley from the revenu[es of Āl-i]rrē, which was disbursed in month VIII of year 3 of Kadašman-Turgu.

| | (meas. by) the big *sūtu* | (meas. by) the *sūtu* of [10] *qû* | Its entry |
|---|---|---|---|
| | 1,121 *sūtu* | | As exchange[?] (of) Bunnanu, son of Nuska-⌜ . . . ⌝; Sîn-išmanni, son of Bussut, and *bēl* . . . received (it); in Dūr-Nuska . . . (given[?]) as production supplies for the miller. |
| | 120 *sūtu* | | Rīmūtu, son of Aḫu-bani, (and) Belānu, son of Innibu. |
| | 90 *sūtu* | | Adāya, *ḫazannu*, in place of his barley that was stored in the granary; his hand is turned. |
| | 30 *sūtu* | | Murānu, *mār bīti*, in place of his *šibšu* of Āl-atḫē; his hand is turned. |
| | [ ] | 943 *sūtu* 5 *qû* | Rations for the inner quarter; the list of names is in accordance with its instructions. |
| | | 360 *sūtu* √[?] | Ḫunābu, *mār bīti*, received as seed of Emūqāt-Marduk as representative of Rīmūtu, son of [Aḫ]u-bani. |
| | [ ] | 150 *sūtu* | Staples (for) Adad-ilu-i[na-māti, *ḫ*]*azannu*. |
| | | 71 *sūtu* √ | Fodder (for) a fattened ox (of) ditto (i.e., Adad-ilu-ina-māti). |
| | | 20 *sūtu* √ | Rations (for) Bunna-Gula, son of Arad-U$_4$.9.KA[M], shepherd of donkeys. |
| | | 15 *sūtu* √ | As rations of the storehouse; Arad-Nergal received (it). |
| Rev. | | 60 *sūtu*, gift | Erība-Šuqamuna, *ṣuḫurtu*. |
| | | 45 *sūtu*, ditto | Rabâ-ša-Marduk, physician. |
| | | 60 *sūtu* | Arad-Marduk, the overseer, as representative of Ninurta-zākir-šumi. |
| | [ ] | 30 *sūtu* | Širištu, son of Šudaḫ-[ . . . ], as representative of ditto (i.e., Ninurta-zākir-šumi). |
| | | 15 *sūtu* | Qišāt-Marduk, son of Bananû, as representative of ditto (i.e., Ninurta-zākir-šumi). |
| | | 11 *sūtu* | *nikis karê* of Adad-ilu-ina-māti, *ḫazannu*. |
| Total | 1,361 *sūtu* | 1,780 *sūtu* 5 *qû* | Grand total: 2,772$^+$ *sūtu* 5 *qû* (measured by) the big *sūtu* after 356 *sūtu* have been deducted, the increase [of the *sūtu*] of 10 *qû* being [at a rate of 1 *pānu* per kor]. |

| | Emmer, (meas. by) the *sūtu* of 10 *qû* | Its entry |
|---|---|---|
| | 72 *sūtu* √ | Fodder for fattened rams (of) Adad-ilu-ina-māti, *ḫazannu*. |
| | 38 *sūtu* √ | Fodder for one fattened ox (of) ditto (i.e., Adad-ilu-ina-māti). |
| Total | 110 *sūtu* | Disbursed emmer, (measured by) the *sūtu* of 10 *qû*. |

Commentary

4. For ŠE.BAL "exchange[?]," see comments to **no. 64**: 2.

8, 10, 17. I do not expect any quantity in the gaps of col. i, since the total in l. 20 corresponds to the sum of the preserved quantities listed in ll. 4–7.

14. This must be the same Erība-Šuqamuna who appears as the recipient of barley as a "gift" also in **nos. 124–125**.

## 151. CUNES 52-10-059

-.XI.3 Kadašman-Turgu

Obv. Š[E $^{giš}$BÁ]N 10 SÌLA *ša* É $^{m}$*I-ri-bu-ni*
*i-n*[*a* $^{it}$]$^{i}$ZÍZ.⸢A.AN⸣ *ša* MU.3.KAM *Ka-dáš-man-Túr-gu*

| | | |
|---|---|---|
| | 4.0.0 | *maš-ši-tu*$_4$ BÀD-$^{d+}$*En-líl*$^{meš.ki}$ |
| | 1.0.0 | NUMUN $^{m}$ÌR-GAŠAN DUMU $^{m}$*Iš-kun*$_8$*-lí-su*<br>$^{m}$*Ba-na-tu-'a-a* DUMU.A.NI *im-ḫur* |
| | 0.2$^{pi}$.0 | ŠE.BA $^{m}$*Il-la-al-lu*$_4$<br>$^{m}$*Ra-ši-lu*$_4$ ŠEŠ.A.NI *im-ḫur* |
| | 0.2.0 | KI.MIN $^{m}$*Ba-bi-la-a-ú*<br>$^{m}$*Ki-din-*$^{d}$*Nin-urta* DUMU.A.NI *im-ḫur* |
| | 0.⸢1⸣$^{pi}$.0 | $^{md}$*Nin-nisi-mu-dam-mi-qí* |
| Rev. | [2].⸢4⸣.4 | ŠE.BA NIBRU$^{ki}$ |
| | 0.3.2 | $^{m}$*Ì-lí-re-man-ni* |
| | 0.0.1 | ÍB.TAK$_4$ ŠE.BA DUMU.MUNUS *Na-am-ri* |
| | 6.2.1 | ÉŠ.GÀR $^{m}$*Lu-da-ri-be-lí*<br>EN 2.1.2 *i-na* ŠÀ ŠE *šub-ti* |
| PAP | 16.0.2 | ŠE SUM-*nu* |

Translation

Obv. Bar[ley, (measured by) the *sū*]*tu* of 10 *qû*, of the House of Irībūni,
in month XI of year 3 of Kadašman-Turgu.

| | | |
|---|---|---|
| | 120 *sūtu* | Delivery (of/for) Dūr-Enlilē. |
| | 30 *sūtu* | Seed (for) Arad-Bēlti, son of Iškun-līssu;<br>his son Banâtū'a received (it). |
| | 12 *sūtu* | Rations (for) Illallu;<br>his brother Rašilu received (it). |
| | 12 *sūtu* | Ditto (i.e., rations) (for) Bābilāyu;<br>his son Kidin-Ninurta received (it). |
| | 6 *sūtu* | Ninnisi-mudammiqī. |
| Rev. | ⸢88⸣ *sūtu* | Rations (for) Nippur. |
| | 20 *sūtu* | Ilī-rēmanni. |
| | 1 *sūtu* | Rest of the rations (for) the daughter of Namru. |
| | 193 *sūtu* | Production supplies (for) Lū-dari-bēlī,<br>including 68 *sūtu* from the barley of the residence$^{?}$/settlement$^{?}$. |
| Total | 482 *sūtu* | Disbursed barley. |

COMMENTARY

5. For the PN Rašilu, cf. Raši-ilu (spelled *Ra-ši-*DINGIR) in MUN 84: i 4 and $^{m}$*Ra-šil* and $^{m}$*Ra-šil-tu* in NB texts (see CAD R, *rašû* 1a 2′, 194; Nielsen 2015, 314–15).

11. For ŠE *šub-ti* "barley of the residence$^{?}$/settlement$^{?}$," see comments to **no. 59**: 2.

## 152. CUNES 52-19-125

-.I.4 Kadašman-Turgu

Allocation of barley as production supplies, fodder, rations, staples, and other expenditures that are not fully preserved.

Obv. ˹ŠE˺ [*ša i-n*]*a* ˹ŠÀ˺ *ša* É NA$_4$.KIŠIB *i-na* $^{iti}$BÁR.Z[AG.GAR]
MU.4.[KAM *K*]*a-dáš-man-Túr-gu* $^{m}$MU-*lí*[*b*$^{?}$-*ši*$^{?}$

| | ŠE $^{giš}$BÁN GAL | $^{giš}$BÁN 10 ˹SÌLA˺ | $^{giš}$BÁN 5 SÌLA | MU.BI.IM |
|---|---|---|---|---|
| | 3.0.0 | | | ˹ÉŠ.GÀR˺ $^{lú}$LUNGA $^{m˹d}$30˺-TI.LA-URU$_4$ *im-ḫur* |
| | | 3.0.0 | | ˹ÉŠ.GÀR˺ $^{m}$*Ṭà-ab-k*[*i-din-*$^{d}$*G*]*u-la* |
| | 0.1$^{pi}$.0 | | | ˹ŠUKU$^{?}$ 1$^{?}$ GU$_4$$^{?}$ $^{md}$30˺-TI-URU$_4$ |
| | | 0.1.[3] | | ˹KI.MIN $^{m}$*Ṭà-ab-ki*˺-[*din-*$^{d}$]*Gu-la* |
| | | | 16.˹0.3˺ | ˹ŠE.BA˺ [x x x x x]˹x˺ |
| | | | 2.0.0 | ˹ŠÁM˺ [<br>$^{m}$[ |
| | | | 0.1.4 | $^{md}$˹x˺[ |
| Rev. | | | 1.0.0 | $^{m}$[x-x]-˹x x˺-[<br>$^{m}$[x]-˹x-*ni*$^{?}$-$^{d}$x˺-[<br>$^{m}$[*Ṭà-a*]*b-ki-din-*[$^{d}$*Gu*$^{?}$*-la*$^{?}$] |
| | | 1.0.0 | | *maš-šar-tu*$_4$ ˹$^{m}$*Tu*˺-[*kul*]-˹*ti*˺-$^{d}$IŠKUR |
| PAP | 3.1$^{pi}$.0 | 4.1.3 | 19./2.1 | ŠU.NIGIN 13.0.4 $^{giš}$BÁN GAL<br>TA *ru-ub-bu-ú*<br>*šu-lu-ú* |

Translation

Obv. Barley, [which] Šumu-li[bši$^{?}$ disbursed$^{?}$ fro]m that of the storehouse in month I,
year 4 of Kadašman-Turgu.

| | Barley, (meas. by) the big *sūtu* | (meas. by) the *sūtu* of 10 *qû* | (meas. by) the *sūtu* of 5 *qû* | Its entry: |
|---|---|---|---|---|
| | 90 *sūtu* | | | ˹Production supplies˺ for a brewer; Sîn-balāṭa-īriš received (it). |
| | | 90 *sūtu* | | ˹Production supplies˺ for Ṭāb-k[idin-G]ula. |
| | 6 *sūtu* | | | ˹Fodder for one$^{?}$ ox$^{?}$ (of) Sîn˺-balāṭa-īriš. |
| | | 9 *sūtu* | | ˹Ditto (i.e., fodder for one ox$^{?}$) (of) Ṭāb-ki˺[din-G]ula. |
| | | | 483 *sūtu* | ˹Ration˺ [ |
| | | | 60 *sūtu* | ˹Price˺ [<br>[ |
| | | | 10 *sūtu* | (For) [PN |
| Rev. | | | 30 *sūtu* | [ . . . ] ˹ . . . ˺ [<br>[ . . . ] ˹ . . . ˺ [<br>[Ṭā]b-kidin-[Gula$^{?}$]. |
| | | 30 *sūtu* | | Staples of Tu[kul]tī-Adad. |
| Total | 96 *sūtu* | 129 *sūtu* | 583 *sūtu* | Grand total: 394 *sūtu* (measured by) the big *sūtu*,<br>after the increase<br>has been deducted. |

## 153. CUNES 52-18-859

-.-.6 Kadašman-Turgu

Allocation of wheat and emmer as production supplies, fodder, and staples (*maššartu*) in different locations.

| | | | |
|---|---|---|---|
| Obv. | GIG | ZÍZ.AN.NA | [M]U.BI.IM |
| | 1.3.2 | 10.4⌜$^{pi}$⌝.0 | [ÉŠ].⌜GÀR LUNGA$^{?}$⌝ $^{md}$30-*iš-man-ni* ⌜*Kar*-$^{d}$*Nuska*⌝$^{ki}$ |
| | 3.1$^{pi}$.0 | | ⌜ÉŠ.GÀR⌝ $^{md}$*Nin-urta*-SAG BÀD-$^{d}$KUR |
| | 4.0.⌜2⌝ | | KI.MIN *Ba-ṣa-a-ti*$^{ki}$ |
| | 0.0.2 | | KI.MIN *Ta-mir-tu*$_{4}$$^{ki}$ |
| | 1.4.2 | 2.0.1 | ÉŠ.GÀR KA.ZÌ.DA BÀD-[$^{d+}$*En-líl*$^{m}$]$^{eš?}$ |
| | 3.0.4 | | ⌜*ša*$^{?}$ URU-*at*⌝-*ḫe-e* ŠU $^{m}$⌜$^{d}$⌝[x-x-x]-⌜x⌝ ⌜EN ZÍZ.AN.NA⌝ *ki-iṣ-rù* |
| L.e. [PAP] | [1]4.0.0 | 12.4.1 | $^{giš}$BÁN GAL |
| Rev. | | 1.1$^{pi}$.0 | ŠUKU 1 UDU.NIGA $^{m}$*A-da-a ḫa-za-n*[*u*] |
| | | 0.4.2 | *m*[*aš*]-*šar-tu*$_{4}$ $^{m}$KI.MIN |
| PAP | | 2.0.2 | $^{g}$[$^{iš}$BÁ]N 10 SÌLA *ša* URU-*ir-re-e* |
| ŠU.NIGIN | 14.0.0 | 14.2.3 | $^{giš}$BÁN GAL TA GAL $^{giš}$BÁN 10 SÌLA *i-na* 1.0.0 0.1$^{pi}$.0 *šu-lu-ú* MU.6.KAM *Ka-dáš-man-Túr-gu* LUGAL |

Translation

| | | | |
|---|---|---|---|
| Obv. | Wheat | Emmer | Its entry |
| | 50 *sūtu* | 324 *sūtu* | [Production] supplies for a brewer$^{?}$; Sîn-išmanni; Kār-Nuska. |
| | 96 *sūtu* | | ⌜Production supplies⌝ (of) Ninurta-ašarēd; Dūr-Amurru. |
| | 122 *sūtu* | | Ditto; Baṣātu. |
| | 2 *sūtu* | | Ditto; Tamirtu. |
| | 56 *sūtu* | 61 *sūtu* | Production supplies for a miller; Dūr-[Enlil]ē$^{?}$. |
| | 94 *sūtu* | | Of$^{?}$ Āl-atḫē; at the disposal of [PN], including emmer (from$^{?}$/as$^{?}$) the *kiṣru*. |
| L.e. [Total] | 420 *sūtu* | 385 *sūtu* | (measured by) the big *sūtu*. |
| Rev. | | 36 *sūtu* | Fodder for one fattened sheep of Adāya, *ḫazannu*. |
| | | 26 *sūtu* | St[apl]es of ditto (i.e., Adāya). |
| Total | | 62 *sūtu* | (measured by) the [*sūt*]*u* of 10 *qû*, of Āl-irrē. |
| Grand total | 420 *sūtu* | 435 *sūtu* | (measured by) the big *sūtu*, after the increase of the *sūtu* of 10 *qû* has been deducted, at a rate of 1 *pānu* per kor. Year 6 of King Kadašman-Turgu. |

## 154. CUNES 52-18-864 (Plate No. 44)

-.XII.6$^?$ Kadašman-Turgu

The tablet, which was too fragile to bake, is still encrusted with dirt in some spots. The bottom right corner of the obverse is a pastiche and must have originally belonged to another tablet (note how the text of the main tablet continues on the bottom edge, while the text on this fragment ends earlier with a horizontal line). The attached fragment is still very dirty and hard to read. The following transliteration refers only to the main tablet, while asterisks indicate the part belonging to the attached fragment.

Obv. [ŠE *ša*] *i-na* ŠÀ 77.0.5 *te-*⌜*li*⌝*-ti* $^{\text{giš}}$BÁ[N
[*š*]*a Ba-ṣa-a-ti*$^{\text{ki}}$ *i-na* MU.⌜6$^?$⌝.KAM *Ka-dáš-m*[*an-Túr-gu*]
*i-na* $^{\text{iti}}$ŠE.[KIN].KU$_5$ *na-ad-*[*nu*]

| | ŠE $^{\text{giš}}$BÁN GAL | $^{\text{giš}}$BÁN 10 SÌLA | MU.BI.IM |
|---|---|---|---|
| | 30.0.0 | | ÉŠ.GÀR $^{\text{md}}$*Nin-urta-*[ |
| | [x].⌜4⌝.3 | | $^{\text{m}}$*Ri-mu-tu*$_4$ DUMU $^{\text{m}}$[x-x-x]-⌜x⌝<br>*ki-mu šib-ši-šu ša Tukul*$^?$*-ti*$^?$-⌜É$^?$⌝.[KUR$^{\text{ki}}$] |
| | [x].⌜3$^?$⌝.2 | | $^{\text{m}}$ZÁLAG-$^{\text{d}}$AMAR.UTU $^{\text{lú}}$[x x] ⌜x x⌝<br>*ki-*⌜*mu* x x *ša* x⌝ ***** |
| | ⌜3$^+$⌝.1.1 | 4.3.1 | ŠE.B[A K]Á-*a-nu* DUMU $^{\text{m}}$⌜*Za*$^?$⌝-******* |
| | | 4.4$^{\text{pi}}$.0 | ⌜ŠUKU⌝ [x] UDU.NIGA *ki-*******<br>[$^{\text{m}}$]⌜*E*⌝*-tel-*KA-$^{\text{d}}$UTU ******* |
| | [ ] | ⌜x.4$^?$.x⌝ | ⌜x x x⌝ *******<br>[$^{\text{m}}$*Eri*$^?$]-*ba-*$^{\text{d}}$I[ŠKUR$^?$] ******* |
| Rev. | [ ] | ⌜1$^?$.0.0⌝ | [ÉŠ$^?$.G]ÀR$^?$ KA.ZÌ.[DA |
| | [ ] | [ ] | ⌜x x⌝ $^{\text{m}}$*Ur-*$^{\text{d}}$⌜IŠKUR$^?$⌝ [ |
| | [ ] | [ ] | [x x] ⌜x x x⌝ [<br>⌜$^{\text{m}}$È⌝-[*a-na*]-⌜ZÁLAG⌝-$^{\text{d+}}$*En-líl* DUMU $^{\text{m}}$[ |
| | [ ] | ⌜0.0.2⌝ | KI.MIN $^{\text{m}}$BA-[*šá*$^?$-$^{\text{d}}$AMA]R.UTU$^?$ DUMU $^{\text{md}}$⌜x⌝[ |
| | [ ] | ⌜1$^?$.2.3⌝ | $^{\text{m}}$⌜*E-tel-*KA⌝-[<br>⌜*ki-i*⌝ ŠU $^{\text{m}}$⌜$^{\text{d}}$*Nin*$^?$*-urta*$^?$-[ |
| | [ ] | ⌜1$^?$.1$^?$.3⌝ | $^{\text{m}}$È-*a-na-*[ZÁLA]G-$^{\text{d+}}$*En-l*[*íl*<br>*ki-i* ŠU $^{\text{m}}$KI.MIN [ |
| | [ ] | | ⌜x ul ú man⌝ [ |
| | [ ] | ⌜0.0.5$^?$⌝ | *ni-ki-is* GU[R$_7$ |
| | [ ] | 27./3.5 | ŠU.NIGIN ⌜77$^?$⌝.[x.x $^{\text{giš}}$BÁN GAL]<br>TA [x.x.x] ⌜$^{\text{giš}}$BÁN⌝ 10 SÌ[LA]<br>*i-na* 1.0.0 0.1$^{\text{pi}}$.0 *šu-*[*lu-ú*] |

Commentary

1–3. "[Barley] from 2,315 *sūtu* of revenues [o]f Baṣātu (measured by) the *sūtu* [. . . , which] was disbursed in year 6$^?$ of Kadaš[man-Turgu], month XII."

19. Perhaps the grand total corresponded to the quantity indicated in the heading (77.0.5—i.e., 2,315 *sūtu*).

## 155. CUNES 53-01-114

-.-.8 Kadašman-Turgu

Summary of barley received by Nuska-nābûšu from Mudammiq-Adad; the purpose is not indicated.

| | |
|---|---|
| Obv. | [Š]E $^{giš}$BÁN 10 SÌLA <*ša*> *i-na* ŠU $^{m}$SIG$_5$-$^{d}$IŠKUR<br>$^{md}$*Nuska-na-bu-šu maḫ-rù* |
| | 0.2.3 ⌜*i*?-*na*?⌝ $^{iti}$GAN.È U$_4$.12.KAM |
| | 0.1.1 5 SÌLA $^{iti}$AB.È U$_4$.16.KAM |
| | 0.1.1 5 SÌLA KI.MIN DUMU $^{lú}$Ì.SUR |
| Rev. | PAP 1 GUR *maḫ-rù*<br>MU.8.[KA]M *Ka-dáš-man-*<br>*Túr-gu* |

COMMENTARY

1–2. "[Barl]ey, (measured by) the *sūtu* of 10 *qû*, <which?> Nuska-nābûšu received from Mudammiq-Adad." The restoration of the relative pronoun *ša* is required by the subordination mark in *maḫru* and supported by the formulation of other texts with a similar phrasing (see, e.g., CUSAS 30 174–76).

5. Perhaps to be corrected to DUMU.<MUNUS> $^{lú}$Ì.SUR "the daughter of Ṣāḫitu," who is often mentioned in these texts (see Index of Personal Names).

## 156. CUNES 52-10-093 (Plate No. 45)

-.-.8 Kadašman-Turgu

Summary of barley given as seed, fodder for oxen, and rations for plowmen in Kār-Nuska, Āl-iššakkī, and Dūr-Enlilē during the 8th year of Kadašman-Turgu. Most of the entries recording rations for the plowmen specify that they refer to a time span of eight months.

Obv. ŠE $^{giš}$BÁN 5 SÌLA *ša a-na* ŠE.NUMUN ŠUKU GU$_4$$^{meš}$ *ù* ŠE.BA $^{lú}$[ENGAR$^{meš}$]
*i-na* MU.8.KAM *Ka-dáš-man-Túr-gu na-ad-nu*

| | *Kar-*$^{d}$*Nuska* | URU-ÉN SI$^{meš}$ | BÀD-$^{d+}$*En-líl*$^{ḫi.a}$ | ŠU.NIGIN | MU.BI.IM |
|---|---|---|---|---|---|
| | 5.0.0 | | | 5.0.0 | $^{md}$*Nin-urta*-MU-MU $^{m}$*Bu-un-na*-$^{d}$AMAR.UTU |
| | 4.0.0 | | | 4.0.0 | $^{m}$KI.MIN $^{m}$GAL-*šá*-GAŠAN |
| | 6.0.0 | | | 6.0.0 | $^{m}$KI.MIN $^{m}$DÙ-*šá*-$^{d}$AMAR.UTU<br>EN 2 GUR AN.ZA.⌜GÀR⌝$^{ki}$ |
| | 4.0.0 | | | 4.0.0 | $^{m}$KI.MIN $^{m}$*A-ḫe-du-tu*$_4$ |
| | 4.0.0 | | | 4.0.0 | $^{m}$KI.MIN $^{m}$*Il-lu-ri-ia* |
| | 4.0.0 | | | 4.0.0 | $^{m}$KI.MIN $^{m}$ZÁLAG-$^{d}$*Iš-tar* |
| | 4.0.0 | | | 4.0.0 | $^{m}$KI.MIN $^{m}$⌜*Ta*?-*a*?⌝-[x-$^{d}$]⌜AMAR?.UTU?⌝ |
| | 4.0.0 | | | 4.0.0 | $^{m}$KI.MIN $^{m}$[x-x]-*ši* |
| | 4.0.0 | | | 4.0.0 | $^{m}$MU-*líb-š*[*i* x x x x] ⌜x⌝ |
| PAP | 39.0.0 | | | 39.0.0 | ŠE.NUMU[N] |
| | | 15.0.0 | | 15.0.0 | ŠUKU 5 ⌜GU$_4$ x⌝ [$^{m}$x-x]-⌜x⌝-$^{d}$AMAR.UTU<br>⌜$^{md}$30-TI-URU$_4$⌝ [x x] EN 18.0.0 *tuḫ-ḫi* |

| | | | | | |
|---|---|---|---|---|---|
| | | | 2.0.0 | 2.0.0 | ⸢ŠUKU 1 GU$_4$ *ša* x⸣ [<br>⸢*ša* ÉRIN$^{meš}$⸣ [x x x] ⸢la$^?$⸣ [<br>⸢x x x $^{d}$x x x⸣[ |
| | | [6.0.0] | | 6.0.0 | ⸢ŠUKU⸣ [ |
| | | ⸢6.0.0⸣ | | 6.0.0 | ⸢ŠUKU 1 GU$_4$⸣ [ |
| Rev. | | ⸢6.0.0⸣ | | 6.0.0 | ŠUKU 2 [GU$_4$<br>EN [ |
| | | [6.0.0] | | 6.0.0 | ŠUKU ⸢2 GU$_4$⸣ $^{m}$*A-ḫe-*⸢*du*⸣-[*tu*$_4$]<br>EN 3 GUR *tuḫ-ḫi* |
| | | 6.0.0 | | 6.0.0 | ⸢ŠUKU 1$^?$ GU$_4$⸣ $^{m}$MU-*líb-ši* EN ⸢4$^?$.2$^?$⸣.[x |
| | | 6.0.0 | | 6.0.0 | ⸢ŠUKU 1$^?$ GU$_4$ $^{m}$GAL-*šá*-GAŠAN⸣ E[N |
| | | 6.0.0 | | 6.0.0 | ⸢ŠUKU 2 GU$_4$ $^{m}$ZÁLAG-$^{d}$*Iš*$^?$⸣-*tar* E[N |
| PAP | | 57.0.0 | 2.0.0 | 59.0.0 | ⸢ŠUKU GU$_4$$^{meš}$⸣ |
| | | | 7.3.4 | 7.⸢3.4⸣ | ⸢ŠE.BA⸣ $^{m}$[x-x]-⸢$^{d}$⸣AMAR.UTU 8 ITI |
| | | | 5.1.4 | 5.⸢1.4⸣ | ⸢ŠE.BA⸣ $^{m}$⸢UŠ$^?$⸣-*a-na*-$^{d}$AMAR.UTU 8 ITI |
| | | | 3.1.0 | 3.1.0 | ⸢ŠE.BA⸣ $^{m}$*I-na-kit-ti-e-le-i* 8 ITI |
| | | | 5.1.4 | 5.1.4 | ŠE.BA $^{m}$*Ri-mu-tu*$_4$ $^{lú}$ENGAR |
| | | | 5.1.4 | 5.1.4 | ŠE.BA $^{m}$*Ta-qí-šu* KI $^{m}$MU-*líb-ši* 8 ITI |
| | | | 5.1.4 | 5.1.4 | ŠE.BA $^{lú}$ENGAR $^{m}$*Il-lu-ri-ia* 8 ITI |
| | | | 5.1.4 | 5.1.4 | ŠE.BA $^{lú}$ENGAR $^{m}$ZÁLAG-$^{d}$*Iš-tar* 8 ITI |
| | | | 5.1.4 | 5.1.4 | ŠE.BA $^{lú}$ENGAR $^{m}$*A-ḫe-du-tu*$_4$ 8 ITI |
| | | | 5.1.4 | 5.1.4 | ŠE.BA $^{m}$*Nin-nu-ú-a* KI $^{m}$GAL-*šá*-GAŠAN 8 ITI |
| PAP | | | 48./1.2 | 48.1.2 ŠE.BA $^{lú}$ENGAR$^{meš}$ | |
| ŠU.NIGIN | | | | 1 ME 46.1.2 ŠE.NUMUN ŠUKU GU$_4$$^{⸢meš⸣}$<br>*ù* ŠE.BA $^{lú}$ENGAR<br>EN 25.4.4 *tuḫ-ḫi* | |

Commentary

1–2. "Barley, (measured by) the *sūtu* of 5 *qû*, that was disbursed as seed, fodder for the oxen, and rations for the [plowmen] in year 8 of Kadašman-Turgu." For the restoration $^{lú}$[ENGAR$^{meš}$] cf. ll. 33–34. Note that the distribution of seed took place in Kār-Nuska, that of fodder for the oxen in Āl-iššakkī (with the exception of the entry in l. 15, which refers to Dūr-Enlilē), and that of rations for the plowmen in Dūr-Enlilē.

6. This amount, associated with Kār-Nuska, includes two kor for Dimtu. On the vicinity of Kār-Nuska and Dimtu, see Introduction §1 (p. 18 n. 1).

34. "Grand total: 4,388 *sūtu* as seed, fodder for the oxen, and rations for the plowmen, including 778 *sūtu* of draff." The draff (*tuḫḫū*) was disbursed as additional fodder for the oxen, cf. ll. 14–22; on the use of draff as fodder for animals, see Stol 1971, 169–71.

## 157. CUNES 52-10-066

-.V.8 Kadašman-Turgu

Obv. ŠE ⸢*ša i-na*⸣ ŠÀ *te-li-ti* ⸢*ša*⸣ URU-⸢*ir-re-e*⸣$^{ki}$
*ša* MU.8.KAM *Ka-dáš-*⸢*man-Túr*⸣*-gu* L[UGAL].E
*i-na* $^{iti}$NE.NE.GAR *na-ad-nu*

| | ŠE $^{giš}$⸢BÁN GAL⸣ | ⸢$^{giš}$BÁN⸣ 10 SÌLA | MU.BI.IM |
|---|---|---|---|
| 5 | 22.0.0 | | *maš-ši-tu*$_4$ URU-ÌR-GAŠAN$^{ki}$<br>$^{m}$⸢ZÁLAG⸣-$^{d}$AMAR.UTU DUMU $^{m}$*Ì-lí-i-da-an-ni* |
| 6 | | 2.2.3 | ŠUKU É.DINGIR$^{didli}$<br>DUMU $^{m}$*Ḫa-am-bi*<br>*i-na* ŠÀ NÍG.KUD.DA *le-qí* |
| Rev. | | 1.0.0 | ŠE.BA $^{m}$UD-*šú*-[ZÁLAG-*ir*] ⸢KI.MIN⸣ |
| PAP | 22.0.0 | 3.2.3 | ŠU.NIGIN 24.4$^{pi}$.0<br>⸢$^{giš}$⸣BÁN GAL<br>⸢TA 0.3.3 GAL $^{giš}$BÁN⸣ 10 SÌLA<br>⸢*i-na*⸣ 1.0.0 0.1$^{pi}$.0 *šu-lu-ú* |

Translation

Obv. Barley which was disbursed in month V from the revenues of Āl-irrē
of year 8 of K[ing] Kadašman-Turgu.

| 4 | Barley (meas. by) the big *sūtu* | (meas. by) the *sūtu* of 10 *qû* | Its entry |
|---|---|---|---|
| 5 | 660 *sūtu* | | Delivery (of/for) Āl-Arad-Bēlti;<br>Nūr-Marduk, son of Ilī-īdânni. |
| 6 | | 75 *sūtu* | Supplies (for) the temples;<br>(to? the) son of Ḫambu;<br>it is taken from the *miksu*. |
| Rev. | | 30 *sūtu* | Ration (for) Aṣûšu-[namir]; ⸢ditto⸣. |
| Total | 660 *sūtu* | 105 *sūtu* | Grand total: 744 *sūtu* (measured by) the big *sūtu*, after 21 *sūtu* have been deducted, the increase of the *sūtu* of 10 *qû* being at a rate of 1 *pānu* per kor. |

COMMENTARY

5. Cf. **no. 123**: 2′–4′ (KT 9), where it is stated that Nūr-Marduk, son of Ilī-īdânni, brought the delivery (*maššītu*) of the town Āl-Arad-Bēlti.

6. Perhaps the same person as Kiribtu, son of Ḫambu, who is mentioned in connection with Āl-irrē in **no. 148**: 5 (KT 2).

7. I restore $^{m}$UD-*šú*-[ZÁLAG-*ir*] because this is the only PN beginning with $^{m}$UD-*šú*- attested in the texts of the Rosen Collection, and the one that appears most frequently in the Nippur texts. Another, less common option would be $^{m}$UD-*šú-ba-ni* (Hölscher 1996, 40; Sassmannshausen 2001, 469; van Soldt 2015, 537).

## 158. CUNES 52-18-824

16.IV.9 Kadašman-Turgu
Sealed by Sîn-balāṭa-īriš.

This account consists of three parts. The first part records amounts of barley that Mudammiq-Adad received at different times from Sîn-balāṭa-īriš (ll. 2–4). The second part states that over several years Mudammiq-Adad "turned the hand of Sîn-balāṭa-īriš" with regard to certain amounts of barley (l. 5); the use of the expression *qāt* PN *turru* "to turn the hand of PN" implies that the barley was given on loan from Sîn-balāṭa-īriš to Mudammiq-Adad and that the latter is now paying back part of his debt (see Paulus forthcoming). The third part gives the balance of the barley that is still at the disposal of Mudammiq-Adad and indicates that Sîn-balāṭa-īriš acknowledged this account by sealing the tablet (l. 6).

| | | | | |
|---|---|---|---|---|
| Obv. | | ŠE $^{giš}$BÁN 10 SÌLA | $^{giš}$BÁN 5 SÌLA | MU.BI.IM |
| 2 | | 3.3.4 | | *i-na ú-ri ša* É $^{m}$*Da-bi-bi* MU.2.KAM *Ka-dáš-man-Túr-gu* |
| 3 | | 1.0.5 | 4.2.5 | *i-na* É $^{m}$KI.MIN ŠE *si-bu-ti* MU.4.KAM |
| 4 | PAP | 4.4.3 | 4.2.5 | *ša i-na* ŠU $^{md}$30-TI-URU$_4$ $^{m}$*Mu-dam-mi-iq*-$^{d}$IŠKUR *maḫ-rù* |
| Rev. | | 3.3.2 | 1.1.3 | $^{m}$*Mu*-SIG$_5$-*iq*-$^{d}$IŠKUR ŠU $^{md}$30-TI-URU$_4$ *ut-te-e-er* TA MU.2.KAM EN MU.8.KAM *Ka-dáš-man-Túr-gu* LUGAL.E |
| 6 | | 1.1.1 | 3.1.2 | ÍB.TAK$_4$ ŠU $^{m}$*Mu*-⸢SIG$_5$-$^{d}$IŠKUR⸣ NA$_4$.KIŠIB $^{md}$30-TI-⸢URU$_4$⸣ |

7 ⸢*i-na* $^{iti}$ŠU⸣.NUMUN.NA U$_4$.16.KAM
L.e. MU.9.KAM *Ka-dáš-man-Túr-gu* LUGAL
NA$_4$.KIŠIB *ṣa-ab-tu$_4$*

Translation

| | | | |
|---|---|---|---|
| Obv. | Barley (meas. by) *sūtu* of 10 *qû* | (meas. by) *sūtu* of 5 *qû* | Its entry |
| | 112 *sūtu* | | On the roof of the house of Dābibī; year 2 of Kadašman-Turgu. |
| | 35 *sūtu* | 137 *sūtu* | In the house of ditto (i.e., Dābibī), barley for brewing; year 4. |
| 4 Total | 147 *sūtu* | 137 *sūtu* | Which Mudammiq-Adad received from Sîn-balāṭa-īriš. |
| Rev. | 110 *sūtu* | 39 *sūtu* | Mudammiq-Adad has turned the hand of Sîn-balāṭa-īriš, from year 2 till year 8 of King Kadašman-Turgu. |
| | 37 *sūtu* | 98 *sūtu* | Rest (which is still) at the disposal of Mudammiq-Adad. Seal of Sîn-balāṭa-īriš. |

7 In month IV, day 16,
L.e. year 9 of King Kadašman-Turgu
the sealed document was drawn up.

COMMENTARY

2. For the roof as a place for storage, see CAD U–W, *ūru* A b, 261.

9. The expression NA$_4$.KIŠIB *ṣabātu* is usually understood as "to seize," "to deposit into custody," or "to take into safekeeping" a sealed document (Brinkman 1976, 392; Gurney 1983, 27; Paulus 2014b, 99 n. 235). However, in my opinion one cannot exclude the meaning "to draw up a sealed document," similar to what has been suggested for the expression *ṭuppa/u ṣabātu* in Assyrian texts (Postgate 2011). Our tablet has been sealed by Sîn-balāṭa-īriš (see l. 6)—i.e., by the person who lent the barley to Mudammiq-Adad and who is now receiving back part of the original amount he lent. The remaining amount that is still with Mudammiq-Adad is also indicated. By sealing the tablet, Sîn-balāṭa-īriš acknowledges simultaneously that he received a certain amount of barley from Mudammiq-Adad, but also that he is still waiting for another amount to be returned to him. Thus, indicating the moment when the sealed document was "drawn up" (rather than "taken into safekeeping") would establish a *terminus post quem* in case future claims should be raised by any of the parties involved in managing the amounts of barley recorded by this text. As noted by Gurney, the plural verbal form *ṣabtū* indicates that NA$_4$.KIŠIB stands here for a *plurale tantum* (Gurney 1983, 27).

### 159. CUNES 52-12-009

-.VI–X.9 Kadašman-Turgu

Summary of barley expenditures that took place from month VI till month X of year 9 of King Kadašman-Turgu.

Obv. ŠE *ša i-na* ŠÀ 48.3.2 *ša* $^{m}$*Ḫu-za-li* [
*i-na* $^{giš}$BÁN GAL *ša* $^{m}$*Ḫu-za-li maḫ-ra-*[*am-ma*]
MU.9.KAM *Ka-dáš-man-Túr-gu* S[UM-*nu*]

| | $^{iti}$KIN | $^{iti}$DU$_6$ | $^{iti}$APIN | $^{iti}$GAN | $^{iti}$AB | ŠU.NIGIN | M[U.BI.IM] |
|---|---|---|---|---|---|---|---|
| | 7.3.5 | | | | | 7.3.5 | Š[E |
| | | 1.4.4 | | 7.0.0 | 1.0.0 | 9.4.4 | ÉŠ.G[ÀR |
| | | 0.2.3 | | | | 0.2.[3] | *a-na* SIS[KUR$^?$ |
| | | | 0.4.3 | | | 0.4.3 | UR$_5$.RA $^{m}$⌜x⌝[ |
| | | | | | 1.0.0 | 1.0.0 | ŠUKU É$^?$ $^{d}$AM[AR.UTU<br>$^{md}$*E-*[*a-*<br>$^{md}$30-T[I$^?$-URU$_4$$^?$ |
| PAP | | | | | | 20.0.3 | $^{giš}$BÁN GA[L] |
| | | 2.0.4 5 | | 6.3.0 | 3.0.0 | 11.3.4 5 SÌLA | ÉŠ.GÀR ⌜DUMU.MUNUS $^{lú}$Ì.SUR⌝ |
| | | 2.0.0 | | | | 2.0.0 | NUMUN $^{m}$*Bu-un-na-*$^{d}$AMAR.UTU<br>[$^{m}$]$^{d}$30-TI-URU$_4$ *im-ḫur* |
| | 0.2$^{pi}$.0 | | | | 0.2.0 | 0.4$^{pi}$.0 | ŠE.BA $^{m}$KI.MIN 2 ITI |
| | 0.2$^{pi}$.0 | | | | 0.2.0 | 0.4$^{pi}$.0 | ŠE.BA $^{m}$*Aq-rù* DUMU.A.NI 2 ITI |
| | 0.3.2 | | | | 0.3.2 | 1.1.4 | ŠE.BA $^{m}$*Ri-mu-tu*$_4$ $^{lú}$ENGAR 2 ITI |
| | 0.3.2 | | | | 0.3.2 | 1.1.4 | ŠE.BA $^{m}$EN-*šu-nu* $^{lú}$ENGAR 2 ITI |
| | | | 4.0.0 | | | 4.0.0 | *ri-mu-tu*$_4$ $^{md}$30-*nap-ši-ra* A.ZU |
| | 0.0.3 | | | | | 0.0.3 | $^{m}$MU-*líb-ši a-na* GU$_4$ *ù* ANŠE$^{meš}$-*šu*<br>TA ŠE *im-ḫu-rù* TA U$_4$.4.KAM EN U$_4$.6.KAM |
| | 0.0.3 | | | | | 0.0.3 | BAPPIR$_x$ 8 ÉRIN$^{ḫi.a}$ TA ŠE *im-ḫu-rù*<br>TA U$_4$.4.KAM EN U$_4$.6.KAM |
| | 0.0.1<br>5 SÌLA | | | | | 0.0.1 5 SÌLA | $^{m}$MU-*líb-ši a-na* KAŠ *ù* Š[UKU ANŠ]E$^{?meš}$-*šu*<br>TA ŠE *a-na* BÀD-$^{d+}$*En-líl*[$^{meš/ḫi.a}$] *iš-šu-ni* |
| | 0.0.1<br>5 SÌLA | | | | | 0.0.1 5 SÌLA | ŠUKU ANŠE$^{meš}$ *ša* ŠE *iš-šu-n*[*i*] |
| | 7 SÌLA | | | | | 7 SÌLA | ŠUKU 3 GU$_4$$^{meš}$ *ša* KI.MIN |

| | | | | | | | |
|---|---|---|---|---|---|---|---|
| | 0.0.1 5 SÌLA | | | | | 0.0.1 5 SÌLA | BAPPIR$_{x}$ 6 ÉRIN$^{ḫi.a}$ *ša* Š[E$^{?}$ U$_{4}$.11.KAM |
| Rev. | | 0.0.1 | | | | 0.0.1 | $^{m}$MU-*líb-ši a-na* KAŠ *ù* Š[UKU$^{?}$ TA ŠE *iš-šu-ni* U$_{4}$.21.[KAM] |
| 25 | | 0.0.1 5 SÌLA | | | | 0.0.1 5 SÌLA | ŠUKU ANŠE$^{meš}$ *ša* ŠE *iš-šu-*[*ni*] U$_{4}$.21.KAM |
| | | 0.0.1 | | | | 0.0.1 | BAPPIR$_{x}$ 6 ÉRIN$^{ḫi.a}$ *ša* ŠE *iš-šu-*[*ni*] U$_{4}$.21.KAM |
| | | | | | 0.2.1 5 | 0.2.1 5 | ŠE.BA É *ša* $^{iti}$ZÍZ.A.AN *ša ki-i at-ri na-ad-nu ša* $^{m}$*Ba-na-nu-ú a-na* URU-*ir-re-e iš-šu-ma ú-ter-ra ù* 0.2.4 5 SÌLA *ú-ma-aṭ-ṭú-ú* |
| | | | | | 0.2.4 5 | 0.2.⌜4⌝ 5 NUMUN $^{m}$*Ba-na-nu-ú* URU-*ir-re-e* | |
| | | | | | 0.2.3 | 0.2.3 | ÉŠ.GÀR $^{m}$È-*a-na*-ZÁLAG-$^{d}$IŠKUR GAR-*nu* $^{md}$30-TI-URU$_{4}$ *i-na* ŠÀ $^{lú}$LUNGA *i-din-ma* ŠU-*su tur-rat* |
| PAP | | | | | | 24.0.0 $^{giš}$BÁN 10 SÌLA | |
| 31 | | | | | 2.0.0 | 2.0.0 | $^{m}$*Bíl-lul-lu*$_{4}$ NAGAR |
| | | | | | 1.0.0 | 1.0.0 | $^{m}$*Ḫu-sa-rak-ku* |
| | | | | | 2.0.0 | 2.0.0 | $^{md}$*Ba-ba*$_{6}$-URU$_{4}$ SIPA LUGAL |
| | | | | | 0.2.3 | 0.2.3 | $^{m}$*Bu-ú-a* SIPA ÁB.GU$_{4}$$^{ḫi.a}$ |
| PAP | | | | | | 5.2.3 | $^{giš}$BÁN 10 SÌLA *ša* ŠE.BA |
| ŠU.NIGIN | | | | | | ⌜40$^{+}$⌝.[x].5 | $^{giš}$BÁN GAL TA GAL-*ú šu-lu-ú* |
| 37 | | | | | | 2.2.1 | $^{giš}$BÁN GAL *ni-ki-i*[*s* GUR$_{7}$] *ù* LA'U$_{4}$ ⌜x⌝[ |

Translation

Obv. Barley from 1,460 *sūtu* of Ḫuzālu [ . . . ]
(measured) by the big *sūtu*, which Ḫuzalu receiv[ed and]
disbursed in year 9 of Kadašman-Turgu:

| | Month VI | Month VII | Month VIII | Month IX | Month X | Grand total | [Its] en[try] |
|---|---|---|---|---|---|---|---|
| 5 | 233 *sūtu* | | | | | 233 *sūtu* | Bar[ley |
| | | 58 *sūtu* | | 210 *sūtu* | 30 *sūtu* | 298 *sūtu* | Production supp[lies |
| | | 15 *sūtu* | | | | 15 *sūtu* | For offer[ing$^{?}$ |
| | | | 27 *sūtu* | | | 27 *sūtu* | Loan [of PN |
| | | | | | 30 *sūtu* | 30 *sūtu* | Supplies for the temple$^{?}$ of Mar[duk E[a- Sîn-ba[lāṭa$^{?}$-īriš$^{?}$ |
| Total | | | | | | 603 *sūtu* | (measured by) the bi[g] *sūtu*. |
| 11 | | 64 *sūtu*, 5 *qû* | | 198 *sūtu* | 90 *sūtu* | 352 *sūtu*, 5 *qû* | Production supplies ⌜for the daughter of Ṣāḫitu⌝. |
| | | 60 *sūtu* | | | | 60 *sūtu* | Seed of Bunna-Marduk; Sîn-balāṭa-īriš received (it). |

| | | | | | | | |
|---|---|---|---|---|---|---|---|
| | 12 *sūtu* | | | | 12 *sūtu* | 24 *sūtu* | Ration of ditto (i.e., Bunna-Marduk), for 2 months. |
| | 12 *sūtu* | | | | 12 *sūtu* | 24 *sūtu* | Ration of Aqru, his son, for 2 months. |
| | 20 *sūtu* | | | | 20 *sūtu* | 40 *sūtu* | Ration of Rīmūtu, plowman, for 2 months. |
| | 20 *sūtu* | | | | 20 *sūtu* | 40 *sūtu* | Ration of Bēlšunu, plowman, for 2 months. |
| | | | 120 *sūtu* | | | 120 *sūtu* | Gift of Sîn-napšira, physician. |
| | 3 *sūtu* | | | | | 3 *sūtu* | (For) Šumu-libši, for (his) ox and his donkeys,<br>after he received the barley; from day 4 till day 6. |
| | 3 *sūtu* | | | | | 3 *sūtu* | Sourdough bread for 8 workmen after he received the barley; from day 4 till day 6. |
| | 1 *sūtu*, 5 *qû* | | | | | 1 *sūtu*, 5 *qû* | (For) Šumu-libši as beer and f[odder for] his d[onkey]s, after they brought the barley here to Dūr-Enlil[ē]. |
| | 1 *sūtu*, 5 *qû* | | | | | 1 *sūtu*, 5 *qû* | Fodder for the donkeys that brought here the barley. |
| | 7 *qû* | | | | | 7 *qû* | Fodder for 3 oxen that ditto (i.e., brought here the barley). |
| | 1 *sūtu*, 5 *qû* | | | | | 1 *sūtu*, 5 *qû* | Sourdough bread for 6 workmen who [ . . . ] the b[arley?]; day 11. |
| Rev. | | 1 *sūtu* | | | | 1 *sūtu* | Šumu-libši as beer and as f[odder . . .], after he/they brought here the barley; day 21. |
| | | 1 *sūtu*, 5 *qû* | | | | 1 *sūtu*, 5 *qû* | Fodder for the donkeys that brought [here] the barley; day 21. |
| | | 1 *sūtu* | | | | 1 *sūtu* | Sourdough bread for 6 workers who brought [here] the barley; day 21. |
| | | | | | 13 *sūtu*, 5 *qû* | 13 *sūtu*, 5 *qû* | Ration of the house of month XI, which was disbursed as additional amount, which Bananû has brought to Āl-irrē and brought back here, and they reduced? 16 *sūtu*, 5 *qû*. |
| | | | | | 16 *sūtu*, 5 *qû* | 16 *sūtu*, 5 *qû*: seed, Bananû, Āl-irrē. | |
| | | | | | 15 *sūtu* | 15 *sūtu* | Production supplies for Lūṣi-ana-nūr-Adad, overseer; Sîn-balāṭa-īriš gave (it) from that of the brewer and his hand is turned. |
| Total | | | | | | 720 *sūtu* | (measured by) the *sūtu* of 10 *qû*. |
| 31 | | | | | 60 *sūtu* | 60 *sūtu* | Billullu, the carpenter. |
| | | | | | 30 *sūtu* | 30 *sūtu* | Ḫusarakku. |
| | | | | | 60 *sūtu* | 60 *sūtu* | Baba-īriš, shepherd of the king. |

| | | | | | | | |
|---|---|---|---|---|---|---|---|
| | | | | | 15 *sūtu* | 15 *sūtu* | Bu'ūa, shepherd of cows and oxen. |
| Total | | | | | | 165 *sūtu*, (meas. by) the *sūtu* of 10 *qû* of the ration. | |
| Grand total | | | | | | ⌜1,205⁺⌝ *sūtu*, (meas. by) the big *sūtu*,<br>after the increase has been deducted. | |
| 37 | | | | | | 67 *sūtu*, (measured by) the big *sūtu*, *nikis* [*karê*]<br>and arrears [ | |

COMMENTARY

1–3. The restoration of the verbal forms is supported by texts with a similar heading, such as CUSAS 30 68, CUSAS 30 71, CUSAS 30 72, CUSAS 30 73, and CUSAS 30 75.

27. This entry is certainly linked to the next one (l. 28), where the quantity recorded as seed of Bananû corresponds to that which has been "reduced" in this line (perhaps better "deducted," but cf. CAD M/I, *maṭû* 3, 433 "to cause a decrease in quantity" and AHw II, *maṭû*(*m*) II D, 636 "mindern, verkürzen": note also that "to deduct, subtract" is usually expressed with the verb *šulû*).

29. On the overseer (*šaknu*) Lūṣi-ana-nūr-Adad, see Introduction §4.2 and §4.6.

30. The correct total would have been 24.0.0 2 SÌLA, but apparently the figure has been rounded to 24.0.0.

35. For the "*sūtu* of 10 *qû* of the ration," see also **no. 160**: 7 and CUSAS 30 85: 21–22; cf. the "*sūtu* of 5 *qû* of the ration" in **no. 70**: 1 and CUSAS 30 194: 2. On the "*sūtu* of the rations" in Nippur texts, see Sassmannshausen 2001, 448–49.

## 160. CUNES 52-12-040 (Plate No. 46)

10⁺.VIII.9 Kadašman-Turgu

Allocation of barley taken from the share of Kār-Nuska of year 8 and from an amount of Ḫuzālu of the town of Mannu-nāṣiršu.

| | | | |
|---|---|---|---|
| Obv. | ŠE *ša i-na*<br>ŠÀ ḪA.LA<br>*ša Kar-*<br>$^{d}$*Nuska*<br>*ša* MU.8.KAM | ŠE *ša i-na*<br>ŠÀ *ša*<br>$^{m}$*Ḫu-za-*<br>*li ša*<br>*Man-nu-*ÙRU-*šu* | MU.BI.I[M] |
| | 1.0.0<br>$^{giš}$BÁN GAL | | ÉŠ.GÀR $^{md}$30-*ib-*⌜*ni* $^{lu}$LUNGA⌝<br>$^{md}$30-TI.LA-URU$_{4}$ *im-ḫur* |
| Rev. | 1.0.0 | 1.0.0 | ÉŠ.GÀR DUMU.MUNUS $^{lú}$Ì.SUR |
| | 0.1.3 | | NUMUN $^{m}$*Bu-un-na-*$^{d}$AMAR.UTU |
| 5 | | 0.0.4 | ŠÁM DUG.GAL<br>*ša* $^{m}$*Ib-ni-*$^{d}$AMAR.UTU *im-ḫu-rù* |
| PAP | 1.1.3 | 1.0.0 | $^{giš}$BÁN 10 SÌLA |
| | | 0.0.5 $^{giš}$BÁN 10 SÌLA *ša* ŠE.⌜BA⌝ [<br>$^{m}$*Bíl-lu*[*l-lu*$_{4}$] | |
| 8 | $^{iti}$APIN.DU$_{8}$.A U$_{4}$.⌜10⁺⌝.[KAM] | | |
| L.e. | MU.9.KAM *Ka-dáš-man-T*[*úr-gu*] | | |

Translation

| | | | |
|---|---|---|---|
| Obv. | Barley which is from the share of Kār-Nuska of the 8th year | Barley which is from that of Ḫuzālu of Mannu-nāṣiršu | Its ent[ry] |
| | 30 *sūtu* (meas. by) the big *sūtu* | | Production supplies (for) Sîn-ibni, the brewer; Sîn-balāṭa-īriš received (it). |
| Rev. | 30 *sūtu* | 30 *sūtu* | Production supplies (for) the daughter of Ṣāḫitu. |
| | 9 *sūtu* | | Seed (for) Bunna-Marduk. |
| | | 4 *sūtu* | Price of a big jar, which Ibni-Marduk received. |
| Total | 40 *sūtu* | 30 *sūtu* | (measured by) the *sūtu* of 10 *qû* |
| | | 5 *sūtu* (measured by) the *sūtu* of 10 *qû* of the ration [ . . . ] Billu[llu]. | |
| | Month VIII, day ⌜10+⌝, | | |
| L.e. | year 9 of Kadašman-T[urgu]. | | |

Commentary

2. Cf. the allocation of 30 *sūtu* of barley, which took place two months later, that is simply described as "production supplies (for) the brewer; Sîn-balāṭa-īriš" in **no. 163**: 6.
4. See also **no. 71**, which records that one month earlier in the same year, Bunna-Marduk received barley as seed for the town of Mannu-[nāṣiršu] from the stocks of Kār-Nuska of year 8.

## 161. CUNES 52-12-024

11.VIII.9 Kadašman-Turgu

| | |
|---|---|
| Obv. | ⌜0.2⌝.3 $^{m}$*Nam-rù* SIPA |
| | 0.0.3 ŠUKU ANŠE$^{meš}$ |
| | PAP 0.3$^{pi}$.0 $^{giš}$BÁN 10 SÌLA |
| 4 | *i-na* URU-*ir-re-e* SUM-*nu* |
| L.e. | $^{iti}$APIN.DU$_{8}$.A U$_{4}$.11.⌜KAM⌝ |
| Rev. | MU.9.KAM |
| | *Ka-dáš-man-Túr-gu* |

Translation

| | |
|---|---|
| Obv. | 15 *sūtu*: Namru, the shepherd. |
| | 3 *sūtu*: fodder for the donkeys. |
| | Total: 18 *sūtu* (meas. by) the *sūtu* of 10 *qû* |
| 4 | have been disbursed in Āl-irrē. |
| L.e. | Month VIII, day 11, |
| Rev. | year 9 |
| | of Kadašman-Turgu. |

## 162. CUNES 52-12-045

28.IX.9 Kadašman-Turgu

Allocation of emmer disbursed as seed, fodder, a loan with interest, and *nikis karê*.

Obv. ZÍZ.AN.NA $^{giš}$BÁN 10 SÌLA *ša i-na te-li-ti*
*ša* URU-*ir-re-e*$^{ki}$
*ša* MU.9.KAM *Ka-dáš-man-Túr-gu* LUGAL.E
*i-na* $^{iti}$GAN.GAN.È U$_4$.28.KAM *na-ad-nu*

| | | |
|---|---|---|
| 1.0.0 | √ | NUMUN $^{md}$*Nin-urta*-MU-MU $^{md}$*Nuska-na-bu-šu* |
| 1.0.0 | √ | NUMUN $^{m}$KI.MIN $^{m}$DÙ-*a-šá*-$^{d}$AMAR.UTU |
| 2.0.0 | √ | NUMUN $^{m}$*Di-mah-di*-$^{d}$*Uraš*<br>$^{m}$*Ku-du-ra-nu* DUMU $^{m}$DINGIR-GAL ⸢*im-hur*⸣ |
| 1.0.0 | √ | NUMUN $^{md}$*Nin-urta-ki-na-i-de*<br>$^{m}$*Bi-in-na-nu* |
| 1.0.0 | √ | NUMUN $^{m}$*Ṭa-bi-ia* DUMU $^{m}$LÚ-$^{d}$INANNA |
| 0.3.5 | √ | NUMUN $^{m}$ZÁLAG-$^{d}$IŠKUR *ha-za-an-nu* |
| 0.2.3 | √ | NUMUN $^{m}$*Iz-kùr*-$^{d}$*Nin-urta*<br>DUMU $^{md}$UTU-ÙRU |
| 0.4.5 | √? | ŠUKU 1 UDU.NIGA $^{m}$ZÁLAG-$^{d}$IŠKUR *ha-za-nu* |
| | | TA 0.0.3 5 SÌLA ŠE.MUŠ$_5$ *mah-rù* |

Rev.

| | | |
|---|---|---|
| 0.2.3 | √? | UR$_5$.RA $^{m}$UŠ-*a-na*-$^{d}$AMAR.UTU $^{lú}$ENGAR<br>⸢*ša*?⸣ $^{md}$*Nin-urta*-⸢MU⸣-MU |
| 0.0.5 | | ⸢ŠUKU ANŠE⸣$^{meš}$ ⸢*ù* DUB.SAR⸣<br>U$_4$.[2]8.KAM ⸢*ù* U$_4$.29.KAM⸣ |
| 0.1.4 | √ | *n*[*i-ki-is* GU]R$_7$ |

PAP 9.1.1 $^{giš}$BÁN [1]0 ⸢SÌLA⸣

⸢ŠU.NIGIN 7⸣.2$^{pi}$.0 $^{giš}$BÁN GA[L]
TA 1.4.1 GAL $^{giš}$BÁ[N 10 SÌLA]
*i-na* 1.0.0 0.1$^{pi}$.0 *šu-lu-ú*

COMMENTARY

1–4. "Emmer, (measured by) the *sūtu* of 10 *qû*, from the revenues of Āl-irrē of year 9 of King Kadašman-Turgu, which was disbursed on the 28$^{th}$ day of month IX." One would expect *i-na* ŠÀ *te-li-ti* instead of *i-na te-li-ti*.

9–11. Since the quantity of seed in l. 9 is the same as in the previous lines, which have two persons as recipients, it seems likely that Ṭābīya and the son of Amīl-Ištar are two different persons (i.e., one should not regard Ṭābīya as the son of Amīl-Ištar). In fact, the next line has a smaller quantity of seed for only one person. Following the same logic, it seems likely that the small amount in l. 11 was assigned to one person (i.e., Izkur-Ninurta, the son of Šamaš-nāṣir).

## 163. CUNES 52-12-031

-.X.9 Kadašman-Turgu

Obv. ŠE *ša i-na* ŠÀ 5.1.⸢4⸣ $^{giš}$BÁN GAL ⸢*maš-ši-ti*⸣
*ša* TA BÀD-$^{d}$⸢KUR⸣ *ša* $^{m}$MU-*líb-ši*
*iš-ša-am-ma* ⸢*id*⸣-*di-nu*
$^{iti}$AB.È MU.9.KAM *Ka-dáš-man-Túr-gu* LUGAL

| | ŠE $^{giš}$⸢BÁN GAL⸣ | $^{giš}$BÁN 10 SÌLA | MU.BI.IM |
|---|---|---|---|
| | 1.0.0 | | ÉŠ.GÀR $^{lú}$LUNGA $^{md}$⸢30-TI-URU$_4$⸣ |
| | | 3.0.0 | ⸢ÉŠ.GÀR DUMU.MUNUS $^{lú}$Ì.SUR⸣ |
| L.e. | | 1.0.0 | *ki-mu* ⸢NUMUN *ša*⸣ [x x x x x]-⸢È?⸣<br>⸢$^{md}$*Nuska-na-b*⸣[*u-šu*]<br>⸢$^{m}$x x x x⸣<br>⸢ŠU? $^{md}$30-TI-URU$_4$⸣<br>⸢ŠU $^{lú}$LUNGA *tur-rat*⸣ |
| Rev. | | 0.2.3 | *ki-*⸢*mu ša*⸣ *a-na* $^{m}$È-[*a-na*]-<br>ZÁLAG-$^{d}$IŠKUR GAR-*ni id-di-n*[*u*]<br>ŠU $^{lú}$LUNGA *tur-rat* |
| | 1.0.0 | | *ki-*⸢*mu ša*⸣ *a-na* É.DINGIR$^{didli}$<br>*ša* ḪUR.SAG.KALAM.MA *id-di-nu*<br>ŠU $^{m}$KI.MIN ⸢*tur*⸣-*rat* |
| PAP | 2.0.0 | 4.2.3 | ŠU.NIGIN 5.⸢1.4⸣ $^{giš}$BÁN GAL<br>TA ⸢GAL?-*ú*?⸣ *šu-lu-ú* |

Translation

Obv. Barley from 160 *sūtu*, (measured by) the big *sūtu*, of the delivery
that is from Dūr-Amurru, which Šumu-libši
brought here and disbursed.
Month X, year 9 of King Kadašman-Turgu.

| | Barley (meas. by) the big *sūtu* | (meas. by) the *sūtu* of 10 *qû* | Its entry |
|---|---|---|---|
| | 30 *sūtu* | | Production supplies (for) the brewer; Sîn-balāṭa-īriš. |
| | | 90 *sūtu* | ⸢Production supplies (for) the daughter of Ṣāḫitu⸣. |
| L.e. | | 30 *sūtu* | In place of the seed that [ . . . ]<br>⸢Nuska-nāb⸣[ûšu]<br>⸢ . . . ⸣<br>⸢at the disposal of Sîn-balāṭa-īriš⸣;<br>⸢the hand of the brewer is turned⸣. |
| Rev. | | 15 *sūtu* | In place of what he/they gave to Lūṣi-[ana]-<br>nūr-Adad, the overseer;<br>the hand of the brewer is turned. |
| | 30 *sūtu* | | In place of what he/they gave<br>to the temples of Ḫursagkalama;<br>the hand of ditto (i.e., the brewer) is turned. |
| Total | 60 *sūtu* | 135 *sūtu* | Grand total: 160 *sūtu* (meas. by) the big *sūtu*,<br>after the increase has been deducted. |

COMMENTARY

6. Cf. **no. 160**: 2, which dates to the same year and records the allocation of 30 *sūtu* of barley as "production supplies (for) Sîn-ibni, the brewer; Sîn-balāṭa-īriš received (it)." In **no. 160**, however, the barley comes from a different source.

4. According to **no. 159**: 11, in the same month of the same year the daughter of the Ṣāḫitu received the same amount of barley as production supplies also from Ḫuzālu.

9. Cf. **no. 159**: 29: "15 *sūtu*: production supplies (for) Lūṣi-ana-nūr-Adad, the overseer; Sîn-balāṭa-īriš gave (it) from that of the brewer and his hand is turned." The two entries are dated to the same month of the same year, but the texts indicate different sources of barley: here it comes from the delivery of Dūr-Amurru and is disbursed by Šumu-libši, while in **no. 159** it is disbursed by Ḫuzālu.

## 164. CUNES 52-12-005

-.XI.9 Kadašman-Turgu

Obv. [ŠE *š*]*a i-na* ŠÀ *te-li-ti ša* ⸢X⸣[

[*š*]*a* MU.9.KAM *Ka-dáš-man-Túr-gu* L[UGAL]

*i-na* $^{iti}$ZÍZ.A.AN *na-ad-*[*nu*]

| | [ŠE] $^{giš}$BÁN GAL | $^{giš}$BÁN 10 SÌLA | | MU.BI.I[M] |
|---|---|---|---|---|
| | | 15.0.0 | | ŠUKU ANŠE.KUR.RA$^{meš}$ $^{m}$*I-la-nu-ú-a* ⸢DUMU $^{m}$⸣[ |
| | | 2.2.3 | | ŠUKU GU$_{4}^{meš}$ DUMU $^{m}$ÌR-$^{d}$KUR |
| | | 2.2.3 | | KI.MIN DUMU DUB.SAR |
| | | 1.0.0 NUMUN | | $^{md}$*Nin-urta*-MU-MU $^{m}$*Bu-un-na*-$^{d}$AMAR.UTU |
| | | 1.0.0 NUMUN | | √ $^{m}$KI.MIN $^{m}$*A-ḫe-du-tu*$_{4}$ |
| | | 1.0.0 NUMUN | | √ $^{m}$KI.MIN $^{m}$*Ba-na-nu-ú* |
| | | 1.0.0 NUMUN | | √ $^{m}$KI.MIN $^{md}$*Nin-nisi-mu*-SIG$_{5}$-*iq* |
| | | 1.0.0 NUMUN | | √ $^{m}$KI.MIN $^{m}$ZÁLAG-$^{d}$*Iš*-⸢*tar*⸣ |
| | | 1.0.0 NUMUN | | √ $^{m}$MU-*líb-ši* $^{m}$*Bi-i'-šu*$_{14}$ |
| | | 1.0.0 NUMUN | √ | $^{m}$È-*a-na*-ZÁLAG-$^{d}$IŠKUR GAR-*nu* |
| | | 6.2.3 | √ | UR$_{5}$.RA $^{m}$È-*a-na*-ZÁLAG-$^{d}$AMAR.UTU DUMU ⸢É⸣ |
| | | 2.0.0 | √ | KI.MIN $^{m}$KAR-*ub*-$^{d}$AMAR.UTU DUMU $^{m}$*Ur*-$^{d}$*Asar-alim-ma* |
| | | 1.0.0 | √ | KI.MIN $^{m}$MU-*líb-ši* $^{m}$*Bi-i'*-⸢*šu*$_{14}$⸣ |
| | | 1.0.0 | √ | KI.MIN $^{m}$*I-din*-$^{d}$U.GUR DUMU $^{m}$*I-din*-$^{d}$U.GUR |
| | | 1.0.0 | √ | KI.MIN $^{md}$*Nin-urta*-ŠEŠ-SUM-*na* DUMU $^{m}$*A-gab-ta-ḫe* |
| Rev. | | 0.1.4 KI.MIN | √ | $^{m}$*Za-ki-rù* ⸢$^{lú}$LUNGA$^{?}$⸣ *ša* $^{md}$*Nin-u*[*rta*$^{?}$- |
| | | 0.1.4 KI.MIN | √ | $^{m}$*I-na-kit-ti-e-le* KI.MIN |
| | 5.0.0 | | | *maš-ši-tu*$_{4}$ BÀD-$^{d+}$*En-líl*$^{meš.ki}$ $^{md}$*Nin-urta*-MU-MU |
| | | 10.0.0 | √ | $^{m}$*Ba-i-rù* $^{lú}$LUNGA-*šu* $^{m}$KI.MIN |
| | | 1.0.0 | √ | $^{md}$*Nuska-na-bu-šu* |
| | | 0.2.3 | | $^{m}$*Ib-ni*-$^{d}$AMAR.UTU DUMU.A.NI |
| | | 0.1.4 | | ŠUKU 2 NÍG.LÁ ANŠE$^{meš}$ TA U$_{4}$.10.KAM [EN] ⸢U$_{4}$.19$^{?}$⸣.[KAM] |
| | | 0.1$^{pi}$.0 | | ŠUKU *ù* BAPPIR$_{x}$ $^{m}$MU-*líb-ši* KI.[MIN$^{?}$] |
| | | 0.0.3 | | KI.MIN $^{m}$*Mu*-SIG$_{5}$-$^{d}$IŠKUR KI.[MIN$^{?}$] |
| | | 0.4$^{pi}$.0 | | KI.MIN 12 ÉRIN$^{ḫi.a\ giš}$MÁ *ša* ŠE ⸢*ù* ZÍZ.AN.⸣[NA] *iš-du-du-ni* TA KI.MIN EN KI.MIN |
| | | 0.0.3 | | KI.MIN 2 MÁ.LAḪ$_{5}^{meš}$ KI.MIN |
| | | 0.3.0 | | Á $^{giš}$MÁ $^{m}$*Ki-din*-$^{d}$IŠKUR |

| | | | |
|---|---|---|---|
| | [0.0.2] | | *ni-ki-is* GUR$_7$ $^{m}$*Il-lul-lu*$_4$ *ḫa-za-nu* |
| [PAP] | 5.0./2 | 52./4$^{pi}$.0 | ŠU.NIGIN 47.1.3 [<br>$^{giš}$BÁN GA[L]<br>TA 10.2.5 GAL [$^{giš}$BÁN 10 SÌLA]<br>*i-na* 1.0.0 0.1[$^{pi}$.0 *šu-lu-ú*] |

Translation

Obv. [Barley] from the revenues of [GN]
of year 9 of K[ing] Kadašman-Turgu,
which was disbursed in month XI.

| | [Barley] (meas. by) the big *sūtu* | (meas. by) the *sūtu* of 10 *qû* | Its entry |
|---|---|---|---|
| 5 | | 450 *sūtu* | Fodder for the horses, Ilānū'a, son of [ . . . ]. |
| | | 75 *sūtu* | Fodder for the oxen, son of Arad-Amurru. |
| | | 75 *sūtu* | Ditto (i.e., fodder for the oxen), son of Tupšarru. |
| | | 30 *sūtu*, seed | Ninurta-zākir-šumi (and) Bunna-Marduk. |
| | | 30 *sūtu*, seed | √ Ditto (i.e., Ninurta-zākir-šumi) (and) Aḫēdūtu. |
| 10 | | 30 *sūtu*, seed | √ Ditto (and) Bananû. |
| | | 30 *sūtu*, seed | √ Ditto (and) Ninnisi-mudammiq. |
| | | 30 *sūtu*, seed | √ Ditto (and) Nūr-Ištar. |
| | | 30 *sūtu*, seed | √ Šumu-libši (and) Bi'šu. |
| | | 30 *sūtu*, seed √ | Lūṣi-ana-nūr-Adad, the overseer. |
| 15 | | 195 *sūtu* √ | Loan, Lūṣi-ana-nūr-Marduk, *mār* ⌜*bīti*⌝. |
| | | 60 *sūtu* √ | Ditto, Šūzub-Marduk, son of Ur-Asaralimma. |
| | | 36 *sūtu* √ | Ditto, Šumu-libši (and) Bi'šu. |
| | | 36 *sūtu* √ | Ditto, Iddin-Nergal, son of Iddin-Nergal. |
| 19 | | 36 *sūtu* √ | Ditto, Ninurta-aḫa-iddina (and?) the son of Agab-taḫe. |
| Rev. | | 10 *sūtu*, ditto √ | Zakīru, brewer? of Ninu[rta- . . .]. |
| | | 10 *sūtu*, ditto √ | Ina-kitti-ele'i, ditto (i.e., brewer? of Ninu[rta- . . .]). |
| | 150 *sūtu* | | Delivery (of/for) Dūr-Enlilē,<br>Ninurta-zākir-šumi. |
| | | 300 *sūtu* √ | Bā'iru, his brewer, ditto (i.e., Ninurta-zākir-šumi). |
| | | 30 *sūtu* √ | Nuska-nābûšu. |
| 25 | | 15 *sūtu* | Ibni-Marduk, his son. |
| | | 10 *sūtu* | Fodder for two teams of donkeys, from day 10 [till]<br>day ⌜19?⌝. |
| | | 6 *sūtu* | Fodder and sourdough bread, Šumu-libši, di[tto?]. |
| | | 3 *sūtu* | Ditto, Mudammiq-Adad, di[tto?]. |
| | | 24 *sūtu* | Ditto for twelve workmen of the boat who towed here barley and emmer, from ditto till ditto. |
| 30 | | 3 *sūtu* | Ditto for two sailors, ditto. |
| | | 18 *sūtu* | Rent of a boat, Kidin-Adad. |
| | [2 *sūtu*] | | *nikis karê* of Illullu, *ḫazannu*. |
| [Total] | 152 *sūtu* | 1,584 *sūtu* | Grand total: 1,419 *sūtu* [<br>(measured by) the big *sūtu*<br>after 317 *sūtu* [have been deducted], the increase<br>[of the *sūtu* of 10 *qû*] being at a rate of 1 [*pānu*] per kor. |

COMMENTARY

6–7. Even if not explicitly identified as such, the son of Arad-Amurru and the son of Tupšarru must be the farmers known from other texts (see the respective entries in the Index of Personal Names).

20–21. KI.MIN in col. ii refers to UR$_5$.RA in l. 15.

32 The quantity restored in col. i is required by the total in l. 33. The *ḫazannu* Illullu is probably the same person as the Ill[ullu] who receives an amount of *nikis karê* in **no. 185**: 9.

## 165. CUNES 52-14-037

-.-.10 Kadašman-Turgu

Summary of amounts of barley received by several individuals in the town of Āl-Sîn-šamuḫ?.

Obv. ŠE $^{giš⌜}$BÁN 5 SÌLA *ša i-na* URU-$^{d}$30-*ša*?-*muḫ*?⌝
*mi-⌜taḫ-ḫu-ra-tu⌝*

| | | |
|---|---|---|
| | 1.0.0 | $^{m}$ÌR-*nu-bat-ti* |
| | 1.0.0 | ⌜$^{md}$30?-ŠEŠ?⌝-SUM-*na* $^{lú}$KÚRUN.NA |
| | 2.0.0 | $^{m}$*Mu*-SIG$_5$-$^{d}$IŠKUR ⌜$^{lú?}$x⌝ |
| | 0.2.4 | $^{m}$DINGIR-*re-man-ni* |
| Rev. | 0.2.1 | $^{m}$*Mar-tu-ku* DUMU $^{m}$*Ḫu-za-lu*$_4$ |
| | 0.1.4 | $^{m}$*E-ri-bu* |
| | 2.0.0 | $^{lú}$ENGAR |
| PAP | 7./1.3 | ŠE $^{giš}$BÁN 5 SÌLA MU.10.KAM $^{d}$*Ka-dáš-man-Tur*$_7$-*gu* LUGAL.E |

## 166. CUNES 52-14-091

-.VI–XII.10 Kadašman-Turgu

Summary of amounts of *arsuppu* (ŠE.EŠTUB), *šeguššu* (ŠE.MUŠ$_5$), and emmer (ZÍZ.AN.NA) received by Nuska-nābûšu from Mudammiq-Adad in different towns.

Obv. ŠE $^{giš}$BÁN 10 SÌLA *i-na* ŠU $^{m}$*Mu*-SIG$_5$-$^{d}$IŠKUR
*i-na* MU.10.KAM *Ka-dáš-man-Túr-gu* $^{md}$*Nuska-⌜na-bu-šu⌝*
*mi-taḫ-ḫu-rù*

| | ŠE.EŠTUB | ŠE.MUŠ$_5$ | ZÍZ.AN.NA | MU.BI.[IM] |
|---|---|---|---|---|
| | 2.0.0 | | | $^{iti}$KIN.$^{d}$INA[NNA] *Tukul-ti*-É.KUR$^{ki}$ |
| | | 1.0.0 | | $^{iti}$APIN.DU$_8$.A BÀD-$^{d+}$*En-líl*$^{ḫi.a}$ |
| Rev. | | 2.0.0 | | $^{iti}$GAN.GAN.È ⌜*i-na*⌝ KI.MIN |
| | | 0.2.3 | | $^{iti}$AB.È KI.MIN |
| | 1.0.0 | | | $^{iti}$ŠE.⌜KIN.KU$_5$⌝ *T*[*ukul-ti*-É].KUR$^{ki}$ |
| | | (eras.) | 1.[0.0] | [$^{iti}$ŠE.KIN].KU$_5$ BÀD-$^{d+}$*En-líl*$^{ḫi.a}$ |
| PAP | 3.0.0 | 3.[2.3] | 1.0.0 | $^{giš}$BÁN 10 SÌLA |

COMMENTARY

1–3. "Grain, (measured by) the *sūtu* of 10 *qû*, which Nuska-nābûšu has been receiving from Mudammiq-Adad in year 10 of Kadašman-Turgu."

7. *ina* KI.MIN (i.e., in Dūr-Enlilē) makes it clear that the GNs in the previous and following lines indicate the towns where Nuska-nābûšu received the cereals from Mudammiq-Adad.

## 167. CUNES 52-00-063

-.XII.[11] Kadašman-Turgu

Obv. ŠE ⸢*ša*⸣ *i-na* ŠÀ *te-li-ti* [
⸢*ša*⸣ MU.11.KAM $^{d}$*Ka-dáš*-[
*i-na* $^{iti}$ŠE.KIN.KU$_5$ [

| | ŠE $^{giš}$BÁN GAL | ŠE $^{giš}$BÁN 10 SÌLA | MU.[BI.IM] |
|---|---|---|---|
| 5 | 6.0.0 | | ÉŠ.GÀR $^{I}$[ú? |
| | | 12.0.0 | ÉŠ.GÀR ⸢x⸣[ |
| | | 2.0.0 | ⸢x x bi?⸣ [ |
| | | 0.3.3 | ⸢x⸣ en? ⸢x⸣ [ |
| | | 2.0.0 | ⸢x⸣ [ |
| Text breaks off (1–2 lines missing) | | | |
| Rev. | | ⸢0.3.1⸣ | ⸢x x⸣ [<br>ŠU $^{m}$[ |
| 9 | 0.1.1 | | ⸢x x⸣ [<br>ŠU $^{m}$[ |
| PAP | 11.1.1 | 18.0.⸢4? 4+⸣ SÌLA | ŠU.[NÍGIN<br>⸢TA⸣ [ |

COMMENTARY

1–3. "Barley from the revenues [of GN] of year 11 of Kadaš[man-Turgu?] which [was disbursed?] in month XII."

## 168. CUNES 52-18-791

-.-.19–20 Nazi-Maruttaš, 11–12 Kadašman-Turgu

Summary of amounts of barley received by Erība-Nergal from Mudammiq-Adad in years 19–20 of Nazi-Maruttaš and 11–12 of Kadašman-Turgu.

Obv. ⸢ŠE *ša*⸣ $^{m}$*Eri-ba*-$^{d}$U.GUR DUMU $^{mf}$⸢*Qa-diš*⸣*-ti*
*i-na* ŠU $^{m}$*Mu*-SIG$_5$-$^{d}$IŠKUR *maḫ-rù*

0.1$^{pi}$.0 MU.19.KAM *Na-zi-Muru*$_4$*-taš*

0.1$^{pi}$.0 MU.20.KAM KI.MIN

5 PAP 0.2$^{pi}$.0 $^{giš}$BÁN GAL *ḫír-ga-lu-ú*

0.0.3 UR$_5$.RA *i-na* ŠÀ ḪA.LA$^{meš}$ *ša* $^{md}$*Nin-urta*-MU-MU

L.e. $^{iti}$AB.È
MU.11.KAM $^{d}$*Ka-dáš-man-Túr-gu*

Rev. 0.0.2 ⸢KI.MIN *i-na* ŠÀ *ša* $^{m}$⸣[$^{d}$30]-EN-IBILA

10 *ša* TA BÀD-$^{d}$*Nuska*$^{ki}$ *iš-šu-ni*
MU.12.KAM

PAP 0.0.5 $^{giš}$BÁN 10 SÌLA
ŠU.NIGIN 1.2.4 ŠE $^{giš}$BÁN 5 SÌLA
*ša* $^{m}$*Eri-ba*-$^{d}$U.GUR *maḫ-rù*

Translation

| | | |
|---|---|---|
| Obv. | Barley which Erība-Nergal, son of Qadištu, received from Mudammiq-Adad: | |
| | 6 *sūtu* | year 19 of Nazi-Maruttaš. |
| | 6 *sūtu* | year 20 of ditto. |
| | Total: 12 *sūtu* of *ḫirgalû*, (measured by) the big *sūtu*. | |
| | 3 *sūtu* | loan from the shares of Ninurta-zākir-šumi; |
| L.e. | | month X, |
| | year 11 of Kadašman-Turgu. | |
| Rev. | 2 *sūtu* | ditto (i.e., loan) from that of [Sîn]-bēl-apli, |
| | who brought it here from Dūr-Nuska; year 12. | |
| | Total: 5 *sūtu*, (measured by) the *sūtu* of 10 *qû*. | |
| | Grand total: 23 *sūtu* of barley, (measured by) the *sūtu* of 5 *qû*, which Erība-Nergal received. | |

### 169. CUNES 52-16-096

-.-.12 Kadašman-Turgu

The text records quantities of *arsuppu* (expended?) to individuals associated with at least three different locations: Tukultī-Ekur, Kār-Nuska, and Dimtu (see ll. 5, 8, 24). Some of the persons are identified as farmers (ÉNSI).

| | | |
|---|---|---|
| Obv. | ŠE.EŠTUB [x-x]-*ú* $^{giš}$BÁN GAL ⸢x x⸣ | |
| | 0.2$^{pi}$.0 | DUMU $^{m}$ÌR-$^{d}$KUR $^{lú}$ÉNSI |
| | 0.2$^{pi}$.0 | DUMU $^{lú}$DUB.SAR KI.MIN |
| | 0.0.3 | $^{m}$*Ba-ti-ia-ú-tu*$_{4}$ |
| | PAP 0.4.3 *Tukul-ti*-É.KUR$^{ki}$ | |
| | 0.1$^{pi}$.0 | $^{m}$⸢*Bi-it-ta*⸣*-a* DUMU DUB.SAR $^{lú}$ÉNSI |
| | [ | ]-$^{d}$IŠKUR |
| | [PAP x.x.x *Kar*-$^{d}$]*Nuska*$^{ki}$ | |
| | [ | ]⸢x⸣-*ti* $^{lú}$ÉNSI |
| | [ | ]-$^{d}$AMAR.UTU KI.MIN |
| | [ | K]I.MIN |
| | [ | K]I.MIN |
| Rev. | [ | ] |
| | [ | ] |
| | [ | ] |
| | [ | ]⸢x⸣ |
| | [ | ]-⸢$^{d}$U.GUR$^{?}$⸣ |
| | 0.0.3 | $^{m}$[ ]⸢x⸣ |
| | 0.0.2 | $^{m}$⸢ZÁLAG$^{?}$⸣-[x] |
| | 0.0.3 | $^{m}$[*Z*]*i-ik-ri*-[$^{d}$IŠ]KUR |
| | 0.0.3 | $^{m}$ŠEŠ-SUM-*na*-$^{d}$AMAR.UTU |
| | 0.0.3 | $^{m}$*Ú-zu-ub-ni-bu* |
| | 0.0.3 | $^{m}$KAL-$^{d}$U.GUR |
| | PAP 2.1$^{pi}$.0 AN.ZA.GÀR$^{ki}$ | |
| L.e. | ŠU.NIGIN 3.2$^{pi}$.0 | |
| | MU.12.KAM | |
| | ⸢$^{d}$⸣*Ka-dáš-man-Túr-gu* | |

COMMENTARY

8. Kār-Nuska is known to be in the same area as Tukultī-Ekur and Dimtu from the topographical map published by Clay 1905. The three towns occur together in several texts; in this corpus, see also **nos. 23, 60, 173**, CUSAS 30 60, CUSAS 30 66, and CUSAS 30 229, and the remarks in van Soldt 2015, 116.
22. This could be explained as a Kassite PN. For the verbal element *uzub*, see Balkan 1954, 153, 187 and cf. Uzub-Ḫala and Usub-Šiḫu (Hölscher 1996, 231, 233), while *nibu* might be a variant of *nibi* (cf. Urpa-nibi and K/Qunanibi in Hölscher 1996, 127, 230, and see also UD-*nibi* in **no. 32**: 15).

## 170. CUNES 52-14-082 (Plate No. 47)

[ . . . ].I.12 Kadašman-Turgu

Allocation of barley as rations, a gift, fodder, and compensation for amounts of barley which Ninurta-ašarēd gave to different people in years 9–10 of Kadašman-Turgu.

Obv. [x x x x] ˹4$^{+}$˺ GUR $^{giš}$BÁN GAL
[*i-na* ŠÀ *maš-ši*]-˹*ti ša* $^{m}$*Ṭà-ab*-IM˺-$^{d}$IŠKUR
[x x x] *i-na* MU.11.KAM *na-ša-am-ma*
[x x x]-*e*$^{ki}$ $^{m}$*Mu*-SI[G$_5$-$^{d}$IŠ]KUR *im-ḫu-ru-m*[*a*]
[*i-na* $^{iti}$BÁR.ZA]G.GAR U$_4$.[x].KAM MU.12.KAM *Ka-dáš-man-T*[*úr-guid-di-nu*]

| | [$^{giš}$BÁN GA]L$^{?}$ | $^{giš}$BÁN [10] SÌLA | MU.BI.I[M] |
|---|---|---|---|
| | [ ] | ˹7$^{?}$.1˺.2 | ŠE.BA ˹*ka-li-i*˺ *ša* $^{iti}$S[IG$_4^{?}$<br>*ša* MU.11.KAM *ša a-na* 4 ˹x˺[ |
| | | 18.˹1.3˺˹4$^{?}$˺ | ŠE.BA *ka-li-i* TA $^{iti}$[<br>EN $^{iti}$SIG$_4$.GA *ša* MU.11.[KAM] |
| | | 3.0.0 | *ri-mu-tu*$_4$ $^{m}$*Ur*-$^{d}$*Nin-ni*[*si* |
| | | 1.1$^{pi}$.0 | ÍB.TAK$_4$ ŠUKU ˹6 UDU.NIGA$^{meš}$˺ $^{m}$˹*E*˺-[*tel*-KA-$^{d}$ . . .]<br>DUMU $^{m}$*Ši-in-na-ni a-na* ˹x˺ [<br>*ša* MU.11.KAM *le-e-qí* |
| | | 6.0.0 | $^{md}$*Nin-urta*-SAG DUMU $^{m}$*Ta-ri-b*[*at*-DINGIR]<br>*ki-mu a-na ri-mu-ti* DUMU $^{m}$BA-*š*[*a*$^{?}$-<br>*i-na* MU.9.KAM *id-di-*˹*nu*˺ ŠU-[*su tur-rat*] |
| | 1.0.0 | | $^{m}$KI.MIN *ki-mu ki-ṣir maḫ-*[*ri*<br>*a-na* $^{m}$*Ì-lí-re-man-ni i*[*d-di-nu*]<br>ŠU-*su tu*[*r-rat*] |
| Rev. | | [0.1.3] | $^{m}$[KI].˹MIN˺ *ki-mu ša a-na* $^{m}$*Ì-l*[*í*-<br>˹*i-na*˺ MU.9.KAM *id-di-nu* ŠU-*s*[*u tur-rat*] |
| | | 0.1.5 | $^{m}$KI.MIN *ki-mu ša* $^{m}$*E-tel*-KA-˹$^{d}$˺[<br>DUMU $^{m}$*Ši-in-na-ni i-na* MU.9.[KAM]<br>*i*[*m*]-*ḫu-ru-ma a-na* $^{f}$TI-*sa*-[GAL$^{?}$]<br>˹*id*˺-*di-nu* ŠU-*su tur-ra*[*t*] |
| | | 1.0.0 | $^{m}$KI.MIN *ki-mu ša a-na* $^{m}$*Ḫu-na-b*[*i*$^{?}$]<br>*i-na* MU.9.KAM *id-di-nu* [<br>ŠU-*su tur-rat* |
| | | 5.0.0 | $^{m}$KI.MIN *ki-mu ša a-na* $^{md+}$*En-*[*líl-*<br>*i-na* MU.10.KAM *id-di-nu* Š[U-*su tur-rat*] |
| | | 2.0.0 | $^{m}$KI.MIN *ki-mu ša a-na* $^{m}$*Bíl-*[<br>*i-na* MU.10.KAM *id-di-nu* Š[U-*su tur-rat*] |
| | | 1.0.0 | $^{m}$KI.MIN *ki-mu ša a-na* $^{m}$*La-*[<br>*i-na* MU.10.KAM *id-di-nu* ŠU-[*su tur-rat*] |

| | | | |
|---|---|---|---|
| | [ ] | 0.0.2 | ŠUKU ANŠE$^{meš}$ *ù* DUB.SAR<br>$U_4$.3.KAM *ù* $U_4$.4.KAM |
| [PAP] | [ ] | 45.2.3 | ŠU.⸢NIGIN⸣ 34.1.5<br>$^{giš}$BÁN GAL<br>TA GAL-*ú šu-lu-ú* |

Translation

Obv. [ . . . ] ⸢4$^{+}$⸣ kor (measured by) the big *sūtu*
[from the delive]ry$^{?}$ of/which Ṭāb-šār-Adad
[ . . . ] in year 11 brought here,
Mudamm[iq-Ad]ad received [in GN] and
[disbursed in month] I, day [x], year 12 of Kadašman-T[urgu].

| | [(meas. by) the bi]g [*sūtu*] | (meas. by) the *sūtu* of [10] *qû* | Its entry |
|---|---|---|---|
| | [ ] | ⸢218$^{?}$ *sūtu*⸣ | Rations of the prisoner(s) of month I[II$^{?}$] of year 11 which [ . . . ] to four [ . . . ]. |
| | | 549 *sūtu* ⸢4$^{?}$⸣ | Rations of the prisoner(s) from month [ . . . ] till month III of year 11. |
| | | 90 *sūtu* | Gift of Ur-Ninni[si |
| | | 36 *sūtu* | Rest of the fodder of 6 fattened sheep: ⸢E⸣[tel-pī-DN], son of Šinnānu, took to/for [ . . . ] of year 11. |
| | | 180 *sūtu* | Ninurta-ašarēd, son of Tarīb[at-ili], in place of (what) he gave in year 9 as gift of the son of Iqīš[a$^{?}$-DN]; [his] hand [is turned]. |
| | 30 *sūtu* | | Ditto (i.e., Ninurta-ašarēd), in place of the *kiṣir maḫ[ri . . .]* he g[ave] to Ilī-rēmanni; his hand is tu[rned]. |
| Rev. | | [9 *sūtu*] | [Di]tto, in place of what he gave to Ilī-[ . . . ] in year 9; hi[s] hand [is turned]. |
| | | 11 *sūtu* | Ditto, in place of what ⸢E⸣[tel-pī-DN], son of Šinnānu, received in year 9 and gave to Bullussa-[rabi$^{?}$]; his hand is turn[ed]. |
| | | 30 *sūtu* | Ditto, in place of what he gave to Ḫunābu in year 9; his hand is turned. |
| | | 150 *sūtu* | Ditto, in place of what he gave to En[lil- . . .] in year 10; [his] ha[nd is turned]. |
| | | 60 *sūtu* | Ditto, in place of what he gave to Bil[lullu$^{?}$] in year 10; [his] ha[nd is turned]. |
| | | 30 *sūtu* | Ditto, in place of what he gave to La[ . . . ] in year 10; [his] hand [is turned]. |
| | [ ] | 2 *sūtu* | Food for the donkeys and the scribe; day 3 and day 4. |
| [Total] | [ ] | 1,365 *sūtu* | Grand [total]: 1,031 *sūtu*, (measured by) the big *sūtu*, after the increase has been deducted. |

COMMENTARY

2. The restoration is tentative, but see also **no. 94**: 1–2 for a sure attestation of the delivery (*maššītu*) of Ṭāb-šār-Adad.

4. The GN at the beginning of the line, ending with *-e*, could have been either Āl-irrē or Āl-atḫē.

5. For the restoration of the verbal form at the end of the line, cf. **no. 179**: 5; another possibility would be *nadnu* (cf. CUSAS 30 74: 3).

7–8. ŠE.BA *ka-li-i* was known so far only from MUN 104: 1, which Sassmannshausen translated "Ration der Kultsänger(?)"; note, however, that the rare attestations of *kalû* "lamentation-priest" in MB sources always use the logogram GALA (Sassmannshausen 2001, 66). Thus, it seems more likely that *ka-li-i* represents here a gen. sg. verbal adjective from *kalû* "to detain"; considering the big amounts of barley assigned as rations, though, one would have rather expected the gen. pl. *kalûti* "of the prisoners" (see ÉRIN$^{meš}$ *ka-lu-ti* in PBS 1/2 43: 11).

10. I understand *le-e-qí* as a 3 sg. stative of *leqû* with active meaning; the spelling *le-e-qí* is less common than *le-qí*, but see Aro 1955, 28 for other cases of unnecessary scriptio plena of *e*.

13. The quantity restored in col. ii is the amount one would expect according to the total.

## 171. CUNES 52-19-145

-.V.12 Kadašman-Turgu

Allocation of barley and wheat as rations, a gift, fodder, and other expenditures that are not fully preserved.

Obv. ŠE *ša i-na* ŠÀ *te-li-ti ša* URU-*ir-re-e*
*ša* MU.12.KAM *Ka-dáš-man-Túr-⸢gu* LUGAL.E⸣
*i-na* $^{iti}$NE.NE.GAR *n*[*a-a*]*d-*[*nu*]

| | ŠE | GIG | MU.[BI.IM] |
|---|---|---|---|
| | 15.2.3 | | [. . .] |
| | | ⸢0.3$^{pi}$.0⸣ | [. . . $^{m}$]EN-SUM-*na im-ḫur* |
| PAP | | | [$^{giš}$BÁN GAL] |
| Rev. | 1.2.3 | | ŠE.BA $^{m}$EN-⸢BA-*šá* $^{lú}$⸣ENGAR 4 ITI *ù* U$_4$.15.KAM |
| | 1.0.0 | | *ri-mu-tu*$_4$ $^{m}$*Ka-gi-ia* $^{lú}$LUNGA *ša* BÁRA.DUMU$^{ki}$ |
| | 0.1.1 | | ŠUKU ANŠE$^{meš}$ $^{m}$*E-ri-bu* U$_4$.17.KAM *ù* U$_4$.18.KAM |
| PAP | 2.3.3 | | $^{giš}$BÁN 10 SÌLA |
| ⸢ŠU.NIGIN⸣ | 17.3.2 5 SÌLA [TA 0.2].⸢4⸣ 5 SÌLA | 0.3$^{pi}$.0 | $^{giš}$BÁN GAL TA GAL $^{giš}$BÁN 10 SÌLA *i-na* 1.0.0 0.1$^{pi}$.0 *šu-lu-ú* |

COMMENTARY

1–3. "Grain from the revenues of Āl-irrē of year 12 of King Kadašman-Turgu, which was [disbu]rs[ed] in month V." As the column headings show, the text records the disbursement of barley and wheat, thus ŠE is used here with its more general meaning "grain, cereals."

8. The entry for the sum was left empty by the scribe, probably because there is only one quantity for each column.

9. "Rations (for) Bēlī-iqīša, plowman, (for) 4 months and 15 days."

10. "Gift (of) Kagiya, brewer of Parak-māri." A PN Kagiya is not attested in the MB onomastic repertoires, but see Dalley 2009, 292 for attestations in documents from the First Sealand Dynasty. An anonymous brewer of Parak-māri receives one kor of barley also in MUN 146, which records disbursements of barley in Dunni-aḫi out of the revenues of the 22nd year of Nazi-Maruttaš.

12. The calculated total should be 2.3.4.

## 172. CUNES 52-14-038

-.VI.12 Kadašman-Turgu

This and the following text (**no. 173**) are almost duplicates, with only minor differences in phrasing and layout.

Obv. 1.0.0 ŠE $^{\text{giš}}$BÁN 10 SÌLA *ša* $^{\text{m}}$⸢*Ṭa*⸣*-bi-ia*
0.4$^{\text{pi}}$.0 ŠE $^{\text{giš}}$BÁN 10 SÌLA ŠUKU ⸢$^{\text{m}}$*Mu*-SIG$_5$⸣-$^{\text{d}}$IŠKUR

PAP 1.4$^{\text{pi}}$.0 ŠE $^{\text{giš}}$BÁN 10 SÌLA
*i-na Tu-kul-ti*-É.KUR$^{\text{ki}}$
$^{\text{m}}$⸢*Mu*-SIG$_5$-$^{\text{d}}$⸣IŠKUR
L.e. ⸢*a-na*⸣ $^{\text{m}}$*Mi-na*-DÙ-DINGIR ⸢AD⸣.KID
Rev. *ip-qí-id-ma*
*a-na pe-ḫe-e i-din-ma it-bal*
$^{\text{iti}}$KIN.$^{\text{d}}$INANNA
MU.12.KAM ⸢$^{\text{d}}$*Ka-dáš-man*⸣*-Túr-gu*
LUGAL.E

Translation

Obv. 30 *sūtu* of barley, (measured by) the *sūtu* of 10 *qû* of Ṭābīya
24 *sūtu* of barley, (measured by) the *sūtu* of 10 *qû*: allocation of ⸢Mudammiq⸣-Adad

Total 54 *sūtu* of barley, (measured by) the *sūtu* of 10 *qû*.
In Tukultī-Ekur
⸢Mudammiq⸣-Adad
6–7 entrusted (it) ⸢to⸣ Mīnâ-ēpuš-ila, the reed-weaver,
Rev. gave (it) in order to place it in storage and took away[?].
Month VI,
year 12 of King ⸢Kadašman⸣-Turgu.

Commentary

2. Here **no. 173**: 3–5 specifies that the food allocation of Mudammiq-Adad is "of Tukultī-Ekur, Kār-Nuska, and Dimtu."

8. The meaning of the last verbal form (*itbal*) in this context is unclear to me; the parallel passage in **no. 173**: 8–11 is phrased differently.

## 173. CUNES 52-18-792

-.VI.12 Kadašman-Turgu

See commentary to **no. 172**.

| | | |
|---|---|---|
| Obv. | ŠE $^{giš}$BÁN 10 SÌLA | |
| | 1.0.0 | *ša* $^{m}$*Ṭa-bi-ia* |
| 3 | 0.4$^{pi}$.0 | ŠUKU $^{m}$*Mu*-SIG$_5$-$^{d}$IŠKUR |
| | | *ša Tukul-ti*-É.KUR$^{ki}$ *Kar*-$^{d}$*Nuska*$^{ki}$ |
| | | *ù* AN.ZA.GÀR$^{ki}$ |
| 6 | PAP 1.4$^{pi}$.0 ŠE $^{giš}$BÁN 10 SÌLA | |
| Rev. | *i-na Tukul-ti*-É.KUR$^{ki}$ | |
| | $^{m}$*Mu*-SIG$_5$-$^{d}$IŠKUR | |
| | *a-na* $^{m}$*Mi-na*-DÙ-*uš*-DINGIR AD.KID | |
| 10 | *a-na pe-he-e* | |
| | *ip-qí-id* | |
| | $^{iti}$KIN.$^{d}$INANNA | |
| | MU.12.KAM $^{d}$*Ka-dáš-man-Túr-gu* LUGAL | |

Translation

| | | |
|---|---|---|
| Obv. | Barley, (measured by) the *sūtu* of 10 *qû*: | |
| | 30 *sūtu* | of Ṭābīya |
| 3 | 24 *sūtu* | food allocation of Mudammiq-Adad |
| | | of Tukultī-Ekur, Kār-Nuska, |
| | | and Dimtu. |
| 6 | Total: 54 *sūtu* of barley, (measured by) the *sūtu* of 10 *qû*. | |
| Rev. | In Tukultī-Ekur | |
| | Mudammiq-Adad | |
| 11 | entrusted (it) | |
| 9 | to Mīnâ-ēpuš-ila, the reed-weaver, | |
| 10 | in order to place it in storage. | |
| | Month VI, | |
| | year 12 of King ⌜Kadašman⌝-Turgu. | |

## 174. CUNES 52-19-123

-.IV.13 Kadašman-Turgu

Obv. ŠE *ša* [*i-n*]*a* ŠÀ *te-li-ti ša Ta-mir-ti*[$^{ki}$]
*š*[*a* M]U.13.KAM *Ka-dáš-man-Túr-gu* LUGAL.E
[*i-na*] $^{iti}$ŠU.NUMUN.NA *na-a*[*d*]*-nu*

| | ŠE $^{giš}$BÁN GAL | $^{giš}$BÁN 10 SÌLA | MU.BI.IM |
|---|---|---|---|
| | 17.1.4 | √ | ÉŠ.GÀR $^{md}$*Nin-urta-*[SA]G |
| | 15.3.1 | √ | ŠUKU É.DINGIR$^{didli}$ $^{m}$KI.MIN |
| | [1]3$^{?}$.3.0 | √ | *ki-is-pu* $^{m}$KI.MIN |
| | | 6.0.0 √ | ŠE.BA DUMU.MUNUS $^{m}$*Be-la-nu* $^{m}$KI.MIN |
| | | 6.0.0 √ | ŠE.BA DUMU.MUNUS $^{mf}$*Ḫa-zi-*$^{d}$AM[AR$^{?}$.UTU$^{?}$] ⌜$^{m}$KI.MIN⌝ |
| | | 6.0.0 √ | ŠE.BA DUMU.MUNUS $^{m}$*Mu-*SIG$_5$-$^{d}$IŠKUR [$^{m}$KI.MIN$^{?}$] |
| Rev. | [ ] | | ÍB.TAK$_4$ *a-na* ŠÀ *maš-ši-t*[*i*] *i-na* NIBRU$^{ki}$ *ta-bi-*⌜*ik*⌝ |
| PAP | [x].3$^{pi}$.0 | 18.0.0 | ŠU.NIGIN 55.0.0 $^{giš}$BÁN ⌜GAL⌝ TA 3.3$^{pi}$.0 GAL $^{giš}$BÁN 10 SÌLA *i-na* 1.0.0 0.1$^{pi}$.0 *šu-lu-ú* |

Translation

Obv. Barley from the revenues of Tamirtu
o[f ye]ar 13 of King Kadašman-Turgu,
which was disbursed [in] month IV.

| | Barley (meas. by) the big *sūtu* | (meas. by) the *sūtu* of 10 *qû* | Its entry: |
|---|---|---|---|
| | 520 *sūtu* | √ | Production supplies; Ninurta-[ašar]ēd. |
| | 469 *sūtu* | √ | Supplies for the temples; ditto (i.e., Ninurta-ašarēd). |
| | 408$^{?}$ *sūtu* | √ | Offering for the cult of the dead ancestors; ditto (i.e., Ninurta-ašarēd). |
| | | 180 *sūtu* √ | Ration (for) the daughter of Bēlanu; ditto (i.e., Ninurta-ašarēd). |
| | | 180 *sūtu* √ | Ration (for) the daughter of Ḫazi-Ma[rduk$^{?}$]; ⌜ditto⌝ (i.e., Ninurta-ašarēd). |
| | | 180 *sūtu* √ | Ration (for) the daughter of Mudammiq-Adad; [ditto$^{?}$, (i.e., Ninurta-ašarēd)]. |
| Rev. | [ ] | | The rest is stored in Nippur together with the delivery. |
| Total | [ . . . ]18$^{+}$ *sūtu* | 540 *sūtu* | Grand total: 1,650 *sūtu* (measured by) the big *sūtu*, after 108 *sūtu* have been deducted, the increase of the *sūtu* of 10 *qû* being at a rate of 1 *pānu* per kor. |

## 175. CUNES 52-18-841 (Plate No. 48)

-.VIa.13 Kadašman-Turgu

Obv. [Š]E *ša i-na* ŠÀ *te-li-ti ša Tukul-ti-*É.[KUR$^{ki}$]
*ša* MU.13.KAM *Ka-dáš-man-Túr-gu* LUGAL.⸢E⸣
*i-na* $^{iti}$KIN.$^{d}$INANNA.2.KAM.MA *na-ad-nu*

| | | ŠE $^{giš}$BÁN GAL | $^{giš}$BÁN 10 SÌLA | MU.BI.IM |
|---|---|---|---|---|
| 5 | | 6.0.4 | | $^{m}$*Be-la-nu* ⸢DUMU $^{m}$*In-ni-bu*⸣<br>*ki-mu* ⸢ḪA⸣.LA-*šu ša* BÀD-$^{d}$KUR$^{ki}$<br>*ša a-na* GUR$_7$ *tab-ku* ŠU-*su* ⸢*tur*⸣-*rat* |
| | | | 6.0.2 | $^{m}$*Ḫa-ni-bu* DUMU $^{m}$DUB.SAR<br>*a-na* ŠE.BA NUMUN *ù* ŠUKU GU$_4$$^{me}$[$^{š}$]<br>*im-ḫur* |
| Rev. | | | 13.0.4<br>5 SÌLA | *ki-mu* NUMUN *es-ri*<br>*ša a-na* ŠÀ NÍG.KUD.DA<br>*tab-ku na-as-ḫa-am-ma*<br>*a-na* NUMUN *ša* BÀD-$^{d+}$*En-líl*$^{meš}$<br>*na-di-in* |
| 8 | PAP | 6.0.4 | 19./1$^{pi}$.0 5 SÌLA | ŠU.NIGIN 21.2.3<br>$^{giš}$BÁN GAL<br>TA 3.4.1 5 SÌLA<br>GAL $^{giš}$BÁN 10 SÌLA<br>*i-na* 1.0.0 0.1$^{pi}$.0 *šu-lu-ú* |

Translation

Obv. [Barl]ey from the revenues of Tukultī-E[kur]
of year 13 of King Kadašman-Turgu,
which was disbursed in month VIa.

| | Barley (meas. by) the big *sūtu* | (meas. by) the *sūtu* of 10 *qû* | Its entry |
|---|---|---|---|
| 5 | 184 *sūtu* | | Belānu, ⸢son of Innibu⸣,<br>in place of his share of Dūr-Amurru<br>that was stored in the granary; his hand is turned. |
| | | 182 *sūtu* | Ḫānibu, son of Tupšarru, received (it) as ration, seed, and fodder for the oxen. |
| Rev. | | 394 *sūtu*<br>5 *qû* | is withdrawn in place of the collected seed, which was stored together with the *miksu*, and is disbursed as seed of Dūr-Enlilē. |
| 8 Total | 184 *sūtu* | 576 *sūtu* 5 *qû* | Grand total: 645 *sūtu*<br>(measured by) the big *sūtu*,<br>after 115 *sūtu* (and) 5 *qû*<br>have been deducted, the increase of<br>the *sūtu* of 10 *qû* being<br>at a rate of 1 *pānu* per kor. |

COMMENTARY

5. Sassmannshausen 2001, 376 notes that the verb *nasāḫu* is rare in MB administrative records. To this line and the occurrences cited by Sassmannshausen add now also CUSAS 30 112: 5.

## 176. CUNES 52-12-017

-.VII.13 Kadašman-Turgu

Obv. ⸢ŠE *ša*⸣ *i-na* ⸢URU-*ir*⸣-*re-e i-na* $^{iti}$[DU$_{6}$].KÙ *na-ad-nu*
MU.13.[KAM] *Ka-dáš-man-Túr-g*[*u*] LUGAL.E

| | | | | |
|---|---|---|---|---|
| | ⸢x x x⸣<br>MU.13.KAM | *te-li-t*[*u*$_{4}$]<br>MU.⸢12⸣.KAM | ⸢ZÍZ.AN.NA⸣<br>MU.13.KAM | MU.BI.IM |
| | 1.2.3 | 2.2.3 | √ | ŠE.NUMUN ŠE.⸢BA⸣ *ù* ŠUKU GU$_{4}$$^{meš}$ $^{m}$GAL-*šá*-$^{d}$*Gu-la* ÉNSI |
| | 1.2.3 | 2.2.3 | √ | KI.MIN $^{m}$UD-*šú*-ZÁLAG-*ir* KI.MIN |
| | 1.2.3 | 2.2.3 | √ | KI.MIN $^{m}$È-*a*-SUD-URU KI.MIN |
| | 3.2.3 | 3.2.3 | √ | UR$_{5}$.RA $^{m}$*Ri-mu-tu*$_{4}$ GAL *za-ra-ti*<br>$^{md}$*Pap-sukkal*-ŠEŠ-SUM-*na* $^{lú}$ENGAR-*šu im-ḫur* |
| | 2.2.⸢3⸣ | | √ | KI.MIN ⸢$^{m}$BA-*šá*-$^{d}$*Nin*⸣-*ìmma*<br>$^{m}$[x]-*ar-ši-kit-tu*$_{4}$ $^{lú}$ENGAR-*šu im-ḫur* |
| | 2.2.3 | | √ | K[I.MI]N $^{m}$*Ṭà-ab*-IM-$^{d}$IŠKUR |
| | 2.2.3 | | √ | [KI.MI]N $^{m}$È-*a-na*-ZÁLAG-$^{d+}$*En-líl* |
| | 2.2.3 | | √ | [K]I.MIN $^{m}$*Za-ki-rù* DUMU $^{m}$*Da-aš-pi* |
| | 2.0.0 | | √ | [K]I.MIN $^{m}$EN-SUM-*na* DUMU $^{m}$*Eri-ba*-DINGIR |
| | 3.2.3 | | √ | KI.MIN $^{m}$*Iz-kùr*-$^{d}$*Nin-urta*<br>DUMU $^{md}$UTU-ÙRU 2 *ḫar-bu* |
| | 1.2.⸢3⸣ | | √ | KI.MIN $^{m}$*Ri-iš-Ak-ka-de* DUMU $^{m}$KI.MIN |
| | [ ] | | √ | KI.MIN $^{m}$*Ta-ri-bat*-$^{d}$UTU DUMU $^{m}$⸢x-x-x⸣ |
| | [ ] | | √ | KI.MIN $^{m}$*Eri-ba*-$^{d}$IŠKUR DUMU $^{m}$ŠEŠ-⸢x-x⸣ |
| | [ ] | | √ | KI.MIN $^{md}$UTU-*qar-rad* LÚ.SAG |
| | [ ] | | √ | KI.MIN $^{m}$LÚ-*ba-n*[*u-ú*] |
| | [ ] | | √ | KI.MIN $^{m}$*Ba*-[ |
| | [ ] | | √ | ⸢KI.MIN⸣ $^{m}$*Mu*-[ |
| Rev. | [ ] | [ ] | | [ |
| | [ ] | [ ] | | [x x x]⸢x⸣ bi ⸢x⸣[<br>[x x x š]U-*su tur-rat*<br>[$^{m}$x]-⸢gu$^{?}$-SUM$^{?}$⸣-MU $^{lú}$ENGAR-*šu im-ḫur* |
| | [ ] | [ ] | | ŠE.NUMUN $^{m}$*Ḫu-na-bi*<br>*i-na Ba-ṣa-a-ti* ŠU *ú-tar* |
| | [ ] | | 2.4.4 | $^{m}$*Iz-kùr*-$^{d}$*Nin-urta ḫa-za-nu*<br>*ma-ḫi-ir* NÍG.KA$_{9}$ *ú-še-ep-peš* |
| | [ ] | ⸢4$^{?}$⸣.1.4 | | $^{m}$⸢*Eri-ba*⸣-$^{d}$IŠKUR MÁ.LAḪ$_{5}$<br>*a-na* $^{lú}$NAGAR *ša* $^{giš}$MÁ<br>*ig-mu-ru i-din* |
| | 2.0.0 | | | $^{m}$*Bíl-lul-lu*$_{4}$ $^{lú}$NAGAR<br>$^{m}$*Ku-du-ra-nu* DUMU.A.NI *im-ḫur* |
| PAP | 44.0.3 | 16.1.4 | 2.4.4 | $^{giš}$BÁN 10 SÌLA |
| PAP | ⸢1.1.2⸣ 2 ½ SÌLA<br>⸢$^{giš}$BÁN⸣ GAL | | | ŠUKU É $^{d}$*Nin-urta ša* BÁRA.DUMU$^{ki}$<br>*ša* $^{iti}$DIRI<br>$^{m}$*Iz-kùr*-$^{d}$*Nin-urta ḫa-za-nu im-ḫur* |
| ŠU.NIGIN | 36./2.5<br>[TA$^{?}$ x x]⸢x⸣ | 13./0.2<br>⸢TA⸣ 3./1.2 | 2.1.4 5<br>SÌLA<br>TA 0.2.5 5<br>SÌLA | $^{giš}$BÁN GAL<br>TA GAL $^{giš}$BÁN 10 SÌLA<br>*i-na* 1.0.0 0.1$^{pi}$.0<br>*šu-lu-ú* |

Translation

| | ⸢. . .⸣ (of) year 13 | reven[ues] (of) year 12 | ⸢emmer⸣ (of) year 13 | Its entry |
|---|---|---|---|---|
| Obv. | Barley that was disbursed in Āl-irrē in month VII; year 13 of King Kadašman-Turgu. | | | |
| | 45 *sūtu* | 75 *sūtu* | √ | Seed, ration, and fodder for the oxen (for) Rabâ-ša-Gula, farmer. |
| | 45 *sūtu* | 75 *sūtu* | √ | Ditto (for) Aṣûšu-namir, ditto (i.e., farmer). |
| | 45 *sūtu* | 75 *sūtu* | √ | Ditto (for) Ūṣâ-rīš-āli, ditto (i.e., farmer). |
| | 105 *sūtu* | 105 *sūtu* | √ | Loan (for) Rīmūtu, *rab zarāti*; Papsukkal-aḫa-iddina, his plowman, received (it). |
| | 75 *sūtu* | | √ | Ditto (for) Iqīša-Ninimma; . . . -kittu, his plowman, received (it). |
| | 75 *sūtu* | | √ | D[it]to (for) Ṭāb-šār-Adad. |
| | 75 *sūtu* | | √ | [Ditt]o (for) Lūṣi-ana-nūr-Enlil. |
| | 75 *sūtu* | | √ | [D]itto (for) Zākiru, son of Dašpu. |
| | 60 *sūtu* | | √ | [D]itto (for) Bēlī-iddina, son of Erība-ilī. |
| | 105 *sūtu* | | √ | Ditto (for) Izkur-Ninurta, son of Šamaš-nāṣir; 2 *ḫarbu*-fields. |
| | 45 *sūtu* | | √ | Ditto (for) Rīš-Akkade, son of ditto. |
| | [. . . *sūtu*] | | √ | Ditto (for) Tarībat-Šamaš, son of . . . |
| | [. . . *sūtu*] | | √ | Ditto (for) Erība-Adad, son of Aḫu- . . . |
| | [. . . *sūtu*] | | √ | Ditto (for) Šamaš-qarrād, *ša rēši*. |
| | [. . . *sūtu*] | | √ | Ditto (for) Amīlu-ba[nû |
| | [. . . *sūtu*] | | √ | Ditto (for) Ba[ |
| | [. . . *sūtu*] | | √ | Ditto (for) Mu[ |
| Rev. | [. . . *sūtu*] | [. . . *sūtu*] | | [. . .] |
| | [. . . *sūtu*] | [. . . *sūtu*] | | [. . .] ⸢. . .⸣[. . .]; his [h]and is turned; [. . .]-⸢nādin?⸣-šumi?, his plowman, received (it). |
| | [. . . *sūtu*] | [. . . *sūtu*] | | Seed of Ḫunābu; he will turn the hand in Baṣātu. |
| | [. . . *sūtu*] | | 88 *sūtu* | Izkur-Ninurta, the *ḫazannu*, has received; he will have the accounting done. |
| | [. . . *sūtu*] | ⸢130?⸣ *sūtu* | | Erība-Adad, the boatman, gave to the carpenter who completed the boat. |
| | 60 *sūtu* | | | Billullu, carpenter; Kudurrānu, his son, received (it). |
| Total | 1,323 *sūtu* | 490 *sūtu* | 88 *sūtu* | (measured by) the *sūtu* of 10 *qû*. |
| Total | 38 *sūtu* 2 ½ *qû* (measured by) the big *sūtu* | | | Supplies for the temple of Ninurta in Parak-māri of month VIa; Izkur-Ninurta, the *ḫazannu*, received (it). |
| Grand total | 1,197 *sūtu* [after? (deducting?) . . .] | 392 *sūtu* after (deducting) 98 *sūtu* | 70 *sūtu* ½ *qû* after (deducting) 17 *sūtu* ½ *qû* | (measured by) the big *sūtu*, after the increase of the *sūtu* of 10 *qû* has been deducted, at a rate of 1 *pānu* per kor. |

Commentary

15–16. These lines end on the reverse; the last signs of the PNs have been obliterated by the text of the reverse.

25. Erība-Adad was a boatman of Ninurta-zākir-šumi, known also from the legal text **no. 327** and from the letter CUSAS 30 31.

28. The temple of Ninurta in Parak-māri appears as a recipient of supplies also in **no. 119**: 3. $^{iti}$DIRI is usually regarded as an abbreviation for $^{iti}$DIRI.ŠE.KIN.KU$_5$—i.e., month XIIa—which is thus far attested only for the early years of Kudur-Enlil; however, it is not always clear whether month XIIa is meant (see Brinkman 1976, 401 with n. 15). Considering that this text records expenditures of barley carried out in month VII of the 13$^{th}$ year of Kadašman-Turgu, it seems more likely that $^{iti}$DIRI here refers to month VIa, which is written $^{iti}$KIN.$^{d}$INANNA.2.KAM(.MA) in other documents from the 13$^{th}$ year of Kadašman-Turgu (**no. 175** and **no. 225**); see also $^{iti}$DIRI in **no. 68**: 1 (KT 7).

## 177. CUNES 52-14-077

-.-.15 Kadašman-Turgu

Summary of barley received by Meli-Šuqamuna from Mudammiq-Adad in different towns.

Obv. ŠE $^{giš⸢}$BÁN 5 SÌLA⸣ *ša i-na* ŠU
$^{m}$*Mu*-SIG$_5$-$^{d}$IŠKUR
$^{m}$*Me-li-*$^{d}$*Šu-qa-mu-na*
*mi-taḫ-ḫu-rù*

---

1.1$^{pi}$.0 BÀD-$^{d+}$*En-líl*$^{ki.a}$ $^{iti}$DU$_6$.KÙ
MU.15 $^{d}$*Ka-dáš-man-Túr-gu* LUGAL

---

L.e. 1.0.0 KI.MIN *i-na* ŠU $^{m}$*Na-siq-*$^{d}$AMAR.UTU UŠ.BAR
[ ] $^{m}$*Ḫal*$^{?}$*-lu*$^{?}$*/ku*$^{?}$-$^{d}$AMAR.UTU ⸢x x⸣
Rev. ⸢x x x x x⸣
⸢x x NIBRU$^{?ki}$ x x⸣

---

[0.4]⸢$^{pi}$.0 *Tukul-ti-*É.KUR$^{ki}$⸣
*i-na* ŠU $^{m}$NÍG.BA-$^{d⸢}$*Sukkal*⸣
⸢x x⸣ *mi-ta-aḫ-ḫur*

---

PAP 3.0.0 ŠE.GUR $^{giš}$BÁN 5 SÌLA
[M]U.15.KAM $^{d}$*Ka-dáš-man-Túr-gu*
LUGAL.E

Commentary

1–4. "Barley, (measured by) the *sūtu* of 5 *qû*, that Meli-Šuqamuna has been receiving from Mudammiq-Adad."

## 178. CUNES 52-16-097 (Plate No. 49)

-.-.15 Kadašman-Turgu

The text records the barley at the disposal of Arad-nubatti, after he gave part of it to Iqīša-Ninimma; Arad-nubatti originally received the barley from Ninurta-zākir-šumi.

The tablet is a pastiche; some of the fake parts have been removed but its obverse is still partially plastered with fake signs, indicated by asterisks.

| | | |
|---|---|---|
| Obv. | ŠE ⸢$^{giš}$BÁN 10 SÌLA⸣ ★ ★ ★ ★ ★ | |
| | *ša* [$^{m⸣}$Ì]R-*nu-bat-ti mi-t*[*aḫ*]-⸢*ḫu-rù*$^?$⸣ | |
| | 0.2.3 | ⸢BÀD?-$^{d+}$*En?-líl?*$^{ḫi.a⸣.ki}$ ⸢x x⸣ |
| | | ★ ★ ★ ★ ★ ★ [*ḫ*]*e-e* $^{iti}$AB.È |
| | | *ša* $^{md}$*N*[*in-ur*]*ta*- ★ ★ ★ ⸢x x x⸣ |
| | 1.0.0 | ⸢KI.MIN x x x⸣ |
| PAP | 1.2.3 | MU.[x.KAM] ⸢$^d$*Ka*⸣-*dáš-man-Túr-gu* LUGAL |
| | 0.2.3 | BÀD-⸢$^{d+}$*En*⸣-[*líl*$^{ḫi.a.ki}$ x x] $^{iti}$Š[E$^?$] x áš |
| | 2.0.0 | B[ÀD$^?$-x-x-x]$^{⸢ki? iti⸣}$[DU$_6^?$].KÙ$^?$ |
| | 1.0.0 | [ ] |
| | ⸢1.0.0⸣ | [x x x x] $^{⸢iti⸣}$[ |
| | 1.0.0 | ⸢KI.MIN $^{iti}$ŠE.KIN.KU$_5$⸣ |
| | ★ ★ ⸢1$^+$⸣.2.3 MU.13$^+$.KAM [ | |
| | ★ ★ ★ ⸢$^{giš}$BÁN⸣ 10 SÌLA *ša i-na* ⸢ŠU $^{md}$*Nin-urta*⸣-MU-MU | |
| L.e. | [$^m$]⸢ÌR-*nu-bat*⸣-*ti maḫ-rù* | |
| Rev. | ⸢*i-na*⸣ BÀD-$^{d+}$*En-líl*$^{ḫi.a.ki}$ | |
| | *i-na* M[U].15.KAM | |
| | *i-na* ⸢ŠU $^{m⸣}$ÌR-*nu-bat-ti* | |
| | $^m$BA-*šá*-$^d$NIN.IMM[A$^?$] *im-ḫur* | |
| | 5.0.0 ÍB.TAK$_4$ ŠE $^{giš}$BÁN 10 SÌLA | |
| | ŠU $^m$ÌR-*nu-bat-ti* | |

COMMENTARY

1–3. "Barley, (measured by) the *sūtu* of 10 *qû* [ . . . ] that Arad-nubatti has been receiving."

4. The original text might have had here the GN [URU-*at*]-*ḫe-e*.

13–19. "45$^+$ *sūtu*, year 13$^+$ [ . . . ], (measured by) the *sūtu* of 10 *qû*, which Arad-nubatti received from Ninurta-zākir-šumi; in Dūr-Enlilē, in year 15, Iqīša-Ninimma received (it) from Arad-nubatti." According to the quantities listed in the previous lines, the total should have been 8.2.3 (255 *sūtu*).

20–21. "150 *sūtu*: remaining barley, (measured by) the *sūtu* of 10 *qû*, (which is still) at the disposal of Arad-nubatti."

## 179. CUNES 52-13-192

-.X.15 Kadašman-Turgu

Account of barley disbursed by Mudammiq-Adad as rations for plowmen, fodder for oxen and donkeys, and "delivery" (*maššītu*) of Dūr-Enlilē.

Obv. ⸢ŠE *ša*⸣ *i-na* ŠÀ 25 GUR [
⸢*ša i-na Tukul-ti*-É.KUR$^{ki}$⸣ [
*ša* MU.15.KAM *Ka-dáš-man-Túr-gu* L[UGAL]
*i-na* $^{iti}$AB.È *ki-i* ŠU $^{md}$[
$^{m}$*Mu*-SIG$_5$-$^{d}$IŠKUR *im-ḫu-ru-ma id*-⸢*di*⸣-*nu*

| | | |
|---|---|---|
| | 1.0.0 | ŠE.BA $^{lú}$ENGAR $^{m}$ZÁLAG-$^{d}$*Iš-tar* ⸢4⸣ ITI |
| | 0.3.4 5 SÌLA | ŠUKU 1 GU$_4$ $^{m}$KI.MIN 3 ITI |
| | 1.0.0 | ŠE.BA $^{lú}$ENGAR $^{m}$*A-ḫe-du-tu*$_4$ ⸢4⸣ ITI $^{m}$*Ki-di-ni-ia* ŠEŠ.A.NI *im-ḫur* |
| | 0.3.4 5 SÌLA | ŠUKU 1 GU$_4$ $^{m}$KI.MIN 3 ITI $^{m}$KI.MIN *im-ḫur* |
| | 1.0.0 | ŠE.BA $^{lú}$ENGAR $^{m}$*Ib-ni-ia* 4 ITI |
| | 0.3.4 5 SÌLA | ŠUKU 1 GU$_4$ $^{m}$KI.MIN 3 ITI |
| | 1.2.3 | ⸢ŠUKU 2⸣ GU$_4$ $^{m}$*Ku-du-ra-nu* $^{m}$É-*ra-bi im-ḫur* 3 ITI |
| | 1.⸢1$^{pi}$.0⸣ | ŠE.BA $^{lú}$ENGAR $^{m}$KI.MIN $^{m}$KI.MIN *im-ḫur* 4 ITI |
| | 1.2.3 | ŠUKU 2 GU$_4$ $^{m}$LÚ-*ba-nu-ú* |
| | 1.0.0 | ⸢ŠE.BA⸣ $^{lú}$ENGAR $^{md}$*Nin-urta*-ÙRU ⸢4$^{?}$⸣ ITI |
| | ⸢0.3.4⸣ 5 SÌLA | ⸢ŠUKU 1 GU$_4$⸣ $^{m}$KI.MIN ⸢3⸣ [ITI] |
| | ⸢x.x.x⸣ | [x x x] ⸢x x⸣ [ |
| Text breaks off (1–2 lines missing) | | |
| Rev. | 1.[x.x] | [ |
| | 0.2.2 | $^{m}$⸢*I*$^{?}$⸣-[ *ki-mu* ⸢x⸣ [ ⸢LÚ x⸣ [x x] ⸢x x⸣ [ |
| | 1.⸢1$^{pi}$.0⸣ | ŠE.BA $^{m}$EN-*šu-nu* $^{lú}$ENGAR 4 ITI |
| | 1.0.0 | ŠE.BA $^{m}$*Pa-ḫal-la-nu* $^{lú}$ENGAR 4 ITI |
| | 0.2.3 | *ri-mu-tu*$_4$ $^{m}$KI.MIN |
| | 0.1$^{pi}$.0 | ŠUKU ANŠE$^{meš}$ ŠUKU *ù* BAPPIR$_x$ $^{m}$*Mu*-SIG$_5$-$^{d}$IŠKUR TA U$_4$.1.KAM EN U$_4$.6.KAM |
| | 3.3.0 | *maš-ši-tu* BÀD-$^{d+}$*En-líl*$^{meš.ki}$ |
| | 1.0.0 | ŠE.BA $^{lú}$ENGAR $^{m}$*Ri-gim*-$^{d}$IŠKUR |
| | 1.2.3 | ŠUKU 2 GU$_4$ $^{m}$KI.MIN |

mu pi ni lu ur ti *ša* $^{d}$AMAR.UTU

2 55

L.e. 22

Translation

Obv. Barley which [ . . . ] from 750 *sūtu* [. . .]
which in Tukultī-Ekur [ . . . ]
of year 15 of K[ing] Kadašman-Turgu,
Mudammiq-Adad received and disbursed
as the representative of [PN] in month X.

| | |
|---|---|
| 30 *sūtu* | Ration (for) a plowman (of) Nūr-Ištar; 4 months. |
| 22 *sūtu* 5 *qû* | Fodder for 1 ox (of) ditto (i.e., Nūr-Ištar); 3 months. |
| 30 *sūtu* | Ration (for) a plowman (of) Aḫēdutu; 4 months.<br>Kidinīya, his brother, received (it). |
| 22 *sūtu* 5 *qû* | Fodder for 1 ox; ditto (i.e., Aḫēdutu); 3 months. Ditto received (it). |
| 30 *sūtu* | Ration (for) a plowman (of) Ibnīya; 4 months. |
| 22 *sūtu* 5 *qû* | Fodder for 1 ox (of) ditto (i.e., Ibnīya); 3 months. |
| 45 *sūtu* | Fodder for 2 oxen (of) Kudurrānu; Bītu-rabi received (it); 3 months. |
| 36 *sūtu* | Ration (for) a plowman (of) ditto (i.e., Kudurrānu); ditto (i.e., Bītu-rabi) received (it); 4 months. |
| 45 *sūtu* | Fodder for 2 oxen (of) Amīlu-banû. |
| 30 *sūtu* | Ration (for) a plowman (of) Ninurta-nāṣir; $4^{?}$ months. |
| 22 *sūtu* 5 *qû* | Fodder for 1 ox (of) ditto (i.e., Ninurta-nāṣir); 3 [months]. |
| ⌜. . .⌝ | [ . . . ] ⌜. . .⌝ [ |

Text breaks off (1–2 lines missing)

| Rev. | | |
|---|---|---|
| | ⌜$30^{+}$ *sūtu*⌝ | [ |
| | 14 *sūtu* | PN [<br>in place of [<br>. . . [ |
| | 36 *sūtu* | Ration (for) Bēlšunu, plowman; 4 months. |
| | 30 *sūtu* | Ration (for) Paḫallanu, plowman; 4 months. |
| | 15 *sūtu* | Gift (for) ditto (i.e., Paḫallanu). |
| | 6 *sūtu* | Fodder for the donkeys, food supplies, and sourdough bread<br>for Mudammiq-Adad; from day 1<br>till day 6. |
| | 108 *sūtu* | Delivery (of/for) Dūr-Enlilē. |
| | 30 *sūtu* | Ration (for) a plowman (of) Rigim-Adad. |
| | 45 *sūtu* | Fodder for 2 oxen (of) ditto (i.e., Rigim-Adad). |

. . . of Marduk.

2 55

L.e. 22

Commentary

6–8. Nūr-Ištar and Aḫēdūtu receive rations for plowmen and fodder for oxen also in **no. 156** (KT 8), where they receive seed as well.

21′. For the PN Paḫallanu, see also **no. 101**: 19 and CBS 3529: 14 ($^{m}$*Pa-ḫal-la-a-nu*).

24′. Cf. the "food allocation for the donkeys and the scribe" in **no. 162**: 14 and **no. 170**: 19; it therefore seems likely that Mudammiq-Adad acts here as a scribe, a function with whom he is explicitly associated in other documents (see **nos. 327, 330, 334** and Introduction § 4.1).

27′. Even though the signs are clear, their interpretation is puzzling. The sign MU at the beginning of the line could mean "year," but one would not expect a year-name formula at this time; even if it were a year-name, I could not interpret the following signs as a sentence. Furthermore, the date is already clearly indicated in the text-heading (year 15 of Kadašman-Turgu). It could be a notation referring to the content of the text, but it does not seem to be a total of the quantities recorded in the previous lines. The line refers to something "of Marduk," perhaps the "command (*urti*) of Marduk" (I thank W. van Soldt for suggesting this possibility). Some calculations follow on the reverse and on the lower edge.

## 180. CUNES 52-18-857 (Plate No. 50)

-.-.2–15$^{?}$ Kadašman-Turgu

Summary of barley received by Sîn-balāṭa-īriš from Mudammiq-Adad over several years of Kadašman-Turgu's reign (from year 2 till at least year 15).

| | | | | |
|---|---|---|---|---|
| Obv. | [ ] | [ŠE$^{?}$ $^{giš}$BÁN<br>10 S]ÌLA | ⸢ZÍZ.AN.NA⸣<br>$^{giš}$BÁN 10 SÌLA | *ša i-na* ŠU $^{m}$*Mu*-SIG$_{5}$-$^{d}$IŠKUR<br>$^{md}$30-TI-URU$_{4}$ *mi-taḫ-ḫu-rù* |
| | [ ] | | | *i-na* ŠÀ ḪA.LA *ša* KI $^{m}$*Ḫu-za-li*<br>$^{iti}$DU$_{6}$.KÙ MU.2.KAM $^{d}$*Ka-dáš-man-Túr-gu* |
| | | 0.3.2 | | *i-na* ŠÀ *maš-ši-ti ša Tukul-ti*-É.KUR *i-na* ŠU $^{m⸢d}$30⸣-*nap-ši-ra*<br>$^{iti}$GU$_{4}$ MU.10.KAM |
| | | 0.1.4 | | *i-na* É GUR$_{7}$ $^{md}$30-ŠEŠ-SUM-*na i-na* ŠU $^{m⸢}$KI.MIN$^{?}$ *im-ḫur*$^{?⸣}$ $^{iti}$DU$_{6}$<br>MU.14.KAM |
| 5 | | 0.1.4 | | *i-na* ŠÀ ŠE *ša* $^{m}$MU-*líb-ši* TA IGI-EDIN *iš*-[<br>$^{iti}$ZÍZ MU.13.KAM |
| | | 0.2.3 | | $^{m}$*Ta-ri-ba*-$^{d}$*Gu-la ka-ṣ*[*i-rù* |
| | | 0.2.3 | | *i-na* ŠU $^{md}$IŠKUR-⸢*di*⸣-[*na*$^{?}$]-⸢*ni*$^{?}$⸣ $^{m}$[<br>$^{iti}$DU$_{6}$ MU.⸢15$^{?}$⸣.[KAM] |
| | [ ] | | 2.0.0 | *i-na* ŠÀ *maš-ši-ti ša Tukul-ti*-[É.KUR] |
| 9 | [ ] | 0.⸢1$^{?pi}$⸣.0 | | *i-na* munus-*bi* $^{m⸢d}$30-ŠEŠ⸣-[SUM-*na* |
| L.e. | [ ] | | | *i-na* ⸢ŠÀ$^{?}$⸣ GUR$_{7}$ *za-ki*-⸢*i* x⸣ [<br>MU.⸢x⸣.K[AM] |
| Rev. | [ ] | ⸢x⸣ | | *i-na* ŠÀ *ša* $^{d}$30-EN-[ |
| 12 | [ ] | 1.0.0 | | *i-na nap-ṭar-ti* $^{m}$KI.[MIN$^{?}$ |
| Several empty lines | | | | |
| | | | | 2 MA.NA SÍG *i-na* ŠÀ *ša* DUMU $^{m}$*A-ḫu-ú-a*<br>MU.9.KAM |
| | [ | | | ] 2 MA.NA SÍG ŠU.NIGIN |

Translation

| | | | | |
|---|---|---|---|---|
| Obv. | [ ] | [Barley$^{?}$, (meas. by) the *sūtu* of 10 *q*]*û* | ⸢Emmer⸣, (meas. by) the *sūtu* of 10 *qû* | which Sîn-balāṭa-īriš has been receiving from Mudammiq-Adad: |
| | [ ] | | | from the share that is with Ḫuzālu;<br>month VII, year 2 of Kadašman-Turgu. |
| | | 20 *sūtu* | | from the delivery of Tukultī-Ekur, from Sîn-napšira;<br>month II, year 10.w |
| | | 10 *sūtu* | | in$^{?}$/from$^{?}$ the granary Sîn-aḫa-iddina received$^{?}$ from ⸢ditto$^{?}$⸣;<br>month VII, year 14. |
| 5 | | 10 *sūtu* | | from the barley that Šumu-libši br[ought$^{?}$] from Pān-ṣēri;<br>month XI, year 13. |
| | | 15 *sūtu* | | Tarība-Gula, kno[tter]. |
| | | 15 *sūtu* | | from Adad-dī[na]nni$^{?}$ [ . . . ];<br>month VII, year 15$^{?}$. |
| | [ ] | | 60 *sūtu* | from the delivery of Tukultī-[Ekur]. |
| 9 | [ ] | 6$^{?}$ *sūtu* | | in$^{?}$ . . . ⸢Sîn-aḫa⸣-[iddina |
| L.e. | [ ] | | | from that of the exempted$^{?}$ granary [<br>year x. |
| Rev. | [ ] | ⸢. . .⸣ | | from that of Sîn-bēl-[apli]. |
| 12 | [ ] | 30 *sūtu* | | in$^{?}$/from$^{?}$ the guest quarter$^{?}$, di[tto]. |
| Several empty lines | | | | |
| | | | | 2 mina of wool from that of the son of Aḫū'a;<br>year 9. |
| | [ | | | ] 2 mina of wool in total. |

Commentary

3. The information in this entry is recorded also in **no. 73**.

5. A form of *našû* "to bring" seems a likely restoration.

9. For *ina* MUNUS-*bi*, see comments to **no. 126**: 6.

12. On *ina napṭarti*, see comments to **no. 81**: 2.

## 181. CUNES 52-13-112 (Plate No. 51)

-.-.15–17 Kadašman-Turgu

Summary of barley received by Ilī-aḫḫē-iddina from Ninurta-kiššat-ilāni between year 15 and year 17 of Kadašman-Turgu. The text is also a balanced account of the barley that is still at the disposal of Ninurta-kiššat-ilāni.

This tablet was already published as CUSAS 30 81, but it is included in this volume because of the date and because, after further cleaning, it was possible to improve several readings.

Obv. [ŠE *ša i-na* ŠU] $^{md}$*Nin-urta*-⌜KIŠ⌝-[DIN]GIR$^{meš}$ DUMU $^{md+}$*En-líl-ki*-⌜*di-ni*⌝
[$^{m}$DIN]GIR-ŠEŠ$^{meš}$-SUM-*na* DUMU $^{m}$[*Lu*]*l-tam-ru-ti*
*ki-mu* ŠE-*šu* *mi-taḫ-ḫu-ru*

| | | ŠE $^{giš}$BÁN GAL | ⌜ŠE $^{giš}$⌝BÁN 5 SÌLA | MU.BI.IM |
|---|---|---|---|---|
| 5 | | ⌜4⌝.0.0 | 14.3.2 | BÀD-$^{d+}$*En-líl*$^{ḫi.a.ki}$ $^{iti}$DU$_6$.KÙ MU.15.KAM $^{d}$*Ka-dáš-man-Túr-gu* LUGAL.E EN 2.0.0 *i-na* ŠU $^{m}$DINGIR.MU-*mu*-SIG$_5$ |
| | | | ⌜6⌝.0.0 | KI.MIN $^{iti}$DU$_6$.KÙ MU.16.KAM *i-na man-de-e ša bi-ri-it bi-né-e* |
| | | | ⌜7⌝.0.0 | URU-$^{lú}$SIMUG$^{ki}$ $^{iti}$APIN.DU$_8$.A MU.17.KAM |
| Rev. | PAP | 4.0.0 | 27./3.2 | ŠU.NIGIN 37.3.2 ŠE $^{giš}$BÁN 5 SÌLA *ša* $^{m}$DINGIR-ŠEŠ$^{meš}$-SUM-*na* *ki-mu* ŠE-*šu il-qú-ú* |
| 9 | | | 2.1.4 | ÍB.TAK$_4$ ŠE $^{giš}$BÁN 5 SÌLA ŠU $^{md}$*Nin*-⌜*urta*-KIŠ⌝-DINGIR$^{meš}$ |

Translation

Obv. [Barley, which I]lī-aḫḫē-iddina, son of [Lu]ltamrūtu, has been receiving [from] Ninurta-kiššat-[il]āni, "son" of Enlil-kidinnī, in place of his barley.

| | | Barley (meas. by) the big *sūtu* | Barley (meas. by) the *sūtu* of 5 *qû* | Its entry |
|---|---|---|---|---|
| 5 | | 120 *sūtu* | 440 *sūtu* | Dūr-Enlilē, month VII, year 15 of King Kadašman-Turgu, including 60 *sūtu* from Ilī-mudammiq. |
| | | | 180 *sūtu* | Ditto (i.e., Dūr-Enlilē), month VII, year 16, in the *mandê*(-field?) that is among the tamarisks. |
| | | | 210 *sūtu* | Āl-nappāḫi, month VIII, year 17. |
| Rev. | Total | 120 *sūtu* | 830 *sūtu* | Grand total: 1,120 *sūtu* of barley, (meas. by) the *sūtu* of 5 *qû*, which Ilī-aḫḫē-iddina took instead of his barley. |
| 9 | | | 70 *sūtu* | Remaining barley, (meas. by) the *sūtu* of 5 *qû*, (which is still) at the disposal of Ninurta-kiššat-ilāni. |

COMMENTARY

1. See van Soldt 2015, 24 for the genealogy of Ninurta-kiššat-ilāni, who probably was the grandson of Enlil-kidinnī.

6. For *i-na man-de-e* "in the *mandê*(-field?)," see comments to **no. 122**: 4.

## 182. CUNES 52-13-100

-.-.[ . . . ] Kadašman-Turgu

Summary of cereals received by Rīš-aṣûšu from Mudammiq-Adad over several months of an unknown year of Kadašman-Turgu.

| | | | | |
|---|---|---|---|---|
| Obv. | [x $^{giš}$BÁN] GAL | [x $^{giš}$]BÁN 10 SÌLA | ⸢ZÍZ.AN.NA⸣ $^{giš}$BÁN G[A]L | *ša i-n[a* ŠU $^{m}$*Mu-da]m-mi-iq*-$^{d}$IŠKUR ⸢$^{m}$*Ri-iš*⸣-UD-*š[ú* DUMU $^{m}$]*Ta-ri-bat*-DINGIR *mi-taḫ-ḫu-ru* |
| | 0.2.3 | | | BÀD-$^{d+}$*En-líl*$^{meš.ki}$ *i-na* ŠU $^{md}$*Nin-urta*-SAG $^{iti}$KIN.$^{d}$INANNA |
| | | 0.2.3 | | KI.MIN *i-na* ŠU $^{m}$BA-*šá*-$^{d}$AMAR.UTU DUMU $^{m}$*Ṭab-bi-ḫi* $^{iti}$KIN.$^{d}$INANNA |
| | | 0.2.3 | | AN.ZA.GÀR$^{ki}$ *i-na* ŠU $^{m}$*Še-mi-i* NU.$^{giš}$KIRI$_6$ $^{iti}$KIN.$^{d}$INANNA |
| | | | 0.1.4 | *Kar*-$^{d}$*Nuska*$^{ki}$ *i-na* ŠU $^{md}$*Nin-urta*-SAG $^{iti}$KIN.$^{d}$INANNA |
| | [ ] | | | URU-*ir-re-e i-na* ŠU $^{md}$*Nin-urta*-SAG $^{iti}$DU$_6$.KÙ |
| Rev. | | [0.2].3 | | NIBRU$^{ki}$ *i-na* ŠÀ *maš-ši-ti* *ša* URU-*ir-re-e i-na* ŠU $^{md}$⸢*Nin-urta*-SAG⸣ $^{iti}$GAN.GAN.È |
| | | 0.1.1 5 SÌLA | | KI.MIN *i-na* ŠU $^{m}$KI.MIN $^{iti}$ŠE.KIN.KU$_5$ |
| | | 0.0.3 | | BÀD-$^{d+}$*En-líl*$^{meš.ki}$ *i-na* ŠU $^{m}$È-*a-na*-ZÁLAG-$^{d}$[IŠ]KUR $^{iti}$ŠE.KIN.KU$_5$ |
| PAP | 0.4.3 | 1.4.1 5 SÌLA | 0.1.4 | ŠU.NIGIN 6.3.4 ŠE $^{giš}$BÁN 5 SÌLA *ša i-na* ŠU $^{m}$*Mu*-SIG$_5$-$^{d}$IŠKUR $^{m}$SUD-UD-*šu* DUMU $^{m}$*Ta-ri-bat*-DINGIR *mi-taḫ-ḫu-ru* |
| L.e. | | [MU.X.KAM] ⸢*Ka-dáš-man-Túr-gu* LUGAL⸣.E | | |

Translation

| | | | | |
|---|---|---|---|---|
| Obv. | [ . . . ] (meas. by) the big *sūtu* | [ . . . ] (meas. by) the *sūtu* of 10 *qû* | ⸢Emmer⸣ (meas. by) the big *sūtu* | which Rīš-aṣûš[u, son of] Tarībat-ili, has been receiving fr[om Muda]mmiq-Adad: |
| | 15 *sūtu* | | | Dūr-Enlilē, from Ninurta-ašarēd; month VI. |
| | | 15 *sūtu* | | Ditto (i.e., Dūr-Enlilē), from Iqīša-Marduk, son of Ṭābiḫu; month VI. |
| | | 15 *sūtu* | | Dimtu, from Šēmû, the gardener; month VI. |
| | | | 10 *sūtu* | Kār-Nuska, from Ninurta-ašarēd; month VI. |

| | | | | |
|---|---|---|---|---|
| | [ ] | | | Āl-irrē, from Ninurta-ašarēd; month VII. |
| Rev. | | 15 *sūtu* | | Nippur, from the delivery of Āl-irrē, from Ninurta-ašarēd; month IX. |
| | | 7 *sūtu* 5 *qû* | | Ditto (i.e., Nippur), from ditto (i.e., Ninurta-ašarēd); month XII. |
| | | 3 *sūtu* | | Dūr-Enlilē, from Lūṣi-ana-nūr-Adad; month XII. |
| Total | 27 *sūtu* | 55 *sūtu* 5 *qû* | 10 *sūtu* | Grand total: 202 *sūtu* of grain, (meas. by) the *sūtu* of 5 *qû*, which Rīš-aṣûšu, son of Tarībat-ili, has been receiving from Mudammiq-Adad. |
| L.e. | [Year x] ⌜of King Kadašman-Turgu. | | | |

## 183. CUNES 52-18-765

14.VIII.[ . . . ] Kadašman-Turgu

Sealed.

| | | |
|---|---|---|
| Obv. | ŠE $^{giš}$BÁN 5 SÌLA MU.BI.IM | |
| | 0.2$^{pi}$.0 | ŠUKU ANŠE.KUR.RA U$_4$.12 U$_4$.14 |
| | 0.1$^{pi}$.0 | ŠUKU ANŠE$^{meš}$ $^{m}$*Ta-ri-bu* |
| | 0.0.3 | $^{md}$IŠKUR-*ša-gim* |
| | 0.3$^{pi}$.0 | *ša ra-ka-si* |
| L.e. | [PAP] | 1.1.3 |
| Rev. | $^{iti}$APIN.DU$_8$.A | |
| | U$_4$.14.KAM | |
| | *Ka-dáš-man-Túr-gu* | |

Commentary

5. *ša rakāsi* "(still) to be assigned" or "for the (work) assignment"? Cf. van Soldt 2015, 34 and CUSAS 30 175: 7, CUSAS 30 277: 6, 13, and CUSAS 30 265: 15–16. Note that the entry mentions neither the person who receives the amount of barley nor the purpose of the disbursement. In other instances, *ša rakāsi* is associated with a trip (*ša rakāsi* KASKAL GN; see **no. 239**: 13, 16 and CUSAS 30 277: 6). There are no elements providing a clear link between these occurrences and the use of the verb *rakāsu* in letters with reference to hiring groups of workers: see most recently the discussion by Sassmannshausen 2001, 123–24, who believes that the use of this verb does not imply the payment of a salary, contra Aro 1957, 86 and AHw II, *rakāsu* 17a, 947, who translate "zur Arbeit mieten"; cf. also CAD R, *rakāsu* 6d, 101 "to assign a person (to a task, a post)."

7–9. It is unusual that date formulae with month, day, and royal name would omit the year (cf. Brinkman 1976, 405–6), but see also **no. 290**.

## 184. CUNES 52-20-307

-.X.[ . . . ] Kadašman-Turgu

Obv. [ŠE . . . *ša i-na*] ŠÀ *te-li-ti ša Kar-*$^{d}$*Nuska*$^{ki}$

[ *ša* MU.X.KAM *Ka*]*-dáš-man-Túr-gu i-na* $^{iti}$AB.È SUM-*nu*

| | [ŠE?] | [GI]G? | ZÍZ.AN.NA | MU.BI.IM |
|---|---|---|---|---|
| | [ ] | | √ | ŠE.BA *ra-ak-si ša* BÀD-*Ku-ri-gal-zu*$^{ki}$ *ša Nam-kar-*$^{d}$*Nuska*$^{ki}$ *iḫ-ru-ú* |
| 5 | 3.1.4 | | √ | ŠE.BA $^{m}$⸢*Ar*⸣*-du-tu*$_4$ DUMU $^{m}$*Iq-bi-ul-i-ni* |
| | ⸢x.1.0⸣ | | √ | ŠUKU 2 ⸢UDU.NIGA⸣ $^{m}$KI.MIN |
| | [x.x].⸢x⸣ | | √ | ŠE.BA $^{m}$*Bu-na-*$^{d}$*Gu-la* DUMU $^{m}$*I-din-*$^{d}$*Nin-urta* |
| | 0.⸢4?.x⸣ | | √ | *ak-lu*$_4$ $^{m}$*Ri-mu-tu*$_4$ GAL *za-ra-ti* $^{m}$*Aš-ri-qu im-ḫur* |
| L.e. | | [x.x].⸢4⸣ 5 S[ÌLA] | [ ] | *ni-ki-is* GUR$_7$ $^{m}$*Iz-kur-*$^{d}$IŠKUR [DU]MU $^{m}$*E-ri-bu* |
| Rev. | 2.0.0 | 1.0.0 | ⸢2?.x⸣.[x] | ⸢$^{m}$*Ku-du-ra-nu* DUMU $^{m}$*Sar-ri-qí*⸣ |
| 11 | 2.0.0 | ⸢1.0.0⸣ | ⸢x.1.1⸣ | $^{m}$*Gu-ub-bu-ḫu* DUMU $^{m}$*Ia-a-a-i* $^{m}$*Ṭa-bu-tu*$_4$ |
| | 2.0.0 | 1.0.0 | [x.x].⸢x⸣ | $^{m}$*Aš-*⸢*ri-qu* $^{m}$*Ša-muḫ-ri-gim-šu*⸣ |
| | [ ] | 1.0.0 | 2.⸢3?.x⸣ | $^{md}$⸢*Nin-urta*-MU-MU $^{m}$*Ṣú*?-*ḫu*?⸣-*tu*$_4$ |
| | [ ] | ⸢0.1.2⸣ | 2.⸢3?.x⸣ | $^{m}$KI.MIN ⸢$^{m}$*La*?-x-x $^{m}$⸣*E-ri-bu* |
| 15 | [ ] | ⸢0.3.2⸣ | 2.2.⸢3?⸣ | $^{md}$⸢x-x-x-x $^{m}$*Ni-ik-ki*⸣ |
| | [ ] | [ ] | [x].⸢2.4⸣ | [$^{giš}$BÁ]N 10 SÌLA |
| | [ ] | [ ] | [ ] | $^{giš}$BÁN GAL [TA X.X.X] GAL $^{giš}$BÁN [10 SÌLA *i-na*] ⸢1⸣.0.0 0.1$^{pi}$.0 [*š*]*u-lu-ú* |

Translation

Obv. [Grain . . . fro]m the revenues of Kār-Nuska

[ of year x of Ka]dašman-Turgu, [which] was disbursed in month X:

| | [Barley?] | [Whea]t? | Emmer | Its entry |
|---|---|---|---|---|
| | [ ] | | √ | Rations for the assigned worker(s?) of Dūr-Kurigalzu who dug the (canal) Namkar-Nuska. |
| 5 | 100 *sūtu* | | √ | Rations (for) Ardūtu, son of Iqbi-ul-īni. |
| | ⸢6+ *sūtu*⸣ | | √ | Fodder for two fattened oxen (of) ditto (i.e., Ardūtu). |
| | [. . .]⸢. . .⸣ | | √ | Rations (for) Bunna-Gula, son of Iddin-Nergal. |
| | ⸢24? *sūtu*⸣ | | √ | *aklu*-expenditure (for) Rimūtu, *rab zarāti*; Ašriqu received (it). |
| L.e. | | [. . .]⸢4 *sūtu*⸣ 5 *q*[*û*] | [ ] | *nikis karê* (for) Izkur-Adad, son of Erību. |
| Rev. | 60 *sūtu* | 30 *sūtu* | ⸢60? *sūtu*⸣ | Kudurrānu, son of Sarriqu. |
| 11 | 60 *sūtu* | 30 *sūtu* | ⸢7+ *sūtu*⸣ | Gubbuḫu, son of Yā'u; Ṭābūtu. |
| | 60 *sūtu* | 30 *sūtu* | [. . .]⸢. . .⸣ | Ašriqu; Šamuḫ-rigimšu. |
| | [ ] | 30 *sūtu* | 78? *sūtu* | Ninurta-zākir-šumi; Ṣuḫḫutu. |
| | [ ] | ⸢8 *sūtu*⸣ | 78? *sūtu* | Ditto (i.e., Ninurta-zākir-šumi); La[. . . , son? of?] Erību. |
| 15 | [ ] | ⸢20 *sūtu*⸣ | 75? *sūtu* | ⸢PN; Nikki⸣. |

| | | | |
|---|---|---|---|
| [ ] | [ ] | ⸢16$^{+}$ *sūtu*⸣ | [(measured by) the *sūt*]*u* of 10 *qû* |
| [ ] | [ ] | [ ] | (measured by) the big *sūtu*<br>[after . . . *sūtu*] have been deducted, the increase of the *sūtu*<br>[of 10 *qû*] being at a rate of 1 *pānu* per kor. |

Commentary

3. For ŠE.BA *ra-ak-si*, cf. ŠE.BA *rak-si* in CUSAS 30 143: 9 and ŠE.BA *ra-ak-su-ti* in PBS 2/2 62: 14. Despite the gen. sg. *raksi*, it seems unlikely that only one person was involved in the digging of a canal; cf., e.g., ŠE.BA ÉRIN$^{ḫi.a}$ *š*[*a*] ⸢ÍD-*Tukul-ti*-É.KUR$^{ki}$⸣ *iḫ-ru-ú* "rations of the workmen w[ho] dug the Nār-Tukultī-Ekur" (**no. 98**: 13 and parallel in CUSAS 30 231: 14). On *rakāsu* meaning "to assign a person (to a task, a post)," see CAD R, *rakāsu* 6d, 101 and the discussion by Sassmannshausen 2001, 123–24, who translates it with "verpflichten" and notes that it remains unclear "in welcher Form Personen für Arbeitstrupps verpflichtet wurden." See also ÌR.É.GAL *ra-ak-su* in BE 15 200: v 5, which Sassmannshausen 2001, 265 translates "verpflichtete Palastdiener."
9. Kudurrānu, son of Sarriqu, could be the same person mentioned also in CUSAS 30 64: 2 (n.d.) and in the Nippur text MUN 10 (accession year of KuE); see also comments to CUSAS 30 233 in van Soldt 2015, 307.

## 185. CUNES 52-20-308

-.-.[ . . . ] Kadašman-Turgu

Obv. [ŠE$^{?}$ . . . *ša i-na* Š]À *te-li-t*[*i*
[ *ša* MU.X.KAM *Ka-dáš-man*]-⸢*Túr*⸣-*gu i-na* $^{i}$[$^{ti?}$
[ ] *na-a*[*d-nu*]

| | | |
|---|---|---|
| | [ ] | [*maš-ši*]-*tu*$_4$ ⸢x x⸣ [ |
| 5 | 1.0.1 | ⸢x x⸣ [<br>⸢x na ta x⸣ [<br>⸢ú gi ig x x *a*$^{?}$-*na*$^{?}$⸣ [ |
| | 19.1.2<br>5 SÌLA | *a-na* ŠE.BA ⸢$^{m}$*Mu*-SIG$_5$-$^{d}$IŠKUR⸣ |
| | 0.1.3 | $^{m}$*A*-⸢*gab-še-en-ni* $^{lú}$LUNGA⸣ *ki-mu* ŠE ⸢x⸣ [<br>⸢*ša*⸣ [x x x] $^{m}$ÌR-GAŠAN DUMU $^{m}$⸢*Iš*$^{?}$-*kun*$_8$$^{?}$⸣-[*li*$^{?}$-*su*$^{?}$]<br>⸢*ša*$^{?}$⸣ [x] ⸢x⸣ [ŠU]-*su tur-rat* |
| Rev. | 4.0.0 | ÉŠ.GÀR $^{m}$*Lu-da-ri*-[*be-lí*] |
| 9 | 0.0.5 | *ni-ki-is* GUR$_7$ $^{m}$*Il-l*[*ul-lu*$_4$] |

PAP 35.4.4 5 SÌLA $^{giš}$BÁN 10 [SÌLA]
ŠU.NIGIN 29.4.4 5 SÌLA $^{giš}$BÁN [GAL]
TA 6.0.0 GAL $^{giš}$BÁN 1[0 SÌLA . . .]

Commentary

1–3. "[Barley$^{?}$ . . . fro]m the revenu[es of . . . of year x of Kadašman]-Turgu, [which] was disbu[rsed] in [month . . .]."
8. For the restoration, cf. Lū-dari-bēlī as recipient of production supplies in **no. 151**: 11.
9. Probably the same Illullu mentioned as recipient of *nikis karê* in **no. 164**: 32, where he is identified as *ḫazannu*.

## 186. CUNES 52-12-047

-.-.[ . . . ] (Kadašman-Turgu)

Even though the date is broken, the text can be assigned to the reign of Kadašman-Turgu on prosopographic grounds. See, e.g., the merchant Tukultu, who appears also in **no. 297** (KT 6), and Ibni-Marduk, son of Nuska-nābûšu, who appears also in **no. 164** (KT 9).

Obv. ⌜ŠE *ša i-na* ŠÀ x⌝ [ ] ⌜x⌝
⌜*ša* MU.X.KAM⌝ [ LUGAL].⌜E⌝
*i-na* $^{iti}$[x x (x)] ⌜*na-ad*⌝*-nu*

| | ŠE ⌜$^{giš}$BÁN GAL⌝ | ŠE $^{giš}$BÁN 10 SÌLA | $^{giš}$BÁN 5 SÌLA ⌜*ša*? ŠE.BA?⌝ | MU.BI.IM |
|---|---|---|---|---|
| | | 0.2$^{pi}$.0 | | ⌜ŠE.BA⌝ $^{f}$*Zu-túr-tu*$_4$ MUNUS.ÀR |
| | | 0.2$^{pi}$.0 | | ŠE.BA $^{f}$*Bal-ti-*$^{d}$KUR MUNUS.ÀR |
| | | 0.2$^{pi}$.0 | | ŠE.BA $^{m}$*Ku-lip*?!*-pi-ri-gi-ir* Ì.DU$_8$ |
| | | 2.3.4<br>⌜5⌝ SÌLA | | ŠUKU ANŠE.KUR.RA$^{meš}$<br>$^{md}$*Nin-urta-kí-pi-šu*<br>*ka-nik* |
| Rev. | 4.4.5 | | | ⌜ŠE.BA⌝ É *ša* $^{iti}$NE.NE.GAR |
| | | | 1.0.0 | *maš-šar-tu*$_4$ $^{m}$*Mi-na-*DÙ*-uš-*DINGIR |
| | | | 0.2.3 | ŠUKU ANŠE.KUR.RA$^{meš}$ $^{md}$30-ŠEŠ-SUM-*na*<br>DUMU MÁ.LAḪ$_5$ |
| | | | 0.2.3 | $^{m}$*Ib-ni-*$^{d}$AMAR.UTU DUMU $^{md}$*Nuska-na-bu-šu* |
| | | | 0.3.0 | ŠÁM 1 PI NU.LUḪ.ḪA.⌜SAR⌝<br>$^{m}$*Tu-kul-tu*$_4$ DAM.GÀR |
| PAP | 4.4.5 | 3.4.4<br>5 SÌLA | 2.3.0 | ŠU.NIGIN 8.4.2 5 SÌLA<br>$^{giš}$BÁN GAL TA GAL-*ú*<br>*šu-lu-ú* |

Translation

Obv. ⌜Barley which was disbursed⌝ in [month x] from [ . . . ]
of year x of [kin]g [ . . . ]:

| | Barley (meas. by) the big *sūtu* | Barley (meas. by) the *sūtu* of 10 *qû* | (meas. by) the *sūtu* of 5 *qû* ⌜of the ration?⌝ | Its entry |
|---|---|---|---|---|
| | | 12 *sūtu* | | Rations (for) Zuturtu, female miller. |
| | | 12 *sūtu* | | Rations (for) Bāltī-Amurru, female miller. |
| | | 12 *sūtu* | | Rations (for) Kulippi-rigir, doorkeeper. |
| | | 82 *sūtu*<br>5 *qû* | | Fodder for the horses<br>(of) Ninurta-kīn-pīšu;<br>it is sealed. |
| Rev. | 149 *sūtu* | | | Rations (for) the house of month V. |
| | | | 30 *sūtu* | Staples (of) Mīnâ-ēpuš-ila. |
| | | | 15 *sūtu* | Fodder for the horses (of) Sîn-aḫa-iddina,<br>son of Malāḫu. |
| | | | 15 *sūtu* | Ibni-Marduk, son of Nuska-nābûšu. |
| | | | 18 *sūtu* | Price for 1 *pānu* of *nuḫurtu*-plant (for)<br>Tukultu, merchant. |
| Total | 149 *sūtu* | 118 *sūtu*<br>5 *qû* | 78 *sūtu* | Grand total: 266 *sūtu* (and) 5 *qû* (meas. by) the<br>big *sūtu*, after the increase<br>has been deducted. |

COMMENTARY

5–7. This might have been the amount for two months, cf. the monthly ration of 6 *sūtu* for *ararratu*-millers attested by **no. 96**.

7. The sign looks more like UK, but cf. the same PN in **no. 291**: 5, where the sign is clearly LUL.

8. Or "Fodder for the horses: Ninurta-kīn-pīšu sealed it."

13. NU.LUḪ.ḪA.SAR (Akk. *nuḫurtu*) is an unidentified medicinal plant, often used against witchcraft, perhaps to be identified with *Asafoetida* (Abusch and Schwemer 2016, 513). See MUN 296: 1 for its mention (*nu-ḫur-tu*) in an administrative text listing quantities of herbs. On the merchant Tukultu, see commentary to **no. 297**.

## 187. CUNES 52-12-012

-.VII.3 Kadašman-Enlil

Obv. ŠE *tab-ku* $^{giš}$BÁN GAL *ša i-na* ŠÀ 46.4.5 5 SÌLA
EN 9.4.1 ḪA.LA DUMU $^{m}$*Ba-bi-la-a-a-i*
EN 0.1.5 LA'U$_4$ *ša ḫa-rab ṭe-mi* [$^{m}$]$^{d}$30-TI-URU$_4$
EN 0.0.5 LA'U$_4$ *ša i-na* ŠU $^{m}$*Ša*-DINGIR-DÙ-*a maḫ-ru*
*na-ad-nu*

| | |
|---|---|
| 4.3.1 | $^{m}$*In-gu-um-gu* |
| 6.2$^{pi}$.0 | ÉŠ.GÀR $^{m}$*É-ra-bi* |
| 2.0.0 | ŠUKU É.DINGIR TA $^{iti}$⸢KIN.$^{d}$INANNA⸣.2.KAM.MA EN $^{iti}$SIG$_4$.GA |
| 11.0.0 | $^{md+}$*En-líl*-MU-SI.SÁ |
| 1.0.0 | $^{m}$⸢*Ki*⸣-*din*-$^{d}$⸢*Gu*⸣-*la* $^{lú}$LUNGA *ša* É.ŠU.ME.ŠA$_4$ |
| 4.0.0 | ⸢x x⸣ DUMU.MUNUS ⸢$^{m}$*Is-ḫu*⸣-*un-ni* |
| 2.[x.x] | $^{m}$⸢x bi? tu?⸣ ⸢x x⸣ i ⸢x x⸣ |
| 2.⸢1?.1⸣ | $^{f}$⸢x x x⸣ [x x x x] ⸢x⸣ 3.⸢x x $^{giš}$⸣BÁN 10 SÌLA |
| 1.⸢1?.x⸣ | [x x x x x x x] ⸢x⸣ |
| 0.3.⸢2⸣ | [x x x x x x x] ⸢x x⸣ |
| 0.3.⸢2⸣ | [x x x x x x x] ⸢x DUMU⸣ $^{md}$30-ŠEŠ-*ub-lam* |
| 0.0.2 | [x x x x x x x] ki |
| 1.⸢3?⸣.[x] | [x x x x x x x] ⸢DUMU $^{m}$x x ti⸣ |
| 2.[x.x] | [x x x x x x x] ⸢x⸣ |
| 0.1.⸢2?⸣ | [x x x x x x x] ⸢x x ti⸣ |
| ⸢x.x.x⸣ | [x x x x] ⸢x ul? x x⸣ |

Rev. PAP 46.4.5 5 SÌLA $^{giš}$BÁN GAL
ŠU $^{md}$30-TI
$^{iti}$DU$_6$.KÙ
MU.3.KAM
$^{d}$*Ka-daš-man*-$^{d+}$*En-líl*
LUGAL.E

COMMENTARY

1–5. "Stored barley, which was disbursed from 1,409 *sūtu* (and) 5 *qû*, including 295 *sūtu* of the share of the son of Bābilāyu, 11 *sūtu* of arrears of the *ḫarab ṭēmi* of Sîn-balāṭa-īriš, and 5 *sūtu* of arrears that were received from Ša-ili-banâ." The meaning of *ḫarab ṭēmi* still needs to be assessed; it can be written also *ḫarbu ṭēmi* and appears in letters (see attestations in Aro 1957, 37 and here text **no. 338**) as well as in legal (CUSAS 30 4) and administrative texts (BE 14 114, CUSAS 30 199, and CUSAS 30 236). In my opinion, it is more likely that it refers to a special type of *ḫarbu*-field (van Soldt 2015, 41) rather than "a plow with which the seed could be planted" (268).

6. This PN is to my knowledge otherwise unattested but cf. perhaps Imgugu in the unpublished Nippur text CBS 7752, quoted by Tenney 2011, 172.

10. Kidin-Gula, the brewer of the Ešumeša, is attested also in CUSAS 30 68: 11 (KuE 9) and perhaps also in CUSAS 30 79: 22 (n.d.; see comments in van Soldt 2015, 135).

## 188. CUNES 52-16-113

-.-.8

The obverse is almost completely lost.

| | | |
|---|---|---|
| Obv. | [ ] | ⸢x⸣ *i*-⸢*na*$^?$ x⸣ ti |
| | [ ] | ⸢x x x⸣ |
| | [ ] | ⸢x *ma-ḫi-ir*⸣ |
| | [ ] | ⸢x⸣ |

Text breaks off

| | | |
|---|---|---|
| Rev. | (1–2 lines missing) | |
| | [ ] | [ ]⸢x⸣ |
| | [ ] | |
| | [ ] | [x $^{giš}$]MÁ$^{meš}$ KÁ$^?$ *Ì-lí*-$^{d}$KUR *ù* ⸢x x⸣ [ |
| | [ ] | [Š]ÁM ḫa x bi *ša* $^{lú}$⸢x x x⸣ |
| | [ ] | ŠÁM KIN $^{lú}$⸢AD$^?$.x⸣ |
| | [PAP] [1]6.0./4 | ŠE $^{giš}$BÁN 10 SÌLA *i-na* ŠÀ *te-li-tu*$_4$ *ša* MU.8.KAM |

*i-na* ŠU $^{m}$*Ì-lí-re-man-ni*
*ù* $^{md}$30-*iš-man-ni*

COMMENTARY

9′. The reading of this line is tentative: the PN *Ì-lí*-$^{d}$KUR is not attested; another possibility would be reading KÁ$^?$-*ì-lí* for Bābili, but this spelling would be unusual in MB texts (see RGTC 5, 47–49).

10′. Perhaps $^{lú}$⸢AD$^?$.KID$^?$⸣, reed-weaver."

## 189. CUNES 52-16-109

-.VI.8

Only the left half of the tablet is preserved, but probably only the MU.BI.IM-column is missing.

Obv. ŠE *ša i-n*[*a*
*ša* MU.⸢8⸣.[KAM
*i-na* $^{iti}$KIN.⸢d⸣[INANNA

| | | |
|---|---|---|
| | ŠE $^{giš}$BÁN GAL | Š[E $^{giš}$BÁN |
| | 14.2.[x] | [ |
| | 6.0.0 | [ |
| | | ⸢x⸣[ |
| Rev. | [ ] | [ |
| | | [ |
| PAP | 21.⸢2$^?$⸣.1 | 8$^+$.[x.x] |

## 190. CUNES 52-16-027

Date not preserved.

Obv. ŠE $^{giš}$BÁN 10 SÌLA *i-na* ⸢*š*⸣[À$^{?}$
*ša* BÀD-$^{d+}$*En-líl*[$^{hi.a/meš}$
2.2.3 $^{md+}$*En-líl*-⸢x⸣[
2.2.3 ŠUKU GU$_4$$^{hi.a}$ ⸢x⸣[
2.4.0 5 SÌLA ⸢ŠUKU$^{?}$ x⸣[
EN $^{iti}$GAN.G[AN.È]
1.0.0 $^{m}$Ì[R$^{?}$
1.0.0 [

The reverse is lost.

COMMENTARY

1–2. "Barley, (measured by) the *sūtu* of 10 *qû*, from [ . . . ] of Dūr-Enlil[ē]."

### 1.3.4 *AKLU*-EXPENDITURES OF FOODSTUFFS

#### i. Single *aklu*-Expenditures

## 191. CUNES 53-01-113

3–5.X.5 Nazi-Maruttaš
Sealed.

Obv. ⸢x x 2$^{?}$ SÌLA⸣ KAŠ
T[A U$_4$].3.KAM
⸢EN U$_4$⸣.5.KAM
⸢*ak*⸣-*lu*$_4$
[ŠU] $^{m}$ZÁLAG-$^{d}$UTU
$^{iti}$AB.È

Rev. [M]U.5.KAM
*Na-zi-Mu-ru-ut-ta-aš*
LUGAL.E

## 192. CUNES 52-17-256

18–[ . . . ].IV.9 Nazi-Maruttaš
Sealed by Enlil-[ . . . ].

Obv. 12.1$^{\text{pi}}$.0 5 SÌLA ZÍZ.A[N.NA]
20 KAŠ.SAG
1 ME 16 ½ KAŠ.ÚS
5 DUG GAL
*ak-lu*$_4$ ŠU $^{\text{md}}$*N*[*in-*
Rev. [B]ÀD-$^{\text{d+}}$*E*[*n*$^{?}$*-líl*$^{\text{ḫi.a.ki?}}$]
_______________
$^{\text{iti}}$ŠU.NUMUN.[NA]
TA U$_4$.18.KAM EN [U$_4$.X.KAM]
MU.9.KAM *Na-zi-Ma-r*[*u-*
NA$_4$.KIŠIB $^{\text{md+}}$*En-lí*[*l-*

## 193. CUNES 52-13-061

30.XI–9.XII.12 Nazi-Maruttaš
Sealed by Rīmūtu.

Obv. 7.3.1 ZÌ.DA $^{\text{giš}}$BÁN 5 SÌLA
17.4.3 ŠE.BAR $^{\text{giš}}$BÁN 5 SÌLA
18 KAŠ.SAG
92 KAŠ.ÚS
*ak-lu*$_4$ *ù* ZI.GA
$^{\text{m}}$*Di-maḫ-di-*$^{\text{d}}$*Uraš*
BÀD-$^{\text{d?}}$KI.ÙR$^{\text{?ki}}$
L.e. [T]A U$_4$.30.KAM *ša* $^{\text{iti}}$ZÍZ.A.AN
EN U$_4$.9.KAM $^{\text{iti}}$ŠE.KIN.KU$_5$
Rev. MU.12.KAM *Na-zi-Ma-ru-ut-taš*
⸢LUGAL⸣.E
NA$_4$.KIŠIB $^{\text{m}}$*Ri-mu-ti*

## 194. CUNES 52-18-789 (Plate No. 52)

7.X.13 Nazi-Maruttaš
Sealed.

Obv. 0.0.3 5 ½ SÌLA ZÌ.DA
0.0.1 3 SÌLA ŠE.BAR
⸢*ak*⸣*-lu*$_4$ $^{\text{giš}}$BÁN 6 SÌLA
ŠU $^{\text{md}}$30-TI.LA-URU$_4$
Rev. $^{\text{iti}}$AB.È
U$_4$.7.KAM
MU.13.KAM
*Na-zi-Ma-ru-ut-taš*
L.e. LUGAL.E

## 195. CUNES 52-16-053

10.X.13 Nazi-Maruttaš
Sealed by Ninurta-zākir-šumi.

Obv. [x x] 6 SÌLA ZÌ.DA
⸢0.1⸣.3 ŠE.BAR
*ak-lu*$_4$ $^{giš}$BÁN 6 SÌLA
ŠU $^{md}$30-TI-URU$_4$-*iš*
5 $^{iti}$AB.È
L.e. U$_4$.10.KAM
Rev. MU.13.KAM
*Na-zi-Ma-ru-ta-aš*
LUGAL.E
NA$_4$.KIŠIB $^{md}$MAŠ-MU-MU

## 196. CUNES 52-13-002

12.X.13 Nazi-Maruttaš
Sealed.

Obv. 0.0.2 2 ½ SÌLA ZÌ.DA
0.0.4 3 SÌLA ŠE.BAR
*ak-lu*$_4$ $^{giš}$BÁN 6 SÌLA
4 ŠU $^{md}$30-TI.LA-URU$_4$
Rev. $^{iti}$AB.È
U$_4$.12.KAM
MU.13.KAM
8 *Na-zi-Ma-ru-u*[*t-ta*]*š*
LUGAL.E

## 197. CUNES 52-19-138

22.X.13 Nazi-Maruttaš
Sealed.

Obv. 0.0.2 KAŠ $^{giš}$BÁN GAL
*ak-lu*$_4$
ŠU $^{m}$ZÁLAG-$^{d}$UTU ud du
4 $^{iti}$AB.È
Rev. U$_4$.22.KAM
MU.13.KAM
*Na-zi-Ma-ru-ut-taš*
8 LUGAL.E

COMMENTARY

3. I believe the correct PN is Nūr-Šamaš, who appears in this position in other *aklu*-texts from the reign of Nazi-Maruttaš (see **no. 191**: 5 and **no. 204**: 5), but the scribe might have been thinking of Ana-nūr-Šamaš-lī/ūṣi ($^{m}$*A-na*-ZÁLAG-$^{d}$UTU-È).

### 198. CUNES 52-19-130

12.IX.15 Nazi-Maruttaš
Sealed.

Obv. 1.2.4 ZÌ.DA
$^{giš}$BÁN 5 SÌLA
*ak-*$lu_4$
$^{m}$*Di-maḫ-di-*$^{d}$*Uraš*
Rev. EN 0.0.4 1 ˹SÌLA˺ [x] ˹x˺
$^{iti}$GAN.GAN.È
$U_4$.12.KAM
MU.15.KAM
*Na-zi-Ma-ru-ut-*
*ta-aš*

### 199. CUNES 52-13-055

26–[ . . . ].VII.16 Nazi-Maruttaš
Sealed by [ . . . ].

Obv. 0.2.2 ŠE.BAR $^{giš}$BÁN [
*ak-*$lu_4$ *ù* Z[I.GA]
TA $U_4$.26 EN ˹$U_4$˺.[x]
ŠU $^{m}$*E-ri-bi*
Rev. $^{iti}$$DU_6$.KÙ
MU.16.KAM
*Na-zi-Ma-ru-ut-ta-a*[*š*]
LUGAL.˹E˺
$NA_4$.KIŠIB $^{md}$[

### 200. CUNES 52-13-063

-.VIII.16 Nazi-Maruttaš
Sealed.

The observe is almost completely lost, with the exception of a few sign traces. A "3," still visible at the beginning of the obverse, suggests that the text recorded items whose quantities are expressed in units (e.g., containers or animals).

Despite the poor state of preservation, the tablet can be tentatively assigned to the *aklu*-expenditures because of its external features (size, shape, and presence of a seal impression) and because Erību appears in two other *aklu*-expenditures dated to NM 16 (**nos. 199** and **201**).

Rev. ŠU $^{m}$*E-ri-bi*  
$^{iti}$APIN.DU$_{8}$.A  
MU.16.KAM  
*Na-zi-Ma-ru-ut-*[  
5′ LUGAL.⸢E⸣

## 201. CUNES 52-13-005

10–16.IX.16 Nazi-Maruttaš  
Sealed.

Obv. 0.1.3 ŠE.BAR $^{giš}$BÁN 6 SÌLA  
*ak-lu*$_{4}$ *ù* ZI.GA  
TA U$_{4}$.10.KAM  
4 EN U$_{4}$.16.KAM  
Rev. [Š]U $^{m}$*E-ri-bi*  
$^{iti}$GAN.GAN.È  
MU.16.⸢KAM⸣  
8 *Na-zi-Ma-ru-ut-ta-aš*  
LUGAL.E

## 202. CUNES 52-13-007

-.XI.18 Nazi-Maruttaš  
Sealed by Rīmūtu.

Obv. ⸢2⸣ UDU.NÍTA  
*ak-lu*$_{4}$ *a-rad* LUGAL  
$^{m}$*Pu-us-su-lu*$_{4}$  
4 $^{iti}$ZÍZ.A.AN MU.18.KAM  
L.e. *Na-zi-Ma-ru-ut-taš*  
Rev. NIBRU$^{ki}$  
NA$_{4}$.KIŠIB $^{m}$*Ri-mu-ti*

COMMENTARY

2. The occasion of the expenditure is the *arād šarri* "coming/going down of the king." This expression seems to refer—together with *elē šarri* "coming/going up of the king"—to the king's travels on the occasion of the New Year festival (Brinkman 1976, 411–14; Sassmannshausen 2001, 10, 302, 324, 335).
3. Pussulu is likely the same person identified as a shepherd (SIPA) in **no. 291**: 4.

## 203. CUNES 52-16-058

-.III.21$^{+}$ Nazi-Maruttaš
Sealed by Rīmūtu.

Obv. ⌜2$^{?}$⌝ SILA$_4$ [
MÁŠ.ŠU.GÍD.GÍD U$_4$.2$^{?}$.KAM
1 UDU.NÍTA $^{m}$BA-*šá*-$^{d}$*Nin-ìmma*
*ak-lu*$_4$ $^{m}$ŠEŠ-*i*
[$^{l}$]$^{ú?}$SIPA
Rev. $^{iti}$SIG$_4$.A.AN
MU.⌜21$^{+}$⌝.KAM
*Na-z*[*i-M*]*a-ru-ut-taš*
[NA$_4$.KIŠIB $^{m}$]*Ri-mu-tu*$_4$

## 204. CUNES 53-02-149

[ . . . ].I.[ . . . ] Nazi-Maruttaš
Sealed.

Obv. 0.4.4 KAŠ $^{giš}$BÁN GA[L]
[E]N 9 DUG.GAL *ša a-na* ⌜x⌝[
[*i*]*š-šu-ú*
*ak-lu*$_4$
ŠU $^{m}$ZÁLAG-$^{d}$UTU
Rev. ⌜$^{iti}$BÁR⌝.ZAG.GAR
[U$_4$.x].KAM
[MU.x].KAM
⌜*Na-zi*⌝-*Mu-ru-ut-ta*-[*aš*]
LUGAL.E

## 205. CUNES 52-13-057

1–30.VII.1 Kadašman-Turgu
Sealed by Ninurta-zākir-šumi.

Obv. 2.4.⌜3⌝ 2 ½ SÌLA ZÌ.DA $^{giš}$BÁN 5 SÌLA
0.1.4 ŠE $^{giš}$BÁN 5 SÌLA
⌜*ak*⌝-*lu*$_4$ $^{m}$*Ṭà-ab-ki-din*-$^{d}$*Gu-la*
*a-ša-bu ù la a-ša-b*[*u*]
$^{iti}$DU$_6$.⌜KÙ⌝
L.e. TA U$_4$.1.KAM EN U$_4$.30.K[AM]
Rev. MU.1.KAM *Ka-dáš-man-Túr*-[*gu*]
LUGAL.E
NA$_4$.KIŠIB $^{md}$*Nin-urta*-
MU-MU

## 206. CUNES 52-13-013

1–29.IV.2 Kadašman-Turgu
Sealed by Ninurta-zākir-šumi.

Obv. 5.2$^{pi}$.0 1 ½ SÌLA ZÌ.DA $^{giš}$BÁN [x] SÌLA
1.2.2 ŠE $^{giš}$BÁN 5 SÌLA
*ak-lu*$_4$ ŠU $^m$*Ṭà-ab-ki-din-*$^d$*Gu-la*
*a-ša-bu*
5 $^{iti}$ŠU.NUMUN.NA
L.e. [T]A U$_4$.1.KAM EN U$_4$.29.KAM
Rev. MU.2.KAM *Ka-dáš-man-Túr-gu*
LUGAL.E
NA$_4$.KIŠIB $^{m⌈d}$*Nin*⌉*-urta*-MU-MU

## 207. CUNES 52-16-055

18$^?$.IX.2 Kadašman-Turgu
Sealed by Ninurta-zākir-šumi.

Obv. 1 SILA$_4$ *a-na* NIBRU[$^{ki}$]
*šu-ul-ma-nu* $^m$*Na-za-lu*$_4$
1 SILA$_4$ *ba-ru-tu*$_4$ U$_4$.18.KAM
4 *ak-lu*$_4$ $^{md}$[*Nin-urta*]-
L.e. MU-MU
Rev. ŠU $^{md}$*Ba-ba*$_6$-URU$_4$
$^{iti}$GAN.GAN.È
MU.2.KAM *Ka-dáš-man-Túr-gu*
LUGAL.E
10 NA$_4$.KIŠIB $^{md}$*Nin-urta-*
L.e. MU-MU

COMMENTARY

6. Considering that this is an expenditure of lambs, which at least in one case are meant for Nippur (l. 1), Baba-īriš could be the homonymous "shepherd of the king" (SIPA LUGAL) mentioned in **no. 159**: 33 (KT 9).

## 208. CUNES 52-13-006

-.XI.2 Kadašman-Turgu
Sealed by Ninurta-kīn-pīšu.

Obv. 2 ½ SÌLA ⌜BÁPPIR$^{?}$⌝
*ak-lu*$_4$ $^{md}$*Nin-urta*-⌜GI-KA-*šu*⌝
ŠU $^{md}$*Nin-urta*-MU-MU
4 $^{iti}$ZÍZ.A.AN
Rev. MU.2.KAM
*Ka-dáš-man-Túr-gu* LUGAL
NA$_4$.KIŠIB $^{md}$*Nin-urta*-
GI-KA-*šu*

## 209. CUNES 52-13-010

1–30$^{?}$.II.2$^{+}$ Kadašman-Turgu
Sealed by Ninurta-zākir-šumi.

Obv. [x (x)] ⌜2$^{?}$⌝ KAŠ.ÚS
[x (x)] DUG.GAL
[*ak-l*]*u*$_4$ *ù* ZI.GA
[ŠU $^{m}$]⌜*A*⌝-*gab-še-en-ni*
[$^{iti}$G]U$_4$.SI.SÁ
L.e. [TA] U$_4$.1.KAM EN U$_4$.⌜30$^{?}$⌝.[KAM]
Rev. [MU].⌜2$^{+}$⌝.KAM *Ka-dáš-man-Túr-gu*
[ LUGAL].⌜E⌝
[NA$_4$.KIŠIB $^{md}$*Nin-u*]*rta*-MU-MU

COMMENTARY
4. Agab-šenni must be the homonymous brewer (see Index of Personal Names).

## 210. CUNES 52-13-014

1–30.VIII.3 Kadašman-Turgu
Sealed by Ninurta-zākir-šumi.

Obv. 6.2.2 NINDA.KAS[KAL]
EN 0.3.0 É.⌜DINGIR$^{didli}$⌝
EN 0.0.4 2 SÌLA *ki-is-p*[*u*]
3.1.2 ŠE.BAR
*ak-lu*$_4$ ŠU DUMU.MUNUS $^{lú}$Ì.[SUR]
*a-ša-bu ù la a-š*[*a-bu*]
Rev. $^{iti}$APIN.DU$_8$.A
TA U$_4$.1.KAM EN U$_4$.⌜30⌝.[KAM]
MU.3.KAM *Ka-dáš-man-Tú*[*r-gu*]
LUGAL.E
NA$_4$.KIŠIB $^{md}$*Nin-urta*-M[U-MU]

## 211. CUNES 53-01-110

24–25.I.4 Kadašman-Turgu
Sealed by Lūṣi-ana-nūr-Marduk.

| | |
|---|---|
| Obv. | 0.0.2 5 ½ SÌLA U$_4$.24.KAM |
| | 0.0.2 U$_4$.25.KAM |
| | PAP 0.0.4 5 ½ SÌLA *ak-lu*$_4$ |
| 4 | $^{iti}$BÁR.ZAG.GAR |
| Rev. | [M]U.4.KAM |
| | [$^{(d)}$*K*]*a-dáš-man-Túr-gu* |
| | NA$_4$.KIŠIB |
| | $^{m}$È-*a-na*-ZÁLAG-$^{d}$AMAR.UTU |

## 212. CUNES 52-15-025 (Plate No. 53)

1–29.III.5 Kadašman-Turgu
Sealed by Ninurta-zākir-šumi.

| | |
|---|---|
| Obv. | 7.3.4 3 ½ SÌLA ZÌ.DA $^{<giš>}$BÁN KIN.SIG |
| | *ak-lu*$_4$ *a-ša-bu* |
| | ŠU DUMU.MUNUS $^{lú}$Ì.SUR |
| | [$^{it}$]$^{i}$SIG$_4$.GA TA U$_4$.1.KAM |
| 5 | [E]N U$_4$.29.KAM |
| | ⸢MU.5⸣.KAM *Ka-dáš-man-Túr-gu* |
| L.e. | LUGAL.E |
| Rev. | [NA$_4$.KIŠIB] $^{md}$*Nin-urta*-MU-MU |

COMMENTARY

1. For the *sūtu naptanu*, see also **no. 232**: 1 and van Soldt 2015, 32 with reference to previous literature.

## 213. CUNES 52-16-051

1–30.VII.7 Kadašman-Turgu
Sealed by Ninurta-zākir-šumi.

| | |
|---|---|
| Obv. | [X X X] ⸢KAŠ.ÚS⸣ |
| | ⸢X⸣ [X X DU]G.GAL |
| | ⸢*ak-lu*$_4$ *a-ša*⸣*-bu* |
| | *ù la a-ša-bu* |
| 5 | ŠU $^{md}$30-TI-URU$_4$ |
| Rev. | $^{iti}$DU$_6$.KÙ |
| | TA U$_4$.1.KAM EN U$_4$.30.KAM |
| | MU.7.KAM *Ka-dáš-man-Túr-gu* |
| | LUGAL.E |
| 10 | NA$_4$.KIŠIB $^{md}$*Nin-urta*-MU-MU |

## 214. CUNES 52-16-045

1–30.XII.7 Kadašman-Turgu
Sealed by Ninurta-zākir-šumi.

Obv. 4.0.1 4 SÌLA ZÌ.DA ⸢KIN.SIG$^{?}$⸣
EN 6 SÌLA ⸢É.DINGIR⸣$^{didli}$
EN 0.0.4 2 SÌLA *ki-is-pi*
⸢*ak-lu*$_4$⸣ *a-ša-bu*
⸢*ù la a-ša-bu*⸣
L.e. ⸢ŠU DUMU⸣.MUNUS <lú>Ì.S[UR]
Rev. ⸢$^{iti}$ZÍZ.A.A⸣[N]
⸢TA⸣ U$_4$.1.KAM EN U$_4$.30.[KAM]
MU.7.KAM *Ka-dáš-man-Túr-gu*
LUGAL.E
NA$_4$.KIŠIB $^{md}$*Nin-urta*-MU-MU

## 215. CUNES 52-15-024

1–29.IV.8 Kadašman-Turgu
Sealed by Ninurta-zākir-šumi.

Obv. [ ]
*ak-*⸢*lu*$_4$ *a*$^{?}$⸣-[*ša*$^{?}$-*bu*$^{?}$]
ŠU $^{m}$*Mu*-S[IG$_5$]-⸢$^{d}$IŠKUR⸣
TA U$_4$.1.[KAM]
EN U$_4$.29.⸢KAM⸣
$^{iti}$ŠU.X.NUMUN.[NA]
Rev. [M]U.8.KAM
*Ka-dáš-man-Túr-gu*
⸢LUGAL.E⸣
NA$_4$.KIŠIB $^{md}$MAŠ-MU-M[U]

COMMENTARY

6. The sign between ŠU and NUMUN in the month name looks like KU; I do not know of any attestation of such a spelling besides **no. 64**: 8.

## 216. CUNES 52-16-054

8.IX.9 Kadašman-Turgu
Sealed.

Obv. 2 ½ KAŠ.ÚS
½ DUG.GAL
*ak-lu*$_4$
NIBRU$^{ki}$
ŠU $^{m}$É-*ra-bi*
Rev. $^{iti}$GAN.GAN.È
U$_4$.8.KAM
MU.9.KAM
*Ka-dáš-man-Túr-gu*
LUGAL.E
L.e. ⸢NA$_4$.KIŠIB x x x⸣

## 217. CUNES 52-16-052

12.VIa.10 Kadašman-Turgu
Sealed by Ninurta-zākir-šumi.

Obv. 1 UDU.NÍTA KIN.SIG U$_4$.12.K[AM]
*ak-lu*$_4$ ŠU $^{m}$*Tukul-ti*-É.UL.MAŠ
$^{iti}$KIN.$^{d}$INANNA.2.KAM
MU.10.KAM
*Ka-dáš-man-Túr-gu*
Rev. NA$_4$.KIŠIB
$^{md}$*Nin-urta*-MU-MU

COMMENTARY

2. Tukultī-Eulmaš must be the same person as Tukultī-Ulmaš, the shepherd responsible for another *aklu*-expenditure involving sheep dated in the 11$^{th}$ year of Kadašman-Turgu (**no. 219**).

## 218. CUNES 52-17-255

1–30.I.11 Kadašman-Turgu
Sealed by Ninurta-zākir-šumi.

Obv. [x x x] SÌLA ŠE $^{giš}$BÁN ⸢5⸣ [SÌLA]
[*ak-l*]*u*$_4^{?}$ *a-ša-bu*
⸢*ù la*⸣ *a-ša-bu*
ŠU $^{m}$*Mi-na-e-pu-uš*-DINGIR
$^{iti}$BÁR.ZAG.GAR
TA U$_4$.1.KAM EN U$_4$.30.KAM
Rev. MU.11.KAM
*Ka-dáš-man-Túr-gu*
NA$_4$.KIŠIB $^{md}$MAŠ-MU-MU

## 219. CUNES 52-16-021

9 and 18.VII.11 Kadašman-Turgu
Sealed by Ninurta-zākir-šumi.

Obv. 1 UDU.NÍTA *maḫ-ru*$^{rù}$
É $^{d}$*Gu-la*
⌜$^{iti}$DU$_{6}$.KÙ⌝ U$_{4}$.9.KAM
1 MÁŠ.TUR KIN.SIG ⌜U$_{4}$⌝.18.KAM
PAP 2 UDU *ak-lu*$_{4}$
ŠU $^{m}$*Tukul-ti*-UL.MAŠ SIPA
Rev. $^{iti}$DU$_{6}$.[K]Ù
MU.11.⌜KAM⌝
⌜*Ka-dáš-man-Túr-gu*⌝
⌜LUGAL⌝.E
⌜NA$_{4}$.KIŠIB $^{md}$*Nin-urta*-MU-MU⌝

## 220. CUNES 52-19-113

1–[ . . . ].IX.11 Kadašman-Turgu
Sealed by [ . . . ].

Obv. ⌜0.4.1 5 SÌLA ⌜GÚ$^{?}$.GAL$^{?}$ $^{giš}$BÁN KIN$^{?}$.SIG$^{?}$⌝
0.1$^{pi}$.0 ⌜ŠE *maḫ-ru* x⌝
1.1.1 4 SÌLA ⌜ŠE $^{giš}$BÁN 5 SÌLA⌝
*ak-lu*$_{4}$ ⌜*la a-ša*⌝*-bu*
ŠU $^{m}$*É-ra-bi a-š*[*a*$^{?}$*-bu*$^{?}$]
$^{iti}$GAN.GAN.È
Rev. ⌜TA⌝ U$_{4}$.1.KAM ⌜EN U$_{4}$⌝.[X.KAM]
MU.11.KAM ⌜*Ka*⌝*-dáš-m*[*an-Túr-gu*]
⌜LUGAL⌝.[E]
NA$_{4}$.KIŠIB $^{m⌜d⌝}$[

## 221. CUNES 52-12-035

1–30.XII.11 Kadašman-Turgu
Sealed by Ninurta-zākir-šumi.

Obv. 8.2.4 4 SÌLA ŠE $^{giš}$BÁN ⌜5⌝ SÌLA
*ak-lu a-ša-bu*
⌜*ù*⌝ *la a-ša-bu*
[Š]U $^{m}$*Mi-na*-DÙ*-uš*-DINGIR
[$^{i}$]$^{ti}$ŠE.KIN.KU$_{5}$
L.e. TA U$_{4}$.1.KAM
EN U$_{4}$.30.KAM
Rev. MU.11.KAM
*Ka-dáš-man-Túr-gu* LUGAL.E
NA$_{4}$.KIŠIB $^{md}$*Nin-urta*-MU-MU

## 222. CUNES 52-13-058

1–30.XI.12 Kadašman-Turgu
Sealed by Ninurta-zākir-šumi.

Obv. 3.2.1 2 SÌLA ŠE $^{giš}$BÁN 5 SÌLA
*ak-lu*$_4$ ⸢ŠU $^{f}$⸣*I-na-A-ka*$^{?}$*-de*$^{?}$-NIN
$^{iti}$ZÍZ.A.AN TA U$_4$.1.KAM
EN U$_4$.30.KAM
⸢MU.12⸣.KAM
Rev. ⸢*Ka-dáš*⸣*-man-Túr-gu*
⸢LUGAL.E⸣
⸢NA$_4$.KIŠIB $^{md}$MAŠ-MU-MU⸣

## 223. CUNES 52-13-004

1–30.XII.12 Kadašman-Turgu
Sealed by Ninurta-zākir-šumi.

Obv. 0.4.0 ŠE 3 ½ KAŠ.ÚS
2 DUG.GAL
*ak-lu a-ša-bu*
⸢*ù*⸣ *la a-ša-bu*
⸢ŠU⸣ $^{m}$*Ṭà-ab-ki-din-*$^{d}$*Gu-la*
$^{iti}$ŠE.KIN.KU$_5$
Rev. [T]A U$_4$.1.KAM EN U$_4$.30.KAM
[M]U.12.KAM *Ka-dáš-man-Túr-gu*
LUGAL.E
NA$_4$.KIŠIB $^{md}$*Nin-urta*-MU-MU

## 224. CUNES 52-15-026

1–[ . . . ].IV.13 Kadašman-Turgu
Sealed by [ . . . ].

Obv. 1.3.1 ZÌ.DA [
0.3.1 ŠE $^{gi}$[$^{š}$BÁN
25 KA[Š
*ak-lu*$_4$ *a-š*[*a-bu*]
*ù la a-*[*ša-bu*]
ŠU $^{m}$É-[*ra-bi*]
Rev. $^{iti}$ŠU.NU[MUN.NA]
TA U$_4$.1.K[AM
MU.13.KAM *K*[*a-*
NA$_4$.KIŠIB $^{m⸢d⸣}$[

## 225. CUNES 52-13-011

1–[ . . . ].VIa.13 Kadašman-Turgu
Sealed by Ninurta-zākir-šumi.

Obv. ⌜43$^{?}$⌝ ½ KAŠ.ÚS
*ak-lu*$_4$
[*a*]*-ša-bu ù la a-ša-bu*
[Š]U $^{m}$*Ṭà-ab-ki-din-*$^{d}$*Gu-la*
⌜$^{iti}$KIN⌝.$^{d}$INANNA.2.KAM
[TA] U$_4$.1.KAM
Rev. EN U$_4$.[x].KAM
MU.13.KAM
*Ka-dáš-man-Túr-gu* LUGAL
NA$_4$.KIŠIB
$^{md}$*Nin-urta*-MU-MU

## 226. CUNES 52-13-001

1–30.IV.14 Kadašman-Turgu
Sealed by Ninurta-zākir-šumi.

Obv. 1.3.4 3 SÌLA ŠE $^{gi}$[$^{š}$BÁN] ⌜5⌝ SÌLA
*ak-lu*$_4$ *a-ša-*[*b*]*u*
*ù la a-ša-bu*
ŠU $^{md}$30-TI-URU$_4$
$^{iti}$ŠU.NUMUN.NA
TA U$_4$.1.KAM
L.e. EN U$_4$.30.KAM
Rev. MU.14.KAM
*Ka-dáš-man-Túr-gu* LUGAL.E
NA$_4$.KIŠIB $^{md}$*Nin-urta*-MU-MU

## 227. CUNES 52-12-034

1–10.V.14 Kadašman-Turgu
Sealed by Ninurta-zākir-šumi.

Obv. 17.1.5 1 ½ SÌLA ZÌ.D[A]
*ak-lu*$_4$ *a-ša-*⌜*bu*⌝
*ù la a-ša-*⌜*bu*⌝
ŠU DUMU.MUNUS $^{lú}$Ì.SUR
$^{iti}$NE.NE.GAR
TA U$_4$.1.KAM EN U$_4$.10.KAM
Rev. [MU].14.KAM
*Ka-dáš-man-Túr-gu* LUGAL.E
NA$_4$.KIŠIB $^{md}$*Nin-urta-*
MU-MU

### 228. CUNES 52-16-047

1–30.VII.14 Kadašman-Turgu
Sealed by Ninurta-zākir-šumi.

Obv. 5.1.2 4 SÌLA ŠE.BAR
*ak-lu*$_4$ *a-ša-bu*
*ù la* ⸢*a*⸣*-ša-bu*
ŠU $^{md}$30-TI-URU$_4$
$^{iti}$DU$_6$.KÙ
Rev. TA U$_4$.1.⸢KAM⸣
EN U$_4$.30.⸢KAM⸣
MU.14.KAM
$^{d}$*Ka-dáš-man-Túr-gu*
LUGAL.E
NA$_4$.KIŠIB $^{md}$*Nin-urta*-MU-MU

### 229. CUNES 52-18-160

1–[ . . . ].X.14 Kadašman-Turgu
Sealed by Ninurta-[zākir$^?$-šumi$^?$].
The right half of the obverse is plastered with clay incised with fake signs, indicated by asterisks.

Obv. [x.x].4$^?$ ½ *
5 * *
*ak-l*[*u*$_4$
4 *a-ša-b*[*u*] * *
L.e. $^{iti}$AB. * *
TA U$_4$.1.KA[M] * *
Rev. [M]U.14.KAM *K*[*a-*
LUGAL.E
⸢NA$_4$.KIŠIB⸣ $^{md}$*Nin-ur*[*ta-*

### 230. CUNES 52-16-020

1–30.II.15 Kadašman-Turgu
Sealed by Ninurta-zākir-šumi.

Obv. 0.4.3 6 SÌLA ZÌ.DA ⸢$^{giš}$BÁN$^?$ KIN.SIG$^?$⸣
0.1$^{pi}$.0 ŠE $^{giš}$BÁN ⸢5⸣ SÌLA
22 ½ KAŠ.ÚS
*ak-lu*$_4$ ŠU $^{m}$É-*ra-bi*
*a-ša-bu*
*ù* ⸢*la a*⸣*-ša-bu*
Rev. $^{iti}$GU$_4$.SI.⸢SÁ⸣
TA U$_4$.1.KAM EN U$_4$.30.KAM
MU.15.KAM *Ka-dáš-man-Túr-gu*
LUGAL.E
NA$_4$.KIŠIB ⸢$^{md}$*Nin*⸣*-urta*-MU-[MU]

## 231. CUNES 52-16-048

1–30.VI.16 Kadašman-Turgu
Sealed by Ninurta-gašir-ilāni.

Obv. 0.4.3 2 SÌLA ZÌ.D[A
1.1.3 2 SÌLA ŠE $^{giš}$[BÁN
EN 1 GUR $^{md}$*Nin*-[
15 KAŠ.ÚS
*ak-lu*$_4$ *a-ša-bu*
*ù la a-ša-bu*
ŠU $^{m}$É-*ra-bi*
Rev. $^{iti}$KIN.$^{d}$INANNA
TA U$_4$.1.KAM EN U$_4$.30.KAM
MU.16.KAM
$^{d}$*Ka-dáš-man-Túr-gu* LUGAL.E
NA$_4$.KIŠIB $^{md}$*Nin-urta-ga-ši-ir*-DINGIR$^{meš}$

COMMENTARY
3. This line has been squeezed in between l. 2 and l. 4, as if it had been added at a later time.

## 232. CUNES 52-20-317

[1]–29.IV.[ . . . ] Kadašman-Turgu
Despite the statement in l. 9, no traces of a seal impression are visible on the surface of the tablet.

Obv. [x x x x] ⸢x ZÌ.DA $^{giš}$BÁN KIN.SIG⸣
[*ak-lu*$_4$ *a-š*]*a-bu*
[*ù la*] ⸢*a*⸣-*ša-bu*
[ŠU DUMU.MUNUS $^{lú}$]Ì.SUR
[$^{iti}$SIG$_4$].GA
[TA U$_4$.1.K]AM EN U$_4$.29
Rev. [MU.x].KAM
[*Ka*]-⸢*dáš-man*⸣-*Túr-gu*
NA$_4$.KIŠIB $^{md}$MAŠ-MU-MU

COMMENTARY
1. For the *sūtu naptanu*, see also **no. 212**: 1 and van Soldt 2015, 32 with reference to previous literature.

## 233. CUNES 52-16-059

[1]–29$^?$.VII$^?$.[ . . . ] Kadašman-Turgu
Sealed by Ninurta-gešir-ilāni.

Obv. ⸢5$^?$⸣.1.2 1 SÌLA ZÌ.DA $^{giš}$BÁN [
0.3.2 1 SÌLA ŠE.BAR $^{giš}$BÁN [
46 ½ KAŠ.ÚS
3 DUG.GAL
*ak-lu*$_4$ *a-ša-bu*
*ù la a-ša-bu*
ŠU $^{m}$*Ṭà-ab-ki-din-*$^{d}$*Gu-la*
Rev. $^{it}$[$^{i}$DU$_6$.K]Ù$^?$
[TA U$_4$.1].⸢KAM EN U$_4$.29$^?$⸣.KAM
[MU.X].KAM
[*Ka-dáš-m*]*an-Túr-gu* LUGAL.E
NA$_4$.KIŠIB $^{md}$⸢*Nin-urta-ge-šìr*-DINGIR$^{meš}$⸣

## 234. CUNES 52-13-012

1–[ . . . ].XII.[ . . . ] Kadašman-Turgu
Sealed.

Obv. 22 ½ KAŠ.ÚŠ
*ak-lu*$_4$
*a-ša-bu*
*ù la a-ša-bu*
ŠU $^{md+}$*En-líl-mu-bal-liṭ*
L.e. $^{iti}$ŠE.KIN.KU$_5$
Rev. [T]A U$_4$.1.KAM
[EN U$_4$.X].KAM
[MU.X.KAM *Ka*]-⸢*dáš-man-Túr*⸣-*gu*
⸢LUGAL.E⸣
[NA$_4$.KIŠIB] ⸢X X X X⸣
⸢X X X X⸣

COMMENTARY
11–12. Very tentatively, one could perhaps read the PN $^{md}$*Nin-urta-ga-ši-ir*-DINGIR$^{meš}$, written on two lines.

## 235. CUNES 53-01-096

Date not preserved.

Obv. 5 ½ KAŠ.SAG
76 ½ KAŠ.ÚS
PAP 82 KAŠ.ÚS
*ak-lu*$_4$ ŠU $^{m}$IBILA-$^{d}$UTU
$^{lú}$LUNGA

The reverse is lost.

## ii. Summaries of *aklu*-Expenditures

### 236. CUNES 52-18-767

11.XII.8 Nazi-Maruttaš

Sealed by Dimaḫdi-Uraš.

| | | |
|---|---|---|
| Obv. | [UDU.NÍTA] | [MU].⸢BI.IM⸣ |
| | [1] | ⸢x⸣ na ḫa *ki-i* |
| | 1 | *ša* $^{m}$*Za-ki-ri* |
| | | $^{md}$AMAR.UTU-*re-man-ni* |
| L.e. | PAP 2 | UDU.NÍTA |
| Rev. | ⸢*ak-lu*$_4$ x⸣ [ | |
| | DUMU $^{m}$*Qa-diš*-⸢*ti*⸣ | |
| | $^{iti}$ŠE.KIN.KU$_5$ U$_4$.11.KAM | |
| | MU.8.KAM *Na-zi-Múru-taš* | |
| | [LUGAL].E | |
| L.e. | [NA$_4$.KIŠ]IB $^{m}$*Di-maḫ*-⸢*di*⸣- | |
| | $^{d}$*Ura*[*š*] | |

COMMENTARY

1. The restoration of the heading in col. i is suggested by the total in l. 5.

### 237. CUNES 52-18-764

-.VI–XI.9 Nazi-Maruttaš

Sealed.

Summary of *aklu*-expenditures issued from month VI till month XI of the 9th year of Nazi-Maruttaš. The obverse is very eroded and the column dividers are barely visible.

| | | | | |
|---|---|---|---|---|
| Obv. | [ ] | [x] | [ŠE].BAR | [MU.BI.IM] |
| | [ ] | | 1.0.1 | $^{m}$⸢x⸣-$^{d}$[<br>⸢x x 4$^?$ x⸣ |
| | [ ] | | 2.2.2 | $^{md}$30-[LU]GAL$^?$-DINGIR$^{meš}$ |
| | 0.2.0 3 SÌLA | | | $^{m}$*Šum-ma-la*-$^{d}$⸢AMAR.UTU⸣ |
| | 0.1$^?$.2$^?$ 4 | 3 | | ŠUKU ⸢x x x⸣ [ |
| | [x].⸢x⸣.2 2 SÌLA | 18 ½ | | ⸢x x x⸣ [<br>⸢x⸣ [ |
| Rev. | [x.x.x] 3 SÌLA | 2 | | ⸢KAŠ$^?$ x⸣ [<br>su$^?$ a[k$^?$ |
| | 0.1.4 5 SÌLA | | | ŠUKU 5 UD[U$^?$<br>TA U$_4$.1.KAM EN ⸢U$_4$⸣.[<br>$^{iti}$ŠU.NUMUN.NA<br>$^{giš}$BÁN ½ SÌLA.TA.ÀM |
| [PAP] | 1.4$^{pi}$.0 | 23 ½ | 3.2.3 | *ak-lu*$_4$ *la-a a-ša*-[*bu*] |
| | TA $^{iti}$NE.GAR EN $^{iti}$ZÍZ ŠE ⸢BÀD$^?$⸣-[ | | | |
| L.e. | MU.9.KAM *Na-zi*-[ | | | |

## 238. CUNES 52-13-060

-.X.19 Nazi-Maruttaš
Sealed by Rīmūtu.

| | UDU.NÍTA | MÁŠ | MU.BI.IM |
|---|---|---|---|
| Obv. | | 2 | *a-na* KÁ$^{meš}$ *mu-uḫ-ḫu-ri* |
| | | 2 | *a-na* GIG$^{meš}$ *a-ka-li* |
| | 1 | | $^{m}$*Ta-qí-šu*$_{14}$ $^{lú}$ḪAL |
| | | 1 | $^{m}$*Ku-ub-bu-t*[*u*] $^{lú}$NAR |
| Rev. PAP | 1 | 5 | *ak-lu*$_{4}$ $^{m}$*Ku-ru-ú* $^{lú}$SIPA |

L.e. $^{iti}$AB.È MU.19.KAM
[*N*]*a-zi-Ma-ru-ut-taš*
LUGAL.E
NA$_{4}$.KIŠIB $^{m}$*Ri-mu-tu*$_{4}$

Translation

| | Male sheep | Male goat | Its entry |
|---|---|---|---|
| Obv. | | 2 | For the gates' offering. |
| | | 2 | For feeding the sick ones. |
| | 1 | | Taqīšu, diviner. |
| | | 1 | Kubbutu, musician. |
| Rev. Total | 1 | 5 | *aklu*-expenditure: Kurû, shepherd. |

L.e. Month X, year 19
of King Nazi-Maruttaš.
Seal of Rīmūtu.

Commentary

2. According to the references quoted in the dictionaries, this would be the first attestation of *muḫḫuru* "offering" in MB texts (CAD M/II, *muḫḫuru*, 176; AHw II, *miḫḫuru*(*m*), *mu/aḫḫurum*(*m*), 651).

## 239. CUNES 53-01-167

-.VIII–XII.22 Nazi-Maruttaš

Summary of *aklu*-expenditures issued over several months (at least from month VIII till month XII) of the 22$^{nd}$ year of Nazi-Maruttaš.

Obv. [ ]
[ ]
[x x x] ⸢x⸣ [
[x x x n]e$^?$ [
0.0.1 $^{m⸢d}$30$^?$-*in*$^{?⸣}$-[
$^{iti}$APIN.DU$_8$.[A
⸢PAP 0.0.2⸣ [
1 SÌLA $^{m⸢d⸣}$AMAR.UTU-MU-MU DUMU ⸢$^m$*Ì-lí-a-a-b*⸣[*a-aš*]
½ SÌLA $^{md}$[*Nin-urta-d*]*i-na-an-ni ka-*⸢*ṣi*⸣*-*[*rù*] ⸢x x x⸣
1 SÌLA $^{m}$⸢x-x⸣-[x]-⸢x⸣$^{meš}$-*šu pi-iš-ša-tu*$_4$
½ SÌLA $^{m}$É-⸢*ra-bi*⸣ *a-na* EDIN *šu-ṣi-i*
PAP 3 SÌLA $^{iti}$GAN.GAN.È
1 SÌLA $^{m}$SU-$^{d}$*Šu-qa-mu-na ṣú-ḫur-tu*$_4$
1 SÌLA *ša ra-ka-*[*si* KASKAL URU-Ì]R-GAŠAN $^{f}$GAŠAN-*ba-rat im-ḫur*
1 SÌLA *pi-iš-*⸢*ša*⸣*-*[*tu*$_4$ $^{m}$]$^{d}$*Nin-urta*-DUGUD-ŠEŠ$^{meš}$-*šu*
PAP 3 SÌLA $^{iti}$AB.È
Rev. 2 SÌLA *ša ra-ka-si* KASKAL URU-ÌR-GAŠAN
2 SÌLA $^{f}$GAŠAN-*ba-rat a-na ra-ma-ni-ša im-ḫ*[*ur*]
1 SÌLA $^{md⸢}$*Nuska*⸣*-na-bu-šu*
PAP 5 [SÌLA $^{iti}$]ZÍZ.A.AN
0.0.1 $^{m⸢}$ÌR-$^{d}$U.GUR⸣ SIPA ANŠE.KUR.RA$^{meš}$
*ša* DUMU.LUGAL
5 SÌLA $^{f}$GAŠAN-*ba-rat*
1 SÌLA $^{md}$*Nuska-na-bu-šu*
PAP 0.0.2 $^{iti}$ŠE.KIN.KU$_5$
ŠU.NIGIN 1 PI *ak-lu*$_4$ $^{md}$*Nin-ur*[*ta*-M]U-MU
MU.22.KAM *Na-*[

COMMENTARY

8. For the restoration of the PN, see **no. 277**: 48′.
9. The PN might have been Ninurta-kabit-aḫḫēšu ($^{md}$*Nin-urta*-DUGUD-ŠEŠ$^{meš}$-*šu*, cf. l. 14).
13. "1 *qû*: to be assigned [(for?) the trip (to?) A]rad-bēlti; Bēltu-bārat received (it)" (cf. CUSAS 30 277: 6). Restorations are based on l. 16. The PN Bēltu-bārat occurs also in CUSAS 30 142: 20 (collated).
17. "2 *qû*: Bēltu-bārat received for herself."

## 240. CUNES 52-18-815

[ . . . ].III.8 Kadašman-Turgu

Sealed by [ . . . ].

The tablet's surface is very eroded and it is not possible to detect the presence of a seal impression.

Obv. ⸢ŠE⸣ $^{giš}$BÁN 5 SÌLA MU.BI.I[M]
9.4.4 2 SÌLA *ak-l*[*u*$_4$]
$^{md}$*Nin-urta*-GI-KA-[*šu*]
[x x] *ak-lu*$_4$ $^{m}$*Ri-mu-*[

0.3$^{?pi}$.0 *ak-lu*$_4$ ⸢$^{md}$⸣[
L.e. PAP 11.⸢x⸣.[x
Rev. [x x] ⸢x x⸣ [
[(x)] ⸢x x⸣ [
[x] ⸢x x x⸣ [
⸢$^{iti}$SIG$_4$.GA⸣ TA U$_4$.12$^+$.[KAM
⸢MU.8.KAM⸣ *Ka-dáš-man-*⸢*Túr*⸣-[*gu*]
[ LUGAL.E]
⸢NA$_4$.KIŠIB⸣ $^{m}$[

## 241. CUNES 52-14-085

-.I–VII.13$^?$ Kadašman-Turgu

Summary of *aklu*-expenditures issued during the 13$^{th?}$ year of the reign of Kadašman-Turgu.

The obverse records quantities of flour and barley and the number of sealed documents concerning beer issued over a timespan that probably covered the first seven months of the year. The reverse records amounts of beer, large jars, and three other items whose nature cannot be established due to the poor state of preservation of the tablet; we can say, though, that the amounts in col. iii–iv were listed in terms of capacity measures and that col. v seems to have had a structure similar to that of the last column of the obverse; the time span covered by the reverse probably corresponded to four months.

Obv. [*a*]*k-lu*$_4$ GABA.RI ⸢*ka*⸣-*ni-ka-a-ti* ⸢MU.13$^?$⸣.[KAM] *Ka-dáš-man-Túr-g*[*u*]

| | ZÌ.DA | ŠE | [*k*]*a-nik-tu*$_4$ KAŠ | |
|---|---|---|---|---|
| | ⸢5$^+$.2⸣.4 4 SÌLA | 3.2.4 3 SÌLA | 1 | $^{iti}$BÁR.ZAG.[GAR] |
| | ⸢5$^+$⸣.4.3 4 SÌLA | 1.3.4 | 1 | $^{iti}$GU$_4$.[SI.SÁ] |
| | ⸢5$^+$⸣.1.4 | 1.1.3 4 SÌLA | 1 | $^{iti}$SIG$_4$.[GA] |
| | ⸢8⸣.1.5 6 ½ SÌLA | 1.0.2 3 SÌLA | 1 | $^{iti}$ŠU.NUMUN.[NA] |
| | ⸢2$^+$.x.4 4⸣ SÌLA | 2.2.2 5 SÌLA | 1 | $^{iti}$NE.N[E.GAR] |
| | 4.⸢0.0⸣ 6 SÌLA | 1.1.4 4 SÌLA | 1 | $^{iti}$KIN.$^{d}$[INANNA] |
| | 4.3.1 ⸢x⸣ SÌLA | 1.1$^{pi}$.0 2 SÌLA | 1 | $^{iti}$⸢DU$_6^?$.K⸣[Ù$^?$ E[N$^?$ |
| PAP | 53.1$^{pi}$.0 ½ SÌLA | 12.3.4 3 SÌLA | ⸢7⸣ [ | |

L.e. ŠU.NIGIN 1-*šu* 5.4.4 [
13.2.4 LA'[U$_4$

| Rev. | KAŠ.ÚS | DUG.G[AL$^?$] | [x x] | [x x] | [ | |
|---|---|---|---|---|---|---|
| | ⸢1-*šu* 1⸣ 4 SÌLA | 1 | | | 1 | [ |
| | 1 ME 2 4 SÌLA | 1 ½ | 0.0.3 1 | 0.1.3 | 1 | $^{i}$[$^{ti}$ |
| | ⸢1-*šu*⸣ 2 | ⸢4$^?$⸣ | | | 1 | $^{i}$[$^{ti}$ |
| | 50$^+$⸢x⸣ | 1 | 2 SÌLA | | 1 | $^{it}$[$^{i}$ |
| | 50$^+$⸢x⸣ | ⸢3$^?$⸣ ½ | 3 SÌLA | | | $^{it}$[$^{i}$ ⸢x⸣[ |
| PAP | 3 ME 26 5 ½ SÌLA | 11 | 0.0.3 6 | 0.1.3 | 4 [ | |

L.e. 12.0.3 1 SÌLA ŠE $^{giš}$BÁN <GAL$^?$> *ak-lu*$_4$
5.4.3 ÍB.TAK$_4$ ŠE $^{giš}$BÁN GAL ŠU ⸢$^{md}$30⸣-TI-U[RU$_4$]

Commentary

1. "*aklu*-expenditure, a copy of the sealed documents of year 13$^?$ of Kadašman-Turgu."

2. The heading of col. iii ("sealed document (concerning) beer") is unusual, but see also DUB *si-bu-*[*ti*] "tablet (concerning) the brewing/tavern" in CUSAS 30 428: 3.
18. "363 *sūtu* (and) 1 *qû* of barley, (measured by) the <big$^{?}$> *sūtu*: *aklu*-expenditure."
19. "177 *sūtu*, remaining barley, (measured by) the big *sūtu*, (which is still) at the disposal of Sîn-balāṭa-ī[riš]."

## 242. CUNES 52-16-056 (Plate No. 54)

-.VI.14 Kadašman-Turgu

Sealed with the seal usually used by Ninurta-zākir-šumi.

| | | | |
|---|---|---|---|
| Obv. | [ŠE $^{giš}$BÁ]N$^{?}$ [KIN$^{?}$].SIG$^{?}$ | ŠE $^{giš}$BÁN 5 SÌLA | MU.BI.IM |
| | [ ]⸢1$^{?}$⸣ | 0.1$^{pi}$.0 | É *pu-uḫ-ri* |
| | | ⸢0.0.2⸣ | *ki-is-pu* ⸢*ša*$^{?}$⸣ SISKUR$^{⸢?⸣}$ |
| | | ⸢x⸣ | DUMU.MUNUS $^{m}$ÁG-⸢*kit*$^{?}$⸣-*ti* |
| | [ ] | [ ] | [$^{m}$]⸢x⸣-$^{d}$50 ŠE.BA ⸢x x x⸣ |
| | [ ] | [ ] | [x x] ⸢x x x x⸣ |
| | [ ] | [ ] | [x] ⸢x x⸣ [x x] |
| L.e. | [ ] | [ ] | [x]$^{meš}$ *ša in-*[ |
| | | | ⸢x x x ZÌ.DA *ša*⸣ *a-na ba*$^{?}$-[ |
| Rev. | [ ] | [ ] | ŠUKU UDU$^{meš}$ ⸢*ša*⸣ $^{m⸢}$*Ki*$^{?⸣}$-[ |
| | | | ŠU$^{?}$ $^{f}$*Ú-ḫa*$^{?}$-*ti* |
| | | | TA NIBRU$^{ki}$ |
| | | | *a-na* BÀD-$^{d+}$*E*[*n-líl*$^{ḫi.a/meš.}$]$^{⸢ki⸣}$ |
| | | | *iš-šu-*⸢*ni*⸣ |
| | [ ] | [ ] | ⸢KI.MIN⸣ *ša* $^{f}$*Qa-diš-*⸢*ta*$^{?}$⸣ |
| | | | TA KI.MIN *a-na* KI.MIN *iš-šu-ni* |
| | [ ] | [x.x].⸢5$^{?}$⸣ | *ak-lu*$_{4}$ ⸢*ša*⸣ $^{m}$É-*ra-bi* |
| L.e. | | | $^{iti}$KIN.$^{d}$INANNA |
| | | | MU.14.KAM |
| | | | *Ka-dáš-man-Túr-gu* LUGAL.⸢E⸣ |

COMMENTARY

2. Until now, the only attestation of *bīt puḫri* "assembly house" in MB sources was in a text from Dūr-Kurigalzu mentioning a "brewer of the assembly house" (cf. Sassmannshausen 2001, 178; CAD P, *puḫru* A 1b 5′, 489).
8. "Fodder for the sheep of Ki[ . . . ]; at the disposal of Uḫatu$^{?}$: they brought here to Dūr-Enlilē from Nippur."
9. "Ditto of Qadištu: they brought (it) here to ditto (i.e., Dūr-Enlilē) from ditto (i.e., Nippur)." One would expect $^{f}$*Qa-diš-ti*.

## 243. CUNES 52-19-141

-.VII–VIII.[ . . . ] Kadašman-Turgu

Account of lambs delivered as *aklu*-expenditures for different purposes (*naptanu*-meals, travel provisions, and an offering) over several months (at least months VII–VIII).

| | | | |
|---|---|---|---|
| Obv. | ⸢SILA$_4$$^{?}$⸣$^{meš}$ MU.BI.I[M] | | |
| | 1 | √ | ⸢KIN.SIG *Ba-ṣa*⸣*-a-ti*$^{ki}$ |
| | 1 | √ | ⸢KIN.SIG x x x⸣ $^{iti}$⸢DU$_6$$^{?}$.KÙ$^{?}$⸣ |
| | 1 | √ | KIN.⸢SIG x x x$^{meš}$⸣ $^{iti}$DU$_6$ |
| | 1 | √ | KIN.SIG KI.MIN $^{iti}$APIN.DU$_8$.A |
| | 1 | | NINDA.KASKAL $^{m}$LÚ-$^{d}$30 ⸢ḪUR.SAG⸣.KALAM.⸢MA⸣ |
| | 1 | √ | NINDA.KASKAL DIRI$^{?}$ $^{m}$ŠEŠ-SUM-*na*-$^{d}$AMAR.UTU $^{iti}$APIN |
| | 1 | √ | SISKUR É $^{d}$*Gu-la* |
| | | | $^{f}$*Bu-un-na*-$^{d}$*Gu-la* $^{iti}$[ |
| Rev. | [1] | | ⸢KIN.SIG x x x x⸣ $^{iti}$⸢DU$_6$.KÙ⸣ |
| | 1 | | KIN.⸢SIG x x x x⸣ $^{iti}$DU$_6$.KÙ |
| PAP | 9 | | *ak*-[*lu*$_4$] |
| | ÍB.⸢TAK$_4$ $^{md}$⸣[x-x]*-ia-tu* ⸢x$^{?}$⸣ | | |
| | [x x x x] x x | | |
| L.e. | [MU.X.KAM *Ka*]*-dáš-man-Túr-gu* | | |

COMMENTARY

7. If the reading DIRI is correct, here it might have had the meaning *atru* "extra, additional."

## 244. CUNES 52-13-079

-.XII.8 Kudur-Enlil

Account of flour and barley issued as *aklu*-expenditures during month XII of the 8$^{th}$ year of Kudur-Enlil.

| | [ZÌ].DA | ŠE | M[U.B]I.I[M] |
|---|---|---|---|
| Obv. | | 0.0.1 | ˹ŠUKU ANŠE˺.KUR.RA x[ |
| | 0.0.1 | 0.0.2 | ŠUKU ANŠE $^{m}$*Qu-nu-nu* [<br>KASKAL *Di-nik-tu*$_4^{ki}$ |
| | 0.0.3 2 SÌLA | | ki ˹x x˺ TA U$_4$.1$^+$.[KAM<br>[EN] U$_4$.21.˹KAM˺ |
| | 0.0.5<br>˹x x x˺ | ˹x x˺ | ˹x x x˺ *ša dul-li*<br>[T]A U$_4$.2.KAM EN U$_4$.21.KAM |
| | ˹x.x.x˺<br>˹x x x˺ | 0.1$^{pi}$.˹x 3$^?$ SÌLA$^?$˺<br>˹x x x˺ | [$^{m}$x-x]-˹*ni*˺-*ia* TA [U$_4$].3.[KAM]<br>[EN] U$_4$.15.KA[M] |
| | | | [$^{m}$KI.MIN$^?$] U$_4$.16.KAM NI[BRU$^?$]$^{˹ki?˺}$ |
| | 0.0.1 1 ½ SÌLA | 0.0.3 3 SÌLA | ˹$^{m}$KI.MIN˺ TA U$_4$.17 EN U$_4$.˹21˺.KAM |
| | 0.0.2 2 SÌLA | | $^{m}$*Ḫu-un-zu-ú*<br>TA U$_4$.3.KAM EN U$_4$.15.KAM |
| | ˹x.x.1$^?$˺ | | $^{m}$KI.MIN U$_4$.16.KAM NIBRU[$^{ki}$] |
| | ˹x.x.x˺ | | $^{m}$KI.MIN EN U$_4$.17.[KAM]<br>EN U$_4$.21.[KAM] |
| Rev. | [x.x].˹x˺ | ˹0.1$^{pi}$.0˺ | DUMU $^{m}$*Ri*$^?$-*ša-tu*$^?$ x [<br>$^{m}$*Qu-nu-nu* ˹x x˺ |
| | | 0.1$^{pi}$.0 | $^{f}$*A-ta-mar*-<ŠU>-*sa* MUNUS.NA[R]<br>U$_4$.2.KAM |
| | | 0.1$^{pi}$.0 | DUMU $^{m}$*Ri-gim*-$^{d}$IŠKUR $^{lú}$ENGAR |
| | 0.0.1 | 0.0.2 | ŠUKU ANŠE $^{m}$*Iz-kùr*-$^{d}$[<br>*a-na Di-nik*-[*tu*$_4^{ki}$] |
| | | 1.1.3 | ŠUKU $^{m}$*Bar-za-m*[*u*$^?$<br>TA U$_4$.3.[KAM]<br>EN U$_4$.15.KAM [x x] x |
| | | ˹x.x.x˺ | ˹x x U$_4$.15$^?$.KAM˺ [x x] ˹x˺ [ |
| | | ˹x.x.x˺ | [x] ˹x TA U$_4$.x.˺[KAM EN] ˹U$_4$.21$^+$.KAM˺ |
| | 2 SÌLA | | ˹$^{m}$*Qu*˺-*nu-nu* [x x x U$_4$].˹16$^+$˺.[KAM] |
| | 0.2.3 | | ˹$^{m}$KI.MIN *a*$^?$-*na*˺ NIBRU$^{˹ki˺}$<br>˹*a-na* x (x)˺ EN É *iš-ši* |
| | | 0.1.4 | ˹ŠUKU ANŠE$^?$ $^{md}$30-x-x˺<br>˹x˺ [ |
| U.e. | [x].˹x˺.3 4 SÌLA | 3.0.5<br>2 SÌLA | *ak-l*[*u*$^?$<br>ŠU [<br>*la* ˹*a*˺-[*ša-bu*<br>$^{iti}$ŠE.K[IN.KU$_5$]<br>MU.8.KAM $^{d}$*Ku-d*[*ur*-$^{d+}$*En-líl*] |

COMMENTARY

11. EN $U_4$.17.[KAM] must be a scribal error for TA $U_4$.17.KAM.

12. The reading of the PN is uncertain: Rīšatu is usually a feminine name, written with -*tu*$_4$ at the end.

13. The musician Ātamar-qāssa occurs frequently in the later texts of the archive; see the attestations in van Soldt 2015, 537.

14. The plowman Rigim-Adad is attested also in CUSAS 30 91: 18 (KuE 6).

20. For the *bēl bīti*, see Sassmannshausen 2001, 144–50; van Soldt 2015, 34, 578–79.

## 245. CUNES 52-12-063

8.II.9 Kudur-Enlil

Obv. 1 ⸢$SILA_4$⸣ KIN.SIG $^{iti}$G[$U_4$.SI.S]Á
$^{m}$*Qu-nu-nu sak-ru-maš*$^{?}$ $^{it}$[$^{i?}$
[1 SI]$LA_4$ *ba-ru-tu*$_4$ *ša* $^{lú}$KID.MAŠ
4 ⸢$^{iti}$⸣$GU_4$.SI.SÁ $U_4$.8.KAM
L.e. PAP 2 *ak-lu*$_4$
Rev. ŠU $^{m}$*Qu-nu-ni*
$^{lú}$SIPA
⸢MU⸣.9.KAM
$^{d}$*Ku-dur-*$^{d+}$*En-líl*
10 LUGAL.E

COMMENTARY

2. The *sakrumaš* Qunnunu occurs also in CUSAS 30 390, an *aklu*-expenditure of rams that dates to the accession year of Šagarakti-Šuriaš.

6–7. The shepherd Qunnunu occurs also in CUSAS 30 391, an account of sheep and goats delivered by him and by another shepherd to a number of individuals, which dates to ŠŠ 1. A Qunnunu, whose profession is not indicated, is responsible for the delivery of sheep also in CUSAS 30 384 (KuE 6$^{?}$) and 386 (KuE 8).

# 2. ADMINISTRATION OF ANIMAL HUSBANDRY

## 2.1 Sheep

### 246. CUNES 53-01-132

3.VI.14 Nazi-Maruttaš
Sealed.

Obv. 1 ⸢UDU x⸣ [
1 ⸢UDU.NÍTA $^{m}$*Bu*$^{?}$-x-x⸣
PAP 2 ⸢x x x⸣
4 ŠU $^{m}$⸢IBILA$^{?}$⸣-[x-x]-⸢x⸣
Rev. $^{iti}$KIN.$^{d}$INANNA
U$_4$.3.KAM
MU.14.KAM
*Na-zi-Ma-ru-ut-ta-aš*
LUGAL.[E]

COMMENTARY
4. The person responsible for these sheep might have been Apil-Nergal ($^{m}$IBILA-$^{d}$U.GUR), known as a shepherd from **no. 251** and mentioned as the person responsible of livestock also in **nos. 250** and **257**.

### 247. CUNES 52-18-771

-.VI.19 Nazi-Maruttaš
Sealed by Rīmūtu.

Obv. 1 UDU.[NÍT]A$^{?}$
$^{m}$*Bíl-lu-lu* $^{lú}$N[AG]AR
1 UDU.NÍTA [$^{m}$]⸢GAL-*a-šá*⸣-$^{d}$AMAR.UTU
4 PAP 2 DUMU $^{m}$*Ṭab-bi-ḫi*
Rev. $^{iti}$KIN.$^{d}$INANNA
MU.19.KAM
*Na-zi-Múru-taš*
⸢LUGAL.E⸣
NA$_4$.KIŠIB $^{m}$*Ri-mu-tu*$_4$

COMMENTARY
4. The son of Ṭābiḫu is probably Iqīša-Marduk, who appears also in another text regarding livestock (**no. 256**: 8–9); cf. Index of Personal Names.

## 248. CUNES 52-16-070

-.VI.21 Nazi-Maruttaš

Sealed.

This document, whose obverse is almost completely lost, has been included in this category because, if the reading 1-⸢*en*$^{?}$ *ba-aq-nu*$^{?}$⸣ in l. 5 is correct, the presence of a form of *baqānu* "to pluck" suggests that the text concerned sheep.

| | | |
|---|---|---|
| Obv. | [x x] | [ |
| | ⸢x⸣ | [x x x x x $^{m}$*E*]*ri*$^{?}$-*bu-ni* |
| | | [x x x x x m]aš$^{?}$ |
| | | 1 [x x x x x] |
| | | 1 [x x x x x-$^{d}$]AMAR.UTU |
| | PAP 2 | 2 ⸢x⸣ [ |
| L.e. | | 1-⸢*en*$^{?}$ *ba-aq-nu*$^{?}$ x x⸣ |
| Rev. | $^{iti}$KIN.$^{d}$INANNA | |
| | MU.21.KAM | |
| | *Na-zi-Múru-taš* | |
| | LUGAL.E | |

COMMENTARY

3–4. The first sign could also be the determinative of a masculine personal name, rather than a numeral.

5. For 1-⸢*en*$^{?}$ *ba-aq-nu*$^{?}$⸣ "once-plucked," see Morrison 1981, 272.

## 249. CUNES 53-01-160

-.-.24 (Nazi-Maruttaš)

The text is assigned to the reign of Nazi-Maruttaš because of the presence of Ninurta-zākir-šumi, who probably appears in this text again as an owner of livestock; here, the person responsible for the flock is Rēš-aṣûšu.

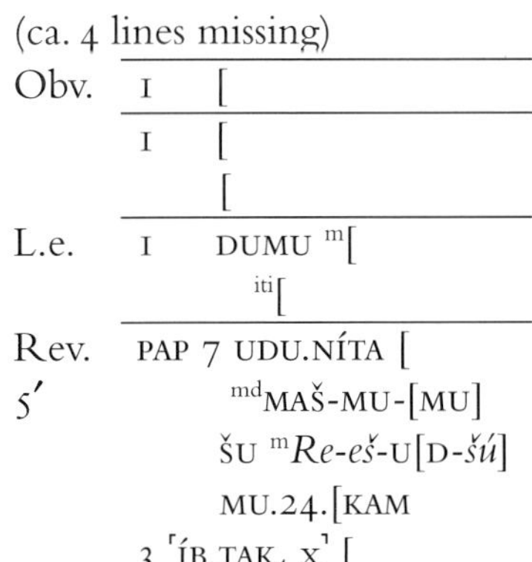

(ca. 4 lines missing)

Obv. 1 [

1 [

[

L.e. 1 DUMU $^{m}$[

$^{iti}$[

Rev. PAP 7 UDU.NÍTA [

$^{md}$MAŠ-MU-[MU]

ŠU $^{m}$*Re-eš*-U[D-*šú*]

MU.24.[KAM

3 ⸢ÍB.TAK$_{4}$ x⸣ [

COMMENTARY

7′. MU is written over an erasure.

## 250. CUNES 52-18-795

1.IV.4$^{?}$ Kadašman-Turgu

Obv. [x] U$_{8}$$^{m}$[$^{eš}$]
[x] ⸢x⸣ nu qu u[š$^{?}$
[š]*a*$^{?}$ MU.⸢24⸣.KAM *Na-z*[*i-*
4 ⸢ŠU⸣ $^{m}$IBILA-$^{d}$U.G[UR]
Rev. $^{iti}$ŠU.NUMUN.NA
U$_{4}$.1.KAM
⸢MU.4$^{?}$.KAM *Ka-daš-man*⸣-[
UMBIN $^{m}$IBI[LA-$^{d}$U.GUR]
*ki-ma* NA$_{4}$.KIŠIB-[*šu*]

Three fingernail impressions on the lower edge of the reverse.

Commentary

4. Apil-Nergal is in charge of sheep also in **no. 251**, where he is identified as shepherd ($^{lú}$SIPA), in **no. 257** and, probably, in **no. 246**.

## 251. CUNES 52-18-798

26.IX.5 Kadašman-Turgu

Sealed by Ninurta-zākir-šumi.

The surface of the obverse is very eroded.

The text's exact content is difficult to assess, but it probably dealt with animals belonging to Ninurta-zākir-šumi that had been entrusted to the shepherd Apil-Nergal; note the remark about Apil-Nergal's hand being "turned" (ll. 9–10).

Obv. ⸢3$^{?}$ MÁŠ$^{?}$⸣ [
⸢*i-na* ŠÀ$^{?}$ x ur$^{?}$⸣ [(x)] ⸢x⸣
⸢x x x⸣ ki ši ⸢x x x⸣
⸢*ki*$^{?}$-*mu*$^{?}$ 2 MÁŠ$^{?}$ x x⸣ [
⸢x x rat$^{?}$⸣
⸢*i-na* ŠU $^{m}$IBILA-$^{d}$U.GUR⸣
L.e. *ša i-na taš-ri-ti*
*ip-šu*
Rev. ŠU $^{m}$IBILA-$^{d}$U.GUR
$^{lú}$SIPA *tur-ra*[*t*]
$^{iti}$GAN.GAN.⸢È⸣
U$_{4}$.26.KAM
MU.5.KAM *Ka-dáš-man-Túr-gu*
LUGAL.E
[NA$_{4}$].KIŠIB $^{md}$*Nin-*[*urta*]-
MU-[MU]

COMMENTARY

7–8. "which he made at the beginning$^?$" or "which he made on the *tašrītu*-festival$^?$": *tašrītu* could indicate either the beginning of a period of time or of a process (e.g., illness or recovery), or a festival (CAD T, *tašrītu*, 297–98; AHw III, *tašrītu(m)*, 1340), but it is not clear what it means in this context. Note that the other MB occurrences listed by CAD are spelled *ta-áš-ri-ti*.

### 252. CUNES 52-12-053 (Plate No. 55)

22.II.14 Kadašman-Turgu

The text certificates that 96 sheep "entered the plucking house" (*bīt buqūni*).

Obv. 6 UDU.NÍTA
84 U$_8$ GAL
6 U$_8$ *na-ḫi-ta-a-tu*$_4$
PAP 96 U$_8$.UDU$^{ḫi.a}$
⸢*ša i-na*⸣ É *bu-qu-ni*
L.e. *i-ru-ba-a-ni*
Rev. $^{iti}$GU$_4$.SI.SÁ
U$_4$.22.KAM
MU.14.KAM
*Ka-dáš-man-Túr-gu*
LUGAL.E

Translation

Obv. 6 rams
84 full-grown ewes
6 ewes with blunted horns$^?$
In total: 96 sheep
5–6 that entered the plucking house.
Rev. Month II,
day 22,
year 14 of
King Kadašman-Turgu.

COMMENTARY

3. Cf. 23 U$_8$ [GA]L EN 4 *na-aḫ*$^?$*-ta-a-ti* EN 2 *ba-aq-na-a-ti* "23 full-grown ewes, including 4 with blunted horns(?) (and) including 2 plucked ones" in CUSAS 30 380: 2–3; van Soldt (2015, 464) comments that "the reading of the sign AḪ is not certain. ḪI is also possible." Both *na-ḫi-ta-a-tu*$_4$ as well as *na-aḫ*$^?$*-ta-a-ti* should be forms related to **naḫātu*, which is attested in the D-stem (*nuḫḫutu*) with the meaning "to trim, clip" (van Soldt 2015, 464; Tropper 1995).

5. According to Sassmannshausen (2001, 177), the only other MB attestation of the "plucking house" (*bīt buqūni*) comes from a text from Ur, which similarly records the plucking of sheep (MBTU 72: 1).

## 253. CUNES 52-13-083

17.II.1 Šagarakti-Šuriaš

Account of ewes belonging to Ninurta-kiššat-ilāni and Nippurītu, two of the "main actors" of the administration in the later phase of the archive (see van Soldt 2015, 24–26).

Obv. 25 U$_{8}$.GAL
*ša* $^{md}$*Nin-urta*-KIŠ-DINGIR$^{meš}$
ŠU $^{m}$*Bu-un-nu-ti*
*it-ti* $^{m}$*I-ri-bi*
⸢DUMU$^{?}$⸣ $^{m}$*Ab*-⸢x⸣-[
$^{iti}$GU$_{4}$.SI.⸢SÁ U$_{4}$.17⸣.[KAM]
MU.1.⸢KAM $^{d}$*Ša*⸣*-garak-t*[*i-Šu*]*-ri-aš*

---

10 U$_{8}$.GAL
*ša* $^{f}$*Ni-ip-pu-ri-ti*
ŠU $^{m}$*Bu-un-nu-ti*
*it-ti* $^{m}$KI.MIN ⸢x⸣[
L.e. $^{iti}$GU$_{4}$.SI.SÁ
U$_{4}$.17.KAM
Rev. MU.1.KAM
$^{d}$KI.MIN

Translation

Obv. 25 full-grown ewes
of Ninurta-kiššat-ilāni,
under the supervision of Bunnūtu,
(are) with Irību,
⸢son$^{?}$ of⸣ Ab[ . . . ];
month II, day 17,
year 1 of Šagarakti-Šuriaš.

---

10 full-grown ewes
of Nippurītu,
under the supervision of Bunnūtu,
(are) with ditto (i.e., Irību) ⸢ . . . ⸣[ . . . ];
month II,
day 17,
year 1
of ditto (i.e., Šagarakti-Šuriaš).

Commentary

3, 10. Bunnūtu is probably the same shepherd who occurs in several other texts dated to the reign of Šagarakti-Šuriaš. See the attestations given by van Soldt 2015, 541.

## 2.2 Goats

### 254. CUNES 52-18-770

-.VIII.19 Nazi-Maruttaš

Sealed by Ninurta-zākir-šumi.

Account of goats belonging to Ninurta-zākir-šumi, which are under the supervision of Sîn-aḫa-iddina, son of Dābibī.

Obv. 3 [

3 [

2 [

3 [

ŠU.NIGIN 11 ⌜ÙZ?⌝$^{\text{ḫi.a}}$

*ša* $^{\text{md}}$MAŠ-MU-MU

ŠU $^{\text{md}}$30-ŠEŠ-SUM-*na*

DUMU $^{\text{m}}$*Da-bi-bi*

Rev. $^{\text{iti}}$APIN.DU$_8$.[A]

MU.19.KA[M]

*Na-zi-Mu-r*[*u-*

UMBIN $^{\text{md}}$30-[ŠEŠ-SU]M-⌜*na*⌝

NA$_4$.KIŠIB

$^{\text{md}}$MAŠ-MU-MU

Four fingernail impressions on left edge of reverse.

## 2.3 Sheep and Goats

### 255. CUNES 52-10-122

-.-.4 Nazi-Maruttaš

The tablet was too fragile to bake and could not be cleaned.

Obv. ⌜6? U$_8$⌝.UDU$^{\text{ḫi.a}}$

$^{\text{md}}$AMAR.UTU-*lí*-⌜*su*⌝

*ki-mu ša* ⌜*si*?⌝-*bu-ti*

*a-na* $^{\text{m}}$*A-ba-ul-i-de*

⌜DUMU $^{\text{md}}$⌝*Uraš-tu*-⌜*kul-ti*⌝

*id*-⌜*din*⌝-*ma*

*ip-ṭú-ur-šu*

Rev. *iš*?-*tu* MU.4.KAM

⌜*Na-zi-Ma-ru-ut-taš*⌝

LUGAL.E

Translation

| | |
|---|---|
| Obv. | Marduk-līssu |
| 6 | gave |
| 4 | to Aba-ul-īde, |
| 5 | son of Uraš-tukultī, |
| 1 | 6? sheep and goats |
| 3 | instead of that of the tavern and |
| 7 | redeemed? it. |
| Rev. | From? year 4 of |
| | King Nazi-Maruttaš. |

COMMENTARY

1–7. The background of this transaction is unclear. Perhaps Marduk-līssu gave the sheep and goats to Aba-ul-īde in order to pay some debts connected to the tavern?

### 256. CUNES 52-16-068

27.VII.9 Nazi-Maruttaš

According to l. 13, the tablet was sealed by Iqīša-Marduk, but no traces of a seal impression are visible on the surface.

| | |
|---|---|
| Obv. | U$_8$.UDU$^{ḫi.a}$ *ša* ⸢x⸣[ |
| | MU.9.KAM *Na-*⸢*zi*⸣*-M*[*a*?- |
| | ⸢5⸣ UDU.NÍTA⸢$^{meš}$⸣ |
| | 7 U$_8^{meš}$ |
| | 1 MÁŠ |
| | 1 ÙZ |
| L.e. | [PAP] 16 U$_8$.UDU$^{ḫi.a}$ |
| Rev. | [*im*?]-⸢*ḫur*?⸣ |
| | ⸢$^m$BA-*šá*⸣-$^d$AMAR.UTU |
| | [DUMU] $^m$*Ṭa-ab-bi-ḫi* |
| | [$^{iti}$]DU$_6$.KÙ |
| | ⸢U$_4$⸣.27.KAM |
| | ⸢MU⸣.9.KAM |
| | NA$_4$.KIŠIB $^m$BA-*šá*-$^d$⸢AMAR.UTU⸣ |

### 257. CUNES 52-12-027 (Plate No. 56)

3.III.17 Nazi-Maruttaš

Account of sheep and goats belonging to Ninurta-zākir-šumi, which are under the supervision of Apil-Nergal; the text also records the fulfillment of Apil-Nergal's obligations toward the flock's owner (see Introduction §2.3).

| | | |
|---|---|---|
| Obv. | 19 | UDU.NÍTA |
| | 1 ME 58 | U$_8^{ḫi.a}$ |
| | 12 | ⸢SILA$_4$.NIM⸣ |

| | | | |
|---|---|---|---|
| | | ⸢36⸣ | [KIR$_{11}$.NIM] |
| 5 | PAP | 2 ⸢ME 2⸣5 | [BABBAR$^{meš?}$] |
| | | ⸢8⸣ | MÁŠ |
| | | ⸢4⸣2 | ÙZ$^{ḫi.a}$ |
| | | 3 | MÁŠ.TUR |
| 9 | | 10 | $^{munus}$<ÁŠ>.GÀR |

Rev. PAP 1-*šu* 3 ÙZ$^{ḫi.a}$
ŠU.NIGIN 2 ME 88 U$_8$.UDU$^{ḫi.a}$
*ša* $^{md}$MAŠ-MU-MU
ŠU $^{m}$IBILA-$^{d}$U.GUR
*i-na* 1 ME 50 *il-da*
15 *i-na* 10 KUŠ $^{uzu}$SA *ù* Ì
⸢*id-di*⸣-*in*
$^{iti}$SIG$_4$.GA U$_4$.3.KAM
MU.17.KAM
*Na-zi-Ma-ru-ut-taš*
20 UMBIN $^{m}$IBILA-$^{d}$U.GUR

6–7 fingernail impressions on left edge of reverse.

Translation

| | | | |
|---|---|---|---|
| Obv. | | 19 | rams |
| | | 158 | ewes |
| | | 12 | male lambs |
| | | 36 | [female lambs] |
| 5 | Total | 225 | [white ones] |
| | | 8 | he-goats |
| | | 42 | she-goats |
| | | 3 | male kids |
| | | 10 | female kids |

Rev. Total: 63 goats.
Grand total: 288 sheep and goats
of Ninurta-zākir-šumi,
under the supervision of Apil-Nergal.
16 He (i.e., Apil-Nergal) gave
14 50 newborns every 100 (and)
15 hide, sinew, and fat every 10 (dead animals).
Month III, day 3,
year 17 of
Nazi-Maruttaš.
20 Fingernail of Apil-Nergal.

Commentary

4–5. KIR$_{11}$.NIM and BABBAR$^{meš}$ are restored after **no. 262**: 4–5 and CUSAS 30 380: 5–6, which list the same types of sheep.

## 258. CUNES 52-18-863

-.-.19 Nazi-Maruttaš

Only the left part of the obverse is preserved; an unknown number of columns is missing after col. v (PAP). For similar ledgers, see **nos. 259–60**.

U.e. [x x] LA'U$_4$ ⸢na$^{?}$ x x⸣

Obv.

| [UDU$^{?}$] | ⸢U$_8$$^{?}$⸣ | ⸢SILA$_4$$^{?}$⸣.NIM | KIR$_{11}$.NIM | PAP |
|---|---|---|---|---|
| [x] | | 29 | ⸢21$^{?}$⸣ | ⸢81⸣ |
| ⸢4$^{?}$⸣ | ⸢14$^{?}$⸣ | 10 | 10 | [ |
| 82 | 14 | 44 | 41 | [ |

Rev. MU.19.KAM

*Na-zi-Ma-ru-[t]a-aš*

LUGAL.E

## 259. CUNES 52-20-311

-.IX$^{?}$/X$^{?}$.20 Nazi-Maruttaš

Only the central portion of the tablet is preserved; an unknown number of columns is missing to the left and to the right of the preserved part.

For similar ledgers, see **nos. 258** and **260**.

U.e. [. . . $^{iti}$GAN$^{?}$/AB$^{?}$].È MU.20.KAM $^{d}$*Na-zi-Ma-ru-*⸢*ta*⸣*-[aš*

Obv.

| PAP | MÁŠ | ÙZ | MAŠ.TUR | MUNUS.ÁŠ.GAR | PAP | ŠU.N[IGIN] |
|---|---|---|---|---|---|---|
| ⸢1$^{+}$⸣ ME 54 | 84 | 2 ME 49 | 55 | 56 | 4 ME 44 | ⸢6$^{?}$ ME⸣ [ |
| ⸢1$^{?}$ ME⸣ 30 | 16 | 1-*šu* ⸢3$^{+}$⸣ | 8 | 9 | ⸢90$^{+}$⸣ | [ |

The text breaks off; the reverse is completely lost.

## 260. CUNES 52-19-142

-.I$^{?}$/V$^{?}$.[ . . . ] Nazi-Maruttaš

This is the best preserved example of a multicolumn ledger summarizing several flocks of sheep and goats entrusted to different shepherds. For similar ledgers, see also **nos. 258–59**.

| | | | | | | | | | | | | |
|---|---|---|---|---|---|---|---|---|---|---|---|---|
| Obv. | ⸢UDU$^{?}$⸣ | ⸢U$_{8}$$^{?}$⸣ | ⸢SILA$_{4}$$^{?}$⸣ | KIR$_{11}$ | PAP | MÁŠ | ÙZ | MÁŠ.TUR | MUNUS.ÁŠ.GÀR | PAP | ŠU.NIGIN | MU.BI.IM |
| | 25 | 1 ME 37 | 10 | 12 ⸢x⸣ | 1 ME 84 | | | | | | 1 ME 1,24 | $^{md}$IŠKUR-[*mu*]*š*-⸢*te-šìr*⸣ ⸢DUMU $^{md}$IŠKUR⸣-*šam-ḫi*-DINGIR$^{meš}$ |
| | 3 | 70 | 1 | 12 | 1-[*šu*] ⸢26⸣ | 2 | 5 | | 2 | 9 | 1 ME 24$^{?}$ | ⸢$^{m}$DÙ-*ša*-$^{d}$*Gu-la*⸣ |
| 4 | [x] | ⸢x x⸣ | 4 | 8 | 1 ME 1-*šu* 6 | 3 | 4 | 1 | | 8 | ⸢1 ME x x⸣ | DUMU $^{m}$⸢x⸣[ |

Rev.

[$^{iti}$x.x].GAR

[MU.x].KAM

[*Na-z*]*i-Ma-ru-ut-taš*

⸢LUGAL⸣.E

COMMENTARY

3. The spelling $^{m}$DÙ-*ša*-DN is unusual; more often one finds $^{m}$DÙ-*šá*-DN or $^{m}$DÙ-*a*-*šá*-DN. Cf., however, ⌜$^{m}$DÙ?-*ša*-$^{d?}$⌝*Gu*-[*la*] in CUSAS 30 6: 15. The figure in col. xi (ŠU.NIGIN) is partially written over an erasure; the correct grand total would be 104.

### 261. CUNES 52-20-310

Date not preserved.

Account of sheep and goats, with totals referring to three different locations: Dūr-bēl-mātāti, Dūr-Enlilē, and Kār-Nin[ . . . ] (see ll. 21, 39, 47).

Obv. [x] ⌜x za? x x⌝ [

| | ⌜UDU.NÍTA⌝ | ⌜U$_8$⌝ | ⌜MÁŠ⌝ | ⌜ÚZ⌝ | ⌜ŠU.NIGIN⌝ | [ |
|---|---|---|---|---|---|---|
| | | | | 1 | | $^{m}$[ |
| | | 1 | | 1 | | $^{m}$[ |
| | | | | 1 | | $^{m}$[ |
| | 1 | | | | | $^{m}$[ |
| | 1 | | | | | $^{m}$[ |
| | | | | 1 | | $^{m}$⌜x⌝[ |
| | 1 | | | | | $^{md}$[ |
| | 1 | | | | | $^{m}$*Bu-u*[*n-na*-$^{d}$ |
| | 1 | | | | | DUMU $^{m}$⌜*N*⌝[*a*?- |
| | 1 | | | | | DUMU $^{m}$*Bar*-[ |
| | 1 | | | | | $^{m}$*Bu-un-n*[*a*-$^{d}$ |
| | 1 | | | | | DUMU.MUNUS x [ |
| | 1 | 1 | | | | $^{m}$KAR-*ub*-[ |
| | 1 | | | | | $^{m}$ZÁLAG-⌜$^{d}$⌝[ |
| | | 1 | | | | $^{m}$ZÁLAG-EN-$^{d}$*Ku-bi* |
| | | 1 | | | | $^{md}$30-URU$_4$-*iš* |
| | | 1 | | | | DUMU $^{m}$*Ta-ḫi-ri-iš-ti* |
| | | 1 | | | | $^{m}$⌜GAL⌝-*šá*-$^{d}$MAŠ |
| [PAP] | 10 | 6 | | 4 | 20 | BÀD-EN-KUR.KUR$^{ki}$ |
| | | 1 | | | | $^{m}$*Šu-ba*?-*gi-ia* |
| | | 2 | | | | DUMU $^{m}$*E-ri-ši* |
| | | | ⌜1⌝ | | | DUMU $^{m}$*Ṭà-ab*-MI-$^{d}$UTU |
| | | | | | | $^{md}$30-*e-pi-rù* |
| | | 2 | | | | $^{m}$*Uz-na-nu* |
| | [ ] | [ ] | | | | $^{m}$*In-nu-un-nu* |
| L.e. | [ ] | [ ] | [ ] | [ ] | [ ] | $^{m}$SUM-$^{d}$AMAR.UTU |
| Rev. | [ ] | [ ] | [ ] | [ ] | [ ] | $^{m}$⌜GAL⌝-*šá*-$^{d}$⌜UTU?⌝ |
| | [ ] | [ ] | [ ] | [ ] | [ ] | $^{md}$U.GUR-DÙ |
| | [ ] | [ ] | [ ] | [ ] | [ ] | [$^{m}$]ÌR-GAŠAN |
| | [ ] | [ ] | [ ] | [ ] | [ ] | [x x] $^{m}$*Šu*-⌜x x⌝ [ |
| | [ ] | [ ] | [ ] | [ ] | [ ] | ⌜$^{md}$⌝[x x] ⌜x⌝ |
| | [ ] | [ ] | [ ] | [ ] | [ ] | [x x $^{m}$]$^{d}$*Nuska-ib-ni* |
| | [ ] | [ ] | [ ] | [ ] | [ ] | ⌜x x x x⌝ *i-na* ŠÀ KI.MIN |
| | 1 [ ] | [ ] | [ ] | [ ] | [ ] | ⌜$^{m}$GAL?⌝-*šá*-$^{d}$⌝MAŠ KI.MIN |
| | [ ] | [ ] | [ ] | [ ] | [ ] | [$^{m}$BA/GAL]-⌜*šá*⌝-$^{d}$U.GUR |
| | [ ] | [ ] | [ ] | [ ] | [ ] | ⌜$^{md}$⌝MAŠ-EN-DINGIR$^{meš}$ |

| | | | | | | |
|---|---|---|---|---|---|---|
| | PAP [ ] | [ ] | [ ] | ⸢4?⸣ | ⸢22?⸣ | [BÀ]D-⸢d+*En-líl*meš.ki⸣ |
| 40 | [ ] | [ ] | [ ] | [ ] | [ ] | [x x x] *ak-lu*$_4$ |
| | [ ] | [ ] | [ ] | [ ] | [ ] | m*Ḫu-un-zu-'u* |
| | 1 | [ ] | | | | ⸢x x x ḫu?⸣ bi [ |
| | [ ] | [ ] | | | | [x x] ⸢x x x⸣ [ |
| | [ ] | [ ] | [ ] | | | [x x] ⸢x x⸣ [ |
| 45 | [ ] | [ ] | [ ] | ⸢1⸣ | [ ] | [ |
| | 1 | [ ] | [ ] | | [ ] | [ |
| | PAP 4 | [2] | | 1 | 7 | *Kar-*⸢*Nin*?⸣-[ |
| | ⸢x 50?⸣ | | | | | |

COMMENTARY

26. A Uznānu is attested as a shepherd (NA.GADA) at Nippur in the 11th year of Kadašman-Turgu (see BE 14 99a: 8).

### 262. CUNES 52-16-112

Date not preserved.
Sealed by Dimaḫdi-Uraš.

| | | |
|---|---|---|
| Obv. | 41 | ⸢UDU.NÍTA x⸣ za ⸢x⸣ |
| | 1 ME 27 | ⸢U$_8$⸣ |
| | 34 | SILA$_4$.NIM |
| | 27 | KIR$_{11}$.NIM |
| 5 | PAP 2 ME 29 | BABBARmeš |
| | 3 | MÁŠ |
| | [x] | ⸢ÙZ⸣ |

Text breaks off

Rev. (few empty lines)

[NA$_4$.KIŠIB m*Di-ma*]*ḫ-di-*d*Uraš*

## 2.4 Cattle

### 263. CUNES 52-16-028

-.-.23 Nazi-Maruttaš

List of cattle belonging to Ninurta-zākir-šumi, which are under the supervision of the shepherd Namru (see also **no. 264**).

| | | |
|---|---|---|
| Obv. | [x | UTUA] |
| | [x] | ⸢ÁB⸣.GAL |
| | [x] | ÁB MU.3 |
| | 10 | ÁB MU.2 |
| 5 | 25 | GU$_4$ MU.4 |
| | 11 | GU$_4$ MU.3 |
| | 9 | GU$_4$ MU.2 |
| | 10 | ÁB.GA |
| L.e. | ⸢10⸣ | AMAR.GA |

Rev. ⸢PAP⸣ 1 ME 23 ⸢ÁB.GU$_4$$^{\text{ḫi.a}}$⸣
*ša* $^{\text{md}}$*Nin-urta*-MU-MU
ŠU $^{\text{m}}$*Nam-rù* $^{\text{lú}}$SIPA
MU.23.KAM *Na-zi-Múru-taš*
LUGAL.E

A small "12" is written at the end of the reverse, after a few empty lines.

Translation

| | | |
|---|---|---|
| Obv. | [x | bull$^?$] |
| | [x] | full-grown cows |
| | [x] | three-year-old cows |
| | 10 | two-year-old cows |
| | 25 | four-year-old oxen |
| | 11 | three-year-old oxen |
| | 9 | two-year-old oxen |
| | 10 | suckling cows |
| L.e. | 10 | suckling calves |

Rev. Total: 123 bovines
of Ninurta-zākir-šumi,
under the supervision of Namru, the shepherd.
Year 23 of King Nazi-Maruttaš.

COMMENTARY

1. The restoration is suggested by comparison with **no. 264**: 1, a list of another cattle herd belonging to Ninurta-zākir-šumi, and with similar cattle lists from Nippur (e.g., MUN 316, 319, 321).

## 264. CUNES 52-13-003 (Plate No. 57)

3.IX.6 Kadašman-Turgu
Sealed by Ninurta-zākir-šumi.

List of cattle belonging to Ninurta-zākir-šumi, under the supervision of the shepherd Namru (see also **no. 263**); note that the latter will have to deliver ghee "according to (the requirements of) the offerings" (ll. 10–11). This cattle herd is much smaller than the one entrusted by Ninurta-zākir-šumi to Namru in the 23$^{\text{rd}}$ year of Nazi-Maruttaš (no. 263).

| | | |
|---|---|---|
| Obv. | 1 | ⸢UTUA⸣ |
| | 20 | ÁB.GAL ⸢*id*$^?$-*din*$^?$⸣ |
| | 1 | Á[B] ⸢MU 3⸣ |
| | 7 | ÁB ⸢MU 2⸣ |
| | 10 | ÁB.GA |
| | 4 | AMAR.⸢GA⸣ |

PAP 43 ÁB.⸢GU$_4$$^{\text{ḫ}}$⸣$^{\text{i.a}}$
*ša* $^{\text{md}}$*Nin-urta*-MU-MU
ŠU $^{\text{m}}$*Nam-rù* $^{\text{lú}}$SIP[A]

Ì.NUN *a-na* KA SISKUR$^{meš}$
[*i*]-*nam-din*
[$^{it}$]$^{i}$GAN.GAN.È
Rev. U$_4$.3.KAM
MU.6.KAM *Ka-dáš-man-Túr-gu*
LUGAL.E
⸢NA$_4$.KIŠIB⸣ $^{md}$*Nin-urta*-MU-MU

Translation

Obv. 1 bull
20 full-grown cows, ⸢he gave$^?$⸣
1 three-year-old cow
7 two-year-old cows
7 suckling cows
4 suckling calves
Total: 43 bovines
of Ninurta-zākir-šumi,
under the supervision of Namru, the shepherd.
11 He (i.e., Namru) will deliver
10 ghee according to (the requirements of) the offerings.
Rev. Month IX,
day 3,
year 6 of King Kadašman-Turgu.
Seal of Ninurta-zākir-šumi.

### 265. CUNES 52-18-136

13.VIa.7 Kadašman-Turgu

Account of cattle belonging to Ninurta-kīn-pīšu, entrusted to the shepherd Namru. The upper half of the tablet is lost.

Obv. (ca. 5–6 lines missing)
⸢x x x x x x⸣
1 GU$_4$.NÍNDA MU.2
*ta*-KAL-*ti* $^{m}$*Ri-iš*-$^{d}$U.GUR
PAP 26 ÁB.GU$_4^{hi.a}$
*ša* $^{md}$*Nin-urta*-GI-KA-*šu*
DUMU $^{md+}$*En-líl-ki-di-ni*
Rev. $^{m}$*Šu-nu-ḫu* ⸢*im*$^?$-*ḫur*$^?$⸣
⸢ŠU$^?$⸣ $^{m}$*Nam-ri* SIPA
$^{iti}$KIN.$^{d}$INANNA.2.⸢KAM.MA⸣
U$_4$.13.KAM
MU.7.KAM *Ka-dáš-man-Túr-gu*
LUGAL.E
[x x (x) *ma*]*ḫ*$^?$-*rù*
Text breaks off

Translation

Obv. (ca. 5–6 lines missing)

⸢. . .⸣

---

1 two-year-old young ox,

. . . of Rīš-Nergal.

---

Total: 26 bovines

of Ninurta-kīn-pīšu,

son of Enlil-kidinnī.

Rev. Šūnuḫu ⸢received?⸣ (them).

[Under the s]upervision? of Namru, the shepherd.

---

Month VIa,

day 13,

year 7 of King Kadašman-Turgu.

[. . . they were recei]ved?.

Text breaks off

Commentary

3′. *ta*-KAL-*ti* could be read either *ta-kal-ti* or *ta-rib-ti*, but neither *takaltu* "bag, pouch, sheath; stomach" nor *tarībtu* "replacement" fits the context convincingly; furthermore, according to the dictionaries *tarībtu* "replacement" is attested only as a component of PNs (see CAD T, 230; AHw III, 1329 s.v.).

### 266. CUNES 52-16-111

Date not preserved.

The upper part of the obverse is missing. In the preserved part, the text records in the first column plow-oxen (GU$_4$.ŠÀ.GU$_4$), associated with individuals and geographic names in the third and last column; the second column, whose heading is missing, probably recorded some other type of bovine.

In the Nippur texts, plow-oxen often occur in connection with *iššakku*-farmers and *ḫarbu*-fields (see the occurrences in CAD K, *kullizu* 2b, 507). Perhaps the personal and geographic names in this document indicate the farmers and the location of the fields where the plow-oxen were to be employed.

(Beginning broken, several lines missing)

| | | | |
|---|---|---|---|
| Obv. | *a-na* ⸢x⸣ [ | | |
| | GU$_4$.ŠÀ.⸢GU$_4$⸣ | ⸢x⸣ [x] | [ |
| | | 2 | [ |
| | | 2 | [<br>[x x (x)] ⸢x⸣ |
| | | 2 | $^{m}$⸢x-x-SUM-*n*⸣[*a*?]<br>*Ba-ṣa-ti*$^{k}$[⸢i⸣] |
| | | 2 | $^{m}$*Ša-muḫ*-$^{d}$U.GUR<br>*Tu-kul-ti*-É.KUR |
| | | 2 | $^{md}$IŠKUR-*za-kir*<br>*Kar*-$^{d}$*Nuska*$^{ki}$ |
| | | 2 EN 1 ÁB | $^{m}$⸢ZÁLAG-GAŠAN⸣-*Ak-k*[*a-de*]<br>BÀD-$^{d+}$*En-líl*[ |
| Rev. | | 2 EN 1 ÁB | $^{m}$*A-ru*-⸢x⸣[<br>BÀD-$^{d+}$*En*-[*líl* |

| | | | |
|---|---|---|---|
| | | 2 EN 1 ÁB | $^{m}$*Ku-uk-ku-*⌜*ú*⌝-[*a*]<br>*Ḫa-am-ri*$^{ki}$ |
| | | 2 | $^{m}$KI-$^{d}$UTU *Kar-*$^{d}$⌜*Nin*⌝-*É-an-*⌜*na*⌝ |
| | | 2 | $^{m}$*Bu-un-*<*na*>-$^{d}$GÌR<br>*Ḫu-uṣ-lu*$_{4}$$^{ki}$ |
| | | 2 | $^{m}$⌜x⌝[ |
| | | 2 | $^{m}$⌜x⌝[<br>⌜x⌝[ |
| | ⌜4$^{?}$⌝ | ⌜2⌝ | [ |
| PAP | ⌜4$^{?}$⌝ | [x] | [ |

Text breaks off

COMMENTARY

6′. Text written over erasure.

12′. Since the GN Ḫuṣlu is, to my knowledge, otherwise unattested, I wonder whether this might be a mistake for Ḫuṣṣu.

## 3.1 Allocation of Wool as Work Material

### 267. CUNES 52-13-109

-.II.16 Nazi-Maruttaš

The text records the work-assignment (*mandattu*, see Introduction §3.2.3) of a group of women in the 16th year of Nazi-Maruttaš, indicating the types of garments they had to produce and the respective quantities of wool they received in order to carry out the work; a quantity of wool assigned to a man has been added at the end of the text (l. 15).

| | | | |
|---|---|---|---|
| Obv. | *man-da-tu*$_4$ MU.16.KAM *Na-zi-Ma-ru-ut-taš* | SÍG$^{ḫi.a}$ | MU.BI.IM |
| | 1 $^{túg}$*ki-iz-zu* KA ⸢GÙN?⸣ 1 $^{túg}$GÚ.È KI.MIN | 4 MA.⸢NA⸣ | ⸢f⸣*Ia-*⸢*e-a*⸣ |
| | 1 $^{túg}$KI.MIN 1 KI.MIN | 4 MA.NA | $^{f}$UD-⸢x-x⸣-*ni* |
| | ⸢1⸣ [$^{túg}$KI.MIN] 1 KI.MIN | 4 MA.NA | $^{f}$*Ú-ru-*⸢*ba*⸣*-tu*$_4$ |
| | [x x x] ⸢1 KI.MIN⸣ | 4 MA.NA | $^{f}$*Ri-ma-a-tu*$_4$ |
| | [x x x] ⸢1? KI.MIN?⸣ | 3 MA.NA | $^{f}$⸢GAŠAN⸣-*ri-šat* |
| | [x x x] | 3 MA.NA | $^{f}$*Ia-nu-*⸢*kit?*⸣*-tu*$_4$ |
| | [x x x] ras.? | 2/3 MA.NA | $^{f}$*Da-a-an-du* |
| | [x x x] ⸢x x⸣ | 1/2 MA.NA | $^{fd}$*Gu-la-šar-at* |
| | [x x x x x] | 1/2 MA.[NA] | $^{f}$*Ba?-ba*$_6$*?-uṣ-*⸢*ri-šu*⸣ |
| Rev. | [x (x)] ⸢KI.MIN?⸣ | ⸢4?⸣ MA.NA | $^{fd}$*Ištar-di-*⸢*ni?*⸣-x-x⸣ |
| | [(x)] 14 TÚG$^{meš}$ | [ŠU.N]IGIN MA.NA<br>⸢x x x⸣<br>⸢x x *i?*⸣*-na* | *man-da-tu*$_4$<br>*lu-bu-uš-tu*$_4$<br>É $^{m}$*Ni-in-nu-ti* |
| | $^{iti}$GU$_4$.SI.SÁ<br>Line erased at end of reverse | 3 MA.NA | $^{md}$*Nuska*-ŠEŠ-SUM *ar-rap?-ḫa?-a?-*[*a?-ú?*] |

COMMENTARY

13–14. Perhaps the finished products were meant as clothes or the clothing allowance of the House of Ninnutu? The dictionaries do not cite any MB occurrence of *lubuštu* (see CAD L, 232ff.; AHw I, 561 s.v.).

### 268. CUNES 52-16-091

3.V.1 Kadašman-Turgu

Obv. 8 MA.NA SÍG.ÙZ
*i-na* ŠU $^{m}$*In-nu-un-nu* SIPA
$^{m}$NÍG.BA-$^{d}$U.GUR
4 *ma-ḫi-ir*
Rev. $^{iti}$NE.NE U$_4$.3.KAM
MU.1.KAM *Ka-dáš-man-Túr-gu*
LUGAL.E

Translation

Obv. 8 minas of goat hair:
3 Qīšat-Nergal
4 received
2 from Innunnu, the shepherd.
Rev. Month V, day 3,
6–7 year 1 of King Kadašman-Turgu.

COMMENTARY

2. An Innunnu, a "shepherd of donkeys" (SIPA ANŠE$^{(meš)}$), is known from other texts of Kadašman-Turgu (see Index of Personal Names); I wonder whether he might be the same person, even though in this text Innunnu seems to have taken care of goats.

### 269. CUNES 52-17-270

-.-.8 Kadašman-Turgu

According to l. 9, the tablet was sealed by Sîn-balāṭa-īriš, but the surface is too poorly preserved to distinguish a sealing.

Obv. [SÍ]G$^{?}$ MU.BI.[IM]
⸢5⸣ MA.NA $^{iti}$SI[G$_4$.G]A$^{?}$
3 1/3 MA $^{iti}$⸢KIN.$^{d}$INANNA⸣.2.KAM
U$_4$.1.KA[M]
5 [PAP] ⸢8⸣ 1/3 MA.N[A]
Rev. [Š]U $^{md}$30-TI-U[RU$_4$]
MU.8.KAM *Ka-dáš-man-⸢Túr⸣-[gu]*
LUGAL.E
NA$_4$.KIŠIB $^{md}$30-
⸢TI-URU$_4$⸣

Translation

Obv. [Woo]l$^{?}$, its ent[ry]:
⸢5⸣ mina, month [II]I$^{?}$
3 1/3 mina, month VIa,
day 1.
5 [Total]: ⸢8⸣ 1/3 min[a].
Rev. [Responsibi]lity of Sîn-balāṭa-īriš.
Year 8 of King Kadašman-Turgu.
9 Seal of Sîn-
balāṭa-īriš.

## 270. CUNES 52-12-033

18.IV.9 Kadašman-Turgu

Obv. ⸢1/3⸣ MA.NA *ta-kil-tu*$_4$
14 GÍN *ḫa-ṣar-tu*$_4$
1/3 MA.NA $^{\text{síg}}$GA.RÍG
*a-na* 3 $^{\text{túg}}$*ḫúl-la-na-ti*
*ša* UDU.NÍTA$^{\text{meš}}$
$^{\text{m}}$*Na-siq*-$^{\text{d}}$AMAR.UTU UŠ.BAR
L.e. *ma-ḫi-ir*
Rev. $^{\text{iti}}$ŠU.NUMUN.[N]A
U$_4$.18.KAM
MU.9.KAM *Ka-dáš-man-Túr-gu*
LUGAL.E

Translation

Obv. 1/3 mina of blue-purple wool,
14 shekels of green? wool, (and)
1/3 mina of combed wool
for 3 *ḫullānu*-garments,
of rams:
Nasiq-Marduk, the weaver,
L.e. received (it).
Rev. Month IV,
day 18,
year 9 of King Kadašman-Turgu.

Commentary

2. Cf. CAD Ḫ, *ḫaṣartu* (1), 130: "wool or cloth made of a certain color, probably green"; see also comments to **no. 273**: 8.

3. This and **no. 272**: 3, 6 are the first attestations of the logographic writing of *pušikku* "combed wool" in Kassite texts (cf. Aro 1970, 29; CAD P, *pušikku* a, 541–42).

5. "of rams" (*ša* UDU.NÍTA$^{\text{meš}}$) must refer to the origin of the wool listed in the previous lines.

## 271. CUNES 52-18-152

10.XI.13 Kadašman-Turgu

Obv. 10 GÍN $^{síg}$ḪÉ.ME.DA
1(AŠ) 8 GÍN $^{síg}$*ta-bar-rù*
½(MAŠ) 2 GÍN $^{síg}$*ta-kil-*$tu_4$
½(MAŠ) 2 GÍN $^{síg}$ZA.[GÌN$^?$] ⸢x⸣[
⸢½$^?$(MAŠ) 2$^?$⸣ [
Text breaks off
Rev. [$^{m}$ÌR]-$U_4$.9.KAM
⸢UŠ⸣.BAR *ma-ḫi-ir*
$^{iti}$ZÍZ.A.AN $U_4$.10.KAM
MU.13.KAM *Ka-dáš-man-⸢Túr-gu⸣*
LUGAL.E

Translation

Obv. 10 shekels of red wool,
8 shekels of red wool,
2 shekels of blue-purple wool,
2 shekels of bl[ue$^?$] wool,
2$^?$ [ . . . ]:
Text breaks off
Rev. [Arad]-$U_4$.9.KAM,
the weaver, received (it).
Month XI, day 10,
year 13 of King Kadašman-Turgu.

COMMENTARY

1. The logogram $^{síg}$ḪÉ.ME.DA may correspond to either *nabāsu* or *tabarru* (MesZl no. 253), both meaning "red wool" (CAD N/1, *nabāsu*, 21; CAD T, *tabarru*, 21; AHw II, *nabāsu*, 697; AHw III, *tabarru*, 1298). According to CAD, "from MB on, the log. SÍG.ḪÉ.ME.DA has the reading *tabarru*" (CAD N/1, *nabāsu*, 22). However, the fact that in this text a quantity of wool is described in l. 1 as $^{síg}$ḪÉ.ME.DA, while another quantity is described in l. 2 as $^{síg}$*tabarru*, suggests that the scribe meant two different types of wool and that here $^{síg}$ḪÉ.ME.DA probably indicates *nabāsu*.

2–5. I cannot explain the AŠ at the beginning of l. 2 and the MAŠ at the beginning of ll. 3–5.

### 272. CUNES 52-18-796

24.VI.17 Kadašman-Turgu

| | | |
|---|---|---|
| Obv. | | 6 GÍN SÍG SA$_5$ *a-na* ⸢x *ša*? x⸣ |
| | | $^{\text{md}}$IŠKUR-*ša-gim ma-ḫi-ir ta-ba-rù* |
| | | 1 MA.NA $^{\text{síg}}$GA.RÍG SA$_5$ ⸢x x ra bu?⸣ |
| | | ⸢x⸣ MA.NA $^{\text{síg}}$ZA.GÌN *a-na ṣa-pe-e* |
| | PAP | $^{\text{md}}$30-TI.LA-URU$_4$ *ma-ḫi-ir* |
| | | ⸢x x en?⸣ $^{\text{síg}}$GA.RÍG SA$_5$ *a-na muš-ṭa-ti* |
| | | $^{\text{md}}$IŠKUR-*ša-gim ma-ḫi-ir* |
| Rev. | | $^{\text{iti}}$KIN.$^{\text{d}}$INANNA U$_4$.24.KAM |
| | | MU.17.⸢KAM⸣ |
| | | *Ka-dáš-man-Túr-gu* LUGAL.E |

Translation

| | | |
|---|---|---|
| Obv. | | 6 shekels of red-brown wool for . . . : |
| | | Adad-šagim received (it); red wool; |
| | | 1 mina of red-brown combed wool . . . , |
| | | ⸢. . .⸣ mina of blue wool for soaking: |
| | Total | Sîn-balāṭa-īriš received (it). |
| | | . . . of red-brown combed wool for combs?: |
| | | Adad-šagim received (it). |
| Rev. | | Month VI, day 24, |
| | | year 17 |
| | | of King Kadašman-Turgu. |

COMMENTARY

1. Neither Aro 1970 nor the dictionaries attest occurrences of SA$_5$ (Akk. *sāmu*) "red, brown" with reference to wool or garments in Kassite texts.

4. *a-na ṣa-pe-e* "for soaking" (CAD Ṣ, *ṣabû*, 45; AHw III, *ṣapû*, 1082; see Quillien 2017, 100 for the transferred meaning "to dye" in texts from 1st mill. Babylonia) or "for the dyer" (CAD Ṣ, *ṣābû*, 55; AHw III, *ṣāpû*, 1082).

## 3.2 Garments and Textiles

### 273. CUNES 52-12-043

11.X.1 Kadašman-Turgu

| | |
|---|---|
| Obv. | 1 ⸢$^{\text{túg}}$*iš*?⸣-*ḫe-na-be gar-rù* |
| | 1 $^{\text{túg}}$KI.MIN SISKUR |
| | 1 $^{\text{túg}}$*su-un* ŠU |
| | 2 $^{\text{túg}}$KI.MIN *šap-ti* |
| | PAP 5 TÚG$^{\text{ḫi.a}}$ *ša* NIBRU$^{\text{ki}}$ |
| | 2 $^{\text{túg}}$GÚ.È SISKUR |
| | 1 $^{\text{túg}}$KI.MIN KA GÙN |
| | 1 $^{\text{túg}}$ÍB.LÁ *ḫa*-⸢*ṣar*?-*ti*⸣ |
| Rev. | 1 $^{\text{túg}}$*in-di-la-rù* |
| | 1 $^{\text{túg}}$*su-un šap-ti* |
| | 1 $^{\text{túg}}$KI.MIN *qer-šu ta*-⸢*kil-tu*$_4$⸣ |
| | 1 $^{\text{túg}}$*na-ak-par-tu*$_4$ SISKUR |

PAP 8 TÚG$^{hi.a}$ *i-na* ⌜ŠÀ⌝
*ša ur-ra-a-ti*
ŠU $^{m}$*Su-un-gi-ir-bu-ni*
$^{iti}$AB.È $U_4$.11.KAM
MU.1.KAM
L.e. *Ka-dáš-man-Túr-gu*
LUGAL.E

Translation

Obv. 1 *išḫenabe*-garment, wavy?
1 ditto (as) votive offering
1 cloth for the hand(s)
2 clothes for the lip(s)
Total: 5 garments of Nippur
2 cloaks (as) votive offering
1 ditto with multicolored trimmings
1 belt (made of) green? wool
Rev. 1 *indilaru*-garment
1 cloth for the lip(s)
1 ditto, with a strip? of blue-purple wool
1 *nakpartu*-garment (as) votive offering
Total: 8 garments from (those)
of the barns?.
Responsibility of Sugir-bunni.
Month X, day 11,
year 1
L.e. of King Kadašman-Turgu.

Commentary

1. The word *gar-rù* appears in these texts usually in connection with *išḫenabe*-garments (see **no. 281**: 1, **no. 287**: 1, 6, **no. 289**: 1, CUSAS 30 365: 24, and CUSAS 30 366: 4); Aro 1970 does not quote any attestation from Nippur. In the dictionaries one finds only the word *garru*, describing some kind of container (AHw I, 282; CAD G, 51 s.v.), and in CUSAS 30 365: 24 it might have had the determinative GIŠ; van Soldt (2015, 447) suggested that it might have been a box used for the *išḫenabe*-garments. I wonder whether it could be a verbal adjective from *q/garāru*, which is attested with the meaning "to be wavy, ribbed" with reference to house roofs (AHw II, *q/garāru(m)* G 4, 902); the same meaning could apply also to fabrics.

8. For *ḫaṣartu*, probably meaning green wool, see AHw I, *ḫaṣa/ertu(m)* 2, 331 and CAD Ḫ, *ḫaṣartu* (1), 130. See also **no. 270**: 2 and probably also CUSAS 30 375: 8, where van Soldt read $^{túg}$ÍB.LÁ *ḫa*-x-*ti*?.

9. The word *indilaru* is attested also in **no. 280**: 3, CUSAS 30 370: 9, CUSAS 30 372: 20, and CUSAS 30 373: 6. See discussion in van Soldt 2015, 455.

11. For *qeršu* referring to textiles, the dictionaries attest only MB examples and suggest the translations "Wollschal" or simply "fabric" (cf. AHw II, *qeršu*, 918; CAD Q, *qiršu* B, 270). Aro 1970, 30 noted that it usually occurs as a part or decoration of garments and cloths. It could be a strip, or perhaps some type of belt (cf. *qaršum* in Durand 2009, 108–9).

12. The only other attestations of this type of garment are in BE 14 157: 15 and CUSAS 30 372: 22; see the remarks in van Soldt 2015, 455.

13–14. For the word *ur-ra-a-ti* as a possible plural form of *urû* or *urrû* "stable, barn," see van Soldt's commentary to CUSAS 30 390: 1; there, however, it occurs in another context ([UDU?].NÍTA$^{meš}$ *i-na* ŠÀ *ša ur-ra-a-*[*t*]*i*?).

## 274. CUNES 52-13-056

-.VIII.2 Kadašman-Turgu
Sealed by Ninurta-zākir-šumi.

Obv. 1 $^{\text{túg}}$GÚ.È SIG KA GÙN
$^{\text{m}}$*Mu*-SIG$_5$-$^{\text{d}}$IŠKUR *ma-ḫi-ir*
1 $^{\text{túg}}$*me-še-en taḫ-ba-a-ti* SISKUR
1 $^{\text{túg}}$*me-še-en* ŠUḪUB
DUMU.MUNUS $^{\text{m}}$È-*a-na*-ZÁLAG-$^{\text{d}}$AMAR.UTU
PAP ŠU $^{\text{f}}$*Bu-un-na*-$^{\text{d}}$*Gu-la*
$^{\text{iti}}$APIN.DU$_8$.A MU.2.KAM
Rev. *Ka-dáš-man-Túr-gu* LUGAL.E
NA$_4$.KIŠIB $^{\text{md}}$*Nin-urta*-MU-MU

Translation

Obv. 1 thin cloak with multicolor trimming:
Mudammiq-Adad received (it);
1 (pair of) shoes with *taḫbātu* (as) votive offering,
1 (pair of) shoes with *šuḫuppatu*:
daughter of Lūṣi-ana-nūr-Adad.
Total, responsibility of Bunna-Gula.
Month VIII, year 2 of
Rev. King Kadašman-Turgu.
Seal of Ninurta-zākir-šumi.

COMMENTARY

3. CAD T, *taḫbātu* 1a, 48 lists only MB occurrences of *mešēn taḫbāti* and regards *taḫbātu* as "a cloth part of footwear"; see also Aro 1970, 27 (s.v. *mešēnu*) and the new attestation in CUSAS 30 364: 6.

4. For ŠÚ.MUL = ŠUḪUB = *šuḫuppatu* "boots," see CAD Š/3, 210 s.v. It is the first attestation in Kassite texts. As a complement of *mešēnu*, *šuḫuppatu* perhaps indicated an item that could be added to shoes in order to better protect the feet or part of the legs (Durand 2009, 168).

## 275. CUNES 52-16-066

-.VIII–IX.5 Kadašman-[Turgu?]

| | | TÚG$^{\text{ḫi.a}}$ | MU.BI.IM |
|---|---|---|---|
| Obv. | | 1 | $^{\text{túg}}$*ḫúl-la-an qú-ma-r*[*i* |
| | | 1 | $^{\text{túg}}$SAGŠU *ki-la-mu*<br>$^{\text{m}}$MU-*líb-ši* $^{\text{iti}}$APIN.DU$_8$.A |
| | | 1 | $^{\text{túg}}$*su-nu* NÍG.LÁM $^{\text{f}}$*Šar*-⸢x⸣[<br>$^{\text{iti}}$GAN.GAN.È |
| | | 1 | $^{\text{túg}}$GU.ZA MUNUS dub bu[r?<br>$^{\text{iti}}$GAN.GAN.⸢È⸣ |
| Rev. | PAP | 4 | TÚG$^{\text{ḫi.a}}$ ZI.GA ŠU ⸢f⸣[*Bu-un-na*-$^{\text{d}}$*Gu-la*]<br>MU.5.KAM *Ka-dáš-man*-[*Túr-gu*]<br>LUGAL.⸢E⸣ |

Translation

| Obv. | | Garments | Its entry |
|---|---|---|---|
| | | 1 | *ḫullānu*-garment with shoulder[s |
| | | 1 | headcloth (with) *kilāmu*<br>(for) Šumu-libši, month VIII. |
| | | 1 | *sūnu* of *lamaḫuššu*-fabric? (for) Šar[ . . . ],<br>month IX. |
| 5 | | 1 | sumptuous garment for a woman . . . [<br>month IX. |
| Rev. | Total | 4 | garments, expenditure; responsibility of [Bunna-Gula].<br>Year 5 of King Kadašman-[Turgu]. |

COMMENTARY

2. *ḫullān qumāri* "*ḫullānu*-garment with shoulders?" is parallel to *ḫullān aḫi* "*ḫullānu*-garment with sleeves," which is much more common. See Aro 1970, 24 for other MB attestations.

4. *sūnu* is "a piece of clothing or part thereof" (CAD S, *sūnu* B, 388–89), while NÍG.LÁM corresponds to *lamaḫuššû*, which could have been a precious garment made of wool (CAD L, *lamaḫuššû*, 59; AHw I, *lam(a)ḫuššû*, 532) or a precious type of wool fabric (Durand 2009, 57; Beaugeard 2013, 284).

5. $^{\text{túg}}$GU.ZA corresponds to Akk. *illūku* or *illukku* "a sumptuous garment" (CAD I/J, *illūku* 2, 86; AHw I, *illu(k)ku, elluku*, 372); to the best of my knowledge, the only other attestations in MB texts are in **no. 278**: 7 and PBS 2/2 121: 4, 6 (cf. Sassmannshausen 2001, 514, read $^{\text{túg}}$GÚ.ZA by Aro 1970, 23).

6. Given the presence of a feminine personal determinative, Bunna-Gula seems a likely restoration because she is responsible for the distribution of garments also in **no. 274**: 6, **no. 276**: 4, **no. 277**: 4, 47′, **no. 278**: 8–9, and **no. 287**: 12–13.

## 276. CUNES 52-16-046

16.III.6 Kadašman-Turgu
Sealed by Ninurta-zākir-šumi.

Obv. 1 $^{\text{túg}}$*me-še-en ka-ba-li*
⸢*ši*?⸣-*p*[*u*] ⸢x x⸣
$^{\text{md}}$⸢x⸣-[x]-⸢x⸣ *im-ḫur*
4 ŠU $^{\text{f}}$*Bu-un-na-*[$^{\text{d}}$*G*]*u-l*[*a*]
Rev. $^{\text{iti}}$SIG$_4$.GA
U$_4$.16.KAM
MU.6.KAM *Ka-dáš-man-Túr-gu*
8 LUGAL.E
NA$_4$.KIŠIB $^{\text{md}}$*Nin-urta-*
MU-MU

Translation

Obv. [PN] received
1 1 (pair of) shoes with leggings
2 (with) ⸢*šipu*-decoration . . .⸣.
4 Responsibility of Bunna-[G]ul[a].
Rev. Month III,
day 16,
year 6 of King Kadašman-Turgu.
Seal of Ninurta-zākir-šumi.

## 277. CUNES 52-10-088

-.-.6$^{?}$ Kadašman-Turgu

Sealed by Ninurta-zākir-šumi.

Long list of different types of garments and textiles, perhaps disbursed on the occasion of a dedication ceremony.

| | | | |
|---|---|---|---|
| Obv. | [x] ⸢x *ša*$^{?}$ NÍG.GA⸣ *te*-⸢*ru-bi-e*⸣-*tu*$_4$ ⸢*ù*$^{?}$⸣[ | | |
| | ⸢*ša*$^{?}$⸣ MU.5.KAM *Ka-dáš-man*-⸢*Túr-gu* LUGAL$^{?}$⸣ | | |
| | [x] $^{\text{iti}}$AB$^{?}$.⸢È⸣ *ša* M[U].⸢1$^{+}$.KAM x⸣ [ | | |
| | [ŠU$^{?}$] $^{\text{f}}$*Bu-un-na*-$^{\text{d}}$*Gu-la* [*ša*] ⸢MU$^{?}$⸣.[x.KAM] | | |
| | [ZI$^{?}$].GA *ša* TA $^{\text{iti}}$AB.È [*ša* MU.x.KAM] | | |
| | [EN $^{\text{iti}}$]AB.È *ša* MU.6.⸢KAM⸣ [x-x]-*ú* | | |
| | 1 | ⸢$^{\text{túg}}$⸣*iš-ḫe-na-be* | ⸢KA GÙN⸣ 2 ⸢x⸣ [(x) *ši*]-*pu ša* NÍTA |
| | 1 | $^{\text{túg}}$KI.MIN | KA GÙN ⸢1 x x⸣ *ši-pu ša* MUNUS |
| | 2 | $^{\text{túg}}$KI.MIN | KA GÙN *gar-rù la ši-pu* |
| | 2 | $^{\text{túg}}$KI.MIN | KA GÙN *su-na-tu*$_4$ *it-ta-tu*$_4$ |
| | 1 | $^{\text{túg}}$KI.MIN | KA G[ÙN x x x] *Tuk-ri-iš* |
| | 3 | [$^{\text{tú}}$]$^{\text{g}}$[K]I.MIN | [ |
| | 30 | [$^{\text{túg}}$]GÚ.È | [ |
| | ⸢30⸣ | [$^{\text{tú}}$]$^{\text{g}}$KI.MIN KA GÙN EN 1 | ⸢x$^{?}$⸣[ |
| | ⸢2$^{?}$⸣ | [$^{\text{t}}$]$^{\text{úg}}$KI.MIN KA GÙN ⸢*ša*$^{?}$⸣ [ | |
| | ⸢4$^{?}$⸣ | [$^{\text{t}}$]$^{\text{úg}}$KI.MIN *mu-ši* KA GÙN ⸢x x⸣ [ | |
| | ⸢1$^{?}$⸣ | [$^{\text{t}}$]$^{\text{úg}}$KI.MIN *ša* GADA ⸢x⸣ [ | |
| | ⸢1$^{?}$⸣ | $^{\text{túg}}$ÍB.[LÁ] | |
| | [ ] | TÚG | ⸢x⸣ [ |
| | [ ] | $^{\text{túg}}$*ḫúl-la-an a-ḫ*[*i*] | |
| | [ ] | $^{\text{túg}}$KI.MIN *ša* | GAD[A |
| | [ ] | ⸢$^{\text{túg}}$⸣[*id*$^{?}$]-*rù* ⸢x⸣[ | |
| | [ ] | ⸢$^{\text{túg}}$⸣*i*[*d*$^{?}$]-*rù ta-bar-r*[*ù*] | |
| | [ ] | [$^{\text{túg}}$]SAGŠU *ki-la-m*[*u*] | |
| | [ ] | $^{\text{túg}}$⸢SAGŠU⸣ | BAB[BAR] |
| | [ ] | $^{\text{túg}}$*tu-un-šu*$_{14}$ GÙN EN 1 *ša* ⸢x⸣ [ | |
| | [ ] | TÚG | KA$^{?}$ [GÙN$^{?}$] |
| | [ ] | TÚG IGI NÍG.BÀRA *ṭe-ḫu-tu*$_4$ SÍG ⸢x⸣ [ | |
| | 1 | TÚG IGI NÍG.BÀRA *ki-iz-zu la ši-pu* | |
| | [ ] | $^{\text{túg}}$AN.TA.DUL *ši-pu* | |
| | [ ] | $^{\text{túg}}$*id-rù* [ | |
| | [ ] | TÚG É *a-ḫ*[*i* x x x] ⸢x⸣ | |
| | [ ] | TÚG É ⸢*a*⸣-[*ḫi* | |
| | [ ] | ⸢TÚG⸣ *ku-ub*-[ | |
| | [ ] | ⸢TÚG x⸣ [ | |
| Text breaks off | | | |
| Rev. | [ ] | ⸢x x x⸣ | [ |
| | [ ] | ⸢x x x⸣ | [ |
| | [ ] | ⸢x x x⸣ | [ |
| | [ ] | ⸢x x x x⸣ | *ša* [ |
| | 1 | [ | ] ⸢x⸣-*tu*$_4$$^{?}$ [ |
| | 1 | [ | ] ša na ba$^{?}$ ⸢x⸣ [ |
| | 2 | [ | ] |

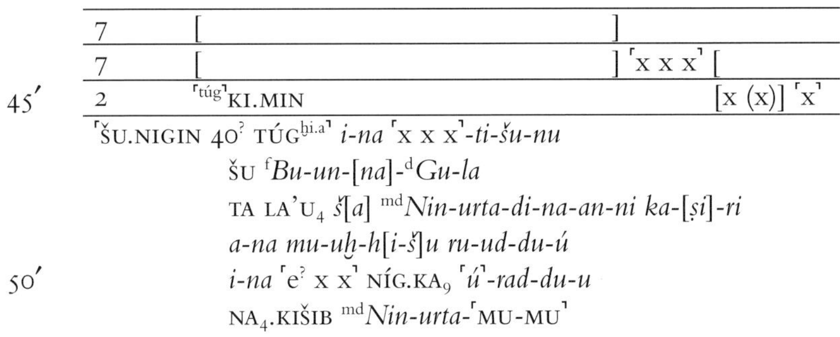

| | | |
|---|---|---|
| 7 | [ ] | |
| 7 | [ ] ⸢x x x⸣ [ | |
| 2 | ⸢túg⸣KI.MIN | [x (x)] ⸢x⸣ |

⸢ŠU.NIGIN 40? TÚG$^{\text{ḫi.a}}$⸣ *i-na* ⸢x x x⸣*-ti-šu-nu*
ŠU ᶠ*Bu-un-*[*na*]*-*ᵈ*Gu-la*
TA LA'U$_4$ *š*[*a*] ᵐᵈ*Nin-urta-di-na-an-ni ka-*[*ṣi*]*-ri*
*a-na mu-uḫ-ḫ*[*i-š*]*u ru-ud-du-ú*
*i-na* ⸢e? x x⸣ NÍG.KA$_9$ ⸢*ú*⸣*-rad-du-u*
NA$_4$.KIŠIB ᵐᵈ*Nin-urta-*⸢MU-MU⸣

Commentary

1. *te-*⸢*ru-bi-e*⸣*-tu$_4$* might be connected with *tērubtu* "ceremony for dedication," for which see the comments to **no. 280**: 7.

5–6. "[Expendi]ture? which [was deduct]ed? from month X [of year x till month] X of year 6"; the verb at the end of l. 6 could have been [*šu-lu*]*-ú*.

7. "1 *išḫenabe*-garment ⸢with multicolored trimmings⸣ 2 ⸢ . . . ⸣ (with) [*ši*]*pu*-decoration for a man." The word spelled *ši*-BU, which occurs in connection with several types of garments, has been interpreted in different ways and read either *ši-bu* or *ši-pu*. AHw III, *šību* A 2, 1128 understands it as "gray" with explicit reference to textiles in MB texts and translates *lā šību* "noch nicht grau geworden"; this interpretation has been followed by Sassmannshausen 2001 in his treatment of MUN 366, 368, 370, and 372. Aro 1970, 32 and CAD Š/3, *šippu*, 72 regard it rather as some kind of decoration, more precisely a "red spot, (red) decoration (on garments)," according to CAD; see also CAD T, *tunšu*, 473, where the word is read *šību*. Van Soldt 2015 reads *ši-pu* (*šīpu*) and leaves it untranslated (CUSAS 30 366: 16, CUSAS 30 370: rev. 3′, 5′). That this term indicated some type of decoration made of red wool is now supported also by the evidence provided by CUSAS 30 375: 2, which records an allocation of red wool (*tabarru*) *a-na* ᵗᵘ́ᵍ*ši-pi ša* ᵗᵘ́ᵍ*iš*!*-ḫe-na-be* "for the *šīpu* of a *išḫenabe*-garment"; the spelling with PI proves that the reading *ši-pu* has to be preferred to *ši-bu*.

8. "1 ditto with multicolored trimmings, 1 ⸢ . . . ⸣ (with) *šīpu*-decoration for a woman."

9. "2 ditto with multicolored trimmings, *garru*, without *šīpu*-decoration."

10. "2 ditto with multicolored trimmings (with) embroidered? *sūnu*-elements." *sunātu ittātu* is probably a further qualification of the *išḫenabe*-garment with multicolored trimmings that is the subject of this entry. *sunātu* should be the plural of *sūnu* B, a term that can be used to indicate a piece of clothing, as well as parts of other garments (CAD S, 388–90 s.v.; Durand 2009, 93–95); here the second meaning seems more likely. *ittātu*, being a plural of *ittu* "mark, sign," could perhaps indicate decorative motifs (see CAD I–J, *ittu* A 1 c 3′, 305 for other attestations in connection with garments, to be integrated with the MB occurrences from Nippur cited by Aro 1970, 25). All this might point, very tentatively, toward *sunātu ittātu* indicating some type of embroidered elements.

11. "1 ditto with multic[olored] trimmings [ . . . ] in the manner of Tukriš."

22. For *idru* as a synonym of *nēbeḫu* "band, belt, sash," see AHw I, *id/tru* III, 364 and CAD I, *idru* B, 10; the word is attested in EA 14, a list of gifts from Egypt to Babylonia. Aro 1970 does not quote any attestations from Nippur; see CUSAS 30 372: 4, 17, 26 for other occurrences in the Rosen texts.

24. For *kilāmu* as a qualification for headcloths, see also **no. 275**: 3, CUSAS 30 364: 5, and CUSAS 30 375: 7; the word is otherwise attested as a qualification of ivory (see AHw I, *g/kilāmu*, 288; CAD G, *gilāmu*, 71).

26. *tunšu* was perhaps a cover, mat, or drapery (CAD T, *tunšu*, 473–74).

28. "Front of a covering? (with) trimming? of wool." For TÚG IGI NÍG.BÁRA, cf. TÚG *ša pān* ⁽ᵗᵘ́ᵍ⁾NÍG.BÀRA at Mari (attestations in Durand 2009, 128). Aro (1970, 29) read ᵗᵘ́ᵍIGI NÍG.KAL BABBAR *ṭe-ḫa-tu$_4$* in PBS 2/2 121: 16′, but collation of the photograph available on CDLI does not exclude that the sign he read as KAL is actually DAG, thus allowing a reading TÚG IGI NÍG.BÁRA there as well; *ṭeḫûtu* and *ṭeḫâtu* are variants of the same word, which perhaps indicated a decoration or trimming (see Aro 1970, 33, and AHw and CAD s.v.; a further attestation of *ṭeḫûtu* is provided also by CUSAS 30 372: 11, there in association with ᵗᵘ́ᵍGÚ.È/*naḫlaptu*). See

also [$^{\text{túg}}$]IGI NÍG.KAL in CUSAS 30 372: 13, perhaps to be read [$^{\text{túg}}$]IGI NÍG.BÁRA. $^{\text{(túg)}}$NÍG.BÀRA is equated with Akk. *muṣû* and *uṣû* in the Mari texts, where it is often described as a cloth having two "fronts" (*pānu*), probably meaning that it was reversible, used to cover pieces of furniture (see most recently Durand 2009, 128; Beaugeard 2013, 284). The $^{\text{(túg)}}$NÍG.BÀRA seems to have had a "front" also in the MB period, but it is uncertain whether it retained its function as a type of covering.

29. "1 front of a covering$^{?}$ (with) *kizzu*, without *šīpu*-decoration$^{?}$." *kizzu* is otherwise attested in connection with $^{\text{túg}}$GÚ.È/*naḫlaptu* "cloak" (see **no. 279**: 1 and **no. 283**: 1); see CAD K, *kizzu* A, 479 and Aro 1970, 26.

32. For TÚG É *aḫi* indicating pieces of clothing for arms, cf. the word compound TÚG.É.Á.MEŠ in the NA period (Gaspa 2017, 78). Aro 1970 and the dictionaries do not mention any attestation in the MB texts from Nippur; see CUSAS 30 372: 5, 28 for other occurrences in the MB texts of the Rosen Collection.

34. "patc[hed$^{?}$] garment": cf. CAD K, *kubbû*, 482 and Durand 2009, 106.

46′–47′. "Total: 40 garments . . . ; responsibility of Bunna-Gula."

48′–50′. "After the arrears of Ninurta-dīnanni, the knotter, have been added to it, in$^{?}$ . . . they will add to$^{?}$ the account."

## 278. CUNES 52-16-050

-.I.7 Kadašman-Turgu
Sealed by Ninurta-zākir-šumi.

Obv. TÚG$^{\text{ḫi.a}}$ MU.BI.IM
1 $^{\text{túg}}$GÚ.È SISKUR
1 $^{\text{túg}}$*in-di-la-rù*
$^{\text{md}}$KUR.GAL-ZI ⸢*im*⸣-[*ḫur*]
1 $^{\text{túg}}$*me-še-en ka-b*[*a-li*]
$^{\text{m}}$*E-ṭi-rù* ⸢*im-ḫur*⸣
[1 $^{\text{t}}$]$^{\text{úg}}$⸢GU.ZA x⸣ [

Rev.
PAP 4 TÚG ZI.GA
ŠU $^{\text{f}}$*Bu-un-na-*$^{\text{d}}$*Gu-la*
$^{\text{iti}}$BÁR.ZAG.GAR

L.e. MU.7.KAM *Ka-dáš-man-Túr-*⸢*gu* LUGAL⸣
NA$_{4}$.KIŠIB $^{\text{md}}$*Nin-urta*-MU-M[U]

Translation

Obv. Garments, its entry:
1 cloak (as) votive offering (and)
1 *indilaru*-garment:
Amurru-napišti recei[ved] (them).
1 (pair of) shoes with legg[ings]:
Ēṭiru received (it).
1 sumptuous garment . . . [ . . . ].

Rev.
Total: 4 garments, expenditure;
responsibility of Bunna-Gula.
Month I,
year 7 of King Kadašman-Turgu.

L.e. Seal of Ninurta-zākir-šu[mi].

Commentary

4. Amurru-napišti occurs in connection with garments also in **no. 288**: 2. To my knowledge, PNs of the type DN-*napišti* are otherwise unattested in Kassite texts (cf., however, Gula-ZI . . . in van Soldt 2015, 544), but see CAD N 1, *napištu* 1a 4′, 299 for oAkk. examples.

7. For $^{\text{túg}}$GU.ZA see **no. 275**: 5.

## 279. CUNES 52-13-059

-.VIII.7 Kadašman-Turgu
Sealed by Ninurta-zākir-šumi.

Obv. 1 $^{\text{túg}}$GÚ.È *ki-iz-zi*
*i-na* ŠÀ *man-da-at-ti*
*ša* MU.6.KAM
*ša* $^{\text{f}}$GAL-*at*-⸢$^{\text{d}}$*Gu-la*⸣
DAM $^{\text{m}}$*Be-la-n*[*i*]
$^{\text{md}}$U.GUR-⸢ŠEŠ-S⸣[UM-*na*]
L.e. DUMU $^{\text{m}}$*Gab*-$^{\text{d+}}$*En-líl* [*ma-ḫir*]
Rev. [$^{\text{iti}}$]APIN.DU$_8$.A
[M]U.7.KAM *Ka-dáš-man-Túr-gu*
LUGAL.E
NA$_4$.KIŠIB $^{\text{md}}$*Nin-urta*-MU-MU

Translation

Obv. 1 cloak (with) *kizzu*
from the work assignment
of year 6
of Rabât-Gula,
wife of Bēlānu:
Nergal-aḫa-id[dina],
L.e. son of Gab-Enlil [received (it)].
Rev. Month VIII,
year 7 of King Kadašman-Turgu.
Seal of Ninurta-zākir-šumi.

Commentary

7. The verbal form could also have been *im-ḫur.*

## 280. CUNES 52-16-081

20.II.9 Kadašman-Turgu

Obv. 1 $^{túg}$*me-še-en ta*[*ḫ*$^{?}$*-ba-ti na*$^{?}$]-⌜*di*$^{?}$⌝-*tu*$_4$
*ša* DUMU $^{m}$*Ḫu-n*[*a*$^{?}$*-bi*$^{?}$]
1 $^{túg}$*in-di-la-rù* aḫ ⌜e$^{?}$⌝ *ḫu-ub-bu-tu*$_4$
*ša zi-ra-ti*
1 TÚG *lab*$^{?}$*-rù* SISKUR ⌜x$^{?}$⌝
*ša* $^{m}$*Na-siq-*$^{d}$AMAR.UTU UŠ.BAR
L.e. ⌜PAP⌝ *te-ru-ub-tu*$_4$
Rev. $^{iti}$GU$_4$.SI.SÁ
U$_4$.20.KAM
MU.9.KAM *Ka-dáš-man-Túr-gu*
LUGAL.E

Translation

Obv. 1 (pair of) shoes with *ta*[*ḫbātu*$^{?}$ (as) gi]ft$^{?}$
of the son of Ḫun[ābu$^{?}$];
1 *indilaru*-garment . . . , a *ḫubbutu*
of *zîru*-fabrics;
1 old$^{?}$ garment (as) votive offering
of Nasiq-Marduk, the weaver.
L.e. ⌜Total⌝: ceremony for dedication.
Rev. Month II,
day 20,
year 9 of King Kadašman-Turgu.

Commentary

3. *ḫubbutu* is known as a type of garment in LB texts (Zawadzki 2006, 131). The word is attested in connection with garments also in CUSAS 30 373: 13, where van Soldt (2015, 457) understands it as a form of *ḫabātu* "to loan" (TÚG$^{ḫi.a}$ *ša i-na* ŠÀ [x x x]*-a*$^{?}$*-ti ḫu-ub-bu-tu*$_4$ "garments that have been borrowed(?) from the . . .").
4. *ša zîrāti* must come from *zîrum*, which might have been a thick fabric used for packaging or for decorating chariots and tents (see Durand 2009, 140–41; Beaugeard 2013, 284).
7. For *tērubtu* "ceremony for dedication" in Kassite texts, see Sassmannshausen 2001, 171 and CAD T, *tērubtu* 1b, 369; one should add now also the administrative text CUSAS 30 212: 13, which mentions ŠUKU UDU.NIGA$^{meš}$ *tērubti* "fodder for fattened sheep for the dedication."

## 281. CUNES 52-14-029

22.VIII.15 Kadašman-Turgu
Sealed by Ninurta-gašir-ilāni.

Obv. [1 TÚG] ⸢*ša*$^{?}$ x x x x⸣ *gar-rù*
⸢$^{m}$LÚ⸣-$^{d}$*Ištar*
1 TÚG *ša* $^{d}$U.GUR KA GÙN$^{?}$
DUMU.MUNUS *Is-ḫu-un-ni*
1 $^{túg}$*me-še-en ka-ba-li taḫ*$^{?}$*-ba*$^{?}$*-ti*
$^{m}$*Be-la-nu* DUMU É
Rev. ⸢PAP⸣ 3 TÚG$^{ḫi.a}$ ZI.GA
ŠU $^{m}$*Su-gi-ir-bu-ni*
$^{iti}$APIN.DU$_{8}$.⸢A⸣ U$_{4}$.22.KAM
MU.15.KAM
$^{d}$*Kad-aš-man-Túr-gu* LUGAL.E
[NA$_{4}$.KIŠ]⸢IB $^{md}$⸣*Nin-urta-ga-ši-ir-*
DINGIR$^{meš}$

Translation

Obv. [1 garment] ⸢. . .⸣, wavy$^{?}$:
Amīl-Ištar;
1 garment of Nergal with multicolored trimming:
the daughter of Isḫunnu;
1 (pair of) shoes with leggings (and) *taḫbātu*:
Bēlānu, *mār bīti*.
Rev. Total: 3 garments, expenditure,
responsibility of Sugir-bunni.
Month VIII, day 22,
year 15 of
King Kadašman-Turgu.
[Sea]l of Ninurta-gašir-ilāni.

## 282. CUNES 52-14-099

-.VII$^{?}$.15$^{?}$ Kadašman-Turgu

Obv. 1 $^{túg}$*tu-un-šu*$_{14}$
LA'U$_{4}$ *man-da-at-ti*
*ša* MU.14.KAM
*ša* $^{f}$*Kir-ta-a-am*
*a-na ma-ši-ri*
L.e. $^{m}$*Su-gi-ir-bu-ni*
*ma-ḫi-[ir]*
Rev. $^{iti}$⸢DU$_{6}$$^{?}$⸣.[KÙ$^{?}$]
MU.15$^{?}$.KAM
$^{d}$*Ka-dáš-man-Túr-gu*

Translation

Obv. 1 *tunšu*-cloth,
arrear of the work
assignment
of year 14
of Kirta
L.e. for a *māširu*-chariot.
Sugir-bunni
Rev. receiv[ed] (it).
Month VII$^{?}$,
year 15$^{?}$
of Kadašman-Turgu.

COMMENTARY

5. See CAD M/1, *mašīru*, 367 and AHw I, *māši/eru*, 626 for other MB texts that record different elements of *māširu*-chariots. Alternatively, *māširu* could indicate here a "teaseler of cloth," but the word is otherwise attested only in OB lexical texts (see CAD M/1, *māširu*, 367).

## 283. CUNES 52-12-062

-.-.15$^{?}$ Kadašman-Turgu

Obv. 1 $^{túg}$GÚ.È *ki-iz-zi* SISKUR
*man-da-at-ti*
$^{f}$*Ri-mu-ti*
$^{m}$IBILA-$^{d}$UTU ⌜$^{lú}$MÁ$^{?}$.LAḪ$_{4}$$^{?}$⌝
*ma-ḫi-ir*
MU.⌜15$^{?}$⌝.KAM
L.e. $^{d}$*Ka-dáš-man-Túr-gu*
LUGAL.E

Translation

Obv. 1 cloak (with) *kizzu* (as) votive offering,
work assignment
of Rīmūtu:
Apil-Šamaš, ⌜the boatman$^{?}$⌝,
received (it).
Year ⌜15$^{?}$⌝ of
L.e. King Kadašman-Turgu.

## 284. CUNES 52-16-092

-.I.16 Kadašman-Turgu

Obv. 3 $^{\text{túg}}$*me-še-en taḫ-ba-ti*
LA'U$_4$ *man-da-ti*
*ša* MU.14.KAM
*ša* $^{\text{m}}$⸢SUD⸣-$^{\text{d}}$AMAR.UTU *ka-ṣi-ri*
⸢$^{\text{m}}$⸣[*Su-gi-ir*]-*bu-ni*
[x x x x] NIBRU$^{\text{ki}}$
L.e. [x x x x] ⸢x⸣
Rev. $^{\text{iti}}$BÁR.ZAG.[GAR]
MU.16.⸢KAM⸣
$^{\text{d}}$*Ka-dáš-man-Túr-gu*
LUGAL.E

Translation

Obv. 2 (pairs of) shoes with *taḫbātu*,
arrears of the work assignment
of year 14
of Rīš-Marduk, the knotter.
[Sugir]-bunni
[ . . . ] Nippur
L.e. [ . . . ].
Rev. Month I,
year 16 of
King Kadašman-Turgu.

COMMENTARY

4. The "knotter" (*kāṣiru*) Rīš-Marduk appears also as recipient of rations in **no. 101**: 16.

## 285. CUNES 52-12-061

-.VI.16 Kadašman-Turgu

Obv. 1 TÚG *iš-ḫe-na-be* SISKUR
*i-na* ŠÀ LA'U$_4$ *man-da-ti*
*ša* $^{\text{f}}$*Bal-ti*-$^{\text{d}}$U.GUR
$^{\text{lú}}$DAM.GÀR
$^{\text{md}}$30-*ú-suḫ$_4$-piš-ti*
*ú-šam-ḫi-ir*
Rev. $^{\text{iti}}$KIN.$^{\text{d}}$INANNA
MU.16.KAM $^{\text{d}}$*Ka-dáš-man-Túr-gu*
LUGAL.E

Translation

| | |
|---|---|
| Obv. | The merchant |
| 5–6 | handed over to Sîn-usuḫ-pišti |
| 1 | 1 *išḫenabe*-garment (as) votive offering |
| 2 | from the arrears of the work assignment |
| 3 | of Bāltī-Nergal. |
| Rev. | Month VI, |
| 8–9 | year 16 of King Kadašman-Turgu. |

Commentary

5. This spelling is a further confirmation that the PN has to be read Sîn-usuḫ-pišti (see Brinkman 2003–4, 400; van Soldt 2015, 402), rather than Sîn-usuḫ-bilti as proposed by Hölscher 1996, 196.

## 286. CUNES 52-15-028

-.VII.16 Kadašman-Turgu

| | |
|---|---|
| Obv. | ⸢1 TÚG *ša muḫ*⸣-*til-le-e* SISKUR |
| | ⸢*i-na* ŠÀ⸣ *man*-⸢*da-at*⸣-*ti* |
| | ⸢*ša*⸣ MU.16.KAM |
| | ⸢DUMU.MUNUS$^{?}$⸣ $^{lú}$Ì.SUR |
| | $^{m}$*Su-gi-ir-bu-ni* |
| | *ma-ḫi-ir* |
| Rev. | [$^{iti}$]DU$_6$.KÙ MU.16.KAM |
| | *Ka-dáš-man-Túr-gu* |
| | LUGAL.E |

Translation

| | |
|---|---|
| Obv. | 1 *muḫtillû*-garment (as) votive offering |
| | from the work assignment |
| | of year 16 |
| | of the daughter of Ṣāḫitu: |
| | Sugir-Bunni |
| | received (it). |
| Rev. | Month VII, year 16 of |
| | King Kadašman-Turgu. |

## 287. CUNES 52-13-107

-.-.17 Kadašman-Turgu

According to l. 16, the tablet was sealed by Ninurta-gašir-ilāni, but no traces of a seal impression are visible on the surface.

Obv. 1 $^{túg}$*iš-ḫe-na-be gar-rù* KA [GÙN]

⸢*i-na*⸣ ŠÀ *man-da-at-ti ša* ⸢MU.17.KAM⸣

[*š*]*a* $^{f}$*Bu-un-na-*$^{d⸢}$*Gu-la*⸣

⸢$^{m}$⸣BA-*šá-*$^{d}$*Nin-imma ma-*[*ḫi-i*]*r*

$^{iti}$DU$_{6}$.KÙ MU.17.K[AM]

---

1 $^{túg}$*iš-ḫe-na-be gar-rù* KA GÙN

1 $^{túg}$*ne-*⸢*be-ḫu*⸣ KA GÙN

⸢*i*⸣*-na* ŠÀ *man-da-at-t*[*i*]

Rev. [*š*]*a* MU.17.K[AM]

[*š*]*a* $^{f}$*Bu-un-na-*$^{d}$*Gu-la*

$^{m}$SU-$^{d}$U.GUR *ma-ḫi-ir*

---

PAP 4 TÚG$^{ḫi.a}$ ZI.GA

ŠU $^{f}$*Bu-un-na-*$^{d}$*Gu-la*

MU.17.KAM $^{d}$*Ka-dáš-man-Túr-gu*

LUGAL.E

NA$_{4}$.KIŠIB $^{md}$*Nin-urta-ga-šir*-DINGIR$^{meš}$

Translation

Obv. 1 *išḫenabe*-garment, wavy?, with [multicolored] trimming

from the work assignment of year 17

[o]f Bunna-Gula:

Iqīša-Ninimma rec[eiv]ed (it).

Month VII, year 17.

---

1 *išḫenabe*-garment, wavy?, with multicolored trimming

1 belt with multicolored trimmings

Rev. from the work assignment

of year 17

[o]f Bunna-Gula:

Erība-Nergal received (it).

---

Total: 4 garments, expenditure;

responsibility of Bunna-Gula.

14–15 Year 17 of King Kadašman-Turgu.

Seal of Ninurta-gašir-ilāni.

Commentary

12. The expected total would be 3.

## 288. CUNES 52-14-043

-.VI.17 Kadašman-Turgu

Very coarse clay. Impressions of a small rope are visible on the lower edge of the reverse.

Obv. 1 TÚG an x di$^?$ x
$^{md}$KUR.GAL-ZI ŠÀ$^?$ ⸢x⸣
⸢*ša*$^?$ *ra*$^?$⸣-*ka-si*
$^{m}$⸢*Bu-un*⸣-*na*-$^{d}$AMAR.UTU
Rev. ⸢PAP$^?$⸣ [x TÚ]G⸢$^{ḫi.a}$⸣ [x x] ⸢x⸣
$^{iti}$KIN.[$^{d}$]INANNA
MU.17.KAM $^{d}$*Ka*-⸢*dáš-man*⸣-*Túr-gu*
LUGAL.⸢E⸣

## 289. CUNES 52-12-057

-.VI.17 (Kadašman-Turgu)
Sealed by Enlil-gešir-ilāni.

Even though the king's name is not mentioned, the text can be dated to the reign of Kadašman-Turgu because of the presence of Enlil-gešir-ilāni, who is the protagonist of a dispute settled in KT 17 (**no. 328**), and of Ekūtu and Arad-U$_4$.9.KAM, who appear also in **no. 101** (KT 15) and **no. 271** (KT 13).

Obv. ⸢1⸣ [$^{túg}$]*iš-ḫe-na-be gar-rù*
⸢*i-na* ŠÀ⸣ *man-da-at-ti*
⸢*ša*⸣ MU.16.KAM
⸢*ša*⸣ $^{f}$*E-ku-tu*$_4$
$^{m}$ÌR-U$_4$.9.KAM
L.e. DUMU $^{m}$*Gu-ub-bu-ḫu*
Rev. $^{iti}$KIN.$^{d}$INANNA
MU.17.KAM
NA$_4$.⸢KIŠIB⸣
$^{md}$50-⸢*ge-šir*⸣-DINGIR$^{meš}$

Translation

Obv. 1 *išḫenabe*-garment, wavy$^?$,
from the work assignment
of year 16
of Ekūtu.
Arad-U$_4$.9.KAM,
L.e. son of Gubbuḫu (received it).
Rev. Month VI,
year 17.
Seal of
Enlil-gešir-ilāni.

Commentary

10. For this PN, see also **no. 328** and cf. Enlil-gešri-ilāni in CUSAS 30 85: 5 (KaE 1). For *gešru* as a variant of *gašru*, see also Ninurta-gešir-ilāni in **no. 233**: 12.

## 290. CUNES 52-15-027

16.I.- Kadašman-Turgu

Obv. 1 $^{\text{túg}}$GÚ.È SIG ⸢SISKUR$^{?}$ $^{\text{m}}$EN-*la-«na»-nu*⸣
1 $^{\text{túg}}$KI.MIN *mu-ši* $^{\text{f}}$*Ba-bu-ú-a* DUMU.MUNUS É$^{?}$
2 $^{\text{túg}}$KI.MIN SIG.GA $^{\text{m}}$*Mu*-SIG$_{5}$-$^{\text{d}}$IŠKUR
1 $^{\text{túg}}$*su-un qa*$^{?}$*-ti* $^{\text{m}}$*Zi-kir*-$^{\text{d}}$IŠKUR
1 $^{\text{túg}}$*me-š[e-en k]a-ba-li* $^{\text{m}}$⸢LÚ⸣-$^{\text{d}}$ŠU.ZI.AN.NA
1 $^{\text{túg}}$⸢*t[u*$^{?}$*-un-š]u*$^{?}$ DUMU $^{\text{m}}$*Ar-di-iu-ú*
PAP 4 TÚG$^{\text{ḫi.a}}$ ⸢SIG$^{?}$ SISKUR$^{?}$⸣
L.e. ŠU $^{\text{m}}$*Su-gi-ir-bu-ni*
Rev. $^{\text{iti}}$BÁR.ZAG.GAR U$_{4}$.16.KAM
*Ka-dáš-man-Túr-gu*
LUGAL.E

Translation

Obv. 1 thin cloak ⸢(as) votive offering$^{?}$⸣: Bēlānu;
1 ditto for the night: Babû'a, *mārat bīti*.
2 thin ditto: Mudammiq-Adad;
1 cloth for the hands: Zikir-Adad;
1 (pair of) sho[es with leg]gings: Amīl-Šuzianna.
1 co[ve]r$^{?}$: son of Ardiyū.
Total: 4 ⸢thin$^{?}$⸣ garments ⸢(as) votive offering$^{?}$⸣,
L.e. responsibility of Sugir-bunni.
Rev. Month I, day 16,
King Kadašman-Turgu.

Commentary

1. I assume an error of the scribe, but note that $^{\text{m}}$EN-*la-nu* would be an unusual spelling of the PN Bēlānu, usually written $^{\text{m}}$*Be-la-nu* (see Hölscher 1996, 48; Sassmannshausen 2001, 471; van Soldt 2015, 539; Index of Personal Names at the end of this volume).

7. The total probably refers only to the garments listed in ll. 1–3, which are qualified as "thin".

9–11. It is unusual for a date formula with month, day, and royal name to omit the year (cf. Brinkman 1976, 405–6), but see also **no. 183**.

# 4. MISCELLANEOUS ADMINISTRATIVE TEXTS

## 4.1 Personnel Lists

### 291. CUNES 53-01-142 (Plate No. 58)

-.-.5–7 Kadašman-Turgu

This tablet records the names and filiation of several young women (MUNUS.TUR) belonging to families (*qinnāti*) of Dūr-Enlilē and Ḫursagkalama. The roster summarizes information concerning years 5–7 of Kadašman-Turgu's reign.

| | | |
|---|---|---|
| Obv. | DUMU.MUNUS$^{meš}$ *qin-na-a-ti ša i-na* BÀD-$^{d+}$*En-líl*$^{meš.ki}$ *ù* ḪUR.SAG.KALAM.MA$^{ki}$ *ṣa-ab-*[ | |
| | MUNUS.TUR GAL-*bat-*$^{d}$*Gu-la* | DUMU.MUNUS $^{m}$*In-na-ni-bu-ú-ti* [ |
| | MUNUS.TUR *Ri-ša-tu*$_4$ | DUMU.MUNUS $^{m}$*Nap-ši-ra-*$^{d}$UTU $^{lú}$[ |
| | MUNUS.TUR *Kal-ba-tu*$_4$ | DUMU.MUNUS $^{m}$*Pu-us-su-li* $^{lú}$SIPA |
| | MUNUS.TUR $^{d}$30-*bal-ti* NIN $^{m}$*In-nu-ni* SIPA ANŠE$^{meš}$ | DAM $^{m}$*Ku-lip-pi-ri-gi-ir* |
| | MUNUS.TUR *Mi-ša-ri-tu*$_4$ | DUMU.MUNUS $^{m}$SU-$^{d}$U.GUR $^{lú}$SI[PA] |
| | ⸢MUNUS.TUR⸣ *Ta-ta-tu*$_4$ | DUMU.MUNUS $^{m}$*Bu-ú-a* SIPA GU$_4$$^{m}$[$^{eš}$] |
| | MUNUS.TUR *Ḫi-in-ni-bu-tu*$_4$ | DUMU.MUNUS $^{m}$*Ki-din-*$^{d+}$*En-líl* $^{lú}$LU[NGA$^?$] |
| | MUNUS.TUR GAŠAN-MUNUS$^{meš}$ | ⸢DUMU.MUNUS⸣ $^{m}$*I-din-*$^{d}$*Gu-la* DUMU $^{f}$*A-bu-ú-ia-ti* |
| | MUNUS.TUR GAL-*bat-a-gal*$^?$-⸢*li*$^?$⸣-*tu*$_4$ ⸢DUMU.MUNUS$^?$⸣ $^{m}$*Muš-tál-*$^{d}$U.[GU]R$^?$ $^{lú}$GÍR DAM $^{m}$*E-muq-*$^{d}$IŠKUR NU.$^{giš}$KIRI$_6$ | |
| | MUNUS.TUR *Ḫu-um-*⸢*mu-ur-tu*$_4$⸣ | NIN $^{m}$*Ḫa-ni-bi* BÀD-$^{d}$KUR$^{ki}$ |
| | MUNUS.TUR $^{d}$30-*a-bu-ša* | DUMU.MUNUS $^{m}$*Bi-it-ta-a* SI[PA$^?$] |
| | MUNUS.TUR.GABA *Ni-ip-*⸢*pu-ri-tu*$_4$⸣ | D[UMU.MUNUS $^{m}$]x-*ni*-x[ |
| | MUNUS.TUR *Ri-ḫe-tu-*⸢*ša*⸣ | DUMU.MUN[US |
| | MUNUS.TUR.TUR *I-na-*ḪUR.SAG.KALAM.MA-*šar-rat* | DUMU.MUNUS [ |
| Rev. | [MUNUS.TUR] ⸢x-x⸣-*i-n*[*a-* | [ |
| | MUNUS.TUR x[ | [ |
| | MUNUS.TUR x[ | [ |
| | ⸢MUNUS.TUR⸣ *na*$^?$-[ | [ |
| | [ ] | [DUMU.MUNUS x x x x]-$^{d}$G[ÌR$^?$ |
| | [ ] ⸢x x x⸣ | [DUMU.MUNUS $^{m}$]$^{d}$*É-*[*a*-x-x DUB$^?$].SAR DAM $^{m}$⸢x⸣[ |
| | [ ] ⸢x x⸣ | [DUMU].MUNUS $^{m}$NÍG.BA-$^{d}$IŠKUR SIPA |
| | [ ] ⸢x x x⸣ ti MÁŠ *ša* ⸢*i-na*⸣ É *a-bi-ši-*⸢*na*⸣ *aš-ba* | |
| | [ ] ⸢x x TA$^?$ $^{iti}$x⸣ *ša* MU.5.KAM EN $^{iti}$KIN.$^{d}$INANNA *ša* MU.⸢7$^?$⸣.KAM $^{d}$*Ka-dáš-man-Túr-gu* LUGAL.E | |

COMMENTARY

1. "Daughters of the families which/who are kep[t] in Dūr-Enlilē and Ḫursagkalama." It is not clear whether the relative pronoun *ša* refers to the daughters or to the families. On *qinnu* in MB society, see Tenney 2011, 97–98 and passim.

4. The shepherd Pussulu had, in addition to this daughter, a son who is mentioned in CUSAS 30 391: 18 (ŠŠ 1).

23–25. "[ . . . ] . . . who live in the houses of their fathers, [ . . . ] from month . . . of year 5 till month VI of year 7 of King Kadašman-Turgu." MÁŠ might be used here as Sumerogramm for the Akk. word *ṣibtu* but I am not sure of its meaning in this context (cf. CAD Ṣ, *ṣibtu* B, 163ff.).

### 292. CUNES 52-19-003

Not dated

Textile impressions on the obverse of the tablet.

| | |
|---|---|
| Obv. | ⸢ÉRIN$^{?}$⸣$^{meš}$ MU.BI.IM |
| | $^{f}$*Bal-ti-*$^{d}$U.GUR |
| | $^{f}$*Bal-ti-*$^{d}$⸢GAŠAN$^{?}$⸣ |
| | $^{m}$*Ul-maš*-ŠEŠ-SUM-*na* |
| | $^{m}$⸢$^{d}$*Nuska*⸣-EN-ÙRU |
| | $^{m}$⸢*E*⸣*-ri-bu* TUR |
| | $^{m}$*Re-eš-*$^{d}$AMAR.UTU |
| | DUMU *I-na*-ŠÀ-*bi*-URU$_4$-*iš* |
| | $^{md}$*Nin-nisi-iš-ti-kal* |
| | $^{f}$⸢*Ia*⸣*-a-u-ú-t*[*u*$_4$] |
| Rev. | $^{m}$*Ša*-DINGIR$^{?}$-DÙ |

The rest of the reverse is blank.

COMMENTARY

8. I am not aware of any other attestation of this PN, but cf. Ina-libbi-eršet in Hölscher 1996, 100.

## 4.2 Beer

### 293. CUNES 53-02-148

10–11.I.5 Nazi-Maruttaš

Sealed.

| | |
|---|---|
| Obv. | 0.0.4 ⸢4$^{?}$⸣ SÌLA KAŠ $^{giš}$BÁN GAL |
| | T[A U$_4$].10.KAM |
| | E[N U$_4$].11.KAM |
| 4 | ⸢ŠU $^{m}$ZÁLAG-$^{d}$UTU⸣ |
| Rev. | $^{iti}$BÁR.ZAG.GAR |
| | MU.5.KAM |
| | *Na-zi-Mu-ru-ut-ta-aš* |
| | LUGAL.E |

## 4.3 Beer and Bread

### 294. CUNES 52-12-051

16.IV$^{?}$.(18)–16.I.19 Nazi-Maruttaš

Despite the statement in l. 8, the tablet does not bear any trace of a seal impression.

Balanced account of the available bread and beer of the inner quarter under the responsibility of Ninurta-nāṣir.

| | | |
|---|---|---|
| Obv. | ⸢7⸣.1$^{pi}$.0 | NINDA |
| | 14.2$^{pi}$.0 | KAŠ |
| | ŠU.NÍGIN 21.3.0 ÍB.TAK$_4$ | |
| | NINDA *u* KAŠ *ša* É-*a-nu* | |
| | ŠU $^{md}$MAŠ-ÙRU | |
| Rev. | $^{m}$*Ri-mu-tu*$_4$ *i-pu-uš* | |
| | TA U$_4$.16.KAM *ša* ⸢$^{iti}$ŠU$^{?}$.⸣[NUMUN.NA$^{?}$] | |
| | *a-di* U$_4$.16.KAM *ša* $^{iti}$BÁR.ZAG.GAR | |
| | MU.19.KAM $^{d}$*Na-zi-Múru-taš* LUGAL.E | |
| | NA$_4$.KIŠIB $^{md}$*Nin-urta*-ÙRU | |

Translation

| | | |
|---|---|---|
| Obv. | 216 *sūtu* | bread |
| | 432 *sūtu* | beer |
| | Total: 648 *sūtu,* remaining | |
| | bread and beer of the inner quarter; | |
| | responsibility of Ninurta-nāṣir. | |
| Rev. | Rīmūtu made (it). | |
| | From day 16 of month I[V$^{?}$] (of year 18) | |
| | till day 16 of month I of | |
| | year 19 of King Nazi-Maruttaš. | |
| | Seal of Ninurta-nāṣir. | |

COMMENTARY

4. For the conjunction *u* written with the sign U, see also CUSAS 30 342: 21.

7–8. For this way of expressing a time span, see also **nos. 63** and **107** and comments there.

## 4.4 Beer and Draff

### 295. CUNES 52-19-120

-.II–IV.9 Kadašman-Turgu

Expenditures of second-quality beer and dry draff over several months of the 9$^{th}$ year of Kadašman-Turgu.

| | | |
|---|---|---|
| Obv. | ⸢KAŠ⸣.ÚS MU.BI.I[M] | |
| | 77 ½ | $^{iti}$GU$_4$.SI.SÁ ⸢EN⸣ [x x] 3.0.0$^?$ |
| | 48 | $^{iti}$SIG$_4$.GA EN 3 KI.MIN |
| 4 | 33 | $^{iti}$ŠU.NUMUN.NA EN 3 KI.MIN |
| | | TA U$_4$.1.KAM |
| | | EN U$_4$.22.KAM |
| Rev. | ⸢PAP 1⸣ ME 58 ½ KAŠ.ÚS | |
| | ⸢4$^+$⸣.0.1 DUḪ ḪÁD.DU.A $^{giš}$BÁN 5 SÌLA | |
| | | ŠU $^{md}$30-⸢TI AD⸣.KID |
| 10 | | NÍG.KA$_9$ *ep*-⸢*šu*⸣ |
| | | TA ZI.GA ⸢*šu*⸣-*lu-ú* |
| | | MU.9.KAM *Ka-dáš-man*-⸢*Túr-gu*⸣ |
| | | ⸢LUGAL.E⸣ |

Translation

| | | |
|---|---|---|
| Obv. | Second-quality beer, i[ts] entry: | |
| | 77 ½ | Month II, including [ . . . ] 90$^?$ *sūtu*$^?$ |
| | 48 | Month III, including 3 of ditto |
| 4 | 33 | Month III, including 3 of ditto |
| | | from day 1 |
| | | till day 22 |
| Rev. | ⸢Total⸣: 158 ½ second-quality beer. | |
| | ⸢121$^+$⸣ *sūtu* of dry draff, (meas. by) the *sūtu* of 5 *qû*, | |
| 10 | | at the disposal of Sîn-muballiṭ, reed-weaver. |
| | | The account was drawn up (lit. done) |
| | | after the expenditure had been deducted. |
| | | Year 9 of King Kadašman-Turgu. |

Commentary

8. On the writing ḪÁD.DU.A for Akk. *ablu* "dry," see CAD A/1, 54.

## 4.5 Pig's Fat

### 296. CUNES 52-10-105

10.II.12 Kadašman-Turgu

Distribution of pig's fat$^{?}$ to women.

| | | |
|---|---|---|
| Obv. | ⸢Ì.ŠAḪ$^{?}$⸣ MU.BI.IM | |
| | 0.0.1 | É $^{m}$*Sa-ar-*<*ri*>*-qí* |
| | 0.0.1 | $^{m}$*Pa-ḫa-rù* |
| | 0.0.1 | $^{f}$*Man-nu-ša-ni-ša* |
| | 0.0.1 | NIN $^{m}$LÚ-*ma* |
| | 0.0.1 | NIN $^{m}$*Ia-ú-ti* |
| | 0.0.1 | $^{fm}$*Ia-a-tu$_4$* |
| Rev. | 0.0.1 | *a*$^{!}$*-na* MUNUS$^{meš}$ |
| | 2 SÌLA *bi*$^{?}$*-i-la-tu$_4$* | |
| | $^{fm}$*Ìš-ḫa-ra-šar-rat* | |
| | PAP 0.1.⸢1⸣ $^{iti}$GU$_4$.SI.SÀ | |
| | U$_4$.10.K[AM] MU.12.KAM | |
| | [*K*]*a-daš-man-Túr-gu* | |

Commentary

1. For another distribution of pig's fat in MB texts, see MUN 279: 4.
7. The use of double gender determinatives was previously known only in the sequence $^{mf}$PN (see Brinkman 2007 for MB texts and Abrahami 2011 for attestations in the Nuzi texts). Yātu is attested elsewhere as a feminine (Hölscher 1996, 114; van Soldt 2015, 570), as well as a masculine name (see attestations in unpublished Nippur ration texts such as Ni. 1391 and Ni. 6670; personal communication of John A. Brinkman).
9. For *billatu* "second-quality beer," one would rather expect the spelling *bi-il-*. This amount is not included in the sum of l. 11.
10. Another PN with double gender determinatives in the sequence $^{fm}$PN. Hölscher 1996, 108 lists Išḫara-šarrat only as a feminine name, but see the unpublished Nippur roster Ni. 6283 i′ 3′ for an attestation with the masculine determinative (personal communication of John A. Brinkman).
11. The total corresponds to the sum of the quantities of pig's fat listed in ll. 2–8.

## 4.6 Receipt of Aromatics and Disbursement of Cereals

### 297. CUNES 52-13-194

-.-.6 Kadašman-Turgu

The text records on the obverse quantities of different commodities (mainly aromatics) received by Ninurta-zākir-šumi from Tukultu, while on the reverse it lists quantities of cereals received by Tukultu from Ninurta-zākir-šumi.

Tukultu, who is identified as a merchant in l. 16 and occurs also in **no. 186**: 13 (n.d.), must be the hypocorism of Tukultī-Marduk, a merchant from whom Ninurta-zākir-šumi acquires sacks (*udû*) of different commodities according to CUSAS 30 377 (n.d.).

Obv. [*ú*]-*du-ú ša i-na* ŠU $^{m}$*Tu-*⸢*kul*⸣-[*tu*$_4$]
[$^{m}$]$^{d}$*Nin-urta*-MU-MU *maḫ-rù*
MU.6.KAM *Ka-dáš-man-Túr-gu* LUGAL.E

5 MA.NA ŠIM$^{ḫi.a}$
⸢4⸣ MA.NA ⸢$^{giš}$⸣ŠUR.⸢MÌN⸣
⸢2/3⸣ MA.NA [x x x]
10 GÍN ⸢GI⸣ DÙG.GA
1/3 MA.NA [x] ⸢x⸣ *ša* ⸢x⸣
1 MA.NA DUḪ.LÀL
PAP ⸢$^{iti}$ŠU.NUMUN.NA⸣
6 1/2 MA.NA ⸢x-x⸣-*tu*$_4$ *ša i*-⸢x-x-x⸣
2 1/3 MA.NA ⸢x x li$^{?}$ bi ra⸣
0.0.3 ⸢x-x⸣$^{sar}$ EN 0.0.1
⸢x x x x x⸣
⸢x x x⸣ *id-di-nu*
L.e. *a-na na-din* di ⸢x⸣
⸢0.0.2 $^{ú}$GAMUN$^{sar}$⸣
$^{iti}$⸢GAN⸣.GAN.È

Rev. ŠE $^{giš}$[BÁN] 5 SÌLA *ša i-na* ŠU $^{md}$*Nin*-⸢*urta*⸣-M[U-MU]
$^{m}$*Tu-kul-t*[*u*$_4$ D]AM.GÀR *mi-taḫ-ḫu-rù*
2.0.0 *i-na* ŠU $^{m}$*É-ra-bi* NIBRU$^{ki}$
$^{iti}$SIG$_4$.GA
1.2.3 *ša* 0.2.⸢3 x⸣ EN 1.3.0 SAR $^{iti}$ŠU.NUMUN.NA
1.0.0 *ša* 2.⸢0.0 ZÍZ$^{?}$.AN.NA⸣
*i-na* ⸢ŠU $^{m}$MU-SIG$_5$-$^{d}$IŠKUR⸣
$^{iti}$Š[U].⸢NUMUN.NA⸣
4.0.0 ⸢x x x x⸣ [
$^{iti}$KIN.$^{d}$IN[ANNA]
⸢8$^{?}$.0.0 x x x x⸣ [
[x] ⸢UDU.NITA$_4$⸣ $^{iti}$⸢x⸣[
PAP 16.2.3 $^{giš}$BÁN KIN.[SIG]
MU.6.KAM *Ka-dáš-man-Túr-gu*
LUGAL.E

COMMENTARY

1–3. "Sacks that Ninurta-zākir-šumi received from Tukultu; year 6 of King Kadašman-Turgu."

4. Cf. CUSAS 30 377: 3, where collation suggests to read 10 MA.NA ŠIM$^{ḫi.a}$ "10 mina of aromatics" instead of 10 MA.NA URUDU$^{ḫi.a}$ "10 mina of copper."

5. For the attestation of cypress as aromatic in economic records, see CAD Š/3, *šurmēnu* c 1′, 351 and Streck 2017, 372; in MB texts it occurs also in a list of herbs and aromatics, written $^{giš}$ŠU.ÚR.MÌN (PBS 2/2 107: 5).

9. For another attestation of wax in a MB economic text, see MUN 406: 1.

19–20. "Barley, (measured by) the *sūtu* of 5 *qû*, that Tukultu, the merchant, has been receiving from Ninurta-zākir-šumi."

## 4.7 Hides

### 298. CUNES 52-16-026

-.-.23 Nazi-Maruttaš

| | | |
|---|---|---|
| Obv. | KUŠ GU$_4$ *ša i-na* MU.22.KAM | |
| | $^{md}$*Nin-urta-ga-mil mi-taḫ-ḫu-ru* | |
| | 10 | *ša* ŠU $^{m}$*Nam-rù* $^{iti}$BÁR.ZAG.[GAR] |
| | 3 | *ša* $^{m}$*Ba-bi-la-a-a-ú* |
| 5 | | *ù* $^{md}$30-EN-NUMUN |
| | | TA ⸢*E-mu-qat*⸣-$^{d}$AMAR.UTU$^{⸢ki?⸣}$ [ |
| | | $^{iti}$NE.NE.GAR |
| L.e | 2 | *ša* $^{m}$GAL-*šá*-GAŠAN ⸢DUMU.A⸣.[NI] |
| 9 | | TA *Za-rat*-⸢x⸣[ |
| Rev. | | $^{iti}$KIN.$^{d}$IN[ANNA] |
| | 2 | *ša* $^{md}$30-⸢ŠEŠ⸣-SUM-*n*[*a*] |
| | 1 | *ša* ÁB *ša* $^{m}$*Ba-bi-la-a*-⸢*ú*⸣ |
| | | |
| | PAP 18 KUŠ GU$_4$ ŠU $^{md}$*Nin-u*[*rta-ga-mil*] | |
| | | MU.23.KAM |
| 15 | | *Na-zi-Ma-ru-ut-ta-aš* |

COMMENTARY

1–2. "Ox hide(s) that Ninurta-gāmil has been receiving in year 22." Ninurta-gāmil might be identified with the homonymous leatherworker mentioned in CUSAS 30 142: 42 (n.d.).

3. Even though Namru's profession is not mentioned, he must be the homonymous shepherd known from other texts dated to the reign of Nazi-Maruttaš (see Index of Personal Names).

### 299. CUNES 52-13-088

8.XII.[ . . . ] Šagarakti-Šuriaš

Cf. CUSAS 30 397 (ŠŠ 2) for another text recording the delivery of hides to Bulālu, probably the same person who is qualified as a "leatherworker (of Nippur)" in CUSAS 30 204: 5 (ŠŠ 1) and CUSAS 30 237: 6 (KuE 9).

| | |
|---|---|
| Obv. | ⸢x⸣ KUŠ GU$_4$ |
| | ⸢30$^{?}$⸣ KUŠ UDU.NÍTA |
| | $^{m}$*Bu-la-lu*$_4$ |
| | ⸢*a-na šu*⸣-*ku-li* |
| 5 | *ma-ḫi-ir* |
| | [$^{iti}$ŠE.KIN].KU$_5$ U$_4$.8.KAM |
| L.e. | [MU.X.KAM] ⸢$^{d}$*Ša-ga-rak*⸣-*ti-Šu-ri-ia-aš* |
| | LUGAL.E |
| Rev. | 57 KUŠ UDU.NÍTA |
| 10 | *a-na* $^{m}$*Ki-din*-$^{d}$*Gu-la* |
| | *pa-aq-du* |
| | $^{iti}$ŠE U$_4$.8.KAM |

Translation

Obv. ⌜x⌝ oxhides,
⌜30?⌝ ram hides:
3–5 Bulālu received for tanning;
[month X]II, day 8,
[year x] of King Šagarakti-Šuriaš.
Rev. 57 ram hides
11 have been consigned
10 to Kidin-Gula;
month XII, day 8.

## 4.8 Bricks

### 300. CUNES 52-18-818

29.IV.3 Kadašman-Turgu

Obv. [x]⌜7⌝ ME 50 SIG$_4$
[*š*]*a* $^{md}$IŠKUR-*šub-ši ù* $^{m}$*A-na-kar-šu-e-mi-id*
ÌR.É.GAL$^{meš}$ *il-bi-nu*
EN 3 ME 30 *ša a-na* ŠÀ É
*iš-šu-ni*
Rev. [$^{it}$]$^{i}$ŠU.NUMUN.NA U$_4$.29.KAM
[M]U.3.KAM *Ka-dáš-man-Túr-gu*
LUGAL.E

Translation

Obv. 750⁺ bricks
that Adad-šubši and Ana-kāršu-ēmid,
*ardū ekalli*, made,
4–5 including 330 that they brought into the house.
Rev. Month IV, day 29,
year 3 of King Kadašman-Turgu.

Commentary

2. The reading Ana-kāršu-ēmid seems more likely than Ana-ēṭiršu-ēmid; both are unattested, but cf. Ana-ṣillīšu-ēmid (Hölscher 1996, 32). For the (rare) use of *kārum* in PNs, see CAD K, *kāru* A 1 c, 233.

3. The fact that the two individuals responsible for the bricks are identified as *ardū ekalli* supports the hypothesis that this title, instead of indicating the status of a palace servant, "may have designated a builder or construction worker" already in MB texts (see Brinkman 2004, 294–95).

## 4.9 Paint

### 301. CUNES 52-12-028

7.XII.3 Kadašman-Turgu

Obv. [x x x MA.N]A ⸢KUŠ.ŠE.GÍN⸣
[x x x] ⸢x⸣
[x] ⸢x⸣ [x] ⸢x x⸣
ŠU.NÍGIN ⸢40 MA.NA⸣ KUŠ.ŠE.GÍN
$^{m}$*Ib-ni-*$^{d}$AMAR.UTU
L.e. *a-píl* KÁ *ša Ì-si-in*
*ma-ḫi-ir*
Rev. $^{iti}$ŠE.KIN.KU$_5$
U$_4$.7.KAM
MU.3.KAM *Ka-dáš-man-Túr-gu* LUGAL

Translation

Obv. [. . . m]inas of paint
⸢. . .⸣
⸢. . .⸣
Total: 40 minas of paint.
Ibni-Marduk,
L.e. the gate keeper of Isin,
received (it).
Rev. Month XII,
day 7,
year 3 of King Kadašman-Turgu.

COMMENTARY

1. For a discussion of KUŠ.ŠE.GÍN (*šimt/du*) "paint" in MB texts, see Sassmannshausen 2001, 410 and the texts MUN 374–88.

## 4.10 Wood

### 302. CUNES 53-01-111

20.V.10 Kadašman-Turgu

This text might be linked to CUSAS 30 422, where one reads that "8 tamarisks were carried to Tukultī-Ekur in the 10$^{th}$ year (to be made) into combs" (ll. 5–7). Nanna-LÚ-SA$_6$, the person who receives the tamarisks in our text, provides the connection with Tukultī-Ekur, since he appears also in **no. 55**: 9, 17, a ledger that records the stored grain of this town (KT 12).

Obv. 8 $^{\text{giš}}$ŠINIG
*i-na* ŠU $^{\text{m}}$*È-ana*-ZÁLAG-$^{\text{d}}$IŠKUR
$^{\text{md}}$*Nanna*-LÚ-SA$_6$
*im-uḫ-ur-ma*
*a-na* 18 *mu-uš-ṭa-*<*ti*>
L.e. *ú-*⸢*na*⸣*-ki-i-is-ma*
Rev. $^{\text{m}}$*Il-lu-lu*$_4$ *ḫa-za-an-nu*
*ù* $^{\text{m}}$*Be-et-ta*
DUMU $^{\text{m.lú}}$DUB.SAR
*a-na Pa-an*-EDIN *iš-šu-ú*
$^{\text{iti}}$NE.NE.GAR
U$_4$.20.KAM MU.10.KAM
$^{\text{d}}$*Ka-dáš-man-Túr-gu*
L.e. LUGAL.E

Translation

Obv. Nanna-LÚ-SA$_6$
4 received
3 from Lūṣi-ana-nūr-Adad
1 8 (pieces of) tamarisks and
5–6 cut (them) into 18 combs, then
Rev. Illullu, *ḫazannu*,
and Bettā,
son of Tupšarru,
10 brought (them) to Pān-ṣēri.
Month V,
day 20, year 10
of King Kadašman-Turgu.

COMMENTARY

8. Despite the different spelling, $^{\text{m}}$*Be-et-ta* must be the same person as $^{\text{m}}$⸢*Bi-it-ta*⸣*-a*, identified as a son of Tupšarru in **no. 169**: 6 (KT 12).

## 4.11 Sickles

### 303. CUNES 52-18-797 (Plate No. 59)

-.-.23 Nazi-Maruttaš

Inventory of copper sickles, indicating their weight and the persons responsible for them.

Obv. $^{\text{urudu}}$[*níg*]*-gál-*<*la*>*-tu*$_4$ *ša i-na* ŠÀ 30 [x x x] x$^{\text{ki}}$
*na-ad-na-ma tur-ra-ni*

---

21 ½ *a-*⌜*na*$^?$ x⌝ *it-ti* ⌜x⌝[
GA.⌜RÍG$^?$ x ša$^?$/da$^?$ x⌝ [
$^{\text{m}}$*Ḫa-*[*aḫ*$^?$]*-ia* ⌜$^{\text{lú?}}$x⌝ [

---

2 *it-ti a-bu-ti* ⌜x⌝[
½ *ma-*⌜*na* KI⌝.LÁ.BI
$^{\text{m}}$ÌR-[GA]ŠAN DUMU $^{\text{m}}$*Iš-kun*$_8$*-*[*lí-su*]

---

2 ½ KI.MIN ⌜1⌝ MA.NA KI.LÁ.BI
L.e. $^{\text{m}}$*Bu-na-*$^{\text{d}}$AMAR.UTU *ma-ḫi-*⌜*ir*⌝

---

Rev. 2 $^{\text{md}}$30*-eri-ba* DUMU $^{\text{m}}$*Da-bi-bi*
*i-na* $^{\text{d}}$*Ìr-ra-ga-mil*$^{\text{ki}}$
*ú-ḫal-li-iq*

---

2 ÍB.TAK$_4$ É NA$_4$.KIŠIB [

---

PAP 30 $^{\text{urudu}}$*níg-gál-l*[*u*$_4$]
L.e. MU.⌜23⌝.KAM
*N*[*a-z*]*i-Múru-taš* LUGA[L.E]

Translation

Obv. Copper [si]ckles that were given out from 30 (sickles) [of GN]
and returned.

---

21 ½ ⌜. . .⌝ [
a rake$^?$ ⌜. . .⌝ [
Ḫa[ḫ]ia$^?$ . . . [

---

2 with an *abūtu*-tool [
their weight is a half mina;
Arad-[Bē]lti, son of Iškun-[līssu].

---

2 ½ Ditto, their weight is a half mina;
L.e. Bunna-Marduk received (them).

---

Rev. 2 Sîn-erība, son of Dābibī,
has lost
in Irra-gāmil.

---

2 Remaining (in/of) the storehouse [

---

Total: 30 copper sickles.
L.e. Year 23
of Kin[g] N[az]i-Maruttaš.

COMMENTARY

1. The GN at the end of the line could have been perhaps [$^{\text{d}}$*Ìr-ra-ga-m*]*il*$^{\text{ki}}$ (cf. l. 12).

4. The reading GA.RÍG (Akk. *mušṭu*) is very tentative; *mušṭu* is attested only with the meaning "comb," but given that the remainder of the document records agricultural tools, the translation "rake" is suggested here. Ḫaḫia might be a hypocoristic form of a PN like Haḫia-Saḫ (MUN 92: 22′).

6. See CAD A/1, *abūtu* B (or *apūtu*), 93 "(a tool)."

12. According to BE 14 18, the village of Irra-gāmil was part of the "province" (*pīḫātu*) Bīt-Sîn, which must have been quite close to Nippur (RGTC 5, 137; see Paulus 2014, 185ff. for a recent discussion on the administrative and geographic meaning of *pīḫātu* in MB sources, esp. pp. 194 and 196 on the "province" Bīt-Sîn).

## 4.12 Sacks

### 304. CUNES 52-13-077

12.VIII.15 Nazi-Maruttaš

Obv. 5 *ú-du-ú la-bi-ru-tu*$_4$
5 KI.MIN *eš-šu-tu*$_4$
$^{\text{m}}$*Bu-un-na-*$^{\text{d}}$AMAR.UTU
5 *ú-du-ú eš-šu-tu*$_4$
⸢2⸣ KI.MIN *la-bi-ru-tu*$_4$
Rev. $^{\text{m}}$30-*eri-ba*
*ma-aḫ-ru*
$^{\text{iti}}$APIN.DU$_8$.A U$_4$.12.KAM
MU.15.KAM
*Na-zi-Mu-ru-ta-aš*

Translation

Obv. 5 old sacks,
5 new ditto (i.e., sacks):
Bunna-Marduk.
5 new sacks,
5 old ditto (i.e., sacks):
Rev. Sîn-erība.
They have been received.
Month VIII, day 12,
year 15
of Nazi-Maruttaš.

COMMENTARY

7. The 3 pl. stative *maḫrū* is understood here as referring to the sacks, but it could also be explained as an active stative referring to the two persons who received them (Bunna-Marduk and Sîn-erība)—i.e., "they received."

## 4.13 Metal

### 305. CUNES 52-13-196

I.XII.11 Kadašman-Turgu

Obv. 1 DÙG.GA *ab-šu*
*ša* ZABAR
*ša* $^{m}$*Ṣíl-lí-Šu-ud*$^{!}$(UŠ)*-da*$^{?}$ SIMUG
4 ⸢*a-na*⸣ ŠÀ-*bi*$^{?}$ *ap-pa-ti*
*ša-qí-li*
L.e. ZABAR
Rev. *i-nam-du-u*
$^{iti}$ŠE.KIN.KU$_5$
U$_4$.1.KAM
10 MU.11.KAM
[*K*]*a-dáš-man-Túr-gu*

Translation

Obv. 1 good strap$^{?}$
of bronze,
which Ṣillī-Šudda, the smith,
7 will fasten
4 to the tip
5–6 of a bronze bolt.
Rev. Month XII,
day 1,
10 year 11
of [K]adašman-Turgu.

Commentary

1. Cf. CAD A/1, *abšu* A, 66 "(a strap or band)" and AHw I, *ab/pšu* I, 7 "eine Art Gurt?," attested only as a synonym of *nēbeḫu*. If it is correct to understand DÙG.GA as an adjective qualifying *abšu*, its position before the noun is unusual.
3. If correct, the PN was previously unattested in MB onomastic repertoires, but see Hölscher 1996, 271 for other PNs with Šudda as a theophoric element.
4. Cf. CAD A/2, *appatu* B, 183 "tip (of metal used on work implements)," which records only NB attestations, and Prechel 2010, 53–54 for several occurrences in the MB inventory texts from Haft Tappeh. The context seems to exclude the word *appatu* "bridle, rein" (CAD A/2, *appatu* A, 181–82; AHw I, *appatu(m)* II, 59).
5. Cf. CAD Š/2, *šāqilu*, 14 "a bolt or lock of a door." Another possible reading would be *ša ki-li* "of the prison," which seems unlikely in this context.
7. Among the several meanings of *nadû*, "to fasten a lock, a mechanical device" seems to be the most fitting in this context (CAD N/1, *nadû* 2 7′, 82); the nasalization of the double consonant (*i-nam-du-u* for *inaddu*) occurs often in MB texts (see Aro 1955, 35–37).

## 4.14 Inventory of Precious Goods

### 306. CUNES 52-12-038 (Plate No. 60)

Not dated.

Inventory of goods, including garments, jewels, and significant amounts of sheep, flour, and malt.

Obv. 2 TÚG$^{\text{ḫi.a}}$ *ṣer-pi*
2 ḪAR.ŠU KÙ.GI SA$_5$ *tu-ru-u'*
⸢5$^?$⸣ GÍN KI.LÁ.BI
1 *ta-*⸢*am*⸣*-lu*$_4$ *in-ṣa-ab-ti* KÙ.GI
3 GÍN KÙ.GI KI.LÁ.BI
6 3 NA$_4$ *ti-ik-ki*
L.e. *ti-ip-ti-tu*$_4$ KÙ.GI
50 UDU.NITA$^{\text{ḫi.a}}$
Rev. 40.0.0 ⸢ZÌ.DA⸣ $^{\text{giš}}$BÁN 5 SÌLA
1 ME 20.0.0 ZÌ.MUNU$_4$ $^{\text{giš}}$BÁN 5 SÌLA
*ša* 1 LIM 2 ME DUG.GAL$^{\text{meš}}$

---

Translation

Obv. 2 garments of red dyed wool,
2 bracelets of red gold . . .
weighing 5$^?$ shekels,
1 stone inlay of a golden ring
weighing 3 shekels of gold,
6 3 stones of a necklace
L.e. (with) openings$^?$ of gold,
50 male sheep,
Rev. 40 kor of flour, (meas. by) the *sūtu* of 5 *qû*,
120 kor of brewing ingredients, (meas. by) the *sūtu* of 5 *qû*,
of (i.e., in?) 1,200 big jars.

---

Commentary

2–6. For an overview of other published and unpublished MB texts listing jewels, see Sassmannshausen 2001, 422, 428, to which one can add now CUSAS 30 376.

2. The word *tu-ru-u'* is to my knowledge unattested; it could be a designation either of the bracelets or of the gold.

6. *ti-ip-ti-tu*$_4$ must be the same word that is spelled *te-ep-te-tu* and [*te*]*-ep-te-e-tu* in MUN 416: 11, 12, 25, a list of precious stones and jewels dating to NM 10. There, it appears in connection with *pappardilû*-stones and gold beads, once with the specification "for the neck" (16 NA$_4$.KÙ.GI *te-ep-te-tu ana* GÚ, MUN 416: 25). Since *teptītu*, the only word recorded by the dictionaries that can correspond to these traces, does not fit the context because of its meaning ("first tilling, clearing of land for cultivation"; see CAD T, 346 and AHw III, 1347 s.v.), Sassmannshausen (2001, 428) suggested that it is a plural form of a thus far unattested singular *teptû*, a nominal form of *petû* "to open." In our text a translation "opening" would be plausible.

# 4.15 Uncertain

## 307. CUNES 52-10-112

-.VI.21 (Nazi-Maruttaš?)

The obverse is almost completely lost; only faint traces of a few signs are still visible. Judging from the final line of the reverse, the text might have recorded the disbursement of foodstuffs to Nippureans (DUMU$^{\text{meš}}$ NIBRU$^{\text{ki}}$). See CUSAS 30 427: 25 for another text of the same archive mentioning Nippureans.

| | | |
|---|---|---|
| Obv. | (ca. 2 lines missing) | |
| | ˹iti?˺ [ | |
| | ˹x˺ [ | |
| | 0.3.0 | [x] ˹x˺ [x x x] ˹x˺ |
| | | ˹x x˺ na ˹x˺ [ |
| | 0.1.[x] | [ |
| | | [ |
| | [x.x.x] | $^{\text{m}}$*Za*-[x x x] ˹x˺ [ |
| | | ˹x˺ [...] |
| Rev. | | ˹$^{\text{m}}$˺*Ba-ḫu-ú* |
| | | DUMU $^{\text{m}}$GAL-*a-šá*-$^{\text{d}}$30 |
| | 0.1.0 | $^{\text{m}}$*Mu-ra-nu* |
| | | DUMU $^{\text{m}}$*A-ḫi-ra-bu-uz-zu* |
| PAP | 1.1.3 | DUMU$^{\text{meš}}$ NIBRU$^{\text{ki}}$ |
| | $^{\text{iti}}$KIN.$^{\text{d}}$INANNA MU.21.[K]AM | |

## 308. CUNES 52-18-867 (Plate No. 61)

-.-.18–22 Nazi-Maruttaš

The exact nature of this text, which probably summarized expenditures dating between year 18 and year 22 of Nazi-Maruttaš, is not clear.

The account is vertically divided into two halves; each half is further divided into several columns. Since the upper part of the tablet, which originally contained the headings of the columns, is missing, it is impossible to assess which kind of goods were counted. According to the grand total at the end of the left half of the tablet, which gives a quantity measured in *sūtu* and mentions seed, this part of the text must have dealt with cereals; note, however, that col. ii records items counted by unit. Also, the first two columns of the right half of the text record goods counted by unit and thus, might have been concerned with, e.g., animals or containers such as pots, jars or tools, while col. iii lists small amounts indicated with capacity measures.

(left half)

| | (i) | (ii) | (iii) | (iv) |
|---|---|---|---|---|
| Obv. | [ ] | [ ] | [ ] | [ ] |
| 2′ | [ ] | [ ] | [ ] | [x x x x x]-*šu*$_4$ |
| 3′ | [ ] | [ ] | [ ] | [x x x] ⸢bi?⸣ |
| 4′ | [ ] | [ ] | [ ] | [x x x x] ⸢$^{iti}$x x⸣ |
| 5′ | [ ] | [ ] | [ ] | [x x x] ⸢x⸣ |
| 6′ | [ ] | [ ] | [ ] | [TA U$_4$.X.KAM] ⸢*ša*?⸣ $^{iti}$AB?⸣<br>[*ša* MU.1]9.KAM<br>[EN U$_4$?].27.KAM ⸢*ša*? x x x⸣<br>⸢*ša*?⸣ MU.20.KAM |
| 7′ | | | | *ka-an-ku*$_8$<br>NA$_4$.KIŠIB $^{md}$*Nin-urta*-MU-MU |
| 8′ | [ ] 4 | | | $^{iti}$ŠE.KIN.KU$_5$ U$_4$.24 U$_4$.27?<br>MU.20.⸢KAM⸣<br>*la ka-an-ku*$_8$ |
| 9′ | [x] ME?<br>[ ]7 | 13 | 0.0.2 | MU.20.KAM |
| 10′ | [ ]4 | | | $^{iti}$ZÍZ.AN U$_4$.18 U$_4$.19? MU.21<br>$^{giš}$KIRI$_6$ $^{uru}$*Ḫi-lu-ni*<br>*ù* $^{giš}$KIRI$_6$-*e*$^{ki}$ |
| 11′ | [ ] | | 1 SÌLA | $^{iti}$GU$_4$ U$_4$.24.KAM |
| 12′ | [ ] | | | $^{iti}$GU$_4$ U$_4$.25 U$_4$.26 |
| 13′ | [ ] | 1 | | $^{f}$*Bar-ma-tu*$_4$ |
| 14′ | [ ] | 1 | 1 ⸢SÌLA⸣ | ⸢$^{iti}$GU$_4$⸣.SI.SÁ MU.21.KAM |
| 15′ | [ ] | | | [TA?] ⸢U$_4$⸣.30 ⸢EN U$_4$⸣.3.KAM<br>[(x) $^{it}$]$^{i}$ZÍZ.A.AN<br>[x x]-*tu*$_4$ É $^{m}$ŠEŠ-SUM-*na*-$^{d}$AMAR.UTU |
| 16′ | [ ] | [ ] | [ ] | [x x] ⸢x a?⸣ EGIR ⸢x⸣ |

(right half)

| (v) | (vi) | (vii) | (viii) | (ix) | |
|---|---|---|---|---|---|
| | [ ] | | | [ | Obv. |
| | [ ] | | | [ | 2′ |
| | ⸢x⸣ | | | [ | 3′ |
| | ⸢2?⸣ | | | [ | 4′ |
| | ⸢1?⸣ | | | [ | 5′ |
| | ⸢2?⸣ | | | $^{iti}$⸢x⸣ [ | 6′ |
| | [ ] | | | $^{iti}$GAN[ | 7′ |
| ⸢PAP⸣ | ⸢3?⸣ | | | $^{iti}$⸢x⸣-[x]-⸢È?⸣ | 8′ |
| | 2 | | 2 SÌLA | $^{iti}$AB.È *a-na ki*-⸢x⸣-[<br>U$_4$.⸢18?.KAM⸣ $^{m}$*Bal*-⸢*lu*⸣-*uk*-[*ku*] | 9′ |
| ⸢PAP⸣ | 2 | | 2 SÌLA | $^{iti}$AB.È | 10′ |
| 1 | | | | $^{iti}$ZÍZ $^{m}$*Ši*-⸢*ri-iš*⸣-*ti*⸣ | 11′ |
| 1 | 1 | | | $^{md+}$*En-líl*-KUR-DINGIR$^{meš}$ | 12′ |
| 1 | 2 | | | $^{m}$ÌR-⸢U$_4$.9⸣.KAM | 13′ |
| 1 ⸢½⸣ | | √ | | $^{m}$*Bal-lu-uk-ku* | 14′ |
| | ⸢3⸣ | √ | | U$_4$.20.KAM | 15′ |
| | 1 | √ | | $^{f}$GAŠAN-*ba-ra*-[*at*] | 16′ |
| | 7 | √ | 1 SÌLA | U$_4$.22.KAM | 17′ |
| | 2 | | | $^{m}$*Mu-ra-nu* DUMU ⸢$^{md}$x-x-x-*ri*⸣<br>$^{m}$*Bi-lak-ku-ul-lu*$_4$ | 18′ |
| PAP ⸢4 ½⸣ | 16 | | 1 SÌLA | ⸢$^{iti}$ZÍZ.⸣A.AN | 19′ |
| | 3 | | | $^{iti}$ŠE.KIN.KU$_5$ U$_4$.10.KAM | 20′ |
| | 13 | 2 | 0.0.1 | MU.⸢21⸣.[KAM] | 21′ |

(left half)

| | (i) | (ii) | (iii) | (iv) |
|---|---|---|---|---|
| Rev. | | | | |
| 17′ | [ŠU].⸢NÍGIN⸣14.3.2 $^{giš}$BÁN ⸢GAL⸣ | | | |
| 18′ | NUMUN *ša a-na* ŠE [x x] | | | |
| 19′ | TA U$_4$.17.KAM *ša* $^{iti}$APIN.⸢DU$_8$⸣.A | | | |
| 20′ | ⸢*ša*⸣ MU.18.KAM EN U$_4$.17.KAM | | | |
| 21′ | *ša* $^{iti}$GAN.GAN.È *ša* MU.22.KAM | | | |
| 22′ | ⸢*Na-zi*⸣-*Ma-ru-taš* LUGAL.E | | | |
| 23′ | [x x x x] ⸢ŠU⸣ $^{m}$*Ṣú-uḫ-ḫu-ti* | | | |

The text breaks off.

(right half)

| (v) | (vi) | (vii) | (viii) | (ix) | |
|---|---|---|---|---|---|
| ⸢I$^{?}$⸣ | 3 | | | [ | Rev. |
| | | 2 | | [ | 23′ |
| | 5 | | | ⸢x⸣ [<br>⸢x x x⸣ [ | 24′ |
| PAP | 8 | 2 | | $^{iti}$BÁR.ZAG.GAR ⸢MU.22⸣.KAM | 25′ |
| | ⸢3⸣ | 1 | | $^{iti}$GU$_4$.SI.SÁ ⸢U$_4$.X U$_4$.24.KAM⸣ | 26′ |
| | ⸢3⸣ | | | $^{iti}$GU$_4$ U$_4$.25 U$_4$.26.KAM | 27′ |
| ⸢PAP⸣ | 6 | 1 | | $^{iti}$GU$_4$.SI.SÁ MU.22.KAM | 28′ |
| | | 2 | | $^{m}$*Bal-lu-uk-ku*<br>TA BÀD-$^{d+}$*En-líl*$^{hi.a}$ ir ⸢x x *iš*$^{?}$⸣-*ši* | 29′ |
| PAP | | 2 | | $^{iti}$SIG$_4$.A.AN ⸢MU.22.⸣[KAM] | 30′ |
| | 8 | | | $^{iti}$⸢ŠU.NUMUN.NA⸣ TA ⸢U$_4$⸣[<br>EN U$_4$.13.KAM | 31′ |
| | 2 | | | $^{iti}$ŠU ⸢x x x⸣ [ | 32′ |
| | 6 | | | $^{iti}$ŠU U$_4$.13 [x x x x] ⸢x x x⸣ | 33′ |
| | 3 | | | $^{iti}$ŠU ⸢x x x⸣ [ | 34′ |
| PAP | 19 | | | $^{iti}$⸢ŠU.NUMUN⸣.NA M[U.22.KAM] | 35′ |
| | 6 | 2 | 1 SÌLA | $^{iti}$⸢NE.NE.GAR⸣<br>U$_4$.20.KAM U$_4$.21.⸢KAM⸣ | 36′ |
| PAP | 6 | 2 | 1 SÌLA | $^{iti}$NE.GAR MU.22.KAM | 37′ |
| | 4 | | | ⸢$^{iti}$KIN.$^{d}$INANNA⸣ [MU.X].⸢KAM$^{?}$⸣ | 38′ |

COMMENTARY

col. iv 7′. "sealed; seal of Ninurta-zākir-šumi." Cf. col. iv 8′ *lā kanku* "not sealed."

col. iv 10′. The "garden" of Ḫilunu and Kirê appears also in PBS 2/2 108: 2–3, a ledger recording amounts of herbs delivered by several "gardens."

col. ix 12′. The PN Enlil-šadî-ilāni is to my knowledge unattested in MB texts; for this type of PN cf., e.g., OB Šamaš-šadî-ilī (Stamm 1968, 226).

## 309. CUNES 52-16-073

3.XII.2 Kadašman-Turgu

| | |
|---|---|
| Obv. | 10 MA.NA *maš-šar-*⌜*ti*?⌝ |
| | ŠÀ *qa-ap-pa-*⌜*ti*⌝ |
| | $^{iti}$ŠE.KIN.KU$_5$ |
| 4 | U$_4$.3.KAM |
| Rev. | MU.2.KAM *Ka-dáš-man-Túr-gu* |
| | LUGAL.E |

Translation

| | |
|---|---|
| Obv. | 10 mina of staples |
| | from the basket. |
| | Month XII, |
| 4 | day 3, |
| Rev. | year 2 of King Kadašman-Turgu. |

COMMENTARY

1. At Nippur (Sassmannshausen 2001, 309–10) as well as in the Kassite texts from the Rosen Collection *maššartu* always refers to amounts of cereals, while here it must have indicated a different commodity that was weighed in minas.
2. ŠÀ can be occasionally used instead of *ina* ŠÀ in order to express "out of, from" (Aro 1955, 103).

## **310. CUNES 52-16-080**

23.II.7 Kadašman-Turgu

Obv. 8 GÍN 3 $^{giš}$GU.ZA$^{meš}$
*ša* ⸢ka$^?$ si$^?$ nun$^?$ ti$^?$ x x ti⸣
$^{md}$30-TI-URU$_4$ ⸢x x⸣
1/3 MA.NA ⸢1 NÍG.LÁ⸣ *ma*-⸢*gar-ri*⸣
*ša* $^{giš}$MAR.GÍD.DA
Rev. [2/3] MA.NA 1 NÍG.LÁ *ma-gar-ri*
[*š*]*a* $^{m}$MU-*líb-ši ša* ba$^?$ ⸢x x⸣

PAP 1 MA.NA 8 GÍN
$^{iti}$GU$_4$.SI.SÀ
L.e. U$_4$.23.KAM
MU.7.KAM *Ka-dáš-man-Túr-gu*

Translation

Obv. 8 shekels (for) 3 chairs
of . . .
Sîn-balāṭa-īriš ⸢. . .⸣;
one-third of a mina (for) a pair of wheels
for a wagon;
Rev. [two-thirds] of a mina (for) a pair of wheels
of Šumu-libši of . . .
In total: one mina (and) 8 shekels.
Month II,
L.e. day 23,
year 7 of Kadašman-Turgu.

COMMENTARY

7. At the end of the line one cannot exclude the reading $^{giš}$⸢GU.ZA⸣.

## **311. CUNES 52-13-131**

-.VII.11 Kadašman-Turgu

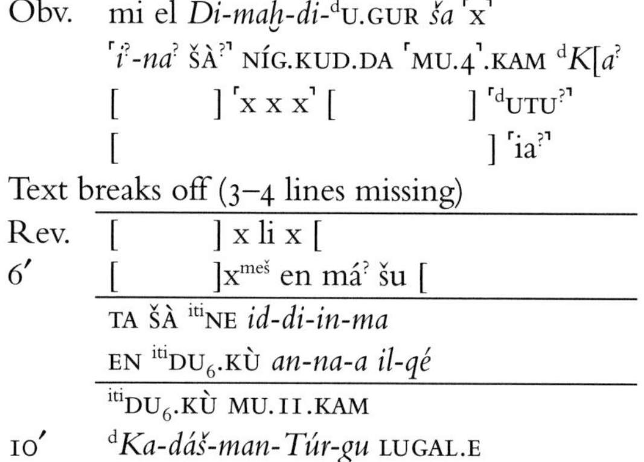
Obv. mi el *Di-maḫ-di*-$^{d}$U.GUR *ša* ⸢x⸣
⸢*i*$^?$-*na*$^?$ ŠÀ$^?$⸣ NÍG.KUD.DA ⸢MU.4⸣.KAM $^{d}$*K*[*a*$^?$
[ ] ⸢x x x⸣ [ ] ⸢$^{d}$UTU$^?$⸣
[ ] ⸢ia$^?$⸣
Text breaks off (3–4 lines missing)

Rev. [ ] x li x [
6′ [ ]x$^{meš}$ en má$^?$ šu [

TA ŠÀ $^{iti}$NE *id-di-in-ma*
EN $^{iti}$DU$_6$.KÙ *an-na-a il-qé*

$^{iti}$DU$_6$.KÙ MU.11.KAM
$^{d}$*Ka-dáš-man-Túr-gu* LUGAL.E

Commentary

1. Or 14.0.0 instead of MI.

## 312. CUNES 52-17-268

-.-.12 Kadašman-Turgu

The obverse is completely lost with the exception of traces of a few signs on the right edge.

Rev. ⸢x x x x⸣
2′ MU.12.KAM
$^{d}$*Ka-dáš-man-*⸢*Túr-gu*⸣
LUGAL.⸢E⸣

## 313. CUNES 52-17-260

-.II.12 Kadašman-Turgu

The tablet was too fragile to bake and its surface is still very encrusted. Scattered sign traces are visible on the obverse and on the right edge, continuing on the reverse.

L.e. PAP ⸢22$^{+}$⸣ [
Rev. $^{iti}$GU$_4$.SI.[SÀ]
3′ MU.12.⸢KAM⸣
⸢*Ka-dáš-man-Túr-gu*⸣

## 314. CUNES 52-18-763

12.IV.12 Kadašman-Turgu

Sealed by Iqīša-Adad.

The tablet is a pastiche, with the obverse plastered with clay and incised with fake signs. Only a few traces of the original signs are still visible on this part of the tablet.

L.e. 1.0.0 ZAG.ḪI.LI ⸢$^{giš}$BÁN 10⸣ [SÌLA]
Rev. ⸢$^{iti}$⸣ŠU.NUMUN.NA
U$_4$.12.KAM
MU.12.KAM
5′ $^{d}$*Ka-dáš-man-Túr-gu*
NA$_4$.KIŠIB $^{m}$BA-*šá*-$^{d}$⸢IŠKUR⸣

## 315. CUNES 52-18-814

5.II.13 Kadašman-Turgu

| | |
|---|---|
| Obv. | $^{md}$IŠKUR-*za-ki-*[*ir* |
| | $^{m}$*Ḫu-ud-di-im-ma-a-nu* ⌜DUMU.A⌝.[NI] |
| | $^{m}$*Ḫu-um-mu-rù* DUMU.A.NI |
| | $^{md}$IŠKUR-MU-*li-ši-ir* DUMU $^{m}$*Ḫu*-⌜x⌝[ |
| | ⌜$^{m}$*Ḫu*$^{?}$-*un*$^{?}$⌝-*nu*-⌜*bu*⌝ ŠEŠ.A.NI |
| | [x x] ⌜x 14$^{?}$.x.x⌝ Í[B$^{?}$.TAK$_{4}^{?}$ |
| | [ŠU$^{?}$] ⌜$^{md}$*Nin*$^{?}$-*urta*$^{?}$⌝-MU-MU |
| | [ ] ⌜x x⌝ [ |
| Rev. | [ ] |
| | [ ] ⌜x ŠEŠ$^{?}$⌝ [ |
| | $^{iti}$GU$_{4}$.SI.SÀ U$_{4}$.5.KAM |
| | MU.13.KAM $^{d}$*Ka-dáš-man-Túr-gu* |
| | LUGAL.E |

## 316. CUNES 52-18-842

-.-.17

Only the right half of the tablet is preserved; an unknown number of columns is missing to the left of the preserved portion.

| | | | |
|---|---|---|---|
| Obv. | [ ] | | MU.BI.IM |
| | [ ]⌜x⌝$^{ḫi.a}$ | ŠU.NÍGIN | MU.17.KAM |
| | [ ]$^{ḫi?.a}$ | | |
| | [ ] | 3.0.0 | $^{m}$*Ta*-TUK-*uš-ši-ni-e*$^{?}$ |
| | [ ] | 2.0.0 | $^{md}$30-*muš-te-šir* |
| | [ ] | 2.0.0 | $^{m}$ŠEŠ-*dam-qu* $^{m}$*Bur-ru-qu*$^{!}$(tum) |
| | [ ] EN 30$^{?}$.0.0 | 5.0.0 | $^{m}$*Bu-un-na*-$^{d}$*Gu-la* |
| | [ ] | 3.0.0 | $^{md}$*Nuska*-ŠEŠ-SUM-*na* |
| | [x.x].2 | 3.0.2 | $^{m}$DÙ-*a-šá*-$^{d}$UTU |
| | [ ] | 2.1.5 | $^{m}$GAL-*šá*-GAŠAN-*ti* |
| Rev. | [ ] | 1.0.0 | $^{md}$30-*eri-ba* |
| | [ ] | 3.0.0 | $^{m}$*E-mi-du* |
| | [ ] | | $^{m}$ZÁLAG-$^{d}$KUR |
| [PAP$^{?}$] | [ ] | 24.2.1 | *šu-ta-pu-ú* |
| | [ ] | ⌜6⌝.2.5 | $^{m}$*I-ku-na* |
| | [ ] | 4.0.0 | $^{m}$KI.MIN $^{md}$MAŠ-*li-su* |
| | [ ] | 4.0.0 | $^{m}$KI.MIN $^{m}$*Ḫu-ud-di-nu* |
| | [ ] | 1.0.0 | $^{m}$*Ib-ni*-$^{d}$AMAR.UTU |
| | [ ] | [0.2].3 | $^{m}$*Ki-din-ni*-$^{d}$UTU |
| [PAP$^{?}$] | [ ] | [1]6.0.2 | |

COMMENTARY

3. The interpretation of the PN escapes me; the last sign could also be KID.

6. EN 30$^{?}$.0.0 is written in a smaller script. EN is clear, but I am not sure that what follows is a quantity.

18. The amount in col. ii is restored after the total in l. 19.

## 317. CUNES 52-13-084

Not dated.

| | |
|---|---|
| Obv. | 10.1.3 *si-ir-im-du* |
| | BÀD-$^{d+}$*En-líl*$^{m[eš].ki}$ |
| | 3.0.2 *Kar-Nin-*⸢*É*⸣*-an-n*[*a*] |
| | PAP 13.1.5 [x x] |

The reverse is blank.

COMMENTARY

1. For *si-ir-im-du*, cf. *si-ir-ri-im-du* in **no. 37**: 37 and see commentary there.

## 318. CUNES 52-12-065

Not dated.

| | |
|---|---|
| Obv. | 9 *tup-pu* SUM-*nu* |
| | *i-na* ŠÀ ŠE ḪA.LA |
| | *ša* KI $^{m}$ÌR-*nu-bat-ti* |
| | EN *ša* 2.2.3 SUM-*ni* |
| L.e. | *maḫ-ri-i* |

The reverse is blank.

## 319. CUNES 52-13-082

Not dated.

| | | |
|---|---|---|
| Obv. | ÚTUL$^{?}$ da ar MU.BI.IM | |
| | 6 | $^{m}$GAL-*šá*-GAŠAN |
| | 6 | DUMU $^{m}$SUM-$^{d}$U.GUR |
| | | *a-na* ⸢a$^{?}$ x x *id*⸣*-din* |
| | 6 | $^{m}$*Za-ki-*[*rù* |
| | | *a-na* ⸢*ki*$^{?}$⸣ [ |
| | 2 | $^{m}$*Mu-*[ |
| | | *a-na* $^{m}$[x x x *id*]*-din* |
| L.e. | 1 | $^{m}$*Il-l*[*u*$^{?}$- |
| | | EN.NU.⸢UN⸣ KÁ.GAL |
| Rev. | PAP 21 ZI.GA | |

COMMENTARY

1. The text records items counted in units, which would fit with the reading ÚTUL, Akk. *diqāru* "bowl." I cannot offer any interpretation for DA AR; instead of AR one could also read *ši-ri* < *šīru* "meat," but that does not seem to make much sense either.

## 320. CUNES 52-00-052

Date not preserved.

Monthly account of unknown items, covering a time span of at least two years. The first part, ending with month XII in l. 3′, probably referred to year 10, while the second part (ll. 4′–11′) concerns months I–VIII of year 11.

Only the right side and the lower part of the obverse are preserved; the number of missing columns is unknown.

Obv. (1–2 lines missing)

| | | | |
|---|---|---|---|
| | [ ] | [x] | [ ] |
| | [ ] | [x] | [$^{iti}$ZÍZ].A.AN |
| | [ ] | [x] | [$^{iti}$]ŠE$^!$.KIN.KU$_5$ |
| | [ ] | [x] | $^{iti}$BÁR.ZAG.GAR MU.11.KAM |
| | [ ] | [x] | ⸢$^{iti}$GU$_4$⸣.SI.SÁ |
| | [ ] | [x] | $^{iti}$SIG$_4$.GA |
| | [ ] | [x] | $^{iti}$ŠU.NUMUN.NA |
| Rev. | [ ] | 1 | $^{iti}$NE.NE.GAR |
| | [ ] | 1 | $^{iti}$KIN.$^{d}$INANNA |
| | [ ] | ⸢1⸣ | $^{iti}$DU$_6$.KÙ |
| | [ ] | [x] | $^{iti}$APIN.DU$_8$.A |
| | [ ] | [x] | [x (x)] ⸢x⸣ ŠU DUMU.MUNUS $^{lú}$Ì.SUR |
| | [ ] | [x] | [x x (x)] ⸢ŠU⸣ DUMU.MUNUS $^{lú}$Ì.SUR |

Text breaks off.

## 321. CUNES 52-00-054

Date not preserved.

Upper right corner of a tablet; it is impossible to assess the size of the missing portion.

Obv. [. . . -$^{d}$N]*in-ìmma*
[. . . -*d*]*in-ma*
[. . . -SUM$^?$]-*at*

---

[. . . DU]MU$^?$ $^{m}$EGIR-DINGIR-⸢SIG$_5$$^?$⸣
[. . .]⸢x⸣ $^{lú}$NAGAR
[. . .] $^{lú}$LUNGA
[. . . $^{m}$*Mu*$^?$-*d*]*a*$^?$-*mi-iq*-⸢$^{d}$⸣[

Text breaks off, unknown number of missing lines

Rev. [. . .] ⸢DINGIR$^?$ na$^?$ x⸣
[. . .]
[. . .] ⸢x-x⸣-*šar-rat*
[. . .] ⸢x x x⸣

## 322. CUNES 52-16-106

Date not preserved.

Only the left portion of the tablet is preserved. It was acquired attached to **no. 123**, with new clay used to fill the gap between the two fragments; it cannot be completely excluded that the two fragments did not originally belong to the same tablet.

The column-headings suggest that the text recorded a monthly account.

Obv. (ca. 2 lines missing)

| | | |
|---|---|---|
| | [x x] | [x] ⸢x⸣ |
| | ⸢$^{iti}$ŠE?⸣ | ⸢$^{iti}$DU$_6$⸣ |
| 2′ | ⸢10$^+$.0.0⸣ | 1 ME 20.0.0 |
| | | |
| | ⸢x⸣ | 1 ME 20.0.0 |

The reverse is blank.

## 323. CUNES 53-01-124

Date not preserved.

Small fragment that was originally attached to **no. 332** and probably also partially plastered with fake signs, here indicated with asterisks. The correct identification of obverse and reverse is not certain.

Obv.? [. . .] ⸢x⸣ rat?
[. . .] ⸢x x⸣
L.e. [. . .] ⸢x⸣ ḫa
[. . .] ⸢x⸣ ar
Rev.? [. . .] ⸢x⸣ ni x *?
[. . .]
[. . .] ⸢x *?⸣

# 5. LEGAL DOCUMENTS

## 5.1 *tuppi aḫūzati*

### 324. CUNES 52-10-089 (Plate No. 62)

29.IX.18 Burna-Buriaš

Sealed by Izkur-Nergal, Ubāru, and Bananâtu.

This tablet, dated to the 18th year of King Burna-Buriaš, represents the oldest MB document in the Rosen Collection kept at Cornell University. It preserves the text of a *tuppi aḫūzati*, a type of document known only for the MB period (see CAD Ṭ, *ṭuppu* A 1a, 134), which was previously attested by only three other examples:

- one from Dūr-Kurigalzu, published as no. 4 in Gurney 1949, 133–34, 144 (henceforth D-K 4)
- one from Tell Zubeidi, published as no. 739 by Kessler 1985, 79, pl. 165 (henceforth Zub. 739)
- one from Nippur, published as MUN 19 by Sassmannshausen 2001, 221.

The surface of the obverse is very worn and one can barely recognize some of the elements already known from the other tablets of the same type. The reverse transmits the names of four witnesses, the date, and the names of the three persons who sealed the tablet.

Tablets of this type were related to those bearing the introductory formula *tuppi zununnê* "tablet of maintenance," with which they partially share the same formulary (see the observations by Gurney 1949, 134 and Gurney 1983, 136–38).

Obv. *tup-pi a-ḫu-za-t*[*i*] ⸢*ša* $^{f}$*Ba-na*$^{?}$*-na*$^{?}$*-ti*⸣
*it-ti* ⸢AMA.A.NI$^{?}$ x⸣ [x] ⸢x x⸣
*it-ti* $^{m}$*Iz-kùr*-⸢$^{d}$U.GUR$^{?}$ x x ni$^{?}$⸣
*ù* ⸢*it-ti* a$^{?}$⸣ [x x x x x] ⸢x⸣
⸢x x x x x li$^{?}$⸣
*a-na* KÙ.BABBAR ⸢*ša*$^{?}$⸣ [x] ⸢*ga-am*⸣*-ru-ti*
2 UDU/TÚG ⸢*ša*$^{?}$⸣ [x x x] 20 ⸢GU$_{4}$$^{?}$⸣$^{meš}$
2 GUR ⸢*ša*$^{?}$⸣ [x x x] ⸢x x⸣
⸢x x x⸣ [x x] ⸢x x x⸣
10 ⸢MA.NA⸣ [x] ⸢x x x⸣
70.0.0 ⸢x x⸣ [x] ⸢ti$^{?}$ x x x⸣
⸢x⸣ [x x x x x *il*$^{?}$]-⸢*qè*$^{?}$⸣
⸢x⸣ [x x x x *id*$^{?}$]-⸢*di*$^{?}$*-in*⸣
[ ]
[ ]

Rev. [*ši*]-*bu* $^{m}$*Šu-ur-ba-a*[*k*-
DUMU $^{m}$*Tu-uḫ*-$^{d+}$*En-lí*[*l*$^{?}$

---

[*ši*]-*bu* $^{m}$*Ḫi-im-ma-tu*$_{4}$
DUMU $^{m}$*Šu-ur-ba-a-a*-x[

---

*ši-bu* $^{m}$[x x]-⸢x⸣-$^{d}$30 le el$^{?}$
DUMU $^{md}$[*Gu*$^{?}$]-⸢*la*$^{?}$-x a$^{?}$ x x x⸣

---

*ši-bu* $^{m}$*Tu-kul-t*[*i-lu-d*]*a*-⸢*ri*⸣
*ḫa-za-an-nu*

---

$^{iti}$GAN.GAN.È U$_{4}$.29.KAM

MU.18.KAM *Bur-na-Bu-ri-ia-*⸢*aš*⸣ LUGAL x⸣
NA$_4$.KIŠIB $^{m}$*Iz-kùr-*$^{d}$U.[GUR$^{?}$]
$^{m}$*U-bar-rù*
*ù* $^{f}$*Ba-na-na-ti*

COMMENTARY

1. The opening line identifies the text as *tuppi aḫūzati ša Bananâti*$^{?}$: if the reading of the PN is correct, Bananâtu must have been the same woman who is mentioned at the end of the reverse as one of the persons who sealed the tablet (see l. 28). However, in the other texts of this type, one finds in the same position the name of a man, who is usually identified as the "bridegroom" (cf. D-K 4: 2 and Zub. 739: 2).

3. Izkur-Nergal probably corresponds to one of the persons who sealed the tablet (see l. 26).

4. Perhaps ⸢*it-ti a*⸣-[*bi-ša*] "with/from [her] fa[ther]"; cf. D-K 4: 3 (KI AD.A.NI) and Zub. 739: 5 (*a-bi-ša*, fragm. context).

5–6. None of the other *tuppi aḫūzati* preserves the verb at the end of the introductory formula. CAD (A/1, *aḫūzatu* 1, 217) proposed that it might have been *īḫuzu*, which is the closing verb of the *tuppi zununnê* D-K 5 (Gurney 1949, 135).

7. Both sheep and garments are plausible, since both items appear in the list of gifts of D-K 4 (cf. ll. 10–13, 41).

12. If it is correct to read GI at the end of the line, then this line could have ended with a 3 sg. preterite G of *leqû* as in D-K 4: 40. Otherwise, one could also restore [KÙ].GI "[go]ld," which often occurs among the gifts listed by D-K 4.

18. For other MB attestations of the spelling *ši-bu*, instead of the more common writing IGI, see also MBTU 15 and MBTU 32 from Ur, and OIC 22, 131 (text no. 19) from Nippur.

23. A *ḫazannu* Tukultī-lū-dāri is known also from BE 15 199: 2, an account of livestock from Nippur that refers to year 15 of an unknown king.

25. The sign after LUGAL looks like the beginning of ŠA.

## 5.2 Contract of Exchange

### 325. CUNES 52-13-101 (Plate No. 63)

-.VIa.14 Nazi-Maruttaš

This text preserves a contract of exchange, like the one from Ur published as MBTU 32 (see Gurney 1983, 8 and 100–101); cf. also 13 N 126, a legal text from Nippur containing an exchange clause (Brinkman 1993, 95–96).

Its structure can be outlined as follows (paragraphs correspond to the actual text divisions indicated by horizontal rulings on the tablet):

§1 ll. 1–3: commodity$_1$
ll. 4–5: PN$_1$ gave (*iddin-ma*) to PN$_2$
l. 6: (PN$_1$) received (*imḫur*) commodity$_2$
ll. 7–12: renunciation of claims by PN$_1$, PN$_2$, and PN$_3$ (see discussion below)
§2 ll. 13–19: witnesses
§3 ll. 20–21: date
ll. 22–23: fingernail impressions of PN$_3$

Obv. [1 G]U$_4$.NÍNDA DIRI
4.0.0 ŠE $^{giš}$BÁN 5 SÌLA
1 TÚG *kab-ru ki* 2 GÍN KÙ.BABBAR
$^{m}$*E-ri-bu a-na* $^{m}$*Man-nu-ki-*$^{d}$*É-a*
*id-di-in-ma*
1 GU$_4$ *ri-it-ti im-ḫu-ur*
*ul i-ta-ar* $^{m}$EN-*šu-nu*
⸢*ù*?$^{m}$⸣*Man-nu-ki-*$^{d}$*É-a*
*a-na* $^{m}$*E-ri-b*[*i ul i-ra-ag-gu-um*]
*ù* $^{m}$⸢*E*⸣*-r*[*i-bu a-na* $^{m}$*Man-nu-ki-*$^{d}$*É-a*]
Rev. ⸢*a-na*⸣ $^{m}$EN-*šu-*[*nu*]
⸢*ul i*⸣*-ra-ag-g*[*u-um*]

---

IGI $^{m}$⸢x-x⸣-[
DUMU $^{m}$*Ba-a*[*q*?*-ni*?]
IGI $^{m}$KAR-*ub-*$^{d}$AMAR.UTU
DUMU $^{m}$*Ur-*$^{d}$*Asar-alim-ma*
IGI $^{m}$*In-na-an-nu*
DUMU $^{m}$*La-qí-pi*
IGI $^{m}$*Ri-iš-*UD*-šú* DUB.SAR

---

$^{iti}$KIN.$^{d}$INANNA.2.KAM.MA
MU.14.KAM *Na-zi-Múru-taš*
L.e. ⸢UMBIN⸣ $^{m}$EN-*šu-nu ki-ma*
NA$_4$.KIŠIB-*šu*

At least 3 fingernail impressions on the left edge of the tablet.

Translation

Obv. Erību gave to Mannu-kī-Ea
1 [one] extra[?] [bu]ll calf,
2 120 *sūtu* of barley (measured by) the *sūtu* of 5 *qû*
3 (and) one thick garment for two shekels of silver,
6 and received one plow-ox.
7 Bēlšunu will not come back (to the contract),
8–9 Mannu-kī-Ea [will not make a claim] against Erīb[u],
10–12 and Er[ību] will not make a cla[im either against Mannu-kī-Ea or] against Bēlšu[nu].

Witness: . . . [ . . . ],
son of Ba[qnu[?]];
15 witness: Šūzub-Marduk,
son of Ur-Asaralimma;
witness: Innannu,
son of Lā-qīpu;
witness: Rīš-aṣûšu, scribe.

20 Month VIa,
year 14 of Nazi-Maruttaš.

L.e. Fingernail (impressions) of Bēlšunu instead
of his seal.

Commentary

1. DIRI probably indicates here the extra ox used as a reserve in plow teams, GU$_4$.(UD.)DIRI(.GA) (see Stol 1995, 191 and Weszeli 2007, 394).

3. I thank Susanne Paulus for having brought to my attention other documents that attest the same value for a thick garment: two shekels of silver in BE 14 128a: 9 and its corresponding value in gold (one half-shekel) in PBS 2/2 27: 10 and D-K 4: 32–33. Alternatively, one could read KI 2 GÍN KÙ.BABBAR "together with two shekels of silver."

6–12. Restorations are tentative. Different types of MB legal documents express the mutual renunciation of claims by the parties involved in the legal transaction through the formula *ul itâr-ma . . . ul iraggum*. Most scholars translate it "he will not return and will not lay a claim" (see translations of MRWH 8: 22–25, MBTU 30: rev. 3–6, MBTU 31: rev. 1–4, MBTU 32: obv. 6–12 and BE 14 123: 9–14, and Sassmannshausen 2001, 209–10), while CAD T, *târu* 5b, 261 understands these cases as occurrences of the use of *târu* in hendiadys and translates them accordingly "to not make a claim again." In our text, a third party comes into play at this point: a certain Bēlšunu, whose relationship to the two other individuals involved in the exchange (Erību and Mannu-kī-Ea) is not clarified, but who clearly had some authority over the exchanged goods, since he is also the person who seals the tablet. Bēlšunu is the postponed subject of *ul itâr*, which is not connected to the following verbal forms (*ul iraggum*) by the enclitic *–ma*, since the subjects of the following sentences are Mannu-kī-Ea and Erību: this seems to confirm that *târu* and *ragāmu* are not used in hendiadys in this formula, contrary to what was proposed by CAD.

19. A scribe named Rīš-aṣûšu is known also from the Nippur text PBS 2/2 133: 32, which dates to the 14[th] year of an unnamed king, identified with Nazi-Maruttaš by Hölscher (1996, 179, s.v. Rīš-aṣûšu 3) and with Kadašman-Turgu by Tsukimoto (1985, 81).

## 5.3 Purchase of an Ox

### 326. CUNES 52-14-030 (Plate No. 64)

20.VI.22 Nazi-Maruttaš
Sealed by Dayyān-Marduk.

The text is a contract for the purchase of an ox; its structure and formulary only partially correspond to the purchases of cattle previously known from Ur, Nippur and the Peiser archive (see Gurney 1983, 3–8; Sassmannshausen 2001, 208–10; PEISER 1905, 30).

After the purchase formula, the document indicates also that the buyer (Ninurta-zākir-šumi) gave the ox to a third individual (the son of Ilī-rēmanni).

Its structure can be outlined as follows:

l. 1: object of the purchase
ll. 2–3: from (*itti*) the seller
l. 4: the purchaser
l. 5: took and (ŠU BA.AN.TI-*ma*)
l. 6: gave (*iddin*) to a third party;
l. 7: for its full price (ŠÁM.TIL.LA.BI.ŠÈ)
ll. 8–9: the purchaser gave (*iddin*) goods in lieu of money
ll. 10–15: sworn statement about the renunciation of future claims
ll. 16–22: witnesses
ll. 23–24: date
ll. 25–26: caption identifying the seal owner (i.e., the seller).

Obv. [1 GU$_4$].⸢Á$^{?}$⸣.ÚR.RA KUŠ-*šu* IGI$^{?}$
[*it*]-*ti* $^{m}$DI.KU$_5$-$^{d}$AMAR.UTU
[DUM]U $^{md}$UTU-ÙRU
[$^{m}$]$^{d}$*Nin-urta*-MU-MU
[Š]U BA.AN.TI-*ma*
*a-na* DUMU $^{m}$*Ì-lí-*⸢*re-man-ni* ÉNSI$^{?}$⸣ *i-din*
ŠÁM.TIL.LA.⸢BI⸣.ŠÈ
8.0.0 ŠE.BAR $^{giš}$BÁN 10 SÌLA
*ki-i* 4 GÍN ⸢KÙ.GI⸣ *i-din*
⸢U$_4$.ME.DA⸣ U$_4$.DA.⸢EGIR.BI⸣.ŠÈ
INIM NU.GÁ.GÁ.A INIM NU.GI$_4$.GI$_4$
[M]U *An-nim* $^{d+}$*En-líl*
[$^{d}$*Ni*]*n-urta* $^{d}$*Nus*[*ka*]
[ ]
Rev. [x x] ⸢x x x⸣ [
[IGI $^{m}$]*Šum-ma-ak-la*-$^{d}$⸢x⸣[
[DU]MU $^{m}$*Me-*⸢*li*⸣-$^{d}$[*Šu-q*]*a-mu-*[*na*]
IGI $^{m}$*Ì-lí-re-man-ni*
[DU]MU $^{m}$*Ì-lí*-BA-*ša*
[IGI] $^{md}$*Nin-urta*-ÙRU
[DUMU] $^{m}$*Ba-ti-ia-ú-tu*$_4$
[IGI] $^{m}$ÌR-GAŠAN DUB.SAR DUMU $^{m}$ÁG-[*kit*]-*ti*
[$^{it}$]$^{i}$KIN.$^{d}$INANNA U$_4$.20.KAM
MU.22.KAM *Na-zi-Ma-ru-ut-ta-aš*
NA$_4$.KIŠIB $^{m}$DI.KU$_5$-$^{d}$AMAR.UTU
DUMU $^{md}$UTU-ÙRU

Translation

Obv. [1] rear-[ox], its hide is . . . ,
[fr]om Dayyān-Marduk,
[so]n of Šamaš-nāṣir,
Ninurta-zākir-šumi
5 [t]ook and
gave to the son of Ilī-rēmanni, the farmer?.
For its full price
8–9 he gave 8 kor of barley (measured by) the *sūtu* of 10 *qû* for 4 shekels of gold.
15 [They swore together]
12 by An, Enlil,
13 [Ni]nurta, Nus[ka],
14 [and by Nazi-Maruttaš]
10 that ⸢at any time⸣, in future days
11 they will not make any claim (and) will not come back (to the contract).
16 [Witness]: Šummak-lā-⸢ . . . ⸣[ . . . ]
[so]n of Meli-[Šuq]amu[na];
witness: Ilī-rēmanni,
[so]n of Ilī-iqīša;
20 [witness]: Ninurta-nāṣir,
[son of] Battiyūtu;
[witness]: Arad-bēlti, scribe, son of Rā'im-[kit]ti.
[Mo]nth VI, day 20,
year 22 of Nazi-Maruttaš.
25 Seal of Dayyān-Marduk,
son of Šamaš-nāṣir.

Commentary

1. The common logographic writing for "rear-ox" would be GU$_4$.(Á).ÙR.RA (see Stol 1995, 191; Weszeli 2007, 394). At the end of the line, one expects an indication of the color of the ox's hide, but the sign, which looks like IGI, does not correspond to any color. Cf. the purchase contracts PBS 2/2 27: 1 (KUŠ *ša* GE$_6$), UDBD 139: 2 ([KU]Š-*šú* GE$_6$), and MRWH 3: 1 (KUŠ-*šu* G[E$_6$]); on the description of cattle by color in administrative texts, see MUN 313, 315, 317, and 322.

5. The verb *ilqe* "he took," here written logographically ŠU BA.AN.TI, is used also in the contract of purchase MBTU 34: obv. 4, where it is spelled syllabically *il-qé*; the other contracts of purchase usually have here the verb *išâm* "he bought" (see variants of logographic and syllabic writings in Sassmannshausen 2001, 205 and 209).

6. The reading of the profession of the son of Ilī-rēmanni is supported by other cases where he is identified as ÉNSI (see Index of Personal Names).

10–15. Such sworn statements about the renunciation of future claims are not attested in the other MB contracts of cattle purchase known to me, but are used in the contracts of purchase of slaves and real estate (Sassmannshausen 2001, 203–8). The number of missing lines is uncertain but the size of the tablet suggests that they cannot be more than one or two. The suggested reconstruction is based on the most "minimalistic" attested formulary: after the gods, one expects at least the name of the ruling king (Nazi-Maruttaš) and the sentence "they swore together," which is usually written logographically (see variants in Sassmannshausen 2001, 206–7).

12. The spelling of the divine name An is unusual; cf. the attestations listed by Sassmannshausen (2001, 206) and also MUN 10: 25 and MUN 11: 6.

16. For PNs of the type Šummak-lā-DN, see van Soldt 2015, 404 (comments to CUSAS 30 321: 11).

## 5.4 Settlements of Disputes

### 327. CUNES 52-16-105 (Plate No. 65)

2.IV.5 Kadašman-Turgu

Settlement of a dispute concerning boat equipment of Erība-Adad, boatman of Ninurta-zākir-šumi.

Obv. 1 *aš-la* 1 *pa-ri-sa-am*
1 $^{giš}$*gi-šal-la ša* $^{m}$*Eri-ba-*⸢$^{d}$IŠKUR⸣
$^{lú}$MÁ.LAḪ$_5$ *ša* $^{md}$*Nin-urta-*MU-MU
$^{md}$*Nin-urta-ki-na-i-de*
DUMU $^{md}$30-LA-*piš-ti*
*ki-i ša* ⸢la$^?$ di iš$^?$ x ma$^?$⸣
*a-na* ŠÀ $^{giš}$MÁ *ša* $^{m}$*Še-*[*le-bi*]
$^{lú}$MÁ.LAḪ$_5$ $^{d+}$*En-líl-mu-kin-*IBI[LA]
*ú-še-li-ma* $^{m}$SU-$^{d}$IŠKUR
$^{md}$*Nin-urta-ki-na-i-de iṣ-bat-ma*
*aš-li pa-ri-si ù gi-*[*šal*]*-li*
*bi-lam-mi*$^!$ *iq-b*[*i-šu*]
⸢x x x x⸣
Text breaks off (1–2 lines missing)
Rev. $^{lú}$MÁ.L[AḪ$_5$
$^{m}$*Eri-ba-*⸢$^{d}$IŠK⸣[UR
*i-šal-ma i-tu-ú-a ia-nu*
$^{md}$*Nin-urta-ki-na-i-de*
*ú-ka-an-na-an-ni-ma*
*ú-nu-ut-ka a-ta-nap-pal-ka*
*a-na* SAG $^{iti}$NE.NE.GAR
*a-dan-ka* ⸢*lu*$^?$*-u*$^?$ *it-*x-x⸣
*mi-it-ḫar i-ta-nap-pal*

---

IGI $^{m}$*Ba-e-ri* DUMU $^{m}$*Ba-ḫe-e*
IGI $^{m}$*Ba-na-ni-i ḫa-za-an-*[*nu*]
IGI $^{m}$*Mu-dam-mi-iq-*$^{d}$IŠKUR
DUB.SAR
L.e. [$^{iti}$]ŠU.NUMUN.NA U$_4$.2.KAM
(7 fingernail impressions)
Le.e. [M]U.5.KAM *Ka-dáš-man-Túr-gu* LUGAL UMBIN $^{m}$*Še-*⸢*le-bi*⸣

Translation

Obv. 1 mooring rope, 1 rudder,
1 boat-pole of Erība-Adad,
boatman of Ninurta-zākir-šumi,
4 Ninurta-kīna-īde,
5 son of Sîn-usuḫ-pišti,
just as . . .

7–9 embarked on the boat of Šē[lebu], boatman of Enlil-mukīn-ap[li], so Erība-Adad
10 seized Ninurta-kīna-īde and
11–12 told [him]: "Bring me my mooring rope, my rudder and my boat-pole!"
13 ⸢. . .⸣
Text breaks off (1–2 lines missing)
Rev. The boat[man
15′ Erība-Ad[ad
asked and (he said): "They are not with me.
Ninurta-kīna-īde
will confirm my statement and
I will pay you back your equipment.
20′ At the beginning of month V
your term . . . ,
he will pay an equal amount (as a fine)."
Witness: Bā'eru, son of Baḫû;
witness: Bananû, *ḫazannu*;
25′ witness: Mudammiq-Adad,
scribe.
L.e. Month IV, day 2,
(7 fingernail impressions)
Le.e. [ye]ar 5 of King Kadašman-Turgu. Fingernail (impressions) of Šēlebu.

Commentary

1–2. According to the dictionaries, these would be the first attestations of *parīsu* "rudder, pole" and *gišallu* "oar, boat-pole" in MB texts from Mesopotamia (see CAD and AHw s.v.).

2. Erība-Adad, the boatman of Ninurta-zākir-šumi, is mentioned also in CUSAS 30 31, a letter of Ninurta-zākir-šumi to his lord, and in the summary of expenditures **no. 176**: 25, where he receives an amount of barley for a carpenter hired to build a boat.

16′–22′. I imagine that the person speaking here is Šēlebu, who commits himself by sealing the tablet (l. 28′), but the exact meaning of this passage escapes me: if Šēlebu does not have Erība-Adad's equipment and Ninurta-kīna-īde will confirm this, why should he pay it back? And then who is the person who will pay the fine?

21′. With *adanka* "your term" as the subject of the sentence, one would expect a form of *etēqu* "to expire" at the end of this line, perhaps *it-ti-iq*.

## 328. CUNES 52-16-069 (Plate No. 66)

19.VI.17 Kadašman-Turgu

Settlement of a dispute arising from a payment owed by Šagarakti to Enlil-gešir$^?$-ilāni$^?$, which is taken over by Iddin-Marduk.

For a similar document in the Rosen Collection, see CUSAS 30 3 (KuE 3).

Obv. [ ]x
*š*[*a*$^?$ $^{md}$50-*ge*]-⌜*šìr*$^?$-DINGIR$^{meš?}$⌝
⌜*i-na*$^?$ UGU$^?$ $^{m}$*Ša-ga*⌝-*rak-ti* ⌜*i-šu-u-ma*⌝
$^{md}$50-*ge-šìr*$^?$-DINGIR$^{meš?}$ $^{m}$*Ša-ga-rak-ti*
⌜*iṣ*$^?$-*bat*$^?$-*ma*$^?$⌝ ŠE.BAR *bi-lam-mi iq-bi-šu*
$^{m}$SUM-$^{d}$AMAR.UTU *a-na* $^{md}$50-*ge-šìr*$^?$-DINGIR$^{meš?}$
*ki-a-a*[*m iq-b*]*i* $^{m}$[*Ša*]-*ga-rak-ti*
*muš-ši*[*r*$^?$ (x) x] ⌜x⌝ *a-na-ku*
2 U$_8$.UDU$^{ḫi.a}$ *lu-ud-di-na-ak-ku*
*a-na* U$_4$.2.KAM *ša* $^{iti}$DU$_6$.KÙ
*a-da-an-na iš-kun*$_8^!$
*a-da-an iš-ku-nu it-ti-iq-ma*
L.e. UDU$^?$ *i-le-eq-qa-am-ma*
*ul im-ma-aḫ-ḫar*
Rev. *ša* 1.2.5 3.0.4 *i-nam-din*
16 IGI $^{m}$MU-*líb-ši*
IGI $^{m}$DINGIR.MU-*mu*-SIG$_5$
IGI $^{md}$30-*nap-ši-ra*

---

$^{iti}$KIN.$^{d}$INANNA U$_4$.19.KAM
MU.17.KAM
*Ka-dáš-man-Túr-gu* LUGAL.E
UMBIN $^{m}$SUM-$^{d}$AMAR.UTU
*ki-ma* NA$_4$.KIŠIB-*šu*

5 fingernail impressions on the left edge of the tablet.

Translation

Obv. [ ]x
w[hich$^?$ Enlil-ge]šir$^?$-ilāni$^?$
had owing from Šagarakti, thus
4–5 Enlil-gešir$^?$-ilāni$^?$ seized Šagarakti and told him: "Bring me the barley!"
6–8 Iddin-Marduk said to Enlil-gešir$^?$-ilāni$^?$ as follows: "Rele[ase$^?$] Šagarakti! [ . . . ] . . . I
9 shall give you 2 sheep."
10–11 He set a term for the second day of month VII.
(If) the term he has set expires and
L.e. the sheep$^?$ he will/should bring
is not accepted,
Rev. he will give 94 *sūtu* for 47 *sūtu*.
16 Witness: Šumu-libši;

witness: Ilī-mudammiq;
witness: Sîn-napšira.

Month VI, day 19,
year 17
of King Kadašman-Turgu.
Fingernail (impressions) of Iddin-Marduk
instead of his seal.

Commentary

1. This line must have recorded the quantity of barley owed by Šagarakti to Enlil-gešir[?]-ilāni[?], which probably amounted to 47 *sūtu* (see l. 14).

2. For the PN Enlil-gešir[?]-ilāni[?], see also **no. 289**: 10.

3. See MUN 16: 4–5 and MUN 18: 2–3 for other occurrences of the formula *ina muḫḫi* PN *išû* "to have (something) owing from PN."

15. If the payment is not performed on time, Iddin-Marduk will have to pay twice as much as the original amount owed by Šagarakti to Enlil-gešir[?]-ilāni[?]. The *poena duplex* as a penalty for failure to fulfil an obligation is attested also at Ur (MBTU 3: rev. 10–13, MBTU 20: rev. 6–9, MBTU 24: rev. 11′–13′) and Nippur (MUN 16: 13–18). Other legal texts from the Rosen Collection mandate instead the payment of an equal amount as a fine (**no. 327**, **no. 331**, and CUSAS 30 3).

## 5.5 Loans

### 329. CUNES 52-16-088

[ . . . ].[ . . . ].5 Kadašman-Turgu

This text is assigned here even though it does not bear all the features of a proper loan contract: the expected list of witnesses is missing and the tablet is not sealed. However, the indication that Arad-nubatti will have to return the barley at harvest time makes it closer to a contract of loan, rather than to a memorandum of barley disbursed as a loan (for which cf., e.g., **no. 121**). On the several possible variations on the standard structure of loan contracts, see Sassmannshausen 2001, 195ff.

Obv. ⸢5$^{+}$⸣.0.0 ŠE.GUR UR$_{5}$.RA $^{giš}$BÁN 10 SÌLA
TA 2 GUR *ša i-na* MU.5.KAM
*i-na* BÀD-$^{d+}$*En-líl*$^{hi.a.ki}$
*id-di-nu šu-lu-ú*
[Í]B.TAK$_{4}$ ŠU $^{m}$ÌR-⸢*nu-bat*⸣*-ti* DUMU $^{m}$*E-la-mi-i*
[*i-n*]*a* U$_{4}$.BURU$_{14}$ Ì.[ÁG].⸢E⸣
[$^{iti}$x U$_{4}$.X.KAM MU].5.KAM
[*Kadašman-Túr-g*]*u* LUGAL.E

The reverse is blank.

Translation

Obv. ⸢150$^{+}$⸣ *sūtu* of barley as loan (measured by) the *sūtu* of 10 *qû*,
2–4 after 60 *sūtu*, which he gave in the 5$^{th}$ year in Dūr-Enlilē, have been deducted:
5 [r]est (still) at the disposal of Arad-nubatti, son of Elamû.
He will deliver (it) at harvest time.
[Month x, day x, year] 5 of
King [Kadašman-Turg]u.

## 330. CUNES 52-10-064 (Plate No. 67)

12.V.14 Kadašman-Turgu

The text is a mix between a loan contract and a balanced account of the barley that Iddin-Nergal received as a loan and has already returned.

Obv. ŠE $^{giš}$BÁN 10 SÌLA UR$_5$.RA *ša* $^{m}$SUM-$^{d}$U.GUR
DUMU $^{m}$SUM-$^{d}$U.GUR *mi-taḫ-ḫu-ru*
⸢6.3⸣.2 ÍB.TAK$_4$ UR$_5$.RA *ša* MU.14.KAM
$^{d}$*Ka-dáš-man-Túr-gu*
TA 4.2.3 *ša* TA BÁRA$^{?}$.⸢DUMU$^{ki?}$ *id-di*⸣-*nu*
*šu-lu-ú*
2.0.0 *Tukul-ti*-É.[KUR]$^{ki}$ *ar*$^{?}$-⸢x-x⸣ $^{iti}$ŠE.KIN.KU$_5$
PAP 8.3.2 UR$_5$.RA *ša* $^{m}$SUM-$^{d}$U.GUR
DUMU $^{m}$SUM-$^{d}$U.GUR *i-na* U$_4$.BURU$_{14}$
Ì.ÁG.E
Rev. IGI $^{m}$KAR-*ub*-[$^{d}$]AMAR.UTU DUMU $^{m}$*Ur*-$^{d}$*Asar-ali*[*m-ma*]
IGI $^{m}$BA-*šá*-$^{d}$*Nin-ìmma* DUMU $^{m}$*E-tel*-KA-$^{d}$*Iš-tar*
IGI $^{m}$*Za-ki-rù man*-⸢*di*⸣-*du*
IGI DUB.SAR $^{m}$*Mu*-⸢SIG$_5$⸣-$^{d}$IŠKUR
$^{iti}$NE.NE.GAR [U$_4$].12.KAM
MU.14.KAM ⸢$^{d}$*Ka-dáš-man-Túr*⸣-*gu* LUGAL.E
UMBIN $^{m}$⸢SUM-$^{d}$U.GUR *ki-ma*⸣ NA$_4$.KIŠIB-*šu*

5 fingernail impressions on the left edge of the obverse.

Translation

Obv. Barley, (measured by) the *sūtu* of 10 *qû*, which Iddin-Nergal,
son of Iddin-Nergal, has been receiving as a loan.
200 *sūtu*: rest of the loan of year 14
of Kadašman-Turgu,
after 135 *sūtu*, which he gave from Parak-māri$^{?}$,
have been deducted.
60 *sūtu*: Tukultī-E[kur] . . . , month XII.
Total: 260 *sūtu* as a loan which Iddin-Nergal,
9–10 son of Iddin-Nergal, will deliver at harvest time.
Rev. Witness: Šuzub-Marduk, son of Ur-Asar-ali[m-ma];
witness: Iqīša-Ninimma, son of Etel-pī-Ištar;
witness: Zākiru, the measuring official;
witness: the scribe Mudammiq-Adad.
Month V, [day] 12,
year 14 of King Kadašman-Turgu.
Fingernail (impressions) of Iddin-Nergal instead of his seal.

COMMENTARY

7. Perhaps *ši-ri*-⸢x-x⸣ instead of *ar*-⸢x-x⸣.

### 331. CUNES 52-18-142 (Plate No. 68)

29.VIII.[ . . . ] Kadašman-Turgu

Textile impressions on the surface of the tablet.

The text is a mixture between a list of quantities disbursed as loans to different people (cf., e.g., **no. 120**) and a contract of loan (see ll. 23–27).

| | | |
|---|---|---|
| Obv. | ⸢ŠE$^{?}$ UR$_5$⸣.RA $^{giš}$B[ÁN 10 SÌLA] | |
| | [x] ⸢x⸣ $^{m}$*Al-*[ | |
| | 0.2.3 | $^{m}$*Ar-*[ |
| | 0.2.3 | $^{m}$*Iz-kùr-*[$^{d}$ |
| | 0.2.3 | $^{m}$*Ba-ni-ia* |
| | 0.2.3 | $^{m}$*Ṭà-ab-*MI |
| | 0.2.3 | $^{m}$*Ki-din-*$^{d}$*Šár-ur*$_4$ |
| | 1.0.0 | $^{m}$*A-*⸢*da-ga*⸣*-*<*al*>-IGI-DINGIR |
| | 0.1.4 | $^{md}$30-ŠEŠ-SUM-*na* |
| | 0.1.4 | $^{m}$IBILA-$^{d}$U.GUR |
| | 0.2.3 | $^{md}$IŠKUR-*šub-ši* |
| | 0.2.3 | $^{m}$*Ri-iš-*È*-šu* |
| | 0.1.4 | $^{m}$*La-te-re-qá-an-ni-*DINGIR |
| | 1 GUR | $^{m}$È*-a-na-nu-ú-a* |
| | 0.2.3 | $^{m}$*Ba-at-ti-i-ú-tu* |
| ⸢PAP⸣ | 7.0.0 | $^{giš}$BÁN 10 SÌLA |
| Rev. | [ | ] ⸢x⸣ *ša* ŠU *di-im-*⸢*ti*⸣ |
| | [ | ]*-na-bi* |
| | [ | $^{m}$*A*]*r-du-tu*$_4$ |
| | [ | *-b*]*i-ir-šu-nu-ti* |

[*i-na* $^{iti}$]⸢APIN⸣ U$_4$.29.KAM
[MU.x.KA]M $^{d}$*Ka-dáš-man-Túr-gu* LUGAL.⸢E⸣
*i-na* U$_4$.BURU$_{12}$ *i-si-ra-am-ma*
*i-nam-di-in*
*i-na* U$_4$.BURU$_{12}$ *ul it-ta-din-ma*
*mi-it-ḫa-ar*
*i-ma-da-ad*
*ṣú-pur* $^{m}$*Ar-du-ti*
*ki-ma* NA$_4$.KIŠIB-*šu*

3 fingernail impressions on the left edge of the tablet.

COMMENTARY

1. $^{giš}$B[ÁN 10 SÌLA] is restored after l. 16.

3. Probably $^{m}$*Ar-*[*du-tu*$_4$]; another possibility would be $^{m}$*Ši-ri-*[*iš-tu*$_4$].

7. To my knowledge, there are no other attestations of MB PNs bearing the theophoric element Šarur; in general, this deified weapon of the god Ninurta appears rarely in documents from the Kassite period, but it is mentioned in the god-list of a *kudurru* from the reign of Nazi-Maruttaš (NM 2 iv 25 in Paulus 2014b, 329 and 333; see Bartelmus 2017, 303).

13. The PN Lā-terêqanni-ilu/ilī "Don't go away from me, (my) god!" was previously unattested in MB onomastic repertoires.

23–29. "(23) On the day of the harvest he will collect (it) and (24) deliver (it). (25) (If) he does not deliver (it) on the day of the harvest, (26–27) he shall pay an equal amount (as fine). (28–29) Fingernail (impressions) of Ardūtu instead of his seal."

## 5.6 Uncertain

### 332. CUNES 53-00-040

-.VI.23 Nazi-Maruttaš

Obv. 1.0.⸢3$^{+}$⸣ [
EN 0.0.2 [
ŠU $^{m}$EN-*šu-nu* ⸢ni$^{?}$⸣ [
$^{iti}$ZÍZ.A.AN
L.e. MU.23.KAM
Rev. *Na-zi-Múru-taš*
LUGAL.E
UMBIN EN-[*šu-nu*]
*ki-ma* [NA$_4$.KIŠIB-*šu*]

2 fingernail impressions and impressions of a thin rope are visible on the left edge of the tablet.

COMMENTARY

3. At the end of the line one could perhaps restore Ì.[SUR], translating "Bēlšunu, the oil-[presser]."

### 333. CUNES 53-02-150 (Plate No. 69)

5.IX.[ . . . ] Nazi-Maruttaš
Sealed by [. . . -Mar]duk$^{?}$.

Obv. [ ]⸢x⸣ *ša* $^{md}$MAŠ-MU-MU
[ ]x$^{ki}$ *e-li-ti*
[ $^{m}$ . . . -SU]M-*na*
[ ]-*ri*
[ ].A.NI *im-ḫu-ur*
[ ]$^{meš}$ *i-na* [U]$_4$.2.KAM
⸢*ša*⸣ $^{iti}$ZÍZ.A.[AN] *i-le-eq-qa-am-ma*
*a-na* $^{md}$MA[Š-MU]-MU
*i-nam-di-in*
[ ]⸢x⸣ *ša* $^{md}$MAŠ-MU-MU

---

IGI $^{m}$*Ap-lu-ti*
[DUMU] $^{md+}$*En-líl-tu-k*[*ul*]-*ti*
IGI $^{m}$*Su*$^{?}$-⸢x⸣[
[DUMU ]
Rev. [IG]I $^{m}$MU-*líb-ši*
DUMU $^{m}$*Ri-iš-*$^{iti}$KIN.$^{d}$INANNA
IGI $^{md}$*Nuska-na-bu-šu*
DUMU $^{m}$*A-a-ri tup-šar-ri*

---

$^{iti}$GAN.GAN.È
[U]$_4$.5.KAM
[MU.x].KAM
[*Na-zi-Ma-ru*]-*ut-taš*
[NA$_4$.KIŠIB $^{m}$x-x-$^{d}$AM]AR.UTU$^{?}$

Translation

Obv. [ . . . ] of Ninurta-zākir-šumi
[in?] Upper [GN]
[. . . . . . -idd]ina
[. . . . . .]
5 [ . . . ] his? [brother?/son?] received.
6–7 On the second day of month XI he will take [the . . .]s and
8–9 give (them) to Ninurta-zākir-šumi.

10 Witness: Aplūtu,
[son] of Enlil-tukultī;
witness: Su[ . . . ],
[son of . . .];
Rev. [wit]ness: Šumu-libši,
15 son of Rīš-Ulūlu;
witness: Nuska-nābûšu,
son of Ayaru, the scribe.

Month IX,
day 5,
20 year [x]
[of Nazi-Mar]uttaš.
[Seal of . . . -Mar]duk?.

## 334. CUNES 52-00-053

Date not preserved.

Obverse completely lost.

Rev. [ . . . ]-*nu* x x [
[ . . . ]-*ar-ra* [
⸢x x⸣ a [

IGI $^{m}$*Iz-kùr*-$^{d}$AMAR.U[TU
5′ IGI $^{m}$⸢NÍG⸣.BA-$^{d}$*Gu-l*[*a*
IGI $^{m}$*Bi-ti-i*[*a*
IGI DUB.SAR $^{m}$*Mu*-S[IG$_5$-$^{d}$IŠKUR]
Text breaks off.

COMMENTARY

7′. The restoration of the PN is suggested by the several attestations of Mudammiq-Adad as a scribe in legal texts (see Index of Personal Names and Introduction §4.1).

## 6. LETTERS

### 335. CUNES 52-12-066 (Plate No. 70)

Letter of Amīl-Marduk to Ninurta-kiššat-ilāni, containing a reprimand and a request for barley.

Ninurta-kiššat-ilāni is probably the same official active in this archive during the reigns of Kadašman-Enlil II, Kudur-Enlil, and Šagarakti-Šuriaš (see van Soldt 2015, 24–25). One cannot exclude that Ninnū'a is a hypochoristic of Ninurta-kiššat-ilāni and that also the letters **nos. 336–37** were sent to him.

Amīl-Marduk must have been higher in rank than Ninurta-kiššat-ilāni, as suggested by the fact that he does not present himself as "your servant/brother" and by the commanding tone he uses in this message. Perhaps he could be identified with the homonymous *šandabakku* of Nippur, who held this position between the 6th year of Kadašman-Enlil II and the 1st year of Kaštiliaš IV (see Redina-Thomas 2015, 15–16).

Obv. *[a-n]a* $^{md}$*Nin-urta*-KIŠ-⸢DINGIR$^{meš}$⸣

*qí-bí-ma*

⸢*um-ma*⸣ $^{m}$LÚ-$^{d}$AMAR.UTU-*ma*

*um-ma-a am-mi-ni a-na dul*$^{!}$*-li*

*e-re-ed-de-e-ma*

*ù at-ta i-na* ŠÀ-*ša*

*aš-ba-ta-ma i-tu-ú-a*

*la ta-al-li-ik*

*e-zi-ib ša* DUMU *šip-ri-ka*

*aš-pu-rak-ku*

Rev. *um-ma-a* LÚ *ša tur-ra ki-i*

*ša aš-pu-rak-ku*

⸢*i*⸣*-na* ŠÀ ŠE.BAR *ša i-na* ŠÀ É.GAL

KI $^{giš}$IG$^{meš}$ *tu-ʾ-a-mi*

*na-aš-ra-tam-ma tab-ka-tu*$_4$

6.3.2 ŠE $^{giš}$BÁN GAL

*mu-du-ud-ma id-na-aš-šu*

*ù* SAG.ÍL *i-na* NA$_4$.KIŠIB-*ka*

⸢*ku*⸣*-nu-uk-ma id-na-aš-šu*

[x x] x NA$_4^{?}$ x *i-na* ⸢x⸣

L.e. [x x (x)] ⸢x x⸣ e ti

[x x (x)] ⸢x uš$^{?}$ x x⸣ [(x)]

Translation

| | |
|---|---|
| 1 | To Ninurta-kiššat-ilāni |
| 2 | say: |
| 3 | thus speaks Amīl-Marduk. |
| 4–5 | Why do I travel for the *dullu*-service |
| 6–8 | and you, you live (in) there but do not come to me? |
| 9–10 | Apart from the fact that I sent to you your messenger |
| 11 | (saying) as follows: "(As for) the man who . . . just |
| 12 | as I am writing to you," |
| 13–15 | (now) from the barley which is deducted from that of the palace by the double doors and is stored, |
| 16–17 | measure 200 *sūtu* of barley (by) the big *sūtu* and give (them) to him, |
| 18–19 | then seal the difference$^{?}$ with your seal and give (it) to him. |
| 20–22 | *Too fragmentary for translation.* |

Commentary

4–5. If it is correct to translate *eredde* according to the meaning "to travel" of *redû* (CAD R, *redû* A 2, 235ff.) and to assume that Amīl-Marduk is a high-ranking official, perhaps even the *šandabakku*, this passage might refer to an inspection of workmen who were carrying out the *dullu*-service. Reading *ki-li* instead of *dul*$^{!}$*-li* (i.e., "Why do I travel to the prison?") seems less convincing.

14. The dictionaries do not mention any MB occurrence of $^{\text{giš}}$IG$^{\text{meš}}$ *tū'ami*, whose function here is unclear; does it indicate a part of a building involved in administration, perhaps some type of storeroom?

15. On the 3$^{\text{rd}}$ sing. fem. stative with the subjunctive marker *–u*, see Aro 1955, 73 and van Soldt 2015, 34.

18. The tentative translation "difference" is based on Veenhof's (1985) assessment of SAG.ÍL(.LA), Akk. *saggilû*, *sangilû* as a term used in OB texts to indicate the "assessed difference, discrepancy" resulting from the measurement of goods with different capacity measures. However, here only one capacity measure is mentioned (the big *sūtu*), thus this letter might attest for a different use of SAG.ÍL(.LA). The request to "seal the difference$^{?}$" suggests that Ninurta-kiššat-ilāni had to seal and deliver either a container holding the intended amount or a document recording it. See also CUSAS 30 89: 15 and CUSAS 30 192: 1 for two further occurrences of SAG.ÍL in these texts (van Soldt 2015, 33).

## 336. CUNES 52-12-030 (Plate No. 71)

Letter of Erība-Marduk to Ninnū'a concerning a horse.

Obv. *a-na* $^{m}$*Nin-nu-ú-a qí-bi-ma*
*um-ma* $^{m}$*Eri-ba-*$^{d}$AMAR.UTU ŠEŠ-*ka-ma*
*um-ma-a a-na* $^{m}$*Nin-nu-ú-a-ma*
ANŠE.KUR.RA *an-na-a*
*at-tu-ka ša ez-zi-ba*
$^{m}$*Ša*-DINGIR-*ba-na-a*
*li-iṣ-ba-ta-ma*
*li-il-qa-am-ma*
L.e. *it-ti* ANŠE.KUR.RA
*at-tu-ú-a*
*lu-uṣ-bat*
*a-di* ANŠE.KUR.RA
*i-pa-ad-du-ni*
*i*$^{!}$*-tu-ú-a li-iz-zi-ba*
*a-na* $u_4$*-um ta-aš-tap-ra*
*li-iṣ-ba-tu*$_4$

Translation

1 To Ninnū'a say:
2 thus (speaks) Erība-Marduk, your brother.
3 (Say) as follows to Ninnū'a:
4–7 Ša-ili-banâ should take this horse of yours, which I am leaving behind,
8 and bring (it) here,
9–11 so that I can keep it with my horse.
12–13 While they are keeping the horse in confinement,
14 he should leave (it) with me.
15 On the day when you will have decided (lit. written),
16 they should take (it).

Commentary

1. Ninnū'a is also the addressee of letter **no. 337** (sent by Enlil-taqīš-bulliṭ). Also a letter from Nippur, sent by Pān-ili-rabî-lūmur, is addressed to a certain Ninnū'a (BE 17 89). Ninnū'a might be the hypochoristic of Ninurta-kiššat-ilāni, who is the addressee of **no. 335**.

13. The verb *pâdu* "to fetter, to put in fetters, to imprison, to take captive, to keep prisoner" is generally used with reference to persons (see CAD P, *pâdu* A, 8ff.), but see UDBD 116: 1–6 for a MB occurrence regarding the detainment of a cow.

14. One would expect *li-zi-ba*.

15. For the use of the perfect tense in order to express the future perfect in temporal clauses introduced by other conjunctions, see Aro 1955, 148 and 151.

## 337. CUNES 52-12-032 (Plate No. 72)

Letter of Enlil-taqīš-bulliṭ to Ninnū'a concerning a legal dispute whose object is not clear.

Obv. *a-na* $^{m}$*Nin-nu-ú-a qí-bi-ma*
*um-ma* $^{md+}$*En-líl-ta-qiš*-TI-*it*
ŠEŠ-*ka-ma um-ma-a*
*a-na* $^{m}$*Nin-nu-ú-a-ma* $^{md}$UTU-BA-*šá*
˹SIPA$^{?}$˺ *ša* $^{md}$*Nin-urta-*˹*re*$^{?}$*-ṣú*$^{?}$*-ú*˺*-a*
˹*ša áš-pu*˺*-rak-*˹*ku* x-x˺*-ka-ti* ˹x x˺
˹*na-ši it*$^{?}$*-ti*˺ $^{m}$ÌR-*nu-bat-ti*
*ḫa-za-an-ni ša* É $^{md+}$*En-líl-ki-di-ni*
*da-ba-ab-šu di-na*
*a-na pa-ni-ka li-id-bu-bu-ma*
*še-mé-ka-ma šu-lim-šu*
Rev. *ù ul ši-mi-ka-ma*
*šu-up-ra-šu-nu-ti-im-ma*
*a-na pa-ni-ia*
*lid-bu-bu*

Translation

1 To Ninnū'a say:
2 thus (speaks) Enlil-taqīš-bulliṭ,
3 your brother.
4 (Say) as follows to Ninnū'a: Šamaš-iqīša,
5 the ˹shepherd$^{?}$˺ of Ninurta-rēṣū'a$^{?}$,
6–7 whom I sent to you, carried . . . :
9 decide his case
7–8 with$^{?}$ Arad-nubatti, the *ḫazannu* of the House of Enlil-kidinnī.
10 They should speak in front of you and
11 (if) he listens to you, pay him in full.
12 But, (if) he does not listen to you,
13 send them to me,
14–15 so that they can speak in front of me.

Commentary

1. On Ninnū'a, see comments to **no. 336**: 1.
6–7. *ša ašpurakku* could also mean "about whom I wrote to you". I take *na-ši* as a 3 sg. stative of *našû* with an active meaning and assume that Šamaš-iqīša is the subject of this sentence, whose complete understanding is, however, hampered by the poor state of preservation of the signs at the end of l. 6, which must have expressed the object of the action.
7–8. On Arad-nubatti, the *ḫazannu* of the House of Enlil-kidinnī, see Introduction §1.3.
11–12. On the use of the stative with an active meaning and direct object in MB texts, see Aro 1955, 79.

## 338. CUNES 52-12-039 (Plate No. 73)

Letter of Ninurta-bēl-mātāti$^{?}$ to his lord concerning agricultural land in Baṣātu and Dūr-Enlilē.

Obv. [*a*]-*na be-lí-ia qí-bí-m*[*a*]  
⸢*um-ma*⸣ $^{md}$*Nin-urta*-EN-⸢KUR$^{?}$.KUR$^{?}$⸣$^{m}$[$^{eš?}$]  
⸢ÌR-*ka-ma*⸣ *aš-šum* A.ŠÀ  
*ša be-lí i-na* $^{uru}$*Ba-ṣa-tì*$^{ki}$  
*iq-ba-a um-ma-a* A.ŠÀ  
*i-ša-ak-ka-nu-nim-ma*  
*a-nam-din-ak-ku*  
*i-na-an-na* A.ŠÀ *a-na be-lí-ia*  
*iš-ta-ak-nu be-lí it*$^{!?}$*-ta-din-ma*  
[*i*]*l*$^{?}$-⸢*ta-ap*⸣*-pa-ra*

Rev. ⸢i ʾ id⸣ nu ⸢x⸣ *um*$^{?}$*-ma-a*  
*la i-ši-im-ma*  
*ù be-lí ḫa-rab ṭe-mi*  
*i-na* BÀD-$^{d+}$*En-líl*$^{meš.ki}$  
⸢*na*$^{?}$⸣*-da-am iq-ba-a*  
*be-lí i-na* BÀD-$^{d+}$*En-líl*$^{meš.ki}$  
⸢*i-nam-din-ma* x-x-*ú*⸣*-a*  
*a-na* ⸢te$^{?}$⸣ [x x x] ⸢x⸣ at  
*be-lí ḫa-rab ṭe-m*[*i*  
⸢ÉNSI⸣ *li-*[  
⸢x x x x⸣

L.e. [*pi*$^{?}$]*-qá-at* A.ŠÀ lu ⸢x⸣ za

Translation

1 To my lord say:  
2 ⸢thus speaks Ninurta-bēl-mātāti$^{?}$⸣,  
3 ⸢your servant⸣. As for the field  
4–5 about which my lord said in Baṣātu as follows:  
5–6 "They will set$^{?}$/prepare$^{?}$ a field for me and  
7 I will give it to you."  
8–9 Now they set$^{?}$/prepared$^{?}$ a field for my lord. My lord gave (it) and  
10 [s]ent$^{?}$  
11 . . . as follows$^{?}$:  
12 "Don't . . ."  
13–15 And my lord said to assign the *ḫarab ṭēmi* in Dūr-Enlilē.  
16–17 My lord will give in Dūr-Enlilē and . . .  
18 . . .  
19 My lord [ . . . ] the *ḫarab ṭēmi*  
20 the farmer [ . . . ]  
21 ⸢ . . . ⸣  
22 [pe]rhaps$^{?}$ the field . . .

Commentary

2. The last signs of the PN are uncertain.

5–6, 8–9. For the expression *eqla* (A.ŠÀ) *šakānu*, see also CUSAS 30 6: 1–2.

9. The first sign of *it*$^{!?}$*-ta-din-ma* looks much more like IA, but *be-lí-ia ta-din-ma* (i.e., "you, my lord, have given") seems unlikely because the syntactical function of "my lord" as the subject of the sentence would require the form *bēlī*, rather than *bēlīya* (cf. ll. 4, 13, 16).

13. On *ḫarab ṭēmi* (a special type of *ḫarbu*-field?), see comments to **no. 187**.

# 7. References


Abrahami, P. 2011. "Masculine and Feminine Personal Determinatives Before Women's Names at Nuzi: A Gender Indicator of Social or Economic Independence?" *CDLI Bulletin* 2011 (1): 1–3.

Abusch, T., and D. Schwemer. 2016. *Corpus of Mesopotamian Anti-witchcraft Rituals.* Vol. 2. Leiden.

Adams, M. M. 1981. *Heartland of Cities: Survey of Ancient Settlements and Land Use on the Central Plain of the Euphrates.* Chicago.

Aro, J. 1955. *Studien zur mittelbabylonischen Grammatik.* StOr 20. Helsinki.

———. 1957. *Glossar zu den mittelbabylonischen Briefen.* StOr 22. Helsinki.

———. 1970. *Mittelbabylonische Kleidertexte der Hilprecht-Sammlung Jena.* Berlin.

Balkan, K. 1954. *Kassitenstudien 1: Die Sprache der Kassiten.* AOS 37. New Haven.

Bartelmus, A. 2017. "Die Götter der Kassitenzeit. Eine Analyse ihres Vorkommens in zeitgenössischen Textquellen." In *Karduniaš: Babylonia Under the Kassites 1. The Proceedings of the Symposium Held in Munich 30 June to 2 July 2011*, edited by A. Bartelmus and K. Sternitzke, 245–312. UAVA 11/1. Boston and Berlin.

Beaugeard, A.-C. 2013. "Les textiles du Moyen-Euphrate à l'époque paléo-babylonienne d'après un ouvrage récent." In *Textile Terminologies from the Orient to the Mediterranean and Europe, 1000 BC to 1000 AD*, edited by S. Gaspa, C. Michel, and M.-L. Nosch, 283–89. http://digitalcommons.unl.edu/zeabook/56.

Beaulieu, P.-A. 2005. "The God Amurru as Emblem of Ethnic and Cultural Identity." In *Ethnicity in Ancient Mesopotamia: Papers Read at the 48th Rencontre Assyriologique Internationale, Leiden, July 1–4, 2002*, edited by W. H. van Soldt, 31–46. PIHANS 102. Leiden.

Boivin, O. 2016. "Agricultural Economy and Taxation in the Sealand I Kingdom." *JCS* 68:45–65.

———. 2018. *The First Dynasty of the Sealand in Mesopotamia.* SANER 20. Boston and Berlin.

Borger, R. 2010. *Mesopotamisches Zeichenlexikon.* AOAT 305. Münster.

Brinkman, J. A. 1976. *A Catalogue of Cuneiform Sources Pertaining to Specific Monarchs of the Kassite Dynasty.* Materials and Studies for Kassite History 1. Chicago.

———. 1993. "Catalogue of Tablets." In *Nippur III: Kassite Buildings in Area WC-1*, edited by R. L. Zettler, 93–111. OIP 111. Chicago.

———. 2003–4. Review of M. Hölscher, *Die Personennamen der kassitenzeitlichen Texte aus Nippur* (Münster 1996). *AfO* 50:396–400.

———. 2004. "Administration and Society in Kassite Babylonia." *JAOS* 124:283–304.

———. 2007. "Masculine or Feminine? The Case of Conflicting Gender Determinatives for Middle Babylonian Personal Names." In *Studies Presented to Robert D. Biggs*, edited by M. T. Roth, W. Farber, and M. W. Stolper, 1–10. AS 27. Chicago.

———. 2017. "Babylonia Under the Kassites: Some Aspects for Consideration." In *Karduniaš: Babylonia Under the Kassites 1. The Proceedings of the Symposium Held in Munich 30 June to 2 July 2011*, edited by A. Bartelmus and K. Sternitzke, 1–44. UAVA 11/1. Boston and Berlin.

Clay, A. T. 1905. "A Topographical Map from Nippur." *Transactions of the Department of Archaeology, Free Museum of Science and Art* 1 (3): 233–35.

———. 1906a. *Documents from the Temple Archives of Nippur Dated in the Reigns of Cassite Rulers (Complete Dates).* BE 14. Philadelphia.

———. 1906b. *Documents from the Temple Archives of Nippur Dated in the Reigns of Cassite Rulers (Incomplete Dates).* BE 15. Philadelphia.

———. 1912a. *Documents from the Temple Archives of Nippur Dated in the Reigns of Cassite Rulers.* PBS 2/2. Philadelphia.

———. 1912b. *Personal Names from Cuneiform Inscriptions of the Cassite Period*. YOS 1. New Haven.

Dalley, S. 2009. *Babylonian Tablets from the First Sealand Dynasty in the Schøyen Collection*. CUSAS 9. Bethesda, MD.

Deheselle, D. 1996. "La distribution aklu à Nippur à l'époque kassite. Approche préliminaire." In *Tablettes et images aux pays de Sumer et d'Akkad*, edited by Ö. Tunca and D. Deheselle, 215–21. Liège.

———. 2004. "Meuniers et brasseurs kassites, travailleurs itinérants." In *Nomades et sédentaires dans le Proche-Orient ancien*, edited by C. Nicolle, 273–85. Amurru 3. Paris.

Del Monte, G. F. 1988. "Razioni e classi d'età in Nippur medio-babilonese." In *Stato Economia Lavoro nel Vicino Oriente antico*, 17–30. Milan.

———. 1994. "Recipienti enigmatici." In *Drinking in Ancient Societies: History and Culture of Drinks in the Ancient Near East*, edited by L. Milano, 187–208. HANE/S 6. Padua.

Devecchi, E. 2018. "The Cultivation of Sesame in Kassite Babylonia: A Note on the Term *naḫḫuḫu*." *Orientalia* n.s. 87:290–293.

———. In press. "Managing the Harvest in Kassite Babylonia: The Evidence for *tēlītu*." In *Babylonia Under the Sealand and Kassite Dynasties*, edited by S. Paulus and T. Clayden. SANER 24. Boston and Berlin.

Dornauer, A. 2016. *Assyrische Nutzlandschaft in Obermesopotamien: Natürliche und anthropogene Wirkfaktoren und ihre Auswirkungen*. Münchner Studien zur Alten Welt 12. Munich.

———. 2018. *Proso, Sorghum, Tiger Nut: Some Minor Crops in the Cuneiform Sources*. BBVO 27. Gladbeck.

Durand, J.-M. 2009. *La nomenclature des habits et des textiles dans les textes de Mari*. ARM 30. Paris.

Edzard, D. O. 1957. *Die "zweite Zwischenzeit" Babyloniens*. Wiesbaden.

Ellis, M. de J. 1976. *Agriculture and the State in Ancient Mesopotamia*. Philadelphia.

Farber, G., and Farber, W. 2018 "The Cuneiform Tablets at Northwestern University Library in Evanston, Illinois." In *Grenzüberschreitungen. Studien zur Kulturgeschichte des Alten Orients. Festschrift für Hans Neumann zum 65. Geburtstag am 9. Mai 2018*, edited by K. Kleber, G. Neumann and S. Paulus, 195-226. Münster.

Finkelstein, J. J. 1962. "Mesopotamia." *JNES* 21:73–92.

Frahm, E. 2009. *Historische und historisch-literarische Texte*. WVDOG 121. Wiesbaden.

Freydank, H. 2009. "Kār-Tukultī-Ninurta als Agrarprovinz." *AoF* 36:16–83.

Gaspa, S. 2017. "Garments, Parts of Garments, and Textile Techniques in the Assyrian Terminology: The Neo-Assyrian Textile Lexicon in the 1st-Millennium BC Linguistic Context." In *Textile Terminologies from the Orient to the Mediterranean and Europe, 1000 BC to 1000 AD*, edited by S. Gaspa, C. Michel, and M.-L. Nosch, 47–90. http://digitalcommons.unl.edu/zeabook/56.

George, A. R. 1993. *House Most High: The Temples of Ancient Mesopotamia*. MC 5. Winona Lake, IN.

Gibson, M. 1978. "Nippur Regional Project: Umm al-Hafriyat." In *The Oriental Institute Annual Report 1977/78*, 20–26. Chicago.

———. 1996. "Nippur and Umm al-Hafriyat." In *Oriental Institute 1995–1996 Annual Report*, edited by W. M. Summer, 70–72. Chicago.

———. 1997. "Nippur and Umm al-Hafriyat." In *Oriental Institute 1996–1997 Annual Report*, edited by W. M. Summer, 62–65. Chicago.

———. 1998. "Nippur and Umm al-Hafriyat." In *Oriental Institute 1997–1998 Annual Report*, edited by G. Gragg, 71–72. Chicago.

———. 2003. "Nippur and Iraq at Time of War." In *Oriental Institute 2002–2003 Annual Report*, edited by G. J. Stein, 88–96. Chicago.

———. 2004. "Nippur and Umm al-Hafriyat." In *Oriental Institute 2003–2004 Annual Report*, edited by G. J. Stein, 116–20. Chicago.

———. 2006. "Nippur and Umm al-Hafriyat." In *Oriental Institute 2005–2006 Annual Report*, edited by G. J. Stein, 86–88. Chicago.

———. 2016. "Nippur." In *Oriental Institute 2015–2016 Annual Report*, edited by G. J. Stein, 128–29. Chicago.

Groneberg, B. 1980. *Die Orts- und Gewässernamen der altbabylonischen Zeit*. RGTC 3. Wiesbaden.

Gurney, O. R. 1949. "Texts from Dur-Kurigalzu." *Iraq* 11:131–49.

———. 1983. *The Middle Babylonian Legal and Economic Texts from Ur*. Oxford.

Hölscher, M. 1996. *Die Personennamen der kassitenzeitlichen Texte aus Nippur*. IMGULA 1. Münster.

Jakob, S. 2009. *Die mittelassyrischen Texte aus Tell Chuēra in Nordost-Syrien*. Wiesbaden.

Joannès, F. 2013. "Textile Terminology in the Neo-Babylonian Documentation." In *Textile Terminologies in the Ancient Near East and Mediterranean from the Third to the First Millennia B.C.*, edited by C. Michel and M.-L. Nosch, 400–408. Oxford.

Johnson, J. C. 2013. "Contractual Formalism and Zukunftsbewältigung in Middle Assyrian Agricultural Accounting." In *Time and History in the Ancient Near East: Proceedings of the 56th Rencontre Assyriologique Internationale at Barcelona 26–30 July 2010*, edited by J. L. L. Feliu, A. Millet Albà, and J. Sanmartín, 525–48. Winona Lake, IN.

Jursa, M. 2011. "Steuer. D. Spätbabylonisch." *RlA* 13:168–75.

Kessler, K. 1982. "Kassitische Tontafeln vom Tell Imlihiye." *BaM* 13:51–116.

———. 1985. "Die Tontafeln." In *Tell Imlihiye, Tell Zubeidi, Tell Abbas*, edited by R. M. Boehmer and H.-W. Dämmer, 74–80, pls. 159–65. BaF 7. Mainz am Rhein.

Kraus, F. R. 1968. "Sesam im Alten Mesopotamien." *JAOS* 88:112–19.

Krebernik, M. 2009a. "Šarrat-Nippur, UN-gal-Nibru." *RlA* 12:76–77.

———. 2009b. "Šēmû." *RlA* 12:389.

Legrain, L. 1922. *Historical Fragments*. PBS 13. Philadelphia.

Levavi, Y. 2017. "Four Middle-Babylonian Legal Documents Concerning Prison." *RA* 111:87–108.

Limet, H. 1971. *Les légendes des sceaux cassites*. Brussels.

Lutz, H. F. 1919. *Selected Sumerian and Babylonian Texts*. PBS 1/2. Philadelphia.

Matthews, D. M. 1992. *The Kassite Glyptic of Nippur.* OBO 116. Freiburg.

Milano, L., and A. Westenholz. 2015. *The "Šuilisu Archive" and Other Sargonic Texts in Akkadian*. CUSAS 27. Bethesda, MD.

Molina, M. 2013. "On the Location of Irisaĝrig." In *From the 21st Century B.C. to the 21st Century A.D.: Proceedings of the International Conference on Sumerian Studies Held in Madrid 22–24 July 2010*, edited by S. Garfinkle and M. Molina, 59–87. Winona Lake, IN.

Morrison, M. A. 1981. "Evidence for Herdsmen and Animal Husbandry in the Nuzi Documents." In *Studies in the Civilization and Culture of Nuzi and the Hurrians: In Honor of Ernest R. Lacheman*, edited by M. A. Morrison and D. I. Owen, 257–96. SCCNH 1. Winona Lake, IN.

Murai, N. 2018. "Studies in the *aklu* Documents of the Middle Babylonian Period." PhD diss., University of Leiden.

Nashef, K. 1982. *Die Orts- und Gewässernamen der mittelbabylonischen und mittelassyrischen Zeit.* RGTC 5. Wiesbaden.

———. 1992. "The Nippur Countryside in the Kassite Period." In *Nippur at the Centennial: Papers Read at the 35e Rencontre Assyriologique Internationale, Philadelphia 1988*, edited by M. de J. Ellis, 151–59. Philadelphia.

Nielsen, J. P. 2015. *Personal Names in Early Neo-Babylonian Legal and Administrative Tablets, 747–626 B.C.E.* NISABA 29. Winona Lake, IN.

Owen, D. I. 2013. *Cuneiform Texts Primarily from Iri-Saĝrig/Āl-Šarrākī and the History of the Ur III Period.* NISABA 15. Bethesda, MD.

Paulus, S. 2007. "'Ein Richter wie Šamaš'—Zur Rechtsprechung der Kassitenkönige." *ZAR* 13:1–22.

———. 2014a. "Die Arbeitskräfte von Nippur: Eine Mikrostudie zum 13. Jh. v. Chr." *ZAR* 20:215–48.

———. 2014b. *Die babylonischen Kudurru-Inschriften von der kassitischen bis zur frühbabylonischen Zeit.* AOAT 51. Münster.

———. In press. "Turn! Turn! Turn!—An Administrative Term with a Legal Connotation." In *Babylonia Under the Sealand and Kassite Dynasties*, edited by S. Paulus and T. Clayden. SANER 24. Boston and Berlin.

Peiser, F. E. 1905. *Urkunden aus der Zeit der dritten babylonischen Dynastie.* Berlin.

Petschow, H. 1974. *Mittelbabylonische Rechts- und Wirtschaftsurkunden der Hilprecht-Sammlung Jena mit Beiträgen zum mittelbabylonischen Recht.* Berlin.

Postgate, N. 2011. "Making Tablets or Taking Tablets? *ṭuppa/u ṣabātu* in Assyria." *Iraq* 73:149–60.

———. 2013. *Bronze Age Bureaucracy: Writing and the Practice of Government in Assyria.* New York.

———. 2014. "Wool, Hair and Textiles in Assyria." In *Wool Economy in the Ancient Near East and the Aegean: From the Beginnings of Sheep Husbandry to Institutional Textile Industry*, edited by C. Breniquet and C. Michel, 401–27. Oxford.

Powell, M. A. 1984. "Sumerian Cereal Crops." *BSA* 1:48–68.

———. 2003. "Obst und Gemüse (Fruits and Vegetables). A. I. Mesopotamien." *RlA* 10:13–22.

Prechel, D. 2010. "Die Tontafeln aus Haft Tappeh 2005–2007." In *Vorbericht der archäologischen Ausgrabungen der Kampagnen 2005–2007 in Haft Tappeh (Iran)*, edited by B. Mofidi-Nasrabadi, 51–57. Münster.

Quillien, L. 2017. "Tools and Crafts, the Terminology of Textile Manufacturing in 1st-Millennium BC Babylonia." In *Textile Terminologies from the Orient to the Mediterranean and Europe, 1000 BC to 1000 AD*, edited by S. Gaspa, C. Michel, and M.-L. Nosch, 91–106. http://digitalcommons.unl.edu/zeabook/56.

Radau, H. 1908. *Letters to Cassite Kings from the Temple Archives of Nippur*. BE 17. Philadelphia.

Reculeau, H. 2011. *Climate, Environment and Agriculture in Assyria in the 2nd Half of the 2nd Millennium BCE.* Studia Chaburensia 2. Wiesbaden.

Redina-Thomas, M. 2015. "Who Governed the Sacred City of Enlil? Shandabakku of Nippur in Written Sources of the Kassite Period" [in Russian]. *Journal of Ancient History* (Вестник древней истории) 4:87–103.

Richter, T. 1998. "Die Lesung des Götternamens AN.AN.MAR.TU." In *General Studies and Excavations at Nuzi 10/2*, edited by D. I. Owen and G. Wilhelm, 135–37. SCCNH 9. Bethesda, MD.

Röllig, W. 2008. *Land- und Viehwirtschaft am Unteren Habur in Mittelassyrischer Zeit.* BATSH 9. Berlin.

Sassmannshausen, L. 1998. Review of M. Hölscher, *Die Personennamen der kassitenzeitlichen Texte aus Nippur* (Münster 1996). *BiOr* 55:824–43.

———. 2001. *Beiträge zur Verwaltung und Gesellschaft Babyloniens in der Kassitenzeit.* BaF 21. Mainz am Rhein.

Selz, G. J. 2008. "The Divine Prototypes." In *Religion and Power: Divine Kingship in the Ancient World and Beyond*, edited by N. Brisch, 13–31. OIS 4. Chicago.

Soden, W. von, and W. Röllig. 1991. *Das akkadische Syllabar.* AnOr 42. Rome.

Soldt, W. H. van. 1988. "Irrigation in Kassite Babylonia." *BSA* 4:105–20.

———. 2015. *Middle Babylonian Texts in the Cornell University Collections I: The Later Kings*. CUSAS 30. Bethesda, MD.

Stamm, J. J. 1968. *Die akkadische Namengebung.* Darmstadt.

Stol, M. 1971. "Zur altmesopotamischen Bierbereitung." *BiOr* 28:167–71.

———. 1995. "Old Babylonian Cattle." *BSA* 8:173–213.

Streck, M. 2004. "Parak-māri." *RlA* 10:334.

———. 2017. "Zypresse." *RlA* 15:371–72.

Tenney, J. S. 2011. *Life at the Bottom of Babylonian Society: Servile Laborers at Nippur in the 14th and 13th Centuries B.C.* Leiden.

———. 2016. "The Elevation of Marduk Revisited: Festivals and Sacrifices at Nippur During the High Kassite Period." *JCS* 68:153–80.

———. 2017. "A Servile Population in Kassite Nippur: A Brief Overview." In *Karduniaš: Babylonia Under the Kassites 1. The Proceedings of the Symposium Held in Munich 30 June to 2 July 2011*, edited by A. Bartelmus and K. Sternitzke, 209–18. UAVA 11/1. Boston and Berlin.

Torczyner, H. 1913. *Altbabylonische Tempelrechnungen umschrieben und erklärt.* Vienna.

Tropper, J. 1995. "Akkadisch *nuḫḫutu* und die Repräsentation des Phonems /ḥ/ im Akkadischen." *ZA* 85:58–66.

Tsukimoto, A. 1985. *Untersuchungen zur Totenpflege (kispum) im alten Mesopotamien.* AOAT 216. Neukirchen-Vluyn.

Van Lerberghe, K., and G. Voet. 2016. "Dūr-Abiešuḫ and Venice. Settlements In-Between Great Rivers." In *Libiamo ne' lieti calici: Ancient Near Eastern Studies Presented to Lucio Milano on the Occasion of His 65th Birthday by Pupils, Colleagues and Friends*, edited by P. Corò, E. Devecchi, N. De Zorzi, and M. Maiocchi, 557–63. AOAT 436. Münster.

Veenhof, K. R. 1985. "SAG.ÍL.LA = saggilû, 'Difference Assessed' on Measuring and Accounting in Some Old Babylonian Texts." In *Miscellanea Babylonica: Mélanges Offerts à Maurice Birot*, edited by J.-M. Durand and J.-R. Kupper, 285–306. Paris.

Viano, M. 2019. "On the Location of Irisagrig Once Again." JCS 71:35–52.

Weszeli, M. 2007. "Rind B. In mesopotamischen Quellen des 2. und 1. Jahrtausends." *RlA* 11:388–406.

Zawadzki, S. 2006. *Garments of the Gods: Studies on the Textile Industry and the Pantheon of Sippar According to the Texts from the Ebabbar Archive.* OBO 218. Freiburg.

# 8. Indexes

## *Personal Names*


**Ab[. . .]** ($^{m}$*Ab*-⸢x⸣-[ . . .])
- father of Irību: **253**: 5 (ŠŠ 1)

**Aba-ul-īde** ($^{m}$*A-ba-ul-i-de*)
- son of Uraš-tukultī: **255**: 4 (NM 4)

**Abbū-dannū** ($^{m}$*Ab-bu-dan-nu*)
- no details: **7**: 18, 19 ([$^{m}$KI.MIN]) (KT 11); **32**: 17, 18 ($^{m}$KI.MIN) (KT 11); **53**: 13 (KT 12)

**Abbū-ṭabū** ($^{m}$*Ab-bu-ú-ṭa-bu*)
- father of Rîmtu: **95**: 7 (KT 6)

**Abī-ul-īde** ($^{m}$*A-bi-ul-i-de*)
- no details: **12**: 10 (KT 13); **35**: 9 (KT 13)

**Abuyatu** ($^{f}$*A-bu-ú-ia-ti*)
- mother of Iddin-Gula **291**: 9 (KT 5–7)

**Adad-[. . .]** ($^{md}$IŠKUR-[ . . .])
- *arad ekalli* (ÌR.É.GAL): **120**: 25 (NM 19$^{?}$)
- no details: **129**: 4 (NM 17); **140**: 26′ (NM 21–KT 3); **149**: 7 (KT 2); **34**: 18′ (KT 12)

**Adad-di . . . , son of** (DUMU $^{md}$IŠKUR-*di*-⸢x-x⸣)
- no details: **120**: 8 (NM 19$^{?}$)

**Adad-dīnanni$^{?}$** ($^{md}$IŠKUR-⸢*di*⸣-[*na*$^{?}$]-⸢*ni*$^{?}$⸣)
- no details: **180**: 7 (KT 2–15$^{?}$)

**Adad-ilu-ina-māti** ($^{md}$IŠKUR-DINGIR-*i-na*-KUR)
- *ḫazannu*: **150**: 10, 11 ($^{m}$KI.MIN), 19, 22, 23 ($^{m}$KI.MIN) (KT 3)
- brother of Daqqatu: **95**: 32 (KT 6)

**Adad-īriš** ($^{md}$IŠKUR-URU$_{4}$)
- no details: **53**: 13 (KT 12)

**Adad-muštešir** ($^{md}$IŠKUR-[*mu*]*š*$^{?}$-⸢*te-šir*⸣)
- son of Adad-šamḫi-ilāni: **260**: 2 (NM x)

**Adad-nāṣir, son of** (DUMU $^{md}$IŠKUR-ÙRU)
- no details: **97**: 7 (KT 9); **98**: 7 (KT 9)

**Adad-qarrād** ($^{md}$IŠKUR-*qar-rad*)
- no details: **4**: 25 (KT 8$^{?}$)

**Adad-ṣillī** ($^{md}$IŠKUR-*ṣíl-lí*)
- no details: **45**: 43 (KT 4)

**Adad-šagim** ($^{md}$IŠKUR-*ša-gim*)
- no details: **130**: 3 (NM 18); **272**: 2, 7 (KT 17); **183**: 4 (KT x)

**Adad-šamḫi-ilāni** (⸢$^{md}$IŠKUR⸣-*šam-ḫi*-DINGIR$^{meš}$)
- father of Adad-muštešir: **260**: 2 (NM x)

**Adad-šār-ilāni** ($^{md}$IŠKUR-LUGAL-DINGIR$^{meš}$)
- no details: **46**: 30 (KT x)

**Adad-šar-m[āti$^{?}$]**

[1] $^{md}$IŠKUR-LUGAL-K[UR$^{?}$]

[2] $^{md}$IŠKUR-LU[GAL$^{?}$-KUR$^{?}$]
- no details: **3**: 9′, 12′ (KT 5) [1, 2]

**Adad-šubši** ($^{md}$IŠKUR-*šub-ši*)
- *arad ekalli* (ÌR.É.GAL): **300**: 2 (KT 3)
- no details: **99**: 7 (KT 9); **331**: 11 (KT x)

**Adad-šumu-līšir** ($^{md}$IŠKUR-MU-*li-ši-ir*)
- son of Ḫu[ . . .], brother of Ḫunnubu: **315**: 4 (KT 13)

**Adad-zākir**

[1] $^{md}$IŠKUR-*za-ki-*[*ir*]

[2] $^{md}$IŠKUR-⸢*za*$^{?}$⸣-*k*[*i*$^{?}$-*ir*$^{?}$]

[3] $^{md}$IŠKUR-*za-kir*
- father of Ḫuddimmānu and of Ḫummuru: **315**: 1 (KT 13) [1]
- no details: **99**: 11 (KT 9) [2]; **266**: 7′ (n.d.) [3]

**Adaggal-pān(i)-ili**

[1] $^{m}$*A-da-gal*-IGI-DINGIR

[2] $^{m}$*A*-⸢*da-ga*⸣-<*al*>-IGI-DINGIR
- no details: **45**: 19 (KT 4) [1]; **331**: 8 (KT x) [2]

**Adāya**

[1] $^{m}$*A-da-a-a*

[2] $^{m}$*A-da-a*
- *ḫazannu*: **150**: 6 (KT 3) [1]; **153**: 9, 10 ($^{m}$KI.MIN) (KT 6) [2]

**Adayūtu** ($^{m}$*A-da-a-a-ú-tu*$_{4}$)
- no details: **46**: 34 (KT x)

**Agab-[. . .]** ($^{m}$*A*-⸢*gab*$^{?}$-x⸣[ . . .])
- no details: **36**: 18 (year 5)

**Agab-šenni** ($^{m}$*A-gab-še-en-ni*)
- brewer ($^{lú}$LUNGA): **110**: 3 (NM 18); **136**: 7 (NM 23); **185**: 7 (KT x)

- probably the brewer: **135**: 6 (NM 21$^{+}$); **149**: 5 (KT 2); **209**: 4 (KT 2$^{+}$)

**Agab-taḫi, son of**
[1] DUMU $^{m}$*A-gab-ta-ḫi*
[2] DUMU $^{m}$*A-gab-ta-ḫe*
- no details: **138**: 6 (NM x) [1]; **164**: 19 (KT 9) [2]

**Agamuza, son of** (DUMU $^{m}$*A-*⌜*ga*⌝*-mu-za*)
- farmer (ÉNSI): **1**: 7 (NM 22)

**Agīya** ($^{m}$*A-gi-ia*)
- father of Damu-nāṣir: **28**: 7 (NM 24)

**Aḫa-iddina, son of** (DUMU $^{m}$ŠEŠ-SUM-[*na*])
- no details: **41**: 10 (NM 18)

**Aḫa-iddina-Marduk** ($^{m}$ŠEŠ-SUM-*na*-$^{d}$AMAR.UTU)
- House (É) of PN: **308**: iv 15′ (NM 22)
- father of Urrāya: **122**: 3, 15 (KT 14)
- no details: **45**: 18 (KT 4); **169**: 21 (KT 12); **243**: 7 (KT x)

**Aḫēdūtu**
[1] $^{m}$ŠEŠ-*du-tu*$_4$
[2] $^{m}$*A-ḫe-du-tu*$_4$
[3] $^{m}$*A-ḫe-du-ti*
- attendant (LÚ.SAG): **45**: 27 (KT 4) [1]
- tax collector (*mākisu*): **122**: 6, 7 (KT 14) [3]
- brother of Kidiniya: **179**: 8, 9 ($^{m}$KI.MIN) (KT 15) [2]
- no details: **2**: 18 (KT 1) [2]; **44**: 10, 11 (KT 1) [2]; **156**: 7, 19, 31 (KT 8) [2]; **164**: 9 (KT 9) [2]; **15**: 7 (KT 14) [2]; **36**: 18 (year 5) [2]

**Aḫ[e . . .], son of** (DUMU $^{m}$*A-ḫ*[*e*$^{?}$- . . .])
- no details: **34**: 14 (KT 12)

**Aḫi** ($^{m}$ŠEŠ-*i*)
- shepherd ([$^{l}$]$^{ú?}$SIPA): **203**: 4 (NM 21$^{+}$)

**Aḫirabuzzu** ($^{m}$*A-ḫi-ra-bu-uz-zu*)
- father of Mūrānu: **307**: 12′ (NM$^{?}$ 21)

**Aḫḫū-dannū** ($^{m}$⌜*Aḫ*$^{?}$⌝*-ḫu-dan-*[*nu*])
- *arad ekalli* (ÌR.É.GAL): **120**: 27 (NM 19$^{?}$)

**Aḫlamû** ($^{m}$*Aḫ-la-mu-ú*)
- no details: **22**: 5 (NM 19); **43**: 7 (KT 1)

**Aḫu-[. . .]** ($^{m}$ŠEŠ-[ . . .])
- no details: **135**: 13 (NM 21$^{+}$); **108**: 9 (KT 3)

**Aḫu- . . .** ($^{m}$ŠEŠ-⌜x-x⌝)
- father of Erība-Adad: **176**: 16 (KT 13)

**Aḫū'a, son of** (DUMU $^{m}$*A-ḫu-ú-a*)
- no details: **180**: 13 (KT 2–15$^{?}$)

**Aḫu-bani**
[1] $^{m}$ŠEŠ-*ba-ni*
[2] $^{m}$[Š]EŠ$^{?}$-DÙ
[3] $^{m}$ŠE[Š-
- father of Rīmūtu: **150**: 5, 9 (KT 3) [1]; **51**: 8 (KT 7) [1]; **45**: 22 (KT 4) [3]
- father of Tarība-Gula: **103**: 12 (KT x) [1]
- no details: **38**: 7 (KT 3) [2]

**Aḫu-damqu**
[1] $^{m}$ŠEŠ-*dam-qu*
[2] $^{m}$ŠEŠ-⌜SIG$_5$$^{?}$⌝
- plowman ($^{lú}$ENGAR): **145**: 2 (KT 2) [1]
- no details: **27**: 7 (NM 20) [2]; **316**: 5 (year 17) [1]

**Aḫūna** ($^{m}$*A-ḫu-na*)
- no details: **31**: 7 (KT 5)

**Aḫūni, son of** (DUMU $^{m}$ŠEŠ-*ni*)
- water drawer (*dālû*): **131**: 17 (NM 18)

**Aḫu-ṣeḫru** ($^{m}$ŠEŠ-⌜TUR⌝)
- no details: **49**: 6 (KT 1)

**Aḫu-ṣīnu** ($^{m}$ŠEŠ-⌜*ṣi*$^{?}$⌝*-nu*)
- no details: **36**: 10, 11 ($^{m}$KI.MIN) (year 5)

**$^{m}$*Ak-ni-*⌜*ša*$^{?}$*-*KÁ$^{?}$-$^{d?}$x-x⌝**
- father of Uballissu-Marduk: **124**: 11 (NM 21)

**Al[ . . .]** ($^{m}$*Al*-[ . . .])
- no details: **331**: 2 (KT x)

**Amīl-Isin** ($^{m}$LÚ-*Ì-si-in*$^{ki}$)
- *arad ekalli* (ÌR.É.GAL): **120**: 32 (NM 19$^{?}$)

**Amīl-Ištar** (⌜$^{m}$LÚ⌝-$^{d}$*Ištar*)
- no details: **281**: 2 (KT 15)

**Amīl-Ištar, son of** (DUMU $^{m}$LÚ-$^{d}$INANNA)
- no details: **162**: 9 (KT 9)

**Amīl-Ištar, daughter of** (DUMU.MUNUS $^{m}$LÚ-INANNA)
- no details: **87**: 2 (KT 15)

**Amīl-Marduk** ($^{m}$LÚ-$^{d}$AMAR.UTU)
- carpenter (NAGAR): **9**: 14, 22 (KT 11)
- sender of letter: **335**: 3 (n.d.)
- no details: **64**: 2 (NM 18); **13**: 9 (KT 13)

**Amīl-Sîn** ($^{m}$LÚ-$^{d}$30)
- no details: **243**: 6 (KT x)

**Amīl-Sîn, son of** (DUMU $^{m}$LÚ-$^{d}$30)
- no details: **113**: 12 (KT 3)

**Amīl-Šuzianna** ($^{m}$⌜LÚ⌝-$^{d}$ŠU.ZI.AN.NA)
- no details: **290**: 5 (KT x)

**Amīlu-banû**
[1] $^{m}$LÚ-*ba-nu-ú*
[2] $^{m}$*A-mi-lu-ú-ba-nu-ú*
- son of Sarriqu, brother of Ēṭiru: **55**: 21 (KT 12) [1]

• no details: **9**: 17 (KT 11) [1]; **12**: 15 (KT 13) [2]; **35**: 14 (KT 13) [2]; **176**: 18 (KT 13) [1]; **179**: 14 (KT 15) [1]

**Amīlūma, sister of** (NIN ᵐLÚ-*ma*)
- no details: **296**: 5 (KT 12)

**Amtu** (ᶠ*A-am-tu₄*)
- daughter of Nin[urta- . . .]: **95**: 5 (KT 6)

**Amurru-[ . . .]** (ᵐᵈKUR-⸢x⸣[ . . .])
- no details: **36**: 13 (year 5)

**Amurru-aḫa-iddina** (ᵐᵈKUR-ŠEŠ-SUM-*na*)
- no details: **45**: 5 (KT 4)

**Amurru-napišti** (ᵐᵈKUR.GAL-ZI)
- no details: **278**: **4 (KT 7); 288**: 2 (KT 17)

**Amurru-nāṣir** (ᵐᵈKUR.GAL-ÙRU)
- father of Arad-Bēlti: **48**: 17 (NM 24); **21**: 5 (n.d.)

**Ana-[. . .], son of** (DUMU ᵐ*A-n*[*a-* . . .])
- no details: **131**: 9 (NM 18)

**Ana-kāršu-ēmid** (ᵐ*A-na-kar-šu-e-mi-id*)
- *arad ekalli* (ÌR.É.GAL): **300**: 2 (KT 3)

**Ana-Namma-taklāku** (⸢*A-na*⸣-ᵈ*Namma-tak-la-k*[*u*])
- DUMU.MUNUS.GABA: **95**: 19 (KT 6)

**Ana-Ninurta-taklāku** (ᵐ*A-na-*ᵈ*Nin-urta-tak-la-ku*)
- farmer (ÉNSI): **2**: 7 (KT 1); **33**: 6 (KT 12?)
- no details: **2**: 40 (KT 1); **13**: 11 (KT 13)

**Ana-nūr-Šamaš-lūṣi** (ᵐ*A-na-*ZÁLAG-ᵈUTU-È)
- brewer (ˡᵘLUNGA): **112**: 2 (NM 19); **114**: 2 (KT 4)

**Ana-Sîn-taklāku, son of** (DUMU ᵐ*A-na-*ᵈ30*-tak-la-ku*)
- farmer (ÉNSI): **1**: 9 (NM 22)
- no details: **40**: 4, 5 ([D]UMU ᵐKI.MIN) (NM 9⁺); **40**: 14′ (NM 9⁺)

**Ana-Šamaš-taklāku** (ᵐ⸢*A-na*⸣-ᵈUTU-⸢*tak-la*⸣*-ku*)
- no details: **28**: 11 (NM 24)

**Apil-[. . .]**
[1] ⸢IBILA?⸣-[x-x]-⸢x⸣
[2] ᵐIBILA-[
- perhaps Apil-Nergal: **246**: 4 (NM 14) [1]
- no details: **140**: 15′ (NM 21–KT 3) [2]

**Apil-Adad** (ᵐIBILA-ᵈIŠKUR)
- no details: **2**: 24 (KT 1); **115**: 7 (KT 6)

**Apil-Marduk** (ᵐ⸢IBILA?-ᵈAMAR.UTU⸣)
- no details: **140**: 13′ (NM 21–KT 3)

**Apil-Nergal** (ᵐIBILA-ᵈU.GUR)
- shepherd (ˡᵘSIPA): **257**: 13, 20 (NM 17)
- probably the shepherd: **250**: 4, 8 (NM 24); **251**: 6, 9 (KT 5)
- no details: **140**: 30′ (NM 21–KT 3); **331**: 10 (KT x)

**Apil-Ninurta** (ᵐIBILA-ᵈ*Nin-urta*)
- no details: **43**: 8 (KT 1)

**Apil-Šamaš** (ᵐIBILA-ᵈUTU)
- brewer (ˡᵘLUNGA): **235**: 4 (n.d.)
- boatman? (⸢ˡᵘMÁ?.LAḪ₄?⸣): **283**: 4 (KT 15?)

**Aplī-id-enši-iš[tu]** (ᵐ*Ap-li-id-en-ši-*⸢*iš*?⸣*-t*[*u₄*])
- no details: **42**: 13 (NM 19)

**Aplūtu**
[1] ᵐ*Ap-lu-tu₄*
[2] ᵐ*Ap-lu-ti*
- partner (*šutāpu*) of Banâ-ša-Šamaš: **22**: 9 (NM 19) [1]
- son of Enlil-tukultī, witness: **333**: 10 (NM x) [2]
- no details: **22**: 19 (NM 19) [1]

**Apparrītu** (ᶠ*Ap-par-ri-tu₄*)
- no details: **136**: 19 (NM 23)

**Aqru** (ᵐ*Aq-rù*)
- son of Bunna-Marduk: **159**: 14 (KT 9)

**Ar[ . . .]** (ᵐ*Ar-*[ . . .])
- no details: **331**: 3, 19 (KT x)

**Arad-[DN]**
- no details: [ᵐÌ]R?-ᵈ[ **10**: 24 (KT 12); ᵐÌR⸢?⸣-[ **108**: 12 (KT 3)

**Arad-[DN], son of** (DUMU ᵐÌR-ᵈ[ . . .])
- no details: **131**: 5 (NM 18)

**Arad-Adad** (ᵐ⸢ÌR?⸣-ᵈIŠKUR)
- no details: **9**: 12 (KT 11)

**Arad-Amurru, son of** (DUMU ᵐÌR-ᵈKUR)
- farmer (⁽ˡᵘ⁾ÉNSI): **147**: 7 (KT 2); **51**: 6 (KT 7); **169**: 2 (KT 12)
- probably the farmer: **164**: 6 (KT 9)

**Arad-Bēlti**
[1] ᵐÌR-GAŠAN
[2] ⸢ᵐÌR⸣-GAŠAN-*ti*
- scribe (DUB.SAR), son of Rā'im-kitti, witness: **326**: 22 (NM 22) [1]
- son of Iškun-līssu and brother of Banâtū'a: **135**: 8 (NM 21⁺) [1]; **303**: 8 (NM 23) [1]; **151**: 4 (KT 3) [1]; **185**: 7 (KT x) [1]
- son of Amurru-nāṣir: **48**: 17 (NM 24) [1]; **21**: 5 (n.d.) [1]
- no details: ᵐÌR-GAŠAN **1**: 17 (NM 22) [1]; **17**: 5 (NM 23) [1]; **29**: 8, 9 (ᵐKI.MIN), 11 (NM

24) [1]; **48**: 8, 9 ($^{m}$KI.MIN), 11, 24, 25 ($^{m}$KI.MIN) (NM 24) [1]; **37**: 8 (KT 1) [1]; **38**: 4, 5 (KT 3) [1]; **261**: 31 (n.d.) [1]; **26**: 7, 8 ($^{m}$KI.MIN) (NM 18) [2]; **2**: 22, 30 (KT 1) [2]

**Arad-Kūbi** ($^{m}$Ì[R]-⌜$^{d}$*Ku-bi*⌝)
- no details: **94**: 10 (KT 2)

**Arad-Marduk** ($^{m}$ÌR-$^{d}$AMAR.UTU)
- overseer (*šaknu*): **150**: 16 (KT 3); **51**: 7 (KT 7); **69**: 3, 9 (KT 9)
- exorcist (*āšipu*), son of Enlil-nāṣir: **124**: 9 (NM 21)
- no details: **31**: 8 (KT 5); **95**: 47′ (KT 6); **51**: 10 (KT 7); **96**: 11 (KT 9); **97**: 6, 7 (KT 9); **98**: 6, 7 (KT 9); **8**: 4, 5 ($^{m}$KI.MIN), 10, 11 ($^{m}$KI.MIN) (KT 11); **10**: 6, 7 ($^{m}$KI.MIN), 10, 13, 14–16 ($^{m}$KI.MIN), 27 (KT 12)

**Arad-Nergal** ($^{m}$ÌR-$^{d}$U.GUR)
- shepherd (SIPA) of the horses of the prince: **239**: 20 (NM 22)
- no details: **150**: 13 (KT 3)

**Arad-nubatti** ($^{m}$ÌR-*nu-bat-ti*)
- *ḫa*[*zannu*?]: **146**: 7 (KT 2)
- *ḫazannu* of the House of Enlil-kidinnī: **337**: 7 (n.d.)
- son of Elamû: **329**: 5 (KT 5)
- father of Nippurû: **138**: 7 (NM x)
- no details: **17**: 7 (NM 23); **139**: 14, 16 (NM x); **37**: 34 (KT 1); **165**: 3 (KT 10); **7**: 17 (KT 11); **32**: 16 (KT 11); **53**: 12 (KT 12); **178**: 2, 15, 18, 21 (KT 15); **318**: 3 (n.d.)

**Arad-Sebetti** ($^{m}$ÌR-$^{d}$IMIN.KAM)
- no details: **45**: 31 (KT 4)

**Arad-$U_4$.9.KAM** ($^{m}$ÌR-$U_4$.9.KAM)
- weaver (UŠ.BAR): **271**: 6′ (KT 13)
- probably the weaver: **101**: 14 (KT 15)
- father of Bunna-Gula: **150**: 12 (KT 3)
- son of Gubbuḫu: **289**: 5 (KT 17)
- no details: **308**: ix 13′ (NM 18–22); **139**: 21 (NM x)

**Ardiyū, son of** (DUMU $^{m}$*Ar-di-ia-ú*)
- no details: **290**: 6 (KT x)

**Ardu** ($^{m}$*Ar-du*)
- gate keeper (*āpil bābi*): **95**: 42′ (KT 6)

**Ardūtu**
[1] $^{m}$*Ar-du-tu*$_4$
[2] $^{m}$*Ar-du-ti*
- son of Iqbi-ul-īni: **184**: 5, 6 ($^{m}$KI.MIN) (KT x) [1]
- *ṣupur* PN: **331**: 28 (KT x) [2]
- no details: **331**: 19 (KT x) [1]

**Arkât-ili-damqā, son of** ([DU]MU? $^{m}$EGIR-DINGIR-⌜SIG$_5$?⌝)
- no details: **321**: 4 (n.d.)

**Aru[. . .]** ($^{m}$*A-ru*-⌜x⌝[ . . .])
- no details: **266**: 9′ (n.d.)

**Aṣûšu-namir** ($^{m}$UD-*šú*-ZÁLAG-*ir*)
- farmer (ÉNSI): **9**: 26 (KT 11); **33**: 9 (KT 12?); **176**: 5 (KT 13)
- GURUŠ, son of Baḫû: **93**: 27′ (KT 2)
- no details: **157**: 7 (KT 8)

**Ašriqu** ($^{m}$*Aš-ri-qu*)
- no details: **4**: 29 (KT 8?); **52**: 11, 22 (KT 11); **14**: 4 (KT 14); **184**: 8, 12 (KT x)

**Aššurāyu, son of** (⌜DUMU? $^{m}$*Aš-šur-a-a-ú*$^{ki}$⌝)
- no details: **47**: 1 (NM 21)

**Ātamar-qāssa**
[1] $^{f}$*A-ta-mar*-ŠU-*sa*
[2] $^{f}$*A-ta-mar*-<ŠU>-*sa*
- musician (MUNUS.NAR): **244**: 13 (KuE 8) [2]
- no details: **100**: 6 (KT 12) [1]; **101**: 7 (KT 15) [1]

**Atkalšu** ($^{m}$*At-kal-šu*)
- no details: **22**: 16, 17–18 ($^{m}$KI.MIN) (NM 19)

**Atta-ilī-ma** ($^{m}$*At-ta*-DINGIR-*ma*)
- farmer (ÉNSI): **15**: 6 (KT 14)

**Ayaru** ($^{m}$*A-a-ri*)
- father of Nuska-nābûšu: **333**: 17 (NM x)

**Ayaru, daughter of** (DUMU.MUNUS $^{m}$*A-a-rù*)
- no details: **139**: 21 (NM x)

**Ba[. . .]** ($^{m}$*Ba*-[ . . .])
- no details: **176**: 19 (KT 13)

**Bā'eru**
[1] $^{m}$*Ba-i-rù*
[2] $^{m}$*Ba-e*-[*rù*]
[3] $^{m}$*Ba-e-ri*
- brewer ($^{lú}$LUNGA): **112**: 2 (NM 19) [1]; **133**: 6 (NM 20) [1]; **114**: 2 (KT 4) [1]; **164**: 23 (KT 9) [1]; **8**: 16 (KT 11) [1]
- son of Baḫû, witness: **327**: 23′ (KT 5) [3]
- no details: **8**: 4, 10 (KT 11) [1]; **10**: 14 (KT 12) [2]

**Baba-asât** ($^{fd}$*Ba-ba*$_6$-*a-sa-at*)
- no details: **101**: 21 (KT 15)

**Baba-šarrat** ($^{fd}$*Ba-ba$_6$-šar-rat*)
- *ararratu*-miller (MUNUS.ÀR), daughter of [. . .]: **96**: 6 (KT 9)
- no details: **100**: 9 (KT 12); **101**: 10 (KT 15)

**Baba-īriš** ($^{md}$*Ba-ba$_6$*-URU$_4$)
- shepherd (SIPA) of the king: **159**: 33 (KT 9)
- probably the shepherd of the king: **207**: 6 (KT 2)

**Baba-uṣrīšu** ($^f$*Ba$^?$-ba$_6^?$-uṣ-*⌜*ri-šu*⌝)
- no details: **267**: 10 (NM 16)

**Bābilāyu**
[1] $^m$*Ba-bi-la-a-ú*
[2] $^m$*Ba-bi-la-a-a-ú*
- father of Kidin-Ninurta: **151**: 6 (KT 3) [1]
- no details: **136**: 15 (NM 23) [2]; **298**: 4, 12 (NM 23) [2, 1]; **2**: 38 (KT 1) [2]; **37**: 5 (KT 1) [2]; **109**: 3 (n.d.) [2]

**Bābilāyu, son of** (DUMU $^m$*Ba-bi-la-a-a-i*)
- no details: **187**: 2 (KaE 3)

**Babû'a** ($^f$*Ba-bu-ú-a*)
- *mārat bīti* (DUMU.MUNUS É$^?$): **290**: 2 (KT x)

**Baḫû**
[1] $^m$*Ba-ḫu-ú*
[2] $^m$*Ba-ḫe-e*
[3] $^m$*Ba-ḫu-*[
- farmer (ÉNSI): **40**: 9 (NM 9$^+$) [1]
- gate keeper (*āpil bābi*): **95**: 41′ (KT 6) [1]
- son of Rabâ-ša-Sîn: **307**: 9′ (NM$^?$ 21) [1]
- father of Aṣûšu-namir: **93**: 27′ (KT 2) [2]
- father of Bā'eru: **327**: 23′ (KT 5) [2]
- no details: **131**: 8 (NM 18) [3]

**Baḫūtu** ($^f$*Ba-ḫu-tu$_4$*)
- *kallātu* (É.GI$_4$.A), mother of Ina-nipḫīša-alsiš: **95**: 30 (KT 6)

**Ballukku** ($^m$*Bal-lu-uk-ku*)
- no details: **308**: ix 9′, 14′, 29′ (NM 18–22)

**Bāltī-Amurru** ($^f$*Bal-ti-*$^d$KUR)
- *ararratu*-miller (MUNUS.ÀR): **186**: 6 (KT x)

**Bāltī-Bēltī** ($^f$*Bal-ti-*$^d$⌜GAŠAN$^?$⌝)
- no details: **292**: 3 (n.d.)

**Bāltī-Nergal** ($^f$*Bal-ti-*$^d$U.GUR)
- no details: **285**: 3 (KT 16); **292**: 2 (n.d.)

**Bananâtu** ($^f$*Ba-na-na-ti*)
- no details: **324**: 1 (BB 18)
- seal (NA$_4$.KIŠIB) of PN: **324**: 28 (BB 18)

**Bananāya** ($^m$*Ba-na-na-a-a*)
- no details: **57**: 16 (KT x)

**Bananû**
[1] $^m$*Ba-na-nu-ú*
[2] $^m$*Ba-na-ni-i*
- *ḫazannu*, witness: **327**: 24′ (KT 5) [2]
- father of Qīšat-Marduk: **150**: 18 (KT 3) [2]
- no details: **44**: 8 (KT 1) [1]; **5**: 15 (KT 8) [1]; **6**: 16 (KT 8) [1]; **159**: 27, 28 (KT 9) [1]; **164**: 10 (KT 9) [1]

**Banâ-ša-Enlil** ($^m$DÙ-*a-šá-*$^{d+}$*En-líl*)
- no details: **2**: 17 (KT 1)

**Banâ-ša-Gula** (⌜$^m$DÙ-*šá-*$^d$*Gu-la*⌝)
- no details: **260**: 3 (NM x)

**Banâ-ša-Marduk**
[1] $^m$DÙ-*šá-*$^d$AMAR.UTU
[2] $^m$DÙ-*a-šá-*$^d$AMAR.UTU
- no details: **27**: 7 (NM 20) [1]; **115**: 5 (KT 6) [1]; **5**: 7 (KT 8) [1]; **6**: 7 (KT 8) [1]; **156**: 6 (KT 8) [1]; **162**: 6 (KT 9) [2]; **7**: 8 (KT 11) [2]; **32**: 7 (KT 11) [2]; **53**: 9 (KT 12) [2]

**Banâ-ša-Papsukkal** ($^m$DÙ-*a-šá-*$^d$⌜*Pap*⌝*-sukkal*)
- no details: **28**: 10 (NM 24)

**Banâ-ša-Šamaš**
[1] $^m$DÙ-*šá-*$^d$UTU
[2] $^m$DÙ-*a-šá-*$^d$UTU
- no details: **22**: 8, 9 ($^m$KI.MIN) (NM 19) [2]; **1**: 18 (NM 22) [1]; **49**: 11 (KT 1) [1]; **316**: 8 (year 17) [2]

**Banâtū'a**
[1] $^m$*Ba-na-tu-'a-a*
[2] $^m$*Ba-na-tu-ú-a*
- son of Iškun-līssu, brother of Arad-Bēlti: **151**: 4 (KT 3)
- no details: **46**: 32 (KT x)

**Banītu**
[1] $^f$*Ba-ni-tu$_4$*
[2] *Ba-ni-tu$_4$*
- MUNUS.TUR, sister of Ima'da: **95**: 40′ (KT 6) [2]
- no details: **101**: 12 (KT 15) [1]

**Banīya** ($^m$*Ba-ni-ia*)
- no details: **331**: 5 (KT x)

**Bānû** ($^m$*Ba-nu-ú*)
- no details: **94**: 18′ (KT 2)

**Bāqilu, son of** (DUMU $^m$*Ba-qí-li*)
- no details: **28**: 6 (NM 24)

**Baqnītu** (*Baq-ni-t*[*i*])
- mother of Ištar-idāya-alki: **95**: 8 (KT 6)

**Baqnītu, son of** ([DUMU $^{mf?}$]⌜*Baq*⌝*-ni-ti*)
- farmer (ÉNSI): **26**: 4 (NM 18)

**Baqnu** ($^{m}$*Ba-a*[*q*$^{?}$*-ni*$^{?}$])
- father of [ . . .]: **325**: 14 (NM 14)

**Baqnu, son of** (DUMU $^{m}$*Ba-aq-ni*)
- no details: **7**: 11 (KT 11); **32**: 10 (KT 11)

**Bar[ . . .], son of** (DUMU $^{m}$*Bar-*[ . . .])
- no details: **261**: 12 (n.d.)

**Bariya, son of** (DUMU $^{m}$*Ba-ri-i*[*a*])
- no details: **46**: 35 (KT x)

**Barmatu** ($^{f}$*Bar-ma-tu*$_{4}$)
- no details: **308**: iv 13′ (NM 18–22)

**Barzamu** ($^{m}$*Bar-za-m*[*u*$^{?}$])
- no details: **244**: 16 (KuE 8)

**Battiyūtu**
[1] $^{m}$*Ba-ti-ia-ú-tu*$_{4}$
[2] $^{m}$*Ba-at-ti-ia-ú-tu*$_{4}$
[3] $^{m}$*Ba-at-ti-i-ú-tu*
[4] $^{m}$*Ba-ti-ia-ú-ti*
- father of Ninurta-nāṣir: **326**: 21 (NM 22) [1]
- father of . . . : **95**: 44′ (KT 6) [4]
- no details: **55**: 9, 17 (KT 12) [2]; **169**: 4 (KT 12) [1]; **331**: 15 (KT x) [3]

**Bēlānu**
[1] $^{m}$*Be-la-nu*
[2] $^{m}$*Be-la-n*[*i*]
[3] ⌜$^{m}$EN-*la-«na»-nu*⌝
- *mār bīti* (DUMU É): **281**: 6 (KT 15) [1]
- son of Innibu: **150**: 5 (KT 3) [1]; **175**: 5 (KT 13) [1]
- husband of Rabât-Gula: **279**: 5 (KT 7) [2]
- no details: **45**: 8, 38 (KT 4) [1]; **57**: 9 (KT x) [1]; **290**: 1 (KT x) [3]

**Bēlānu, daughter of** (DUMU.MUNUS $^{m}$*Be-la-nu*)
- no details: **174**: 8 (KT 13)

**Bēlessunu**$^{?}$ ([$^{f}$x-x]*-su-nu*)
- sister of Enlil-[ . . .]: **95**: 22 (KT 6)

**Bēlet-sinnišāti** (GAŠAN-MUNUS$^{meš}$)
- MUNUS.TUR, daughter of Iddin-Gula: **291**: 9 (KT 5–7)

**Bēlī-iddina** ($^{m}$EN-SUM-*na*)
- father of Taqīšu: **37**: 21 (KT 1)
- son of Erība-ilī: **176**: 12 (KT 13)
- no details: **171**: 6 (KT 12)

**Bēlī-iqīša** ($^{m}$EN-BA-*šá*)
- plowman ($^{lú}$ENGAR): **171**: 8 (KT 12)
- no details: **11**: 11 (KT 12); **54**: 11 (KT 12); **46**: 10 (KT x)

**Bēlī-kitti** ($^{m}$EN-*kit-ti*)
- son of Qiltu: **71**: 6 (KT 9)

**Bēliyātu, son of** (DUMU $^{m}$*Be-lí-ia-a-tu*$_{4}$)
. no details: **131**: 13 (NM 18)

**Bēl-qali**$^{?}$ ($^{m}$EN-*qa-li*)
- GURUŠ, son of Enlil-tukultī and brother of Rīš-Nergal: **93**: 24′ (KT 2)

**Bēlšunu**
[1] $^{m}$EN-*šu-nu*
[2] EN-[*šu-nu*]
- plowman ($^{lú}$ENGAR): **159**: 16 (KT 9) [1]; **179**: 20′ (KT 15) [1]
- no details: **325**: 7, 11, 22 (NM 14) [1]; **332**: 3, 8 (NM 23) [1]; **10**: 21, 27 (KT 12) [1]

**Bēltu-bārat**
[1] $^{f}$GAŠAN-*ba-rat*
[2] $^{f}$GAŠAN-*ba-ra-*[*at*]
- no details: **239**: 13, 17, 21 (NM 22) [1]; **308**: ix 16′ (NM 18–22) [2]

**Bēltu-irīša** (⌜$^{f}$GAŠAN⌝*-iri-*[*š*]*a*)
- *ararratu*-miller (MUNUS.ÀR), daughter of Paḫāru: **96**: 7 (KT 9)

**Bēltu-rīšat** ($^{f}$⌜GAŠAN⌝*-ri-šat*)
- no details: **267**: 6 (NM 16)

**Bēltu-terēmanni** ($^{f}$GAŠAN-*te-re-m*[*an*$^{?}$*-ni*$^{?}$])
- no details: **95**: 13 (KT 6)

**Bēlu-mušallim** ($^{m}$*Be-lu*$_{4}$*-mu-šal-lim*)
- no details: **57**: 15 (KT x)

**Bi'šu** ($^{m}$*Bi-i'-šu*$_{14}$)
- no details: **1**: 14 (NM 22); **2**: 23 (KT 1); **5**: 6 (KT 8); **6**: 13 (KT 8); **164**: 13, 17 (KT 9); **7**: 13 (KT 11); **32**: 12 (KT 11); **53**: 10 (KT 12); **56**: 13 (KT 13)

**Bil[. . .]** ($^{m}$*Bíl-*[ . . .])
- no details: **170**: 17 (KT 12)

**Bilakkullu** ($^{m}$*Bi-lak-ku-ul-lu*$_{4}$)
- no details: **308**: ix 18′ (NM 18–22)

**Biliya** ($^{m}$*Bi-l*[*i-ia*])
- no details: **99**: 14 (KT 9)

**Billullu**
[1] $^{m}$*Bíl-lu-lu*
[2] $^{m}$*Bíl-lul-lu*$_{4}$
[3] $^{m}$*Bíl-*⌜*lu*⌝*-u*[*l*$^{?}$*-lu*$_{4}$$^{?}$]
[4] $^{m}$*Bíl-lu*[*l-lu*$_{4}$]
- carpenter ($^{(lú)}$NAGAR): **247**: 2 (NM 19) [1]; **159**: 31 (KT 9) [2]
- carpenter ($^{lú}$NAGAR), father of Kudurrānu: **176**: 26 (KT 13) [2]

- son of Šamaš-kīna-īde: **124**: 8 (NM 21) [3]
- no details: **160**: 7 (KT 9) [4]

**Biltī-marṣāt** ($^{f}$*Bì-il-ti-mar-ṣa-at*)
- no details: **131**: 15 (NM 18)

**Binnānu** ($^{m}$*Bi-in-na-nu*)
- no details: **3**: 15′ (KT 5); **162**: 8 (KT 9); **9**: 15 (KT 11)

**Bitiya** ($^{m}$*Bi-ti-i*[*a*])
- witness: **334**: 6′ (n.d.)

**Bittā, Bettā**
[1] $^{m}$*Bi-it-ta-a*
[2] $^{m}$*Be-et-ta*
- farmer ($^{lú}$ÉNSI), son of Tupšarru: **302**: 8 (KT 10) [2]; **169**: 6 (KT 12) [1]
- shepherd$^{?}$ (SI[PA$^{?}$]), father of Sîn-abūša: **291**: 12 (KT 5–7) [1]
- no details: **2**: 41 (KT 1) [1]; **50**: 8, 17 (KT 1) [1]

**Bītu-rabi** ($^{m}$É-*ra-bi*)
- no details: **239**: 10 (NM 22); **297**: 21 (KT 6); **68**: 7 (KT 7); **216**: 5 (KT 9); **220**: 5 (KT 11); **224**: 6 (KT 13); **242**: 10 (KT 14); **102**: 8′ (KT 15); **179**: 12, 13 ($^{m}$KI.MIN) (KT 15); **230**: 4 (KT 15); **231**: 7 (KT 16); **187**: 7 (KaE 3)

**Bu . . .** (⌜$^{m}$*Bu*$^{?}$-x-x⌝)
- no details: **246**: 2 (NM 14)

**Bugaš-Ḫa[rbe$^{?}$]** ($^{m}$⌜*Bu-ga-áš*$^{?}$⌝-*Ḫa*[*r*$^{?}$*-be*$^{?}$])
- no details: **27**: 8 (NM 20)

**Bugurrānu** ($^{m}$*Bu-gur-ra-nu*)
- no details: **4**: 32 (KT 8$^{?}$)

**Buḫiru** ($^{m}$*Bu-ḫi-ri*)
- father of Dilbat-bāni: **94**: 11 (KT 2)

**Bulālu** ($^{m}$*Bu-la-*$lu_4$)
- no details: **299**: 3 (ŠŠ x)

**Bullussa-[rabi$^{?}$]** ($^{f}$TI-*sa*-[GAL$^{?}$])
- no details: **170**: 14 (KT 12)

**Bunna-[DN]**
[1] ⌜$^{m}$*Bu*$^{?}$*-na*⌝-[
[2] $^{m}$*Bu-un-na-*$^{d}$[
[3] $^{m}$*Bu-u*[*n-na-*$^{d}$
[4] $^{m}$*Bu-un-n*[*a-*$^{d}$
- *arad ekalli*$^{?}$ (ÌR.É.GAL$^{?}$): **137**: 3 (NM x) [1]
- no details: **40**: 6 (NM 9$^{+}$) [2]; **135**: 14 (NM 21$^{+}$) [2]; **18**: 7 (KT 3) [2]; **5**: 11 (KT 8) [2]; **6**: 12 (KT 8) [2]; **261**: 10, 13 (n.d.) [3, 4]

**Bunna-[DN], son of** (DUMU $^{m}$*Bu-un-n*[*a-* . . .])
- no details: **147**: 8 (KT 2)

**Bunna-Adad** ($^{m}$*Bu-un-na-*$^{d}$IŠKUR)
- farmer (ÉNSI): **34**: 7, 19′ (KT 12)

**$^{m}$Bunna-Gula**
[1] $^{m}$*Bu-un-na-*$^{d}$*Gu-la*
[2] $^{m}$*Bu-na-*$^{d}$*Gu-la*
- shepherd (SIPA) of donkeys, son of Arad-$U_4$.9.KAM: **150**: 12 (KT 3) [1]
- son of Innibu, father of Enlil-taklāku: **121**: 7 (NM 23$^{?}$, KT 3$^{?}$) [1]
- son of Iddin-Ninurta: **184**: 7 (KT x) [2]
- son of Nūr-Bēlet-Akkade: **103**: 10 (KT x) [1]
- GURUŠ.TUR, escapee (ZÁḪ): **95**: 45′ (KT 6) [1]
- no details: **57**: 10 (KT x) [1]; **316**: 6 (year 17) [1]; **109**: 6 (n.d.) [2]

**$^{f}$Bunna-Gula** ($^{f}$*Bu-un-na-*$^{d}$*Gu-la*)
- no details: **274**: 6 (KT 2); **275**: 4 (KT 5); **276**: 4 (KT 6); **277**: 4, 47′ (KT 6); **278**: 9 (KT 7); **100**: 4 (KT 12); **101**: 6 (KT 15); **287**: 3, 10, 13 (KT 17); **243**: 8 (KT x); **104**: 4 (ŠŠ 2)

**Bunna-Marduk**
[1] $^{m}$*Bu-un-na-*$^{d}$AMAR.UTU
[2] $^{m}$*Bu-na-*$^{d}$AMAR.UTU
- son of Ubbuttu: **136**: 29 (NM 23) [1]
- father of Aqru: **159**: 12, 13 ($^{m}$KI.MIN) (KT 9) [1]
- no details: **304**: 3 (NM 15) [1]; **303**: 10 (NM 23) [2]; **141**: 7 (NM 24–KT 3) [2]; **142**: 3 (NM 24–KT 3) [1]; **2**: 34 (KT 1) [1]; **37**: 4 (KT 1) [1]; **50**: 4, 13 (KT 1) [2, 1]; **108**: 5 (KT 3) [1]; **156**: 4 (KT 8) [1]; **72**: 5 (KT 9) [1]; **160**: 4 (KT 9) [1]; **164**: 8 (KT 9) [1]; **12**: 7 (KT 13) [1]; **35**: 6 (KT 13) [1]; **79**: 2 (KT 13) [1]; **288**: 4 (KT 17) [1]

**Bunna-Nergal**
[1] [$^{m}$]*Bu-un-na-*$^{d}$GÌR
[2] $^{m}$*Bu-un-*<*na*>*-*$^{d}$GÌR
- no details: **40**: 10 (NM 9$^{+}$); **266**: 12′ (n.d.)

**Bunnanu** ($^{m}$*Bu-un-*[*n*]*a-nu*)
- son of Nuska- . . . šu: **150**: 4 (KT 3)

**Bunnūtu** ($^{m}$*Bu-un-nu-ti*)
- no details: **253**: 3, 10 (ŠŠ 1)

**Burna-Buriaš** (*Bur-na-Bu-ri-ia-*⌜*áš*$^{?}$⌝)
- king: **324**: 25 (BB 18)

**Burra-Saḫ** ($^{m}$*Bur-ra-Saḫ*)
- no details: **26**: 10 (NM 18)

**Burruqu**
[1] $^{m}$*Bur-ru-qu*
[2] $^{m}$*Bur-ru-qu*$^{!}$
- no details: **99**: 3 (KT 9) [1]; **316**: 5 (year 17) [2]

**Bur-Sîn** (mBur-d30)
- no details: **99**: 18 (KT 9)

**Bussut** (mBu-su-ut)
- father of Sîn-išmanni: **150**: 4 (KT 3)

**Bušaršu** (m⌈Bu?⌉-šar-šu)
- farmer (ÉNSI): **46**: 14 (KT x)

**Bu'ūa** (mBu-ú-a)
- shepherd (SIPA) of bovines, father of Tatatu: **291**: 7 (KT 5–7); **159**: 34 (KT 9)

**Dābibī** (mDa-bi-bi)
- House (É) of PN: **158**: 2, 3 (mKI.MIN) (KT 9)
- father of Sîn-aḫa-iddina: **254**: 8 (NM 19)
- father of Sîn-erība: **303**: 11 (NM 23)

**Damu-nāṣir** (mdDa-mu-ÙRU)
- son of Agīya: **28**: 7 (NM 24)
- son of Elamû: **28**: 8 (NM 24)
- no details: **44**: 8, 9, 12 (KT 1)

**Dān-Nergal** (mKAL-dU.GUR)
- no details: **169**: 23 (KT 12)

**Daqqatu** (fDaq-qá-tu4)
- sister of Adad-ilu-ina-māti, mother of Rabâ-ša-Šēmû: **95**: 32 (KT 6)

**Dašpu** (mDa-aš-pí)
- father of Zākiru: **176**: 11 (KT 13)

**Dayyān-Marduk** (mDI.KU5-dAMAR.UTU)
- son of Šamaš-nāṣir: **326**: 2 (NM 22)
- seal (NA4.KIŠIB) of PN (= son of Šamaš-nāṣir): **326**: 25 (NM 22)

**Dayyantu**
[1] fDa-a-an-du
[2] fDa-a-a-an-du
- no details: **267**: 8 (NM 16) [1]; **100**: 8 (KT 12) [2]; **101**: 9 (KT 15) [2]

**Di . . .** (⌈fDi?-x-x⌉)
- daughter of Bēlessunu?: **95**: 28 (KT 6)

**Dilbat-bāni** (md⌈Dil-bat⌉-ba-ni)
- son of Buḫiru: **94**: 11 (KT 2)
- no details: **120**: 7 (NM 19?); **94**: 7 (KT 2)

**Dimaḫdi-Nergal** (Di-maḫ-di-dU.GUR)
- no details: **311**: 1 (KT 11)

**Dimaḫdi-Uraš** (mDi-maḫ-di-dUraš)
- seal (NA4.KIŠIB) of PN: **236**: 11 (NM 8); **262**: 8′ (n.d.)
- no details: **193**: 6 (NM 12); **198**: 4 (NM 15); **47**: 8, 11 (NM 21); **162**: 7 (KT 9); **9**: 16, 23, 24 (mKI.MIN), 29, 30 (mKI.MIN) (KT 11); **11**: 8, 9–13 (mKI.MIN) (KT 12); **54**: 8, 9–13 (mKI.MIN), 16 (KT 12); **12**: 17 (KT 13); **35**: 16 (KT 13); **46**: 7 (KT x)

**Ea-[. . .]**
[1] [m]dÉ-[a-
[2] mdE-[a-
- scribe? ([DUB?].SAR): **291**: 21 (KT 5–7) [1]
- no details: **159**: 9 (KT 9) [2]

**Ea- . . . , son of** (DUMU mdÉ-a-⌈x-x⌉-[. . .])
- no details: **5**: 13 (KT 8)

**Ea-aḫa-iddina** (mdé-a-ŠEŠ-SUM)
- no details: **139**: 10 (NM x)

**Ekūtu** (fE-ku-tu4)
- no details: **101**: 11 (KT 15); **289**: 4 (KT 17)

**Elamû** (mE-la-mi-i)
- father of Ēmidu: **120**: 36 (NM 19?)
- father of Damu-nāṣir: **28**: 8 (NM 24)
- father of Arad-nubatti: **329**: 5 (KT 5)

**Ēmid-ana-Marduk** (mUŠ-a-na-dAMAR.UTU)
- plowman (lúENGAR) of Ninurta-zākir-šumi: **156**: 25 (KT 8); **162**: 13 (KT 9)

**Ēmidu** (mE-mi-du)
- son of Elamû: **120**: 36 (NM 19?)
- no details: **45**: 8 (KT 4); **4**: 21 (KT 8?); **7**: 22 (KT 11); **32**: 21 (KT 11); **316**: 11 (year 17)

**Ēmuq-Adad** (mE-muq-dIŠKUR)
- gardener (NU.gišKIRI6): **136**: 23 (NM 23)
- gardener (NU.gišKIRI6), husband of Rabât-agallitu?, son-in-law of Muštāl-Nergal: **291**: 10 (KT 5–7)

**Enki-MU.PÀ.DA** (md+En-ki-MU.PÀ.DA)
- no details: **4**: 26 (KT 8?); **56**: 12 (KT 13); **14**: 4 (KT 14)

**Enlil-[. . .]** (md+En-líl-[. . .])
- seal (NA4.KIŠIB) of PN: **192**: 10 (NM 9)
- GURUŠ.TUR: **95**: 16, 38′ (KT 6)
- brother of Bēlessunu?: **95**: 22 (KT 6)
- no details: **170**: 16 (KT 12); **190**: 3 (n.d.)

**Enlil-aḫa-iddina** (md+En-líl-ŠEŠ-SUM-na)
- son of [. . .]: **95**: 4 (KT 6)

**Enlil-alsa, son of** (DUMU md+En-líl-AL.SA6)
- no details: **96**: 1, 11 (KT 9)

**Enlil-apla-iqīša** (md50-IBILA-[BA]-šá)
- no details: **104**: 8 (ŠŠ 2)

**Enlil-gešir-ilāni** (md50-⌈ge-šìr⌉-DINGIRmeš)
- seal (NA4.KIŠIB) of PN: **289**: 10 (KT 17)
- no details: **328**: 2, 4, 6 (KT 17)

**Enlil-kidinnī** ($^{md+}$*En-líl-ki-di-ni*)
- House (É) of PN: **81**: 3 (KT 14); **337**: 8 (n.d.)
- father of Ninurta-kīn-pīšu: **265**: 6′ (KT 7)
- father of Ninurta-kiššat-ilāni: **181**: 1 (KT 15–17)

**Enlil-m[u . . .]** ($^{md+}$*En-líl-m*[*u*$^{?}$- . . .])
- GURUŠ.TUR: **95**: 14 (KT 6)

**Enlil-muballiṭ** ($^{md+}$*En-líl-mu-bal-liṭ*)
- no details: **234**: 5 (KT x)

**Enlil-mukīn-apli** ($^{d+}$*En-líl-mu-kin*-IBI[LA])
- no details: **327**: 8 (KT 5)

**Enlil-MU.PÀ.DA** ($^{md+}$*En-líl*-MU.PÀ.DA)
- brother of Nanna-šar-dīni: **139**: 32 (NM x)

**Enlil-mutakkil** ($^{md+}$*En-líl-mu-tak-kil*)
- no details: **22**: 14 (NM 19); **31**: 6 (KT 5); **51**: 11 (KT 7)

**Enlil-nāṣir** ($^{md+}$*En-líl*-ÙRU)
- father of Arad-Marduk: **124**: 9 (NM 21)

**Enlil-ṣulūlī** ($^{md+}$*En-líl-ṣú-lu-li*)
- no details: **45**: 30 (KT 4)

**Enlil-šadî-ilāni** ($^{md+}$*En-líl*-KUR-DINGIR$^{meš}$)
- no details: **308**: ix 12′ (NM 18–22)

**Enlil-šumu-līšir** ($^{md+}$*En-líl*-MU-SI.SÁ)
- no details: **187**: 9 (KaE 3)

**Enlil-taklāku** ($^{md+}$*En-líl-tak-la-ku*)
- son of Bunna-Gula: **121**: 9 (NM 23$^{?}$, KT 3)

**Enlil-taqīš-bulliṭ** ($^{md+}$*En-líl-ta-qiš*-TI-*it*)
- sender of letter: **337**: 2 (n.d.)

**Enlil-tukultī**
[1] $^{md+}$*En-líl-tu-k*[*ul*]-*ti*
[2] ⌜$^{md+}$*En-líl-tukul*⌝-*ti*
- father of Aplūtu: **333**: 11 (NM x) [1]
- father of Rīš-Nergal and of Bēl-qali$^{?}$: **93**: 22′ (KT 2) [2]

**Erēmšē'a** ($^{m}$*E-re-e*[*m*]-*še-e-a*)
- no details: **77**: 3 (KT 12)

**Erība-Adad**
[1] $^{m}$*Eri-ba*-$^{d}$IŠKUR
[2] $^{m}$SU-$^{d}$IŠKUR
- boatman ($^{lú}$MÁ.LAḪ$_{5}$) of Ninurta-zākir-šumi: **327**: 2, 9, 15′ (KT 5) [1, 2, 1]; **176**: 25 (KT 13) [1]
- son of Aḫu-. . . : **176**: 16 (KT 13) [1]
- no details: **45**: 7, 30 (KT 4) [2]; **3**: 17′ (KT 5) [1]; **154**: 10 (KT 6$^{?}$) [1]; **34**: 8 (KT 12) [1]; **12**: 8 (KT 13) [1]; **13**: 10 (KT 13) [1]; **35**: 7 (KT 13) [1]; **46**: 20 (KT x) [1]

**Erība-ilī** ($^{m}$*Eri-ba*-DINGIR)
- father of Bēlī-iddina: **176**: 12 (KT 13)

**Erība-Marduk**
[1] $^{m}$*Eri-ba*-$^{d}$AMAR.UTU
[2] $^{m}$SU-$^{d}$AMAR.UTU
- sender of letter: **336**: 2 (n.d.) [1]
- no details: **30**: 10 (KT 4) [1]; **45**: 17, 31 (KT 4) [2]; **7**: 10 (KT 11) [1]; **9**: 21 (KT 11) [2]; **32**: 9 (KT 11) [1]; **34**: 15′ (KT 12) [1]; **101**: 15 (KT 15) [1]

**Erība-Nergal**
[1] $^{m}$*Eri-ba*-$^{d}$U.GUR
[2] $^{m}$SU-$^{d}$U.GUR
- shepherd ($^{lú}$SI[PA]), father of Mīšarītu: **291**: 6 (KT 5–7) [2]
- son of Qadištu: **168**: 1, 14 (NM 19–20, KT 11–12) [1]
- no details: **287**: 11 (KT 17) [2]

**Erība-Nin$^{?}$ . . .** ($^{m}$⌜SU$^{?}$⌝-$^{d}$⌜*Nin*$^{?}$-x⌝)
- no details: **45**: 16 (KT 4)

**Erība-Ninurta**
[1] $^{m}$*Eri-ba*-$^{d}$*Nin-urta*
[2] $^{m}$*Eri-ba*-$^{d}$⌜MAŠ$^{?}$⌝
- brewer ($^{lú}$LUNGA): **133**: 7 (NM 20) [1]
- probably the brewer: **135**: 7 (NM 21$^{+}$) [1]
- no details: **33**: 15 (KT 12$^{?}$) [2]

**Erība-Šamaš** ($^{m}$*Eri-ba*-$^{d}$UTU)
- *elamû*: **95**: 52′ (KT 6)

**Erība-Šuqamuna**
[1] $^{m}$*Eri-ba*-$^{d}$*Šu-qa-mu-na*
[2] $^{m}$SU-$^{d}$*Šu-qa-mu-na*
- *ṣuḫurtu*: **239**: 12 (NM 22) [2]; **150**: 14 (KT 3) [2]
- probably *ṣuḫurtu*: **124**: 7 (NM 21) [2]; **125**: 2, 6 (NM 21–23) [1]
- no details: **29**: 10 (NM 24) [2]; **48**: 10 (NM 24) [1]; **36**: 9 (year 5) [2]

**Erībātu** ($^{m}$*Eri-ba-a*-[*tu*$_{4}$])
- no details: **4**: 30 (KT 8$^{?}$)

**Erību, Irību**
[1] $^{m}$*E-ri-bu*
[2] $^{m}$*E-ri-bi*
[3] $^{m}$*I-ri-bu*
[4] $^{m}$*I-ri-bi*
- farmer (ÉNSI): **34**: 9 (KT 12) [3]
- son of Šamaš-nāšir: **42**: 9, 10 ($^{m}$KI.MIN) (NM 19) [1]

- father of Izkur-Adad: **14**: 9 (KT 14) [2]; **184**: 9 (KT x) [1]
- son of Ab[ . . .]: **253**: 4, 11 (ᵐKI.MIN) (ŠŠ 1) [4]
- TUR: **292**: 6 (n.d.) [1]
- no details: **325**: 4, 9, 10 (NM 14) [1, 2, 1]; **199**: 4 (NM 16) [2]; **200**: 1′ (NM 16) [2]; **201**: 5 (NM 16) [2]; **140**: 23′ (NM 21–KT 3) [3]; **145**: 7 (KT 2) [1]; **165**: 8 (KT 10) [1]; **171**: 10 (KT 12) [1]; **184**: 14 (KT x) [1]

**Erību, son of** (DUMU ᵐ*E-ri-bu*)
- no details: **3**: 19′ (KT 5)

**Erībūni, Irībūni**
[1] ᵐ*E*[*ri*]-⌜*bu-ni*⌝
[2] [ᵐ*E*]*ri*?-*bu-ni*
[3] ᵐ*I-ri-bu-ni*
- House (É) of PN: **151**: 1 (KT 3) [3]
- no details: **22**: 6, 7 (ᵐKI.MIN) (NM 19) [1]; **248**: 2 (NM 21) [2]; **57**: 8 (KT x) [3]

**Ērišti-Adad** (*E-riš-ti-*ᵈIŠKUR)
- *ararratu*-miller (MUNUS.ÀR), daughter of Kubbutu: **96**: 5 (KT 9)

**Ērišu, son of** (DUMU ᵐ*E-ri-ší*)
- no details: **261**: 23 (n.d.)

**Esagila-līdiš** (ᵐÉ.SAG.ÍLA-*l*[*i-d*]*i-iš*)
- no details: **66**: 3 (NM 20)

**Etel-pī-[DN]** (ᵐ*E-tel*-KA-⌜ᵈ⌝[ . . .])
- son of Šinnānu: **170**: 10, 14 (KT 12)
- no details: **154**: 15 (KT 6?)

**Etel-pī-Ištar** (ᵐ*E-tel*-KA-ᵈ*Iš-tar*)
- father of Iqīša-Ninimma: **330**: 12 (KT 14)

**Etel-pī-Ninurta**
[1] ᵐ*E-tel*-KA-ᵈMAŠ
[2] ᵐ*E-tel*-KA-ᵈ*Nin-urta*
- no details: **26**: 9 (NM 18) [1]; **48**: 20, 21 (ᵐKI.MIN) (NM 24) [2]

**Etel-pī-Šamaš** ([ᵐ]⌜*E*⌝-*tel*-KA-ᵈUTU)
- no details: **154**: 9 (KT 6?)

**Etel-pû** (ᵐ*E-tel-pu*)
- no details: **31**: 10 (KT 5)

Ēṭiranni-Marduk see Šūzibanni-Marduk
Ēṭiranni-Šamaš see Šūzibanni-Šamaš

**Ēṭiru** (ᵐ*E-ṭi-rù*)
- son of Sarriqu, brother of Amīlu-banû: **55**: 21 (KT 12)
- no details: **278**: 6 (KT 7); **52**: 10, 21 (KT 11); **10**: 28 (KT 12)

**(E)ulmaš-aḫa-iddina** (ᵐUL.MAŠ-ŠEŠ-SUM-*na*)
- no details: **292**: 4 (n.d.)

**Eulmaš-iqīša** (ᵐÉ.UL.MAŠ-BA-*šá*)
- knotter (*kāṣiru*): **101**: 17 (KT 15)

**Ēz-u-pāšir**
[1] ᵐ*E-zu-ú-pa-ši-ir*
[2] ᵐ*E-zi-ù-pa-ši-ir*
[3] ᵐ⌜*E-ez-ù-pa*⌝-[*ši-ir*]
- no details: **45**: 42 (KT 4) [1]; **4**: 28 (KT 8?) [2]; **14**: 7 (KT 14) [2]; **36**: 11 (year 5) [3]

**Gab-Enlil** (ᵐ*Gab*-ᵈ⁺*En-líl*)
- father of Nergal-aḫa-iddina: **279**: 7 (KT 7)

**Gimil-Adad** (ᵐŠU-ᵈIŠKUR)
- farmer (ˡᵘÉNSI): **45**: 10 (KT 4)

**Gimillu** (ᵐ*Gi-mil-lu*₄)
- weaver (UŠ.BAR), brother of Bēlessunu?: **95**: 24 (KT 6)

**Gubbuḫu**
[1] ᵐ*Gu-ub-bu-ḫu*
[2] ᵐ*Gu-ub-*<*bu*>-*ḫu*
[3] ᵐ*Gu-bu-ḫu*
- leather-worker (ˡᵘAŠGAB): **48**: 19 (NM 24) [2]
- father of Arad-U₄.9.KAM: **289**: 6 (KT 17) [1]
- son of Yaya'u: **184**: 11 (KT x) [1]
- no details: **29**: 8 (NM 24) [1]; **48**: 8 (NM 24) [1]; **3**: 21′ (KT 5) [1]; **46**: 38 (KT x) [1]; **26**: 10, 11–12 (ᵐKI.MIN) (NM 18) [3]

**Gula- . . .** (ᵐᵈ[*Gu*?]-⌜*la*?-x)
- father of . . . -Sîn: **324**: 21 (BB 18)

**Gula-balāṭa-īriš** (ᵐᵈ*Gu-la*-TI-URU₄)
- no details: **91**: 3 (ŠŠ x)

**Gula-īriš** (ᵐᵈ*Gu-la*-URU₄)
- no details: **33**: 12 (KT 12?)

**Gula-šarrat** (ᶠᵈ*Gu-la-šar-at*)
- no details: **267**: 9 (NM 16)

**Guraš** (ᵐ*Gu*-⌜*ra-aš*⌝)
- no details: **27**: 6 (NM 20)

**Ḫaḫia** (ᵐ*Ḫa*-[*aḫ*?]-*ia*)
- ⌜ˡᵘ?x⌝: **303**: 5 (NM 23)

**Ḫaldīya** (ᵐ*Ḫal-di-ia*)
- father of Tarība-Gula: **120**: 42 (NM 19?)
- father of Illullu: **50**: 7, 14 (KT 1); **147**: 10 (KT 2)

**ᵐ*Ḫal*?-*lu*?/*ku*?-ᵈAMAR.UTU**
- no details: **177**: 8 (KT 15)

**Ḫambu**
[1] $^{m}$*Ḫa-an-bu*
[2] $^{m}$*Ḫa-am-bu*
[3] $^{m}$*Ḫa-am-bi*
- farmer (ÉNSI): **13**: 5, 7 (KT 13) [1]
- father of Kiribtu: **148**: 5 (KT 2) [1]
- father of Iqīša-Adad: **97**: 2 (KT 9) [2]
- no details: **27**: 6 (NM 20) [2]; **66**: 4 (NM 20) [2]; **120**: 34 (NM 19$^{?}$) [3]; **139**: 34 (NM x) [3]

**Ḫambu, son of** (DUMU $^{m}$*Ḫa-am-bi*)
- no details: **157**: 6 (KT 8)

**Ḫananaya, son of** (DUMU $^{m}$*Ḫa-na-na-a-a*)
- no details: **33**: 7 (KT 12$^{?}$)

**Ḫānibu**
[1] $^{m}$*Ḫa-ni-bu*
[2] $^{m}$*Ḫa-ni-bi*
- farmer (ÉNSI): **55**: 7 (KT 12) [1]; **15**: 5 (KT 14) [1]
- *arad ekalli* (ÌR.É.GAL): **120**: 26 (NM 19$^{?}$) [1]
- son of Tupšarru: **175**: 6 (KT 13) [1]
- brother of Ḫummurtu: **291**: 11 (KT 5–7) [2]
- no details: **26**: 8 (NM 18) [1]; **106**: 24 (NM 23) [1]; **107**: 4 (KT 2) [1]

**Ḫannabu** ($^{m}$*Ḫa-an-na-bu*)
- no details: **10**: 13 (KT 12)

**Ḫašmar** ($^{m}$*Ḫaš-mar*)
- House (É) of PN: **16**: 7 (KT x)

**Ḫazi-M[arduk$^{?}$], daughter of** (DUMU.MUNUS $^{mf}$*Ḫa-zi*-$^{d}$AM[AR$^{?}$.UTU$^{?}$])
- no details: **174**: 9 (KT 13)

**Ḫildiya, son of** (DUMU $^{m}$*Ḫi-il-di-ia*)
- no details: **131**: 14 (NM 18)

**Ḫimmatu** ($^{m}$*Ḫi-im-ma-tu*$_{4}$)
- son of Šurbā[ . . .], witness: **324**: 18 (BB 18)

**Ḫinnibūtu** (*Ḫi-in-ni-bu-tu*$_{4}$)
- MUNUS.TUR, daughter of Kidin-Enlil: **291**: 8 (KT 5–7)

**Ḫu[. . .]** ($^{m}$*Ḫu*-⸢x⸣[ . . .])
- father of Adad-šumu-līšir and of Ḫunnubu: **315**: 4 (KT 13)

**Ḫuddimmānu** ($^{m}$*Ḫu-ud-di-im-ma-a-nu*)
- son of Adad-zākir, brother of Ḫummuru: **315**: 2 (KT 13)

**Ḫuddinu** ($^{m}$*Ḫu-ud-di-nu*)
- no details: **316**: 16 (year 17)

**Ḫudiya, son of** (DUMU $^{m}$*Ḫu-di-ia*)
- no details: **31**: 11 (KT 5)

**Ḫummurtu** (*Ḫu-um*-⸢*mu-ur-tu*$_{4}$⸣)
- MUNUS.TUR, sister of Ḫānibu: **291**: 11 (KT 5–7)

**Ḫummuru** ($^{m}$*Ḫu-um-mu-rù*)
- son of Adad-zākir, brother of Ḫuddimmānu: **315**: 3 (KT 13)

**Ḫumurbiya-[Saḫ$^{?}$], son of** (DUMU $^{m}$*Ḫu-mur-bi-i*[*a-Saḫ*$^{?}$])
- no details: **46**: 23 (KT x)

**Ḫunābu**
[1] $^{m}$*Ḫu-na-bu*
[2] $^{m}$*Ḫu-na-bi*
- *ḫazannu*: **19**: 8 (KT 12) [2]
- *mār bīti* (DUMU É): **150**: 9 (KT 3) [1]
- ⸢lú?⸣[ . . .]:**127**: 3 (NM 10$^{+}$) [2]
- no details: **3**: 11′ (KT 5) [1]; **4**: 19, 20–21 ($^{m}$KI.MIN), 27, 36 (KT 8$^{?}$) [1]; **57**: 11 (KT x) [1]; **65**: 4 (NM 18) [2]; **70**: 3 (KT 9) [2]; **170**: 15 (KT 12) [2]; **126**: 4 (KT 13) [2]; **176**: 23 (KT 13) [2]

**Ḫunābu, son of** (DUMU $^{m}$*Ḫu-n*[*a*$^{?}$*-bi*$^{?}$])
- no details: **280**: 2 (KT 9)

**Ḫunbī-ina-Uruk** ($^{f}$*Ḫu-un-bi*-⸢*i-na*-UNUG$^{?}$⸣[$^{ki}$])
- mother of Ina-Sagila-kabtat: **96**: 10 (KT 9)

**Ḫunnubu**
[1] $^{m}$*Ḫu-un-nu-bu*
[2] ⸢$^{m}$*Ḫu*$^{?}$*-un*$^{?}$⸣*-nu*-⸢*bu*⸣
[3] ⸢$^{m}$*Ḫu*$^{?}$⸣-[*un*]-⸢*nu*$^{?}$*-bu*$^{?}$⸣
[4] [$^{m}$*Ḫu*$^{?}$*-u*]*n*$^{?}$*-nu-bi*
- son of Ḫu[ . . .], brother of Adad-šumu-līšir: **315**: 5 (KT 13) [2]
- no details: **2**: 32 (KT 1) [1], **13**. 12 (KT 13) [1]; **57**: 17 (KT x) [1]; **10**: 20 (KT 12) [3]; **10**: 25 (KT 12) [4]

**Ḫunzu'u**
[1] $^{m}$*Ḫu-un-zu-ú*
[2] $^{m}$*Ḫu-un-zu-'u*
- no details: **22**: 11 (NM 19) [1]; **2**: 28 (KT 1) [1]; **244**: 9, 10–11 ($^{m}$KI.MIN) (KuE 8) [1]; **261**: 41 (n.d.) [2]

**Ḫurtu** ($^{m}$*Ḫu-ur-ti*)
- no details: **62**: 2 (NM 7)

**Ḫusarakku** ($^{m}$*Ḫu-sa-rak-ku*)
- no details: **159**: 32 (KT 9); **77**: 4 (KT 12)

**Ḫuzālu**
[1] $^{m}$*Ḫu-za-lu*$_{4}$
[2] $^{m}$*Ḫu-za-li*
- father of Martuk(k)u: **165**: 7 (KT 10) [1]

- no details: **2**: 14, 15–18 ($^{m}$KI.MIN) (KT 1) [1]; **49**: 8 (KT 1) [1]; **38**: 6 (KT 3) [1]; **159**: 1, 2 (KT 9) [2]; **160**: 1 (KT 9) [2]; **39**: 4 (KT 10) [2]; **180**: 3 (KT 2–15$^{?}$) [2]

**Ibbaši-ma-rūq** ($^{m}$*Ib*$^{!}$*-ba-ši-ma-ru-uq*)
- no details: **9**: 15 (KT 11)

**Ibni-[DN]** ($^{m}$*Ib-ni-*$^{d}$[ . . .])
- no details: **40**: 11 (NM 9$^{+}$); **9**: 19 (KT 11); **140**: 24′ (NM 21–KT 3)

**Ibni-Adad** ($^{m}$*Ib-ni-*$^{d}$IŠKUR)
- carpenter ($^{lú}$NAGAR): **12**: 19 (KT 13); **35**: 18 (KT 13); **103**: 6 (KT x)

**Ibni-Marduk** ($^{m}$*Ib-ni-*$^{d}$AMAR.UTU)
- gate keeper (*āpil bābi*) of Isin: **138**: 11, 12 (NM x); **113**: 11 (KT 3); **301**: 5 (KT 3)
- son of Nuska-nābûšu: **164**: 25 (KT 9); **186**: 12 (n.d.)
- no details: **160**: 5 (KT 9); **316**: 17 (year 17)

**Ibnīya** ($^{m}$*Ib-ni-ia*)
- no details: **37**: 30, 33 (KT 1); **148**: 9 (KT 2); **149**: 10, 11–12 ($^{m}$KI.MIN) (KT 2); **179**: 10, 11 ($^{m}$KI.MIN) (KT 15)

**Ibnûtu** ($^{m}$*Ib-nu-tu*$_{4}$)
- carpenter (NAGAR): **57**: 18 (KT x)
- no details: **7**: 19 (KT 11); **32**: 18 (KT 11)

**Iddin-Adad**
- [1] $^{m}$*I-din-*$^{d}$IŠKUR
- [2] $^{m}$SUM-$^{d}$IŠKUR
  - no details: **47**: 13, 17, 18 ([$^{m}$KI.MI]N$^{?}$), 27 (NM 21) [2]; **21**: 8 (n.d.) [1]

**Iddin-Adad, son of** (DUMU $^{m}$*I-din-*$^{d}$IŠKUR)
- no details: **46**: 28 (KT x)

**Iddin-Eulmaš** ($^{m}$*I-din-*É.U[L.MAŠ])
- no details: **102**: 4′ (KT 15)

**Iddin-Gula** ($^{m}$*I-din-*$^{d}$*Gu-la*)
- father of Bēlet-sinnišāti, son of Abuyatu: **291**: 9 (KT 5–7)

**Iddin-Marduk** ($^{m}$SUM-$^{d}$AMAR.UTU)
- cook$^{?}$ ($^{lú⸢}$MUḪALDIM$^{?⸣}$): **9**: 10 (KT 11)
- no details: **328**: 6, 22 (KT 17); **261**: 28 (n.d.)

**Iddin-Marduk, daughter of** (DUMU.MUNUS $^{m}$*I*$^{?}$*-din-*$^{d⸢}$AMAR.UTU$^{⸣}$)
- no details: **95**: 45′ (KT 6)

**Iddin-Nergal**
- [1] $^{m}$*I-din-*$^{d}$U.GUR
- [2] $^{m}$SUM-$^{d}$U.GUR
  - son of Iddin-Nergal: **164**: 18 (KT 9) [1]; **330**: 1, 8, 17 (KT 14) [2]
  - father of Iddin-Nergal: **164**: 18 (KT 9) [1]; **330**: 2, 9 (KT 14) [2]
  - no details: **9**: 13, 14 ($^{m}$KI.MIN) (KT 11) [2]; **57**: 9, 10 ($^{m}$KI.MIN), 25 (KT x) [1]

**Iddin-Nergal, son of** (DUMU $^{m}$SUM-$^{d}$U.GUR)
- no details: **319**: 3 (n.d.)

**Iddin-Ninurta** ($^{m}$*I-din-*$^{d}$*Nin-urta*)
- father of Bunna-Gula: **184**: 7 (KT x)

**Iddinu** ($^{m}$*Id-di-nu*)
- no details: **57**: 18 (KT x)

**Ikkaru**
- [1] $^{m}$*Ik-ka-rù*
- [2] $^{m}$*Ik-ka-ri*
  - father of Ina-Sagila-bāltī: **96**: 8 (KT 9) [2]
  - no details: **33**: 8, 13 (KT 12$^{?}$) [1]

**Ikūna** ($^{m}$*I-ku-na*)
- no details: **8**: 11 (KT 11); **316**: 14, 15–16 ($^{m}$KI.MIN) (year 17)

**Ilānū'a** ($^{m}$*I-la-nu-ú-a*)
- son of Lū-dari-bēlī: **116**: 2, 7 (KT 9)
- son of [ . . .]: **164**: 5 (KT 9)
- no details: **47**: 16 (NM 21); **45**: 19 (KT 4); **52**: 27 (KT 11)

**Ilī-aḫa-[. . .]** ($^{m}$DINGIR-⸢ŠEŠ⸣-[ . . .])
- GURUŠ.TUR: **95**: 15 (KT 6)

**Ilī-aḫḫē-iddina** ($^{m}$DINGIR-ŠEŠ$^{meš}$-SUM-*na*)
- son of Lultamrūtu: **181**: 2, 8 (KT 15–17)

**Ilī-ayabaš** ($^{m}$*Ì-lí-a-ba-aš*)
- father of Marduk-zākir-šumi: **239**: 7 (NM 22); **139**: 11 (NM x)
- father of [ . . .] **136**: 24 (NM 23)

**Ilī-īdânni** ($^{m}$*Ì-lí-i-da-an-ni*)
- father of Nūr-Marduk: **157**: 5 (KT 8); **123**: 3′ (KT 9)

**Ilī-iddina** ($^{m}$DINGIR-SUM-⸢*na*⸣)
- no details: **2**: 15 (KT 1)

**Ilī-ippašra** ($^{m}$DINGIR-*ip-pa-aš-ra*)
- no details: **4**: 8, 17, 22 (KT 8$^{?}$)

**Ilī-iqīša** ($^{m}$*Ì-lí-*BA-*ša*)
- father of Ilī-rēmanni: **326**: 19 (NM 22)
- no details: **57**: 15 (KT x)

**Ilīma-Adad** ($^{m}$DINGIR-*ma-*$^{d}$IŠKUR)
- no details: **47**: 13, 27 (NM 21)

**Ilīma-ilu** ($^{m}$*Ì-lí-ma-*DINGIR)
- no details: **2**: 31 (KT 1)

**Ilī-mudammiq** ($^{m}$DINGIR.MU-*mu-*SIG$_{5}$)
- witness: **328**: 17 (KT 17)
- no details: **181**: 5 (KT 15–17)

**Ilī-rabi** (mDINGIR-GAL)
- father of Kudurrānu: **162**: 7 (KT 9); **54**: 16 (KT 12)

**Ilī-rabi, daughter of** (DUMU.MUNUS mDINGIR-GAL)
- no details: **9**: 12 (KT 11)

**Ilī-rēmanni**
[1] mÌ-lí-re-man-ni
[2] mDINGIR-re-man-ni
- son of Ilī-iqīša, witness: **326**: 18 (NM 22) [1]
- seal (NA4.KIŠIB) of PN: **145**: 15 (KT 2) [1]
- no details: **2**: 31 (KT 1) [1]; **37**: 9, 25 (KT 1) [1]; **50**: 5 (KT 1) [1]; **145**: 4 (KT 2) [1]; **108**: 8 (KT 3) [1]; **151**: 9 (KT 3) [1]; **165**: 6 (KT 10) [2]; **170**: 12, 13 (KT 12) [1]; **188**: 13′ (year 8) [1]

**Ilī-rēmanni, son of** (DUMU mÌ-lí-re-man-ni)
- farmer (ÉNSI): **1**: 10 (NM 22); **326**: 6 (NM 22); **33**: 7 (KT 12?)
- no details: **40**: 3, 15′ (NM 9+)

**Ilī-rigim . . . , daughter of** (DUMU.MUNUS mDINGIR-ri-gim?-⌜x⌝)
- no details: **46**: 38 (KT x)

**Ilīya** (Ì-lí-ia)
- no details: **104**: 7 (ŠŠ 2)

**Illallu** (mIl-la-al-lu4)
- brother of Rašilu: **151**: 5 (KT 3)

**Illīya** (mIl-li-ia)
- no details: **48**: 21 (NM 24)

**Illīya, son of** (DUMU mIl-li-ia)
- no details: **64**: 3 (NM 18)

**Ill[u . . .]** (mIl-l[u?- . . .])
- gate guard (EN.NU.⌜UN⌝ KÁ.GAL): **319**: 9 (n.d.)

**Illullu**
[1] mIl-lul-lu4
[2] mIl-lu-lu4
[3] mIl-lul-lu
[4] mIl-lu-ul-lu4
- *ḫazannu*, probaby identical with the son of Ḫaldīya: **164**: 32 (KT 9) [1]; **302**: 7 (KT 10) [2]
- son of Ḫaldīya, probaby identical with the *ḫazannu*: **50**: 7, 14 (KT 1) [1]; **147**: 10 (KT 2) [3]
- probably *ḫazannu:* **185**: 9 (KT x) [1]
- no details: **2**: 39 (KT 1) [1]; **45**: 21 (KT 4) [4]; **99**: 16 (KT 9) [4]

**Illurīya** (mIl-lu-ri-ia)
- no details: **5**: 18 (KT 8); **6**: 6 (KT 8); **156**: 8, 29 (KT 8); **7**: 12 (KT 11); **32**: 11 (KT 11)

**Ilqāšu-ilī?** (mIl-qa-šu-DINGIR)
- GURUŠ.TUR, son of Išemmūtu and brother of Tarībtu: **93**: 30′ (KT 2)

**Ilulūtu** (mI-lu-lu-tu4)
- no details: **56**: 10 (KT 13)

**Ima'da** (mI-ma-a'-da)
- GURUŠ.TUR.TUR, brother of Banītu: **95**: 39′ (KT 6)

**Imbu(b)bu** (mIm-bu-⌜ub?⌝-bu)
- no details: **33**: 14 (KT 12?)

**Imguru, son of** ([DUMU m]⌜Im⌝-gu-ri)
- no details: **123**: 7′ (KT 9)

**Ina-Akkade-bēlet** (⌜f⌝I-na-A-ka?-de?-NIN⌝)
- no details: **222**: 2 (KT 12)

**Ina-Egalmaḫ-šarrat** ([fI]-na-É.GA[L.MAḪ]-šar-rat)
- daughter of . . . : **95**: 49′ (KT 6)

**Ina-Ekur-dan[nāt?]** (fI-na-É.KUR-⌜dan?⌝-[ . . .])
- escapee (ZÁḪ): **95**: 12 (KT 6)

**Ina-Ḫursagkalama-šarrat** (I-na-ḪUR.SAG.KALAM.MA-šar-rat)
- MUNUS.TUR.TUR, daughter of [ . . .]: **291**: 15 (KT 5–7)

**Ina-Isin-bā'ilat** (fI-na-Ì-si-in-ba-'i-lat)
- *ararratu*-miller (MUNUS.ÀR), daughter of [ . . .]: **96**: 4 (KT 9)

**Ina-kitti-elê/ele'i**
[1] mI-na-kit-ti-e-le
[2] mI-na-kit-ti-e-le-i
[3] mI-na-kit-ti-e-l[e]
- brewer (lúLUNGA) of Ninu[rta?- . . .]: **164**: 21 (KT 9) [1]
- no details: **4**: 33 (KT 8?) [1]; **156**: 26 (KT 8) [2]; **102**: 6′ (KT 15) [3]

**Ina-libbi-īriš, son of** (DUMU I-na-ŠÀ-bi-URU4-iš)
- no details: **292**: 8 (n.d.)

**Ina-nipḫīša-alsiš**
[1] fI-na-ni-ip-ḫi-ša-al-si-iš
[2] ⌜fI-na⌝-KUR-ša-[al?]-⌜si?⌝-[iš?]
- daughter of Baḫūtu: **95**: 31 (KT 6) [1]
- no details: **95**: 20 (KT 6) [2]

**Ina-Sagila-bāltī** (⌜fI?-na?⌝-SAG.ÍLA-ba[l-t]í)
- *ararratu*-miller (MUNUS.ÀR), daughter of Ikkaru: **96**: 8 (KT 9)

**Ina-Sagila-kabtat** (⌜fI-na⌝-SAG.ÍLA-DUGUD-at)

- *ararratu*-miller (MUNUS.ÀR), daughter of Ḫunbī-ina-Uruk: **96**: 10 (KT 9)

**Ina-ṣilli-Ea-lubluṭ** (ᵐ*I-na-ṣíl-lí-ᵈÉ-a-lu-ub-lu-uṭ*)
- no details: **13**: 8, 11 (KT 13)

**Ingumgu** (ᵐ*In-gu-um-gu*)
- no details: **187**: 6 (KaE 3)

**Innanibūtu**
[1] ᵐᶠ*In-na-ni-bu-ti*
[2] ᵐ*In-na-ni-bu-ú-ti*
- father/mother of Marduk-zākir-šumi: **93**: 5 (KT 2) [1]
- father of Rabât-Gula: **291**: 2 (KT 5–7) [2]

**Innanibūtu, son of**
[1] DUMU ᵐᶠ*In-na-ni-bu-ti*
[2] DUMU ᵐ*In-na-ni-bu-ti*
- farmer (ÉNSI): **1**: 11 (NM 22) [1]; **2**: 8 (KT 1) [1]
- probably the farmer: **2**: 37 (KT 1) [1]
- no details: **131**: 6 (NM 18) [2]

**Innannu** (ᵐ*In-na-an-nu*)
- son of Lā-qīpu, witness: **325**: 17 (NM 14)

**Innibu** (ᵐ*In-ni-bu*)
- father of Bunna-Gula: **121**: 8 (NM 23?, KT 3)
- father of Bēlānu: **150**: 5 (KT 3); **175**: 5 (KT 13)
- no details: **21**: 6 (n.d.)

**Innū'atu, daughter of**
[1] DUMU.MUNUS ᵐ*I*[*n*?-*nu*?]-⌜*a*?-*ti*?⌝
[2] DUMU.⌜MUNUS?⌝ *In-nu-ú-a-ti*
- no details: **136**: 11, 20 (NM 22) [1, 2]

**Innunnu**
[1] ᵐ*In-nu-un-nu*
[2] ᵐ*In-nu-nu*
[3] ᵐ*In-nu-ni*
[4] ᵐ*In-nu-un-nu-«nu»*
[5] ᵐ*In-nu-un-«un»-nu*
- *mandidu*: **17**: 6 (NM 23) [1]
- shepherd (SIPA), sometimes identified as shepherd of donkeys: **268**: 2 (KT 1) [1]; **35**: 15 (KT 13) [1]; **46**: 12 (KT x) [1]
- shepherd (SIPA) of donkeys, brother of Sîn-bāltī, brother-in-law of Kulippi(-)rigir: **291**: 5 (KT 5–7) [3]
- farmer (ÉNSI): **46**: 13 (KT x) [4]
- no details: **37**: 31 (KT 1) [1]; **5**: 13 (KT 8) [1]; **6**: 15 (KT 8) [1]; **9**: 17 (KT 11) [5]; **11**: 14 (KT 12) [2]; **54**: 14 (KT 12) [1]; **12**: 16 (KT 13) [1]; **261**: 27 (n.d.) [1]

**Ipputu**? (ᵐ*Ip*?-*pu-t*[*u*₄?])
- no details **58**: 3 (NM 18?)

**Iqbi-ul-īni** (ᵐ*Iq-bi-ul-i-ni*)
- father of Ardūtu: **184**: 5 (KT x)

**Iqīša-[DN]**
[1] ᵐ*I-qí-*[
[2] ᵐ*I-qí-ša-*ᵈ[
[3] ᵐBA-*šá*-ᵈ[
- no details: **44**: 11 (KT 1) [1]; **3**: 22′ (KT 5) [3]; **24**: 8 (KT 15?) [3]; **36**: 13 (year 5) [2]

**Iqīša-[DN], son of** (DUMU ᵐBA-*š*[*á*?- . . .])
- no details: **170**: 11 (KT 12)

**Iqīša-Adad** (ᵐBA-*šá*-ᵈIŠKUR)
- son of Ḫambu: **97**: 2, 21 (KT 9); **98**: 1 (KT 9)
- probably the son of Ḫambu: **138**: 8 (NM x)
- seal (NA₄.KIŠIB) of PN: **314**: 6′ (KT 12)

**Iqīša-Amurru** (ᵐBA-*šá*-ᵈKUR)
- farmer (ÉNSI): **55**: 6 (KT 12)
- no details: **57**: 17 (KT x)

**Iqīša-Dilbat** (ᵐBA-⌜*šá*⌝-ᵈ*Dil-bat*)
- carpenter (ˡᵘNAGAR): **80**: 8 (KT 13⁺)

**Iqīša-Marduk** (ᵐBA-*šá*-ᵈAMAR.UTU)
- son of Ṭābiḫu: **256**: 9 (NM 9); **89**: 4 (KT x); **182**: 3 (KT x)
- seal (NA₄.KIŠIB) of PN (= son of Ṭābiḫu): **256**: 14 (NM 9)
- son of Qadištu: **148**: 8 (KT 2)
- son of Kunzubu: **97**: 8 (KT 9)
- son of [ . . .]: **154**: 14 (KT 6?)

**Iqīša-Nergal** (ᵐBA-*ša*-ᵈU.GUR)
- GURUŠ.TUR, son of Rīš-Nergal: **93**: 23′ (KT 2)

**Iqīša-Ninimma** (ᵐBA-*šá*-ᵈ*Nin-ìmma*)
- son of Etel-pī-Ištar, witness: **330**: 12 (KT 14)
- no details: **203**: 3 (NM 21⁺); **3**: 18′ (KT 5); **4**: 14 (KT 8?); **33**: 17 (KT 12?); **176**: 8 (KT 13); **178**: 19 (KT 15); **287**: 4 (KT 17)

**Iqīša-Ninurta** (ᵐBA-*šá*-ᵈ*Nin-urta*)
- son of [ . . .]: **97**: 14 (KT 9)
- no details: **12**: 18 (KT 13); **35**: 17 (KT 13); **103**: 3 (KT x)

**Iqīša-Papsukkal** (ᵐBA-*šá*-ᵈ*Pap-sukkal*)
- no details: **57**: 12, 21 (KT x)

**Irēmanni-Adad** (ᵐ*I-re-man-ni*-ᵈIŠKUR)
- no details: **29**: 7 (NM 24); **48**: 7 (NM 24)

**Irēmanni-ilī** (ᵐ*I-re-man-ni*-DINGIR)
- no details: **120**: 35 (NM 19?); **11**: 15 (KT 12); **54**: 15 (KT 12)

Irību see Erību

Irībūni see Erībūni
**Īriš-Ea** ($^{m}$URU$_{4}$-$^{d}$*É-a*)
- no details: **112**: 2 (NM 19)

**Isḫunnu, daughter of**
[1] DUMU.MUNUS *Is-ḫu-un-ni*
[2] DUMU.MUNUS $^{m}$*Is-ḫu-un-*⌜*ni*⌝
- no details: **281**: 4 (KT 15) [1]; **102**: 9′ (KT 15) [2]; **187**: 11 (KaE 3) [2]

**Iš[ . . .]** ($^{m}$*Iš-*⌜x⌝[ . . .])
- father of Tunami-Saḫ: **137**: 10 (NM x)

**Išemmi-ina-Esagila**
[1] $^{m}$*I-ši-im-me-i-na*⌝-É.SAG.ÍLA
[2] $^{m}$*I-še-em-mi-i-na*-É.SAG.ÍLA
- GURUŠ: **93**: 8 (KT 2) [1]
- no details: **44**: 7 (KT 1) [2]

**Išemmūtu** ($^{m}$*E-še-mu-ti*)
- father of Tarībtu and of Ilqāšu-ilī: **93**: 29′ (KT 2)

**Išḫara-šarrat** ($^{fm}$*Ìš-ḫa-ra-šar-rat*)
- no details: **296**: 10 (KT 12)

**Iškun-līssu**
[1] $^{m}$*Iš-kun$_{8}$-lí-su*
[2] $^{m}$*Iš-kun$_{8}$-*[*lí-su*]
[3] $^{m}$⌜*Iš*$^{?}$*-kun$_{8}$*$^{?}$⌝*-*[*lí*$^{?}$*-su*$^{?}$]
- father of Arad-Bēlti and of Banâtū'a: **135**: 8 (NM 21$^{+}$) [1]; **303**: 8 (NM 23) [2]; **151**: 4 (KT 3) [1]; **185**: 5 (KT x) [3]

**Išriqu** ($^{m}$*Iš-ri-qu*)
- no details: **45**: 39 (KT 4)

**Ištar-dīnī$^{?}$- . . .** ($^{fd}$*Ištar-di-*⌜*ni*$^{?}$-x-x⌝)
- no details: **267**: 11 (NM 16)

**Ištar-idāya-alkī** ($^{fd}$*Iš-tar-i-da-a-a-al-ki*)
- daughter of Baqnītu: **95**: 8 (KT 6)

**Itti-ilīya-aḫbut** ($^{m}$KI-DINGIR-*ia-aḫ-b*[*u-u*]*t*)
- no details: **49**: 9 (KT 1)

**Itti-Marduk** ($^{m}$KI-$^{d}$AMAR.UTU)
- no details: **9**: 11 (KT 11)

**Itti-Šamaš** ($^{m}$KI-$^{d}$UTU)
- no details: **266**: 11′ (n.d.)

**Ittīša-aḫbut** (*It-ti-ša-*⌜*aḫ-bu-ut*⌝)
- DUMU.GABA: **95**: 35 (KT 6)

**Izkur-[DN]** ($^{m}$*Iz-kùr-*$^{d}$[ . . .])
- no details: **41**: 14 (NM 18); **3**: 16′ (KT 5); **46**: 4 (KT x); **331**: 4 (KT x); **244**: 15 (KuE 8); **36**: 14 (year 5)

**Izkur-Adad**
[1] $^{m}$*Iz-kùr-*$^{d}$IŠKUR
[2] $^{m}$*Iz-kur-*$^{d}$IŠKUR
- *arad ekalli* (ÌR.É.GAL): **120**: 38 (NM 19$^{?}$) [1]
- builder ($^{lú}$DÙ): **12**: 13 (KT 13) [1]
- ⌜$^{lú}$x⌝: **9**: 20 (KT 11) [1]
- son of Erību: **14**: 9 (KT 14) [1]; **184**: 9 (KT x) [2]
- no details: **30**: 11 (KT 4) [1]; **45**: 41 (KT 4) [1]; **9**: 18 (KT 11) [1]; **52**: 11, 22 (KT 11) [1]; **12**: 11 (KT 13) [1]; **35**: 10, 12 (KT 13) [1]; **46**: 9 (KT x) [1]

**Izkur-Dilbat** ($^{m}$*Iz-kùr-*$^{d}$*Dil-*[*bat*])
- no details: **36**: 12 (year 5)

**Izkur-Marduk** ($^{m}$*Iz-kùr-*$^{d}$AMAR.UTU)
- witness: **334**: 4′ (n.d.)
- son of Nergal-nāṣir: **42**: 8 (NM 19)
- son of Tarībat-ilī: **28**: 15 (NM 24)
- no details: **55**: 11 (KT 12)

**Izkur-Nergal**
[1] $^{m}$*Iz-kùr-*⌜$^{d}$U.GUR$^{?}$⌝
[2] $^{m}$*Iz-kùr-*$^{d}$GÌR
- seal (NA$_{4}$.KIŠIB) of PN: **324**: 26 (BB 18) [1]
- no details: **324**: 3, 30 (BB 18) [1, 2]

**Izkur-Ninurta** ($^{m}$*Iz-kùr-*$^{d}$*Nin-urta*)
- *ḫazannu*: **176**: 24, 28 (KT 13)
- son of Šamaš-nāṣir: **162**: 11 (KT 9); **176**: 13 (KT 13)
- no details: **9**: 29 (KT 11); **11**: 8 (KT 12); **54**: 8 (KT 12); **12**: 9, 16 (KT 13); **35**: 8, 18 (KT 13)

**Izkur-Sîn** ($^{m}$*Iz-kùr-*$^{d}$30$^{?}$)
- no details: **12**: 19 (KT 13)

**Izkur-Šamaš**
[1] $^{m}$*Iz-kùr-*$^{d}$UTU
[2] $^{m}$*Iz-kur-*$^{d}$UTU
- GURUŠ.TUR, weaver (UŠ.BAR), son of Bēlessunu$^{?}$: **95**: 25 (KT 6) [1]
- no details: **3**: 20′ (KT 5) [2]

**Kadašman-Enlil** ($^{d}$*Ka-daš-man-*$^{d+}$*En-líl*)
- king: **187**: 26 (KaE 3)

**Kadašman-Turgu**
[1] *Ka-dáš-man-Túr-gu*
[2] $^{d}$*Ka-dáš-man-Túr-gu*
[3] $^{d}$*Kad-*<*aš*>*-man-Túr-gu*
[4] $^{d}$*Kad-aš-man-Túr-gu*
[5] $^{d}$*Ka-dáš-man-Tur$_{7}$-gu*
[6] [*K*]*a-dáš-man-*⌜*Du-ur-gu*⌝
[7] $^{m}$*Ka-da-áš-man-Du-gu*
[8] $^{m}$*Ka-dáš-man-Túr-gu*
- king: [1] and [2] passim in date formulae; **43**: 13 (KT 1) [6]; **44**: 2 (KT 1) [7]; **165**: 11 (KT 10) [5]; **9**: 1 (KT 11) [3]; **83**: 8 (KT 14) [8];

**87**: 8 (KT 15) [8]; **102**: 16′ (KT 15) [4]; **281**: 11 (KT 15) [4]
**Kagiya** (ᵐ*Ka-gi-ia*)
- brewer (ˡᵘ́LUNGA) of Parak-māri: **171**: 9 (KT 12)
**Kakkiya, son of** (DUMU ᵐ*Ka-ak-ki-i-*[*ia*])
- no details: **7**: 14 (KT 11); **32**: 13 (KT 11)
**Kalbatu** (*Kal-ba-tu₄*)
- MUNUS.TUR, daughter of Pussulu: **291**: 4 (KT 5–7)
**Kalbu** (ᵐ*Kal-bu*)
- *arad ekalli* (ÌR.É.GAL): **120**: 29 (NM 19?)
- son of Šamaš-nāṣir: **42**: 6 (NM 19)
- no details: **1**: 15 (NM 22); **2**: 21 (KT 1); **37**: 7 (KT 1); **94**: 6 (KT 2); **108**: 6 (KT 3)
**Karamdari**? (ᵐ*Ka-ra-am-da-ri-*⸢x⸣)
- father of Usātū'a: **49**: 17 (KT 1)
**Ki[. . .]** (ᵐ*Ki-*[ . . .])
- no details: **112**: 8 (NM 19); **106**: 3 (NM 23); **242**: 8 (KT 14); **36**: 16 (year 5)
**Ki . . . tu** (ᵐ⸢*Ki-*x-x-*tu₄*⸣)
- no details: **109**: 4 (n.d.)
**Kidin- . . . , Kidin-[ . . .]**
[1] ᵐ⸢*Ki-din*?-x-x⸣
[2] ᵐ⸢*Ki-di*⸣[*n-*
- no details: **94**: 16′ (KT 2) [2]; **45**: 12 (KT 4) [1]
**Kidin-Adad** (ᵐ*Ki-din-*ᵈIŠKUR)
- no details: **164**: 31 (KT 9)
**Kidin-Amurru** (ᵐ*Ki-din-*ᵈMAR.TU)
- farmer (ÉNSI): **34**: 10 (KT 12)
**Kidin-Dilbat** (ᵐ*Ki-din-*ᵈ*Dil-bat*)
- *arad ekalli* (ÌR.É.GAL): **120**: 39 (NM 19?)
**Kidin-Enlil** (ᵐ*Ki-din-*ᵈ⁺*En-líl*)
- brewer? (ˡᵘ́LU[NGA?]), father of Ḫinnibūtu: **291**: 8 (KT 5–7)
- son of Sāmu: **134**: 5′, 6′ (ᵐKI.MIN) (NM 21)
- no details: **31**: 7 (KT 5); **51**: 12 (KT 7)
**Kidin-Gula** (ᵐ*Ki-din-*ᵈ*Gu-la*)
- brewer (ˡᵘ́LUNGA) of the Ešumeša: **187**: 10 (KaE 3)
- knotter (*kāṣiru*): **90**: 3 (KT x)
- no details: **135**: 9 (NM 21⁺); **99**: 4 (KT 9); **102**: 3′ (KT 15); **299**: 10 (ŠŠ x)
**Kidiniya** (ᵐ*Ki-di-ni-ia*)
- brother of Aḫēdūtu: **179**: 8, 9 (ᵐKI.MIN) (KT 15)
**Kidin-Latarak** (⸢ᵐ*Ki-din*⸣-ᵈ*La-ta-*⸢*ra*⸣*-ak*)
- GURUŠ.TUR, son of Bēlessunu?: **95**: 26 (KT 6)
**Kidin-Marduk** (ᵐ*Ki-din-*ᵈAMAR.UTU)
- no details: **4**: 29 (KT 8?)
**Kidin-Ninurta** (ᵐ*Ki-din-*ᵈ*Nin-urta*)
- son of Bābilāyu: **151**: 6 (KT 3)
**Kidinnī-Šamaš** (ᵐ*Ki-din-ni-*ᵈUTU)
- no details: **316**: 18 (year 17)
**Kidinnītu** (ᶠ*Ki-di-ni-tu₄*)
- no details: **100**: 2 (KT 12); **101**: 3 (KT 15)
**Kidinnû** (ᵐ*Ki-di-nu-ú*)
- *amurrû*: **43**: 4 (KT 1)
- no details: **10**: 26 (KT 12)
**Kidin-Sîn** (ᵐ*Ki-*[*din*]-ᵈ30)
- no details: **49**: 10 (KT 1)
**Kidin-Šarur** (ᵐ*Ki-din-*ᵈ*Šár-ur₄*)
- no details: **331**: 7 (KT x)
**Kidiya** (ᵐ*Ki-di-ia*)
- *elamû*: **95**: 51′ (KT 6)
**Kiribti-[DN]** (ᵐ⸢*Ki-rib-ti*⸣-[ . . .])
- no details: **94**: 17′ (KT 2)
**Kiribti-Enlil, son of** (DUMU ᵐ*Ki-rib-ti-*ᵈ⁺*En-líl*)
- no details: **1**: 18 (NM 22)
**Kiribti-Marduk** (ᵐ*Ki-rib-ti-*ᵈAMAR.UTU)
- no details: **9**: 19 (KT 11)
**Kiribtu** (ᵐ*Ki-rib-tu₄*)
- son of Ḫambu: **148**: 5, 6–7 (ᵐKI.MIN) (KT 2)
- no details: **17**: 7 (NM 23); **2**: 30 (KT 1); **36**: 7 (year 5)
**Kirta(m)** (ᶠ*Kir-ta-a-am*)
- no details: **282**: 4 (KT 15?)
**Kittu-līšir, son of**
[1] DUMU ᵐ*Kit-t*[*u₄-li-š*]*ir*
[2] DUMU ᵐ*Kit-tu-*x-[x]
- no details: **29**: 10 (NM 24) [2]; **48**: 10 (NM 24) [1]
**Kubbutu**
[1] ᵐ*Ku-ub-bu-t*[*u*]
[2] ᵐ*Ku-ub-bu-ti*
- musician (ˡᵘ́NAR): **238**: 5 (NM 19) [1]
- father of Ērišti-Adad: **96**: 5 (KT 9) [2]
**Kubbutu, son of** (DUMU ᵐ*Ku-ub-bu-ti*)
- farmer (ÉNSI): **1**: 12 (NM 22); **2**: 9 (KT 1); **147**: 6 (KT 2); **33**: 10 (KT 12?)
- no details: **48**: 26 (NM 24); **2**: 42 (KT 1); **50**: 6, 16 (KT 1)
**Kudur-Enlil** (ᵈ*Ku-dur-*ᵈ⁺*En-líl*)

- king: **244**: 22 (KuE 8); **245**: 9 (KuE 9)

**Kudurrānu** (ᵐ*Ku-du-ra-nu*)
- son of Ilī-rabi: **162**: 7 (KT 9); **54**: 16 (KT 12)
- son of Billullu: **176**: 26 (KT 13)
- son of Sarriqu: **184**: 10 (KT x)
- no details: **30**: 8 (KT 4); **4**: 7, 16 (KT 8?); **179**: 12, 13 (ᵐKI.MIN) (KT 15)

**Kukkū'a** (ᵐ*Ku-uk-ku-*⌈*ú*⌉*-[a]*)
- no details: **266**: 10′ (n.d.)

**Kulippi(-)rigir** (ᵐ*Ku-lip-pi-ri-gi-ir*)
- porter (Ì.DU₈): **186**: 7 (KT x)
- husband of Sîn-bāltī, brother-in-law of Innunnu: **291**: 5 (KT 5–7)

**Kunzubu** (ᵐ*Kun₈-zu-b[i]*)
- father of Iqīša-Marduk: **97**: 8 (KT 9)

**Kuppitātu, son of**
[1] DUMU ᵐ*Ku-up-pí-ta-ti*
[2] DUMU ᵐᶠ*Ku-up-pi-ta-ti*
- farmer (ÉNSI): **26**: 3 (NM 18) [1]; **27**: 4 (NM 20) [1]; **29**: 3 (NM 24) [2]; **48**: 3 (NM 24) [2]

**Kurû** (ᵐ*Ku-ru-ú*)
- shepherd (ˡᵘ́SIPA): **238**: 6 (NM 19)

**La[ . . .], La . . .**
[1] ᵐ⌈*La*?⌉-[
[2] ⌈ᵐ*La*?-x-x⌉
- no details: **170**: 18 (KT 12) [1]; **184**: 14 (KT x) [2]

**Lā-qīpu**
[1] ᵐ*La-qí-pu*
[2] ᵐ*La-qí-pi*
- miller (KA.ZÌ.DA): **112**: 2 (NM 19) [1]
- father of Innannu: **325**: 18 (NM 14) [2]
- no details: **47**: 12, 28 (NM 21) [1]

**Larsû**
[1] ᵐ*La-ar-su-ú*
[2] *La-ar-su-ú*
- no details: **11**: 14, 15 (KT 12) [2, 1]; **54**: 14, 15 (KT 12) [1]

**Latarak-bāni** (ᵐᵈ*La-ta-ra-ak-ba-ni*)
- farmer (ÉNSI): **28**: 4 (NM 24)

**Latarak-šemi** (ᵐᵈ*La-ta-rak-še-mi*)
- no details: **57**: 6, 11 (KT x)

**Lā-terêqanni-ilu/ilī** (ᵐ*La-te-re-qá-an-ni-*DINGIR)
- no details: **331**: 13 (KT x)

**Libāšu, daughter of** (DUMU.MUNUS ᵐ*Li-ba-šu*)
- no details: **1**: 17 (NM 22)

**Līširanni-Šamaš** (ᵐ*Li-ši-*⌈*ra-an-ni*⌉-ᵈUTU)
- no details: **120**: 12 (NM 19?)

**Lū-d[a? . . .]** (ᵐ*Lu-d[a?- . . .]*)
- father of Taklāku: **89**: 5 (KT x)

**Lū-dān-nēmedī** (⌈*Lu*⌉*-da-an-né-me-di*)
- MUNUS.TUR.TUR: **95**: 43′ (KT 6)

**Lū-dari-bēlī** (ᵐ*Lu-da-ri-be-lí*)
- father of Ilānū'a: **116**: 2 (KT 9)
- no details: **151**: 11 (KT 3); **185**: 8 (KT x)

**Lū-dari-bēlī, son of** (⌈DUMU⌉ ᵐ*Lu-da-[ri-be]-lí*)
- no details: **57**: 8 (KT x)

**Ludmiq** (ᵐ*Lu-*⌈*ud*?⌉*-mi-i[q]*)
- no details: **10**: 16 (KT 12)

**Lultamar-Sîn** (ᵐ*Lul-ta-mar-*ᵈ30)
- ˡᵘ́⌈x⌉: **136**: 13 (NM 23)

**Lultamar-zikirša** (*Lul-ta-mar-zi-kir-ša*)
- MUNUS.TUR: **95**: 46′ (KT 6)

**Lultamrūtu** (ᵐ*[Lu]l-tam-ru-ti*)
- father of Ilī-aḫḫē-iddina: **181**: 2 (KT 15–17)

**Lūṣi-ana-nūr-Adad**
[1] ᵐÈ-*a-na*-ZÁLAG-ᵈIŠKUR
[2] ᵐÈ-*ana*-ZÁLAG-ᵈIŠKUR
- overseer (*šaknu*): **159**: 29 (KT 9) [1]; **163**: 9 (KT 9) [1]; **164**: 14 (KT 9) [1]
- no details: **45**: 9 (KT 4) [1]; **302**: 2 (KT 10) [2]; **7**: 17 (KT 11) [1]; **32**: 16 (KT 11) [1]; **56**: 9 (KT 13) [1]; **86**: 2 (KT 15) [2]; **182**: 9 (KT x) [1]

**Lūṣi-ana-nūr-Enlil** (ᵐÈ-*a-na*-ZÁLAG-ᵈ⁺*En-líl*)
- son of [ . . .]: **154**: 13 (KT 6?)
- no details: **154**: 16 (KT 6?); **176**: 10 (KT 13)

**Lūṣi-ana-nūr-Gula** (ᵐ⌈È-*a-na*-ZÁLAG⌉-ᵈ*Gu-la*)
- no details: **45**: 11 (KT 4)

**Lūṣi-ana-nūr-Marduk** (ᵐÈ-*a-na*-ZÁLAG-ᵈAMAR.UTU)
- *mār bīti* (DUMU É): **144**: 9 (KT 1); **164**: 15 (KT 9)
- seal (NA₄.KIŠIB) of PN: **211**: 8 (KT 4)
- no details: **40**: 19′ (NM 9⁺); **22**: 13 (NM 19); **29**: 12 (NM 24); **48**: 12 (NM 24); **45**: 34 (KT 4); **3**: 14′ (KT 5); **4**: 12, 18 (KT 8?); **34**: 7 (KT 12); **16**: 5 (KT x)

**Lūṣi-ana-nūr-Marduk, daughter of** (DUMU.MUNUS ᵐÈ-*a-na*-ZÁLAG-ᵈAMAR.UTU)
- no details: **274**: 5 (KT 2)

**Lūṣi-ana-nūr-Sîn** (ᵐÈ-*a-na*-ZÁLAG-ᵈ30)
- no details: **44**: 6, 7 (ᵐKI.MIN) (KT 1)

**Malāḫu** (MÁ.LAḪ₅)

- father of Sîn-aḫa-iddina: **186**: 11 (KT x)

**Maluktu** ($^{f}$*Ma-lu-uk-tu*$_4$)
- no details: **100**: 7 (KT 12); **101**: 8 (KT 15)

**Mandidâya** ($^{m}$*Man-di-i-da-a-a*)
- knotter (*kāṣiru*): **101**: 13 (KT 15)

**Mannu-balu-Šamaš** ($^{m}$*Man-nu-ba-lu-*$^{d}$⌜UTU$^{?}$⌝)
- no details: **26**: 11 (NM 18)

**Mannu-kī-Ea** ($^{m}$*Man-nu-ki-*$^{d}$*É-a*)
- no details: **325**: 4, 8 (NM 14)

**Mannu-šāninša** ($^{f}$*Man-nu-ša-ni-ša*)
- no details: **296**: 4 (KT 12)

**Marduk-[. . .]** ($^{md}$AM[AR.UTU-. . .])
- no details: **140**: 31′ (NM 21–KT 3)

**Marduk-līssu** ($^{md}$AMAR.UTU-*lí-su*)
- no details: **255**: 2 (NM 4); **46**: 29 (KT x)

**Marduk-muballiṭ** ($^{md}$AMAR.UTU-*mu-bal-liṭ*)
- no details: **140**: 17′, 29′ (NM 21–KT 3); **30**: 4, 5–6 ($^{m}$KI.MIN) (KT 4); **45**: 10 (KT 4); **4**: 14, 20 (KT 8$^{?}$); **52**: 7, 8 ($^{m}$KI.MIN), 9, 15, 17–18, 19 ($^{m}$KI.MIN) (KT 11); **14**: 5, 6–8 ($^{m}$KI.MIN) (KT 14)

**Marduk-rēmanni** ($^{md}$AMAR.UTU-*re-man-ni*)
- no details: **236**: 4 (NM 8); **46**: 19 (KT x)

**Marduk-rē'û[a]/Marduk-rē'û[ni]** ($^{md}$AMAR.UTU-*re-ú-*[ . . .])
- no details: **42**: 12 (NM 19)

**Marduk-šūzibanni** ($^{md}$AMAR.U[TU-K]AR-*an-n*[*i*])
- father of Nanna-šar-dīni: **149**: 7 (KT 2)

**Marduk-zākir-šumi** ($^{md}$AMAR.UTU-MU-MU)
- farmer$^{?}$ (ÉNSI$^{?}$): **34**: 8 (KT 12)
- son of Ilī-ayabaš: **239**: 7 (NM 22); **139**: 11 (NM 22)
- GURUŠ, son of Innannibutu: **93**: 5 (KT 2)

**Martuk(k)u** ($^{m}$*Mar-tu-ku*)
- *ḫazannu*: **51**: 13 (KT 7)
- son of Ḫuzālu: **165**: 7 (KT 10)
- no details: **40**: 16′ (NM 9$^{+}$); **7**: 9, 20, 21 ($^{m}$KI.MIN) (KT 11); **32**: 8, 19, 20 ($^{m}$KI.MIN) (KT 11); **46**: 31 (KT x)

**Meli-Šuqamuna** ($^{m}$*Me-li-*$^{d}$*Šu-qa-mu-na*)
- father of Šummak-lā-⌜ . . . ⌝[ . . .]: **326**: 17 (NM 22)
- no details: **177**: 3 (KT 15)

**Me[li-Šuqamuna], daughter of** (DUMU.MUNUS ⌜$^{m}$*Me*⌝-[ . . .])
- no details: **104**: 2 (ŠŠ 2)

**Mīnâ-ēgu-[. . .]** ($^{f}$*Mi-na-a-e-*⌜*gu*$^{?}$⌝-[ . . .])
- no details: **95**: 11 (KT 6)

**Mīnâ-ēgu-ana-ili** ($^{m}$*Mi-na-e-gu-a-na-*DINGIR)
- no details: **46**: 18 (KT x)

**Mīnâ-ēpuš-ila**
[1] $^{m}$*Mi-na-*DÙ-*uš*-DINGIR
[2] $^{m}$*Mi-na-e-pu-uš*-DINGIR
- reed-weaver (AD.KID): **172**: 6 (KT 12) [1]; **173**: 9 (KT 12) [1]
- no details: **144**: 7 (KT 1) [1]; **218**: 4 (KT 11) [2]; **221**: 4 (KT 11) [1]; **186**: 10 (KT x) [1]

**Mīšarītu** (*Mi-ša-ri-tu*$_4$)
- MUNUS.TUR, daughter of Erība-Nergal: **291**: 6 (KT 5–7)

**Mu[. . .]** ($^{m}$*Mu-*[ . . .])
- no details: **176**: 20 (KT 13); **319**: 7 (n.d.)

**Mu[ . . .], son of** (DUMU $^{m}$⌜*Mu*$^{?}$⌝-[ . . .])
- no details: **36**: 10 (year 5)

**Mudammiq-[. . .]** ([$^{m}$*Mu*$^{?}$*-d*]*a*$^{?}$*-mi-iq-*⌜$^{d}$⌝[ . . .])
- no details: **321**: 7 (n.d.)

**Mudammiq-Adad**
[1] $^{m}$*Mu-dam-mi-iq-*$^{d}$IŠKUR
[2] $^{m}$MU-SIG$_5$-$^{d}$IŠKUR
[3] $^{m}$*Mu*-SIG$_5$-*iq*-$^{d}$IŠKUR
[4] $^{m}$*Mu-da-mi-iq-*$^{d}$IŠKUR
[5] $^{m}$SIG$_5$-$^{d}$IŠKUR
- scribe (DUB.SAR), witness: **327**: 25′ (KT 5) [1]; **330**: 14 (KT 14) [2]; **334**: 7′ (n.d.) [2]
- ⌜lú$^{?}$ . . . ⌝: **165**: 5 (KT 10) [2]
- no details: **135**: 10 (NM 21$^{+}$) [2]; **141**: 15 (NM 24–KT 3) [2]; **142**: 5 (NM 24–KT 3) [2]; **37**: 42 (KT 1) [4]; **274**: 2 (KT 2) [2]; **297**: 25 (KT 6) [2]; **155**: 1 (KT 8) [5]; **215**: 3 (KT 8) [2]; **158**: 4, 5–6 (KT 9) [1, 3]; **164**: 28 (KT 9) [2]; **73**: 3 (KT 10) [2]; **74**: 5 (KT 10) [2]; **166**: 1 (KT 10) [2]; **168**: 2 (NM 19–20, KT 11–12) [2]; **53**: 15, 16 ($^{m}$KI.MIN) (KT 12) [2]; **76**: 5 (KT 12) [2]; **170**: 4 (KT 12) [2]; **172**: 2, 5 (KT 12) [2]; **173**: 3, 8 (KT 12) [2]; **56**: 18 (KT 13) [2]; **126**: 6 (KT 13) [2]; **81**: 4 (KT 14) [2]; **83**: 2 (KT 14) [2]; **84**: 6 (KT 14) [2]; **122**: 12 (KT 14) [2]; **177**: 2 (KT 15) [2]; **179**: 5, 23′ (KT 15) [2]; **180**: 1 (KT 2–15$^{?}$) [2]; **88**: 2 (KT x) [5]; **90**: 4 (KT x) [2]; **182**: 1, 10 (KT x) [1, 2]; **185**: 6 (KT x) [2]; **290**: 3 (KT x) [2]

**Mudammiq-Adad, daughter of** (DUMU.MUNUS $^{m}$*Mu*-SIG$_5$-$^{d}$IŠKUR)
- no details: **174**: 10 (KT 13)

**Multēa** ([$^{m}$*Mul-te*]-⌜*e*⌝*-a*)
- no details: **49**: 12 (KT 1)

**Mun[. . .]** ($^{m}$*Mu-un-*[ . . .])

- no details: **136**: 17 (NM 23)

**Mūrānu** (mMu-ra-nu)
- *mār bīti* (DUMU É): **48**: 16 (NM 24); **150**: 7 (KT 3)
- son of Aḫirabuzzu: **307**: 11′ (NM? 21)
- son of . . . ri: **308**: ix 18′ (NM 18–22)
- no details: **29**: 7 (NM 24); **48**: 7 (NM 24); **45**: 33 (KT 4); **19**: 5 (KT 12)

**Muštāl-Nergal** (m*Muš-tál*-dU.[GU]R?)
- butcher (lúGÍR), father of Rabât-agallitu?, father-in-law of Ēmuq-Adad: **291**: 10 (KT 5–7)

**Muštālu** (m*Muš-ta-lu*4)
- shepherd (SIPA): **55**: 10 (KT 12)

**Muštešīm/Multešim-ilī**
[1] m*Muš-te-šim*-DINGIR
[2] m*Mu-u*[*l-te-šim*-DINGIR]
- no details: **44**: 10 (KT 1) [2]; **13**: 12 (KT 13) [1]

**Muštēšir-[DN]** (m*Muš-te-ši-*⌈*ir*⌉-[. . .])
- no details: **46**: 27 (KT x)

**Muštēšir-Adad** (m*Muš-te-ši-ir*-dIŠKUR)
- no details: **28**: 9 (NM 24)

**Muštēšir-Marduk** (m*Muš-te-ši-ir*-dAMAR.UTU)
- no details: **33**: 18 (KT 12?)

**Na[. . .], son of** (DUMU m⌈*N*⌉[*a*?- . . .])
- no details: **261**: 11 (n.d.)

**Nabû-nāṣir** (mdAG-ÙRU)
- no details: **46**: 16 (KT x)

**Nabûnātu, son of** (DUMU m*Na-bu-na-a-tu*4)
- no details: **7**: 21 (KT 11); **32**: 20 (KT 11)

**Nāḫiru** (m*Na-ḫi-rù*)
- no details: **26**: 7 (NM 18)

**Naḫzi-Marduk** (m⌈*Na*?*-aḫ*?⌉*-zi*-dAMAR.UTU)
- no details: **45**: 15 (KT 4)

**Naḫzutu** (m*Na-aḫ-zu-tu*4)
- no details: **33**: 19 (KT 12?)

**Nam[. . .]** (m*Nam*-[. . .])
- no details: **34**: 15 (KT 12)

**Namru**
[1] m*Nam-rù*
[2] m*Nam-ri*
- shepherd ((lú)SIPA): **263**: 12 (NM 23) [1]; **264**: 9 (KT 6) [1]; **161**: 1 (KT 9) [1]; **265**: 8′ (KT 7) [2]; **71**: 5 (KT 9) [2]
- probably the shepherd: **298**: 3 (NM 23) [1]
- no details: **45**: 29 (KT 4) [1]; **34**: 20′ (KT 12) [1]

**Namru, daughter of** (DUMU.MUNUS *Na-am-ri*)
- no details: **151**: 10 (KT 3)

**Nanna-LÚ-SA6** (md*Nanna*-LÚ-SA6)
- no details: **45**: 18 (KT 4); **302**: 3 (KT 10); **55**: 9, 10 (mKI.MIN), 17 (KT 12)

**Nanna-šar-dīni** (md*Nanna*-LUGAL-DI)
- brother of Enlil-MU.PÀ.DA: **139**: 32 (NM x)
- son of Marduk-šūzibanni: **149**: 7 (KT 2)

**Nannaya**
[1] m*Na-an-na-a-a*
[2] m*Na-na-a-a*
- brewer (lúLUNGA) of the Ekur: **65**: 2 (NM 18) [1]
- no details: **102**: 5′ (KT 15) [2]

**Napšira-Šamaš** (m*Nap-ši-ra*-dUTU)
- father of Rīšatu: **291**: 3 (KT 5–7)
- no details: **4**: 9, 24 (KT 8?)

**Nasiq-Marduk** (m*Na-siq*-dAMAR.UTU)
- weaver (UŠ.BAR): **270**: 6 (KT 9); **280** 6 (KT 9); **177**: 7 (KT 15)

**Nazalu** (m*Na-za-lu*4)
- no details: **207**: 2 (KT 2)

**Nazi-Maruttaš**
[1] *Na-zi-Ma-ru-ut-ta-aš*
[2] d*Na-zi-Ma-*⌈*ru-ut-ta*?*-aš*?⌉
[3] *Na-zi-Ma-ru-ta-aš*
[4] d*Na-zi-Ma-ru-*⌈*ta*⌉-[*aš*]
[5] *Na-zi-Ma-ru-taš*
[6] *Na-zi-Mu-ru-ut-ta-aš*
[7] *Na-zi-Mu-ru-ta-aš*
[8] *Na-zi-Múru-taš*
[9] d*Na-zi-Múru-taš*
[10] *Na-zi-Muru*4*-taš*
[11] *Na-zi-Mu-r*[*u-*
[12] [*Na-zi-Ma*]-⌈*ru*?*-taš*?⌉
[13] ⌈d⌉[*Na-zi-Ma-ru*]-*taš*
- king: [1] passim in date formulae; **191**: 8 (NM 5) [6]; **293**: 8 (NM 5) [6]; **236**: 9 (NM 8) [8]; **127**: 7 (NM 10+) [6]; **195**: 8 (NM 13) [3]; **325**: 21 (NM 14) [8]; **304**: 10 (NM 15) [7]; **110**: 1 (NM 18) [8]; **42**: 1 (NM 19) [2]; **132**: 1 (NM 19) [5]; **247**: 7 (NM 19) [8]; **254**: 11 (NM 19) [11]; **258**: 7 (NM 19) [3]; **294**: 9 (NM 19) [9]; **259**: 1 (NM 20) [4]; **124**: 1 (NM 21) [8]; **248**: 8 (NM 21) [8]; **308**: 22′ (NM 18–22) [5]; **136**: 1 (NM 23) [8]; **263**: 13 (NM 23) [8]; **303**: 17

(NM 23) [8]; **332**: 6 (NM 23) [8]; **28**: 1 (NM 24) [9]; **141**: 19 (NM 24–KT 3) [9]; **142**: 8 (NM 24–KT 3) [8]; **168**: 3 (NM 19–20, KT 11–12) [10]; **137**: 15 (NM x) [8]; **138**: 11 (NM x) [13]; **139**: 1 (NM x) [5]; **204**: 9 (NM x) [6]; **147**: 10 (KT 2) [12]

**Nergal-aḫa-iddina** ($^{md}$U.GUR-ŠEŠ-SUM-*na*)
- son of Gab-Enlil: **279**: 6 (KT 7)
- no details: **44**: 14 (KT 1)

**Nergal-bāni** ($^{md}$U.GUR-DÙ)
- no details: **261**: 30 (n.d.)

**Nergal-mušallim** ($^{md}$U.GUR-*mu-š*[*al*$^?$-*lim*$^?$])
- no details: **99**: 15 (KT 9)

**Nergal-nāṣir**
[1] $^{md⸢}$U.GUR⸣-ÙRU
[2] $^{md}$IGI.DU-ÙRU
- father of Izkur-Marduk: **42**: 8 (NM 19) [1]
- father of . . . : **4**: 11 (KT 8$^?$) [1]
- no details: **3**: 15′ (KT 5) [2]

**Nikki** (⸢$^{m}$*Ni-ik-ki*⸣)
- no details: **184**: 15 (KT x)

**Nin[. . .]**
[1] $^{md}$*N*[*in*-
[2] $^{md}$*Nin*-[
- no details: **192**: 5 (NM 9) [1]; **231**: 3 (KT 16) [2]

**Nin[. . .], son of** (⸢DUMU $^{md}$*Nin*$^?$⸣-[ . . .])
- no details: **1**: 21 (NM 22)

**Ninnū'a** ($^{m}$*Nin-nu-ú-a*)
- plowman$^?$ (ENGAR$^?$): **156**: 32 (KT 8)
- addressee of letter: **336**: 1, 3 (n.d.); **337**: 1, 4 (n.d.)

**Ninnuti** ($^{m}$*Ni-in-nu-ti*)
- House (É) of PN: **267**: 12 (NM 16)

**Ninnisi-[ . . .]** ($^{md}$*Nin-nisi*-[ . . .])
- son of Ubbuttu: **136**: 18 (NM 23)

**Ninnisiš-tikal** ($^{md}$*Nin-nisi -iš-ti-kal*)
- no details: **63**: 4 (NM 8); **292**: 9 (n.d.)

**Ninnisi-mudammiq**
[1] $^{md}$Nin-*nisi-mu*-SIG$_5$-*iq*
[2] $^{md}$*Nin-nisi-mu-dam-mi-qí*
- no details: **151**: 7 (KT 3) [2]; **5**: 9 (KT 8) [1]; **6**: 9 (KT 8) [1]; **164**: 11 (KT 9) [1]; **7**: 7 (KT 11) [1]; **32**: 6 (KT 11) [1]; **55**: 22 (KT 12) [1]; **56**: 11 (KT 13) [1]

**Ninurta-[. . .]**
[1] $^{md}$*Nin*$^?$-*urta*$^{?⸣}$-[
[2] $^{md}$*Nin*$^?$-*u*[*rta*$^?$-
[3] $^{md}$*Nin-urta*-⸢x⸣-[
[4] $^{md}$*Nin-urta*-[
[5] $^{md}$*Nin*-[*urta*$^?$]-⸢x⸣-[
[6] $^{md}$*N*[*in-ur*]*ta*-[
- seal (NA$_4$.KIŠIB) of PN: **80**: 12 (KT 13$^+$) [1]
- father of Amtu: **95**: 5 (KT 6) [2]
- no details: **137**: 13 (NM x) [3]; **140**: 12′ (NM 21–KT 3) [3]; **143**: 11 (KT 1) [1]; **154**: 5, 15, 16 ($^{m}$KI.MIN) (KT 6$^?$) [4, 1]; **60**: 7 (KT 12) [1]; **80**: 7 (KT 13$^+$) [5]; **178**: 5 (KT 15) [6]

**Ninurta-aḫa-[. . .]** ($^{md}$*Nin-urta*-ŠEŠ-[ . . .])
- no details: **36**: 8 (year 5)

**Ninurta-aḫa-iddina** ($^{md}$*Nin-urta*-ŠEŠ-SUM-*na*)
- no details: **115**: 6 (KT 6); **164**: 19 (KT 9); **46**: 39 (KT x)

**Ninurta-āpil-idīya** ([$^{m}$]$^{⸢d}$*Nin*⸣-*urta-a*-⸢*pil*-Á-*ia*⸣)
- no details: **102**: 11′ (KT 15)

**Ninurta-ašarēd**
[1] $^{md}$MAŠ-SAG
[2] $^{md}$*Nin-urta*-SAG
- son of Tarībat-ili: **64**: 6 (NM 18$^?$) [1]; **138**: 5 (NM x) [2]; **143**: 1 (KT 1) [2]; **147**: 5 (KT 2) [2]; **113**: 2 (KT 3) [2]; **170**: 11, 12–18 ($^{m}$KI.MIN) (KT 12) [2]
- seal (NA$_4$.KIŠIB) of PN (identical with the son of Tarībat-ili): **143**: 14 (KT 1) [2]
- seal (NA$_4$.KIŠIB) of PN: **88**: 8 (KT x) [2]
- no details: **120**: 37 (NM 19$^?$) [1]; **111**: 6 (NM 18) [1]; **133**: 8 (NM 20) [2]; **139**: 9, 18–20 ($^{m}$KI.MIN), 33 (NM x) [2]; **37**: 39 (KT 1) [2]; **143**: 12 (KT 1) [2]; **146**: 4 (KT 2) [2]; **113**: 13 (KT 3) [2]; **153**: 3 (KT 6) [2]; **51**: 20 (KT 7) [2]; **54**: 26 (KT 12) [2]; **174**: 5, 6–9 ($^{m}$KI.MIN) (KT 13) [2]; **182**: 2, 5–7, 8 ($^{m}$KI.MIN) (KT x) [2]; **88**: 4 (KT x) [2]

**Ninurta-bāni** ($^{md}$*Nin-urta*-DÙ)
- GURUŠ.TUR.TUR, son of [ . . .]: **95**: 34 (KT 6)

**Ninurta-bēl-apli** ($^{md}$*Nin-urta*-EN-IBILA)
- no details: **144**: 10 (KT 1)

**Ninurta-bēl-ilāni** (⸢$^{md}$⸣MAŠ-EN-DINGIR$^{meš}$)
- no details: **261**: 38 (n.d.)

**Ninurta-bēl-mātāti**$^?$ ($^{md}$*Nin-urta*-EN-⸢KUR$^?$.KUR$^{?⸣m}$[$^{eš?}$])
- sender of letter: **338**: 2 (n.d.)

**Ninurta-bēlī-uṣrī** (⸢$^{md}$*Nin-urta*⸣-EN-*uṣ-rí*)
- no details: **95**: 47′ (KT 6)

**Ninurta-dī[nanni**$^?$] ($^{md}$MAŠ-*di*-[ . . .])
- no details: **63**: 2 (NM 8)

**Ninurta-dīnanni**

[1] $^{md}$*Nin-urta-di-na-an-ni*
[2] $^{md}$MAŠ-*di-na-an-ni*
- knotter (*kāṣiru*): **239**: 8 (NM 22) [1]; **277**: 48′ (KT 6$^?$) [1]
- *arad ekalli* (ÌR.É.GAL): **120**: 28 (NM 19$^?$) [2]

**Ninurta-gamil** ($^{md}$*Nin-urta-ga-mil*)
- no details: **298**: 2, 13 (NM 23)

**Ninurta-gašir/gešir-ilāni**
[1] $^{md}$*Nin-urta-ga-ši-ir*-DINGIR$^{meš}$
[2] $^{md}$*Nin-urta-ge-šìr*-DINGIR$^{meš}$
- seal (NA$_4$.KIŠIB) of PN: **281**: 12 (KT 15) [1]; **231**: 12 (KT 16) [1]; **287**: 16 (KT 17) [1]; **233**: 12 (KT x) [2]
- no details: **102**: 18′ (KT 15) [1]

Ninurta-gešir-ilāni see Ninurta-gašir-ilāni

**Ninurta-ibni** ($^{md}$*Nin-urta-ib-ni*)
- House (É) of PN: **95**: 55′ (KT 6)

**Ninurta-iddina** ($^{md⌜}$*Nin-urta*⌝-SUM-*na*)
- no details: **94**: 8 (KT 2)

**Ninurta-kabit-aḫḫēšu** ([$^{m}$]$^{d}$*Nin-urta*-DUGUD-ŠEŠ$^{meš}$-*šu*)
- no details: **239**: 14 (NM 22)

**Ninurta-kīna-īde**
[1] $^{md}$*Nin-urta-ki-na-i-de*
[2] $^{md}$*Nin-urta-kí-na-i-de*
- son of Sîn-usuḫ-pišti: **327**: 4, 10, 17′ (KT 5) [1]
- no details: **162**: 8 (KT 9) [1]; **9**: 18, 26 (KT 11) [1]; **11**: 9 (KT 12) [1]; **54**: 9, 22 (KT 12) [1]; **12**: 9, 18 (KT 13) [1]; **35**: 8, 17 (KT 13) [2, 1]; **46**: 8 (KT x) [1]

**Ninurta-kīn-pīšu**
[1] $^{md}$*Nin-urta*-GI-KA-*šu*
[2] $^{md}$*Nin-urta-ki-pi-šu*
[3] $^{md}$*Nin-urta-kí-pi-šu*
[4] $^{md}$*Nin-urta-ki-in-pi-šu*
- son of Enlil-kidinnī: **265**: 5′ (KT 7) [1]
- seal (NA$_4$.KIŠIB) of PN: **208**: 7 (KT 2) [1]
- no details: **44**: 6 (KT 1) [2]; **208**: 2 (KT 2) [1]; **4**: 6, 7–8 ($^{m}$KI.MIN), 12, 15, 16–18 ($^{m}$KI.MIN) (KT 8$^?$) [1]; **240**: 3 (KT 8) [1]; **9**: 5, 8 (KT 11) [1]; **16**: 4, 5–6 ($^{m}$KI.MIN), 9 (KT x) [1]; **186**: 8 (KT x) [3]; **36**: 7, 8 ($^{m}$KI.MIN) (year 5) [4];

**Ninurta-kīn-pīšu, son of** (DUMU $^{md}$*Nin-urta-ki*-KA-*šu*)
- no details: **139**: 34 (NM x)

**Ninurta-kiššat-ilāni** ($^{md}$*Nin-urta*-KIŠ-DINGIR$^{meš}$)
- son of Enlil-kidinnī: **181**: 1, 9 (KT 15–17)
- addressee of letter: **335**: 1 (n.d.)
- no details: **94**: 21′ (KT 2); **253**: 2 (ŠŠ 1)

**Ninurta-muballiṭ** ($^{md}$*Nin-urta-mu-ba*[*l-liṭ*])
- no details: **34**: 17′ (KT 12)

**Ninurta-mutēr-gimilli** ($^{md}$*Nin-urta-mu-ter*-ŠU)
- no details: **9**: 13 (KT 11)

**Ninurta-nāṣir**
[1] $^{md}$*Nin-urta*-ÙRU
[2] $^{md}$MAŠ-ÙRU
- son of Battiyūtu, witness: **326**: 20 (NM 22) [1]
- seal (NA$_4$.KIŠIB) of PN: **294**: 10 (NM 19) [1]
- no details: **42**: 4 (NM 19) [1]; **294**: 5 (NM 19) [2]; **179**: 15, 16 ($^{m}$KI.MIN) (KT 15) [1]

**Ninurta-qarrād**
[1] $^{md}$*Nin-urta-qar-rad*
[2] $^{md}$MAŠ-*qar-rad*
- no details: **26**: 12 (NM 18) [2]; **1**: 16 (NM 22) [1]; **29**: 11 (NM 24) [1]; **48**: 11, 18 (NM 24) [1]; **3**: 22′ (KT 5) [1]

**Ninurta-rā'im-kitti** ($^{md}$*Nin-urta*-ÁG-*kit*-[*ti*])
- no details: **36**: 12 (year 5)

**Ninurta-rēmanni** ($^{md}$*Nin-urta-re-man-ni*)
- no details: **49**: 10 (KT 1); **33**: 15 (KT 12$^?$)

**Ninurta-rēṣū'a**$^?$ ($^{md}$*Nin-urta-*⌜*re*$^?$*-ṣú*$^?$*-ú*⌝*-a*)
- no details: **337**: 5 (n.d.)

**Ninurta-rēṣūšu**
[1] $^{md}$*Nin-urta-re-ṣú-šu*
[2] $^{md}$MAŠ-*re-ṣu-ú-šu*
- no details: **45**: 23 (KT 4) [2]; **52**: 6, 14, 20, 29 (KT 11) [1]

**Ninurta-rīm-ilāni** ($^{md⌝}$*Nin-urta*-AM-DINGIR$^{meš}$)
- no details: **139**: 23 (NM x)

**Ninurta-zākir-šumi**
[1] $^{md}$*Nin-urta*-MU-MU
[2] $^{md}$MAŠ-MU-MU
- seal (NA$_4$.KIŠIB) of PN: **195**: 10 (NM 13) [2]; **254**: 6, 14 (NM 19) [2]; **205**: 9–10 (KT 1) [1]; **206**: 9 (KT 2) [1]; **207**: 10–11 (KT 2) [1]; **209**: 9 (KT 2$^+$) [1]; **274**: 9 (KT 2) [1]; **210**: 11 (KT 3) [1]; **59**: 3, 4–7 ($^{m}$KI.MIN) (KT 4) [1]; **212**: 8 (KT 5) [1]; **251**: 15 (KT 5) [1]; **277**: 51′ (KT 5) [1]; **264** 8, 16 (KT 6) [1]; **276**: 9 (KT 6) [1]; **213**: 10 (KT 7) [1]; **214**: 11 (KT 7) [1]; **278**: 12 (KT 7) [1]; **279**: 11 (KT 7) [1]; **215**: 10 (KT 8) [2]; **218**: 9 (KT 11) [2]; **219**: 11 (KT 11) [1]; **221**: 10 (KT 11) [1]; **222**: 8

(KT 12) [2]; **223**: 10 (KT 12) [1]; **225**: 11 (KT 13) [1]; **226**: 10 (KT 14) [1]; **227**: 9 (KT 14) [1]; **228**: 11 (KT 14) [1]; **229**: 10 (KT 14) [1]; **230**: 11 (KT 15) [1]; **232**: 9 (KT x) [2]

- no details: **40**: 11 (NM 9$^{+}$) [2]; **127**: 1 (NM 10$^{+}$) [2]; **128**: 4 (NM 17$^{?}$) [2]; **257**: 12 (NM 17) [2]; **58**: 6, 8 (NM 18$^{?}$) [2]; **110**: 9 (NM 18) [1]; **111**: 7 (NM 18) [2]; **41**: 11 (NM 18) [2]; **22**: 3, 4 ($^{m}$KI.MIN) (NM 19) [2]; **112**: 14 (NM 19) [1]; **135**: 2 (NM 21$^{+}$) [1]; **1**: 15, 19 (NM 22) [1]; **239**: 24 (NM 22) [1]; **326**: 4 (NM 22) [1]; **308**: iv 7′ (NM 18–22) [1]; **263** 11 (NM 23) [1]; **17**: 4, 5 ($^{m}$KI.MIN) (NM 23) [1]; **141**: 18 (NM 24–KT 3) [1]; **142**: 7 (NM 24–KT 3) [1]; **249**: 5′ (NM 24) [2]; **333**: 1, 8 (NM x) [2]; **2**: 19, 20–22 ($^{m}$KI.MIN), 42, 43 ($^{m}$KI.MIN), 47 (KT 1) [1]; **144**: 2 (KT 1) [1]; **145**: 6, 10 (KT 2) [1]; **149**: 1 (KT 2) [1]; **207**: 4–5 (KT 2) [1]; **208**: 3 (KT 2) [1]; **18**: 4, 5 ($^{m}$KI.MIN) (KT 3) [1]; **38**: 1 (KT 3) [1]; **108**: 5, 6–12 ($^{m}$KI.MIN) (KT 3) [1]; **150**: 16, 17–18 ($^{m}$KI.MIN) (KT 3) [1]; **45**: 12 (KT 4) [1]; **59**: 1, 3, 4–7 ($^{m}$KI.MIN), 10 (KT 4) [1]; **3**: 13′ (KT 5) [1]; **327**: 3 (KT 5) [1]; **115**: 4, 5–7 ($^{m}$KI.MIN) (KT 6) [1]; **297**: 2, 19 (KT 6) [1]; **68**: 2 (KT 7) [1]; **4**: 19, 20–21 ($^{m}$KI.MIN), 36 (KT 8$^{?}$) [1]; **5**: 7, 8–12 ($^{m}$KI.MIM), 18 (KT 8) [1]; **6**: 6, 7–12 ($^{m}$KI.MIN) (KT 8) [1]; **156**: 4, 5–11 ($^{m}$KI.MIN) (KT 8) [1]; **162**: 5, 6 ($^{m}$KI.MIN), 13 (KT 9) [1]; **164**: 8, 9–12 ($^{m}$KI.MIN), 22, 23 ($^{m}$KI.MIN) (KT 9) [1]; **39**: 1 (KT 10) [1]; **74**: 3 (KT 10) [1]; **217**: 7 (KT 10) [1]; **7**: 6, 7–12 ($^{m}$KI.MIN), 25 (KT 11) [1]; **9**: 9, 10 ($^{m}$KI.MIN) (KT 11) [1]; **32**: 5, 6–11 ($^{m}$KI.MIN), 23 (KT 11) [1]; **52**: 6, 7 ($^{m}$KI.MIN), 14, 15 ($^{m}$KI.MIN), 19, 20, 27 (KT 11) [1]; **168**: 6 (NM 19–20, KT 11–12) [1]; **10**: 17, 18–19 ($^{m}$KI.MIN) (KT 12) [1]; **53**: 6, 7–9 ($^{m}$KI.MIN), 11 (KT 12) [1]; **55**: 8, 12, 13 ($^{m}$KI.MIN), 18, 19 ($^{m}$KI.MIN), 29 (KT 12) [1]; **56**: 7, 8–12 ($^{m}$KI.MIN), 15 (KT 13) [1]; **315**: 7 (KT 13) [1]; **84**: 3 (KT 14) [1]; **178**: 14 (KT 15) [1]; **57**: 6, 7 ($^{m}$KI.MIN) (KT x) [1]; **184**: 13, 14 ($^{m}$KI.MIN) (KT x) [1]

**Nippurītu**

[1] $^{f}$*Ni-ip-pu-ri-tu*$_{4}$

[2] *Ni-ip-pu-ri-tu*$_{4}$

[3] $^{f}$*Ni-ip-pu-ri-ti*

- MUNUS.TUR.GABA: **291**: 13 (KT 5–7) [2]
- no details: **100**: 5 (KT 12) [1]; **101**: 5 (KT 15) [1]; **253**: 9 (ŠŠ 1) [3]

**Nippurû** ($^{m}$*Ni-ip-pu-ru-ú*)

- son of Arad-nubatti: **138**: 7 (NM x)

**Nukarribu, daughter of** (DUMU.MUNUS $^{lú}$NU.$^{giš}$KIRI$_{6}$)

- no details: **115**: 4 (KT 6)

**Nūra-līmur** ($^{m}$ZÁLAG-*li-m*[*ur*$^{?}$])

- no details: **124**: 3 (NM 21)

**Nūr-[DN]** ($^{m}$ZÁLAG-$^{d}$[ . . .])

- no details: **108**: 10 (KT 3); **39**: 7 (KT 10); **10**: 18 (KT 12); **169**: 19 (KT 12); **261**: 16 (n.d.)

**Nūr-Adad** ($^{m}$ZÁLAG-$^{d}$IŠKUR)

- *ḫazannu*: **162**: 10, 12 (KT 9)

**Nūr-Amurru** ($^{m}$ZÁLAG-$^{d}$KUR)

- no details: **316**: 12 (year 17)

**Nūr-Bēlet-Akkade** ($^{m}$ZÁLAG-GAŠAN-*Ak-ka-de*)

- father of Bunna-Gula: **103**: 10 (KT x)
- no details: **22**: 7 (NM 19); **49**: 8 (KT 1); **266**: 8′ (n.d.)

**Nūr-Bēl-Kubi** ($^{m}$ZÁLAG-EN-$^{d}$*Ku-bi*)

- no details: **261**: 17 (n.d.)

**Nūr-Bēlti** ([$^{m}$]ZÁLAG-$^{d}$GAŠAN)

- no details: **45**: 43 (KT 4)

**Nūr-Ištar**

[1] $^{m}$ZÁLAG-$^{d}$*Ištar*

[2] $^{m}$ZÁLAG-$^{d}$*Iš-tar*

- no details: **1**: 16 (NM 22) [1]; **2**: 25, 29 (KT 1) [2]; **50**: 3 (KT 1) [1]; **38**: 8 (KT 3) [1]; **115**: 4 (KT 6) [1]; **5**: 10 (KT 8) [2]; **6**: 10 (KT 8) [2]; **156**: 9, 22, 30 (KT 8) [2]; **159**: 29 (KT 9) [2]; **7**: 6 (KT 11) [2]; **32**: 5 (KT 11) [2]; **53**: 8 (KT 12) [2]; **76**: 4 (KT 12) [2]; **179**: 6, 7 ($^{m}$KI.MIN) (KT 15) [2]

**Nūr-Ištar-Akkade** ($^{m}$ZÁLAG-$^{d}$INANNA-*A-ga-dè*)

- no details: **2**: 26 (KT 1)

**Nūr-Marduk** ($^{m}$ZÁLAG-$^{d}$AMAR.UTU)

- water drawer (*dālû*): **131**: 16 (NM 18)
- son of Ilī-īdânni **157**: 5 (KT 8); **123**: 3′ (KT 9)
- son of Za[ . . .]: **46**: 26 (KT x)
- $^{lú}$[x x]: **154**: 7 (KT 6$^{?}$)
- no details: **17**: 10 (NM 23); **2**: 14, 36 (KT 1); **49**: 9 (KT 1); **30**: 7 (KT 4); **9**: 9 (KT 11); **35**: 9, 10 ($^{m}$KI.MIN) (KT 13); **12**: 10, 11 ($^{m}$KI.MIN) (KT 13); **102**: 7′ (KT 15); **140**: 27′ (NM 21–KT 3)

**Nūr-Nergal** (mZÁLAG-dU.GUR)
- no details: **37**: 27 (KT 1); **147**: 9 (KT 2)

**Nūr-Šamaš** (mZÁLAG-dUTU)
- *arad ekalli* (ÌR.É.GAL): **120**: 30 (NM 19?)
- no details: **191**: 5 (NM 5); **293**: 4 (NM 5); **197**: 3 (NM 13); **204**: 5 (NM x)

**Nurzannu** (m*Nu-ur-za-nu*)
- no details: **99**: 5 (KT 9)

**Nu[ska?- . . .]** (md*Nu[ska?- . . .]*)
- no details: **10**: 19 (KT 12)

**Nuska- . . .**
[1] md*Nuska*-⸢x-*šu*?⸣
[2] ⸢md*Nuska*-x-x-x⸣
- father of Bunnanu: **150**: 4 (KT 3) [1]
- no details: **10**: 24 (KT 12) [2]

**Nuska-aḫa-iddina**
[1] md*Nuska*-ŠEŠ-SUM
[2] md*Nuska*-ŠEŠ-SUM-*na*
- *arrapḫāyu*: **267**: 13 (NM 16) [1]
- no details: **316**: 7 (year 17) [2]

**Nuska-bēla-uṣur** (m⸢d*Nuska*⸣-EN-ÙRU)
- no details: **292**: 5 (n.d.)

**Nuska-ibni** (md*Nuska-ib-ni*)
- no details: **141**: 17 (NM 24–KT 3); **142**: 7 (NM 24–KT 3); **2**: 20, 29 (KT 1); **37**: 6 (KT 1); **147**: 9 (KT 2); **261**: 34 (n.d.)

**Nuska-mudammiq** (md*Nuska*-MU-SIG5)
- no details: **42**: 3 (NM 19)

**Nuska-nābûšu** (md*Nuska-na-bu-šu*)
- scribe (DUB.SAR), son of Ayaru, witness: **333**: 16 (NM x)
- father of Ibni-Marduk: **164**: 25 (KT 9); **186**: 12 (KT x)
- no details: **63**: 5 (NM 8); **112**: 7 (NM 19); **239**: 18, 22 (NM 22); **141**: 10 (NM 24–KT 3); **142**: 4 (NM 24–KT 3); **155**: 2 (KT 8); **162**: 5 (KT 9); **163**: 8 (KT 9); **166**: 2 (KT 10); **7**: 18 (KT 11); **32**: 17 (KT 11); **53**: 7 (KT 12); **56**: 14, 15 (mKI.MIN) (KT 13)

**Nuska-nāṣir** (md*Nuska*-ÙRU)
- *ḫazannu*: **97**: 20 (KT 9); **98**: 18 (KT 9)

**Payanu?** (m*Pa-a-a-ni-i*)
- no details: **16**: 4 (KT x)

**Paḫallanu** (m*Pa-ḫal-la-nu*)
- plowman (lúENGAR): **179**: 21′, 22′ (mKI.MIN) (KT 15)

**Paḫallanu, sister of** (NIN m*Pa-ḫal-la-ni*)
- no details: **101**: 19 (KT 15)

**Paḫāru**
[1] m*Pa-ḫa-rù*
[2] m*Pa-ḫa-ri*
- father of Bēltu-irīša: **96**: 7 (KT 9) [2]
- no details: **296**: 3 (KT 12) [1]

**Pān-Marduk-lūmur** (mIGI-dAMAR.UTU-*lu-mur*)
- son of Zāninu: **46**: 33 (KT x)

**(Pap)sukkal-aḫa-iddina**
[1] md*Pap-sukkal*-ŠEŠ-SUM-*na*
[2] md*Sukkal*-ŠEŠ-SUM-*na*
- plowman (lúENGAR) of Rīmūtu *rab zarāti*: **176**: 7 (KT 13) [1]
- no details: **124**: 10 (NM 21) [2]

**Papsukkal-zākir-šumi** (md*Pap-sukkal*-MU-MU)
- no details: **33**: 10 (KT 12?)

**Paqqāyu** (m*Pa-qa-a-a-i*)
- no details: **139**: 28 (NM x)

**Pussulu**
[1] m*Pu-us-su-lu*4
[2] m*Pu-us-su-li*
- shepherd (lúSIPA), father of Kalbatu: **291**: 4 (KT 5–7) [2]
- probably the shepherd: **202**: 3 (NM 18) [1]

**Qadištu**
[1] m*Qa-diš-ti*
[2] mf*Qa-diš-ti*
[3] f*Qa-diš*-⸢*ta*?⸣
- father of Šarratu: **96**: 9 (KT 9) [1]
- father/mother of Iqīša-Marduk: **148**: 8 (KT 2) [2]
- father/mother of Erība-Nergal: **168**: 1 (NM 19–20, KT 11–12) [2]
- no details: **242**: 9 (KT 14) [3]

**Qadištu, son of** (DUMU m*Qa-diš*-⸢*ti*⸣)
- no details: **236**: 7 (NM 8)

**Qiltu** (DUMU m*Qí-il-ti*)
- no details: **71**: 7 (KT 9)

**Qīšat-Adad** (mNÍG.BA-dIŠKUR)
- shepherd (SIPA): **291**: 22 (KT 5–7)

**Qīšat-Gula** (mNÍG.BA-d*Gu-la*)
- witness: **334**: 5′ (n.d.)
- no details: **2**: 35 (KT 1); **45**: 24 (KT 4)

**Qīšat-Marduk** (mNÍG.BA-dAMAR.UTU)
- son of Bananû: **150**: 18 (KT 3)
- no details: **12**: 14 (KT 13); **35**: 13 (KT 13)

**Qīšat-Nergal** (ᵐNÍG.BA-ᵈU.GUR)
- carpenter (⁽ˡᵘ́⁾NAGAR): **45**: 26 (KT 4); **4**: 25, 26 (ᵐKI.MIN) (KT 8ˀ)
- no details: **2**: 37 (KT 1); **268**: 3 (KT 1); **94**: 5 (KT 2); **10**: 29 (KT 12)

**Qīšat-(Pap)sukkal**
[1] ᵐNÍG.BA-ᵈ*Pap-sukkal*
[2] ᵐNÍG.BA-ᵈ⌜*Sukkal*⌝
- no details: **45**: 20 (KT 4) [1]; **4**: 27 (KT 8ˀ) [1]; **55**: 23 (KT 12) [1]; **15**: 7 (KT 14) [1]; **177**: 13 (KT 14) [2]

**Qunnunu**
[1] ᵐ*Qu-nu-nu*
[2] ᵐ*Qu-nu-ni*
[3] ᵐ*Qu-un-nu-ni*
- *sakrumaš*: **245**: 2 (KuE 9) [1]
- shepherd (ˡᵘ́SIPA): **245**: 6 (KuE 9) [2]
- GURUŠ, son of Marduk-zākir-šumi: **93**: 7 (KT 2) [1]
- no details: **11**: 12 (KT 12) [1]; **54**: 12 (KT 12) [1]; **85**: 3 (KT 14) [3]; **86**: 3 (KT 15) [1]; **46**: 6 (KT x) [1]; **244**: 3, 12, 19, 20 (ᵐKI.MIN) (KuE 8) [1]

**Qurunnu** (⌜ᵐˀ⌝*Qù-ru-un-ni*)
- no details: **19**: 3 (KT 12)

**Rabâ-ša-Bēlti**
[1] ᵐGAL-*šá*-GAŠAN
[2] ᵐGAL-*a-šá*-GAŠAN
[3] ᵐGAL-*šá*-GAŠAN-*ti*
- son of . . .ˀ: **298**: 8 (NM 23) [1]
- no details: **49**: 12 (KT 1) [1]; **146**: 6 (KT 2) [2]; **108**: 7 (KT 3) [1]; **115**: 6 (KT 6) [1]; **5**: 12 (KT 8) [1]; **6**: 11 (KT 8) [1]; **156**: 5, 21, 32 (KT 8) [1]; **55**: 12, 18, 20, 29 (KT 12) [1]; **33**: 16 (KT 12ˀ) [1]; **316**: 9 (year 17) [3]; **319**: 2 (n.d.) [1]

**Rabâ-ša-Gula**
[1] ᵐGAL-*šá*-ᵈ*Gu-la*
[2] ᵐGAL-*a-šá*-ᵈ*Gu-la*
- farmer (ÉNSI): **176**: 4 (KT 13) [1]
- no details: **26**: 9 (NM 18) [1]; **42**: 7 (NM 19) [2]; **99**: 2 (KT 9) [1]

**Rabâ-ša-Marduk**
[1] ᵐGAL-*a-ša*-ᵈAMAR.UTU
[2] ᵐGAL-*šá*-ᵈAMAR.[UTU]
- physician (A.ZU): **150**: 15 (KT 3) [1]
- no details: **247**: 3 (NM 19) [1]; **124**: 5 (NM 21) [2]; **139**: 33 (NM x) [2]

**Rabâ-ša-Nergal** (ᵐGAL-*šá*-ᵈU.GUR)
- plowman (ˡᵘ́ENGAR): **148**: 10 (KT 2)

**Rabâ-ša-Ninurta**
[1] ᵐGAL-*šá*-ᵈ*Nin-urta*
[2] ᵐ⌜GAL⌝-*šá*-ᵈMAŠ
- plowmanˀ (ˡ[ᵘ́EN]GARˀ): **94**: 19′ (KT 2) [1]
- no details: **261**: 20, 36 (n.d.) [2]

**Rabâ-ša-Sîn** (ᵐGAL-*a-šá*-ᵈ30)
- *ṣuḫurtu*: **43**: 5, 9 (KT 1)
- father of Baḫû: **307**: 10′ (NMˀ 21)

**Rabâ-ša-Šamaš** (ᵐ⌜GAL⌝-*šá*-ᵈ⌜UTUˀ⌝)
- no details: **261**: 29 (n.d.)

**Rabâ-ša-Šēmû** (ᶠGAL-*šá*-ᵈ*Še-em-me*-⌜*i-u*⌝)
- daughter of Daqqatu: **95**: 33 (KT 6)

**Rabât-agallituˀ** (GAL-*bat-a-gal*ˀ-⌜*li*ˀ⌝-*tu₄*)
- MUNUS.TUR, daughter of Muštāl-Nergal, wife of Emūq-Adad: **291**: 10 (KT 5–7)

**Rabât-Gula**
[1] ᶠGAL-*at*-⌜ᵈ*Gu-la*⌝
[2] GAL-*bat*-ᵈ*Gu-la*
- wife of Bēlānu: **279**: 4 (KT 7) [1]
- MUNUS.TUR, daughter of Innannibūtu: **291**: 2 (KT 5–7) [2]

**Rabâtūtu** (ᶠ*Ra-ba*-⌜*tu*⌝-*tu*)
- no details: **115**: 5 (KT 6)

**Rā'im-kitti** (ᵐÁG-[*kit*]-*ti*)
- father of Arad-Bēlti: **326**: 22 (NM 22)

**Rā'im-kitti, daughter of** (DUMU.MUNUS ᵐÁG-⌜*kit*ˀ⌝-*ti*)
- no details: **242**: 3 (KT 14)

**Rašilu** (ᵐ*Ra-ši-lu₄*)
- brother of Illallu: **151**: 5 (KT 3)

**Rigim-Adad** (ᵐ*Ri-gim*-ᵈIŠKUR)
- no details: **179**: 25′, 26′ (ᵐKI.MIN) (KT 15)

**Rigim-Adad, son of** (DUMU ᵐ*Ri-gim*-ᵈIŠKUR)
- plowman (ˡᵘ́ENGAR): **244**: 14 (KuE 8)

**Riḫêtûša** (ᵐ*Ri-ḫe-tu-ša*)
- MUNUS.TUR: **291**: 14 (KT 5–7)
- no details: **99**: 6 (KT 9)

**Rimātu** (ᶠ⌜*Ri*⌝-*ma-a-tu₄*)
- no details: **267**: 5 (NM 16)

**Rîmtu** (ᶠ*Ri-im-tu₄*)
- daughter of Abbū-ṭabū: **95**: 7 (KT 6)

**ᵐRīmūtu**
[1] ᵐ*Ri-mu-tu₄*
[2] ᵐ*Ri-mu-ti*
[3] ᵐ*Ri*-<*mu*>-*ti*
[4] ᵐ*Ri*-⌜*mu*ˀ-*ti*ˀ⌝

[5] $^{m}$*Ri-mu-*[
- *ṣuḫurtu*: **4**: 31 (KT 8$^{?}$) [1]
- *rab zarāti*: **176**: 7 (KT 13) [1]; **184**: 8 (KT x) [1]
- brewer ($^{lú}$LUNGA): **112**: 2 (NM 19) [1]; **146**: 5 (KT 2) [1]; **114**: 2 (KT 4) [1]
- plowman ($^{lú}$ENGAR): **156**: 27 (KT 8) [1]; **159**: 15 (KT 9) [1]
- seal (NA$_4$.KIŠIB) of PN: **193**: 12 (NM 12) [2]; **202**: 7 (NM 18) [2]; **238**: 10 (NM 19) [2]; **247**: 9 (NM 19) [1]; **203**: 9 (NM 21$^{+}$) [1]
- son of Aḫu-bani: **150**: 5, 9 (KT 3) [1]; **45**: 22 (KT 4) [1]; **51**: 8 (KT 7) [1]
- son of [ . . .]:**154**: 6 (KT 6$^{?}$) [1]
- no details: **294**: 6 (NM 19) [1]; **2**: 27 (KT 1) [1]; **49**: 5 (KT 1) [1]; **30**: 4 (KT 4) [4]; **45**: 6, 17, 29, 32 (KT 4) [1]; **51**: 9 (KT 7) [1]; **240**: 4 (KT 8) [5]; **70**: 5 (KT 9) [2]; **97**: 11 (KT 9) [1]; **98**: 11 (KT 9) [2]; **122**: 5 (KT 14) [2]; **123**: 6′ (KT 9) [1]; **19**: 7 (KT 12) [1]; **33**: 16 (KT 12$^{?}$) [1]; **34**: 11, 12 ($^{m}$KI.MIN) (KT 12) [1]; **46**: 36 (KT x) [1]; **57**: 12, 13–14 ($^{m}$KI.MIN), 21, 22–23 ($^{m}$KI.MIN) (KT x) [1, 3]

**$^{f}$Rīmūtu** ($^{f}$*Ri$^{?}$-mu-tí*)
- no details: **283**: 3 (KT 15$^{?}$)

**Rī[š- . . .]** ($^{m}$*Ri-i*[*š*- . . .])
- no details: **108**: 11 (KT 3)

**Rīš-Adad**
[1] $^{m}$*Ri-iš*-$^{d}$IŠKUR
[2] $^{m}$SUD-$^{d}$IŠKUR
- *arad ekalli* (ÌR.É.GAL): **120**: 31 (NM 16) [1]
- no details: **120**: 9 (NM 19$^{?}$) [1]; **45**: 4, 37 (KT 4) [2]; **12**: 12 (KT 13) [1]; **35**: 11 (KT 13) [1]

**Rīš-Akītu** ($^{m}$*Ri-iš-Á-ki-tu$_4$*)
- GURUŠ.TUR.TUR, son of Šimê-suppâya: **95**: 54′ (KT 6)
- no details: **49**: 7 (KT 1)

**Rīš-Akkade** ($^{m}$*Ri-iš-Ak-ka-de*)
- son of Šamaš-nāṣir: **176**: 14 (KT 13)

**Rīš-aṣûšu**
[1] $^{m}$*Ri-iš*-UD-*šú*
[2] $^{m}$*Ri-iš*-È-*šu*
[3] $^{m}$*Re-eš*-U[D-*šú*]
[4] $^{m}$*Re-eš*-È-*šu*
[5] $^{m}$SUD-UD-*šu*
- scribe (DUB.SAR), witness: **325**: 19 (NM 14) [1]
- son of Tarībat-ili: **49**: 18 (KT 1) [1]; **103**: 5, 12 (KT x) [1]; **182**: 2, 12 (KT x) [1, 5]
- ⌜$^{lú?}$ x a x⌝: **99**: 17 (KT 9) [4]
- no details: **249**: 6′ (NM 24) [3]; **10**: 8, 12 (KT 12) [1]; **331**: 12 (KT x) [2]

**Rīšatu**
[1] *Ri-ša-tu$_4$*
[2] $^{f}$⌜*Ri-ša-tu$_4$*⌝
- MUNUS.TUR, daughter of Napšira-Šamaš: **291**: 3 (KT 5–7) [1]
- no details: **100**: 3 (KT 12) [2]; **101**: 4 (KT 15) [2]

**Rīšatu, son of** (DUMU $^{m}$*Ri$^{?}$-ša-tu$^{?}$*)
- no details: **244**: 12 (KuE 8)

**Rīš-Ekur** ($^{m}$*Ri-iš*-É.KUR)
- plowman ($^{lú}$ENGAR): **94**: 20′ (KT 2)
- no details: **52**: 10, 21 (KT 11)

**Rīš-ikkillašu**
[1] $^{m}$*Ri-iš-ik-kil-la-šu*
[2] $^{m}$SUD-*ik-ki*-⌜*la*⌝-[*šu*]
- no details: **45**: 15 (KT 4) [2]; **3**: 23′ (KT 5) [1]

**Rīš-ilāni** ($^{m}$*Ri-iš*-DINGIR$^{meš}$)
- no details: **57**: 14, 23 (KT x)

**Rīš-Marduk**
[1] $^{m}$*Ri-iš*-$^{d}$AMAR.UTU
[2] $^{m}$*Re-eš*-$^{d}$AMAR.UTU
[3] $^{m}$⌜SUD⌝-$^{d}$AMAR.UTU
- knotter (*kāṣiru*): **101**: 16 (KT 15) [1]; **284**: 4 (KT 16) [3]
- no details: **94**: 9 (KT 2) [1]; **292**: 7 (n.d.) [2]

**Rīš-napāḫšu, daughter of** (DUMU.MUNUS $^{m}$*Ri-iš-na-pa-aḫ-šu*)
- no details: **136**: 12 (NM 23)

**Rīš-Nergal**
[1] $^{m}$*Ri-iš*-$^{d}$U.GUR
[2] $^{m}$*Re-eš*-$^{d}$U.[GUR]
- farmer (ÉNSI): **10**: 8, 12 (KT 12) [1]
- GURUŠ, son of Enlil-tukultī, father of Iqīša-Nergal and brother of Bēl-qali: **93**: 22′ (KT 2) [1]
- no details: **27**: 8 (NM 20) [2]; **29**: 12 (NM 24) [2]; **48**: 12 (NM 24) [1]; **265**: 3′ (KT 7) [1]

**Rīš-Ulūlu** ($^{m}$*Ri-iš*-$^{iti}$KIN.$^{d}$INANNA)
- father of Šumu-libši: **333**: 15 (NM x)

**Rišûtu** ([$^{m}$]*Ri-šu-tu*)
- no details: **16**: 7 (KT x)

**Rišûtu, son of** (DUMU $^{m}$*Ri-šu-ti*)
- no details: **28**: 4 (NM 24); **13**: 5, 7, 10 (KT 13)

**Sāmidu** ($^{m}$*Sa-mi-du*)
- no details: **99**: 9 (KT 9)

**Sāmu** ($^{m}$*Sa-a-mi*)
- father of Kidin-Enlil: **134**: 5′ (NM 21)

**Saniq-pī-Ištar, son of** (DUMU $^{m}$*Sa-niq*-KA-$^{d}$*Ištar*)
- no details: **51**: 12 (KT 7)

**Sarriqu**
[1] $^{m}$*Sar-ri-qu*
[2] $^{m}$*Sar-ri-qí*
[3] $^{m}$*Sa-ar-*<*ri*>*-qí*
- House (É) of PN: **296**: 2 (KT 12) [3]
- father of Ēṭiru and of Amīlu-banû: **55**: 21 (KT 12) [1]
- father of Kudurrānu: **184**: 10 (KT x) [2]
- no details: **3**: 11′, 12′ ($^{m}$KI.MIN) (KT 5) [1]; **140**: 3′, 22′, 28′, 32′, 33′ (NM 21–KT 3) [1, 2]

**Sibutu** ($^{m}$*Si-bu-tu$_4$*)
- no details: **13**: 8 (KT 13)

**Sikiltu** ($^{m}$*Si-kil-t*[*i*$^{?}$])
- no details: **140**: 25′ (NM 21–KT 3)

**Sîn- . . .** (⸢$^{md}$30-x-x⸣)
- no details: **244**: 21 (KuE 8)

**Sîn-abūša** ($^{d}$30-*a-bu-ša*)
- MUNUS.TUR, daughter of Bittā: **291**: 12 (KT 5–7)

**Sîn-aḫ[a- . . .] or Sîn-nāṣ[ir]** ($^{md}$30-ŠE[Š$^{?}$- . . .])
- no details: **50**: 18 (KT 1)

**Sîn-aḫa-iddina** ($^{md}$30-ŠEŠ-SUM-*na*)
- innkeeper ($^{lú}$KÚRUN.NA): **165**: 4 (KT 10); **84**: 8 (KT 14)
- son of Malāḫu: **186**: 11 (KT x)
- son of Dābibī: **254**: 7, 12 (NM 19)
- no details: **298**: 11 (NM 23); **45**: 33 (KT 4); **126**: 8 (KT 13); **81**: 6 (KT 14); **180**: 4, 9 (KT 2–15$^{?}$); **331**: 9 (KT x)

**Sîn-aḫa-ublam, son of** (DUMU $^{md}$30-ŠEŠ-*ub-lam*)
- no details: **187**: 16 (KaE 3)

**Sîn-balāṭa-īriš**
[1] $^{md}$30-TI-URU$_4$
[2] $^{md}$30-TI-URU$_4$-*iš*
[3] $^{md}$30-TI.LA-URU$_4$
- seal (NA$_4$.KIŠIB) of PN: **269**: 9 (KT 8) [1]; **158**: 6 (KT 9) [1]
- no details: **195**: 4 (NM 13) [2]; **194**: 4 (NM 13) [3]; **196**: 4 (NM 13) [3]; **136**: 21 (NM 23) [3]; **28**: 12 (NM 24) [1]; **152**: 4, 6 (KT 4) [3, 1]; **213**: 5 (KT 7) [1]; **310**: 3 (KT 7) [1]; **156**: 14 (KT 8) [1]; **269**: 6, 9 (KT 8) [1]; **158**: 4, 5 (KT 9) [1]; **159**: 9, 12, 29 (KT 9) [1]; **160**: 2 (KT 9) [1]; **163**: 6, 8 (KT 9) [1]; **73**: 5 (KT 10) [1]; **74**: 6 (KT 10) [1]; **7**: 22 (KT 11) [1]; **32**: 21 (KT 11) [1]; **76**: 6 (KT 12) [1]; **126**: 7 (KT 13) [1]; **241**: 19 (KT 13$^{?}$) [1]; **226**: 4 (KT 14) [1]; **81**: 5 (KT 14) [1]; **84**: 5 (KT 14) [1]; **228**: 4 (KT 14) [1]; **180**: 1 (KT 2–15$^{?}$) [1]; **272**: 5 (KT 17) [3]; **90**: 2 (KT x) [1]; **187**: 3 (KaE 3) [1]

**Sîn-bāltī** ($^{d}$30-*bal-ti*)
- MUNUS.TUR, sister of Innunnu, wife of Kulippi-rigir: **291**: 5 (KT 5–7)

**Sîn-bēl-[. . .]** ([$^{d}$30-EN-[. . .])
- no details: **180**: 11, 12 ($^{m}$KI.MIN) (KT 2–15$^{?}$)

**Sîn-bēl-apli** ($^{md}$30-EN-IBILA)
- no details: **74**: 2 (KT 10); **10**: 22 (KT 12); **168**: 9 (NM 19–20, KT 11–12);

**Sîn-bēl-zēri**
[1] $^{md}$30-EN-NUMUN
[2] $^{md}$<30>-EN-NUMUN
- no details: 136: 14 (NM 23) [1]; 298: 5 (NM 23) [1]; 2: 38 (KT 1) [2]; 109: 5 (n.d.) [1]

**Sîn-ēpiru** ($^{md}$30-*e-pi-rù*)
- no details: **261**: 25 (n.d.)

**Sîn-erība** ($^{m}$30-*eri-ba*)
- son of Dābibī: **303**: 11 (NM 23)
- no details: **304**: 6 (NM 15); **43**: 3 (KT 1); **316**: 10 (year 17)

**Sîn-ibni** ($^{md}$30-*ib-*⸢*ni*⸣)
- brewer ($^{lú}$LUNGA): **160**: 2 (KT 9)

**Sîn-iddina** ($^{md}$30-SUM-*na*)
- no details: **134**: 3′ (NM 21); **4**: 23 (KT 8$^{?}$)

**Sîn-in$^{?}$[ . . .]** ($^{m⸢d}$30$^{?}$-*in*$^{?}$⸣-[ . . .])
- no details: **239**: 5 (NM 2)

**Sîn-īriš** ($^{md}$30-URU$_4$-*iš*)
- no details: **261**: 18 (n.d.)

**Sîn-išmânni** ($^{md}$30-*iš-man-ni*)
- son of Bussut: **150**: 4 (KT 3)
- no details: **37**: 23 (KT 1); **30**: 6 (KT 4); **3**: 17′ (KT 5); **153**: 2 (KT 6); **4**: 22, 23 ($^{m}$KI.MIN) (KT 8$^{?}$); **33**: 17 (KT 12$^{?}$); **188**: 14′ (year 8)

**Sînma-ilu, son of** (DUMU $^{md}$30-*ma*-DINGIR)
- farmer (ÉNSI): **3**: 24′ (KT 5); **33**: 11 (KT 12$^{?}$)
- no details: **93**: 13 (KT 2)

**Sîn-muballiṭ**
[1] $^{md}$30-TI
[2] $^{md}$30-*mu-bal-liṭ*
• reed-weaver (AD.KID): **295**: 9 (KT 9) [1]
• miller (KA.ZÌ.DA): **112**: 2 (NM 19) [2]
• no details: $^{md}$30-TI **187**: 23 (KaE 3) [1]
**Sîn-mušallim** ($^{md}$30-*mu-*⸢*šal*⸣*-l*[*im*])
• no details: **124**: 4 (NM 21)
**Sîn-muštēšir** ($^{md}$30-*muš-te-šìr*)
• no details: **47**: 12 (NM 21); **316**: 4 (year 17)
**Sîn-napšira**
[1] $^{md}$30-*nap-ši-ra*
[2] $^{m}$[$^{d}$30$^{?}$]-⸢*nap*⸣*-ši-*⸢*ra*$^{?}$⸣
• physician (A.ZU): **159**: 17 (KT 9) [1]
• witness: **328**: 18 (KT 17) [1]
• no details: **136**: 27 (NM 23) [2]; **73**: 4 (KT 10) [1]; **79**: 4 (KT 13) [1]; **83**: 3 (KT 14) [1]; **180**: 3 (KT 2–15$^{?}$) [1]; **57**: 7 (KT x) [1]
**Sîn-rēmni**$^{?}$**, son of** (DUMU $^{md}$30-*re-mì-ni*)
• no details: **28**: 5 (NM 24)
**Sîn-šadûni** ($^{md}$30-KUR-*ni*)
• carpenter ($^{lú}$NAGAR): **46**: 15 (KT x)
**Sîn-šadûni, son of** (DU[MU] $^{md}$30-KUR-*ni*)
• no details: **9**: 22 (KT 11)
**Sîn-šarru** ($^{md}$30-*šar-rù*)
• no details: **134**: 4′ (NM 21)
**Sîn-šar-ilāni** ($^{md}$30-[LU]GAL$^{?}$-DINGIR$^{meš}$)
• no details: **237**: 3 (NM 9)
**Sîn-taklāku, son of** (DUMU $^{md}$30-*tak-la-ku*)
• farmer (ÉNSI): **10**: 6, 10 (KT 12)
**Sîn-usuḫ-pišti**
[1] $^{md}$30-LA-*piš-ti*
[2] $^{md}$30-*ú-suḫ*$_4$*-piš-ti*
• father of Ninurta-kīna-īde: **327**: 5 (KT 5) [1]
• no details: **285**: 5 (KT 16) [2]
**Siyātu**
[1] $^{m}$*Si-ia-a-tu*$_4$
[2] $^{m}$*Si-ia-tu*$_4$
[3] $^{m}$*Si-ia-ti*
• boatman ($^{lú}$MÁ.LAḪ$_5$): **44**: 13 (KT 1) [1]
• probably the boatman: **28**: 14 (NM 24) [2]
• no details: **139**: 35 (NM x) [2]; **57**: 13, 20, 22 (KT x) [2, 3]
**Su[. . .]** ($^{m}$*Su*$^{?}$-⸢x⸣[ . . .])
• witness: **333**: 12 (NM x)
**Sugir-bunni**
[1] $^{m}$*Su-un-gi-ir-bu-ni*
[2] $^{m}$*Su-gi-ir-bu-ni*
• no details: **273**: 15 (KT 1) [1]; **281**: 8 (KT 15) [2]; **282**: 6 (KT 15$^{?}$) [2]; **284**: 5 (KT 16) [2]; **286**: 5 (KT 16) [2]; **290**: 8 (KT x) [2]
**Ṣāḫitu, daughter of** (DUMU.MUNUS $^{lú}$Ì.SUR)
[1] DUMU.MUNUS $^{lú}$Ì.SUR
[2] ⸢DUMU⸣.MUNUS $^{<lú>}$Ì.S[UR]
[3] ⸢DUMU.MUNUS$^{?}$⸣ $^{lú}$Ì.SUR
• no details: **210**: 5 (KT 3) [1]; **212**: 3 (KT 5) [1]; **214**: 6 (KT 7) [2]; **159**: 11 (KT 9) [1]; **160**: 3 (KT 9) [1]; **163**: 7 (KT 9) [1]; **78**: 5 (KT 13) [1]; **79**: 3 (KT 13) [1]; **227**: 4 (KT 14) [1]; **286**: 4 (KT 16) [3]; **232**: 4 (KT x) [1]; **320**: 12′, 13′ (n.d.) [1]
**Ṣāḫitu, son of** (DUMU $^{lú}$Ì.SUR)
• no details: **155**: 5 (KT 8)
**Ṣillī-[. . .], son of** ([D]UMU $^{m}$*Ṣíl-*⸢*li*$^{?}$⸣-[ . . .])
• no details: **34**: 9 (KT 12)
**Ṣillī-Ea-šarru, son of** (DUMU $^{m}$*Ṣíl-lí-*$^{d}$*É-a*-LUGAL)
• no details: **131**: 15 (NM 18)
**Ṣillī-Nergal** ($^{m}$*Ṣíl-li-*$^{d}$IGI.DU)
• ⸢GURUŠ$^{?}$.TUR⸣: **95**: 50′ (KT 6)
**Ṣillī-Šudda** ($^{m}$*Ṣíl-lí-Šu-ud*$^{!}$*-da*$^{?}$)
• smith (SIMUG): **305**: 3 (KT 11)
**Ṣillūtu** ($^{m}$*Ṣíl-lu-t*[*u*$_4$])
• no details: **34**: 20′ (KT 12)
**Ṣīssu-namrat**
[1] $^{m}$*Ṣi-*⸢*is-su*$^{!}$⸣*-nam-rat*
[2] $^{m}$*Ṣi-is-su-nam-rat*
• no details: **47**: 14, 24 (NM 21) [1, 2]
**Ṣuḫartu** (⸢$^{f}$*Ṣú*⸣*-ḫar-tu*$_4$)
• no details: **101**: 20 (KT 15)
**Ṣuḫḫutu**
[1] $^{m}$*Ṣú-ḫu-tu*$_4$
[2] $^{m}$*Ṣú-uḫ-ḫu-tu*$_4$
[3] $^{m}$*Ṣú-uḫ-ḫu-ti*
• brewer ($^{lú}$LUNGA): **112**: 2 (NM 19) [1]; **114**: 2 (KT 4) [1]; **133**: 5 (NM 20) [2]; **138**: 4 (NM x) [2]
• no details: **308**: iv 23′ (NM 18–22) [3]; **184**: 13 (KT x) [1]
**Ṣuppuru**
[1] $^{m}$*Ṣú-up-pu-rù*
[2] $^{m}$*Ṣú-up-pu-ri*
• no details: 47: 9, 14, 15 ([$^{m}$]⸢KI.MIN⸣), 18, 25 (NM 21) [2, 1]
**Šabayutu** ($^{m}$*Ša-ba-a-a-ú-t*[*u*$_4$])
• no details: **34**: 16′ (KT 12)

**Ša-DI-mi**
[1] ᵐ*Ša*-DI-*mi*
[2] <ᵐ>*Ša*-DI-*mi*
• no details: **54**: 13 (KT 12) [1]; **11**: 13 (KT 12) [2]

**Šagarakti** (ᵐ*Ša-ga-rak-ti*)
• no details: **7**: 15 (KT 11); **32**: 14 (KT 11) [1]; **328**: 3, 4, 7 (KT 17) [1]

**Šagarakti-Šuriaš**
[1] ᵈ*Ša-garak-t*[*i-Šu*]*-ri-aš*
[2] ᵈ*Ša-ga-rak-ti-Šu-ri-ia-aš*
[3] [*Šagarakti*]*-Šu-ri-aš*
• king: **253**: 7, 15 (ᵈKI.MIN) (ŠŠ 1) [1]; **104**: 12 (ŠŠ 2) [2]; **91**: 7 (ŠŠ x) [3]; **299**: 7 (ŠŠ x) [2]

**Šagi[ . . .]** (ᵐ*Ša-gi-*⸢x⸣[ . . .])
• no details: **40**: 9 (NM 9⁺)

**Ša-ili, son of** (DUMU ᵐ*Ša-i-li*)
• no details: **22**: 6 (NM 19)

**Ša-ili-banâ**
[1] ᵐ*Ša*-DINGIR-DÙ-*a*
[2] ᵐ*Ša*-DINGIR?-DÙ
[3] ᵐ*Ša*-DINGIR-*ba-na-a*
• no details: **187**: 4 (KaE 3) [1]; **292**: 11 (n.d.) [2]; **336**: 6 (n.d.) [3]

**Šā'iltu, daughter of** (DUMU.MUNUS *Ša-il-ti*)
• no details: **104**: 3 (ŠŠ 2)

**Šamaš-[. . .]** (ᵐᵈUTU-⸢x⸣[ . . .])
• no details: **131**: 7 (NM 18)

**Šamaš-aḫa-[ . . .]** (ᵐᵈUTU-ŠEŠ-x[ . . .])
• no details: **97**: 12 (KT 9)

**Šamašālitu** (ᶠ*Ša-ma-ša-li-tu₄*)
• no details: **95**: 6 (KT 6)

**Šamaš-amīla-uballiṭ** (ᵐᵈUTU-LÚ-TI.LA)
• no details: **94**: 13 (KT 2)

**Šamaš-bēl-kitti** (ᵐᵈUTU-EN-*ú-kit-ti*)
• no details: **21**: 9 (n.d.)

**Šamaš-dayyān** (ᵐᵈ⸢UTU⸣-DI.KU₅)
• son of Ištar-idāya-alki: **95**: 9 (KT 6)

**Šamaš-iqīša** (ᵐᵈUTU-BA-*šá*)
• shepherd? (⸢SIPA?⸣) of Ninurta-rēṣū'a?: **337**: 4 (n.d.)

**Šamaš-kīna-īde** (ᵐᵈ⸢UTU-*ki*⸣*-na-i-de*)
• father of Billullu: **124**: 8 (NM 21)

**Šamaš-muballiṭ** (ᵐᵈUTU-*mu-bal-liṭ*)
• no details: **31**: 6 (KT 5); **51**: 9, 11 (KT 7)

**Šamaš-nādin-aḫḫē** (ᵐᵈ⸢UTU⸣-SUM-ŠEŠ⸢ᵐᵉˢ⸣)
• no details: **57**: 16 (KT x)

**Šamaš-nāṣir** (ᵐᵈUTU-ÙRU)
• father of Kalbu: **42**: 6 (NM 19)
• father of Erību: **42**: 9 (NM 19)
• father of Dayyān-Marduk: **326**: 3, 26 (NM 22)
• father of Izkur-Ninurta: **162**: 11 (KT 9); **176**: 13 (KT 13)
• father of Rīš-Akkade: **176**: 14 (ᵐKI.MIN) (KT 13)

**Šamaš-qarrād** (ᵐᵈUTU-*qar-rad*)
• attendant (LÚ.SAG): **176**: 17 (KT 13)
• no details: **33**: 19 (KT 12?)

**Šamaš-šarru** (ᵐᵈUTU-LUGAL)
• no details: **107**: 2 (KT 2); **146**: 8 (KT 2)

**Šamuḫ-Nergal** (ᵐ*Ša-muḫ*-ᵈU.GUR)
• no details: **45**: 6 (KT 4); **266**: 6′ (n.d.)

**Šamuḫ-Ninurta** (ᵐ*Ša-m*[*uḫ*?]-⸢ᵈ*Nin-urta*⸣)
• GURUŠ.TUR.TUR, son of Bēlessunu?: **95**: 29 (KT 6)

**Šamuḫ-rigimšu** (ᵐ*Ša-muḫ-ri-gim-šu*)
• no details: **30**: 5 (KT 4); **4**: 6, 15 (KT 8?); **52**: 8, 17 (KT 11); **14**: 5 (KT 14); **184**: 12 (KT x)

**Šan(n)abu**
[1] ᵐ*Ša-an-na-bu*
[2] ᵐ*Ša-na-bu*
• no details: **2**: 33, 34 (ᵐKI.MIN) (KT 1) [1]; **50**: 12 (KT 1) [1]; **50**: 4 (KT 1) [2]

**Šar[. . .]** (ᶠ*Šar-*⸢x⸣[ . . .])
• no details: **275**: 4 (KT 5)

**Šarratu** (ᶠ*Šar-ra-tu₄*)
• MUNUS.⸢ÀR, daughter of Qadištu: **96**: 9 (KT 9)

**Šaruku . . . ?, son of** (DUMU ᵐ*Ša-ru-ku*?-⸢x⸣)
• no details: **46**: 24 (KT x)

**Šēlebu** (ᵐ*Še-*⸢*le-bi*⸣)
• boatman (ˡᵘMÁ.LAḪ₅) of Enlil-mukīn-apli: **327**: 7, 28′ (KT 5)

**Šēmû** (ᵐ*Še-mi-i*)
• gardener (NU.ᵍⁱˢKIRI₆): **182**: 4 (KT x)
• no details: **136**: 25 (NM 23)

**Šimdi-Šuqamuna** (ᵐ*Šim-di*-ᵈ*Šu-qa-mu-na*)
• no details: **39**: 6 (KT 10)

**Šimê-suppâya** (ᶠ*Ši-me-e-su-up-pa-*⸢*a-a*⸣)
• *lullubītu*, mother of Rīš-Akītu: **95**: 53′ (KT 6)

**Šinnānu** (ᵐ*Ši-in-na-ni*)
• father of Etel-pī-[ . . .]: **170**: 10, 14 (KT 12)

**Širištu**
[1] ᵐ*Ši-ri-iš-tu*₄
[2] ᵐ*Ši-ri-iš-ti*
- weaver (*māḫiṣu*): **3**: 16′ (KT 5) [1]
- son of [ . . .]-Enlil: **149**: 9 (KT 2) [1]
- son of Šudaḫ[ . . .]: **150**: 17 (KT 3) [1]
- no details: **308**: ix 11′ (NM 18–22) [2]; **146**: 9 (KT 2) [2]; **30**: 12 (KT 4) [2]

**Šu . . . , Šu[ . . .]**
[1] ᵐ*Šu*-⸢x-x⸣
[2] ᵐ*Šu*-[
- no details: **133**: 12 (NM 20) [2]; **261**: 32 (n.d.) [1]

**Šu[. . .], son of** (DUMU ᵐ⸢*Šu*?⸣-[ . . .])
- *arad ekalli* (ÌR.É.GAL?): **137**: 5 (NM x)

**Šubagīya** (ᵐ*Šu-ba*?*-gi-ia*)
- no details: **261**: 22 (n.d.)

**Šudaḫ[ . . .]** (ᵐ*Šu-da-aḫ*-x-[(x)])
- father of Širištu: **150**: 17 (KT 3)

**Šummak-lā-[DN]** ([ᵐ]*Šum-ma-ak-la*-ᵈ⸢x⸣[ . . .])
- son of Meli-Šuqamuna, witness: **326**: 16 (NM 22)

**Šumma-lā-Marduk** (ᵐ*Šum-ma-la*-ᵈ⸢AMAR.UTU⸣)
- no details: **237**: 4 (NM 9)

**Šumuḫ-Nergal**? (ᵐ*Šu-muḫ*-ᵈ⸢U?⸣.[GUR?])
- no details: **45**: 32 (KT 4)

**Šumuḫ-rigimšu** (ᵐ*Šu-muḫ-r*[*i-gim*]*-šú*)
- no detailas: **45**: 44 (KT 4)

**Šumu-libši** (ᵐMU-*líb-ši*)
- son of Rīš-Ulūlu, witness: **333**: 14 (NM x)
- witness: **328**: 16 (KT 17)
- no details: **92**: 3 (NM 19); **1**: 14 (NM 22); **17**: 4, 8, 9 (ᵐKI.MIN) (NM 23); **141**: 3 (NM 24–KT 3); **142**: 2 (NM 24–KT 3); **2**: 16, 23, 24–26 (ᵐKI.MIN), 43, 44 (ᵐKI.MIN) (KT 1); **37**: 11 (KT 1); **50**: 3, 11 (KT 1); **144**: 8 (KT 1); **18**: 5, 8, 9 (KT 3); **108**: 4 (KT 3); **275**: 3 (KT 5); **310**: 7 (KT 7); **5**: 6, 8, 14 (KT 8); **6**: 8, 13, 14 (ᵐKI.MIN) (KT 8); **156**: 12, 20, 28 (KT 8); **159**: 18, 20, 24 (KT 9); **163**: 2 (KT 9); **164**: 13, 17, 27 (KT 9); **7**: 13, 14–16 (ᵐKI.MIN) (KT 11); **32**: 12, 13–15 (ᵐKI.MIN) (KT 11); **53**: 10, 11–12 (ᵐKI.MIN) (KT 12); **55**: 8, 13, 19 (KT 12); **33**: 6, 13 (KT 12?); **56**: 8, 13 (KT 13); **126**: 2 (KT 13); **180**: 5 (KT 2–15?); ᵐMU-*lí*[*b*?*-ši*?] **152**: 2 (KT 4)

**Šūnuḫu** (ᵐ*Šu-nu-ḫu*)
- no details: **45**: 40 (KT 4); **265**: 7′ (KT 7)

**Šuqa[muna- . . .]** (ᵐᵈ*Šu-qa*-[ . . .])
- no details: **36**: 14 (year 5)

**Šuqamuna-īriš**
[1] ᵐᵈ*Šu-qa-mu-na*-URU₄
[2] ᵐᵈ*Šu-qa-mu-na*-URU₄-*iš*
- no details: **29**: 9 (NM 24) [2]; **48**: 9 (NM 24) [1]; **16**: 6 (KT x) [2]

**Šurbā[. . .]** (ᵐ*Šu-ur-ba-a-a*-x[ . . .])
- father of Ḫimmatu: **324**: 19 (BB 18)

**Šurba[k . . .]** (ᵐ*Šu-ur-ba-a*[*k*- . . .])
- son of Tuḫ-Enlil, witness: **324**: 16 (BB 18)

**Šuri, son of** (⸢DUMU?⸣ ᵐ*Šu*-⸢*ri-i*⸣)
- no details: **129**: 4 (NM 17)

**Šurīḫa-īli, son of** (DUMU ᵐ*Šu-ri-ḫa*-DINGIR)
- farmer (ÉNSI): **29**: 3, 13 (NM 24); **48**: 3, 13 (NM 24); **2**: 11 (KT 1); **33**: 8 (KT 12?)
- no details: **50**: 15 (KT 1); **2**: 39 (KT 1)

**Šūzibanni-[DN]** (ᵐ*Šu-zi-ib-a*[*n-ni*-ᵈ . . .])
- DUMU.GABA: **95**: 17 (KT 6)

**Šūzibanni-Marduk (or Ēṭiranni-Marduk)** (ᵐKAR-*ni*-ᵈAMAR.UTU)
- no details: **4**: 28 (KT 8?)

**Šūzibanni-Šamaš (or Ēṭiranni-Šamaš)** (ᵐKAR-*an-ni*-ᵈUTU)
- no details: **46**: 11 (KT x)

**Šūzub-[DN]** (ᵐKAR-*ub*-[ . . .])
- no details: **261**: 15 (n.d.)

**Šūzub-Marduk** (ᵐKAR-*ub*-ᵈAMAR.UTU)
[1] ᵐKAR-*ub*-ᵈAMAR.UTU
[2] ᵐKAR-[ᵈAMA]⸢R.UTU⸣
[3] ⸢ᵐKAR⸣-[*ub*-ᵈAMAR.UTU]
- son of Ur-Asaralimma, witness: **325**: 15 (NM 14) [1]; **330**: 11 (KT 14) [1]
- son of Ur-Asaralimma: **49**: 16 (KT 1) [1]; **119**: 11 (KT 9) [1]; **164**: 16 (KT 9) [1]
- no details: **47**: 8, 11, 23 (NM 21) [1]; **49**: 5 (KT 1) [2]; **5**: 14, 15 (ᵐKI.MIN) (KT 8) [1]; **6**: 14 (KT 8) [3]; **9**: 5, 8 (KT 11) [1]; **33**: 14 (KT 12?) [1]

**Šūzub?-Šamaš** (ᵐKAR?-ᵈUTU?)
- no details: **70**: 12 (KT 9)

**ᵐ⸢*Ta*?*-a*?⸣[-x-ᵈ]⸢AMAR?.UTU?⸣**
- no details: **156**: 10 (KT 8)

**Tabnî-bulliṭī** (ᵐ*Tab-ni-i-bu-li-ṭí*)
- no details: **31**: 10 (KT 5)

**Taḫirištu son of** (DUMU ᵐ*Ta-ḫi-ri-iš-ti*)
- no details: **261**: 19 (n.d.)

**Taklāku** ($^{m}$*Tak-la-ku*)
- son of Lū-d[a . . .]: **89**: 6 (KT x)
- no details: **95**: 3, 48′, 55′ (KT 6)

**Taklāku-ana-Ninurta** ($^{m}$*Tak-la-ku-a-na-*$^{d}$*Nin-urta*)
- no details: **43**: 6 (KT 1)

**Taqīšu**
[1] $^{m}$*Ta-qí-šu*$_{14}$
[2] $^{m}$*Ta-qí-šu*
- diviner ($^{lú}$ḪAL): **238**: 4 (NM 19) [1]
- plowman$^{?}$ ($^{lú}$ENGAR$^{?}$): **156**: 28 (KT 8) [2]
- son of Bēlī-iddina: **37**: 21 (KT 1) [2]
- no details: **131**: 13 (NM 18) [1]; **37**: 22 (KT 1) [2]; **44**: 9, 12 (KT 1) [2]; **94**: 14 (KT 2) [2]; **52**: 9, 18 (KT 11) [2]; **13**: 9 (KT 13) [2]; **14**: 6 (KT 14) [2]

**Taqulu** ($^{m}$*Ta-qu-li*$^{?}$)
- no details: **83**: 4 (KT 14)

**Tarība-Gula** ($^{m}$*Ta-ri-ba-*$^{d}$*Gu-la*)
- knotter (*kāṣiru*): **180**: 6 (KT 2–15$^{?}$)
- son of Ḫaldīya: **120**: 42 (NM 19$^{?}$)
- GURUŠ.TUR, son of Aṣûšu-namir: **93**: 28′ (KT 2)
- son of Aḫu-bani: **103**: 12 (KT x)

**Tarībat-ili** ($^{m}$*Ta-ri-bat*-DINGIR)
- House (É) of PN: **120**: 37 (NM 19$^{?}$)
- father of Ninurta-ašarēd: **64**: 6 (NM 18$^{?}$); **138**: 5 (NM x); **143**: 1 (KT 1); **147**: 5 (KT 2); **113**: 2 (KT 3); **170**: 11 (KT 12)
- father of Rīš-aṣûšu: **49**: 18 (KT 1); **103**: 5, 12 (KT x); **182**: 1, 10 (KT x)
- father of Izkur-Marduk: **28**: 15 (NM 24)
- no details: **39**: 6 (KT 10)

**Tarībat-ili, son of** (DUMU $^{m}$*Ta-ri-bat*-DINGIR)
- no details: **128**: 6, 12 (NM 17$^{?}$)

**Tarībat-Šamaš** ($^{m}$*Ta-ri-bat-*$^{d}$UTU)
- son of . . . : **176**: 15 (KT 13)

**Tarībti-Adad** ($^{m}$*Ta-rib-ti-*$^{d}$IŠKU[R])
- no details: **46**: 22 (KT x)

**Tarībtu** ($^{m}$*Ta-rib-tu*$_{4}$)
- GURUŠ, son of Išemmūtu and brother of Ilqašu-ilī: **93**: 29′ (KT 2)

**Tarību** ($^{m}$*Ta-ri-bu*)
- attendant (LÚ.SA[G$^{?}$]): **41**: 17 (NM 18)
- miller (KA.ZÌ.DA): **112**: 2 (NM 19)
- no details: **2**: 28 (KT 1); **31**: 9 (KT 5); **99**: 13 (KT 9); **85**: 2 (KT 14); **183**: 3 (KT x)

**Tarzame, son of** (DUMU $^{m}$*Tar-za-me*)
- no details: **4**: 9, 10$^{?}$ (DUMU $^{m}$KI.MIN) (KT 8$^{?}$)

**Tatatu** (*Ta-ta-tu*$_{4}$)
- ⸢MUNUS.TUR⸣, daughter of Bu'ūa: **291**: 7 (KT 5–7)

$^{m}$***Ta*-TUK-*uš-ši-ni-e***$^{?}$
- no details: **316**: 3 (year 17)

**Tuḫ-Enlil** ($^{m}$*Tu-uḫ-*$^{d+}$*En-lí*[*l*$^{?}$])
- father of Šurba[k . . .]: **324**: 17 (BB 18)

**Tukultī-Adad**
[1] $^{m}$*Tukul-ti-*[$^{d}$IŠKU]R
[2] ⸢$^{m}$*Tu*⸣-[*kul*]-⸢*ti*⸣-$^{d}$IŠKUR
- no details: **49**: 6 (KT 1) [1]; **152**: 12 (KT 4) [2]

**Tukultī-Enlil** ($^{m}$*Tukul-ti-*$^{d+}$*En-líl*)
- no details: **99**: 10 (KT 9); **57**: 19 (KT x)

**Tukultī-Marduk** ($^{m}$*Tukul-ti-*$^{d}$AMAR.UTU)
- no details: **3**: 18′ (KT 5)

**Tukultī-Nergal** ($^{m}$*Tukul-ti-*$^{d}$U.GUR)
- no details: **4**: 32 (KT 8$^{?}$)

**Tukultī-lū-dāri** ($^{m}$*Tu-kul-t*[*i-lu-d*]*a-*⸢*ri*⸣)
- *ḫazannu*, witness: **324**: 22 (BB 18)

**Tukultu** ($^{m}$*Tu-kul-tu*$_{4}$)
- merchant (DAM.GÀR): **297**: 1, 20 (KT 6); **186**: 13 (KT x)

**Tunami-Saḫ**
[1] $^{m}$*Tu-nam-is-Saḫ*
[2] $^{m}$*Tu-na-mi-Saḫ*
- $^{(lú)}$Ì.SUR: **9**: 24, 25 (KT 11) [1]; **54**: 21 (KT 12) [2]; **46**: 17 (KT x) [3]
- son of Iš[ . . .]:**137**: 10 (NM x) [2]

**Tuni[ . . .]** ($^{m}$*Tu-ni-*⸢x⸣[ . . .])
- no details: **40**: 10 (NM 9$^{+}$)

**Tupšarru**
[1] $^{m.lú}$DUB.SAR
[2] $^{m}$DUB.SAR
[3] DUB.SAR
- brewer ($^{lú}$LUNGA): **114**: 2 (KT 4) [1]
- father of Bittā/Bettā: **302**: 9 (KT 10) [1]; **169**: 6 (KT 12) [3]
- father of Ḫānibu: **175**: 6 (KT 13) [2]

**Tupšarru, son of**
[1] DUMU $^{m}$DUB.SAR
[2] DUMU $^{lú}$DUB.SAR
[3] DUMU DUB.SAR
- farmer (ÉNSI): **1**: 8 (NM 22) [1]; **2**: 10 (KT 1) [1]; **169**: 3 (KT 12) [2]
- probably farmer: **164**: 7 (KT 9) [3]

**Turrat$^{?}$- . . .** ($^{m}$⸢*Tur*$^{?}$*-rat*$^{?}$⸣-[x]$^{meš?}$)
- no details: **149**: 8 (KT 2)

**ᵐTuša-iballuṭ** (ᵐ*Tu-ša*-TI.LA)
- no details: **2**: 27, 35 (KT 1)

**ᶠTuša-iballuṭ** (ᶠ*Tu-ša*-TI.L[A])
- daughter of Bēlessunu?: **95**: 27 (KT 6)

**Ṭā[b- . . .], son of** (⸢DUMU ᵐ*Ṭà*⸣-[*ab*- . . .])
- *arad ekalli* (ÌR.É.GAL?): **137**: 4 (NM x)

**Ṭābiḫu**
[1] ᵐ*Ṭa-ab-bi-ḫi*
[2] ᵐ*Ṭab-bi-ḫi*
- father of Iqīša-Marduk: **256**: 10 (NM 19) [1]; **89**: 4 (KT x) [2]; **182**: 3 (KT x) [2]

**Ṭābiḫu, son of** (DUMU ᵐ*Ṭab-bi-ḫi*)
- probably identical with Iqīša-Marduk, son of Ṭābiḫu: **247**: 4 (NM 19)

**Ṭābīya** (ᵐ*Ṭa-bi-ia*)
- no details: **45**: 4, 5 (ᵐKI.MIN), 16, 37 (KT 4); **162**: 9 (KT 9); **34**: 14′ (KT 12); **172**: 1 (KT 12); **173**: 2 (KT 12)

**Ṭāb-kidin-[DN]** (ᵐ*Ṭà-ab-ki-din*-ᵈ[ . . .])
- no details: **102**: 10′ (KT 15)

**Ṭāb-kidin-Gula** (ᵐ*Ṭà-ab-ki-din*-ᵈ*Gu-la*)
- no details: **133**: 10 (NM 20); **136**: 9 (NM 23); **205**: 3 (KT 1); **149**: 6 (KT 2); **206**: 3 (KT 2); **152**: 5, 7, 11 (KT 4); **52**: 28 (KT 11); **223**: 5 (KT 12); **225**: 4 (KT 13); **82**: 3, 10 (KT 14); **87**: 3 (KT 15); **233**: 7 (KT x)

**Ṭāb-kidin-Ninurta** (ᵐ*Ṭà-ab-ki-din*-ᵈ*Nin-urta*)
- no details: **49**: 7 (KT 1); **33**: 12 (KT 12?)

**Ṭāb-ṣilli-Eulmaš** (ᵐ*Ṭà-ab-ṣíl-lí*-É.UL.MAŠ)
- no details: **31**: 8 (KT 5); **51**: 10 (KT 7)

**Ṭāb-ṣilli-(E)ulmaš, son of** ([DU]MU? ᵐ*Ṭà-ab*-ᵍⁱˢMI-⸢UL⸣.MAŠ)
- no details: **10**: 23 (KT 12)

**Ṭāb-ṣilli-Šamaš, son of** (DUMU ᵐ*Ṭà-ab*-MI-ᵈUTU)
- no details: **261**: 24 (n.d.)

**Ṭāb-ṣillu**
[1] ᵐ*Ṭà-ab-ṣíl-lu₄*
[2] ᵐ*Ṭà-ab*-ᵍⁱˢMI
[3] ᵐ*Ṭà-ab*-MI
- gardener (⁽ˡᵘ́⁾NU.ᵍⁱˢKIRI₆): **136**: 21 (NM 23) [1]; **45**: 25 (KT 4) [2]
- no details: **2**: 44 (KT 1) [1]; **331**: 6 (KT x) [3]

**Ṭāb-šār-Adad** (ᵐ*Ṭà-ab*-IM-ᵈIŠKUR)
- no details: **94**: 2 (KT 2); **31**: 9 (KT 5); **97**: 6 (KT 9); **98**: 6 (KT 9); **33**: 11 (KT 12?); **170**: 2 (KT 12); **176**: 9 (KT 13); **80**: 6 (KT 13⁺)

**Ṭābūtu** (ᵐ*Ṭa-bu-tu₄*)
- no details: **184**: 11 (KT x)

**Uballissu-[DN]** (ᵐTI-*su*-⸢ᵈ⸣[ . . .])
- no details: **40**: 16′ (NM 9⁺)

**Uballissu-Marduk**
[1] ᵐTI-*su*-ᵈAMAR.UTU
[2] ᵐ*Ú-bal-liṭ-su*-ᵈA[MAR.UTU?]
- son of ᵐ*Ak-ni*-⸢*ša*?-KÁ?-ᵈ?x-x⸣: **124**: 11 (NM 21) [1]
- no details: **42**: 11 (NM 19) [2]

**Uballissu-Marduk, son of** (DUMU ᵐTI-*su*-ᵈAMAR.UTU)
- no details: **22**: 14 (NM 19)

**Ubartu** (ᶠ*U-bar-tu₄*)
- no details: **101**: 22 (KT 15)

**Ubāru** (ᵐ*U-bar-rù*)
- seal (NA₄.KIŠIB) of PN: **324**: 27 (BB 18)

**Ubbuttu**
[1] ᵐᶠ*Ub-bu-ut-ti*
[2] ᶠ*Ub-bu-ti*
- father/mother of Ninnisi-[ . . .]: **136**: 18 (NM 23)
- father/mother of Bunna-Marduk: **136**: 28 (NM 23)
- no details: **61**: 8 (n.d.)

**ᶠ⸢UD?-x-x-⸣-*ni***
- no details: **267**: 3 (NM 16)

**UD-*nibi*** (ᵐUD-*ni-bi*)
- no details: **7**: 16 (KT 11); **32**: 15 (KT 11)

**Uḫatu?** (ᶠ*Ú-ḫa*?-*ti*)
- no details: **242**: 8 (KT 14)

Ulmaš-aḫa-iddina see (E)ulmaš-aḫa-iddina

**Ur-[ . . .]** (ᵐ*Ur*-[x-x-x]-⸢x⸣)
- no details: **89**: 2 (KT x)

**Ur-Adad** (ᵐ*Ur*-ᵈ⸢IŠKUR?⸣)
- no details: **154**: 12 (KT 6?)

**Ur-Asaralimma** (ᵐ*Ur*-ᵈ*Asar-alim-ma*)
- father of Šūzub-Marduk: **325**: 16 (NM 14); **49**: 16 (KT 1); **119**: 11 (KT 9); **164**: 16 (KT 9); **330**: 11 (KT 14)

**Uraš-Tukultī** (⸢ᵐᵈ⸣*Uraš-tu*-⸢*kul-ti*⸣)
- father of Aba-ul-īde: **255**: 5 (NM 4)

**Urḫabu, son of** (DUMU ᵐ*Ur*-⸢*ḫa*⸣-*bu*)
- *arad ekalli*? (ÌR.É.GAL?): **137**: 2 (NM x)

**Ūrīya-Marduk** (ᵐ⸢*Ú-ri-a*-ᵈAMAR⸣.UTU)
- no details: **2**: 36 (KT 1)

**Ur-Ninnisi** (ᵐ*Ur*-ᵈ*Nin-ni*[*si*])
- no details: **170**: 9 (KT 12)

**Urrāya** (ᵐ*Ur-ra-a-a*)
- son of Aḫa-iddina-Marduk: **122**: 3, 15 (KT 14)

**Ur-Sîn** (ᵐ*Ur-*ᵈ30?)
- no details: **101**: 18 (KT 15)

**Urubātu** (ᶠ*Ú-ru-*⌜*ba*?⌝*-tu*₄)
- no details: **267**: 4 (NM 16)

**Usātū'a** (ᵐ*Ú-sa-tu-ú-a*)
- *arad ekalli* (ÌR.É.GAL): **120**: 40 (NM 19?)
- son of Karamdari?: **49**: 17 (KT 1)
- no details: **49**: 11 (KT 1); **12**: 8 (KT 13); **35**: 7 (KT 13)

**Usub-Šipak** (ᵐ⌜*Ú*⌝*-su-ub-Ši-pak*)
- no details: **4**: 24 (KT 8?)

**Ūṣâ-rīš-āli**
[1] ᵐÈ*-a-ri-iš*-URU
[2] ᵐÈ*-a*-SUD-URU
[3] ᵐÈ*-a-ri-*<*iš*>-URU
- farmer (ÉNSI): **10**: 7, 11 (KT 12) [1]; **176**: 6 (KT 13) [2]
- GURUŠ.TUR, son of Rīš-Nergal: **93**: 25′ (KT 2) [3]

**Ūṣi-annû'a**? (ᵐÈ*-a-na-nu-ú-a*)
- no details: **331**: 14 (KT x)

**Uznānu** (ᵐ*Uz-na-nu*)
- no details: **261**: 26 (n.d.)

**Uzub-nibu** (ᵐ*Ú-zu-ub-ni-bu*)
- no details: **169**: 22 (KT 12)

**Yaē'a** (⌜ᶠ⌝*Ia-*⌜*e-a*⌝)
- no details: **267**: 2 (NM 16)

**ᶠYānu-kittu** (ᶠ*Ia-nu-*⌜*kit*?⌝*-tu*₄)
- no details: **267**: 7 (NM 16)

**ᵐYānu-kittu, son of** (DUMU ᵐ*Ia-nu-kit-tu*₄)
- no details: **4**: 33 (KT 8?)

**Yātu** (ᶠᵐ*Ia-a-tu*₄)
- no details: **296**: 7 (KT 12)

**Yā'um** (ᵐ*Ia-ù'-um*)
- no details: **2**: 32 (KT 1)

**Yaya'u**? (ᵐ*Ia-a-a-ú*)
- father of Gubbuḫu: **184**: 11 (KT x)

**Yaya'u**?**, son of** (DUMU ᵐ*Ia-a-a-*⌜*ú*?⌝)
- no details: **3**: 10′ (KT 5)

**ᵐYā'ūtu, sister of** (NIN ᵐ*Ia-ú-tú*)
- no details: **296**: 6 (KT 12)

**ᶠYā'ūtu** (⌜ᶠ*Ia*⌝*-a-u-ú-t*[*u*₄])
- no details: **292**: 10 (n.d.)

**Za[ . . .]**
[1] ⌜ᵐ*Za*-x⌝-[
[2] ᵐ*Za*-[
- father of Nūr-Adad?: **46**: 26 (KT x) [1]
- no details: **307**: 7′ (NM? 21) [2]

**Za[ . . .], son of** (DUMU ᵐ⌜*Za*?⌝-[ . . .])
- no details: **154**: 8 (KT 6?)

**Zākiru**
[1] ᵐ*Za-ki-rù*
[2] ᵐ*Za-ki-ri*
- *mandidu*, witness: **330**: 13 (KT 14) [1]
- carpenter ((lú)NAGAR): **47**: 9, 15, 26 (NM 21) [1]; **2**: 33 (KT 1) [1]
- brewer? (⌜lúLUNGA?⌝) of Ninu[rta?- . . .]: **164**: 20 (KT 9) [1]
- son of Dašpu: **176**: 11 (KT 13) [1]
- no details: **236**: 3 (NM 8) [2]; **9**: 16 (KT 11) [1]; **11**: 10 (KT 12) [1]; **54**: 10 (KT 12) [1]; **12**: 7 (KT 13) [1]; **35**: 6 (KT 13) [1]; **46**: 5 (KT x) [1]; **319**: 5 (n.d.) [1]

**Zāninu** (ᵐ*Za-nin-ní*)
- father of Pān-Marduk-lūmur: **46**: 33 (KT x)

**Zikir-Adad**
[1] ᵐ*Zi-ik-ri-*ᵈIŠKUR
[2] ᵐ*Zi-kir-*ᵈIŠKUR
- no details: **99**: 8 (KT 9) [1]; **169**: 20 (KT 12) [1]; **290**: 4 (KT x) [2]

**Zuturtu** (ᶠ*Zu-túr-tu*₄)
- *ararratu*-miller (MUNUS.ÀR): **186**: 5 (KT x)

**ᶠᵈ⌜x⌝-[x]-*a*?*-bíl-ti***
- no details: **95**: 21 (KT 6)

**. . .-Adad, [ . . .]-Adad**
[1] [ᵐx-x]*-ir-*ᵈIŠKUR
[2] ⌜ᵐx-x-x⌝-ᵈIŠKUR
[3] ᵐ⌜x-x⌝-ᵈIŠKUR
[4] [ . . .]-ᵈIŠKUR
- *arad ekalli* (ÌR.É.GAL): **103**: 9 (KT x) [4]
- no details: **120**: 5, 10 (NM 19?) [1, 2]; **124**: 6 (NM 21) [3]; **169**: 7 (KT 12) [4]; **89**: 3 (KT x) [4]

**. . .-aḫa-īriš** (⌜ᵐᵈx-ŠEŠ⌝-URU₄)
- GURUŠ.TUR, son of Marduk-zākir-šumi: **93**: 6 (KT 2)

**ᵐ[x]*-ar-ši-kit-tu*₄**
- plowman (lúENGAR) of Iqīša-Ninimma: **176**: 8 (KT 13)

**[ . . .]-Dilbat**? ([ᵐx-x]-⌜x⌝-⌜ᵈ*Dil*?*-bat*?⌝)
- no details: **120**: 6 (NM 19?)

**. . . din** (${}^{m}$˹x-x-x-*din*?˺)

- no details: **180**: 4 (KT 2–15?)

**. . .-Enlil, [ . . .]-Enlil**

[1] [${}^{m}$]˹x˺-${}^{d}$50

[2] ${}^{m}$[x-(x)]-˹${}^{d+}$*En-líl*˺

- father of Širištu: **149**: 9 (KT 2) [2]
- no details: **242**: 4 (KT 14) [1]

**[ . . .]ḫiru** ([${}^{m}$x]-*ḫi-rù*)

- no details: **21**: 7 (n.d.)

**[ . . .]iatu** (˹${}^{md}$˺[x-x]-*ia-tu*)

- no details: **243**: 8 (KT x)

**. . .-iddina, [ . . .]-iddina**

[1] ${}^{m}$˹x-x-SUM-*n*˺[*a*?]

[2] [${}^{m}$ . . . -SU]M-*na*

- no details: **333**: 3 (NM x) [2]; **266**: 5′ (n.d.) [1]

**[ . . .]-ilumma** (${}^{m}$[x-x-(x)]-DINGIR-*ma*)

- farmer (${}^{lú}$ÉNSI): **45**: 13 (KT 4)

**. . .-Ištaran** (${}^{m}$˹x x x x ${}^{d}$˺KA.DI)

- no details: **8**: 5 (KT 11)

**[DN- . . . m]anni**

[1] ${}^{mfd}$[x x x x-m]*an*?-*ni*

[2] ${}^{md}$[x-x-x-*ma*]*n-ni*

- no details: **115**: 5 (KT 6) [1]; **33**: 9 (KT 12?) [2]

**[ . . .]-Marduk**

[1] [${}^{m}$x-x-${}^{d}$AM]AR.UTU?

[2] [${}^{m}$ . . .]-${}^{d}$AMAR.UTU

[3] [${}^{m}$x-x]-˹x˺-${}^{d}$AMAR.UTU

[4] ˹${}^{m}$˺[x-x]-${}^{d}$A[MAR.UT]U?

- seal ($NA_4$.KIŠIB) of PN: **333**: 22 (NM x) [1]
- farmer (${}^{lú}$ÉNSI): **169**: 10 (KT 12) [2]
- no details: **248**: 4 (NM 21) [2]; **136**: 16 (NM 23) [2]; **37**: 32, 33 (${}^{m}$KI.MIN) (KT 1) [4]; **156**: 14 (KT 8) [3]

**[DN]-mutakkil** ([${}^{md}$x-x-*m*]*u-tak-kil*)

- no details: **10**: 22 (KT 12)

**. . . na** (˹${}^{m}$x-x-*na*?˺)

- no details: **120**: 11 (NM 19?)

**[ . . .]-˹nādin?˺-šumi?** ([${}^{m}$x]-˹*gu*?-SUM?˺-MU)

- plowman (${}^{lú}$ENGAR): **176**: 22 (KT 13)

**. . .-Nergal, [ . . .]-Nergal**

[1] ˹${}^{m}$x-x-x-${}^{d}$U.GUR?˺

[2] [${}^{m}$ . . .]-˹${}^{d}$U.GUR?˺

- no details: 120: 13 (NM 19?) [1]; 169: 17 (KT 12) [2]

**[ . . .]-Ninimma** ([${}^{m}$ . . . -${}^{d}$N]*in-ìmma*)

- no details: **321**: 1 (n.d.)

**[ . . .]-Ninnisi** (˹${}^{m}$˺[x-x-(x)]-˹x˺-${}^{d}$*Nin-nisi*)

- no details: **10**: 21 (KT 12)

**[ . . .]niya** ([${}^{m}$x-x]-˹*ni*˺-*ia*)

- no details: **244**: 6 (KuE 8)

**[ . . .]-remanni** (${}^{m}$[x x x]-˹*re-man*˺-*ni*)

- no details: **136**: 26 (NM 23)

**. . . ri** (˹${}^{md}$x-x-x-*ri*˺)

- father of Mūrānu: **308**: ix 18′ (NM 18–22)

**. . .-Sîn** (${}^{m}$[x-x]-˹x˺-${}^{d}$30)

- son of Gula-. . . , witness: **324**: 20 (BB 18)

**[ . . .]-Šamaš** ([${}^{m}$x]-${}^{d}$UTU)

- son of Bēlessunu?: **95**: 23 (KT 6)

**[Iqī]ša-Nergal or [Rabâ]-ša-Nergal** ([${}^{m}$BA/GAL]-˹*šá*˺-${}^{d}$U.GUR)

- no details: **261**: 37 (n.d.)

**. . .-šarrat** (˹x-x˺-*šar-rat*)

- no details: **321**: 10′ (n.d.)

**[ . . .]ši** (${}^{m}$[x-x]-*ši*)

- no details: **156**: 11 (KT 8)

**. . . šu** (${}^{m}$˹x-x˺-[x]-˹x˺${}^{meš}$-*šu*)

- no details: **239**: 9 (NM 22)

**[ . . .]ti** ([ . . .]˹x˺-*ti*)

- farmer (${}^{lú}$ÉNSI): **169**: 9 (KT 12)

**. . . ti, son of** ([DU]MU ${}^{m}$˹x-x-*ti*˺)

- no details: **22**: 4 (NM 19)

## *Professions*

AD.KID see *atkuppu*

***amtu*** (GÉME) "maid, female servant"

- anonymous ˹GÉME${}^{?meš}$˺: **97**: 7

***āpil bābi*** (*a-píl* KÁ) "gate keeper"

- see: Ardu; Baḫû; Ibni-Marduk

***arad ekalli*** (ÌR.É.GAL, ÌR.É.GAL${}^{meš}$) "lit. palace servant, perhaps construction worker"

- see: Adad-[ . . .]; Adad-šubši; Aḫḫū-dannū; Amīl-Isin; Ana-kāršu-ēmid; Ḫānibu; Izkur-Adad; Kalbu; Kidin-Dilbat; Ninurta-dīnanni; Nūr-Šamaš; Rīš-Adad; son of Šu[ . . .]; son of Ṭāb-[ . . .]; son of Urḫabu; Usātū'a; . . .-Adad
- anonymous ÌR.˹É?˺.[GAL?]: **137**: 6
- anonymous ÌR.É.GAL${}^{meš}$: **120**: 33, 41; **300**: 3

***ararratu*** (MUNUS.ÀR) "a type of miller"

- see: Baba-šarrat; Bāltī-Amurru; Bēltu-irīša; Ērišti-Adad; Ina-Isin-bā'ilat; Ina-Sagila-bāltī; Ina-Sagila-kabtat; Zuturtu
- anonymous MUNUS.ÀR$^{meš}$: **96**: 11

***asû*** (A.ZU) "physician"
- see: Rabâ-ša-Marduk; Sîn-napšira

AŠGAB see *aškāpu*

***āšipu*** (*a-ši-pu*) "exorcist"
- see: Arad-Marduk

***aškāpu*** ($^{lú}$AŠGAB) "leather-worker"
- see: Gubbuḫu

***ašlāku*** ($^{lú}$ÁZLAG, $^{lú}$ÁZLAG$^{meš}$) "washerman, fuller"
- anonymous $^{⌜lú⌝}$ÁZLAG: **51**: 17
- anonymous $^{lú}$ÁZLAG$^{meš}$: **139**: 31

***atkuppu*** (AD.KID) "reed-weaver"
- see: Mīnâ-ēpuš-ila; Sîn-muballiṭ
- anonymous AD.KID$^{meš}$: **139**: 28

***atû*** (Ì.DU$_8$) "porter"
- see: Kulippi(-)rigir

ÁZLAG see *ašlāku*

A.ZU see *asû*

***bānû*** ($^{lú}$DÙ) "builder"
- see: Izkur-Adad

***bārû*** ($^{lú}$ḪAL, MÁŠ.ŠU.GÍD.GÍD) "diviner"
- see: Taqīšu ($^{lú}$ḪAL)
- MÁŠ.ŠU.GÍD.GÍD: **203**: 2

***bēl bīti*** (EN É)
- anonymous: **244**: 20

***bēl parṣi*** (EN MAR.ZA)
- anonymous: **69**: 6

***bēl pīḫāti*** (EN *pi-ḫa-ti*) "provincial governor"
- anonymous: **8**: 14; **51**: 16

***dālû*** (*da-lu-ú*) "water drawer"
- see: son of Aḫūni; Nūr-Marduk

DAM.GÀR see *tamkāru*

$^{lú}$DÙ see *bānû*

DUB.SAR see *tupšarru*

DUMU É see *mār bīti*

DUMU.MUNUS É see *mārat bīti*

EN É see *bēl bīti*

EN MAR.ZA see *bēl parṣi*

ENGAR see *ikkaru*

EN.NU.UN KÁ.GAL see *maṣṣar abulli*

ÉNSI see *iššakku*

ÉRIN$^{ḫi.a/meš}$ see *ṣābu*

GÉME see *amtu*

$^{lú}$GÍR see *ṭābiḫu*

$^{lú}$ḪAL see *bārû*

***ḫazannu*** (*ḫa-za-nu, ḫa-za-an-nu, ḫa-za-an-ni*)
- see: Adad-ilu-ina-māti; Adāya; Arad-nubatti; Bananû; Ḫunābu; Illullu; Izkur-Ninurta; Martuk(k)u; Nūr-Adad; Nuska-nāṣir; Tukultī-lū-dāri
- [PN]: **133**: 15

Ì.DU$_8$ see *atû*

***ikkaru*** ($^{lú}$ENGAR) "plowman"
- see: Aḫu-damqu; Bēlī-iqīša; Bēlšunu; Ēmid-ana-Marduk; Ninnū'a; Paḫallanu; (Pap)sukkal-aḫa-iddina; Rabâ-ša-Nergal; Rabâ-ša-Ninurta; son of Rigim-Adad; $^{m}$Rīmūtu; Rīš-Ekur; Taqīšu; . . . -kittu
- anonymous $^{lú}$ENGAR: **149**: 11, **156**: 29–31, 34; **165**: 9; **179**: 6, 8, 10, 13, 15, 25′
- anonymous $^{lú}$ENGAR$^{meš}$: **134**: 2′; **136**: 11; **156**: 33

ÌR.É.GAL see *arad ekalli*

$^{(lú)}$Ì.SUR see *ṣāḫitu*

***išparu*** (UŠ.BAR, UŠ.BAR$^{meš}$) "weaver"
- see: Arad-U$_4$.9.KAM; Gimillu; Izkur-Šamaš; Nasiq-Marduk
- anonymous UŠ.BAR$^{meš}$: **97**: 19; **98**: 17; **139**: 29

***iššakku*** ($^{(lú)}$ÉNSI, $^{(lú)}$ÉNSI$^{meš}$) "farmer"
- see: son of Agamuza; Ana-Ninurta-taklāku; son of Ana-Sîn-taklāku; son of Arad-Amurru; Aṣûšu-namir; Atta-ilī-ma; Baḫû; son of Baqnītu; Bittā/Bettā; Bunna-Adad; Bušaršu; Erību, Irību; Gimil-Adad; Ḫambu; Ḫānibu; son of Ilī-rēmanni; son of Innanibūtu; Innunnu; Iqīša-Amurru; Kidin-Amurru; son of Kubbutu; Kuppitātu, son of; Latarak-bāni; Marduk-zākir-šumi; Rabâ-ša-Gula; Rīš-Nergal; son of Sînma-ilu; son of Sîn-taklāku; son of Šurīḫa-ili; son of Tupšarru; Ūṣâ-rīš-āli; [ . . .]-ilumma; [ . . .]-Marduk; [ . . .]ti
- anonymous ÉNSI: **19**: 4; **40**: 6
- anonymous ÉNSI$^{meš}$: **1**: 13; **2**: 13; **20**: 7; **21**: 2; **29**: 3; **48**: 3

KA.KÉŠ$^{me}$ see *kāṣiru*

***kāṣiru*** (*ka-ṣi-rù, ka-ṣi-ri*, KA.KÉŠ$^{meš}$) "knotter"
- see: Eulmaš-iqīša; Kidin-Gula; Mandidâya; Ninurta-dīnanni; Rīš-Marduk; Tarība-Gula
- anonymous KA.KÉŠ$^{meš}$: **139**: 30

***kaṣṣidakku*** ($^{(lú)}$KA.ZÌ.DA, $^{(lú)}$KA.ZÌ.DA$^{meš}$) "miller"
- see: Lā-qīpu; Sîn-muballiṭ; Tarību

- anonymous $^{(lú)}$KA.ZÌ.DA: **112**: 16; **150**: 3; **153**: 6; **154**: 11
- anonymous $^{(lú)}$KA.ZÌ.DA$^{meš}$: **111**: 5; **139**: 18–19, 20 (KI.MIN)

KA.ZÌ.DA see *kaṣṣidakku*

$^{lú}$KID.MAŠ see *šangû*

$^{lú}$KÚRUN.NA see *sābû*

$^{(lú)}$LUNGA see *sīrāšû*

LÚ.SAG see *ša rēši*

***māḫiṣu*** (*ma-ḫi-ṣu*) "weaver"
- see: Širištu

***mākisu*** (*ma-ki-si*) "tax collector"
- see: Aḫēdūtu
- in the compound ŠE *ma-ki-si*: **1**: 5; **2**: 5, 13; **4**: 4, 13; **8**: 6, 12; **9**: 6, 7; **10**: 4, 9; **11**: 5, 7; **12**: 4, 5; **26**: 6; **29**: 6; **31**: 5; **33**: 5; **34**: 5; **35**: 5; **36**: 6; **44**: 15; **47**: 7; **48**: 6; **49**: 13; **51**: 5; **53**: 5; **54**: 6; **55**: 5; **56**: 6; **57**: 5
- in the compound ÉSAG *ma-ki-si*: **11**: 6; **51**: 5; **54**: 7

$^{(lú)}$MÁ.LAḪ$_5$, MÁ.LAḪ$_4$ see *malāḫu*

***malāḫu*** ($^{(lú)}$MÁ.LAḪ$_5$, ⸢$^{lú}$MÁ$^?$.LAḪ$_4$$^?$⸣, MÁ.LAḪ$_5$$^{meš}$) "boatman"
- see: Apil-Šamaš; Erība-Adad; Siyātu; Šēlebu
- anonymous $^{(lú)}$MÁ.LAḪ$_5$: **139**: 24, 25 (KI.MIN); **327**: 14′
- anonymous MÁ.LAḪ$_5$$^{meš}$: **164**: 30
- cf. also PN Malāḫu

***mandidu*** (*man-di-du*)
- see: Innunnu; Zākiru

***mār bīti*** (DUMU É)
- see: Bēlānu; Ḫunābu; Lūṣi-ana-nūr-Marduk; Mūrānu

***mārat bīti*** (DUMU.MUNUS É$^?$)
- see: Babû'a

***mār šipri*** (DUMU *šip-ri*) "messenger"
- anonymous: **137**: 11, 12; **335**: 9

***maṣṣar abulli*** (EN.NU.⸢UN⸣ KÁ.GAL) "gate guard"
- see: Ill[u . . .]

MÁŠ.ŠU.GÍD.GÍD see *bārû*

$^{lú}$MUḪALDIM see *nuḫatimmu*

MUNUS.ÀR see *ararratu*

MUNUS.NAR see *nârtu*

$^{(lú)}$NAGAR see *nagāru*

***nagāru*** ($^{(lú)}$NAGAR) "carpenter"
- see: Amīl-Marduk; Billullu; Ibni-Adad; Ibnûtu; Iqīša-Dilbat; Qīšat-Nergal; Sîn-šadûni; Zākiru
- anonymous $^{(lú)}$NAGAR: **45**: 35; **176**: 25; **321**: 5

***nappāḫu*** (SIMUG) "smith"
- see: Ṣillī-Šudda

$^{lú}$NAR see *nâru*

***nârtu*** (MUNUS.NAR) "musician"
- see: Ātamar-qāssa

***nâru*** ($^{lú}$NAR) "musician"
- see: Kubbutu

$^{(lú)}$NU.$^{giš}$KIRI$_6$ see *nukarribu*

***nuḫatimmu*** (⸢$^{lú}$MUḪALDIM$^?$⸣) "cook"
- see: Iddin-Marduk

***nukarribu*** ($^{(lú)}$NU.$^{giš}$KIRI$_6$) "gardener"
- see: Ēmuq-Adad; Šēmû; Ṭāb-ṣillu
- cf. also PN Nukarribu

***rab zarāti*** (GAL *za-ra-ti*) (lit. "chief of the tents")
- see: $^{m}$Rīmūtu

***rē'û*** ($^{(lú)}$SIPA, SIPA$^{meš}$) "shepherd"
- see: Aḫi; Apil-Nergal; Arad-Nergal; Baba-īriš; Bittā/Bettā; $^{m}$Bunna-Gula; Bu'ūa; Erība-Nergal; Innunnu; Kurû, Muštālu; Namru; Pussulu; Qīšat-Adad; Qunnunu; Šamaš-iqīša; Tukultī-(E)ulmaš
- anonymous SIPA: **106**: 4; **107**: 5
- anonymous SIPA$^{meš}$: **103**: 5

***sābû*** ($^{lú}$KÚRUN.NA) "innkeeper"
- see: Sîn-aḫa-iddina
- anonymous $^{lú}$KÚRUN.NA: **46**: 7

***sakrumaš*** (*sak-ru-maš*) "a chariot officer"
- see: Qunnunu

SIMUG see *nappāḫu*

$^{(lú)}$SIPA see *rē'û*

***sīrāšû*** ($^{(lú)}$LUNGA, $^{lú}$LUNGA$^{meš}$) "brewer"
- see: Agab-šenni; Ana-nūr-Šamaš-lūṣi; Apil-Šamaš; Bā'eru; Erība-Ninurta; Ina-kitti-elê/ele'i; Kagiya; Kidin-Enlil; Kidin-Gula; Nannaya; $^{m}$Rīmūtu; Sîn-ibni; Ṣuḫḫutu; Tupšarru; Zākiru
- anonymous $^{(lú)}$LUNGA: **112**: 16; **152**: 4; **153**: 2; **159**: 29; **163**: 6, 8–9; **321**: 6
- anonymous $^{lú}$LUNGA$^{meš}$: **114**: 1

***ṣābu*** (ÉRIN$^{ḫi.a}$, ÉRIN$^{meš}$) "workmen"
- ÉRIN$^{ḫi.a}$: **35**: 4; **94**: 4; **97**: 14, 15 (KI.MIN), 17; **98**: 13, 15; **103**: 5; **159**: 19, 23, 26; **164**: 29
- ÉRIN$^{meš}$: **99**: 19; **120**: 37; **156**: 15, **292**: 1

***ṣāḫitu*** ($^{(lú)}$Ì.SUR, $^{lú}$Ì.ŠUR$^{meš}$) "oil-presser"
- see: Tunami-Saḫ
- anonymous $^{lú}$Ì.ŠUR$^{meš}$: **139**: 27

- cf. also PN Ṣāḫitu

***ṣuḫurtu*** (*ṣú-ḫur-tu*$_4$) "(an official)"
- see: Erība-Šuqamuna; Rabâ-ša-Sîn; $^{m}$Rīmūtu

***ša rēši*** (LÚ.SAG) "attendant"
- see: Aḫēdūtu; Šamaš-qarrād; Tarību

***ša rukūbi*** ([*š*]*a*$^?$ *ru-ku-bi*) "boatman of a cargo boat"
- anonymous: **103**: 10

***šaknu*** (*šak-nu*, GAR-*nu*, GAR-*ni*) "overseer"
- see: Arad-Marduk; Lūṣi-ana-nūr-Adad

***šangû*** ($^{lú}$KID.MAŠ) "priest"
- anonymous: **245**: 3

***tamkāru*** ($^{(lú)}$DAM.GÀR) "merchant"
- see: Tukultu
- anonymous $^{lú}$DAM.GÀR: **285**: 4

***tupšarru*** (DUB.SAR, *tup-šar-ri*) "scribe"
- see: Arad-Bēlti; Ea-[ . . .]; Mudammiq-Adad; Nuska-nābûšu; Rīš-aṣûšu
- anonymous DUB.SAR: **162**: 14; **170**: 19

***ṭābiḫu*** ($^{lú}$GÍR) "butcher"
- see: Muštāl-Nergal
- cf. also PN Ṭābiḫu

***ummānu*** (*um-ma-nu*) "workmen"
- **94**: 22′; **103**: 6

UŠ.BAR see *išparu*


## *Geographic Names and Ethnonyms*


**Akkad**
- see PNs Ina-Akkade-bēlet, Nūr-Bēlet-Akkade, Nūr-Ištar-Akkade, Rīš-Akkade

**Āl-Arad-Bēlti**
- URU-ÌR-GAŠAN$^{ki}$: **42**: 2; **97**: 17; **157**: 5
- URU-ÌR-[GAŠAN$^{ki}$]: **98**: 15
- URU-ÌR-⸢GAŠAN⸣[$^{ki}$]: **123**: 2′
- URU-ÌR-GAŠAN: **239**: 13, 16

**Āl-Arad-bīt-Kiš** (URU-ÌR-É-*Kiš*$^{ki}$)
- **112**: 6, 14

**Āl-atḫē**
- URU-*at-ḫe-e*$^{ki}$: **16**: 1; **19**: 1; **23**: 9; **24**: 4; **26**: 1; **29**: 1; **60**: 4; **98**: 12; **150**: 7
- URU-*at-ḫe-e*: **36**: 1; **48**: 1; **97**: 13; **118**: 1; **119**: 2; **125**: 3, 4 (KI.MIN); **153**: 7

**Āl-irrē**
- URU-*ir-re-e*$^{ki}$: **11**: 1, 17; **23**: 7; **25**: 6; **60**: 8; **97**: 9, 14; **111**: 4; **139**: 22; **157**: 1; **162**: 2
- [URU-*i*]*r-re-e*$^{ki}$: **150**: 1
- URU-*ir-re-e*[$^{(ki)}$]: **124**: 10
- URU-*ir-re-e*: **9**: 1, 28; **12**: 21; **22**: 18–20; **35**: 1; **46**: 1, 21, 40; **54**: 1; **98**: 9, 13; **112**: 4; **113**: 4; **119**: 2; **148**: 5, 6; **153**: 11; **159**: 27, 28; **161**: 4; **171**: 1; **176**: 1; **182**: 6, 7
- URU-*ir-re*-[*e*]: **37**: 23

**Āl-iššakkī** (URU-ÉNSI$^{meš}$)
- **39**: 7; **156**: 2

**Āl-Mār-Bā'ili** (URU-DUMU-*Ba-'i-li*)
- **97**: 20; **98**: 18; **113**: 6

**Āl-Mār-Kāri** (URU-DUMU-*Ka-a-ri*)
- **98**: 19

**Āl-Mīna-ēpuš-ila** (URU-*Mi-na*-DÙ-DINGIR$^{ki}$)
- **113**: 11

**Āl-nappāḫi** (URU-$^{lú}$SIMUG$^{ki}$)
- **181**: 7

**Āl-Sîn-šamuḫ**$^?$ (URU-$^{d}$30-*ša*$^?$-*muḫ*$^{?!}$)
- **165**: 1

**Āl-ṣalamti** (URU-*ṣa-lam-ti*$^{ki}$)
- **119**: 6; **138**: 2

**Āl-šēlebi** (URU-*še-le-bi*)
- **140**: 35′

**amurrû** (*a-mur-ru-ú*)
- **43**: 4

**AN.AN.MAR.TU$^{ki}$** (AN.AN.MAR.TU$^{ki}$)
- **69**: 4; **97**: 7

**arrapḫāyu** (*ar-rap*$^?$-*ḫa*$^?$-*a*$^?$-[*a*$^?$-*ú*$^?$])
- **267**: 13

**Babylon**
- see PN Bābilāyu

**Baṣātu**
- *Ba-ṣa-a-ti*$^{ki}$: **33**: 1; **57**: 21; **60**: 3; **153**: 4; **154**: 2; **243**: 2
- *Ba-ṣa-a-t*[*i*$^{ki}$]: **49**: 1
- *Ba-ṣa-ti*$^{k}$[$^{i}$]: **266**: 5′
- *Ba-ṣa-a-ti*: **176**: 23
- $^{uru}$*Ba-ṣa-ti*$^{ki}$: **338**: 4

**Bīt-bēri** (É.DANNA$^{ki}$)
- **119**: 5; **138**: 3

**Burrānu**
- $^{uru}$*Bur-ra-nu*$^{ki}$: **119**: 4
- $^{uru}$*Bur-r*[*a-nu*$^{ki}$]: **118**: 2

**Di . . .** (⸢*Di*-x-x⸣$^{k}$[$^{i?}$])
- **124**: 1

**Dikirtu**
- *Di-kir-tu*$_4$$^{ki}$: **13**: 1, 14; **23**: 10

- *Di-⸢kir-tu*$_{4}$⸣[$^{ki}$]: **28**: 1
- $^{uru}$*Di-ki-ir-tu*$_{4}$: **44**: 1

**Dimtu**
- AN.ZA.GÀR$^{ki}$: **23**: 3; **34**: 1; **60**: 5; **97**: 4, 10; **98**: 4, 10, 11 (KI.MIN); **156**: 6; **169**: 24; **173**: 5; **182**: 4
- ⸢$^{uru}$⸣AN.ZA.GÀR$^{ki}$: **45**: 36

**Diniktu**
- *Di-nik-tu*$_{4}^{ki}$: **244**: 3
- *Di-nik-*[*tu*$_{4}^{ki}$]: **244**: 15

**Dunni-Isin**
- $^{uru}$*Du-un-ni-Ì-si-in*$^{ki}$: **119**: 7
- $^{u}$[$^{ru}$]⸢*Du-un-n*⸣[*i-Ì-si-in*$^{ki}$]: **118**: 3

**Dū[r?- . . .]** (B[ÀD?-X-X-X]⸢$^{ki?}$⸣)
- **178**: 9

**Dūr-Amurru**
- BÀD-$^{d}$KUR$^{ki}$: **8**: 1; **10**: 1, 31; **25**: 8; **27**: 1; **31**: 1; **37**: 39; **143**: 6; **175**: 5; **291**: 11
- BÀD-$^{d}$KUR: **153**: 3; **163**: 2
- $^{uru}$BÀD-$^{d}$KUR$^{ki}$: **24**: 5
- BÀD-$^{d}$MAR.TU: **22**: 17, 20
- BÀD-$^{d}$⸢MAR.TU⸣$^{ki}$: **51**: 1

**Dūr-Bēl-mātāti**
- BÀD-EN-KUR.KUR$^{ki}$: **25**: 4; **37**: 38; **110**: 6, 7 (KI.MIN); **130**: 2; **148**: 1; **149**: 2; **261**: 21
- BÀD-EN-KUR.KUR[$^{(ki)}$]: **112**: 18
- [BÀD-E]N-KUR.KUR$^{ki}$: **139**: 5
- BÀD-EN-KUR.KUR: **120**: 4

**Dūr-(E)ki'ur** (BÀD-$^{d?}$KI.ÙR$^{?ki}$)
- **193**: 7

**Dūr-Enlilē**
- BÀD-$^{d+}$*En-líl*$^{meš.ki}$: **6**: 1; **7**: 1; **18**: 1; **23**: 6; **32**: 1; **52**: 28; **53**: 1; **56**: 1; **113**: 6, 7–10 (KI.MIN); **121**: 2, 4 (KI.MIN); **122**: 2; **144**: 3; **147**: 1; **164**: 22; **179**: 24′; **182**: 2, 3 (KI.MIN), 9; **261**: 39; **291**: 1; **317**: 2; **338**: 14, 16
- BÀD-$^{d+}$*En-líl*$^{meš}$: **22**: 10; **119**: 2; **120**: 42; **151**: 3; **175**: 7
- BÀD-[$^{d+}$*En-líl*$^{m}$]$^{eš?}$: **153**: 6
- BÀD-$^{d+}$*En-líl*$^{ḫi.a.ki}$: **1**: 1; **2**: 1, 46; **5**: 1; **25**: 3; **37**: 14, 29; **38**: 2; **48**: 26; **88**: 3; **108**: 2; **110**: 4; **112**: 7; **133**: 1; **135**: 3; **143**: 7, 8 (KI.MIN); **149**: 9; **178**: 8, 16; **181**: 5, 6 (KI.MIN); **329**: 3
- BÀD-$^{d+}$*En-líl*$^{ḫi.a}$: **17**: 1; **112**: 5, 17; **131**: 2; **137**: 12; **156**: 3; **166**: 6, 7–8 (KI.MIN), 10; **177**: 5, 7 (KI.MIN); **308**: col. ix 29′
- BÀD-$^{d+}$*En-líl*$^{ḫi.}$[$^{a.(ki)}$]: **50**: 1
- [BÀD-$^{d+}$*En-lí*]*l*$^{ḫi.a}$: **1**: 28
- BÀD-$^{d+}$*E*[*n-líl*$^{ḫi.a/meš.}$]⸢$^{ki}$⸣: **242**: 8, 9 (KI.MIN)
- BÀD-$^{d+}$*En-líl*[$^{ḫi.a/meš.ki}$]: **39**: 5, 6 (KI.MIN); **119**: 9; **159**: 20; **190**: 2; **266**: 8′, 9′
- [B]ÀD-$^{d+}$*E*[*n*?-*líl*$^{ḫi.a.ki?}$]: **192**: 6

**Dūr-Ištar** (BÀD-$^{d}$INANNA)
- **95**: 1

**Dūr-Kurigalzu**
- BÀD-*Ku-ri-gal-zu*: **123**: 5′
- BÀD-*Ku-ri-gal-zu*$^{ki}$: **184**: 4

**Dūr-Nuska** (BÀD-$^{d}$*Nuska*$^{ki}$)
- **113**: 5; **150**: 4; **168**: 10

**Dūr-Pa(p)-niĝara** (BÀD-$^{d}$*Pa*$_{4}$*-nig*$_{6}$*-gar-ra*$^{ki}$)
- **75**: 2

**Elamû** (*e-la-mu-ú*)
- **95**: 51′, 52′ (KI.MIN)

**Emūqāt-Marduk**
- $^{uru}$*E-mu-qat-*$^{d}$AMAR.UTU$^{ki}$: **150**: 9
- ⸢*E-mu-qat*⸣-$^{d}$AMAR.UTU⸢$^{ki?}$⸣: **298**: 6

**Ḫa[ . . .]** (⸢$^{uru?}$⸣*Ḫa-*[ . . .])
- **132**: 1

**Ḫamru**
- *Ḫa-am-ri*$^{ki}$: **22**: 16, 20; **110**: 5; **112**: 9, 11; **266**: 10′
- $^{uru}$*Ḫa-am-r*[*i*]: **127**: 2

**Ḫilunu** ($^{uru}$*Ḫi-lu-ni*)
- **308**: iv 10′

**Ḫurādu** ($^{uru}$*Ḫu-ra-du*)
- **46**: 16

**Ḫursagkalama**
- ḪUR.SAG.KALAM.MA$^{ki}$: **144**: 11; **291**: 1
- ḪUR.SAG.KALAM.MA: **163**: 10; **243**: 6
- ḪUR.SAG.K[ALAM.MA$^{(ki)}$]: **119**: 8
- see PN Ina-Ḫursagkalama-šarrat

**Ḫuṣlu?** (*Ḫu-uṣ-lu*$_{4}^{ki}$)
- **266**: 12′

**Ḫuṣṣu** (*Ḫu-uṣ-ṣu*$^{ki}$)
- **22**: 15; **25**: 5; **120**: 4, 14

**Irra-gāmil** ($^{d}$*Ìr-ra-ga-mil*$^{ki}$)
- **303**: 12

**Isin**
- *Ì-si-in*$^{ki}$: **113**: 11
- *Ì-s*[*i-in*$^{ki}$]: **138**: 11
- ⸢$^{uru?}$⸣*Ì-si-in*$^{ki}$: **138**: 12
- *Ì-si-in*: **301**: 6
- see PNs Amīl-Isin, Ina-Isin-bā'ilat

**Kār-Nin-[Eanna?]** (*Kar-*⸢*Nin*?⸣-[ . . .])

- **261**: 47

**Kār-Nin-Eanna** (*Kar-dNin-É-an-na*)
- **22**: 11; **112**: 13; **266**: 11′; **317**: 3

**Kār-Nuska**
- *Kar-dNuska*ki: **3**: 1, 27′; **4**: 1, 35; **14**: 1; **23**: 5; **52**: 1; **60**: 6; **71**: 2; **72**: 2; **78**: 3; **112**: 10; **135**: 2; **140**: 5′, 11′, 12′–17′ (KI.MIN), 34′, 36′; **153**: 2; **169**: 8; **173**: 4; **182**: 5; **184**: 1; **266**: 7′
- *Kar-dNuska*[ki]: **140**: 38′
- *Ka*[*r-dNuska*ki]: **140**: 2′, 3′ (KI.MIN)
- *Kar-dN*[*usk*]*a*ki: **140**: 7′, 8′ (KI.MIN)
- *Kar-dNuska*: **14**: 10; **30**: 1; **41**: 12, 16; **156**: 3; **160**: 1

**Kirê** (gišKIRI6-eki)
- **308**: iv 10′

**lullubû** (*lul-lu-bi-tu*4)
- **95**: 53′

**Mannu-nāṣiršu** (*Man-nu*-ÙRU-*šu*)
- **39**: 4; **72**: 4; **160**: 1

**Mê-Zurud** (*Me-e-Zu-ru-ud*ki)
- **125**: 5

**Namkar-Nuska (canal)** (*Nam-kar-dNuska*ki)
- **184**: 4

**Nār-ḫaḫḫi (canal)** (ÍD-*ḫa-aḫ-ḫi*)
- **94**: 4

**Nār-Tukultī-Ekur (canal)** (⌈ÍD-*Tukul-ti*-É.KURki⌉)
- **98**: 13

**Nippur**
- NIBRUki: **64**: 5; **90**: 4; **96**: 2; **139**: 20, 21, 23; **149**: 7; **151**: 8; **174**: 11; **177**: 11; **182**: 7, 8 (KI.MIN); **202**: 6; **207**: 1; **216**: 4; **242**: 8, 9 (KI.MIN); **244**: 10, 20; **273**: 5; **284**: 6; **297**: 21; **307**: 13′
- NI[BRU?]⌈ki?⌉: **244**: 7
- see PNs Nippurītu, Nippurû

**Pān-ṣēri**
- IGI-EDIN: **180**: 5
- *Pa-an*-EDIN: **302**: 10

**Parak-māri**
- BÁRA.DUMUki: **119**: 3; **171**: 10; **176**: 28
- BÁRA.DUM[Uki]: **137**: 7
- BÁRA?.⌈DUMUki?⌉: **330**: 5

**Pī-nāri**
- KA-ÍD.DAki: **143**: 4
- ⌈KA⌉-ÍD.DA: **96**: 11
- K[A-ÍD.DA?]: **96**: 1

**Sikila** (uru*Si-ki-la*)
- **97**: 5; **98**: 5

**Tamirtu**
- *Ta-mi-ir-tu*4ki: **24**: 6; **25**: 7; **153**: 5
- *Ta-mi-ir*-⌈*tu*4⌉[ki]: **143**: 5
- ⌈*Ta-mir-tu*4ki⌉: **23**: 8
- *Ta-mir-ti*[ki]: **174**: 1

**Tâmtu**? (*ta-an-ti*)
- **64**: 4

**Tukriš** (*Tuk-ri-iš*)
- **277**: 11

**Tukultī-Ekur**
- *Tukul-ti*-É.KURki: **15**: 1, 8; **23**: 4; **41**: 7, 15; **55**: 1; **60**: 7; **97**: 8, 12, 15 (KI.MIN); **98**: 8, 13, 14–17 (KI.MIN); **99**: 24; **112**: 3, 8, 12, 15, 19; **116**: 5, 6; **119**: 2; **120**: 41; **126**: 2; **166**: 5, 9; **169**: 5; **172**: 4; **173**: 4, 7; **175**: 1; **177**: 12; **179**: 2; **330**: 7
- *Tukul-ti*-É.KUR: **73**: 2; **140**: 4′, 6′, 9′, 37′; **180**: 3, 8; **266**: 6′
- uru*Tukul-ti*-É.KUR⌈ki⌉: **45**: 28
- *Tukul*?-*ti*?-⌈É?⌉.[KURki]: **154**: 6

**Tukultī-(E)ulmaš**

[1] m*Tukul-ti*-UL.MAŠ

[2] m*Tukul-ti*-É.UL.MAŠ
- shepherd (SIPA): **219**: 6 (KT 11) [1]
- probably the shepherd: **217**: 2 (KT 10) [2]

**Uruk**
- see PN Ḫunbī-ina-Uruk

**Zarāt-[ . . .]** (*Za-rat*-⌈x⌉[ . . .])
- **298**: 9

**Zarāt-šarri** (*Za-rat*-LUGALki)
- **37**: 20; **112**: 14


## *Temples*


**Akītu**
- see PN Rīš-Akītu

**Egalmaḫ**
- see PN Ina-Egalmaḫ-šarrat

**Ekiur** (KI.ÙR)
- **24**: 13

**Ekur** (É.KUR)
- **24**: 11, 12; **65**: 2

- see also PNs Ina-Ekur-dan[nāt?] and Rīš-Ekur, and GN Tukultī-Ekur

**Esagila**
- see PNs Esagila-līdiš, Ina-Sagila-bāltī, Ina-Sagila-kabtat, Išemmi-ina-Esagila

**Ešumeša** (É.ŠU.ME.ŠA$_4$)
- **187**: 10

**Eulmaš**
- see PNs (E)ulmaš-aḫa-iddina, Eulmaš-iqīša, Iddin-Eulmaš, Tukultī-(E)ulmaš, Ṭāb-ṣilli-Eulmaš

**Temple, temples**
- É.DINGIR: **187**: 8
- É.DINGIR$^{didli}$: **110**: 7; **119**: 1; **139**: 35; **157**: 6; **174**: 6; **214**: 2
- temples (É.DINGIR$^{didli}$) of Ḫursagkalama: **163**: 10

**Temple of Gula** (É $^{d}$*Gu-la*)
- of Dū[r-Enlilē?]: **119**: 9
- no details: **219**: 2; **243**: 8

**Temple of Ištar** (É $^{d}$*Iš-tar*)
- of Ḫursagkalama: **119**: 8

**Temple of Ninnisi** (É $^{d}$*Nin-nisi*)
- **97**: 18; **98**: 16; **119**: 11

**Temple of Ninurta** (É $^{d}$*Nin-urta*)
- of Āl-ṣalamti: **119**: 6; **138**: 2
- of Bīt-bēri: **119**: 5; **138**: 3
- of Burrānu: **118**: 2; **119**: 4
- of Dunni-Isin: **118**: 3; **119**: 7
- of Parak-māri: **119**: 3; **176**: 28

**Temple of Šarrat-[Nippur?]** (É $^{d}$*Šar-ra*[*t*-NIBRU$^{ki?}$])
- **119**: 10


## *Cuneiform Sources*


13 N 126: p. 326
BE 14 16: p. 124
BE 14 18: p. 311
BE 14 43: pp. 151–152
BE 14 57: p. 172
BE 14 78: p. 40
BE 14 81: p. 48
BE 14 88: p. 26 n. 3
BE 14 99a: p. 275
BE 14 114: p. 237
BE 14 118: pp. 19, 26, 99
BE 14 123: p. 327
BE 14 127: p. 44
BE 14 128a: p. 327
BE 14 137: p. 132
BE 14 148: p. 80
BE 14 157: p. 285
BE 14 166: p. 89
BE 14 167: p. 181
BE 15 59: p. 64
BE 15 91: pp. 26, 99
BE 15 110: p. 168
BE 15 131: p. 22 n. 2
BE 15 199: pp. 48, 325
BE 15 200: p. 235
BE 17 39: p. 79
BE 17 40: p. 124
BE 17 89: p. 341
CBS 7752: p. 237
CBS 10434: p. 18 n. 1
CBS 13885: p. 18 n. 1
CUSAS 30 1: pp. 38, 41, 45 n. 1
CUSAS 30 3: pp. 38, 332–333
CUSAS 30 4: pp. 78, 237
CUSAS 30 6: pp. 273, 344
CUSAS 30 16: p. 41 n. 2
CUSAS 30 17: pp. 39, 41 n. 2, 43
CUSAS 30 27: p. 122
CUSAS 30 31: pp. 40, 225, 331
CUSAS 30 34: pp. 62–63, 86–87
CUSAS 30 35: pp. 21 n. 3, 52, 65–66, 101
CUSAS 30 36: p. 78
CUSAS 30 40: pp. 23 n. 8, 55, 84, 93
CUSAS 30 43: p. 23 n. 8
CUSAS 30 44: p. 23 n. 8
CUSAS 30 45: pp. 23 n. 8, 84
CUSAS 30 46: p. 27 n. 1
CUSAS 30 53: p. 95
CUSAS 30 60: p. 216
CUSAS 30 64: pp. 40 n. 2, 79, 235
CUSAS 30 66: p. 216
CUSAS 30 67: pp. 83, 98
CUSAS 30 68: pp. 36, 48, 207, 237
CUSAS 30 71: p. 207
CUSAS 30 72: p. 207
CUSAS 30 73: p. 207

CUSAS 30 74: p. 218
CUSAS 30 75: p. 207
CUSAS 30 81: p. 231
CUSAS 30 85: pp. 207, 298
CUSAS 30 89: pp. 174, 340
CUSAS 30 91: p. 263
CUSAS 30 92: p. 78
CUSAS 30 112: p. 222
CUSAS 30 131: p. 288
CUSAS 30 134: p. 48 n. 4
CUSAS 30 135: pp. 40, 45, 175
CUSAS 30 138: pp. 151, 181
CUSAS 30 139: pp. 102, 162, 192
CUSAS 30 141: pp. 40, 114
CUSAS 30 142: pp. 19 n. 4, 44 n. 2, 258, 306
CUSAS 30 143: pp. 40 n. 4, 156, 235
CUSAS 30 144: pp. 40 n. 2, 156, 158
CUSAS 30 150: pp. 44 n. 2, 82, 117, 131
CUSAS 30 161: p. 114
CUSAS 30 162: pp. 26 n. 3, 127
CUSAS 30 165: p. 181
CUSAS 30 174–76: p. 200
CUSAS 30 175: p. 233
CUSAS 30 192: p. 240
CUSAS 30 194: p. 207
CUSAS 30 204: pp. 20 n. 4, 306
CUSAS 30 206: p. 20 n. 4
CUSAS 30 212: p. 292
CUSAS 30 228: p. 106
CUSAS 30 229: p. 216
CUSAS 30 231: pp. 20 n. 1, 43, 45, 142–146, 181, 235
CUSAS 30 233: p. 235
CUSAS 30 237: p. 306
CUSAS 30 240: p. 165
CUSAS 30 247: p. 165
CUSAS 30 256: p. 102
CUSAS 30 257: p. 104
CUSAS 30 263: p. 115
CUSAS 30 265: p. 233
CUSAS 30 267: p. 115
CUSAS 30 269: p. 115
CUSAS 30 274: pp. 26 n. 3, 115
CUSAS 30 277: pp. 42, 233, 258
CUSAS 30 280: p. 159
CUSAS 30 309: p. 127
CUSAS 30 311: p. 141
CUSAS 30 313: p. 160
CUSAS 30 317: p. 150
CUSAS 30 318: p. 150
CUSAS 30 319: p. 20 with n. 5
CUSAS 30 321: pp. 45, 329
CUSAS 30 326: p. 20
CUSAS 30 342: p. 151
CUSAS 30 360: p. 150
CUSAS 30 362: p. 20
CUSAS 30 364: pp. 286, 289
CUSAS 30 365: p. 285
CUSAS 30 366: pp. 37 n. 1, 150, 285, 289
CUSAS 30 370: pp. 285, 289
CUSAS 30 371: pp. 37 n. 9, 138
CUSAS 30 372: pp. 37 nn. 8–9, 289–290
CUSAS 30 373: pp. 285, 292
CUSAS 30 375: pp. 285, 289
CUSAS 30 376: p. 313
CUSAS 30 377: p. 304
CUSAS 30 380: pp. 267, 271
CUSAS 30 383: p. 35
CUSAS 30 384: pp. 35, 263
CUSAS 30 386: p. 263
CUSAS 30 387: p. 35
CUSAS 30 390: pp. 263, 285
CUSAS 30 391: p. 263
CUSAS 30 394: p. 47
CUSAS 30 397: p. 306
CUSAS 30 400: p. 136
CUSAS 30 412: p. 33 n. 3
CUSAS 30 413: p. 33 n. 2
CUSAS 30 422: p. 309
CUSAS 30 427: pp. 136, 314
CUSAS 30 428: pp. 46, 78, 260
D-K 4: pp. 324–325, 327
D-K 5: p. 325
EA 14: p. 289
Iml. 4: p. 129
Iml. 20: p. 129
MBTU 3: p. 333
MBTU 15: p. 325
MBTU 20: p. 333
MBTU 24: p. 333
MBTU 30: p. 327
MBTU 31: p. 327
MBTU 32: pp. 325, 327
MBTU 34: p. 329
MBTU 65: p. 129
MBTU 72: p. 267

MRWH 3: p. 329
MRWH 8: p. 327
MUN 10: pp. 235, 329
MUN 11: p. 329
MUN 16: p. 333
MUN 18: p. 333
MUN 19: p. 324
MUN 31: p. 93
MUN 46: p. 78
MUN 62: pp. 21 n. 3, 23, 55
MUN 64: pp. 21 n. 3, 22 n. 2, 23, 27 n. 4, 48–49, 55, 104–105
MUN 68: p. 69
MUN 69: p. 78
MUN 72: p. 101
MUN 73: p. 101
MUN 84: p. 196
MUN 92: p. 311
MUN 97: p. 151
MUN 98: p. 129
MUN 104: p. 218
MUN 118: p. 129
MUN 121: pp. 50, 103
MUN 134: pp. 117, 128
MUN 138: p. 41
MUN 140: pp. 118, 130
MUN 146: p. 218
MUN 159: p. 40
MUN 162: p. 31 n. 1
MUN 164–80: p. 39 n. 5
MUN 173: p. 57
MUN 177: p. 117
MUN 181–86: p. 39 n. 5
MUN 187: p. 80
MUN 240: p. 117
MUN 269: p. 134
MUN 279: p. 304
MUN 296: p. 237
MUN 307: p. 46–47, 50, 162
MUN 313: p. 329
MUN 315: p. 329
MUN 316: p. 276
MUN 317: p. 329
MUN 318: p. 32
MUN 319: pp. 32, 276
MUN 321: pp. 32, 276
MUN 322: p. 329
MUN 329: pp. 32, 33 n. 1
MUN 330: pp. 32, 33 n. 1
MUN 345: p. 37 n. 7
MUN 350: p. 37 n. 1
MUN 351: p. 37 n. 1
MUN 355: p. 37 n. 7
MUN 366: p. 289
MUN 368: p. 289
MUN 370: p. 289
MUN 372: p. 289
MUN 374–88: p. 308
MUN 395: p. 138
MUN 406: p. 305
MUN 416: p. 313
MUN 463: p. 78
Ni. 1391: p. 304
Ni. 2221: p. 117
Ni. 5920: p. 117
Ni. 6283: p. 304
Ni. 6670: p. 304
PBS 1/2 43: p. 218
PBS 1/2 54: p. 134
PBS 2/2 27: pp. 327, 329
PBS 2/2 34: p. 181
PBS 2/2 53: p. 139
PBS 2/2 58: p. 127
PBS 2/2 62: p. 235
PBS 2/2 91: p. 101
PBS 2/2 103: p. 122
PBS 2/2 107: p. 305
PBS 2/2 108: p. 317
PBS 2/2 112: p. 69
PBS 2/2 121: p. 287
PBS 2/2 133: p. 327
PBS 13 70: p. 124
UDBD 96: p. 44
UDBD 116: p. 341
UDBD 139: p. 329
UM 29-15-684: pp. 23 n. 7, 26 n. 3
VAT 15420: p. 97
Zub. 739: pp. 324–325

# *9. Plates*

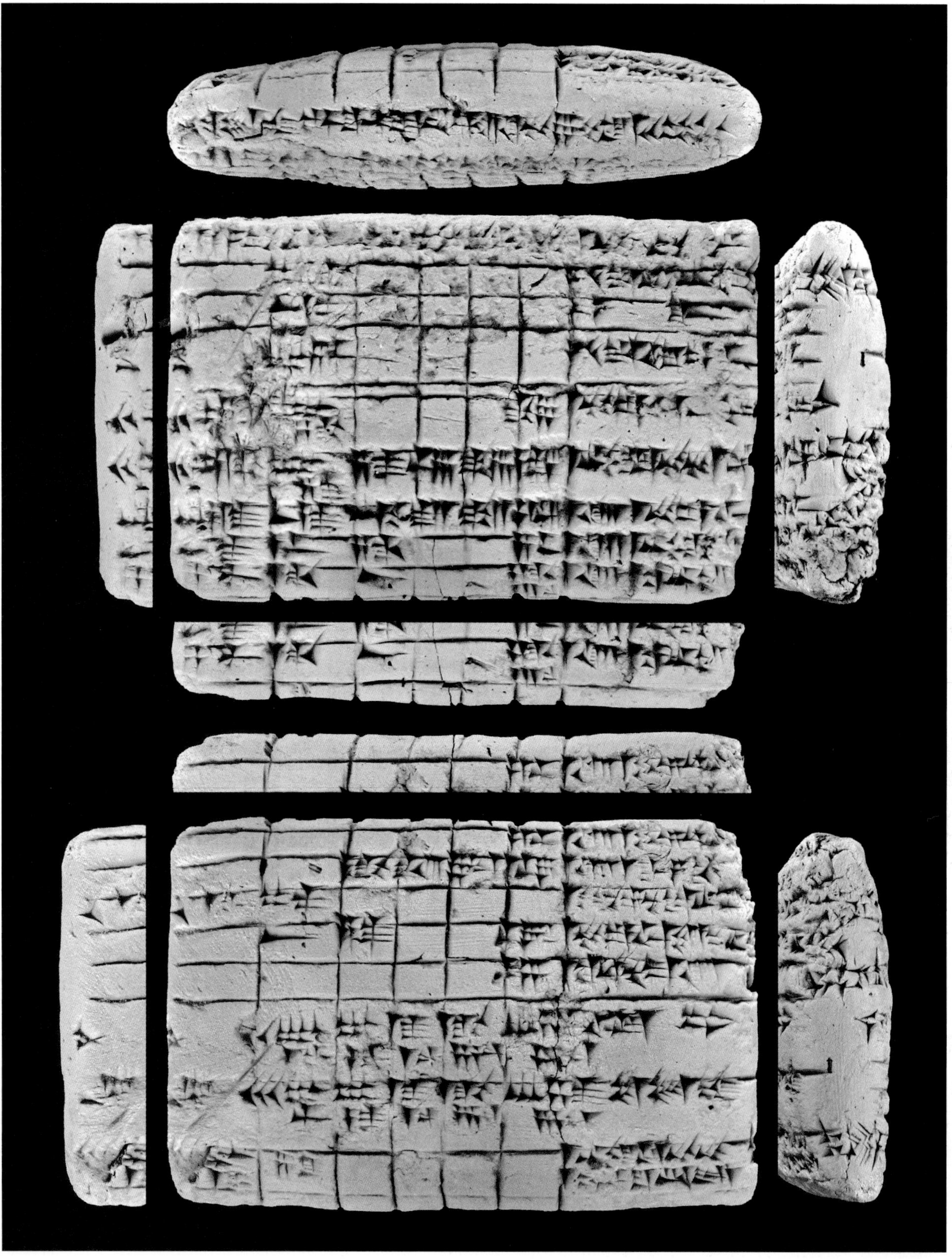

TEXT 5

Text 6

Text 8

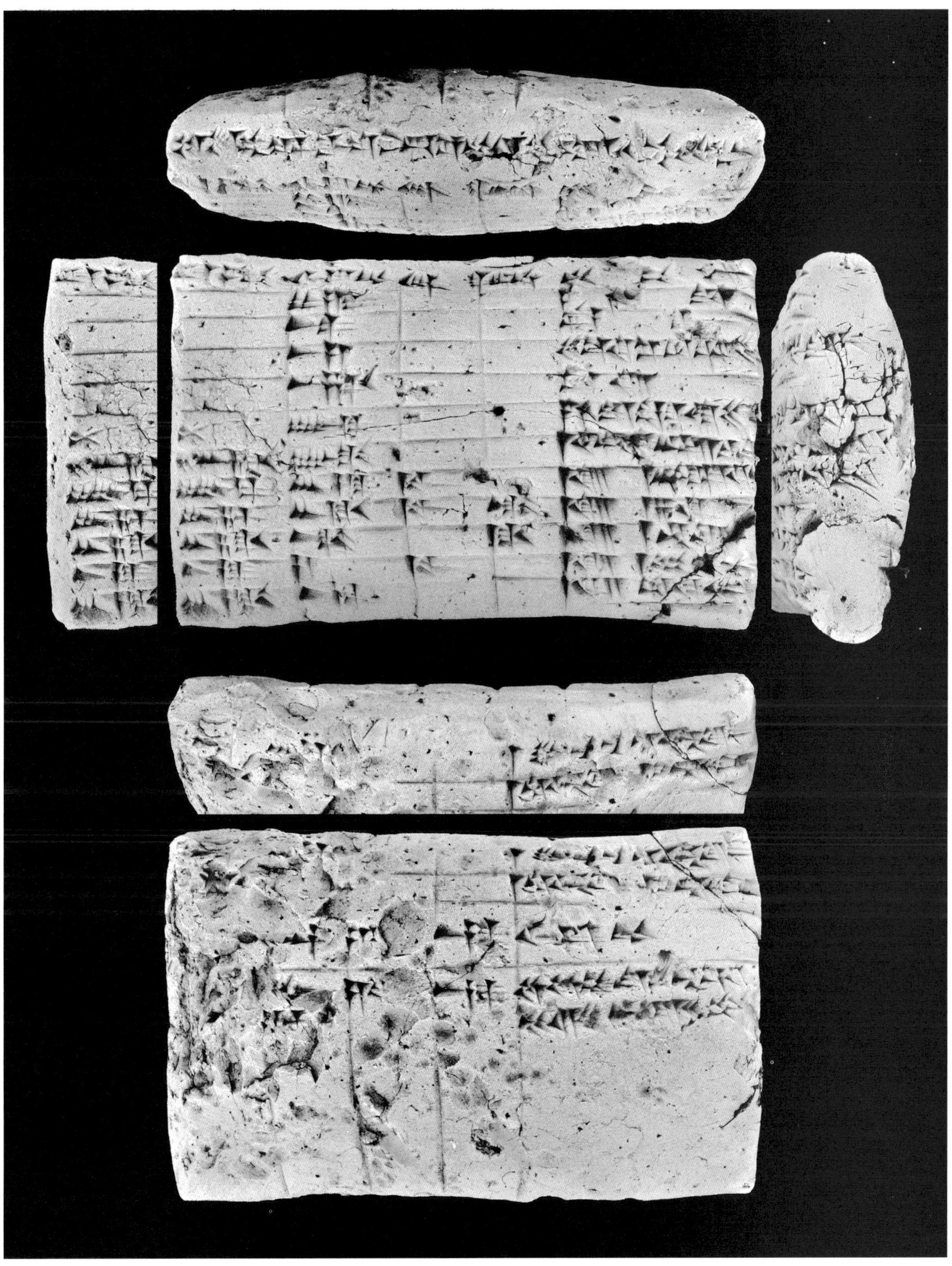

TEXT 11

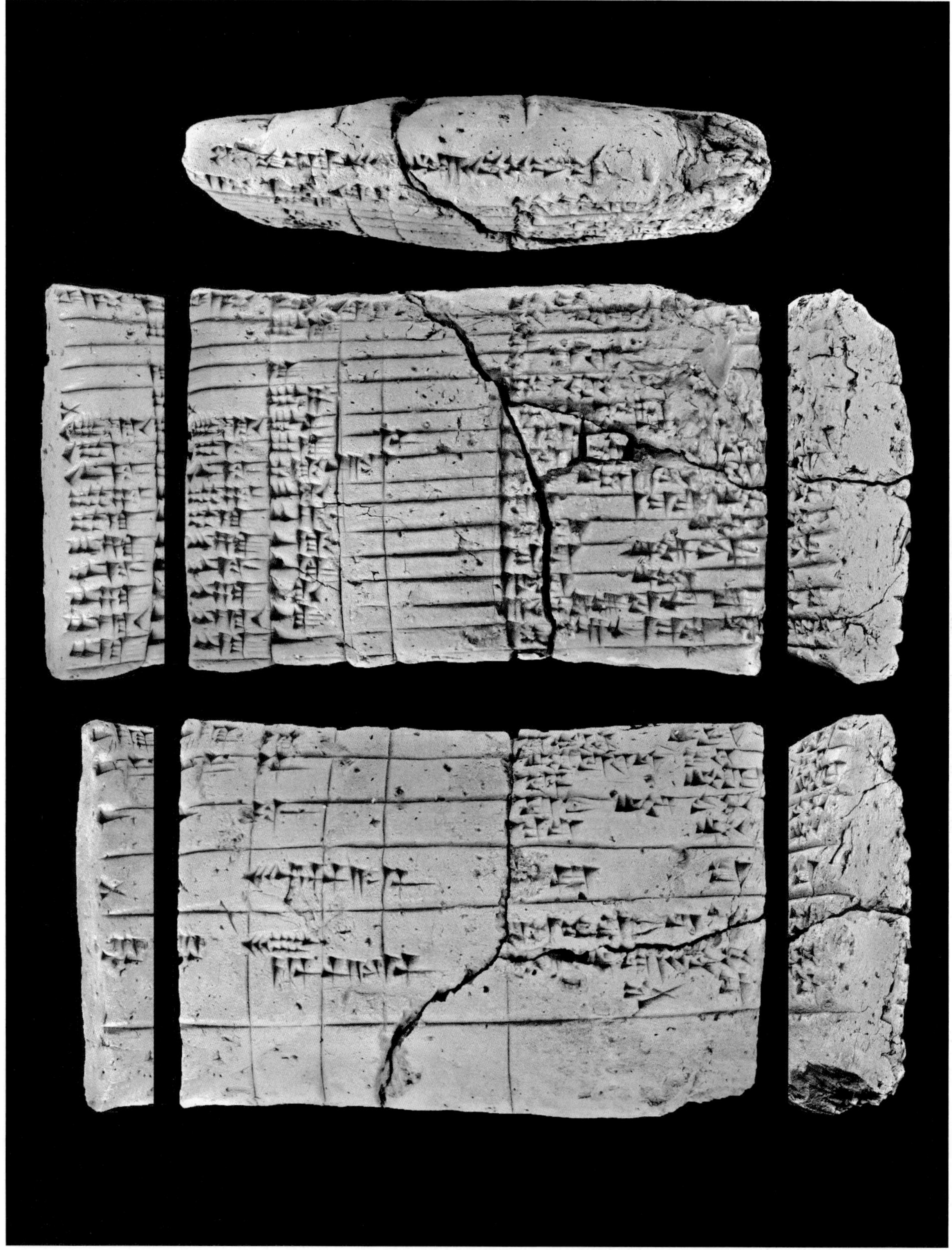

Text 12

# Plate 6

Text 17

Text 18

Text 19

TEXT 20

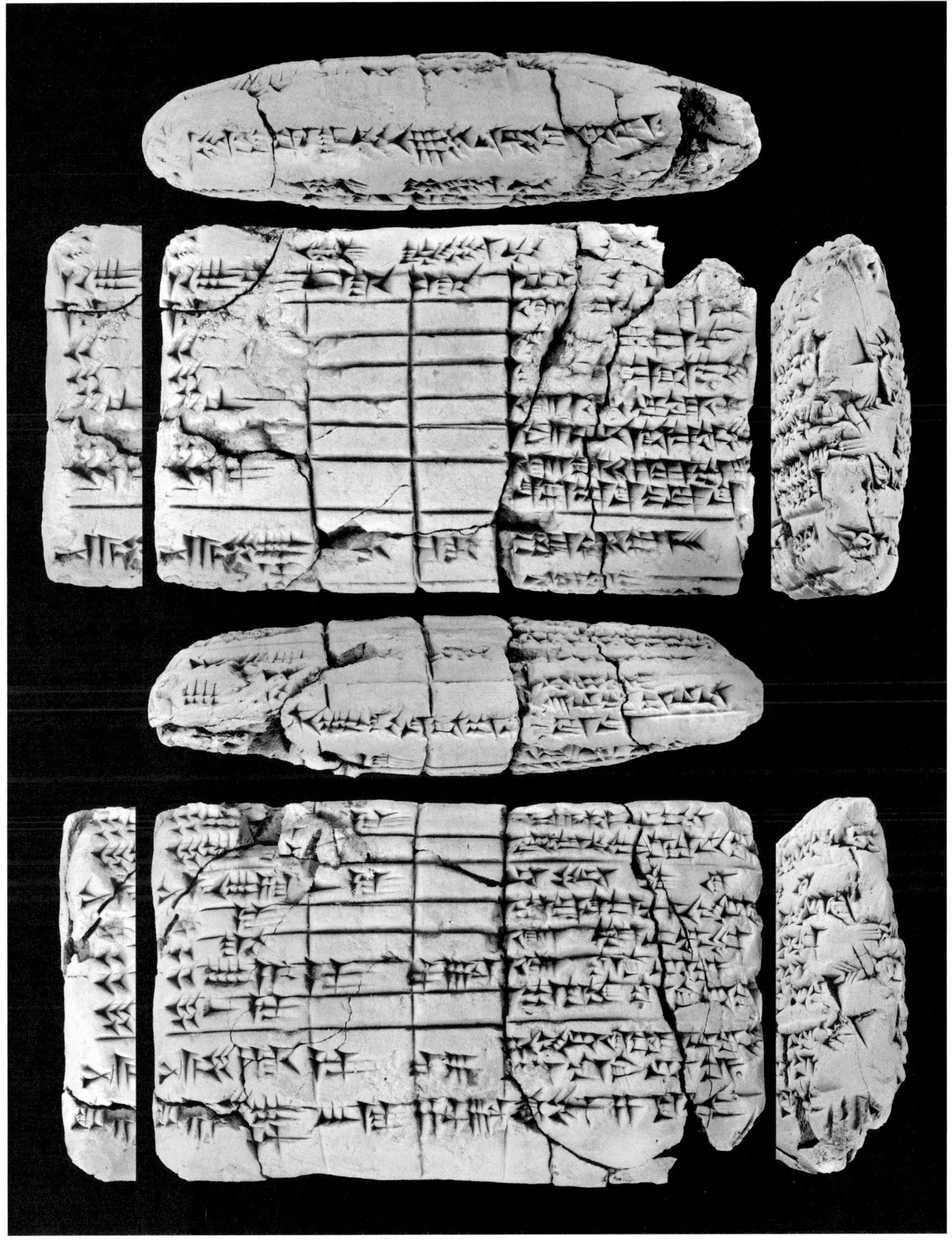

TEXT 22

# Plate 11

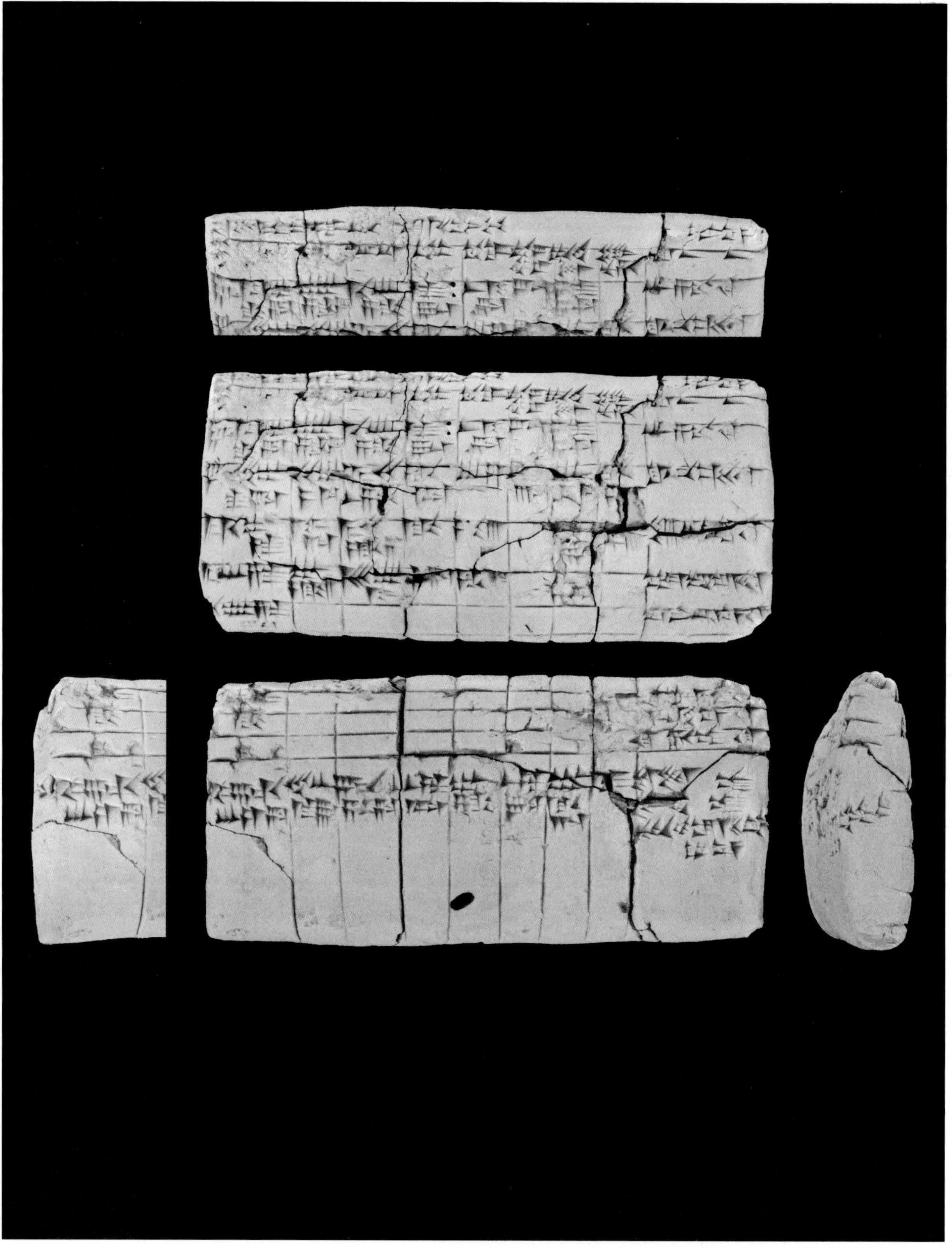

Text 23

TEXT 25

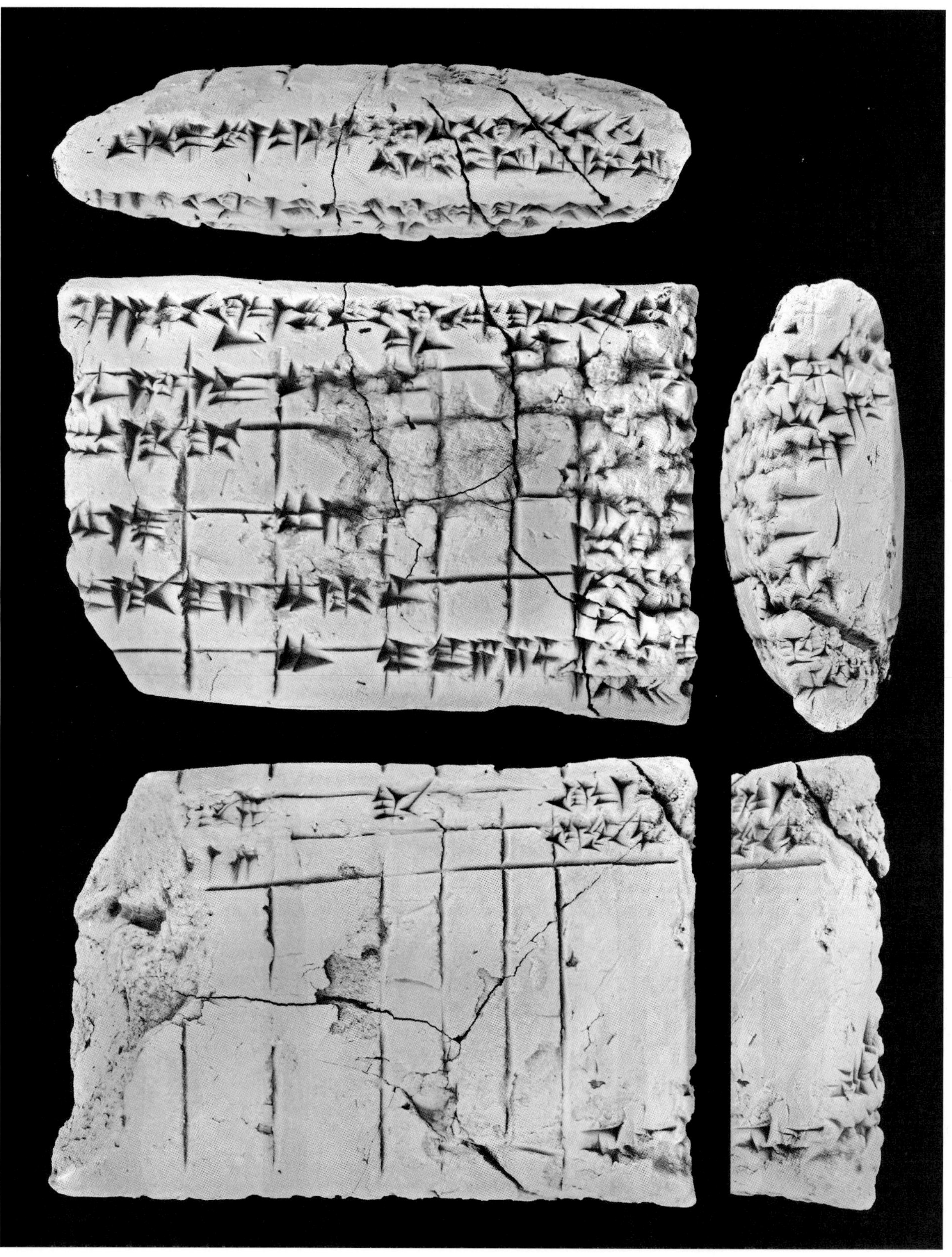

Text 27

Text 31

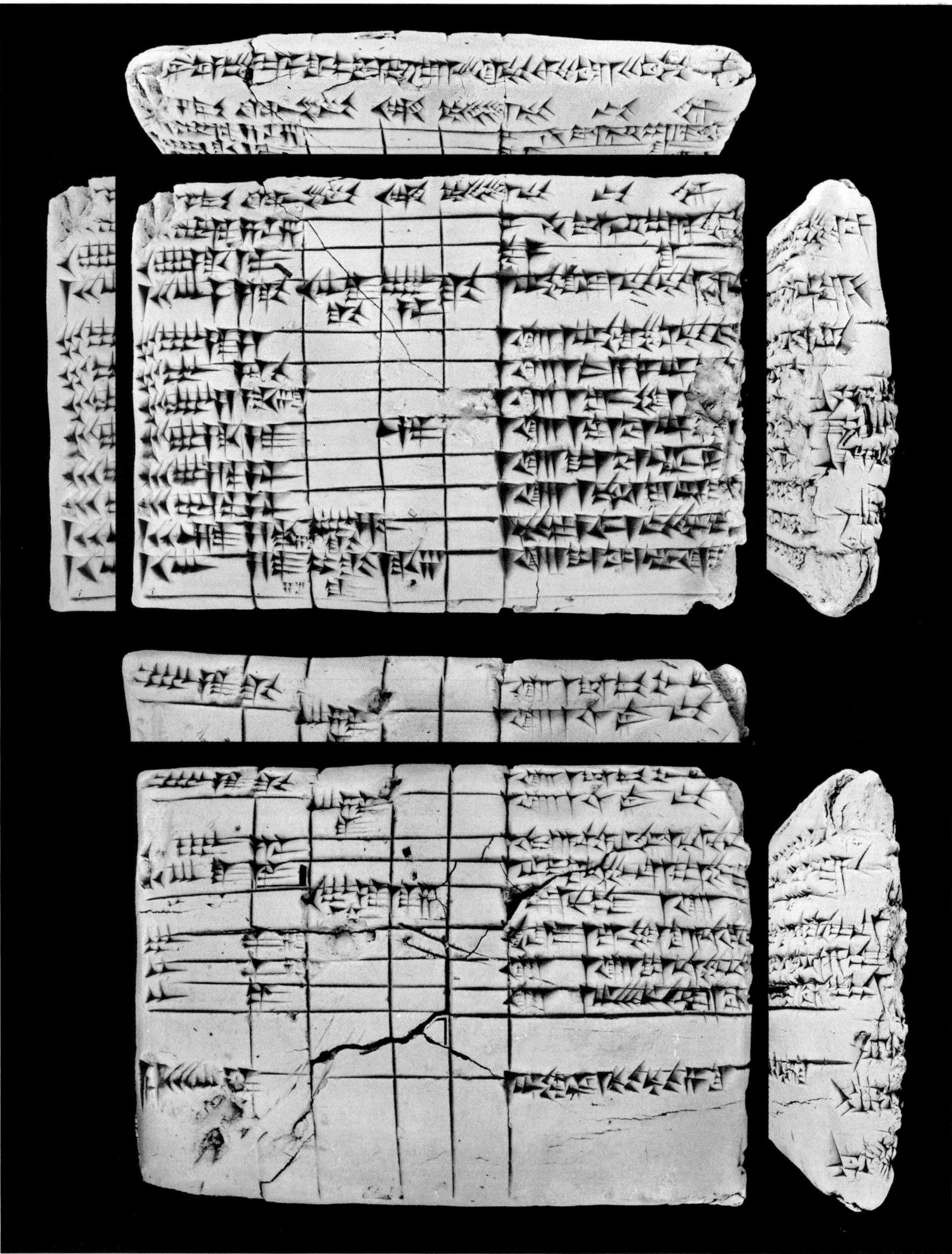

TEXT 32

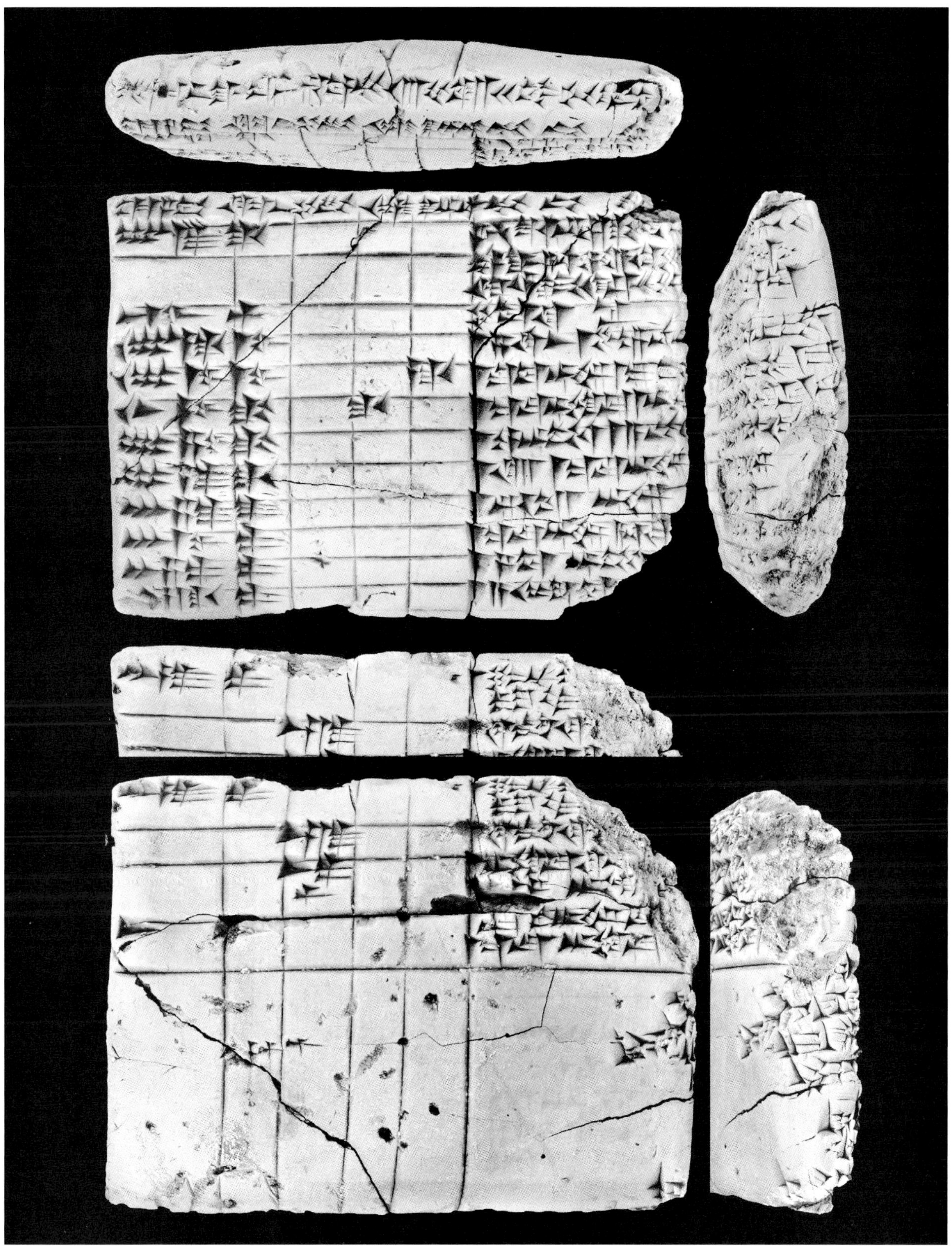

TEXT 35

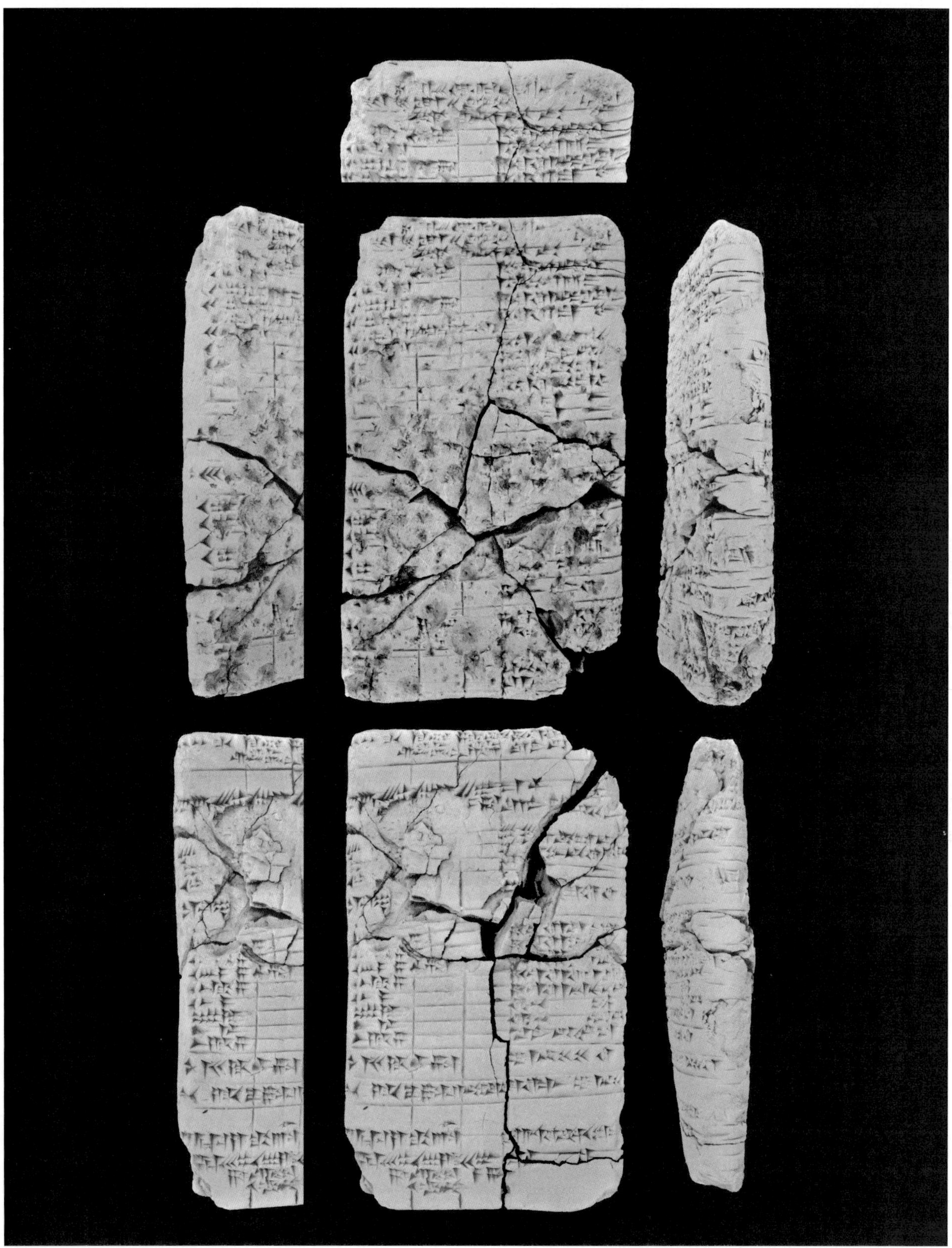

TEXT 37

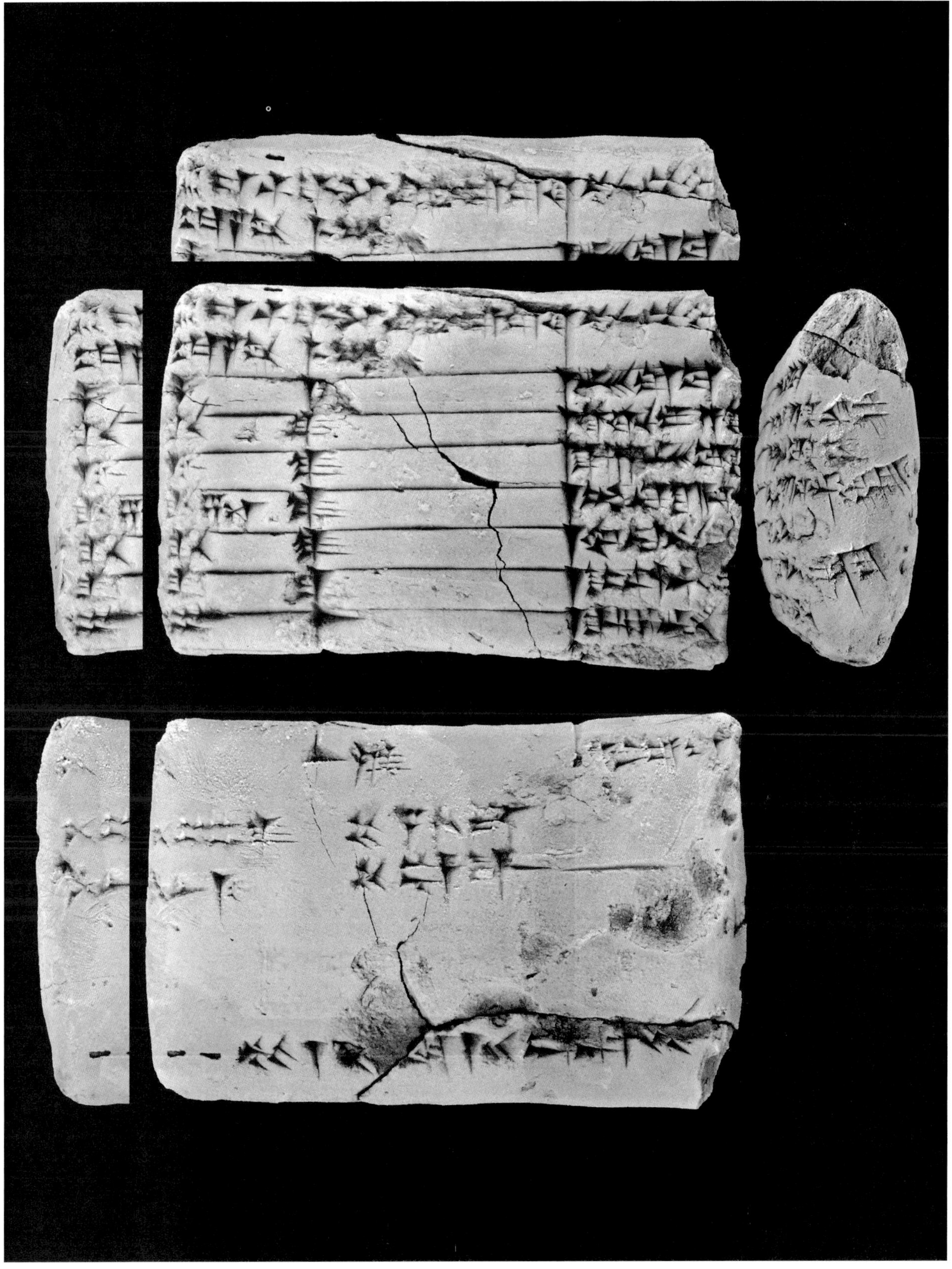

TEXT 43

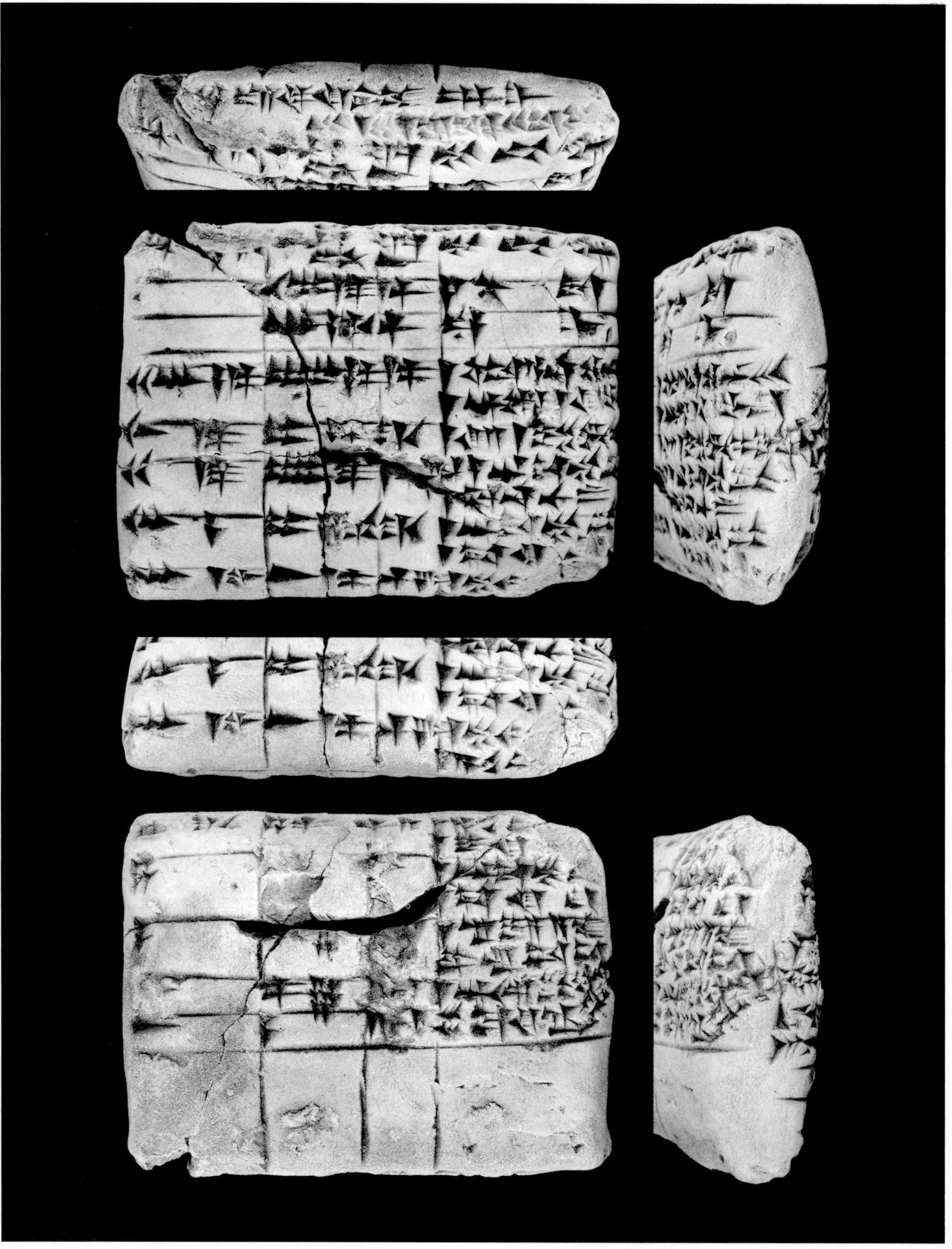

Text 44

TEXT 46

TEXT 48

Text 49

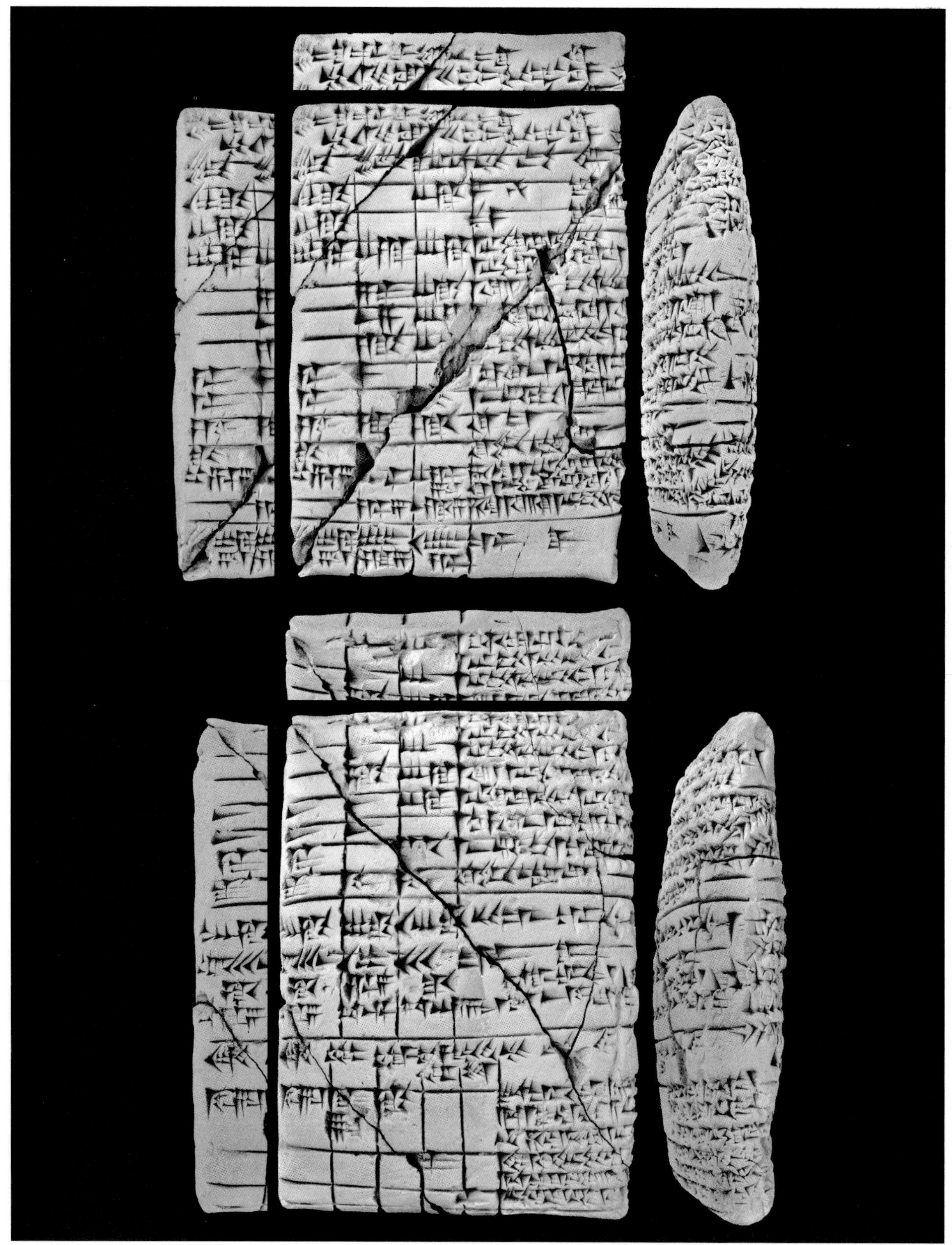

Text 52

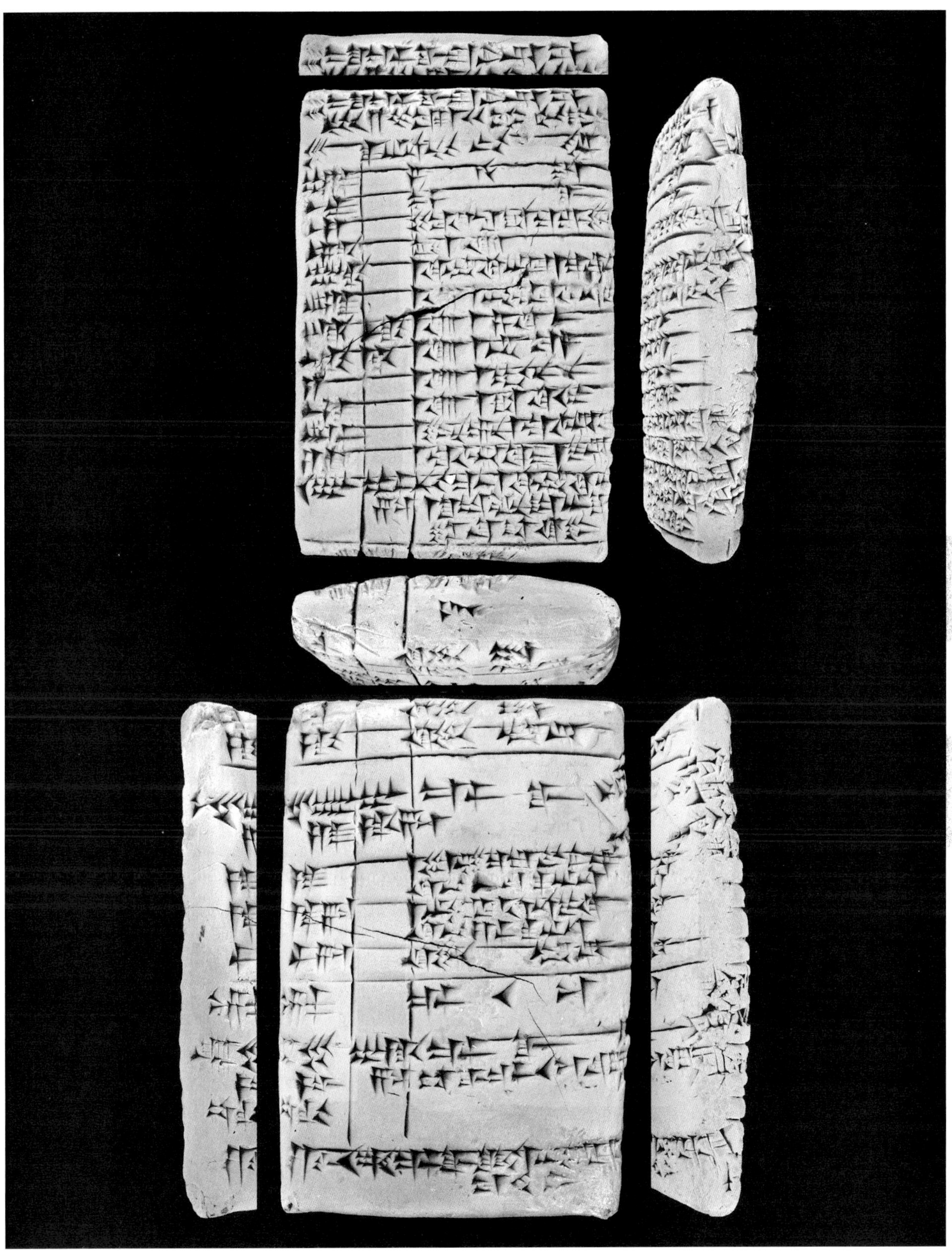

Text 54

Text 59

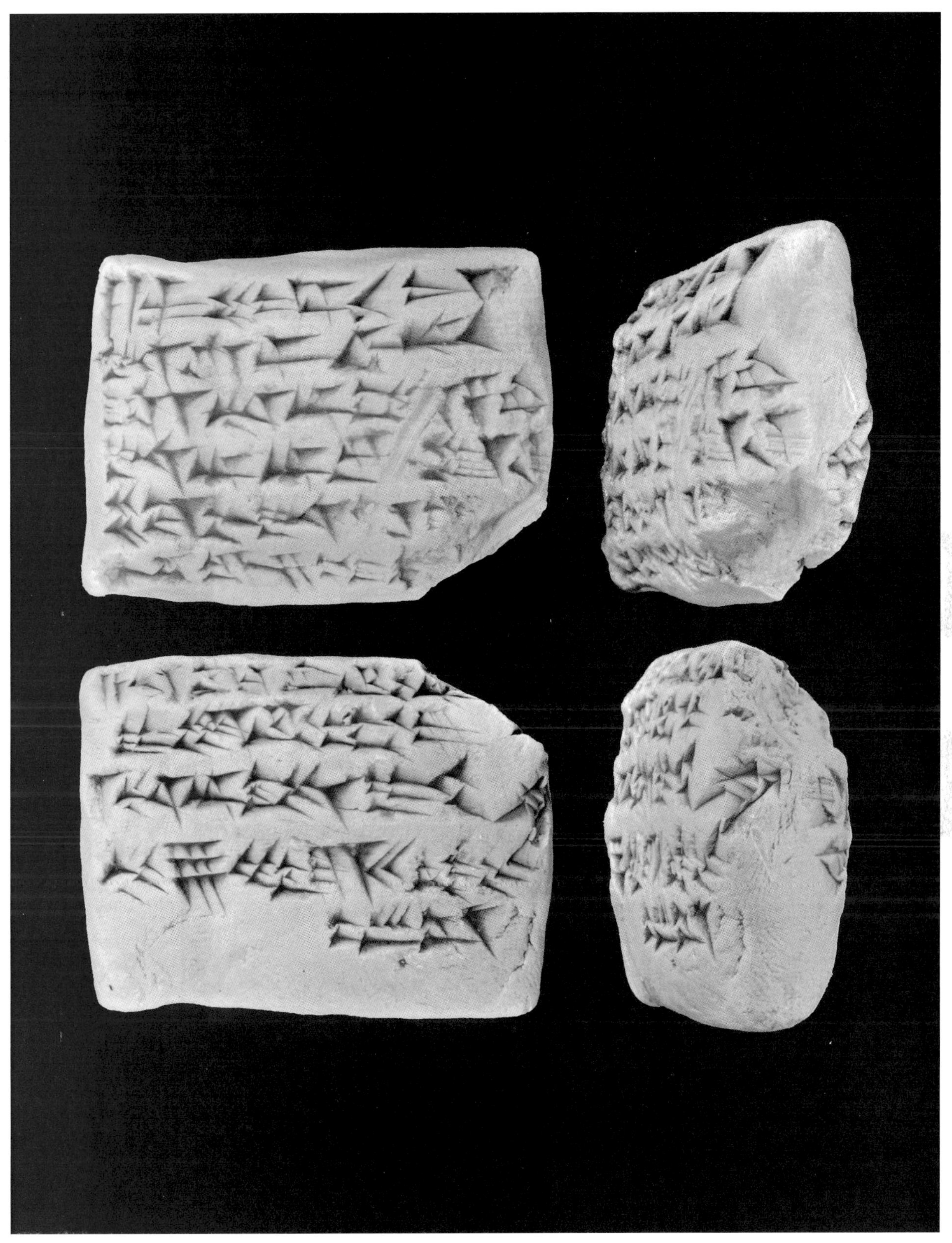

Text 69

Text 81

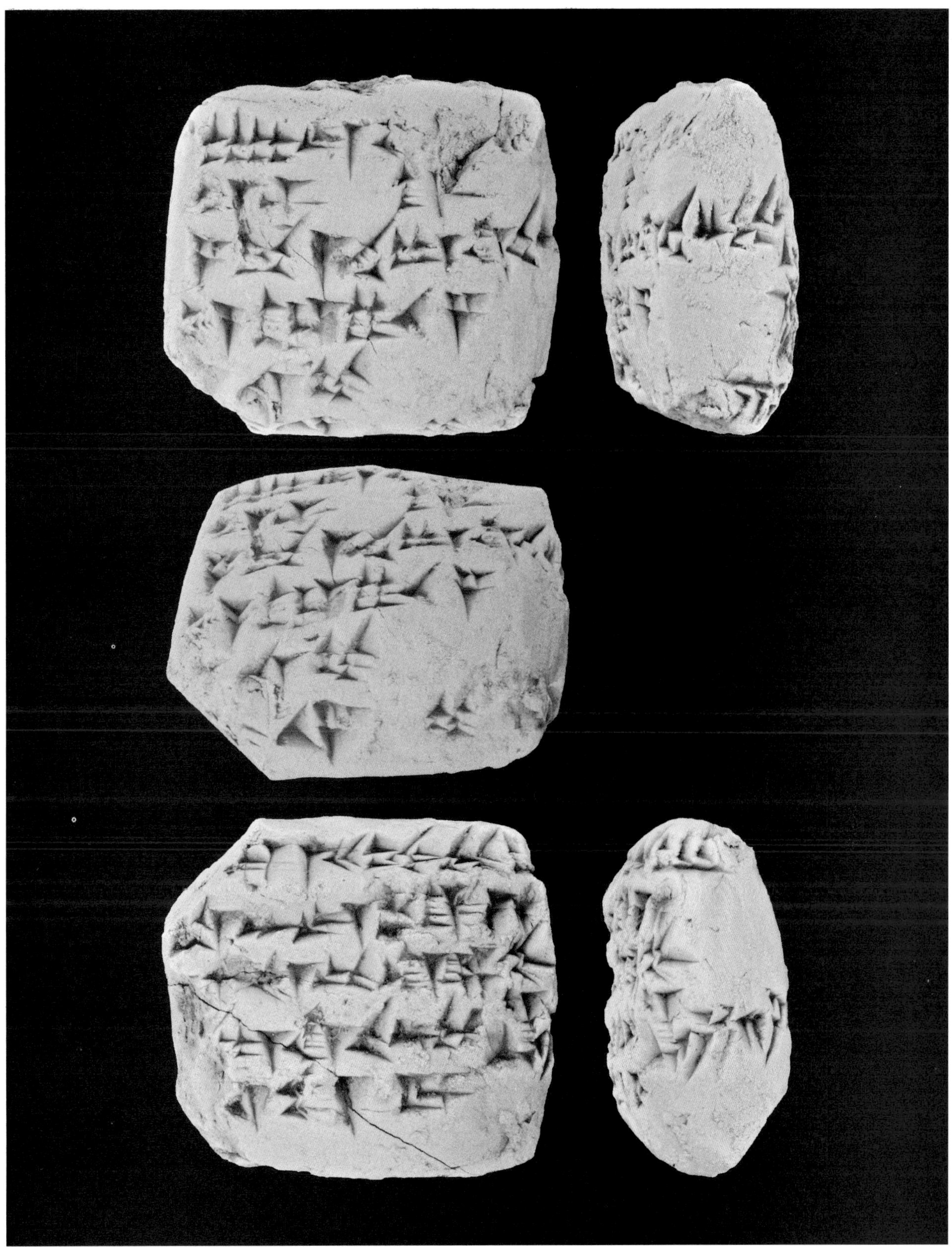

TEXT 82

Text 87

TEXT 93

TEXT 95

Text 96

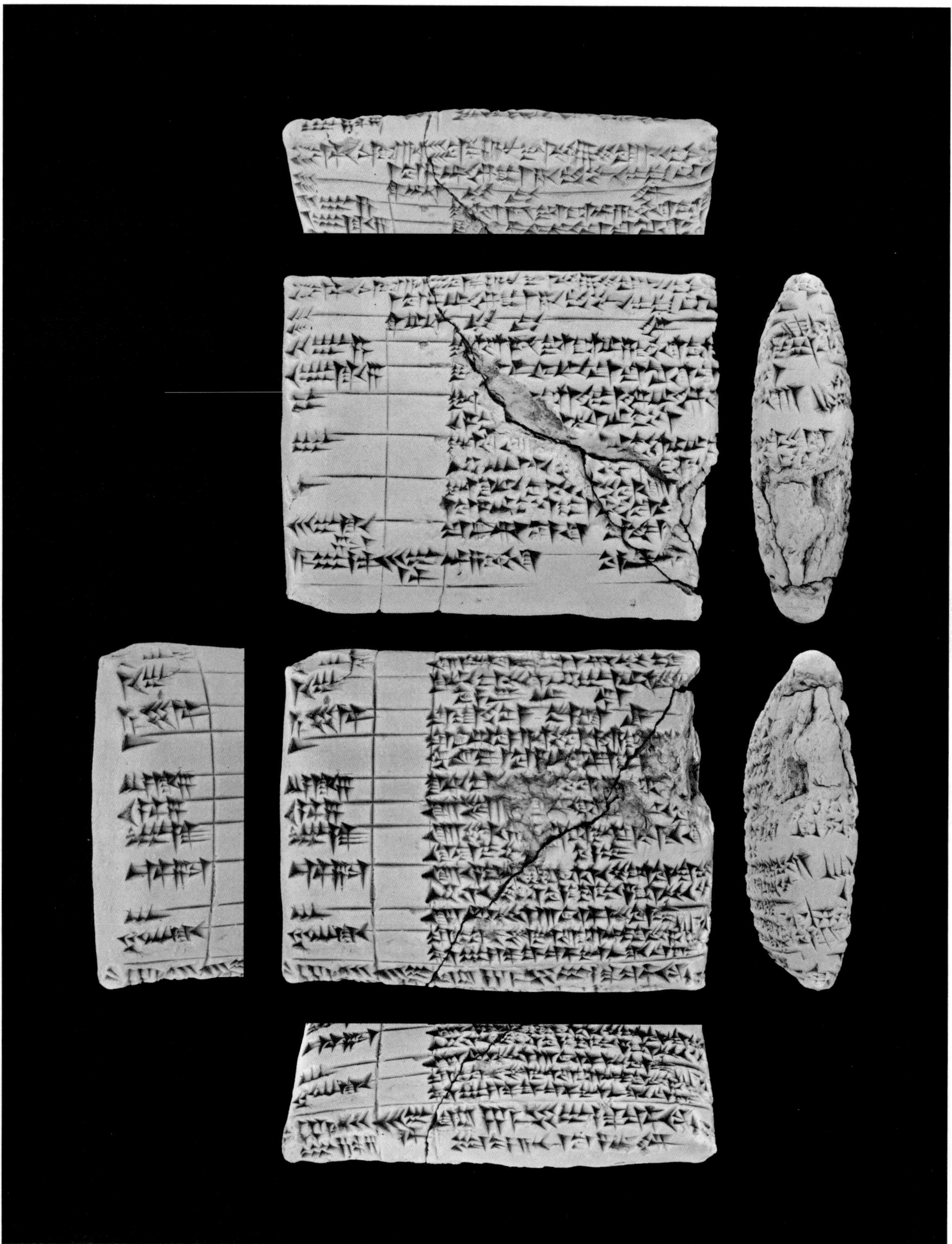

TEXT 97

Text 98

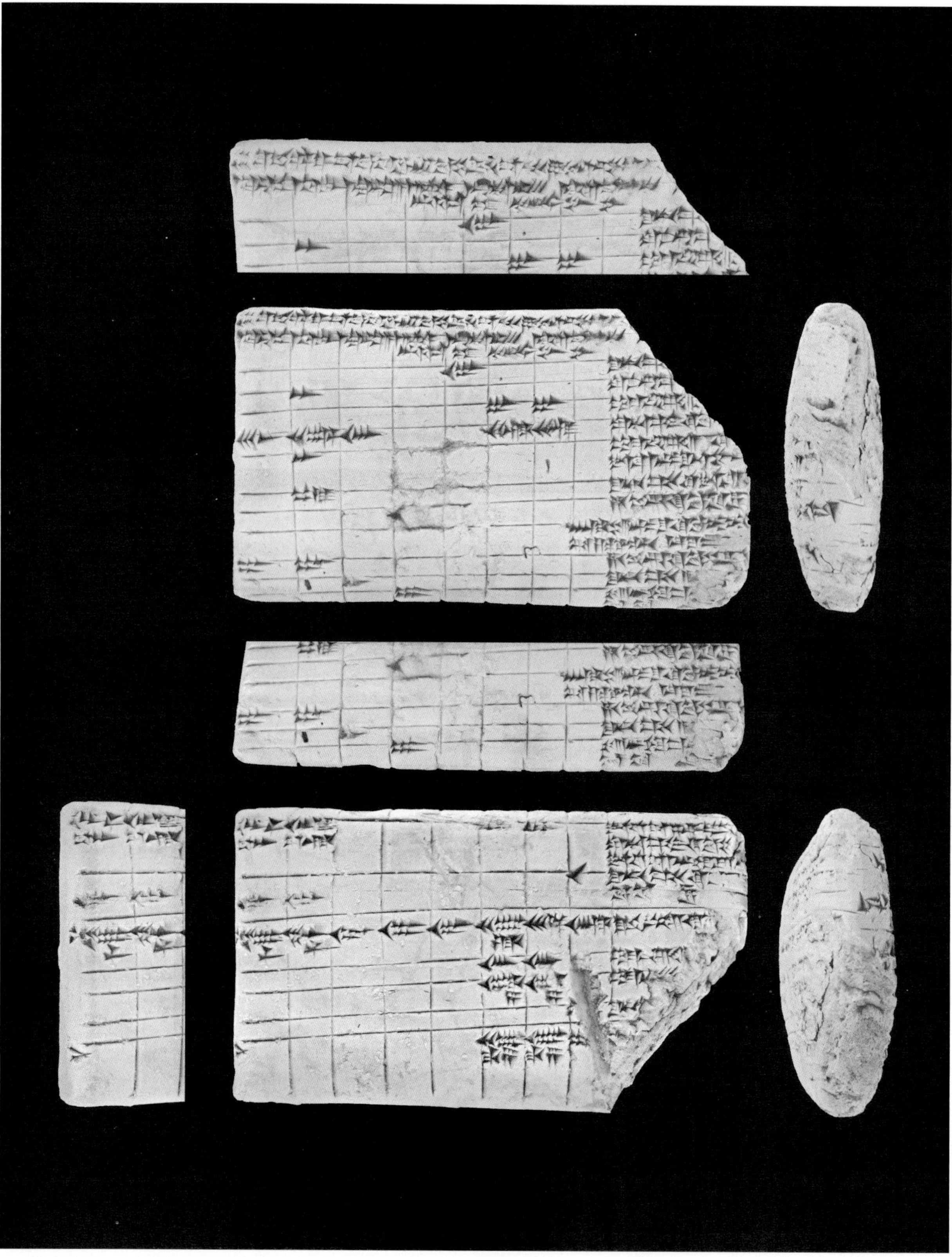

Text 112

TEXT 118

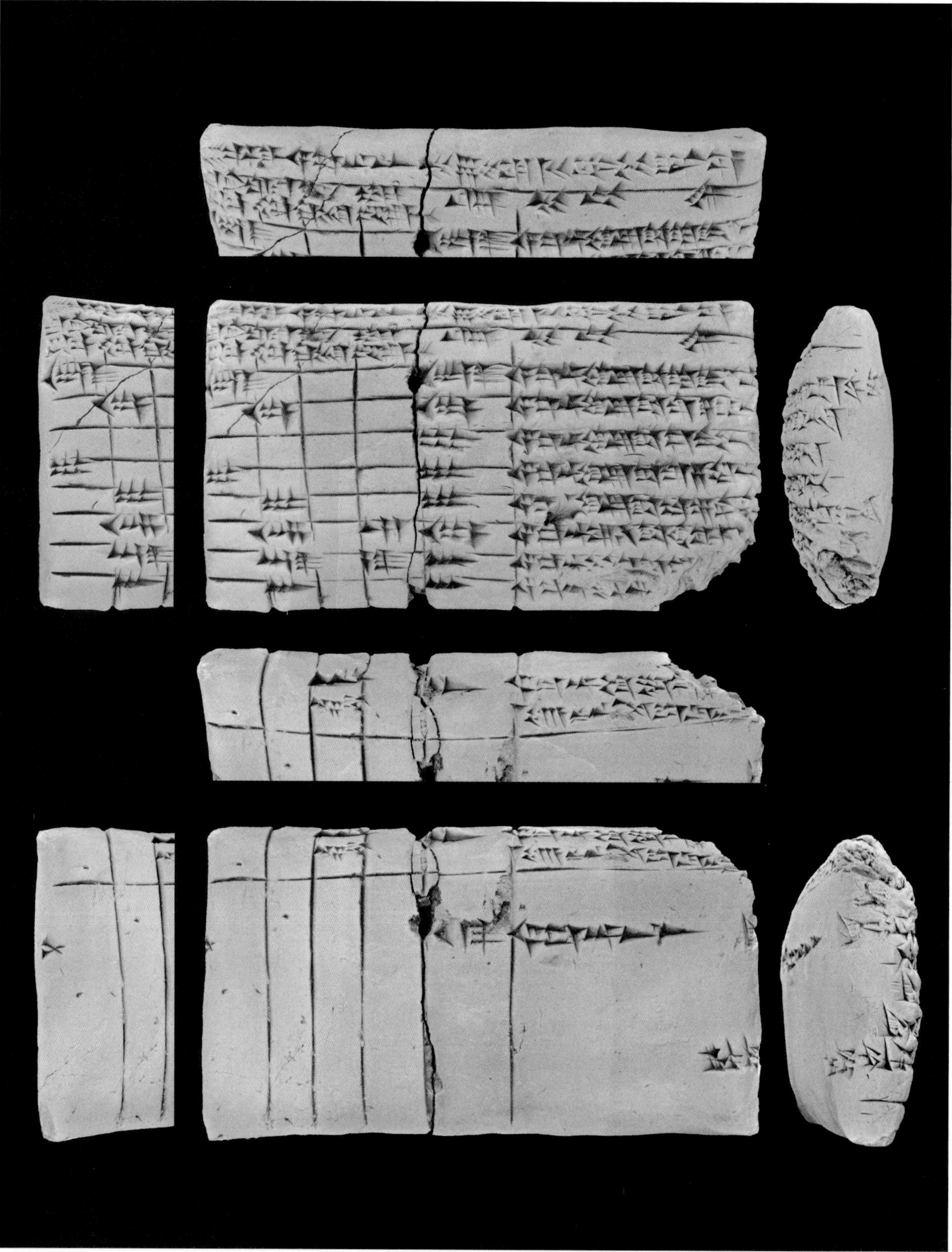

TEXT 119

Text 122

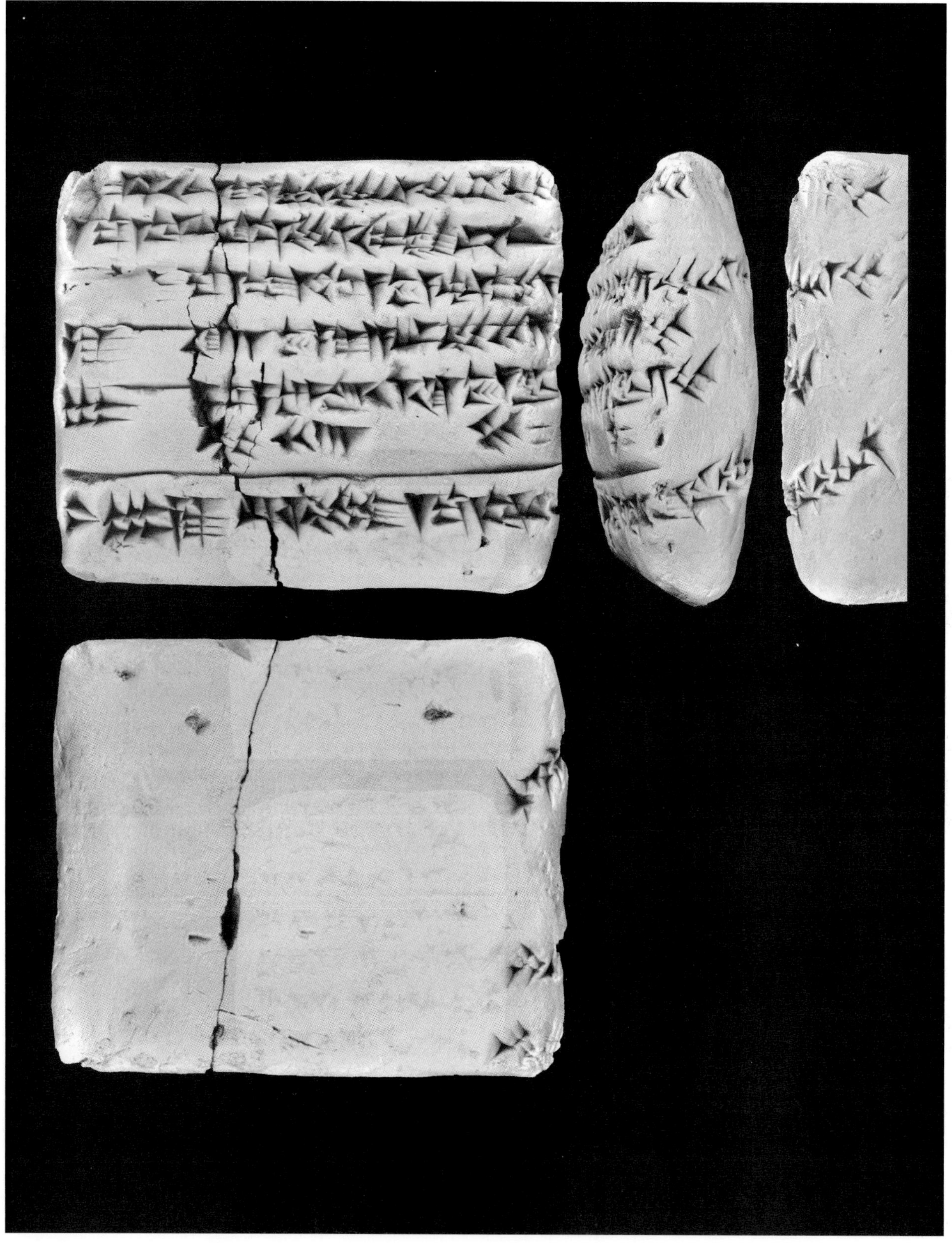

Text 125

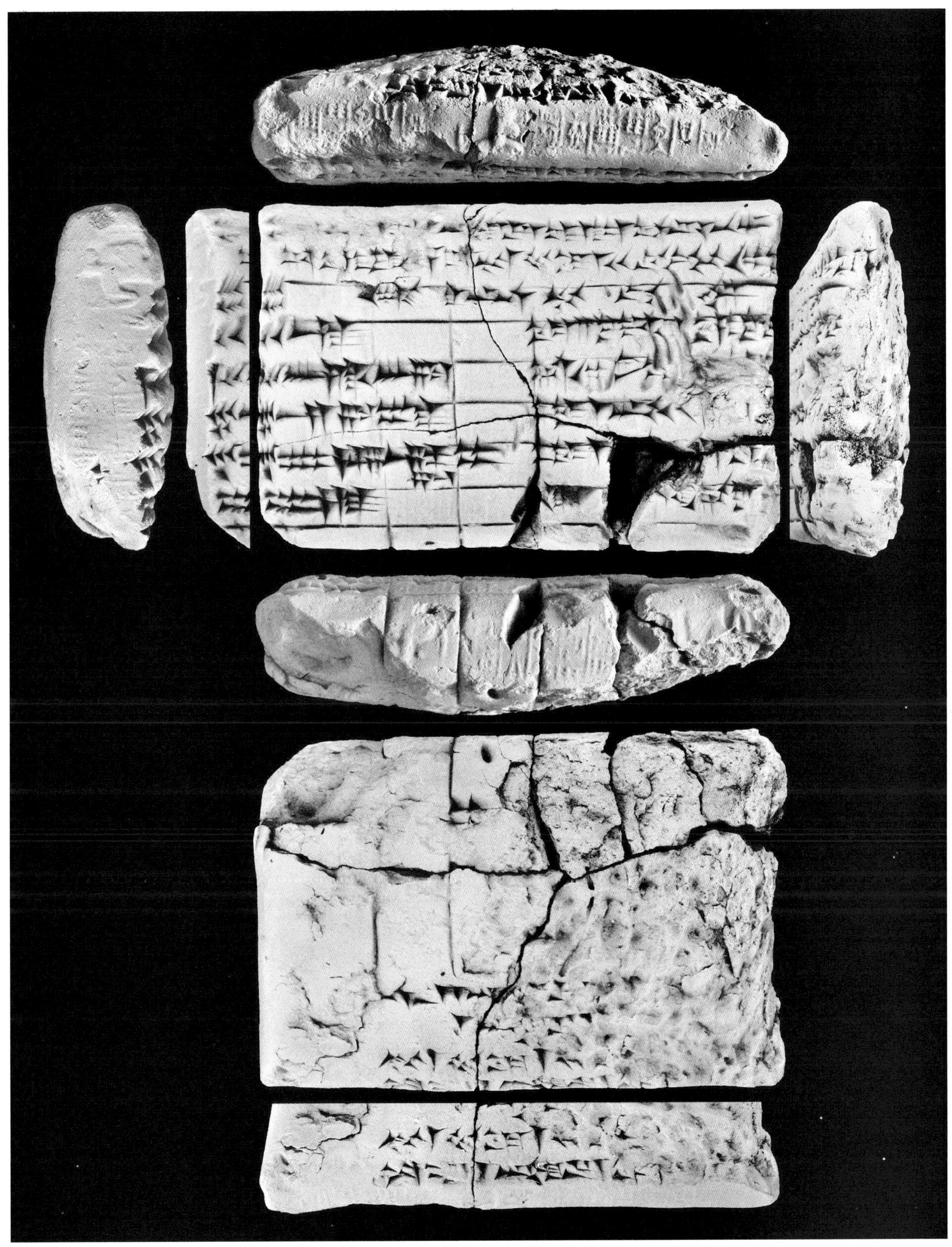

Text 143

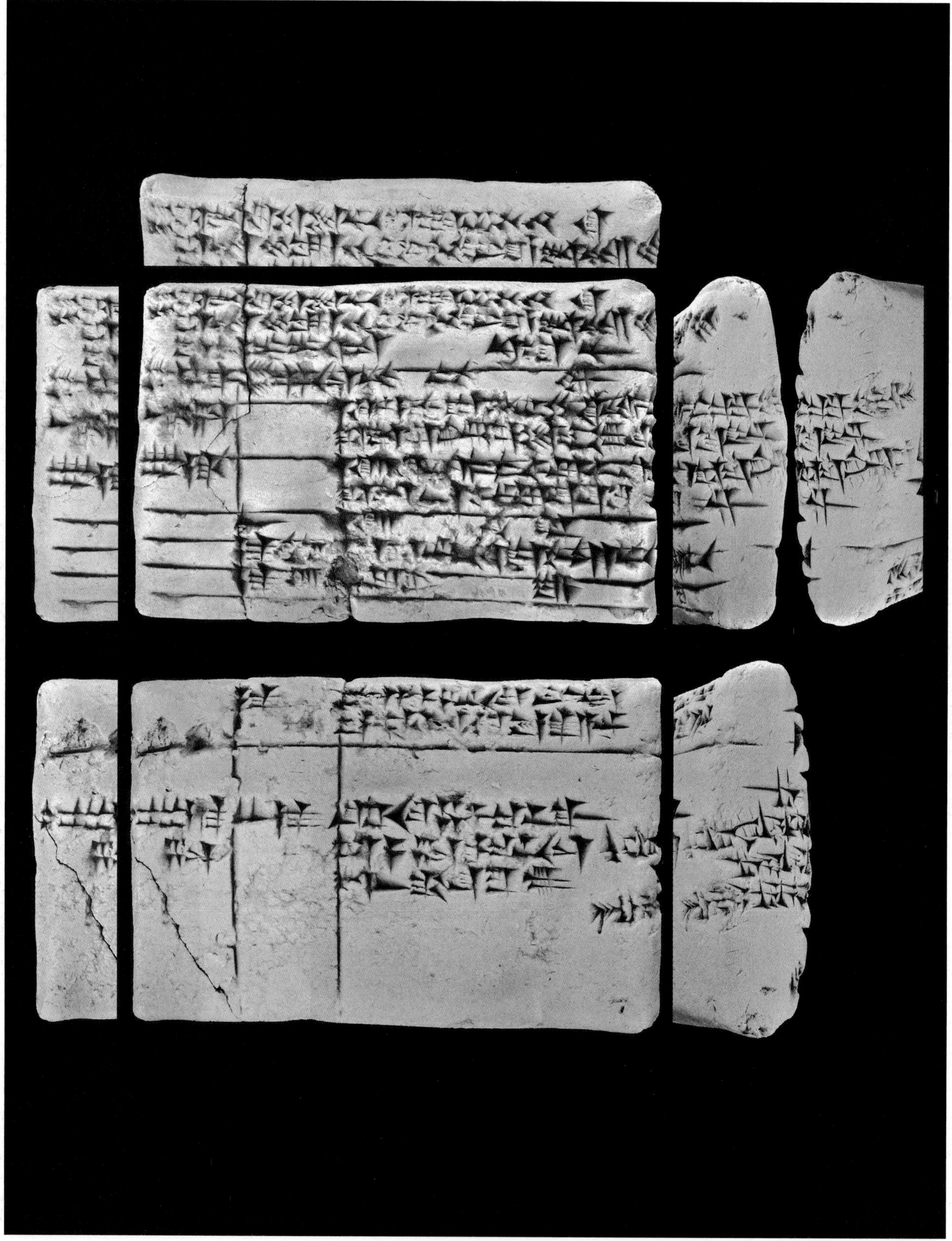

Text 148

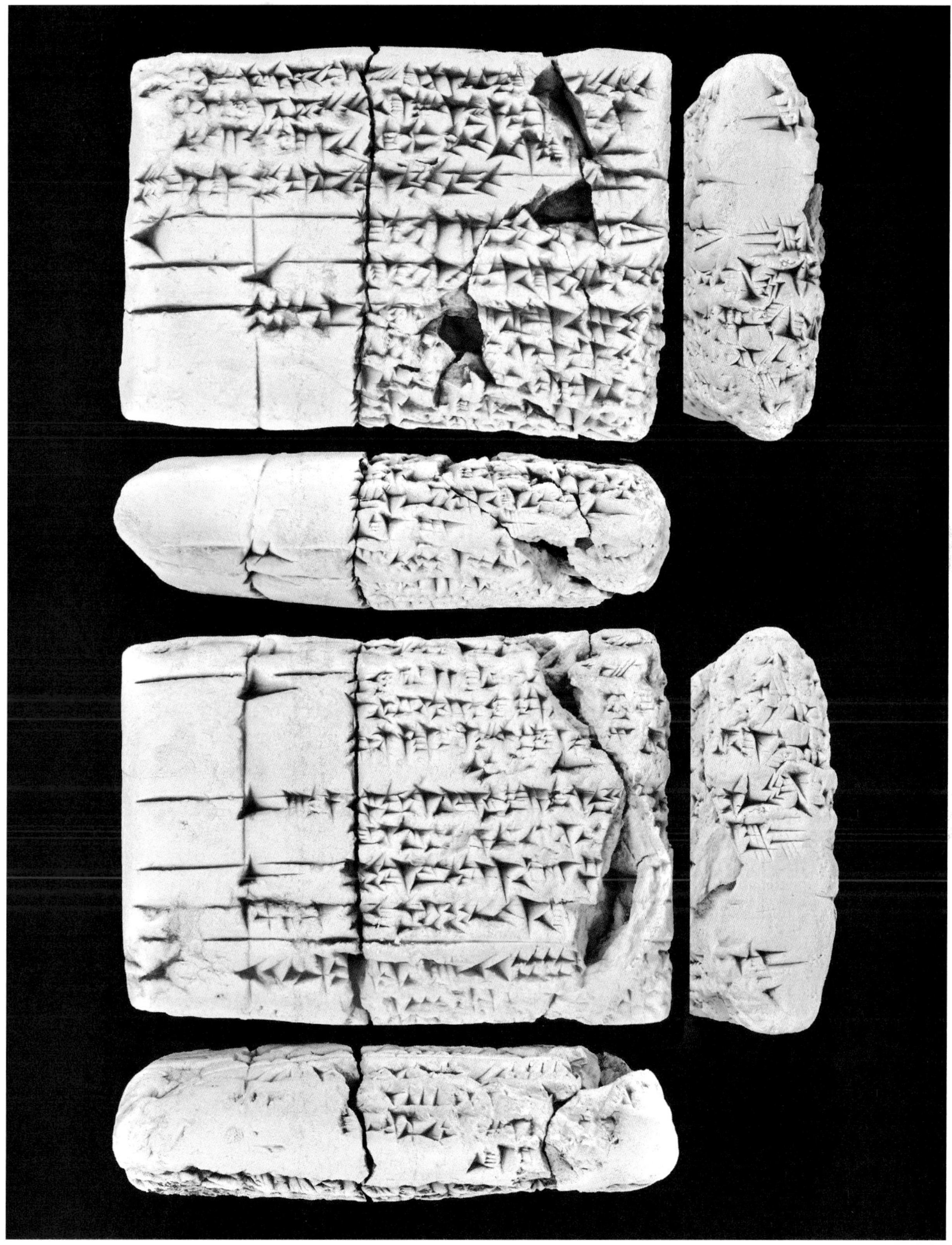

Text 149

Text 150

TEXT 154

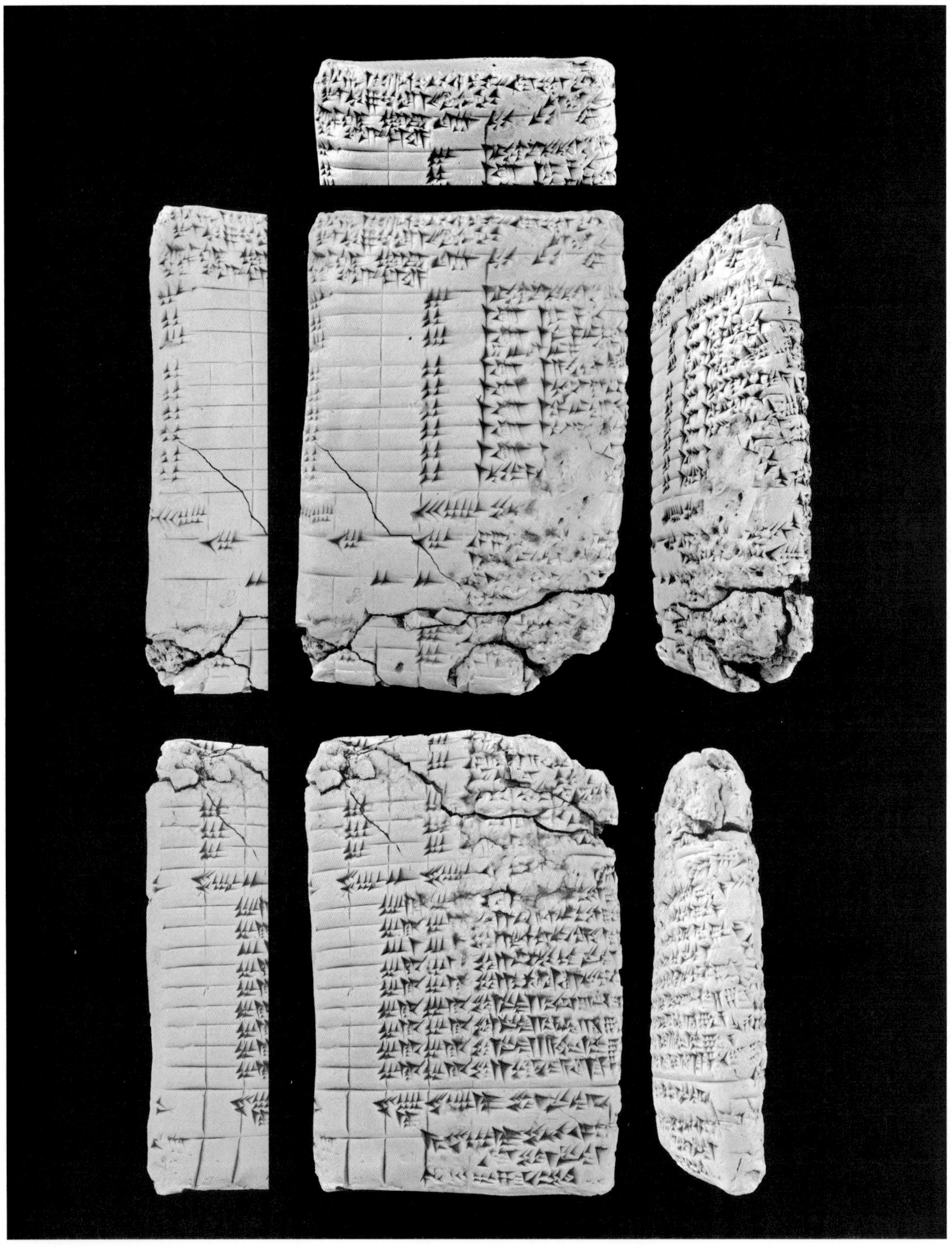

TEXT 156

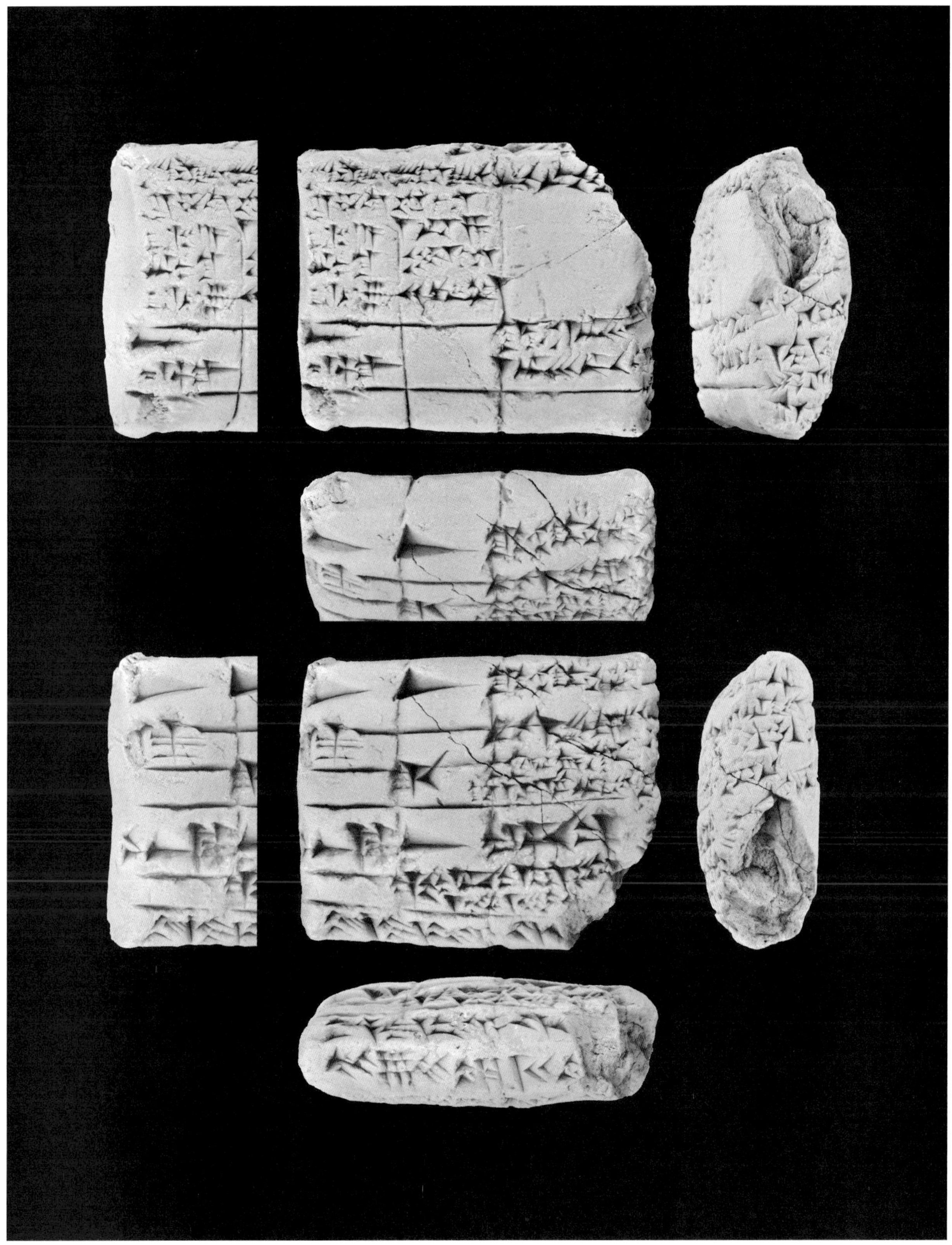

TEXT 160

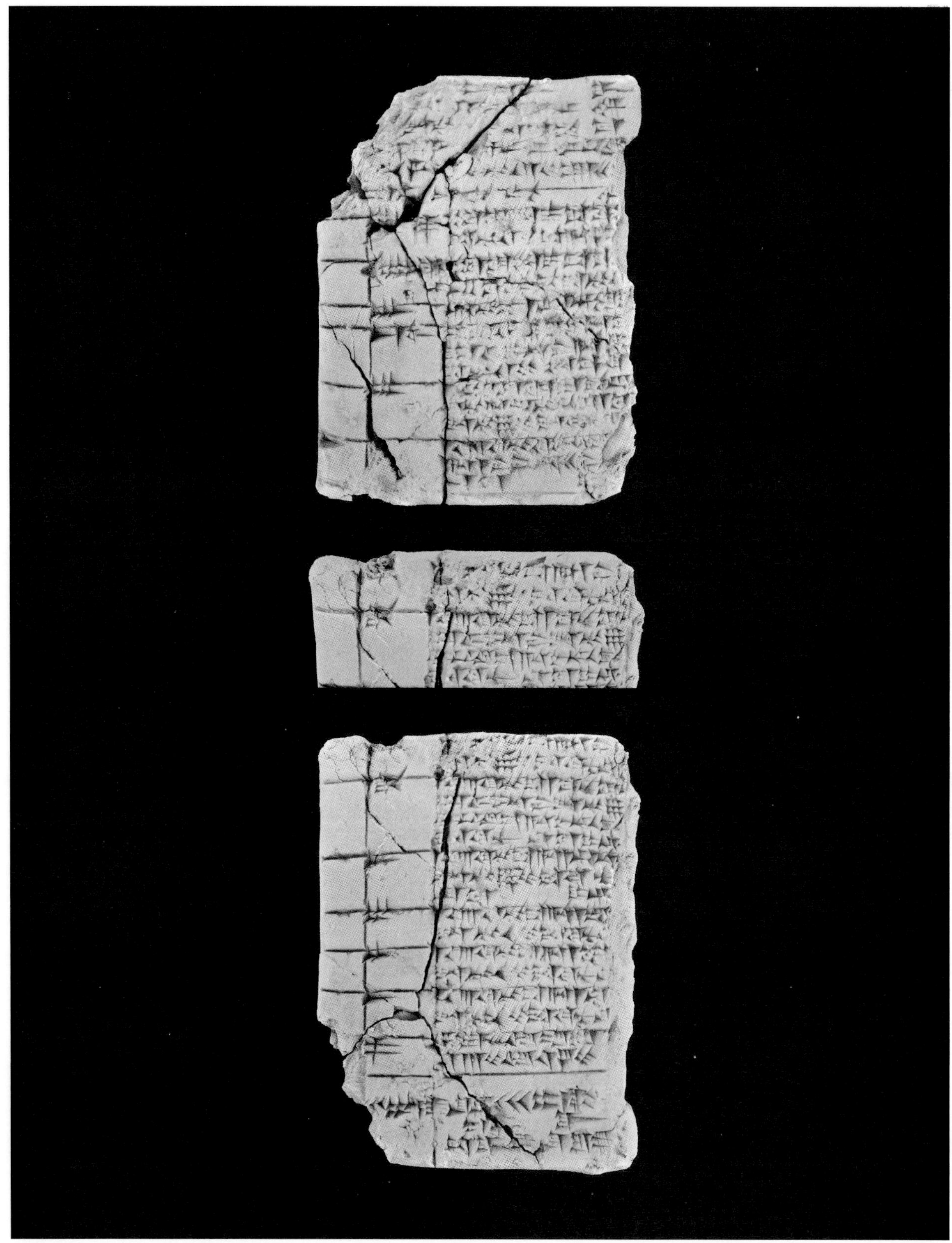

TEXT 170

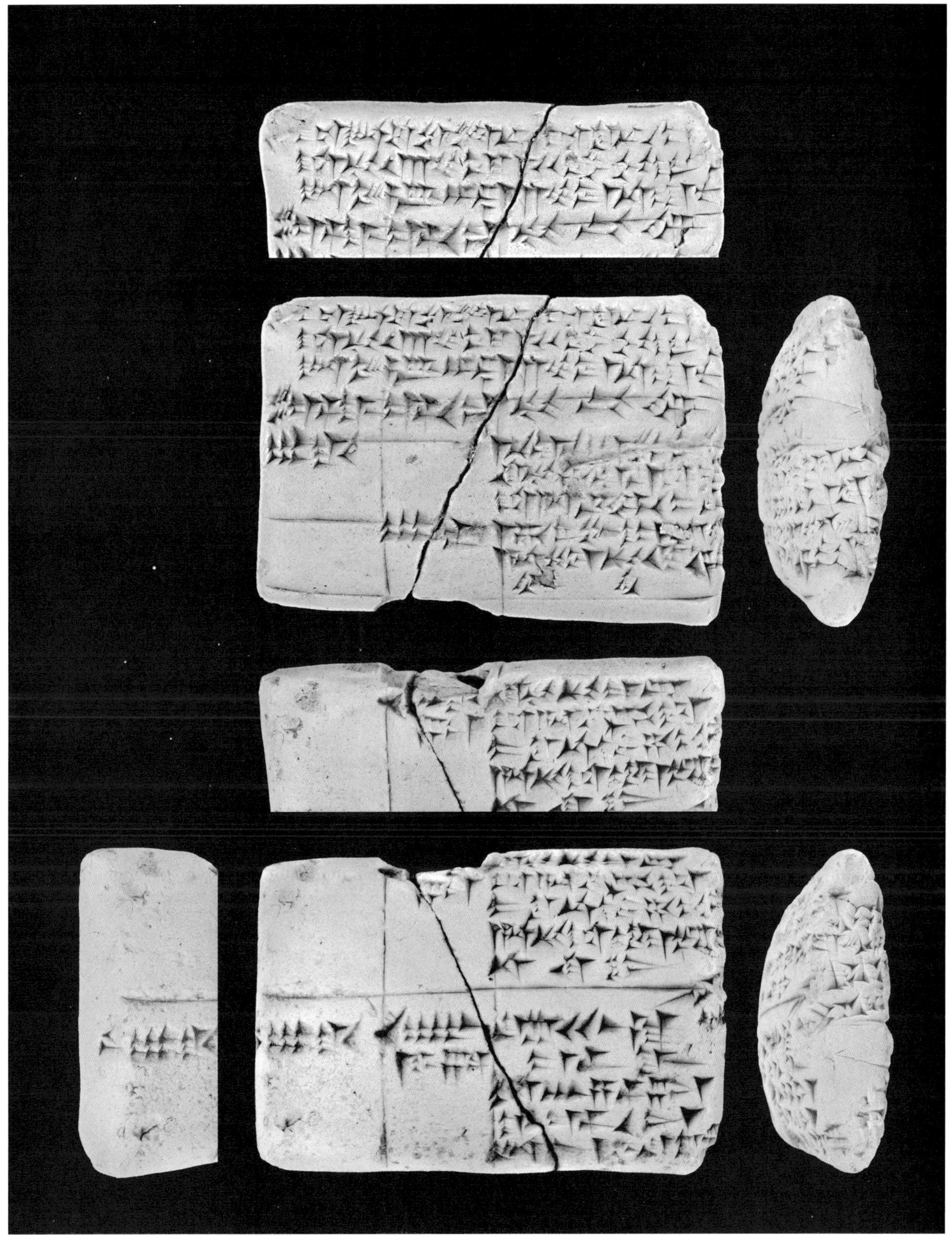

Text 175

# PLATE 49

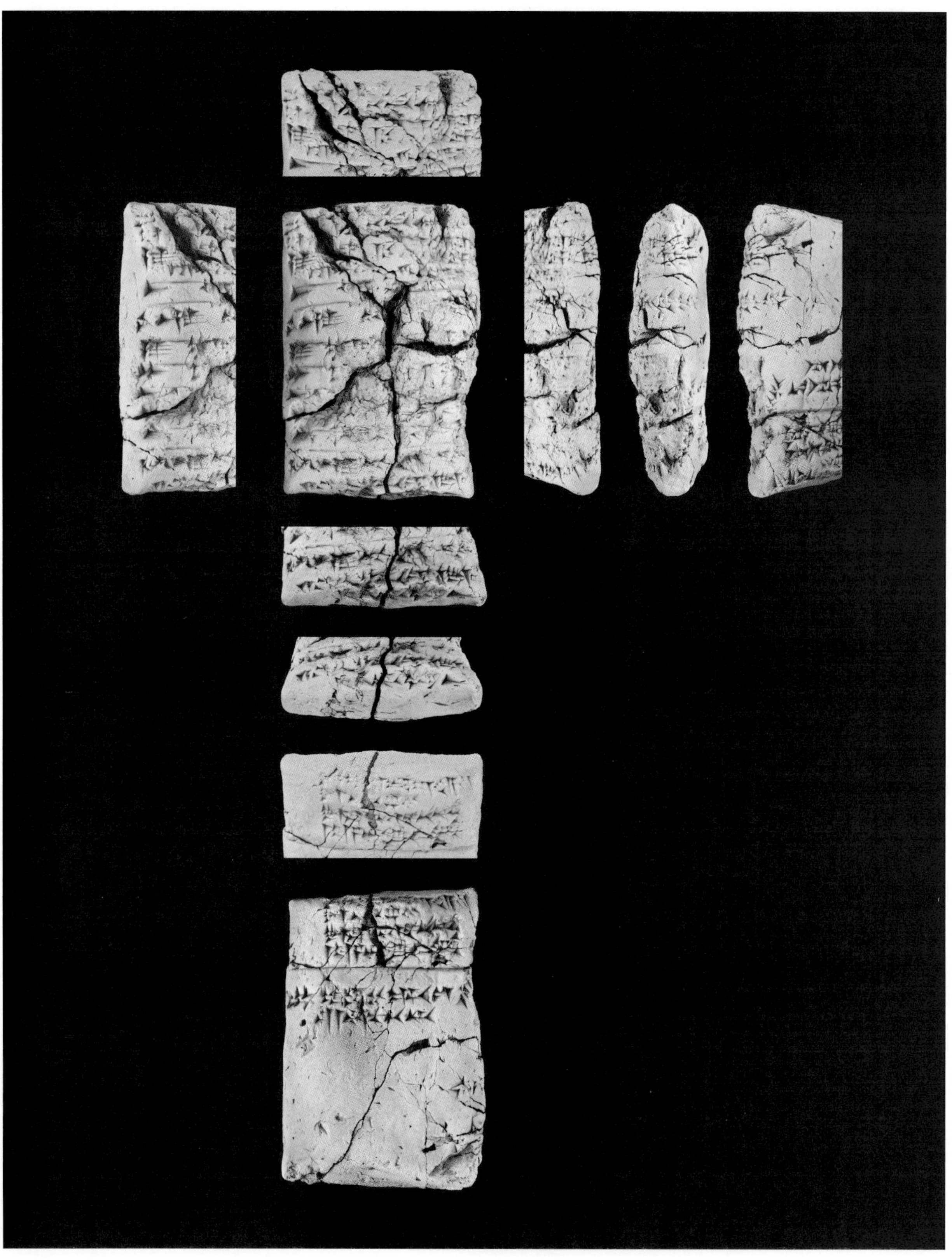

TEXT 178

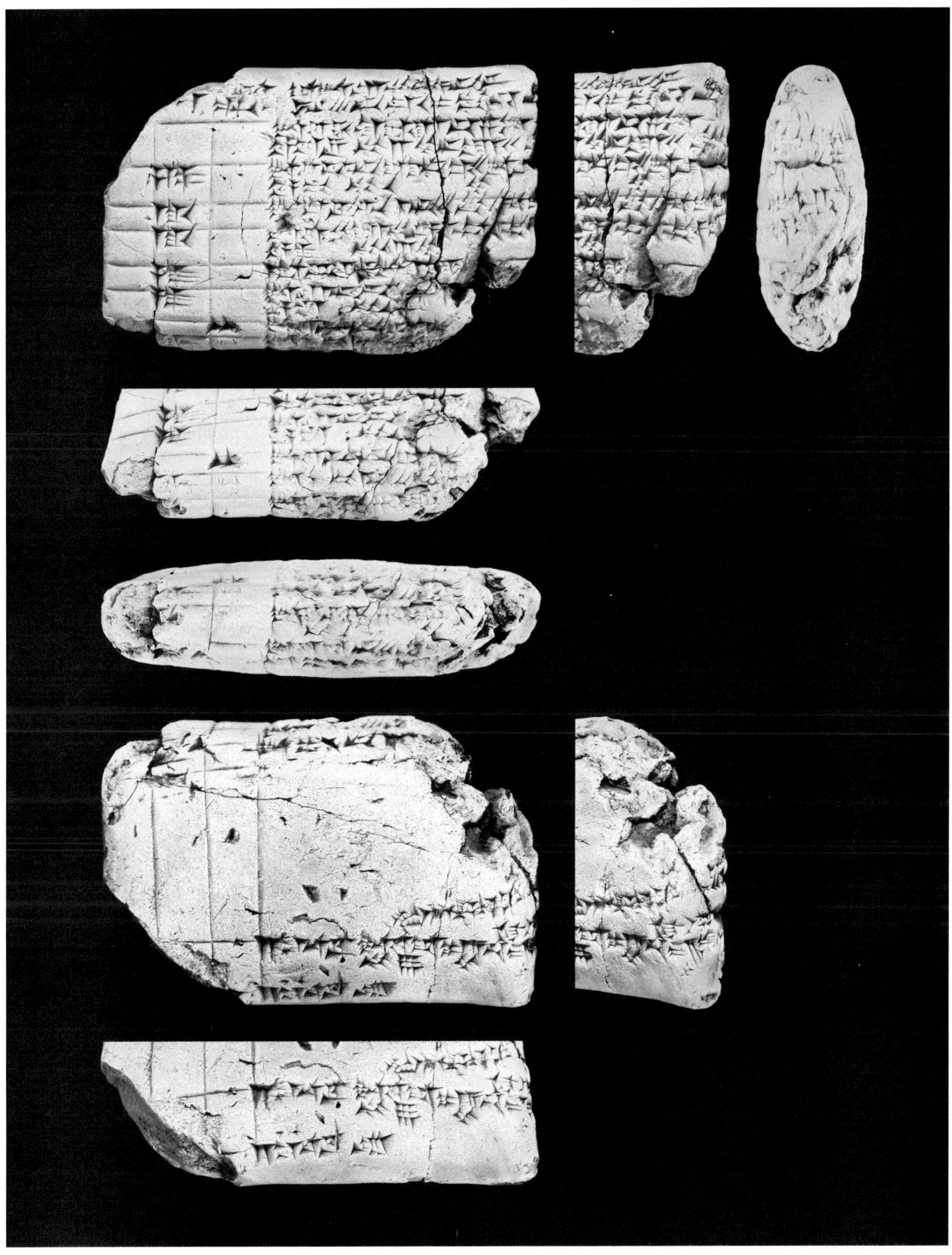

Text 180

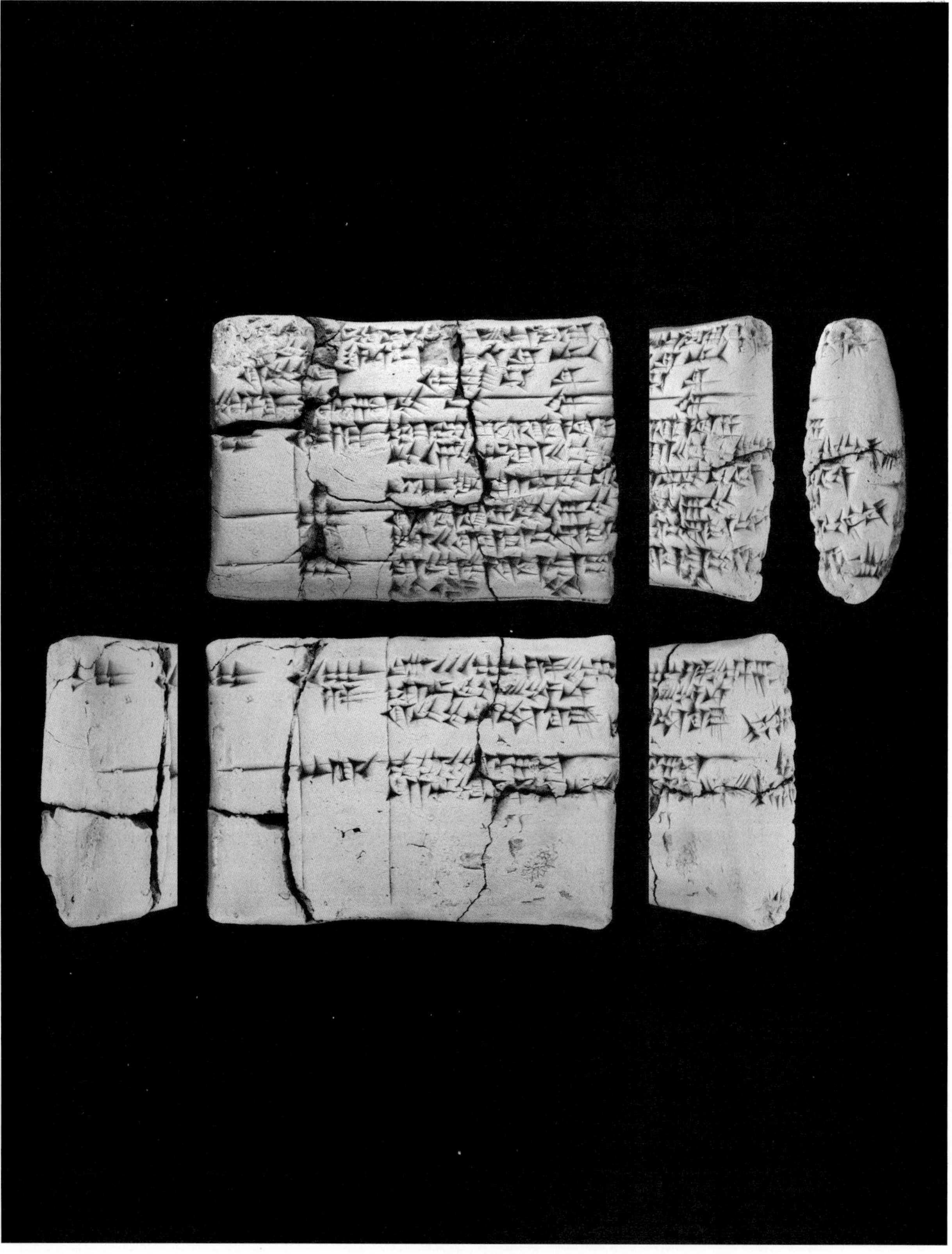

Text 181

Text 194

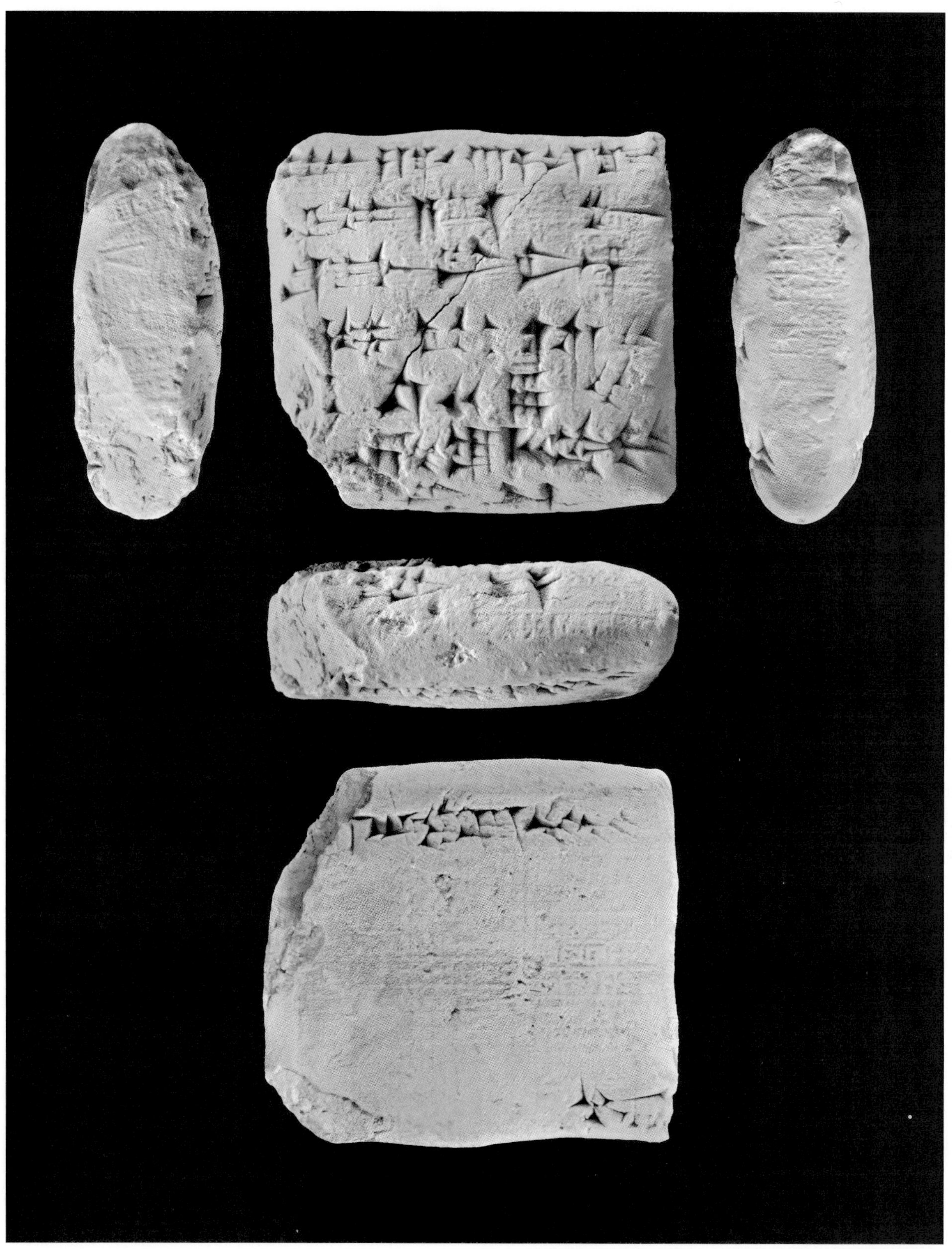

TEXT 212

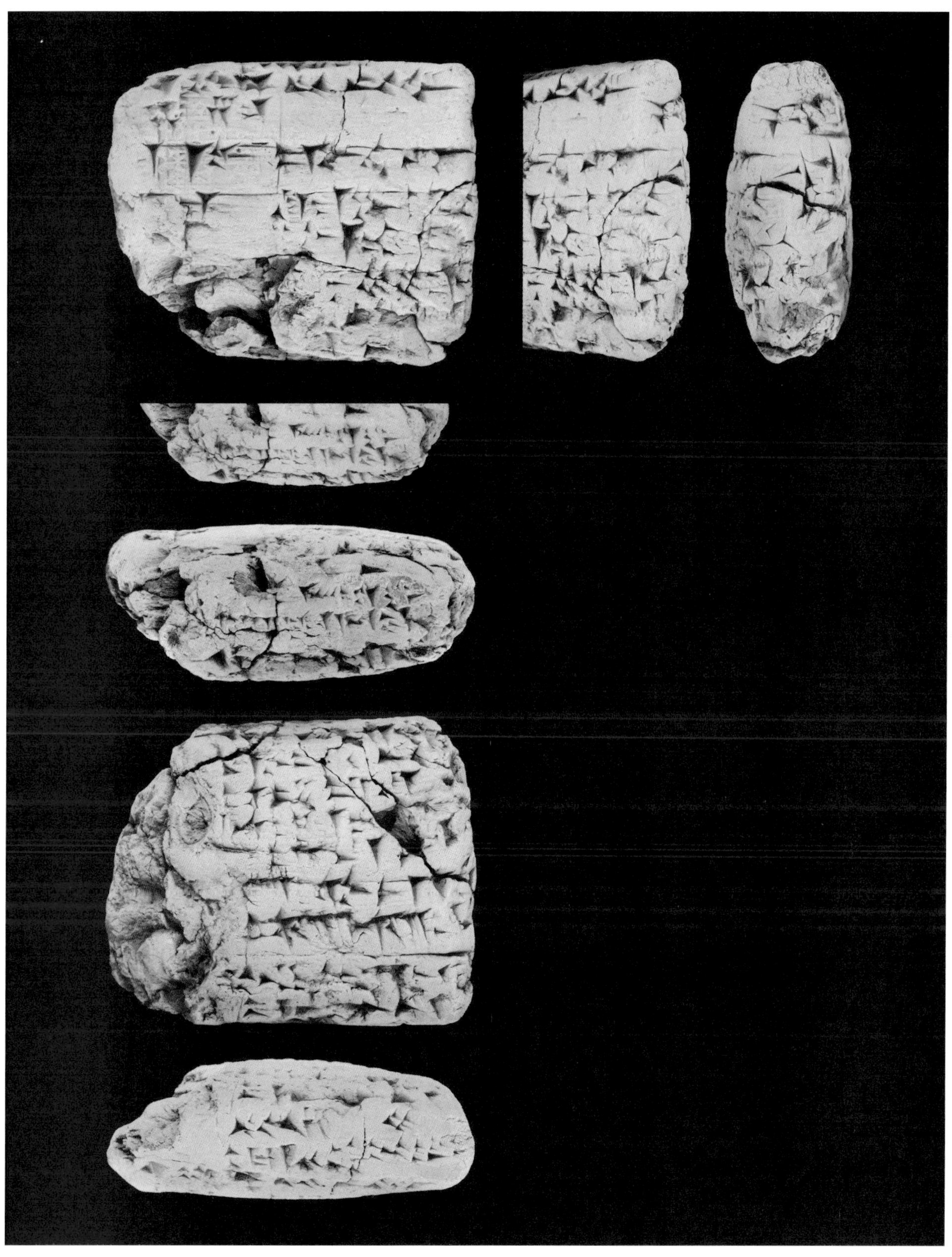

TEXT 242

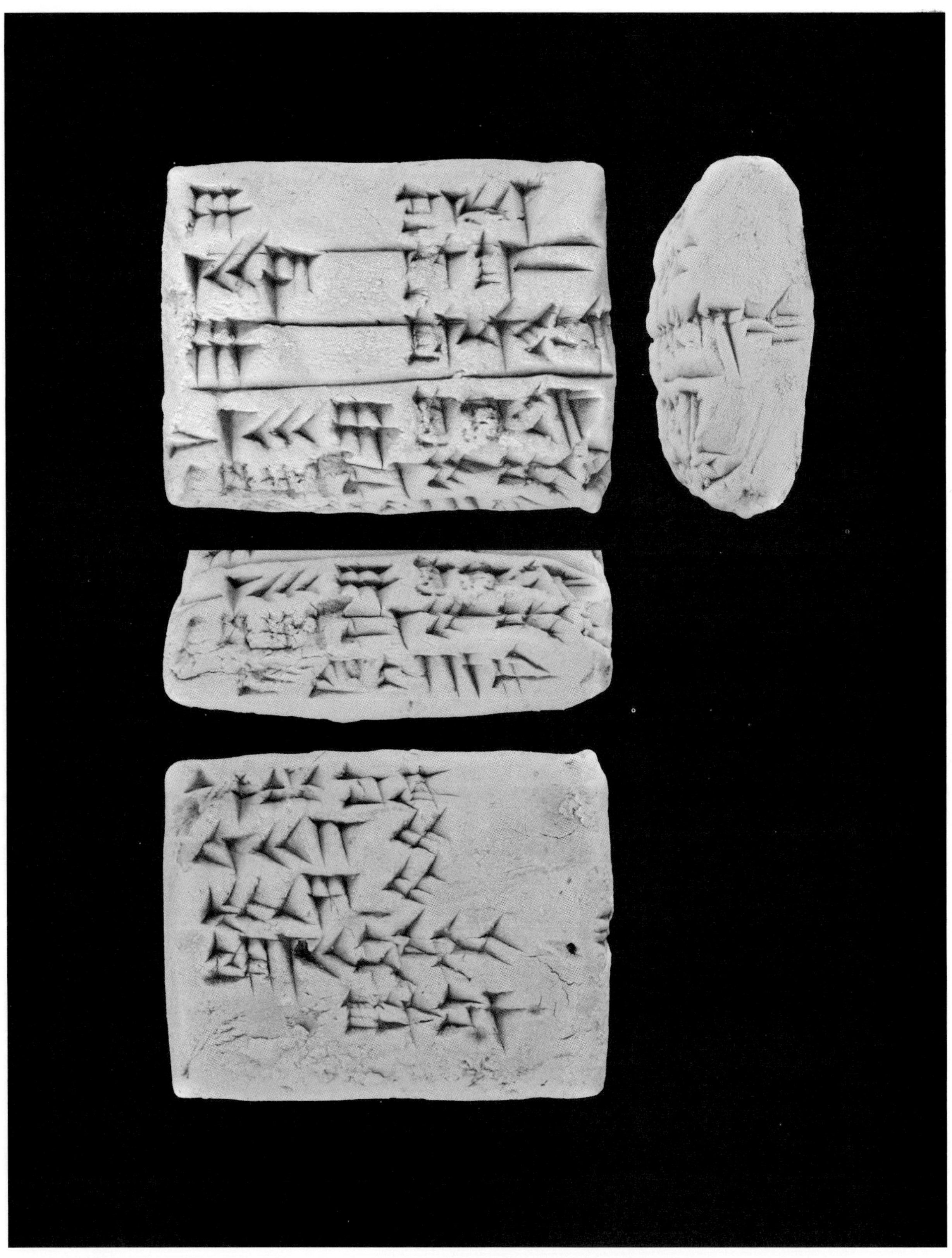

TEXT 252

Text 257

TEXT 264

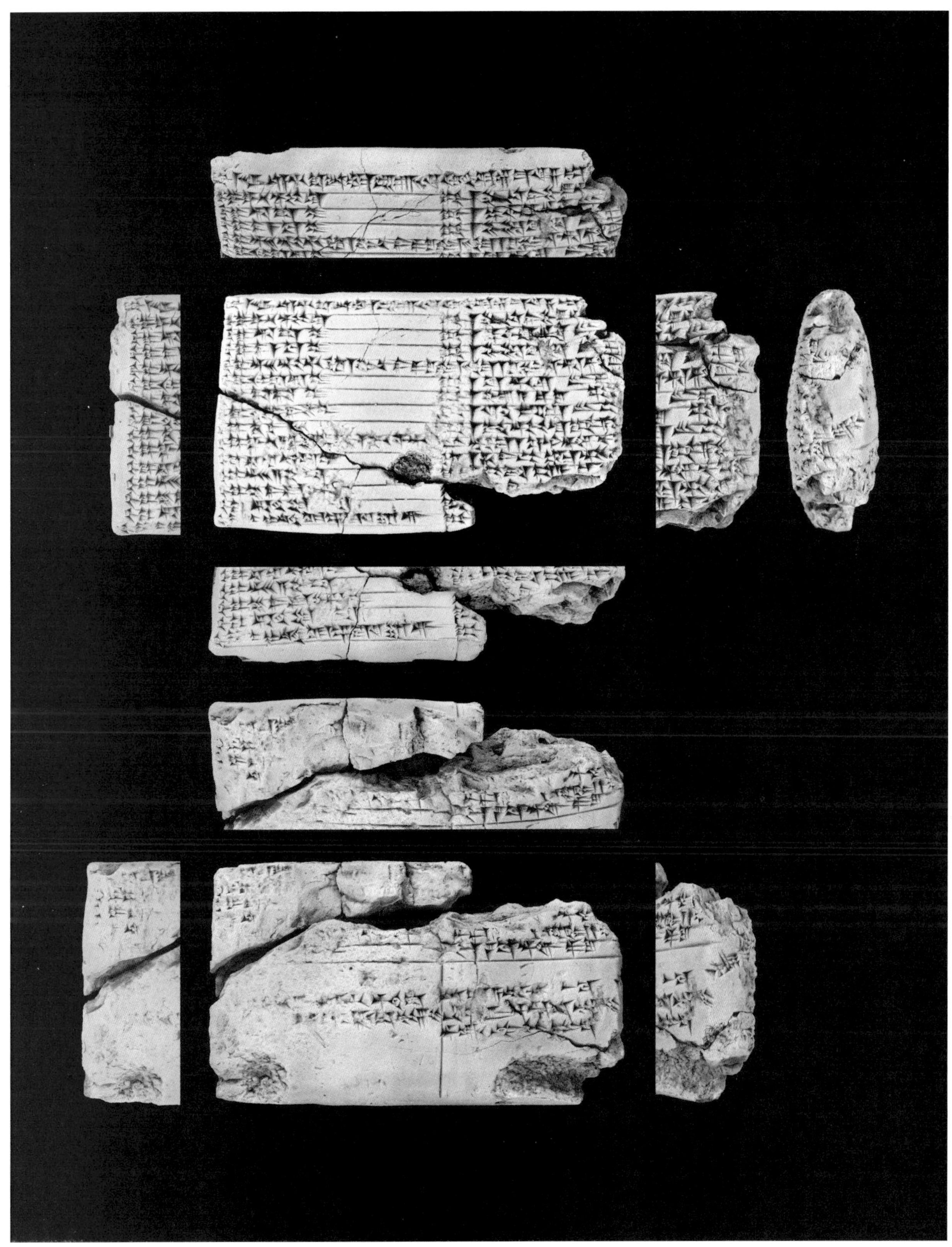

TEXT 291

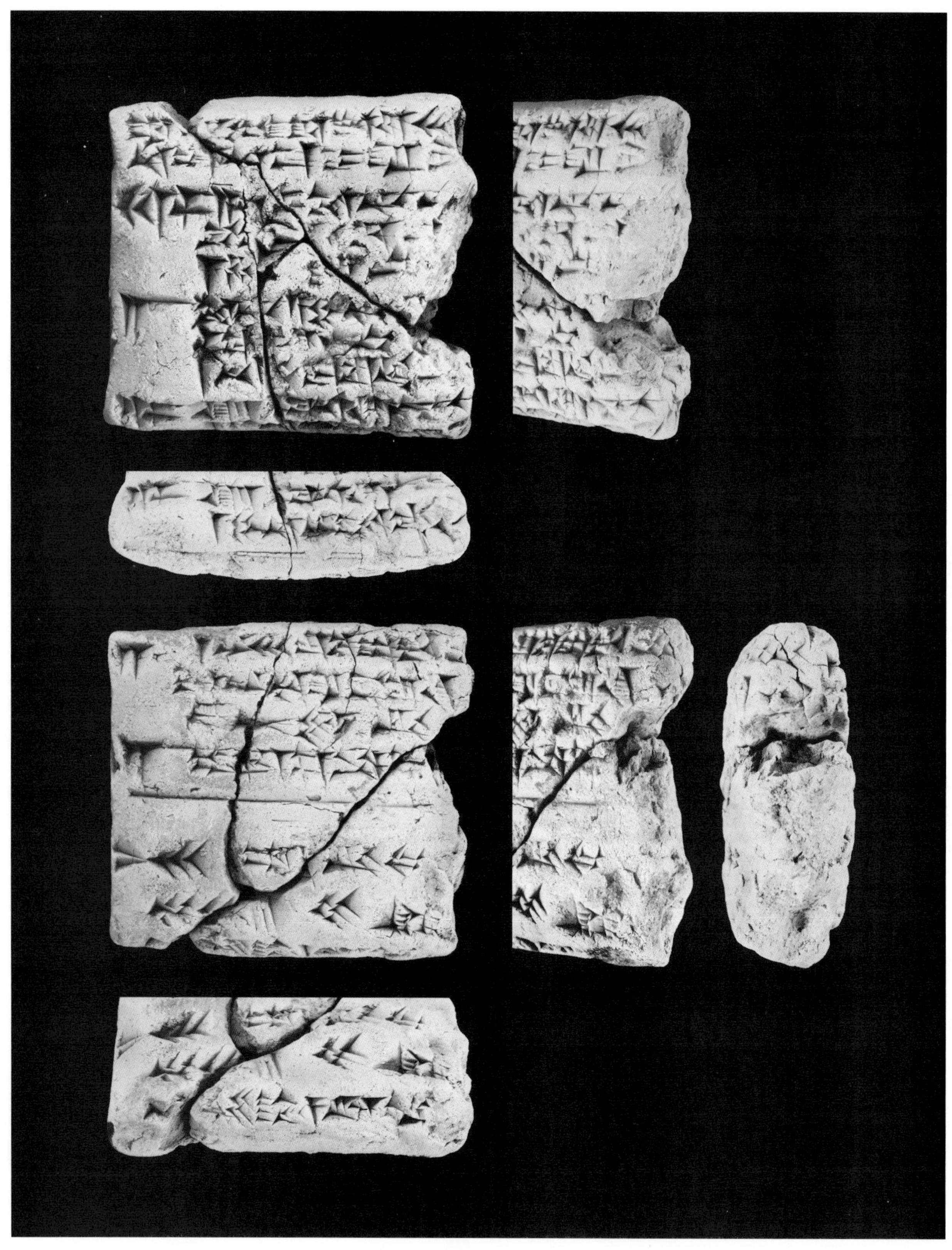

Text 303

Text 306

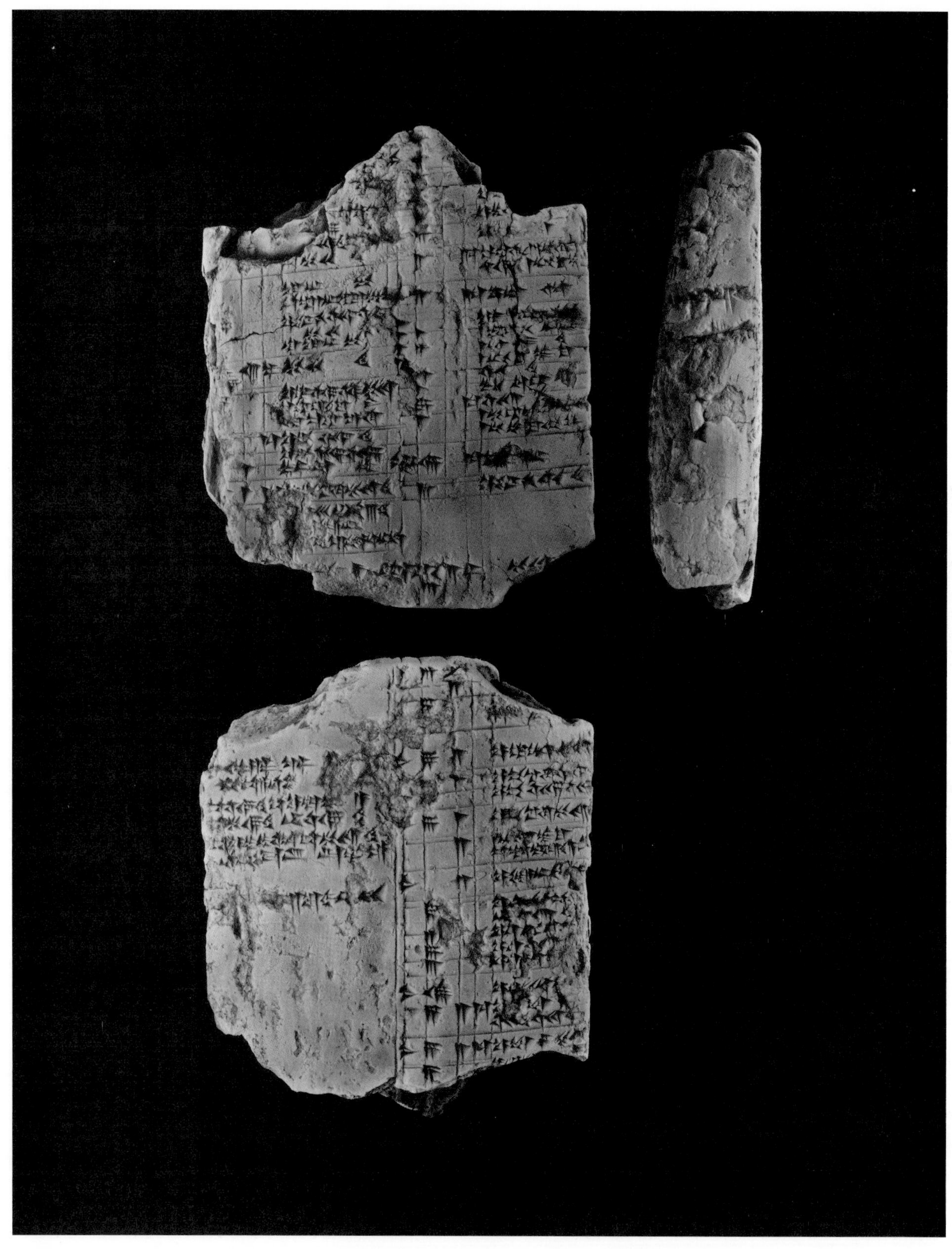

Text 308

Text 324

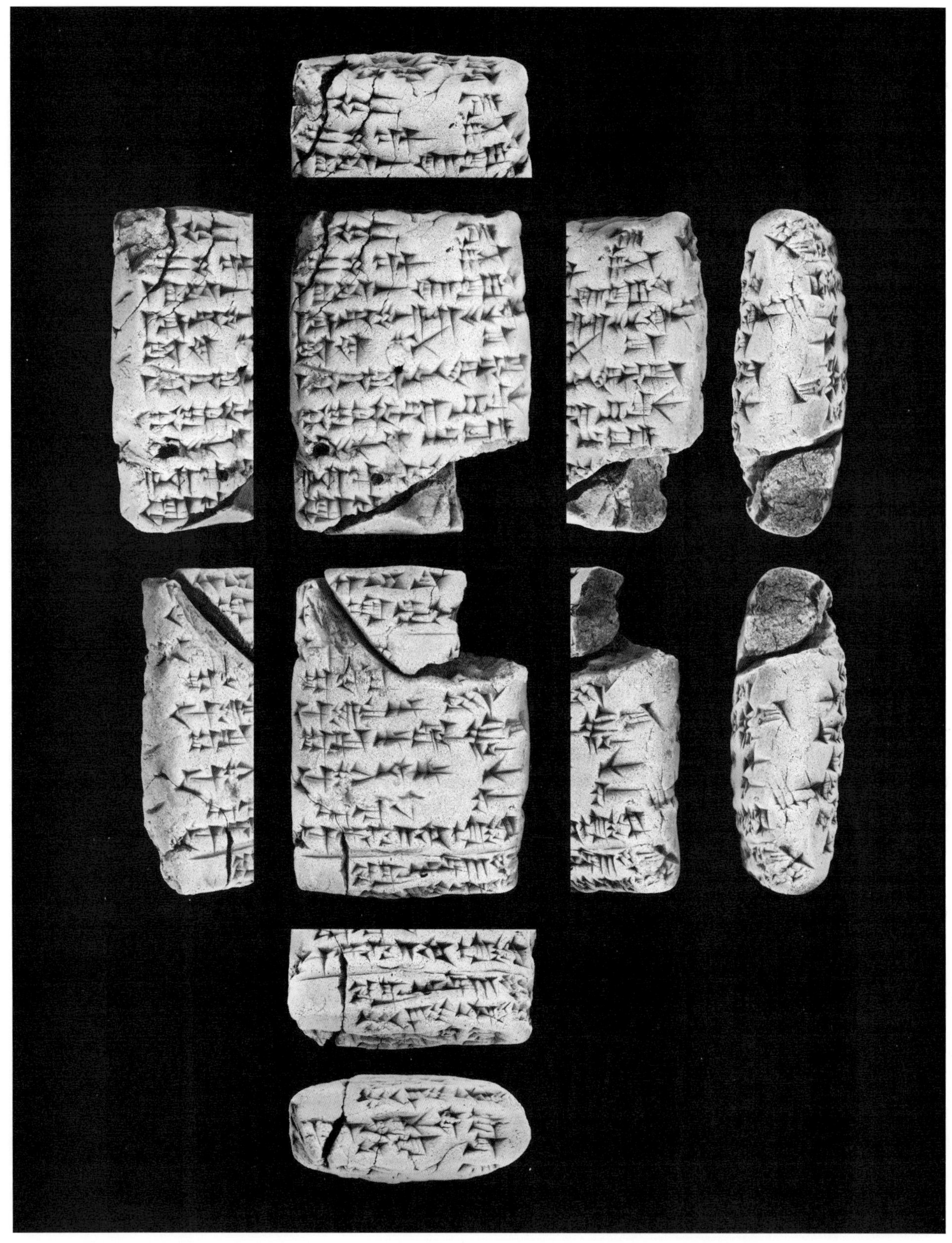

Text 325

Text 326

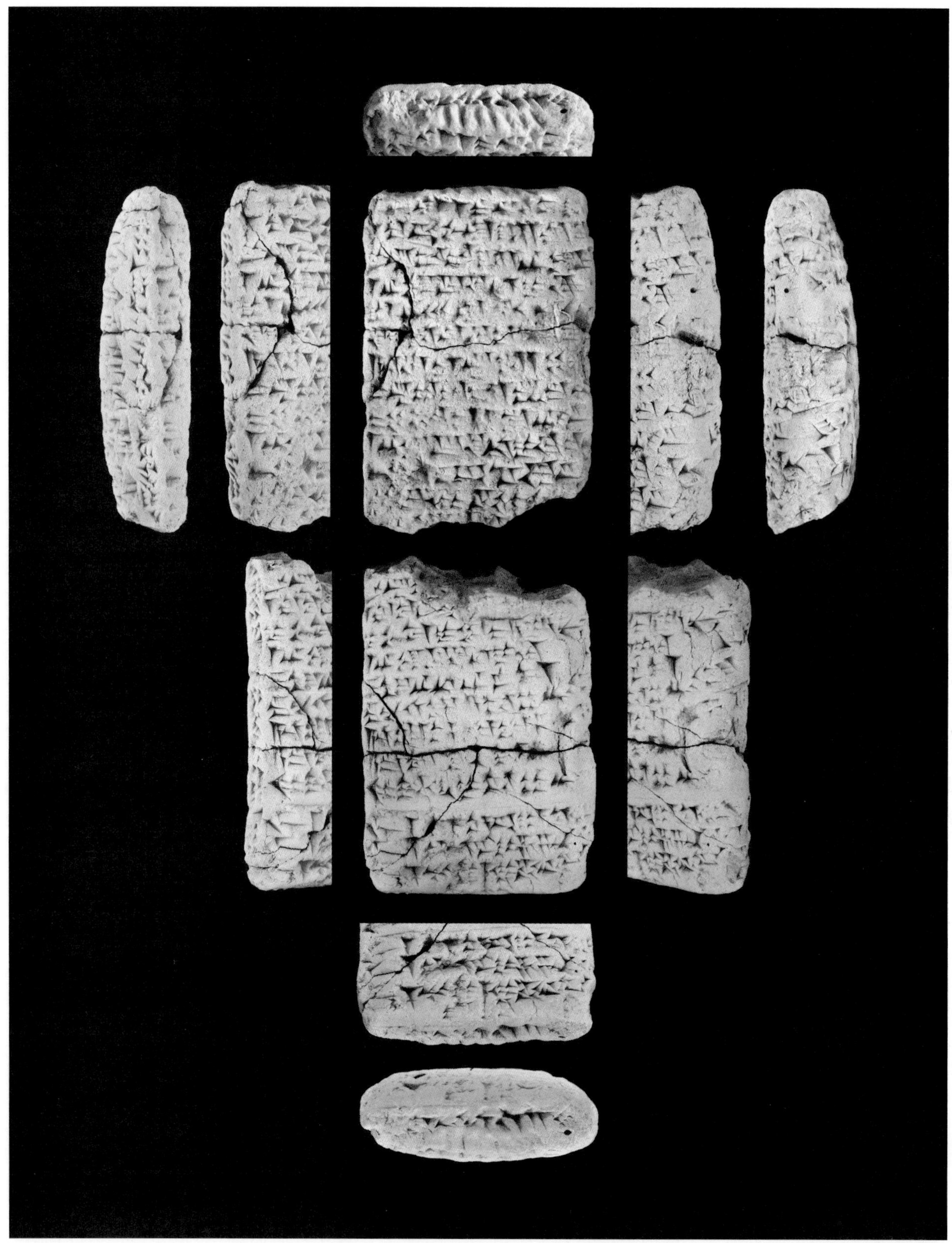

Text 327

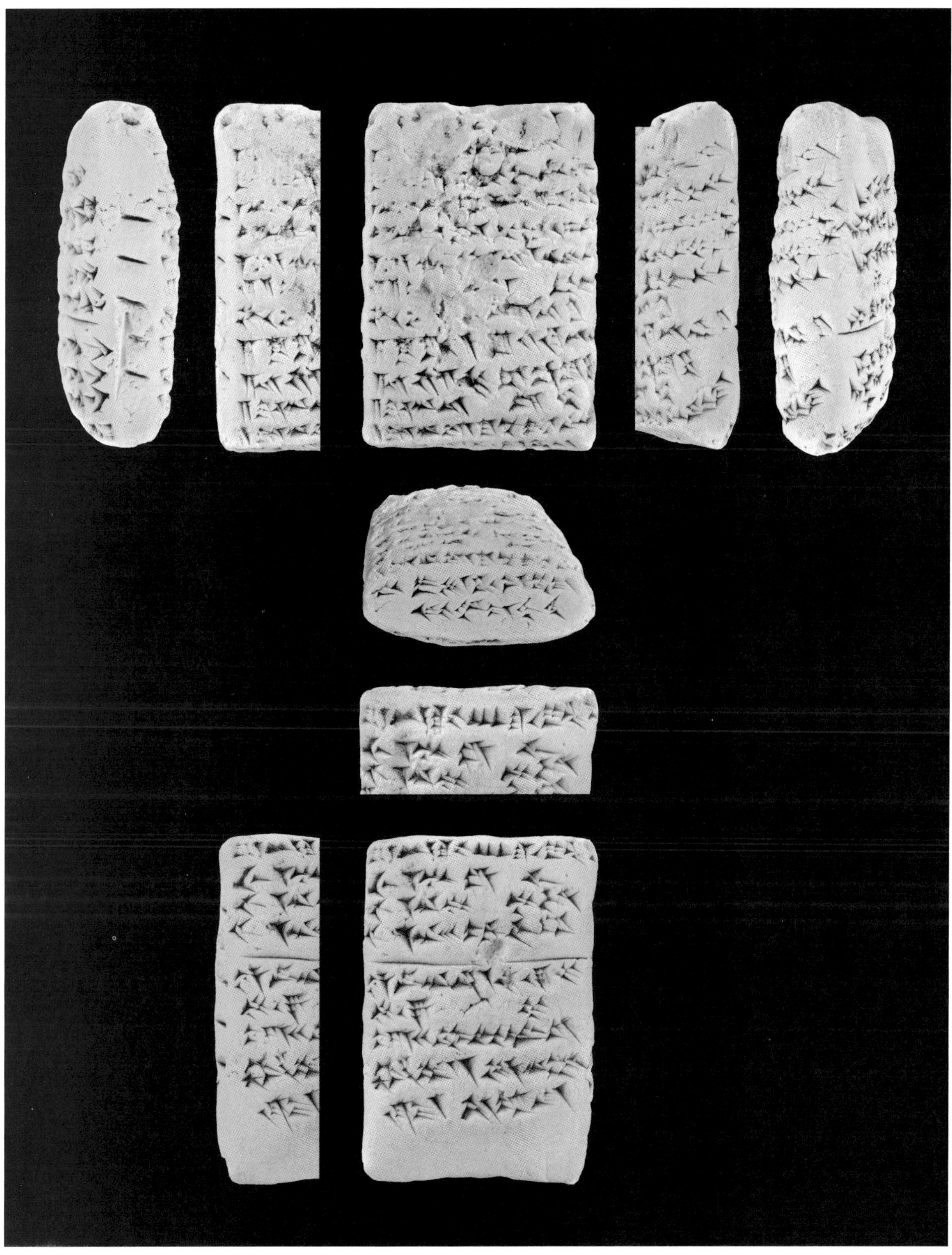

Text 328

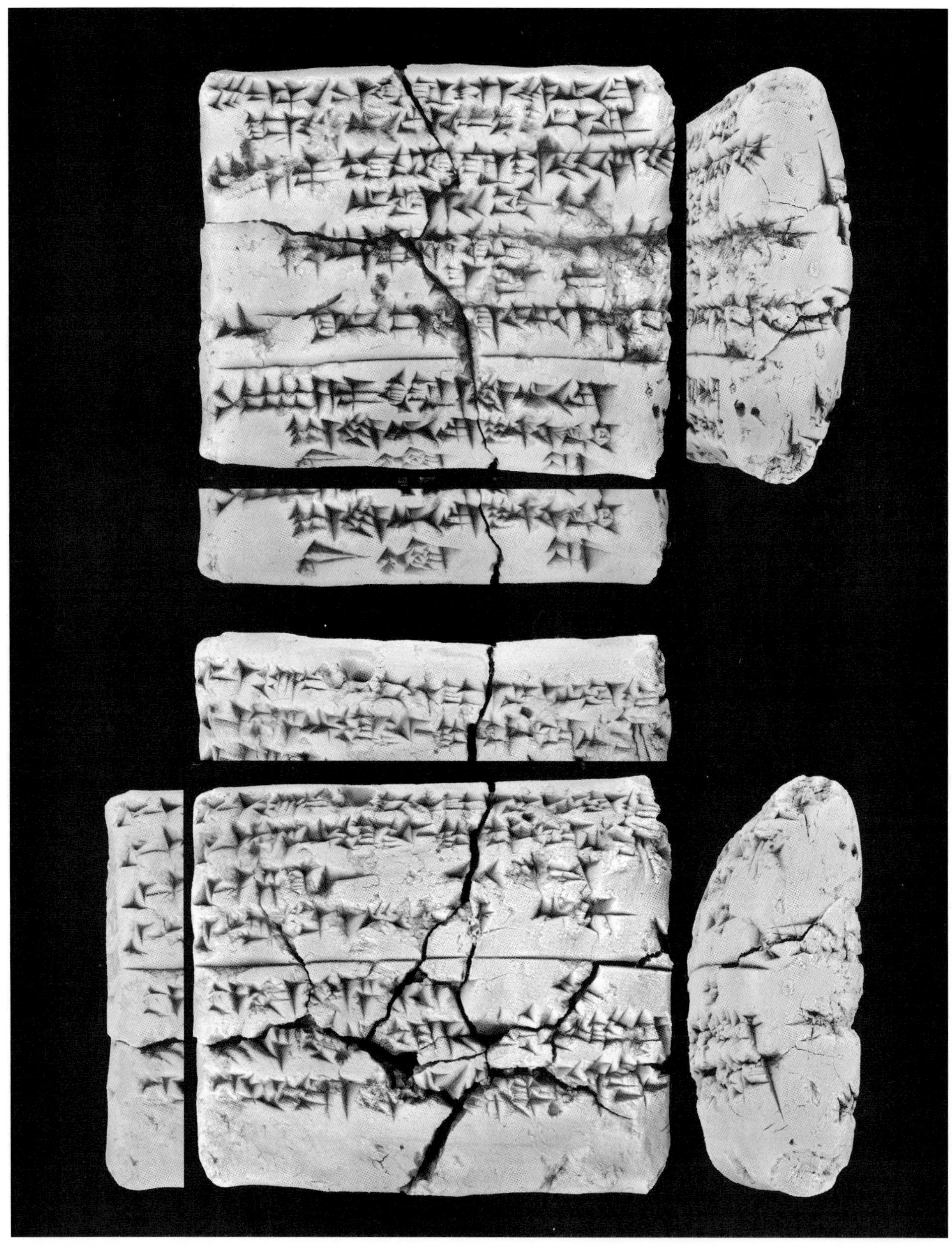

Text 330

Text 331

# Plate 69

Text 333

Text 335

TEXT 336

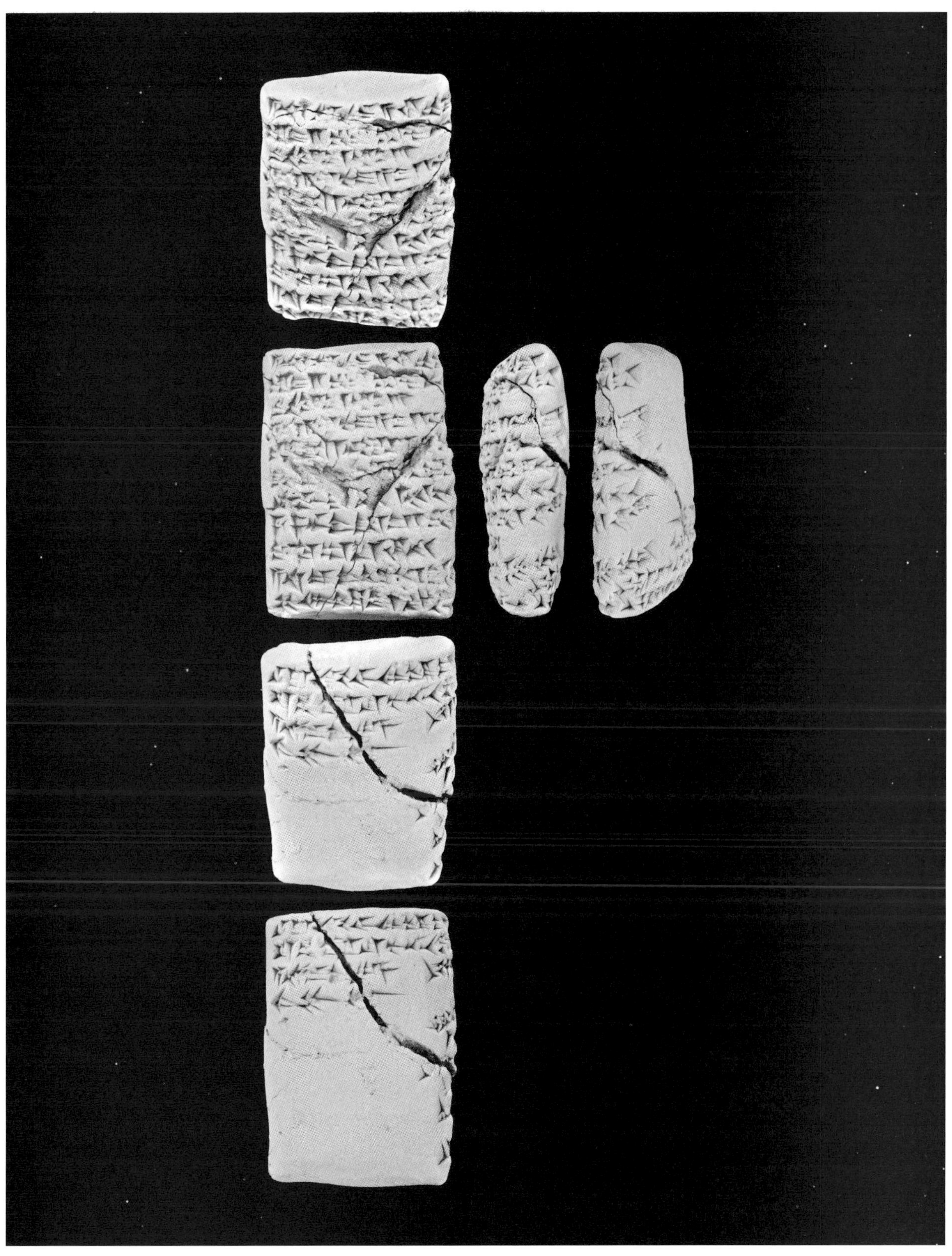

Text 337

TEXT 338